Perry A. Massey

Geographic Perspectives on America's Past

Geographic Perspectives on America's Past

Readings on the Historical Geography of the United States

Edited by
DAVID WARD

With the assistance of Thomas S. Flory

New York, OXFORD UNIVERSITY PRESS, 1979

Library of Congress Cataloging in Publication Data

Main entry under title:

Geographic perspectives on America's past.

Bibliography: p.
1. United States—Historical geography—Addresses, essays, lectures. I. Ward, David, 1938-
E179.5.G46 911'.73 77-28302
ISBN 0-19-502353-6

Printed in the United States of America

In Memory of
ANDREW HILL CLARK
Scholar, Teacher, Friend

Preface

This anthology was conceived by the late Andrew Clark and myself shortly before his death in May 1975, and, although it may be different from what he had in mind, it is dedicated to his memory. Most contributors are familiar with his works, many have encountered his interest in their work, some were his students; this collection would, I am sure, have stimulated and provoked him. I hope these selections have the same effect on the reader.

In keeping with Clark's interest in Canada and in comparative historical geography, our original plan was to include Canadian material; however, the growing volume of publications persuaded me to limit this selection to the United States alone. Barely a decade ago the selection process for an anthology of this kind would have been difficult because of the diminutive stock of available material on some topics; this problem is now less critical and painful choices had to be made in assembling this collection. It is hoped that the bibliographic sections will direct the reader's attention to many contributions which would have been equally appropriate for inclusion.

The author of each article has allowed me the liberty to make substantial reductions in the length of the material, and the reader should keep in mind that cuts have been made. For this freedom and for the privilege of using this research, I offer each author my appreciation. Finally, I would like to record my debt to Tom Flory who assisted me so effectively.

D.W.

Madison, Wisconsin
May 1978

Contents

II. *The Regional Mosaic*

III. *Urbanization*

Geographic Perspectives on America's Past

Introduction

Geographic Perspectives on the Past

Whenever sensitivity to the regional environmental settings and locational patterns of past human behavior is displayed in historical studies, a geographic perspective is consciously or unconsciously employed. These geographic perspectives on the past have been grouped in almost as many different classifications as there are approaches. For long, however, a simple if exaggerated distinction was drawn between studies that aimed to reconstruct the distinctive geography of a particular place for specific periods and those that examined the changing distributions of features selected because of their prevalence in current geographic patterns. The former approach viewed a reasonably well defined period of the past in much the same way that a regional geographer might view a foreign area today, emphasizing the individuality of the period and place. The latter approach has related the persistence or change in the locational patterns of settlements, economic activities, and social groups to critical processes in the development of a region or several regions. These processes include migration, industrialization, and urbanization. Of course, the two approaches are not mutually exclusive; reconstructions of a sequence of past geographies have been used as a basis for a synoptic viewpoint.

These different perspectives may also be rephrased to express a more fundamental distinction in approaches. Studies in which interest in the past is directly subservient to an explanation of current or universal conditions may be contrasted with studies which examine the past as distinctive contexts in which many assumptions based upon modern conditions must be relaxed or abandoned. The former approach views the past selectively, either to the degree that past conditions contribute to current geographic patterns, or as an alternative context to the present—to test the universality of generalizations or theories founded upon current behavior. The latter approach assumes that only from a comprehensive knowledge of past periods is it possible to determine those aspects of past conditions that have relevance to the present. Consequently, to this viewpoint, the uncritical retrospective application of generalizations based on modern life is likely to be unrewarding.

It would be appealingly simple to describe these different approaches as approximations of the generalist and particularist traditions in human geography as a whole. Both approaches refer to generalizations: those orientated to present conditions use generalizations derived from contemporary human geography; those focused on the past use generalizations derived from the historiographic or interpretative works on a specific period and place. These historiographic generalizations have no pretensions to formal theoretical consistency or universality but, nevertheless, they represent a common body of interpretative statements to which individual studies may be related. For example, studies of traditional or mercantile cities may find historiographic generalizations about these societies, despite their neglect of geographic patterns, a more useful source of hypotheses than the more explicitly geographic formulations about modern cities. For these reasons nongeographers have at times made impressive contributions to historical geography.

Some geographers believe that all geography is historical geography. This conviction implies that historical geography is a contrived subdiscipline which thrives because too many contemporary geographers neglect the historical dimension. The belief, however, that all geography is historical geography is but a narrow expression of a more general proposition, perhaps even a truism, that the past is inextricably part of the present. Of late, attempts have been made to cross-fertilize the concepts and methods of the social sciences with history, but, despite much hybrid research, traditional disciplines do not seem to be about to merge. Similarly, geographic interest in the past has been enriched by the retrospective application of the concepts and methods of current human geography. However, until there is a convincing synthesis of historical studies and of social sciences, historical geography will remain a distinctive part of the repertoire of a geographic education.

This anthology attempts to reveal the range and versatility of geographic perspectives in the American past, to which the contributions of specifically historical geographers represent but one tradition. The articles are grouped into three sections:

I. The Land and Its People
II. The Regional Mosaic
III. Urbanization

The first section confronts the distinctiveness of the landscape and of the people of the United States; the second emphasizes the uneven distribution of these distinctive traits and records the divergent experiences of different regions; the third section presents the cityward movement of people and activities as convergent processes occurring in all regions but at different rates and with different periodicities.

I. The Land and Its People

The individuality of American culture or subculture raises many challenging problems, not the least of which is that of synthesizing the environmental variety of the land and the complex impact of diverse cultural groups on that land. Curiosity about the meaning of the adjective "American" has stimulated many seminal interpretative works on the United States. Some of these writings have explicitly stressed the impact of the geographic isolation of pioneers in the formation of American institutions and the effects of an abundance of resources on American attitudes and values. In short, a distinctive culture was attributed to an experience of remote pioneering subsequently rewarded by material abundance. Although many Americans never directly experienced either remoteness or abundance, they certainly experienced directly the institutions and values which were presumed to be rooted in these attributes. Geographers have, however, only rarely ventured large-scale definitions of American culture and have tended to be somewhat indifferent to if not skeptical of generalizations with implied environmental explanations. Whether this reluctance is a matter of discretion or a failure of imagination is open to question, but in the reciprocal relationships between a plural society and a varied physical environment, common denominators may be among the most trivial indications of American individuality.

Geographic contributions to general interpretations about the United States are perhaps most graphically illustrated in examinations of the landscape; how it has been perceived and how it has been transformed. A belief in the value of improvement and newness are celebrated American traits and "change" itself, rather than identifiable fixed features, often dominates the American landscape. The vast dimensions of the country are to some degree made manageable when change is viewed as a process creating a landscape of monotonous similarity. To be sure, there are rich and varied provincial landscapes in the United States, but both popular and academic perceptions are rarely sensitive to their subtle forms.

Indeed, the complex and overlapping territorial patterns of different ethnic, racial, religious, and linguistic groups may be detected in the landscape only after the less visible attributes of each group are well known. This relationship between landscapes and cultural identities is especially complex when a population is migratory. A substantial proportion of the American population moves from place to place with great frequency. These movements are not purposeless wanderings; they have destinations made familiar by the information circulated among employers, family, and friends. These networks of destinations may vary from group to group, or may overlap to create a plural society. The resulting plural society is defined by the differing social and economic relationships of the member groups. This diversity of people may be diminished either through assimilation to the culture of the locally dominant resident or immigrant group or through the fusion of different groups to create a new culture. Alternatively, group differences may be maintained either by the voluntary retention of inherited cultural traits or by the association of immigrant groups with strata in American society. For example, the over- and under-representation of ethnic, racial, or other groups in occupational categories remain a constant pre-occupation of public policy. Although many of the original cultural traits of ethnic groups disappeared, employment patterns continue to define the distinctive place of some groups in American society.

II. The Regional Mosaic: Divergent Processes of Change

The uneven distribution and distinctive combinations of different ethnic groups in the United States create well defined regional differences in the kind and degree of pluralism. Variations based on resource endowments and/or regional economic development are emphasized by the selective migrations of several ethnic, racial, religious, and linguistic groups. Accordingly, the second group of articles is devoted to those divergent processes of change that contribute to striking regional variation in the American society and economy. The words "section" and "minority" have become indispensable parts of the vocabulary used in describing American life, and terms like "East," "West," "Midwest," and "South" imply divergent patterns of life to most Americans. The differences often are related to the region's specialized economic interests or to some peculiarity in the make-up of its population; certainly national elections are always accompanied by speculations about regional voting patterns. The definitions and boundaries of East, West, Midwest, and South are vague, but their content and form have changed markedly over the past three and a half centuries. The United States as a nation-state was formed by the federation of at least three divergent regional economies with distinctive provincial sub-cultures in New England, the Middle Colonies, and the South. The first two generations of the new nation saw the emergence of additional regional variations as the newly settled sections in the lower and upper Mississippi Valley followed divergent courses of development. Beyond the Mississippi, the presence of resident and relocated native Americans, Spanish-speaking people, and the distinctive patterns of Mormon settlement complicated the effects of later migrations and regional economic specialization.

The special mark of a geographic perspective on the formation of distinctive regional economies and sub-cultures is, however, its emphasis on their internal complexity. The inter-regional contrasts by which large-scale regions are perceived and defined often obscure intra-regional variations. Distinctions have been drawn between the coastal and backcountry areas of colonial settlement, between the upland and lowland South, between the upper and lower Midwest while the West almost loses its overall identity once it is demarcated into numerous, separate localities. The effects of ethnic population differences within regions has also attracted geographic scrutiny; in particular, those between Scotch-Irish and Germans in colonial Pennsylvania, between Yankees and Germans of the Midwest, between yeoman and planter in the South, and between Anglo and Hispano in the West. Although the effects of cultural pluralism are not necessarily consistent from region to region, differences in the kind of pluralism provide a more satisfactory basis for regional definition than a principle of group dominance or homogeneity.

III. Urbanization: Convergent Processes of Change

Regional economic specialization and selective migration stimulated regional differences, but the concurrent process of urbanization eventually diminished these differences. The coordination of the varied but often complementary resources of different regions and the creation of national markets for consumer goods and services led to the partitioning of the country into metropolitan regions. The growth of a dominant regional metropolis and the development of a system of subordinate service centers within the metropolitan hinterland was a familiar sequence in most newly settled regions. The sizes and densities of such service centers and the rate at which they developed varied according to the region's economic specializations and to local patterns of consumption, but since the late nineteenth century, there has been a striking convergence in regional levels of urbanization. The precise levels of regional urbanization prior to that time have not been clearly established since published census returns and readily accessible colonial records rarely reveal the complexity of the system of lower-order service centers. The rapid growth of the northeastern seaports and the emergence of large interior cities have been well documented, but the selective growth of smaller centers has only recently attracted attention.

The development of metropolitan regions represents a convergent process in the spatial organization of the national economy, but differences in regional economies and population composition exert persistent divergent influences on urban life. These influences are rarely dominant for the large American metropolis has become the subject of many generalizations about modern urban life. The internal spatial arrangement of land use and of social groups, the journey to work or to play, the locational preferences of consumers for goods, services, and housing have all been formulated into models which seek to be universal. Further, the formation of a central business district and specialized industrial areas, the clustering and dispersal of minority groups, and the growth of suburbs are all presumed to have followed a broadly similar sequence resulting in a striking uniformity of the appearance of American cities. Our image of uniformity, which is derived from the generic models of the social sciences, is reinforced by an indifference, if not a hostility, to cities that has marked American literary and political thought. Age, location, and symbolic reputation do differentiate some American cities, but these differences are confined to a limited number of cities; divergent patterns have rarely attracted serious attention.

The three themes in this anthology should help us to understand how a geographic perspective contributes to our appreciation of the American past. The first section defines the environment and population of the United States and charts their change. A geographic perspective which emphasizes how diverse and changing culture groups perceived and then transformed the environment often challenges generalizations about national identities. Conflicting and complementary relationships emerge between region and nation, and between minority group and host society rather than a well-articulated synthesis. The second and third sections deal with this problem by identifying both diverging and converging processes in the changing geography of the United States. The challenge of geographic interpretation is the simultaneous study of generic locational patterns of human behavior and the distinctive identities of places resulting from interaction between a particular environment and its residents. The second section stresses those processes which had particular manifestations in specific regions. The third section emphasizes those processes which had similar results in most places. The choice of processes discussed is necessarily affected by the material available and to some degree reflects the focus of recent research. However, the anthology's structure is general enough so that other processes and other routes might supplement those suggested in this introduction.

Suggested Additional Reading

A. Methodology

Baker, Alan R. H., et al., "The Future of the Past," *Area* 1 (1969):46-50.
Baker, Alan R. H., ed., *Progress in Historical Geography* (London: David & Charles, 1970).
Harris, R. Colebrook, "Theory and Synthesis in Historical Geography," *Canadian Geographer* 15 (1971):157-72.
———, "Reflections on the Fertility of the Historical Geographic Mule," (Toronto: University of Toronto, Department of Geography, Discussion Paper, No. 10, 1970).
Jakle, John, "Time, Space, and the Geographic Past: A Prospectus for Historical Geography," *American Historical Review* 76 (1971):1084-1103.
Kulikoff, Alan, "Historical Geographers and Social History: A Review Essay," *Historical Methods Newsletter* 6 (1973):122-28.
Langton, John, "Potentialities and Problems of Adopting a Systems Approach to the Study of Change in Human Behavior," *Progress in Geography* 4 (1972):125-79.
Meinig, Donald W., "Environmental Appreciation: Localities as a Humane Art," *The Western Humanities Review* 25 (1971):1-11.
Mikesell, Marvin W., "The Rise and Decline of 'Sequent Occupance': A Chapter in the History of American Geography," pp. 149-69 in, David Lowenthal and Martyn J. Bowden, eds., *Geographies of the Mind* (New York: Oxford University Press, 1976).
Patten, John H. C., "The Past and Geography Reconsidered," *Area* 2 (1970):37-39.
Prince, Hugh C., "Three Realms of Historical Geography," *Progress in Geography* 3 (1971):1-86.
Swierenga, Robert P., "Towards the 'New Rural History': A Review Essay," *Historical Methods Newsletter* 6 (1973):111-22.
Tuan, Yi Fu, *Topophilia: A Study of Environmental Perception, Attitudes and Values* (Englewood Cliffs, N.J.: Prentice-Hall, 1976).
Ward, David, "The Debate on Alternative Approaches in Historical Geography," *Historical Methods Newsletter* 8 (1975):82-87.
Zelinsky, Wilbur, "In Pursuit of Historical Geography and Other Wild Geese," *Historical Geography Newsletter* 3 (1973):1-5.

B. The Land and its People

Billington, Ray A., *The Genesis of the Frontier Thesis: A Study in Historical Creativity* (San Marino, Cal.: Huntington Library, 1971).
Brown, Ralph H., *Historical Geography of the United States* (New York: Harcourt Brace, 1948).
———, *Mirror for Americans: Likeness of the Eastern Seaboard, 1810* (New York: American Geographical Society, 1943).
Graber, Linda, *Wilderness as Sacred Space* (Washington, D.C.: Association of American Geographers, Monograph No. 7, 1977).
Hart, John F., *The Look of the Land* (Englewood Cliffs, N.J.: Prentice-Hall, 1975).

Hartz, Louis, *The Founding of New Societies* (New York: Harcourt Brace, 1964).

Kammen, Michael, *People of Paradox: An Inquiry Concerning the Origins of American Civilization* (New York: Knopf, 1972).

Mead, William R., ed., *The American Environment* (London: University of London, Athlone Press, 1974).

Potter, David M., "Abundance and the Turner Thesis," in his *People of Plenty* (Chicago: University of Chicago Press, 1954).

Paullin, Charles O. and John K. Wright, eds., *Atlas of the Historical Geography of the United States* (Washington and New York: Carnegie Institution and American Geographical Society, 1932).

U.S. Bureau of the Census, *Historical Statistics of the United States, Colonial Times to 1970* (Washington, D.C.: Government Printing Office, 1976, vol. 1: esp. "Population," 1-43; "Vital Statistics," 44-86; and "Migration," 87-120; vol. 2: "Colonial and Pre-Federal Statistics," 1152-1174).

———, *Indian Population in the United States and Alaska, 1910* (Washington, D.C.: Government Printing Office, 1915).

———, *Negro Population, 1790-1915* (Washington, D.C.: Government Printing Office, 1918).

———, *A Century of Population Growth from the First Census of the United States to the Twelfth, 1790-1900* (Washington, D.C.: Government Printing Office, 1909).

Watson, J. Wreford and Timothy O'Riordan, eds., *The American Environment: Perceptions and Policies* (New York: Wiley, 1976).

C. The Regional Mosaic

Gaustad, Edwin, *Historical Atlas of Religion in America,* rev. ed. (New York: Harper and Row, 1972).

Gastil, Raymond D., *Cultural Regions of the United States* (Seattle: University of Washington Press, 1975).

Greeley, Andrew M., *Ethnicity in the United States: A Preliminary Reconnaissance* (New York: Wiley, 1974).

Gillin, John, "National and Regional Cultural Values in the U.S.," *Social Forces* 34 (1955):107-13.

Hart, John F., ed., *Regions of the United States* (New York: Harper and Row, 1972).

Jackson, John B., *American Space: The Centennial Years, 1865-1976* (New York: Norton, 1972).

Perloff, Harvey S., et al., *Regions, Resources and Economic Growth* (Baltimore: The Johns Hopkins University Press, 1960).

Perloff, Harvey S., and Lowden Wingo, Jr., "Natural Resource Endowment and Regional Economic Growth," pp. 191-212, in J. J. Spengler, ed., *Natural Resources and Economic Growth* (Washington, D.C.: Resources for the Future, 1961).

Russo, David J., *Families and Communities: A New View of American History* (Nashville: American Association for State and Local History, 1974).

Sutter, Ruth E., *The Next Place You Come To* (Englewood Cliffs, N.J.: Prentice-Hall, 1973).

Zelinsky, Wilbur, *The Cultural Geography of the United States* (Englewood Cliffs, N.J.: Prentice-Hall, 1973).

D. Urbanization

Clay, Grady, *How to Read the American City* (New York: Praeger, 1974).

Gutman, Herbert G., "Work, Culture, and Society in Industrializing America" in his *Work, Culture, and Society in Industrializing America* (New York: Knopf, 1976).

Lampard, Eric E., "The Evolving System of Cities in the United States," pp. 81-138, in, Harvey S. Perloff and Lowden Wingo, Jr., eds., *Issues in Urban Economics* (Baltimore: The Johns Hopkins University Press, 1968).

Pred, Allan R., *The Spatial Dynamics of U.S. Urban-Industrial Growth, 1806-1914* (Cambridge, Mass.: M.I.T. Press, 1966).

Vance, James E. Jr., *The Merchants World: The Geography of Wholesaling* (Englewood Cliffs, N.J.: Prentice-Hall, 1970).

Wade, Richard C., *The Urban Frontier: The Rise of Western Cities, 1790-1830,* Cambridge, Mass.: Harvard University Press, 1959).

Ward, David, *Cities and Immigrants: A Geography of Change in Nineteenth-Century America* (New York: Oxford University Press, 1971).

Warner, Sam B., Jr., *The Urban Wilderness: A History of the American City* (New York: Harper and Row, 1972).

I The Land and Its People

A study of the relationship between Americans and their environment requires careful qualification of the terms "American" and "environment." The papers in this section illuminate the complexity of these terms. The first group confronts the varied and changing meaning of the American landscape and environment and the degree to which it displays a distinctive American identity. The second group examines the changing composition and distribution of the American population, focusing upon both the ethnic pluralism and the proverbial mobility of American society.

A. Landscape and Identity

Interpretors of the American landscape often view its distinctiveness as one of two extremes. The first was uninhabited wilderness at a scale unmatched in other industrialized countries and displays an almost sacred attitude to unchanged nature. The other extreme views the American landscape as intensively occupied tracts from which all traces of the original natural environment have been removed and applauds the ingenuity by which nature has been altered. These irreconcilable viewpoints contribute to the confused and fragile responses to environmental problems. The American landscape does not express a single conception of the relationship between a people and their land, but rather does express the conflict within and among Americans about their environment. Only in the context of American "extremes" would Leopold's concept of a landscape where human ingenuity is restrained be called a "middle" landscape. In other developed nations, the extremes of perception are more muted and there is less need of a metaphorical "middle" landscape. David Lowenthal examines these issues in his article on "The American Scene" by elaborating terms such as size, wilderness, extremes, and formlessness. These terms are a kind of language designed to convey idealized images or stereotypes of how Americans perceive their landscape. Their perceptions reveal attitudes toward change and the past which are more revealing of an American identity than the "scene" itself. These same perceptions also affect how the future is imagined. In "Geographical Knowledge and American Images of the Louisiana Territory," John Allen documents the changing impressions and images that Americans had of their newly acquired western inheritance. In part because of incomplete knowledge, but also because of unrestrained aspirations, the West was imagined as an "inland garden" and a route to the Indies. Only later were the subhumid conditions and mountain barriers of the Far West fully appreciated.

Images of the West also reinforced the growing national consciousness of the new republic, strongly influencing ideologies and interpretations of the distinctiveness of American society. Robert Berkhofer in "Space, Time, Culture, and the New Frontier" examines Frederick Jackson Turner's frontier thesis, the most familiar and controversial of the interpretative schemes. Turner related the distinctiveness of American institutions to the experience of frontier pioneering. Berkhofer views Turner's ideas in the context of the time at which they were formulated; he argues that Turner's thesis was sustained by concerns of the late nineteenth century—with the closing of the frontier—rather than the realities of the frontier experience. Although the frontier thesis superficially recognizes the geographic factors of relative isolation and environmental adaptation, Berkhofer shows that it is in fact insensitive to differences of culture and environment which affected the pioneer experience.

This kind of insensitivity also characterized efforts to define the identity of the subhumid West. Walter Prescott Webb in *The Great Plains* attributed the distinctiveness of western American life to the breakdown of old ways of pioneering adapted to the humid East. Unlike Turner, Webb was directly concerned with the determining effects of the physical environment, but specified this environment so generally that many so-called adaptations were actually made under very different environmental circumstances. Some adaptations to new conditions were common to all westward moving pioneers, but others were strongly influenced by the peculiarities of local environments. The common reactions of several different ethnic groups to specific local environments are explored by Terry Jordan in "Between Forest and Prairie." Assertions have been made that early settlers preferred woodland environments over prairies and that Yankee settlers were more likely to colonize prairies than were European, especially German, pioneers. After examining both the effects of ethnic background and the differences in vegetation type in the settlement of the Midwest, Jordan concludes that a dichotomous classification of the midwestern environment into woodland and prairie is too simplistic: it rarely captures other equally influential locational considerations such as drainage and accessibility. In addition, he discovered no evidence that ethnic differences between settlers influenced their judgments on natural vegetation in relation to settlement priorities.

National aspirations or ideologies prevalent at a particular time affect the images or interpretative schemes which express the American identity in terms of large scale perspectives on environment and landscape. These images and schema rarely reveal the ambiguities and conflicts which are also apparent in the American scene, nor do they define environments or localities on a scale appropriate to the evaluation of human responses to new surroundings. These responses are further complicated by the cultural pluralism and mobility of the American population, to which the second group of papers in this first section are devoted.

B. Migrants in a Plural Society

By the end of the seventeenth century the ethnic and religious diversity of the European settlers, the removal and resettlement of the aboriginal Indian population, and the early importation of slave labor from Africa had created a plural society in the American colonies. From the establishment of the new nation-state until the mid-nineteenth century, the ethnic diversity of European immigrants did not attract much attention. Up to that time the overwhelming majority of Americans of European descent were from the British Isles, and almost all, irrespective of country of origin, were of the Protestant faith. With the arrival of large numbers of Catholic Irish immigrants, and Catholic and Jewish immigrants from southern and eastern Europe, differences were highlighted and the question of how these exotic people were to be assimilated into American society was raised. Of course, the relationships of aboriginal and black Americans to European Americans had for long been a serious issue, but Indian reservations and racial segregation indicated that the host society did not envisage the assimilation of these groups.

Francis Femminella in "The Immigrant and the Urban Melting Pot" reviews various conceptions of assimilation. These conceptions reveal different images of American society rather than mutually exclusive immigrant experiences. If the United States was envisaged as a homogenous society, then either assimilation to an Anglo-American norm or a selective fusion of diverse groups into a new American norm was desired. If it was viewed as a plural society, then the retention of some immigrant cultural traits or the maintenance of group consciousness might be preferred. If differences among European immigrant groups aroused concern about the nature of American society, clearly the placement of aboriginal Americans, Afro-Americans, and Oriental immigrants posed special problems, which many of those who envisaged a homogeneous society never confronted. Wilbur Jacobs in "The Indian and the Frontier in American History," and Richard Morrill and O. F. Donaldson in "Geographical Perspectives on the History of Black America" address these issues. Jacobs stresses the reciprocal relationships between European and Indian in frontier situations. Rather than recording the saga of displacement and demoralization, he emphasizes the Indian contribution to European adaptations to the land. Morrill and Donaldson record the four major geographic aspects of the black experience in America: first, their settlement as slaves in the southern colonies; second, their forced redistribution within the South with the expansion of cotton production; third, their dispersal into the rural South following emancipation; and fourth, their movement, initially to border cities and later to northern and western cities.

The pluralism of the American population is a consequence of the convergence of free and forced migrations from several continents. These movements to the United States were not simple ventures from an origin to a destination. There was an ebb as well as a flow along migration routes, and many Americans frequently migrated within the country. Recent documentations of high rates of population turnover during the nineteenth century in both urban and frontier settlements suggest that Americans, proportionately, moved as frequently then as they do today. Some contemporary observers assume that the high mobility of modern America has contributed to the disintegration of "communities." Vance Packard for example, has argued that high mobility has created a nation of "strangers," but population turnover was also high a century ago. This historical research questions the assumption, implicit in many modern community studies, that the quality of human interaction is dependent upon the propinquity of the participants. Nineteenth-century migrants maintained personal connections over long distances and moved along well-traveled routes to destinations charted by friends and relatives. John Hudson in "Migration to an American Frontier" examines the movement patterns of several ethnic groups who moved to North Dakota in the late nineteenth century. He relates both turnover and seasonal migration to the changing pattern of employment opportunities: the high levels of migration among most ethnic groups recorded their common predicament in the market economy. Although groups often clustered in well-defined localities, there was inevitably considerable interspersal. Certain cultural traits and territorial patterns may have defined some groups, but selective and frequent migration in response to employment opportunities probably characterized the distinctively American aspect of their experience.

A. Landscape and Identity

The American Scene* / *David Lowenthal*

Face to face with the look of his own country, the well-traveled American is characteristically dismayed. Henry James, more than most others, viewed the American scene at the turn of the century with outright distaste. After his twenty-five years abroad, America seemed bleak and raw, except at Harvard College, where the mellow tones of the older buildings allowed him to hope that "we are getting almost ripe, . . . beginning to begin, and we have that best sign of it, . . . that we make the vulgar, the very vulgar, think we are beginning to end."[1] If the American scene was elsewhere deplorable, it was because American society was unformed, American taste untutored. James attributed the sordid shabbiness of New Hampshire's wayside farms and people to "the suppression of the two great factors of the familiar English landscape, the squire and the parson."[2] That America seemed such "an ugly . . . wintering, waiting, world" was a consequence, he believed, of "the vast general unconsciousness and indifference"[3] about its appearance; things looked as they did because almost no one cared.

A pioneer conservationist decided a century ago that although others "think that the earth made man, man in fact made the earth."[4] This insight was ecological, but the statement is as true esthetically. Landscapes are formed by land-

---

* This paper is condensed and revised from a lecture delivered at the Graduate School of Design, Harvard University, in November 1966. It is part of a longer work in preparation. The author acknowledges with gratitude the assistance of the John Simon Guggenheim Memorial Foundation, for a fellowship in 1965-66; and his indebtedness for the title to Henry James's book (see footnote 1 below).

1. Henry James, *The American Scene* (New York and London, 1907), p. 61. See also Donald Emerson, "Henry James: A Sentimental Tourist and Restless Analyst," *Trans. Wisc. Acad. of Science* 52 (1963):17-25.

2. James, *American Scene,* p. 23.

3. Henry James, *The American Scene,* edited by W. H. Auden (New York, 1946), pp. 461, 464. These phrases were omitted from the original American edition.

4. George Perkins Marsh, letter to Spencer Fullerton Baird, May 21, 1860, as quoted in David Lowenthal, *George Perkins Marsh: Versatile Vermonter* (New York, 1958), p. 248.

Reprinted (with omissions) from the *Geographical Review* 58 (1968):61-88.

scape tastes. People see their surroundings through preferred and accustomed glasses and tend to make the world over as they see it. Such preferences long outlast geographical reality. Thus the English, although now mainly "town-birds through and through," still think of rural England as their true home; for them, Browning's chaffinch still sings on an orchard bough.[5]

Images and Stereotypes

The American scene, as much as any other, mirrors a long succession of idealized images and visual stereotypes. Let us examine a few historic responses to that scene and see how they are reflected in contemporary landscape and townscape.

A literary historian has categorized typical Eastern reactions to Western landscapes in terms of *vastness, astonishment, plenitude* (owing to the apparent inexhaustibility of wildlife), *incongruity* (the contrast between landscapes fit for the gods and their mean and petty human inhabitants), and *melancholy* (owing to the absence or transience of man and his works).[6] But such responses were not new, nor were they confined to the West. They were equally appropriate in early settlements in the East, in forest as in prairie, in the salt marshes of Massachusetts as in the Sierras. America has usually struck visitors as vast, wild, and empty, formless and unfinished, and subject to violent extremes. A few examples will illustrate each trait.

Size

No aspect of the American scene is more notorious than the scale of the landscape and the size of objects in it. Eyes accustomed to European vistas and artifacts may take years to adjust, as one visitor put it, to "the unnerving bigness of everything"[7] in America. " 'Too big,' said one of our Frenchmen, peering a mile down into the Grand Canyon; but he was wrong. In England something of that size would be absurd, but there it is in scale (although the American woman who wrote in the visitors' book before us 'Very pretty' was probably cutting it down to size too far)."[8] The initial shock is the same in every kind of landscape; "the streets remain streets, the mountains mountains, and the rivers rivers–and yet one feels at a loss before them, simply because their scale is such that the normal adjustment of man-to-environment becomes impossible."[9]

So it has seemed from the start. Weary weeks on the Atlantic, eyes strained between sky and ocean, did not habituate travelers to the continental scale of America. They expected monotony from the sea, but not from the land. West Indian landforms contrasted pleasantly with the solitude of the voyage. But the continent itself dismayed them; instead of circumnavigable islands, America proved to be an intractable hunk of land, more and more alien, interminable, and unrewarding the farther they moved into it. And it conformed less and less with European preconceptions about promised lands, visions chiefly Arcadian, insular, and small-scale. The long search for the Northwest Passage was more than a yearning for the fabled East; it was also an expression of active distaste for the American impedi-

5. David Lowenthal and Hugh C. Prince: English Landscape Tastes, *Geographical Review* 55 (1965):186-222; reference on p. 187.
6. Howard Mumford Jones, *O Strange New World* (New York, 1964), pp. 379-86.

7. Peter Shepheard, "A Philadelphia Enquirer," *Listener* (May 9, 1963):787-89; reference on p. 787.
8. George Seddon, "Hurricane View of U.S.," *Observer* (London, Nov. 18, 1962).
9. C. Lévi-Strauss, *Tristes tropiques,* tr. John Russell (New York, 1961), p. 83.

ment. Only the trapper, the lumberman, the religious fanatic, and the most optimistic imperialist waxed enthusiastic over the endless forests and swamps, the prairies and deserts, of North America.

Limitless frontiers did attract a few. Jefferson thought the "smooth blue horizon" seen where the Potomac clove the Blue Ridge was a view "worth a voyage across the Atlantic."[10] Eighteenth-century fashion admired panoramic views and primitive nature; many paid homage to America on both counts. But they enjoyed landscapes more as set pieces than as real places. The botanist Bartram dutifully gazed "with rapture and astonishment . . . [at the] amazing prospect of grandeur" in the southern Appalachians yet confided he felt as lonely as Nebuchadnezzar, "constrained to roam in the mountains and wilderness."[11] . . .

"The American imitates nature, with whose great works he is in constant communication," said an observer a century ago. "Only an appreciation of the grandeur of such a fall as that of Niagara, could fit a man to construct the bridge that spans its river."[12] Eighteenth-century European scientists had earlier asserted that nature and man in the New World were more puny than in the Old. "In America, there is not an animal that can be compared to the elephant," asserted Buffon, and "all the animals which have been transported from Europe . . . the horse, the ass, the sheep, the goat, the hog, etc., have become smaller . . . [All species] shrink and diminish under a niggardly sky and an unprolific land, thinly peopled with wandering savages."[13] Jefferson and others took great pains to refute these taunts, citing the elk and the moose, and mammoth bones discovered in Ohio.

Pride thus paved the way for a cult of bigness. The dinosaur became emblematic. Americans soon boasted that they had the largest animals, the longest rivers, the highest mountains, the tallest trees. And they created gargantuan structures to match. New York skyscrapers and the Golden Gate and Verrazano bridges reflect ambitions of the same order as that of the medieval cathedral builders who aimed at record heights. The best-known American structures are monumental. Boulder Dam, Fort Knox, the Mormon Temple, the Empire State Building are admired less for their efficiency or beauty than for their size. Size is preferred even in things that might be better small. But local planners can hardly be blamed for thinking big when the biggest projects get the largest federal allocations. They "want to see big, really important open spaces," as one planner put it, lest their funds be "wasted and frittered away on a bunch of little playgrounds and parks."[14] . . .

The prevailing gridiron pattern, with straight streets at right angles, also accentuates size and space. In New York, Sartre's "glance met nothing but space. It

---

10. Thomas Jefferson, *Notes on the State of Virginia* (1787), ed. William Peden (Chapel Hill, N.C., 1955), p. 19.

11. William Bartram, *Travels of William Bartram* (1791), ed. Mark Van Doren (New York: Dover Publications, n.d.), pp. 292-93.

12. Quoted in Perry Miller, *The Life of the Mind in America* (New York, 1965), p. 304.

13. Count de Buffon, *Natural History, General and Particular,* tr. William Smellie, 3rd ed., 9 vols. (London, 1791), as quoted in Gilbert Chinard, "Eighteenth Century Theories on America as a Human Habitat," *Proc. Amer. Phil. Soc.* 91 (1947):27-57; reference on pp. 30-31.

14. William H. Whyte, "The Politics of Open Space," in *Resources, the Metropolis, and the Land-Grant University: Proceedings of the Conference on Natural Resources,* University of Massachusetts, January-May 1963 (edited by A. J. W. Scheffey), *Univ. of Massachusetts, College of Agriculture, Cooperative Extension Service, Publ. 410,* n.d., pp. 22-27; reference on p. 26.

slid over blocks of identical houses . . . to lose itself in empty space, at the horizon. . . . The moment you set foot on" a Manhattan avenue "you understand that it has to go on to Boston or Chicago."[15] In smaller towns the grid emphasizes every aspect of the terrain and draws the eye away from the houses out to the lonely horizon.

Wildness

The nature of America, like its scale, leaves the spectator alone in an alien world—alien both in what it contains and in what it lacks. America is still full of unfamiliar, undomesticated, unclassifiable things, "a waste and howling wilderness," as Michael Wigglesworth described it in the seventeenth century, "where none inhabited but hellish fiends, and brutish men."[16] Even more than these strange shapes and species, the virtual absence of man's artifacts appalled viewers. Indians were few, nomadic, ephemeral; their works scarcely detracted from the powerful impression of emptiness. . . .

Perhaps the most cogent summary of American wildness is Gertrude Stein's: "In the United States there is more space where nobody is than where anybody is. That is what makes America what it is."[17] To be sure, other countries have uninhabited wildernesses; those of Tibet, of Chile, of Algeria, for example, may be more extensive. What gives American emptiness its special poignance is its pervasiveness in ordinary landscapes. In a night train on the outskirts of a Kansas town, the traveler realizes that "beyond is America . . . and no one there. . . . It's only ten, fifteen minutes since you've left a thriving town but life has already been swallowed up in that ocean of matter which is and will remain as wild as it was made"[18] (Fig. 1).

Over much of the country, man and his structures seem to be insignificant or temporary features of the landscape (Fig. 2). Even the sturdy New England farmhouse looks to many Europeans "like a temporary wooden structure hastily erected against the elements and marauding savages."[19] But it is in the metropolis that impermanence is most sharply felt. An English essayist recalls "lonely moments in some American city at night when you are on the edge of nightmare" and begin to fear that the place is "no more than a huddle of people . . . round a camp fire who will have packed up and moved on . . . in the morning."[20]

Formlessness

Compared with Old World landscapes, those of America appear generally ragged, indefinite, and confused; parts stand out at the expense of a unified whole. Over much of the country topographic features are large, vague, and indefinitely structured, and vegetation tends to cloak patterns of terrain. The quality of American light is also partly responsible for the absence of clearly defined structure. Frequently bright, hard, undiminished by moisture, it seems to separate and isolate

15. Jean-Paul Sartre, "New York, the Colonial City," in *Literary and Philosophical Essays,* tr. Annette Michelson (New York, 1955), pp. 118-24; reference on pp. 119 and 122.
16. Michael Wigglesworth, "God's Controversy with New-England (1662), *Proc. Massachusetts Hist. Soc.,* 1871-1873, p. 83. See also Alan Heimert, "Puritanism, the Wilderness, and the Frontier," *New England Quarterly* 26 (1953): 361-82.
17. Gertrude Stein, *The Geographical History of America* (New York, 1936), pp. 17-18.
18. Jacques Barzun, *God's Country and Mine* (Boston, 1954), p. 3.
19. Stewart Alsop, "America the Ugly," *Saturday Evening Post* (June 23, 1962), pp. 8 and 10; reference on p. 10.
20. V. S. Pritchett, "Second Steps," *New Statesman* (July 30, 1965), pp. 155-56; reference on p. 155.

FIG. 1. Relics of transient occupance—an abandoned cement works near Snelling, California.

FIG. 2
Thomas Hart Benton's "Boom Town." Rochester Memorial Art Gallery.

features rather than to join and compose them.

Man's structures mirror nature. Boundaries between city and county are blurred and smudged. Localities neither begin nor end, and little seems fixed. Unfenced, "the little houses sit lightly, barely engaged with the ground and the landscape," as Banham has put it.[21] Le Corbusier felt that the absence of framing walls and fences gave the American landscape a pleasing amplitude.[22] But most observers tend, with Henry James, to inveigh against "this diffused vagueness of separation . . . between the . . . [place] you are in and the . . . [place] you are not in," and to deplore "the indefinite extension of all spaces . . . ; the enlargement of every opening, . . . the substitution of . . . far perspectives and resounding voids for enclosing walls."[23]

Visual flux, with continual rebuilding, is the rule in the skyscraper city. As Kouwenhoven argues, "the logic of cage construction" is that of something "always complete but never finished." He concludes that America "is not an artifact; . . . America is process."[24]

But the process produces artifacts, even they are not rooted in place. They create America's most distinctive look—casual chaos (Fig. 3). A French anthropologist provides a classic account of the genesis of the vacant lot: "Patches of dead ground . . . were once owned, and once briefly worked, by Man. Then he went off somewhere else and left behind him a battleground strewn with the relics of his brief tenure. . . . [On it] there has arisen a new, disorderly, and monotonous vegetation."[25] From railroad cutting to riverbank, from city park to town dump, this landscape engulfs the country. More ragged than the primeval wilderness, it divides and subverts any ordered scene. Hence Dickens' description of an open space in Washington as "a melancholy piece of waste ground with frowzy grass, which looks like a small piece of country that has taken to drinking, and has quite lost itself."[26]

Extremes

America also strikes observers as subject to terrifying—or exhiliarating—extremes. Nature here is not only on a larger scale but more violent than the early settlers had ever experienced. They endured torrid summers and bitter winters and despairingly noted savage vagaries of climate. Within this framework of excess, tornado, flood, and drought often wreaked havoc. And extremes are not confined to climate and weather; a modern visitor remarks that "the whole of American life is tempered by the threats of . . . overwhelming natural excesses. . . . In almost every State there are turbulences of scenery, grotesque formations or things of feverishly exaggerated size."[27] . . .

To the excesses of nature have been added those of man. In their buildings, as in their behavior, Americans resemble the

21. Reyner Banham, "Urbanism: USA," *Architectural Rev.* 130 (London, 1961):303-5; reference on p. 305.
22. [Charles-Edouard] Le Corbusier, *When the Cathedrals Were White,* tr Francis E. Hyslop, Jr. (New York, London, Toronto: McGraw-Hill Paperbacks, 1964).
23. James, *American Scene,* pp. 161-162.
24. John A. Kouwenhoven, "What's 'American' about America," in *The Beer Can by the Highway* (Garden City, N.Y., 1961), pp. 39-73; reference on pp. 49-50 and 72-73. See also Jean Gottmann, "Why the Skyscraper?" *Geogr. Rev.* 56 (1966):190-212.
25. Lévi-Strauss, *Tristes tropiques,* p. 99.
26. Charles Dickens, *American Notes, and Pictures from Italy* (1842 and 1846) (London, New York, Toronto, 1957), p. 116.
27. James Morris, *Coast to Coast* (London, 1962), p. 41.

FIG. 3. Decoration begins somewhere else. Fresno, California.

landscape they inhabit—exaggerated, vehement, powerful, unpredictable.

Insiders and Outsiders

Vast and wild, teeming yet lonely, formless, violent, and extreme—no wonder America seemed to the first Europeans like the original Creation, now chaos, now garden. "In the beginning all the world was America," John Locke said;[28] the phrase conveys the threat as well as the promise of the New World. This was a land that simultaneously attracted and repelled, but in the end had to be brought to terms. Empty, it must be filled; unfinished, it must be completed; wild, it must be tamed.

To the Elizabethans, America was simply a vision; to the settlers that vision was a challenge requiring action. Action became so strong a component of the American character that landscapes were often hardly seen at all; they were only acted on. Immediate necessity made a mockery of mere contemplation. To wrest a living from the soil, to secure frontiers against hostile forces, seemed to demand full attention. Appreciation of the landscape itself, apart from its practical uses, was disdained as pointless and effete.

The irrelevance of "scenic values" to real life is dramatized by Mark Twain. After a typical tourist blurb about majestic panoramas, Twain turns around and derides the tourist view as artificial, self-conscious, above all ignorant. The tourist only enjoys the view because he is an outsider and doesn't understand it. Before he becomes familiar with the Mississippi, Twain's pilot enjoys the stock re-

28. John Locke, "Essay Concerning the True Original Extent and End of Civil Government," in *Two Treatises of Government* (1690) (Everyman edit.; London, 1924), p. 140.

sponses to a glowing sunset on the silvery water. But after he learns the river, he looks at the same scene "without rapture" and comments, "This sun means that we are going to have wind tomorrow; . . . that slanting mark on the water refers to a bluff reef which is going to kill somebody's steamboat one of these nights; . . . that silver streak in the shadow of the forest is the 'break' from a new snag."[29] . . .

In short, the landscape is worthy of its hire. Its ultimate critics are its residents, not its visitors. Such is the lesson of William James's "On a Certain Blindness in Human Beings."

> Journeying in the mountains of North Carolina, I passed by a large number of "coves" . . . which had been newly cleared and planted. The impression on my mind was one of unmitigated squalor. The settler had . . . cut down the more manageable trees, and left their charred stumps. . . . The larger trees he had girdled and killed . . . and had set up a tall zigzag rail fence around the scene of his havoc. . . . Finally, he had irregularly planted the intervals between the stumps and trees with Indian corn. . . . The forest had been destroyed; and what had "improved" it out of existence was hideous, a sort of ulcer, without a single element of artificial grace to make up for the loss of Nature's beauty.

Then a mountaineer told James, "Why, we ain't happy here, unless we are getting one of these coves under cultivation."

> I instantly felt that I had been losing the whole inward significance of the situation. . . . To me the clearings [were] . . . naught but . . . a mere ugly picture on the retina. . . . But, when *they* looked on the hideous stumps, what they thought of was personal victory. The chips, the girdled trees, and the vile split rails spoke of honest sweat, persistent toil and final reward. (Fig. 4)

29. Mark Twain, *Life on the Mississippi* (1875) (New York and London, 1929), pp. 79-80.

And he points his moral: "The spectator's judgment is sure to miss the root of the matter, and to possess no truth."[30]

Many Americans would still agree. The editor of *Landscape* derides "beautification" as empty and idle. Abandon "the spectator stance," he urges, and ask instead what chances the landscape offers "for making a living . . . for freedom of choice of action . . . for meaningful relationships"–all emphatically *non*visual standards. And he concludes that "we should never tinker with the landscape without thinking of those who live in the midst of it. . . . What the spectator wants or does not want is of small account."[31] . . .

Ideal versus Reality

Most Americans reserve such esthetic considerations for select landscapes only. Thus the comment of a visitor from the Great Plains on first seeing the Hudson River Highlands: "It looks like scenery should look!"[32] The gulf between ideal and reality, between "how things *ought* to look" and the easy acceptance of surroundings not remotely resembling that ideal–this cleavage takes many forms. Each illumines a facet of national behavior of value for environmental design and planning. (I do not mean to imply that any of these is unique to this country,

30. William James, "On a Certain Blindness in Human Beings," in *Talks to Teachers on Psychology: and to Students on Some of Life's Ideals* (1899) (New York: The Norton Library, 1958), pp. 149-69; reference on pp. 150-52. I have developed this theme elsewhere ("Not Every Prospect Pleases: What is Our Criterion for Scenic Beauty?" *Landscape* 12 (Winter 1962-63):19-23; reference on pp. 21-22).

31. [J. B. Jackson] "Notes and Comments," *Landscape* 13 (Winter 1963-64):1-3; references on pp. 1-2.

32. E. J. Kahn, Jr., "The Hudson River," *Holiday* 40 (1966):40-55 and 83-89; reference on p. 42.

FIG. 4. The pioneer's delight. Near Monticello, Virginia.

only that they are clearly recognizable as American attitudes.) Let us look briefly at a few of them.

The Present Sacrificed to the Glorious Future

. . . Americans build for tomorrow, not for today. They *"love* their country, not, indeed, *as it is,* but *as it will be,"* a traveler noted in the 1830's; "they do not love the land of their fathers; but they are sincerely attached to that which their children are destined to inherit."[33] A New York State settler challenged an eighteenth-century visitor to "return in ten years and you will not recognize this . . . wild and savage . . . [district]. Our humble log houses will be replaced by fine dwellings. Our fields will be fenced in, and the stumps will have disappeared."[34] . . .

The current American scene is not a finished landscape, but an embryo of future greatness. Meanwhile we endure protracted labor pains. Vast areas of our cities are occupied by wrecking crews and bulldozers, sand and gravel, rubble and structural elements—semipermanent wastelands dedicated to Tomorrow. A large proportion of the cityscape is in painful gestation at any time. The vaguest tidings of Urban Renewal, if sufficiently sweetened and signposted, persuade the citizen to suffer the laying waste of his city for years on end (Fig. 5). . . .

Living in the future, Americans are

33. Francis J. Grund, *The Americans in Their Moral, Social, and Political Relations,* 2 vols. (London, 1837), vol. 2, pp. 263-64.

34. Michel-Guillaume St. Jean de Crèvecoeur, *Journey into Northern Pennsylvania and the State of New York* (in French, 1801), tr. Clarissa Spencer Bostelmann (Ann Arbor, Mich., 1964), p. 493.

FIG. 5. The present yields to the envisaged future. The Embarcadero, San Francisco, California.

predisposed to accept present structures that are makeshift, flimsy, and transient, obsolete from the start. "Downtowns and suburbs still bear the imprint of frontier-camp design," Pushkarev points out.[35] Elevated transit lines, overhead wiring, exterior fire escapes, are among the fixtures that stem from that spirit. We live in throwaway stage sets.

But the habit of discarding buildings almost as soon as they are put up has its compensations. "If something is built wrong," writes an observer of Los Angeles, "it doesn't matter much. Everyone expects it to come down in a decade or two."[36] Because we invest so lightly in our buildings, we can–and do–experiment easily. Innovations embellish the whole countryside.

The Present Diminished by Contrast with an Idealized Past[37]

Old Sturbridge Village, the Minute Man National Historic Monument, the Trustees of Reservations, the Society for the Preservation of New England Antiquities–such Massachusetts-based institutions all testify to our wish to preserve, and if necessary to manufacture, an idealized Historyland as a sanctuary from the awful present. That past includes not only historic buildings and places but also

35. Boris Pushkarev, "Scale and Design in a New Environment," in *Who Designs America?*, ed. Laurence B. Holland (Garden City, N.Y.: Anchor Original, 1966), pp. 86-119; reference on p. 111.
36. Quoted in Christopher Rand, "L.A., The Ultimate City: I–Upward and Outward," *New Yorker* (Oct. 1, 1966), pp. 56-65+; reference on p. 56.
37. See David Lowenthal, "The American Way of History," *Columbia University Forum* (1966):27-32.

a pastoral countryside and a sublime wilderness.

These romantic tastes are by no means unique to America. What is striking is how fast they took root here, after our initial rejection of whatever was old or natural. As early as 1844 the American Art Union promoted the sale of Hudson River School paintings as an antidote to the abysmal environment of city folk: "a painted landscape is almost essential to preserve a healthy tone to the spirits, lest they forget in the wilderness of bricks . . . the pure delights of nature and a country life."[38] And this at a time when the countryside was half an hour's walk from New York City! . . .

The visitor to historic sites seldom cares whether he is looking at a real relic or a fake. A Charleston resident contends that "if you point to an alley and say 'Catfish Row,' visitors are perfectly satisfied and return North happy."[39] As a promoter of Lincoln's supposed birthplace remarked in the 1890's, "Lincoln was born in a log cabin, weren't he? Well, one cabin is as good as another."[40] Even a replica of Uncle Tom's fictional cabin meets the demand for historic atmosphere.

As treasured heritages, History and Nature are not only altered to fit "a dream-image of an immutable past";[41] they have also become objects of isolated pleasure and reverence, fenced off and enshrined in historical museums and wilderness preserves, out of touch with the rest of the landscape (Fig. 6). By contrast with the idealized past, the present workaday environment is considered not worth looking at.

Nature is likewise thought preferable to artifice. The favored landscapes are wild; landscapes altered or disturbed or built on by man are considered beneath attention or beyond repair. Adoration of the wilderness, like idealization of the past, focuses attention on the remote and the special to the neglect of the nearby and the familiar[42] (Fig. 7). . . .

Individual Features Emphasized at the Expense of Aggregates

"Featurism," as defined by an Australian architect, is "the subordination of the essential whole and the accentuation of selected separate features. . . . A featurist city has little or no consistency of atmospheric quality and plenty of numbers on the guide map directing the visitor to features of interest. . . . Each new building is determined to be arresting."[43]

Accentuation of features is perhaps less deliberate in America than in Australia. But it has been pervasive since the first settlements. Weak relationships mark even the old New England clustered villages. The houses may be homogeneous in style, but they are fragmented by distance and by the absence of any binding framework. As an English observer put it, they stand out around their central greens "like plucked chickens." Other

38. "Annual Report, Transactions of the American Art Union for the Promotion of Fine Arts in the United States for the Year 1844" (New York, n.d.), pp. 6-8, as quoted on p. 64 in John William Ward, "The Politics of Design," in *Who Designs America?*, pp. 51-85.

39. Philip Hamburger, *An American Notebook* (New York, 1965), p. 32.

40. David R. Barbee, letter to the editor, *Washington Post,* Oct. 11, 1948, as quoted in Charles B. Hosmer, Jr., *Presence of the Past* (New York, 1965), p. 141.

41. Walter Muir Whitehill, "Promoted to Glory . . . ," in *With Heritage So Rich: A Report of a Special Committee on Historic Preservation . . .* (New York, 1966), pp. 35-44; reference on p. 44.

42. David Lowenthal, "Is Wilderness 'Paradise Enow'? Images of Nature in America," *Columbia University Forum* 7 (1964):34-40.

43. Robin Boyd, *The Australian Ugliness* (Melbourne, 1960), pp. 9-11.

FIG. 6. America's historylands are typically trim, well-kept, and protected. Smith's Clove, Orange County, New York.

FIG. 7
Man and Nature compete for attention near Aaronsburg, Pennsylvania.

places are only collections of heterogeneous buildings marooned in wastelands (Figs. 8 and 9). It is the same in cities. No office structure in New York lines up its cornice or parapet with another. New York's Lever and Seagram buildings are "each elegantly and humanely designed within its boundaries," but they are separated, the visitor notes, by "a rush of cars, browbeaten shrubs, dumb pavements. . . . The art of making a pattern in the environment is entirely neglected."[44] . . .

Noting the contrast between our new buildings and the subtopia around them, an English architect asked his American colleagues "how it was that they could see their splendid, shining buildings put up in surroundings that would make a Balkan sanitary inspector blench." They replied that "it was surprising what you could get used to, and anyway they were so busy doing architecture they had not yet had the time to worry about the spaces between."[45] But the condition has other roots: our fluid social structure, our disposable dwellings, the absence of strong local ties. . . .

But American structures sometimes fit together in an unselfconscious manner. House types in a small town (Fig. 10), neon signs along a highway, the skyscrapers of Manhattan, relate to one another in a fashion celebrated in the paintings of Charles Demuth, Stuart Davis, and Robert Rauschenberg,[46] which organize a large number of seemingly unrelated things in a single comprehensive design.

44. Ian Nairn: The American Landscape (New York, 1965), pp. 13 and 3, respectively.
45. Sir Hugh Casson, "Critique of Our Expanding 'Subtopia,'" *New York Times Magazine* (Oct. 27, 1957), pp. 31+; reference on p. 36.
46. G. A. Jellicoe, *Studies in Landscape Design,* 2 vols. (London, New York, Toronto, 1966), vol. 2, caption to Plate 80.

The Nearby and the Typical Neglected for the Remote and the Spectacular

The National Parks were originally set up to enshrine the freaks and wonders of nature, and park literature still touts the Grand Canyon, the Grand Tetons, Yellowstone, and Yosemite as unique. If they were typical, who would bother to go and see them? And so with the works of man. If they are not unique, they are valueless, quickly passed by and soon forgotten. Litchfield, in the western Connecticut highlands, is heralded as the *ne plus ultra* of Federalist gracious living, while a score of nearby villages of almost equal grace go nearly unnoticed. Their counterparts in neighboring New York State, crossroad and railroad villages with massive, high-gabled roofs, remain unappreciated as visual entities because no architectural accolade has come to the individual houses.

In the West, neglect of the general in favor of a single focus of merit goes further still. Half a century ago Puget Sound boasted several attractive cities and many livable towns. Seattle alone is still alive. Up and down the coast the moribund harbors and decayed buildings of Bellingham and Port Angeles, Everett and La Conner, speak not only of the passing of enterprise, but of the feebleness of local spirit. The sense of neglect and abandonment is keenest in Tacoma, the region's second city, which used to be thought of as a Boston to Seattle's New York. The Tacoman sense of identity is now about on a par with that of Yonkers or Hoboken. Once the most glamorous city in the Pacific Northwest, Tacoma today appeals to one refugee from the East mainly "because it's such a *nothing* town. This gives it a real charm."[47]

47. Charles T. Michener, "Why Would Anyone Want to Live in Tacoma?" *Seattle* 3 (1966):

FIG. 8. Assorted objects on a village green. Ancram, New York.

FIG. 9. Village panorama from above the railroad tracks. Croton-on-Hudson, New York.

FIG. 10. Proportion without pretentiousness. Ancram, New York.

Where urban visual qualities *are* a matter of pride, Americans are apt to allude to the general setting rather than to anything near at hand. Seattleites daily admire Mount Rainier, fifty miles away, while ignoring the tawdriness under their noses. Above the smog in the Berkeley Hills people enjoy the lights of San Francisco, fifteen miles across the Bay. The greatest feature of Jersey City is the New York skyline. And New Yorkers themselves appreciate Gotham mainly when they desert the squalid streets to circumnavigate Manhattan at fifty miles an hour on an elevated parkway. . . .

18-25 and 46-47; reference on p. 46. See also M. R. Wolfe, *Towns, Time, and Regionalism* (Seattle: University of Washington, Department of Urban Planning, Urban Planning and Development Series, 1963).

Scenic Appreciation Serious and Self-Conscious

For many people "seeing" is an activity of specific purpose and fixed duration, as in the cartoon of the maid, about to draw curtains across the window, who turns to ask, "Is Madam through with the moon?" We dichotomize experience as we zone places: certain intervals are set aside for looking at things; the rest of the time we are blind.

From these habits of mind and sight scenic views inevitably take their character. Americans enhance preferred views by landscaping and highlight them with identifying markers. But scenic promoters do not merely inform the traveler that he is now crossing Chipmunk Creek or ascending Hogback Hill; they give him a thumbnail sketch of the geology and natural history of the area, a disquisition on the domestic economy of the Indians, and an arrow on a trunk pointing out the route of Washington's retreat or Grant's advance. The signs along Virginia's Skyline Drive are so numerous, prominent, artful, and information-laden that the conscientious traveler is not so much seeing a landscape as reading a book or viewing a museum diorama.

Like exits from a modern highway, the scenic experience is not only signposted but numbered; to get the most out of a landscape, one is supposed to see a prearranged sequence, as along Boston's Freedom Trail. But the art of ordering experience is most fully developed for views of nature. "A trail should have a definite purpose," the Forest Service notes. "Upon reaching his goal, the traveler should have a feeling of accomplishment . . . of having 'found' most of the interest points along the way, of having struggled to the top of the overlook where he can rest and enjoy his prize—the scenic view spread out before him."[48] . . .

The well-blazed trail, the obstacle-course mentality, and the segregation of scenery within quotation marks tend ultimately to make any scenic view appear contrived. In such circumstances, to "beautify" is merely to plug in replicas of esthetic treasures, like the giant-size billboard copy of Gainsborough's "Blue Boy" along a New Jersey highway. We destroy by overemphasis as surely as by neglect and vandalism.

Comments on the American scene are often doctrinaire and imprecatory. City and country, suburb and slum, whatever critics see appalls them. The loss of natural and historic treasures; the ubiquity of litter, both the used-up old and the shoddy new; the absence of vital or well-integrated human landscapes—these are defects on which designers have moralized at length. Many of the remedies they recommend would require wholesale reform of American character and behavior. But values are no easier to alter than habitats. . . .

It used to be said that "the views of nature held by any people determine all their institutions."[49] But it may make more sense to stand this statement on its head: our whole way of life determines our views of nature. To be effective, therefore, planning and design should be grounded on intimate knowledge of the ways people think and feel about environment; this calls for a substantial familiarity with social and intellectual history, with psychology and philosophy, with art and anthropology. All these fields contribute to our knowledge of how we see the world we live in, how vision and value affect action, and how action alters institutions. . . .

48. "The American Outdoors," *U.S. Forest Service Misc. Publ. No. 1000* (Washington, D.C., 1965), p. 51.

49. Ralph Waldo Emerson, "English Traits" (1856), in *The Selected Writings of Ralph Waldo Emerson* (Modern Library T14; New York, 1950), pp. 523-690; reference on p. 548.

Geographical Knowledge and American Images of the Louisiana Territory / *John L. Allen*

On July 4, 1803, through the medium of the public press, the news that the United States had gained possession of that vast territory comprising much of the western drainage of the Mississippi River and known as Louisiana[1] burst upon an American populace almost totally unprepared to understand what they had acquired. One observer, writing to a major Washington newspaper, said of Louisiana geography that "all is vague conjecture and uncertain calculation."[2] And another writer of the same time noted that "there are vast regions . . . of which no nations know anything . . . there is no certainty whether it be land or sea, mountain or plain."[3] Even Thomas Jefferson, unwitting architect of the purchase, could say only that the "information as to the country is very incomplete."[4]

Despite the fuzziness and inadequacy of geographical lore on Louisiana, the experience of more than a century of exploration in that area was not completely lost to literate Americans of 1803-1804. Ever since the French missionary-explorer Jacques Marquette discovered the Missouri River and named it as the logical pathway to the Pacific Ocean,[5] explorers operating with the sanctions of French, British, and Spanish colonial authority had penetrated the trans-Mississippi region, hoping to find—by way of the Missouri River and its hypothetical connections with westward-flowing waters—the fabled passage across North America that had been the goal of exploration since the New World was first recognized as a barrier in Europe's path to the Orient. Other rivers of the territory, such as the Red and Arkansas, were partially explored, often with the hope that they might provide trade connections with the assumed rich Kingdom of New Mexico. This drive of the European colonial powers toward the west provided experiences and literature which were vital in establishing the images or patterns of belief about the nature and content of Louisiana in American minds.

1. Although neither term is completely accurate in a purely historical sense, "Louisiana" and "Louisiana Territory" will be used to refer only to that portion of the Mississippi basin between the Continental Divide and the Mississippi itself.
2. *The National Intelligencer* (Washington), August 10, 1803.
3. Charles B. Brown, "An Address to the Government of the United States on the Cession of Louisiana," (Philadelphia, 1803), p. 16.
4. Jefferson to Governor Breckinridge, 12 August 1803, Jefferson Papers, Library of Congress, 134: fols. 23144-46.
5. Marquette began the chain of exploration up the Missouri when he described that river as heading in an area close to another river which flowed to the Pacific. See R. G. Thwaites, ed., *The Jesuit Relations,* 72 vols. (Cleveland, 1907), 59:87-163.

Reproduced (with omissions) by permission from *Western Historical Quarterly* 2 (1971):151-70. For elaboration see also the author's *Passage through the Garden: Lewis and Clark and the Image of the American Northwest* (Urbana: University of Illinois Press, 1975).

Geographical lore that was characteristically American was mingled with the French, British, and Spanish geographical knowledge of the continent.[6] Like the European powers, the young republic was interested in the passage to India.[7] Her motives were both commercial and territorial. While the explorers of France, Britain, and Spain had sought the will-o'-the-wisp that was the Northwest Passage, the frontier society that became the United States had been "realizing westward." By the time of the purchase of Louisiana, the vanguard of the American migration had already reached the eastern border of that new territory. . . .

The way that men perceive or understand their environment is significant for explanations of human spatial activity. At no time in the history of the United States had this statement been more true than it was at the opening of the nineteenth century. By the time that American acquisition of a major portion of the trans-Mississippi West became a reality through the purchase of Louisiana, many elements of the American population were already advocating expansion of the republic into that territory.[8] What would later be called "manifest destiny" was becoming a force in American thought and action; the expansion of America into the West, hesitant at first and then gaining momentum, began. In all its phases, this expansion was conditioned by the geographical images that had formed in American minds relative to the lands beyond the frontier of the Mississippi, particularly those images that dealt with the agricultural potential of the West and with the prospects of an easy transcontinental communication system via the western rivers.

As is the case with so many geographical ideas, those images of the West that formed first were among the last to fade. An examination of American geographical thought about Louisiana for the period during which Americans were beginning to articulate their views of the area may help to interpret the conditioning influence of the initial images of the West on later exploration and settlement. . . .

The United States in 1804 was an agricultural nation with an administration in Washington based on the Jeffersonian assumptions of the ideal agrarian republic. In spite of the fact that among some segments of American society—particularly in the urban centers of the Northeast—agrarian expansionism was viewed with disfavor,[9] most American images of the

6. This lore was not necessarily different in content from other lore on the West. It was, however, "geoamerican" knowledge, interpreted by Americans in ways that were distinctly different from the interpretations given it by other peoples. See John K. Wright, "What's American about American Geography," in *Human Nature in Geography* (Cambridge, 1966), 124-39.

7. American interest in the passage is nowhere more evident than in the objective of the Lewis and Clark Expedition of 1804-06 as stated by Jefferson: "The object of your mission is to explore the Missouri river, & such principal stream of it, as, by it's course and communication with the waters of the Pacific ocean, whether the Columbia, Oregan, Colorado or any other river may offer the most direct & practicable water communication across this continent for the purposes of commerce." Jefferson to Lewis, 20 June 1803, Jefferson Papers, 132: fols. 22884-87.

8. An authority on America's attitudes about manifest destiny has written that "sober-minded elements in both political parties in the period prior to the War of 1812 consigned such revealers of God's purpose [those who favored western expansion as the natural right of the Republic] to the outer edge of the lunatic fringe." Frederick Merk, *Manifest Destiny and Mission in American History* (New York, 1963), p. 13. This might well be an accurate statement but it is misleading. Many historians have failed to recognize the difference between opinion of the elite which was nonexpansionist and the opinion of the nonelite or folk opinion which tended to be expansionist in nature.

9. The greatest volume of criticism of the administration's action in acquiring Louisiana was found in the newspapers and pamphlets of Bos-

Louisiana territory seem to have been colored by the feeling that the United States must maintain vast areas for the expansion of an agricultural population if she were to remain a republic. The majority opinions among Americans on the land quality of the West, then, were based on hope and optimism—a hope that the lands to the west would provide a firm base for the agrarian republic and an optimism that this must be the case.

Detractors had put forth the view that the West was "an absolute barren" or a "dreary tract" and indeed, some of the reports of the most recent explorers in the West (insofar as these reports were available) could have substantiated this notion. But these critics were not in the majority. The predominating concept of the West was that it was indeed a garden, with extremely fertile soil, climates benign, soft, and salubrious.[10] Immense plains might, as many accounts put it, stretch as far as the southern ocean, but these plains were not barren, sandy nor even partially arid. They were verdant, lush, teeming with game and, most important, available for the spread of an agricultural population. The rivers flowed among the most beautiful dales; the Mississippi and other rivers of Louisiana were analogous to Niles which diffused the fertility of Egypt from their banks. The West was full of hope.

Like the views of the land itself, the ideas on what the land contained were seemingly based on this agrarian tradition. For centuries, wealth in gold, gems, and other precious minerals had been sought toward the sunset, but in the American images of the West in 1804, few elements of the eldorado remained. The choicest luxuries of the West were the lush vegetation and the salubrious climate. Some authorities might have held that the lands of the West contained precious minerals in their bowels, but the folk emphasis on mineral wealth was more practical.[11] The West contained lead, iron, and salt, basic needs of a frontier agricultural people; gold and silver and gems could come later.

According to what seems to have been the majority opinion, the area of Louisiana was a well-watered region, with many streams available for millsites, and rivers available for transportation.[12] Little was actually known about major rivers such as the Red, the Arkansas, the Missouri or the Columbia; virtually nothing was known of the Kansas, Platte, Yellow-

ton, Hartford, New York, and Philadelphia. Slightly less than 25 percent of the references to the territory in those papers commented on any advantages to be gained by an expansion of American population into the purchase lands. The picture is different for newspapers from rural locations in the same general area of the Northeast. More than two-thirds of the references to the value of the purchase in those papers viewed the acquisition of new agricultural territories favorably.

10. Out of a total of 134 items related to Louisiana or the West in the 1804 materials consulted, 54 items made direct reference to land quality. In these 54 items, the word "fertile" appeared 36 times; "benign," 14 times; "salubrious," 27 times. "Verdant," "fine," "beautiful," each appeared between 5 and 10 times, and "lush" was used 3 times. By contrast, the words "barren," "sterile," or "waste" appeared twice, three times, and once respectively. The word "desert" was not used in any of the 54 land quality descriptions.

11. In spite of the fact that some of the more important source materials mentioned the wealth of precious and semiprecious minerals to be found in the West, only five out of twenty-nine references to minerals in the 1804 publication referred to precious metals or stones.

12. A total of twenty-one items provided some description of the rivers and streams of Louisiana and in these twenty items, "well-watered" appeared thirteen times. In none of the twenty-one items was it suggested that Louisiana was water deficient. Fifteen of the items mentioned either long-range navigation or millsite location as advantages of the rivers of Louisiana.

stone, Snake, and others.[13] Americans tended to think about the western rivers in general terms, and all the rivers of Louisiana were apparently accorded the same characteristics of length, size, and navigability that had been mentioned in accounts of the Mississippi and Missouri.[14] Like many other things in the West, the rivers were seen as having majestic proportions:[15]

> Each step which one takes from East to West, the size of all objects increases tenfold in volume. It seems that nature has made this corner of the terrestrial globe the most favorite of its immense sphere. The products which one discovers there in proportion as one goes into the interior are more majestic, more beautiful than elsewhere.

There was also a gap in American geographic knowledge relative to the lakes of western North America. The concepts of great lakes or inland seas in the western interior, an important feature in the geographical lore of earlier times, does not seem to have formed a major element in the American images of Louisiana.[16] The fact that some few Americans held to the earlier notions of huge inland seas was important to the overall nature of the patterns of belief about the territory, for from the inland lakes emanated the mythical and the fantastic. Associated with the inland seas of earlier lore and still a partial feature of American thought about the West were tribes of white Indians, bearded Indians, civilized Indians, Welsh Indians, golden cities, alabaster cities, mythical beasts and all the hosts of fancy that have always been part of the literature of the American West.

American ideas about the symmetrical drainage patterns of North America were more important. The tenets of theoretical geography had provided a common source area for the major North American rivers somewhere in the interior, and it is possible that this concept was widely accepted.[17] When it was combined with the theoretical assumptions of the long-range navigational possibilities of the western rivers, it provided a rational basis for the hope of establishing an all-water communication from the Atlantic to the Pacific.[18]

---

13. A total of eighty-six items mentioned (although not necessarily described) rivers by name; in each of these items the Mississippi was mentioned. The Missouri was mentioned in all but four, the Red River appeared in thirty-two items and the Arkansas in nineteen. The Columbia or "Oregan" was mentioned eleven times, the Kansas and Platte once each.

14. The overenthusiastic estimates of the size and navigability of western rivers did not begin to erode until after the Lewis and Clark Expedition and even then slowly. Even such careful observers as Lewis and Clark consistently overestimated the length and degree of navigability of the rivers they passed. John L. Allen, "Geographical Images of the American Northwest, 1673-1806" (Ph.D. dissertation, Clark University, 1969), chaps. 6-8.

15. From a letter written by Louis Vilemont, a traveler in Spanish Louisiana during the opening years of the nineteenth century. Cited in A. P. Nasatir, *Before Lewis and Clark: Documents Illustrating the History of the Missouri,* 2 vols. (St. Louis, 1952), 2:690-703.

16. Great lakes or huge inland seas in the lands west of the Mississippi were mentioned in only 4 of the 134 items consulted.

17. Only 4 items out of the 134 that related to Louisiana or the West described the source area of the major rivers; each of these 4, however, gave a description based on either Morse or Pinkerton. In spite of the lack of commentary on the common source area in the 1804 material, it would seem logical to assume that the notion was well-fixed since the common source area was described in so many of the geographical writings of the period.

18. This type of rationalization led Thomas Jefferson to plan and sponsor the Lewis and Clark Expedition of 1804-06. Prior to his first term as president, Jefferson had made several attempts to have the connection between the Missouri and the Columbia located for the purposes of establishing an all-water transportation route between the Atlantic and Pacific. His plans

This all-water communication, like the notions on land quality, was an important feature of the optimism with which Americans viewed the newly acquired territory. Through the channels of communication with which the West was blessed, the agricultural produce that was a necessary adjunct of the great fertility of the western lands might find new outlets—even into the shores of China and Japan:[19]

Rejoice, ye too, rejoice ye swains,
Increasing commerce shall reward your
cares.
A day will come if not too deep we drink
The cup which luxury on careless wealth
Pernicious gift bestows; a day will come
When through new channels we shall clothe
The California coast, and all the realms
That stretch from Anian's Streights to proud
Japan.

Certain agreements might have prevailed in the images regarding the fertility of the West or the size and navigability of western rivers. No such agreement pertained to the view of the western mountains. Called by various names, the western mountains were shifting, misty, and illusory features. They were viewed as an unbroken chain running three thousand miles north from Mexico. Or they terminated around the forty-seventh or forty-eighth parallel of latitude and left the way open to the Pacific. They were a very high range of mountains, perhaps highest on the continent or maybe even in the world. Or they were simple ridges or hills of no great size and extent. The concept of the mountains as a continental divide which separated the "rivers and streams, sending some to the Atlantic and others to the Pacific,"[20] seems to have been grasped by some. But even this notion was a contradiction in the face of the conflicting view that the major rivers of the continent had their sources in an area that could best be described as a pyramidal height-of-land.

The opposing views on the mountains as either source or separator of the western rivers were made less contradictory by several theories on the nature of the mountains themselves. Some believed it possible that the Shining Mountains ran without break from north to south. Alexander Mackenzie, the British explorer whose widely read journals fixed the nature of the mountains in the minds of many, admitted that he did not know how far south of this crossing the mountains extended, and that it was therefore possible that breaks in the backbone of the continent might be found below the fiftieth parallel.[21] Jonathan Carver, another traveler and also a primary source of information, reported (and American geography books relayed the information) that a southern range of mountains called "the mountains of New Mexico" terminated between forty-seven and forty-eight degrees north latitude and that between them and the Shining Mountains on the north there might be an area of level ground.[22] It was in this area of level ground that, in Carver's theoretical

were never carried through until he dispatched Lewis and Clark to find "the most direct & practicable water communication across this continent for the purposes of commerce" via the Missouri and Columbia rivers.

19. This poem, possibly by Isaiah Thomas of Worcester and Boston, first appeared in the *Royal American Magazine* (Boston), January 1774. During 1803 and 1804 it was reprinted in broadside form and circulated widely, particularly in New England.

20. *The Medical Repository* (second hexad), I: (1804), 393.

21. Alexander Mackenzie, *Voyages from Montreal . . . to the Frozen and Pacific Oceans* (London, 1801), 2:346-48.

22. Jonathan Carver, *Travels Through the Interior Parts of North America* (London, 1781), p. 121.

scheme, the common source area for the "capital" North American rivers—including the Columbia and Missouri—would be found. This view, probably accepted by many Americans, including some of the best informed,[23] made possible both the recognition of a range of mountains that acted as a continental divide and the retention of the concept of a common source area for the major rivers of the West. The implications of such a rationalization for those who desired the all-water route to the Pacific are obvious.

Perhaps the most inaccurate notions about the western mountains were those relative to size, extent, and location. The altitude of the Shining Mountains was a matter of great conjecture and although some unreliable sources had reported extreme elevation, few specific measurements were available. The most widely read and reliable scientific periodical of the day, the *Medical Repository,* reported that the Shining Mountains were "in some places as much as 3250 feet high above the level of their base which is, perhaps, 3000 feet above the sea."[24] It is clear that the true height of the Rockies (either in terms of their vertical rise or of their base height above sea level) was not even remotely grasped.

Also inaccurate was the popular conceptualization of the mountains as a single ridge. Most of the travel accounts which had reported the crossing of the mountains—and it matters not whether those reports were fictional, as most of them certainly were—described the passage as one of relative ease. Even the accurate and factual journals of Alexander Mackenzie who had indeed crossed the Rocky Mountains spoke in terms of a simple portage of 817 paces across a slight ridge of land as the only break in water transportation from the Atlantic to the Pacific drainage. Mackenzie's information was accurate for the area between the headwaters of the Mackenzie-Athapasca and the Fraser River, but Mackenzie and virtually everyone else believed the river he discovered on the western side of the divide to be the upper Columbia. If only a simple ridge separated the Peace River from the Columbia, so the theoretical reasoning went, then it was likely that only a simple ridge lay between the head of the Missouri and the source region of the southern branches of the Columbia. In the minds of many Americans, the crossing of the Shining Mountains would certainly not be an insurmountable or even difficult task, and if the great navigability of the streams which flowed from the mountains were considered, then the crossing could be viewed with even more optimism.[25]

The location of the mountains relative to the Pacific Coast was a matter for conjecture also, and the Shining Mountains shifted from east to west and back again, depending on the authority. From much of the British information, it was clear that the mountains lay somewhere between the 112th and 115th meridians, and this view appeared on many available maps. . . . But other popular sources of

23. A close examination of the correspondence among Thomas Jefferson, Albert Gallatin, and the members of the American Philosophical Society indicates such a conception among the best scientists of the day. Allen, "Geographical Images," pp. 401-8.

24. *The Medical Repository* (first hexad) 5: (1802), p. 462. The same information is noted in caption form on Aaron Arrowsmith's maps of North America published in 1796 and 1802.

25. It is true that, in many cases, only a slight height-of-land separates the furthermost sources of the western rivers. But the great difference between reality and what was imagined in 1804 to be reality is that by no wild stretching of the imagination can mountain rivers be considered navigable. It took exploration into the west to destroy the illusions of the theoretical geographers that rivers such as the Missouri were navigable nearly to their sources.

information pushed the mountains farther west, toward the Pacific. Reports from the Spanish officials in Louisiana during the last decade of the eighteenth century had entered American geographical lore through correspondence from Americans living on the western frontier, and many of those reports indicated that the western ranges could not be far from the shores of the South Sea—perhaps as close as forty leagues or about one hundred miles. Alexander Mackenzie, always the primary authority on western geography, added that the mountains he had crossed in Canada closely paralleled the coast.[26] The generalized image of the Shining Mountains was of a low, single ridge which was fairly close to the Pacific and which might well have breaks in the chain where the sources of the Atlantic waters approached those of the Pacific. If one view were held in common about the mountains of the West, it was that they provided no greater barrier to the expansion of American commerce and population toward the Pacific.

If geographical knowledge of the West can be envisioned as three-dimensional, then the Louisiana territory in American lore of 1804 can best be described as a basin, surrounded by ridges of better knowledge and grading into a vast, flat interior surface of pure conjecture, broken here and there by peaks of better understanding or more information. Exploration by the French and Spanish in the lower reaches of the Mississippi's western tributaries, by the British across the continent north of the lands encompassed in the purchase, and by the British and Spanish along the coast of the Pacific Northwest meant that fairly reliable geographical information was available for the periphery of Louisiana. The quality of absolute knowledge graded downward swiftly toward the interior, into those areas contacted briefly by the fur trade or partially known through Indian information and finally into those areas of the interior that were virtually unknown. Some islands of better information, such as the Great Bend of the Upper Missouri that was reached by both the British from the north and the Spanish-sponsored explorers from the south, appeared as enclaves of higher quality knowledge within the partially known or unknown area.

From this geographical lore, literate Americans developed patterns of belief about the nature and content of Louisiana, images that were accurate for some sections of the territory but imperfect when applied, as they were, to the Northwest as a whole.[27] If Americans tended to view the Louisiana territory as a garden, it was because the greatest volume of geographical information—that obtained from the lands bordering the Mississippi—presented such a picture. If the rivers were considered as oversized, it was because they had been observed only in their lower reaches. If the mountains were seen as low, single ridges that were close to the Pacific, it was because the only mountains with which most Americans were familiar fit such a description, as did the mountains which were crossed by the British fur trade in Canada. Like geographic knowledge itself, the images can be graded for quality. In the gradation can be seen the impact of the geography of hope and desire. . . .

26. Mackenzie, *Voyages from Montreal,* 2:346.

27. People do not like blank spaces in their images any more than cartographers like blank spaces on maps and therefore tend to take information from "known" areas and expand it into areas for which information is not available or is nonexistent.

Space, Time, Culture, and the New Frontier

Robert F. Berkhofer, Jr.

Every historian is as much a product of history as he is an interpreter of it; for, according to the "truths" of his time, he frames the questions he asks of his sources and fashions the organization of his material. Of no American historian is this more true than Frederick Jackson Turner, whose frontier interpretation has probably been the single most important key to an understanding of American civilization. His triumphant synthesis depended more upon the social theory and myth current in his day than upon the facts of frontier life. The seventy years which have passed since Turner delivered his now-classic paper have seen the maturation of the social sciences with a new body of theory. Yet we find the teaching of the West and the use of the frontier hypothesis too little influenced by the enormous changes in theory which have occurred. To show how dependent Turner was upon contemporary thought, and how the American frontier should be viewed in the new perspective afforded by modern social theory, constitutes the principal tasks of this article.

Fundamental to Turner's concern about the nature of civilization and why it changed was his theory of society, reflected by such words as "germs," "growth," or "organs."[1] Although Turner only once explicitly stated that "society is an organism, ever growing,"[2] the organismic theory so prevalent in his day was the foundation of the frontier hypothesis.[3] It was a theory based on the biological analogy of society as a living organism. As a result, the most prominent feature of society is "growth" by which

1. For the use of these terms in his classic essay, see Frederick Jackson Turner, *The Frontier in American History* (New York: H. Holt and Co., 1920), pp. 2, 3, 4, 9, 15. Henchforth referred to as *Frontier*.

2. Fulmer Mood, ed., *The Early Writings of Frederick Jackson Turner* (Madison: University of Wisconsin Press, 1938), p. 57. Cf. Ibid., p. 73.

3. These influences came from both German scholarship and Herbert Spencer. For these influences on one of Turner's mentors and friends, see Richard T. Ely, *An Introduction to Political Economy* (New York: Chautauqua Press, 1889), pp. 14-17; *Studies in the Evolution of Industrial Society* (New York: Macmillan, 1903), chaps. 1, 2. The vogue of Spencer is treated in Richard Hofstadter, *Social Darwinism in American Thought,* rev. ed. (Boston: Beacon Press, 1955), pp. 30-50. German influence is touched upon by Richard T. Ely, "The Past and Present of Political Economy," *Johns Hopkins University Studies in Historical and Political Science,* II (1884), paper no. 3. For an example of this thinking, see Herbert Spencer, *Principles of Sociology* (New York: D. Appleton and Co., 1876-1897), 1, Part I. Section 9, 10, 15-21; Part II.

Reproduced (with omissions) by permission from *Agricultural History* 38 (1964):21-30. For elaboration see also the author's, *A Behavioral Approach to Historical Analysis* (New York: The Free Press, 1969).

the societal organism evolves from a simple undifferentiated structure to a highly differentiated structure of many "organs" with specialized functions, as represented by political, economic, and social institutions. As differentiation occurs, there is a continuous adjustment of the internal organs within the society, as well as the constant adaptation of the whole organism to its external environment of soil, climate, and other physical factors of contact. These changes are passed on to the future in accordance with the theory of Lamarck that an organism can inherit acquired characteristics. Eventually, as the result of the continuous growth and differentiation inherent in the social organism a new "species" evolves. With this conception of society, Turner could say:

> The history of our political institutions, our democracy, is not a history of imitation, of simple borrowing; it is a history of the evolution and adaptation of organs in response to changed environment, a history of the origin of new political species.[4]

Since the social organism, like all living things, obeyed the law of evolution, Turner was little interested in the normal historian's preoccupation with "history conceived as a succession of events in a time series."[5] He wrenched his material loose from specific time, and, for that matter, place, in his attempt to synthesize history.[6] Thus Turner maintained, "The factor of time in American History is insignificant when compared with the factors of space and social evolution."[7] In saying this, Turner again subscribed to a dominant doctrine of his day, namely, the idea of social progress in which cultural changes were viewed as gradual, continuous, and following a fixed and determined order.[8] Society in all its many forms must go through essentially the same stages. Differences between societies resulted from the speed with which they passed through stages. Thus, still-existing primitive societies demonstrated prior stages of social evolution. Such an assumption lay in back of the widespread use of the comparative method in this period.[9]

For this type of comparative approach, the United States offered a unique study for the evolutionist, because the stages of development presumably existed spatially as well as temporally. Turner pointed this out in his oft-quoted statement: "The United States lies like a huge page in the history of society. Line by line as we read this Continental page from West to East we find the record of social evolution."[10] Furthermore, Turner, like his contemporaries, assumed that societal stages were characterized by certain modes of technology and economic production. Thus, the page of American history revealed the advance from hunter to cattlemen through farmer to robber baron.[11] Operating upon the basic assumption that the growth of

4. *Frontier,* pp. 205-6. Cf. Ibid., p. 2.
5. According to Carl Becker in Howard W. Odum, ed., *American Masters of Social Sciences* (New York, H. Holt & Co., 1927), p. 313.
6. Ibid., pp. 305, 313.
7. Turner, *The Significance of Sections in American History* (New York: H. Holt and Co., 1932), p. 6. Henceforth referred to as *Sections.*
8. J. B. Bury, *The Idea of Progress, An Inquiry into Its Origin and Growth,* Intro. Charles A. Beard (New York: Macmillan, 1932), pp. 334-41. For Turner's great faith in progress, see Fulmer Mood, "The Development of Frederick Jackson Turner as a Historical Thinker," *Publications of the Colonial Society of Massachusetts* 34 (1937-1942):292. Henceforth referred to as "Development of Turner."
9. The best analysis of the doctrines of social evolution is the brief article by Alexander Goldenweiser, "Evolution, Social," in E. R. A. Seligman and A. Johnson, eds., *Encyclopedia of Social Sciences,* V (New York: Macmillan Co., 1930-1934), 656-62.
10. *Frontier,* p. 11.
11. Ibid. For the background of Turner's evolutionary theory, see Mood, "Development of Turner," pp. 304-7.

complex institutions depended upon the size of the population to staff the organs, Turner then correlated the westward spread of societal evolution with the density of population.[12]

Reasoning in this manner Turner would have demonstrated that American history was European history. This would not have satisfied the patriotic Wisconsin historian, whose fundamental preconception, according to Carl Becker, was a deep-seated loyalty to the United States.[13] All patriots knew instinctively that America was different from Europe, and that the United States had been unique since its founding. With this prejudice the question posed for Turner, with his social theory, was how to account for the development of this unique society. While America had originated from European "germs," its history could not be explained by this genesis; the causative agent must be found in America itself. Thus he turned to an environmental interpretation of American history. The answer was found in the interaction between the social organism and American space.[14]

American space, according to Turner, was divided into physiographic provinces or areas.[15] From our point of view, the most important feature of these provinces was the environmental bases they provided for independent economic and social evolution. In this vein Turner wrote:

> The American physical map may be regarded as a map of potential nations and empires, each to be conquered and colonized, each to achieve a certain social and industrial unity, each to possess certain fundamental assumptions, certain psychological traits, and each to interact with the others, and in combination to form that United States, the explanation of which is the task of the historian.[16]

An examination of Turner's actual use of this concept reveals that he thought of the provinces as regions bounded by mountains and unified by rivers and their valleys.[17] In his overall thinking the most prominent river was the Mississippi and its tributaries, and the most significant mountain range was the Allegheny.[18] Though Turner recognized its subregions, he tended to think of the Mississippi Valley as one province.[19] This great "heartland of America" was the "economic and political center of the Republic."[20] This Valley provided the base for a new society. When settlers moved into it "a real national activity, a genuine American cul-

12. Turner gives his most explicit correlation in his brief article "Frontier in American Development" in Andrew C. McLaughlin and Albert Bushnell Hart, eds., *Cyclopedia of American Government,* III (New York: Peter Smith, 1914; reprinted, 1949), p. 62. Again for background, consult Mood, "Development of Turner," pp. 315-318. Cf. Ely, *Introduction,* pp. 35-54, for stages of economy as a teacher and friend saw them.
13. Becker, p. 300.
14. Ellen C. Semple maintained that Friedrich Ratzel got the basis for his system of Anthropogeography from Spencer's ideas on the interaction of the social organism and environment in *Influences of Geographic Environment on the Basis of Ratzel's System of Anthropo-geography* (New York: H. Holt & Co., 1911), pp. vi-vii.
15. Again for background, see Mood, "Development of Turner," pp. 313-15. The same author has written on "The Origin, Evolution, and Applications of the Sectional Concept, 1750-1900," in Merrill Jensen, ed., *Regionalism in America* (Madison: University of Wisconsin Press, 1951), pp. 5-98.
16. *Sections,* pp. 8-9. Cf. *Frontier,* pp. 127, 158.
17. E.g., *Sections,* pp. 93-94, 133-34.
18. In the colonial struggle between the French and English, he points out how the Mississippi Valley forced the French to view the whole interior as a "unity" in spite of their efforts to bound Louisiana by the Mississippi River rather than the Allegheny Mountains. On the other hand the English regarded the Alleghenies as a boundary to their area, especially as seen in the Proclamation Line of 1763. *Frontier,* p. 186; *Sections,* p. 139.
19. See especially *Frontier,* pp. 126-27.
20. Ibid. For the parallel of Turner and Halford Mackinder, see James C. Malin, *Essays on Historiography* (Lawrence: Author, 1946), pp. 1-44.

ture began."[21] The Alleghenies divided East from West, hence Europe from America. As he said in his famous 1893 essay: "From the time the mountains rose between the pioneer and the seaboard, a new order of Americanism arose. The West and the East began to get out of touch with each other."[22] The migration across the mountains, he rhapsodized, "put new fire into its veins—fires of militant expansion, creative social energy, triumphant democracy. A new section was added to the American nation, a new element was infused into the combination we call the United States, a new flavor was given to the American spirit."[23] Here was the West defined as geographical space, or as Turner called it, a section.[24]

The question remained as to the specific nature of this new environment that caused it to produce a new social species, the *Homo Americanus*. First of all, the American continent was an enormous storehouse of resources which Turner subsumed under the rubric "free land."[25] More important was the abundance of vacant land with its resources, a whole continent, a "vast space," empty of population.[26] His attitude is well summarized when he wrote:

> The very fact of the wilderness appealed as a fair blank page on which to write a new chapter in the story of man's struggle for a higher type of society. The Western wilds, from the Alleghenies to the Pacific, constituted the richest free gift that ever spread out before civilized man.[27]

Presumably, the abundance of resources available at low cost, or even free, and the empty spaces, invited settlement. But the relatively low density of population in the newly settled areas forced, according to the social organism theory, a reversion to a society of fewer organs, hence a society of earlier evolutionary stage. Thus the West was an area of re-evolving society with opportunity for a different growth resulting in a new species. As Turner maintained:

> The West, at bottom, is a form of society rather than an area. It is the term applied to the region whose social conditions result from the application of older institutions and ideas to the transforming influences of free land. By this application, a new environment is suddenly entered, freedom of opportunity is opened, the cake of custom is broken, and new activities, new lines of growth, new institutions and new ideals are brought into existence[28]

Here was the West defined as processes. Eventually all Wests evolved to modern civilization, but what distinguished them from the East were the slightly primitive "survivals"[29] of frontier experience. . . .

The frontier hypothesis was a fascinating fusion of the popular myth and social theory of Turner's day. The frontier was more than an area or a process; it was, in its deepest sense, an interaction of space as nature and of society as an evolutionary organism to produce those virtues upon which Americans prided themselves most.

21. *Frontier,* p. 190.
22. Ibid., p. 18.
23. Ibid., p. 166.
24. For the definition of section, see *Sections,* p. 103; Turner, "Sectionalism in the United States," McLaughlin and Hart, eds., vol. 3, p. 280. The differences between East and Wset are treated ibid., pp. 281-82.
25. Lee Benson has gathered his two important articles on this subject and much relevant to other parts of this paper in his *Turner and Beard, American Historical Writing Reconsidered* (Glencoe, Ill.: 1960), pp. 1-91.
26. *Frontier,* pp. 2, 128, 260-61, 269, 293. The Indians were considered among the environmental factors to be overcome in good American fashion.
27. Ibid., p. 261. Cf. p. 212.
28. Ibid., p. 205. Cf. pp. 38, 261.
29. For use of the term, see ibid., p. 205. On the concept of survivals, consult Margaret T. Hodgen, *The Doctrine of Survivals* (London: Allenson and Co., 1936).

Turner, in other words, held a mirror to the prejudices of America, and she was utterly captivated by her image. In order to interpret the uniqueness of American history from the theoretical viewpoint, he had to put space as the primary determinant and time and society in secondary positions, for otherwise the evolving social organism would have duplicated European society in the West—a conclusion abhorrent to his in-grained provincialism and patriotism. Space was the only factor that could modify what we call culture today, for culture was assumed by Turner to be an inherited part of the social organism. For this reason, Turner found the real clue to American history in the West.

In order to explain the West and American Civilization in terms of today's social theory, we would have to reverse the order of space, time, and culture. In the development of institutions in any new area, the prevailing cultural system is considered a far more fundamental influence than physical environment. The response to environment is considered to be highly conditioned by the cultural screen through which the stimulus passes.

In the past two decades the concept of culture has increasingly come to mean a normative system rather than the total social heritage so often used in older textbooks. As such, it is the blueprint or design for behavior rather than the artifacts themselves. Thus a person's culture prescribes what ought to be done, delimits what may be done, and defines what exists, or concerns what are frequently called values, norms, and beliefs. Culture, then, shapes the nature of the institutions in a society and the roles a person plays in them. Culture also filters the perception of reality. What a person accepts as "fact" is highly conditioned by his value-orientation. It is assumed that the various cultural by-patterns, such as subsystems and institutions, fit into an overall configuration that provides that culture's unique integration.[30]

It is important for the frontier historian to distinguish between culture as a normative system as used here and culture as behavior and artifact as was the older interpretation, for the distinction is vital in properly assessing the influence of environment. Climate, terrain, and other physical factors of space affect behavior far more than they do culture. Man adapts his inherited institutions and ways to a new environment only begrudgingly. While his behavior may change, he may not approve of it. A frontiersman may build a log cabin, but that does not mean he will not build a substantial frame house the first chance he gets. For the frontier to have influence, it must change the conception of what is desirable as well as behavior. The impact of environment, furthermore, is proportionate to the technological level of the society. The more technology a society possesses, the less it has to bend its institutions to the dictates of natural environment. Technology as a function of culture can create a secondary environment more powerful than the natural in affecting men's lives, as any mod-

30. Much writing exists on the definition of culture. I have found the following most useful for these paragraphs: for the history and general use of the term, Alfred L. Kroeber and Clyde Kluckhohn, *Culture: A Critical Review of Concepts and Definitions in Papers of the Peabody Museum of American Archaeology and Ethnology* 47 (Cambridge: The Museum, 1952); on culture as a normative system, Florence R. Kluckhohn and Fred L. Strodtbeck, *Variations in Value Orientations* (Evanston, Ill.: Row, Peterson, 1961), esp. pp. 1-48; Philip E. Jacob and James J. Flink, "Values and Their Function in Decision-Making," *American Behavioral Scientist* 5 (Supplement, May 1962):7-27; on the attempt to apply social theory to a complex society, Robin M. Williams, Jr., *American Society, A Sociological Interpretation* (New York: Knopf, 1951), pp. 19-35.

ern city proves. At the same time, the distinction between normative system and behavior also means that certain institutions and customs are more subject to environmental modification than others. The less an institution or custom results in behavior or artifacts dependent upon environmental products, the less the environment can influence it. Diet and clothing are far more subject to environment than prayerbooks and church admission. Thus, it would seem that political, social, and religious institutions would be far less influenced by frontier experience than economic ones.[31]

While this article can not draw all the implications of modern cultural theory for frontier history, it can by a brief and highly selective survey of westward expansion point up some of the consequences in two spheres deemed significant to Turnerian interpretation—the political and economic. We will concentrate on (1) the connection between cultural perception, technology, economic organization and the exploitation of resources, and (2) the bearing of the theory of society at a given time on frontier social and political democracy. By focusing on these two areas, we can see the differential effect of the frontier on institutions more and less dependent upon environment as well as the overall interrelationship of institutions due to cultural configuration and integration.

The economic potential of an area is a cultural as well as a physical phenomenon. Natural resources, as David Potter points out in his *People of Plenty: Economic Abundance and the American Character,* are not merely "a storehouse of fixed and universally recognizable assets reposing on shelves until humanity by a process of removal strips them bare. Rather abundance resides in a series of physical potentialities, which have never been inventoried at the same value for any two cultures in the past and are not likely to seem of identical worth to different cultures in the future."[32] The economic value of resources, then, is a matter of what people *want* to exploit and what they *can* exploit. On one hand, the economic organization and technology of a culture at a given time determine the possibility of utilization. On the other hand, the relation of the economic institutions to the overall configuration of cultural values and institutions also determines what may be used in what manner. This is seen on the Atlantic seaboard of the seventeenth century as well as on the plains of the nineteenth. . . .

The English colonists brought a conception of society inherited from the Middle Ages, embodying a hierarchal social structure. Although mobility existed, the stratification was believed rightfully rigid, even God-ordained. A man's status determined his obligations and rights. State and society seemed one, for social respect and political authority reinforced one another. Naturally, political privileges were determined by social status which was in turn connected with economic foundations. Wealth, rank, and power all went together in the same person, and to everyone this unity seemed right. Mobility consisted in obtaining one and getting all three.[33]

31. The best analysis of culture and geography is C. Daryll Forde, *Habitat, Economy, and Society, A Geographical Introduction to Ethnology* (London: Methuen & Co., 1934). A critique of geographical determinism from a historical viewpoint is Franklin Thomas, *The Environmental Basis of Society, A Study in the History of Sociological Theory* (New York: Century Co., 1925).

32. (Chicago: University of Chicago Press, 1954), p. 164.

33. For analysis of social structure see for New England, Perry Miller and Thomas H. Johnson,

On the colonial frontier, the settlers did not abandon this conception of society, but rather filled the structure with new people. The whole English population did not duplicate itself in North America. Rather certain classes came over in numbers disproportionate to others. "Dukes don't emigrate" runs an old proverb, and even most gentlemen would rather risk their purses than their persons. The bulk of English settlers were from the "middling classes" of farmers and skilled laborers.[34] For colonial society to stratify according to the English pattern, this middling class had to fill all levels. Small wonder, then, that the colonial aristocracy was a working one and at best a pale imitation of the mother country's, nor is it strange that Americans possessed those virtues of aggressive individualism that Turner ascribes to the frontier, for they brought these traits from overseas.[35]

The attitude towards land further abetted this process of societal expansion. The social theory that Englishmen held on the eve of settlement was based originally on medieval land tenure. Although other factors had supplemented land as the sole determinant of status in Elizabethan England, still its possession was *the* symbol of rank. Under the medieval agrarian system, emphasis was placed upon rendering subsistence for the servile population and a living for their lords, but in the new age of agricultural capitalism, stress was more and more laid upon land producing a profit. Land possessed market value, besides determining status, and so speculation in land and leases was prevalent. Not only did large landowners deal in the land market, but so did the yeoman—all the while trying to wring the greatest crop yield, hence profit, from their acres.[36]

This dual attitude of land as commodity and as status determinant sailed with the acquisitive middling class across the Atlantic, where it was reflected in the relationship of economic, political, and social institutions in the Colonial period and goes far to show the importance of land in American history. On the one hand, commercial farming and profit were coincident with settlement, and land-jobbing and speculation were not far behind.[37] On the other hand the abundance of American acres offered the colonists a greater chance than in England to move up the social ladder and gain political rights in line with contemporary social theory. Land made possible a middle class dis-

The Puritans (New York: American Book Co., 1938), pp. 17-18, 181-84; for the South, Louis B. Wright, *The First Gentlemen of Virginia* (San Marino, Calif.: Huntington Library 1940), esp. chap 1; in general for colonies, Leonard W. Larabee, *Conservation in Early American History* (New York: New York University Press, 1948), pp. 105-7; for England, Wallace Notestein, *The English People on the Eve of Colonization, 1603-1630* (New York: Harper and Brothers, 1954). For the significance of the concept of order and hierarchy, see the brilliant little book by E. M. W. Tillyard, *The Elizabethan World Picture* (New York: Macmillan, 1944).

34. A brief but detailed study is Mildred Campbell, "Social Origins of Some Early Americans," in James M. Smith, *Seventeenth-Century America, Essay in Colonial History* (Chapel Hill: University of North Carolina Press, 1959), pp. 63-76.

35. Everett S. Lee suggested that aggressiveness, self-confidence, individualism, and other character traits ascribed to frontiersmen by Turner may be found as part of the personality of all migrants. See Everett S. Lee, "A Theory of Migration," *Demography* 3 (1966):47-57.

36. This paragraph is based mainly on Mildred Campbell, *The English Yeoman Under Elizabeth and the Early Stuarts* (New Haven: Yale University Press, 1942), pp. 64-104, 156-220; and Richard H. Tawney, *The Agrarian Problem in the Sixteenth Century* (London: Longmans, Green and Co., 1912).

37. Even in early New England there was speculation and the extended farm pattern, see Darrett B. Rutman, *Winthrop's Boston* (Chapel Hill, N.C.: University of North Carolina Press, 1965).

proportionately large compared to Europe's. The unity of rank, wealth, and power was retained, but the frontier gave the colonist the opportunity to reduplicate it with many new people at a higher level.[38] It was this colonial base of newly risen people and the larger middle class that appears to have laid the foundations for the unique society that Turner attributed to the Western frontier of the later period.

During the same period in which settlement flowed into the Trans-Appalachian West, a major shift occurred in American ideology. Thus Turner's perception of a new western society was really the recognition of a new social and political outlook which justified self-sufficient farms, social and economic equality, and democracy—not the actual creation of a simplified economic system and elementary democracy as he thought. Historians reconstructing the past of the Old Southwest and the Old Northwest find the extension of the complex institutions and societal network of the East into the new areas of settlement. Cotton grower and grain farmer marched westward with the speculator in the vanguard. Slavery and tenancy likewise travelled over the mountains. So did most of the occupations of the time. All these men were aggressive, and all were looking for the main chance. Forests were cleared and fields cultivated according to the technology and economic organization of the time. If a farmer was self-sufficient, it was only because he had no access to market.[39] In reality, a much more stratified social system and more complex economic system existed from the earliest settlement west of the mountains than Turner's hypothesis allowed.[40]

At the same time historians no longer find the democratic innovations that Turner did in this area. After an examination of Western state constitutions, Benjamin Wright concluded that the familiar pattern of executive, bicameral legislature, hierarchy of courts, and even local government was copied from Eastern models. Thus he asserts that Western citizens were "imitative not creative. They were not interested in making experiments. Their constitutional, like their domestic, architecture was patterned after that of communities from which they had moved westward."[41] Likewise, with the

38. Support for this conclusion relative to the 17th Century may be found in Bernard Bailyn's stimulating essay on "Politics and Social Structure in Virginia," in James M. Smith, ed., pp. 90-115. Also see Thomas J. Wertenbaker, *The Planters of Colonial Virginia* (Princeton: Princeton University Press, 1922); Susie M. Ames, *Studies of the Virginia Eastern Shore in the Seventeenth Century* (Richmond: Dietz Press, 1940); Thomas P. Abernethy, *Three Virginia Frontiers* (Baton Rouge: Louisiana State University Press, 1940), pp. 1-62, for material relevant to this paragraph. For the 18th Century see Charles S. Grant's admirable monograph, *Democracy in the Connecticut Frontier Town of Kent* (New York: Columbia University Press, 1961).

39. Rodney C. Loehr, "Self-Sufficiency on the Farm," *Agricultural History* 26 (April 1952): 37-45.

40. Among many, consult Abernethy, pp. 63-96; and his *From Frontier to Plantation in Tennessee: A Study in Frontier Democracy* (Chapel Hill: University of North Carolina Press, 1932); Harriette Arnow, *Seedtime in the Cumberland* (New York: Macmillan, 1960); James A. Frost, *Life on the Upper Susquehanna, 1783-1860* (New York: King's Crown Press, 1951); Paul W. Gates, *The Farmer's Age, Agriculture, 1815-1860* (New York: Holt, Rinehart, and Winston, 1960); Neil McNall, *An Agricultural History of the Genessee Valley, 1790-1860* (Philadelphia: University of Pennsylvania Press, 1952); Richard L. Power, *Planting Corn Belt Culture; the Impress of the Upland Southerner and Yankee in the Old Northwest* (Indianapolis: Indiana Historical Society, 1953); William B. Hamilton, "The Southwestern Frontier, 1795-1817: An Essay in Social History," *Journal of Southern History* 10 (November 1944):389-403.

41. Benjamin F. Wright, Jr., "Political Institutions and the Frontier," in Dixon R. Fox, ed., *Sources of Culture in the Middle West* (New York: D. Appleton-Century Co., 1934), pp. 15-

liberalization of suffrage requirements, some Eastern states led the way, although the West followed quickly.[42] Western political institutions reflected the trends of the time, though perhaps slightly accelerated in the Western states as opposed to the Eastern states as a whole. . . .

The history of the West in every period must also be placed in a larger economic context. This view of frontier economy strips such stalwarts as the miscegenetic fur trader, the lonesome cowboy, and the hardy pioneer of their picturesque garb to reveal them for the petty capitalists they were. The fur trapper becomes the minor agent in an economic organization stretching from his canoe to Philadelphia, New York, Montreal, and overseas. The cowboy on the long trail was but the link between the range and packing plant in the cattle industry. Lastly, the pioneer farmer ceases his pose of self-subsistence and eagerly seeks a market. At the same time other occupations join Turner's pioneers on the frontier as extensions of the economic institutions of the time.

Frontier capitalism thus was part of the economic development of the United States. As such, it was subject to the vicissitudes of provincial, national, and international markets depending upon the transportation and economic organization of the time.[43] Frontiersmen had economic opportunity to the extent of their technology and economic institutions. At the same time, the frontier offered an opportunity closed to a society without it. America possessed a geographical frontier that could be exploited by the current level of technology and economic institutions without innovation, thereby decreasing the investment risk from one of invention to one of timing. Moreover, a geographical frontier presented opportunity for profit on "once-and-for-all" investments such as transportation systems and public buildings which everyone knew were needed but which yielded profit only once at the critical moment.[44] . . .

. . . The American frontier meant opportunity in the broadest sense, for not only did it mean the possibility for the extension of institutions and trends in the society at the time, but the proliferation and constant founding of institutions enabled a greater number of people to participate at a higher level in them than would have been possible in a society without a frontier. The institutions that sprang up depended more upon the cultural baggage of the migrants than upon the influence of the frontier whether as geography or unpopulated space. Yet, this did not mean the exact duplication of European or Eastern society, for such selective factors as nationality, class background, and the period of time of settlement provided differential cultural bases for institutional growth. Thus German or English heritage, arisocrat or yeoman, 1760 or 1860, accounts more for institu-

---

38. John D. Barnhart in an extended analysis. *Valley of Democracy, The Frontier Versus the Plantation in the Ohio Valley, 1775-1818* (Bloomington: Indiana University Press, 1953), confirms Wright's conclusions, although his Turnerian prejudice blinds him to the implications of his facts.

42. Chilton Williamson, *American Suffrage from Property to Democracy, 1760-1860* (Princeton: Princeton University Press, 1960), pp. 208-222.

43. An interesting series of articles dealing with Western economics from this viewpoint is "The American West as an Underdeveloped Region," *Journal of Economic History* 16 (December 1956).

44. This idea and other valuable insights may be found in George Murphy and Arnold Zellner, "Sequential Growth, the Labor-Safety-Value Doctrine, and Development of American Unionism," *Journal of Economic History* 19 (September 1959):402-21.

tions in a newly settled area as to both similarities and differences from older areas than does forest or climate or terrain. This does not imply that geographical environment played no part; it operated as a limiting factor rather than as a determinant. The limitations were most felt in the speed and direction of settlement and economic activity, but even here, technology modified space.

In this attempt at redefinition, the frontier is viewed not as an area demanding innovation, but as an opportunity for the proliferation of old institutions. The uniqueness of the frontier is basically not one of place, but of time, making possible the rapid extension of certain trends prevailing in Anglo-American society during a given period. To the extent that the frontier afforded this opportunity, it possesses validity as an explanatory factor in American history.

Between the Forest and the Prairie / *Terry G. Jordan*

Much has been written about the advance of the frontier westward from the Appalachians and the contrast between forest and prairie that was encountered, and many writers have recognized that the nature of the vegetational cover was often a factor influencing the distribution of settlement. The classic picture is that of the woodland pioneers emerging from the shade of the trees that had sheltered them and shaped their culture for many generations and entering, somewhat hesitantly, the vast expanses of the grassland. . . .

In an effort to emphasize the effects of the obvious contrast between forest and prairie, many scholars have created the erroneous impression that there were only two types of land—that covered with timber and that devoid of timber. In fact, however, there was a land between the forest and the prairie, a land which shared the attributes of both, where the settler could have timber as well as grass on his land.

The present paper centers about the following questions: what was the influence of the mixed prairie-forest areas on the initial choice of settlement sites, and were these areas evaluated differently (1) from one period of time to another or (2) by settlers of different origins? The answers will be sought in the area of the Old Northwest and in Kentucky.

Patterns and Types of Vegetation

. . . For the purposes of the present paper, the following vegetational patterns and types will be recognized: (1) the *openings,* those areas where trees were more widely spaced than in the true forest and where grass grew among the trees; (2) the *fringes of small dry prairies,* island-like in the sea of forests and generally situated in interfluvial areas; (3) the *fringes of small, wet prairies,* identical in pattern with type two, but covered for at least part of the year by standing water and situated usually in low-lying areas subject to flooding; (4) the *fringes of large prairies,* wet or dry, identical with types two and three except that the woodland, rather than the prairie, was island-like, appearing in isolated groves and *galeria* forests along the streams; (5) *large, dry prairies,* treeless and not adjacent to woodland; (6) *large, wet prairies,* like type five except that standing water was present for part of the year; (17) *interfluvial forests,* devoid of any prairie; and (8) *fluvial forests,* located in valleys and lowlands. It can be seen that three, not two, major vegetational patterns are represented by these eight types—the *prairie-forest mixture,* encompassing types one through four; the *open prairies,* including types five and

Reproduced (with omissions) by permission from *Agricultural History* 38 (1964):205-16. For elaboration in a different regional context, see also the author's *German Seed in Texas Soil: Immigrant Farmers in Nineteenth-Century Texas* (Austin: University of Texas Press, 1966).

six; and the *forests,* as represented by types seven and eight. The basic point to be understood is that there was an extensive transition zone between the forest and the prairie. . . .

Some Proposed Answers to the Problem

Since there are three variables involved—vegetation, origin of settlers, and period of settlement—a large number of hypotheses is possible. The one which has gained the widest acceptance proposes that settlers in Kentucky and the Old Northwest in the period before about 1830 avoided the prairie in all its many forms, and that settlement of the grasslands did not take place until necessitated by population pressures. In particular, the practice of prairie avoidance has been attributed to the southerners from Kentucky, North Carolina, and Virginia who dominated the settlement of considerable portions of the Old Northwest before 1830.[1] The Yankee New Englanders, who settled the Old Northwest in large numbers after about 1830, were supposedly the first to "conquer" the small prairies, a feat that escaped their southern predecessors.[2] Confusion reigns with regard to the European settlers. On the one hand they are pictured as quite willing to settle in mixed prairie-forest areas, arriving "without the prejudices of forest-trained American frontiersmen,"[3] while in contrast other Europeans, in particular the Germans, are said to have preferred the forests for, among others, "sentimental reasons."[4]

At first glance, the theory of pioneer prairie avoidance seems valid, especially if the consideration is limited simply to "prairie" and "forest." The disadvantages of settlement on the open prairies have often been listed, the major ones being (1) the absence of timber for construction, fencing, and fuel; (2) the lack of usable surface water for household and livestock use or to power mills; and (3) the necessity of breaking a tough sod of grass. This latter difficulty was, however, offset by the fact that the back-breaking job of forest clearance was unnecessary, and pastures were "ready made." Nevertheless, if the choice was to be made between areas of exclusively forest or grass, it is clear that the former was the better choice. . . .

Instead of only two vegetational choices, however, many pioneers in the period before 1850 had a third—the areas of mixed prairie and forest, areas that offered a number of the advantages of both forest and prairie settlement with a minimum of disadvantages (Table 1). In these mixed regions, the settlers could have the timber needed for construction and fuel, while at the same time avoiding the drudgery of years of forest clearance. Contem-

1. Southerner prairie-avoidance is discussed in the following basic sources: Frederick J. Turner, *The Frontier in American History* (New York, 1920), pp. 134-36; Carl O. Sauer, *Geography of the Upper Illinois Valley and History of Development,* Illinois State Geological Survey, Bulletin 27 (Urbana, 1916), p. 150; Harlan H. Barrows, *Geography of the Middle Illinois Valley,* Illinois State Geological Survey, Bulletin 15 (Urbana, 1910), p. 66. General avoidance of the grasslands by nearly all pioneers in the pre-1830 period is proposed in Ray A. Billington, *Westward Expansion, a History of the American Frontier* (2nd edition; New York, 1960), pp. 294, 296; and Percy W. Bidwell, and John L. Falconer, *History of Agriculture in the Northern United States 1620-1860* (Washington, D.C., 1925), p. 158.

2. Barrows, *Geography of the Middle Illinois Valley,* p. 79.

3. Billington, *Westward Expansion,* p. 296. The reference is to English immigrants who settled on the fringe of a small, dry prairie in southern Illinois in 1818.

4. Elfrieda Lang, "Some Characteristics of German Immigrants in Dubois County, Indiana," *Indiana Magazine of History* 42 (1946):37.

TABLE 1. Comparative Advantages for Settlement of the Various Types and Patterns of Vegetation

Advantages for Settlement	*Prairie-Forest Mixture*				*Open Prairie*		*Forest*	
	1	2	3	4	5	6	7	8
Timber available	×	×	×	×			×	×
Clearing unnecessary	+	×	×	×	×	×		
Healthful site	×	×		×	×		×	
Protection from wind, storms	×	×	×	×			×	×
Drainage unnecessary	×	×	○	×	×		×	×
Pastures ready-made	×	×	×	×	×	×		
No thick sod to break							×	×
Freedom from grass fires							×	×
Woods available for hunting	×	×	×				×	×
Mast available for swine	×	×	×	×			×	×

Key to the patterns and types of vegetation: 1 = openings; 2 = fringe of small, dry prairie; 3 = fringe of small, wet prairie; 4 = fringe of large prairie; 5 = large, dry prairie; 6 = large, wet prairie; 7 = interfluvial forest; 8 = fluvial (bottom) forest.

Key to symbols: × = as a rule; ○ = often; + = less clearing needed than in true forest. A blank indicates a negative value for the particular advantage under consideration.

porary accounts indicate that breaking the prairie sod was much easier than removing a cover of timber, and the job of initial plowing was quite often done by experienced hired labor equipped with the necessary horses or oxen. Certainly, the prairies of the mixed vegetational areas were being plowed long before the introduction of the steel plow. In addition, the natural grasslands were available immediately upon settlement for grazing purposes.

These considerations lead to a second hypothesis, that the mixed prairie and forest areas were very desirable as sites for settlement and must, therefore, have played an important role in shaping the pattern of initial settlement. It also follows that the mixed areas would have been most desirable for *all* pioneers, be they from the South, New England, or Europe, and that these areas would have continued to exert an attractive power as long as they were accessible and available, conditions which existed during most of the first half of the nineteenth century in many areas. . . . The major problems of prairie settlement did not begin in the mixed areas, but the major problem of woodland settlement—clearing—ended there. The Indian old fields which were so welcome a sight to the first settlers on the Atlantic Coast can scarcely have offered more advantages than the ready-made clearings and abundant timber of the mixed forest-prairie country.

Nor were men slow to recognize the advantages of the mixed areas. . . . In 1811, an English traveller in the Old Northwest recommended that new settlers would do best to locate on the edge of a prairie, making use of the timber while raising crops and grazing livestock on the prairie.[5] In 1817 the *Western Gazetteer* advised its readers, "In choosing a situation for a farm it is important so to locate a tract as to have half prairie and half wood land. . . ."[6] D. Thomas observed in 1816 on the watered fringe of a small, dry prairie in southeastern Illinois that "Several families have erected huts in the edge of woodlands. The inducement has been the convenience of timber and

5. John Bradbury, *Travels in the Interior of America in the Years 1809, 1810, and 1811;* . . . (Liverpool and London, 1817), p. 308.
6. Samuel R. Brown, *The Western Gazetteer; or Emigrant's Directory* (Auburn, N.Y., 1817), p. 48.

fire wood, a supply of water, and land adjoining ready cleared."[7] B. Harding noted the identical situation several years later, also in Illinois, and commented: "At present the new settler builds his cabin in the edges of the timbered land, and fences in the prairie ground, sufficient for his tillage, which he has no trouble of clearing."[8] Some twenty years later, this same settlement procedure was described by an anonymous author, who observed in Illinois that "the settlements are at present chiefly confined to the margins of the timber and prairie. . . ."[9]

However desirable the mixed vegetational areas might have been in actuality, there is some indication of the existence of a prejudice against all non-forested areas, a prejudice that seemingly might have reduced the attractive force of the mixed areas. It is often the case that what people *thought* an area to be was far more influential than how it *actually was.* . . . That such prejudice did exist is indicated by many of the travel accounts and immigrant handbooks, whose authors take pains to dispel any fears the reader might have regarding the grassland. M. Birkbeck, an early English settler in Edwards County, Illinois, discussed the prejudice as follows:

> The people to the east of us are incapable of imagining a dry and rich wholesome country, where they may enter at once on the fine lands prepared for cultivation, without the enormous expense of time and labour in *clearing*. . . . The inhabitants of the old States are profoundly and *resolutely* ignorant of the advantages of our prairie country. Books are written in the east to prove the wretchedness of the prairies. . . . (May, 1821)[10]
>
> An erroneous opinion has generally prevailed, both in England and the Eastern States, that all prairies partake more or less of the nature of swamps: that they are, in fact, morasses too wet for the growth of timber. (January, 1819)[11]

The indication is, then, that the characteristics of some types of prairie were being applied to all types.

Apparently there were no misgivings about the fertility of the natural grasslands, as is shown as early as the 1780's by A. Fitzroy's comment on the Kentucky Barrens: "The country, in general, is well timbered, and exceeded by none in variety. Where it is not so, the land is still fine, and covered with a rich grass, which serves for excellent provinder."[12] Very few guidebooks or travel accounts fail to mention the fertility of the prairies.

A very casual survey of the existing contemporary literature leads to the tentative conclusions that, although the prejudice did exist, (1) it was directed primarily at the large expanses of open prairie, where wood and water were absent, rather than at the mixed areas, (2) it did not have its basis in a belief of prairie infertility, (3) it was more the result of the belief, held by persons who had little or no contact with the grasslands, that *all* prairies were devoid of timber and water and were quite extensive. To be sure, the early pioneers must have had initial doubts about the grasslands, doubts

7. David Thomas, *Travels Through the Western Country in the Summer of 1816* . . . (Auburn, N.Y., 1819), p. 185.
8. Benjamin Harding, "A Tour Through the Western Country, A. D. 1818 & 1819," a pamphlet (New London, 1819), p. 9.
9. *Illinois in 1837* . . . (Philadelphia, 1837), p. 14.
10. Birkbeck, Morris, letter of May 7, 1821, as quoted in Sparks, Edwin Erle (ed.), *The English Settlement in the Illinois* (London & Cedar Rapids, 1907), p. 51.
11. Ibid., pp. 5, 6.
12. Fitzroy, Alexander, "The Discovery, Purchase, and Settlement of the Country of Kentuckie in North America, . . ." (a pamphlet), London, 1786, p. 8.

which were only natural for a woodland people, but these were quickly dispelled by experience, and the advantages of the mixed areas were soon fully realized. . . .

The two hypotheses are, then, (1) that different groups interpreted the prairie-forest mixture in different ways at different periods of history and (2) that the mixed areas were very advantageous for settlement and must have exerted an attractive force to settlement by *all* groups during all of the lengthy period during which such areas were accessible and available to the settlers. . . .

The study has been limited to a search for as many actual firsthand accounts of settlement in the area under consideration as can be found. These are in the form of letters, travel accounts, reminiscences, and the like. They do not represent a random sampling or an adequately large one, and it is not maintained that they offer conclusive proof or disproof of the hypotheses. However, it is expected that they will lend support to one or the other and give some possible indication of the correct answer. . . . The samples have been arranged by groups on the basis of origins.

Southerners

The task of subduing the wilderness and preparing the way of civilization in the Ohio valley before 1830 was undertaken largely by pioneers from the South. These settlers came from three major areas, (1) the Piedmont, (2) the southern Appalachian highlands, and (3) the Great Valley, and were generally of two types: (1) the hunters or backwoodsmen, who built log cabins, relied to a great extent on hunting for their livelihood, but also raised a little corn and vegetables, and kept some hogs, a cow or two, and several horses, and (2) the class of settlers who followed the backwoodsmen into an area, differing from their predecessors in that they depended to a greater degree on farming, kept more livestock, and had more conveniences.[13] As was indicated earlier, these southerners supposedly avoided the grasslands.

The first important trans-Appalachian experience that the southerners had with prairies was in the Barrens of Kentucky. Sauer, in his study on the Pennyroyal, reached the conclusion that the fringe of the Barrens attracted settlement quite early, even before 1790, and that the settlers recognized the obvious value of the grassland as pasture.[14] It was, in fact, the pastoral function of the grassland that served as the major attraction to settlement in Kentucky. . . . On the fringe of the Barrens, the settlers generally planted their corn and tobacco in the woodlands, often in Indian old fields, and used the grassland only for grazing. The development and prosperity of many settlements was dependent on their location on the fringes of the Barrens.[15]

Nor were southerners slow to seek out the mixed vegetational areas beyond the Ohio River, and to use the grassland for crops as well as pasture. G. Flower observed on the fringe of a small, dry prairie in southeastern Illinois in 1817 that "it was being settled exclusively by small corn-farmers from the slave states."[16] A map of the nearby English settlement in

---

13. Elias Pym Fordham, *Personal Narrative of Travels . . . and of a Residence in the Illinois Territory: 1817-1818,* ed. Frederick A. Ogg (Cleveland, 1906), pp. 125, 126.
14. Carl O. Sauer, *Geography of the Pennyroyal,* Kentucky State Geological Survey. Series 6, Vol. 25 (Frankfort, 1927), pp. 134, 135, 137.
15. Samuel N. Dicken, "The Kentucky Barrens," *Bulletin of the Geographical Society of Philadelphia* 33 (1935):50.
16. George Flower, *History of the English Settlement in Edwards County, Illinois* (Chicago, 1882), p. 63.

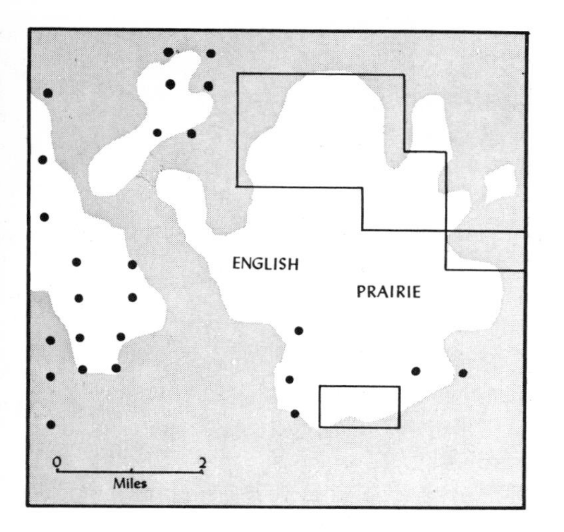

FIG. 1. Map of the English settlement in Edwards County, in 1818. Unshaded areas represent prairie, shaded areas forest. The holdings of the English colony are outlined, while the locations of land entries made by American backwoodsmen are indicated by dots. Map taken from E. P. Fordham, "Personal Narrative of Travels . . . and of a Residence in the Illinois Territory: 1817-1818," ed. F. A. Ogg (Cleveland, 1906), p. 113.

Edwards County revealed that southern backwoodsmen were settled on the fringes of the small dry prairies thereabouts in 1818 (Fig. 1).[17] Farther to the west, a Kentuckian named Reynolds, one of the earliest settlers in Madison County, Illinois located his farm on the fringe of a small, dry prairie, with his fields in the grassland and his house just within the woods.[18] One year later, a native of North Carolina wrote from Hillsborough, in nearby Montgomery County, Illinois, that he had 240 acres of land and planned to get 100 more, "about 40 acres of perraria, the balance timbered land."[19] He was breaking the sod with "4 horses in one plow."[20] A sketch map drawn by an original settler in the Princeville, Peoria County, Illinois, settlement revealed that J. Nixon and B. Slane, two natives of Virginia, located on the fringe of a large, dry prairie. They settled there in 1831 on the edge of a grove and were engaged in farming.[21] Finally, an anonymous author wrote that the small, dry Allison's Prairie in Lawrence County, Illinois, was settled in part by Kentuckians in 1816 and 1817.[22]

The small prairies of southwestern Michigan also received a number of southerners. In 1833 an observer reported a Kentuckian, two "suckers" from southern Illinois, and a "hoosier" from Indiana settled on the fringe of small, dry Prairie Ronde in Kalamazoo County, and added that southerners and westerners outnumbered New Yorkers there.[23] . . . Fuller remarked that southerners were dominant on all of the eight major small, dry prairies of Kalamazoo County by 1831.[24]

Though the preceding accounts represent only a small, unscientific sampling, it is obvious from them that southerners were using the grassland of the mixed areas at an early date, both for grazing and for cropland, and that the prairie fringes were exerting an attraction upon them. . . . It may well have been the

17. Fordham, *Personal Narrative of Travels,* map on p. 113.
18. Salomon Köpfli, "Die Schweizer-Kolonie Highland in Illinois," *Deutsch-Amerikanische Geschichtsblätter* (5, 1905), Heft 2, p. 17.
19. James W. Patton, ed., "Letters From North Carolina Emigrants in the Old Northwest, 1830-1834," *Mississippi Valley Historical Review* 47 (1960-1961):270.
20. Ibid., p. 273.
21. Old Settlers' Union of Princeville and Vicinity, vol. 1 of *History and Reminiscences* (Peoria, 1912), pp. 20, 21; the map can be seen in vol. 2 (Peoria, 1915), opp. p. 4.
22. *Illinois in 1837,* p. 86.
23. Charles Fenno Hoffman, *A Winter in the West* (New York, 1835), vol. 1, pp. 176, 177, 181.
24. George N. Fuller, *Economic and Social Beginnings of Michigan* (Lansing: Michigan Historical Publications, 1916), p. 315.

adjacent location of the forests of the Old Northwest to Kentucky and the guiding function of the rivers that led the bulk of the southerners to settle in forested areas. The southerners came into contact with the mixed vegetational areas of Illinois and Indiana *later* than they did the forests, and the evidence seems to indicate that once this contact was made, they were quick to realize the advantages of the mixed areas. . . .

Northerners

In the period following the opening of the Erie Canal, from about 1830 to 1850, there was a flood of immigration into the Old Northwest from New York and New England. The flow of northern settlers was further supplemented by Pennsylvanians and Ohioans moving to the west along the roads and rivers, and within a twenty-year period they had settled most of northern Indiana and Illinois, southern Michigan, and southern Wisconsin. In so doing, they were presented with a vegetational choice, and a sample of their reaction follows.

The small, dry prairie rondes of southwestern Michigan were one of the first areas where the Yankees encountered the mixed vegetational areas. E. Lothrop of Massachusetts settled on the south margin of Prairie Ronde, Kalamazoo County, in 1830, and built his home in the shelter of the woods. The larger part of his 720 acres, including the fields, lay in the prairie.[25] A traveller on Prairie Ronde in 1834 quoted one of the southern settlers there as having said "we can winter our cows . . . on wooden clocks, there's so many Yankees among us."[26] Natives of Vermont and Maine were reportedly settled on White Pigeon and Sturgis Prairies in the St. Joseph Valley as early as 1827.[27] Fuller, a student of Michigan settlement history, reached the conclusion that New Englanders, and indeed, all settlers, preferred these mixed vegetational areas and occupied them before the forests were taken.[28]

In an early account, dated 1818, a Vermonter wrote from near Edwardsville, Madison County, Illinois, that he had purchased 264 acres, "part Prairie and part timbered land." He mentioned that it required three yoke of oxen or six horses to break the sod.[29] Some years later, near Boyd's Grove, which lay southeast of Dixon, Illinois, a traveller reported in 1834 that a New York farmer had settled "along the edge of a beautiful and well watered grove."[30] S. Dodge found the identical arrangement around Princeton, Bureau County, Illinois, where New Englanders built their homes in the margin of the woods.[31]

In 1836 a group of New Yorkers under the leadership of Reverend George W. Gale founded a religious settlement in Knox County, Illinois, the present-day Galesburg. The site for settlement was carefully chosen to include both prairie and forest, and the farms of two south-

25. G. V. N. Lothrop, "Edwin Howard Lothrop," *Historical Collections, Pioneer Society of the State of Michigan* (2nd edition, 1908), pp. 234, 235.

26. Hoffman, *A Winter in the West,* vol. 1, p. 178.

27. Fuller, *Economic and Social Beginnings of Michigan,* p. 263.

28. Ibid., p. 311.

29. Solon J. Buck, ed., "Pioneer Letters of Gershom Flagg," *Transactions of the Illinois State Historical Society for the Year 1910* (Springfield, 1912), pp. 155, 157.

30. Hoffman, *A Winter in the West,* vol. 1, pp. 239, 240.

31. Stanley D. Dodge, "Bureau and the Princeton Community," *Annals of the Association of American Geographers* 22 (1932):184, 185, 192.

erners who lived between the prairie and forest were bought in order that the woodland and grassland holdings of the colony might be contiguous.[32]

B. Bryant recalled that emigrants from Knox County, Ohio, wintered on Morgan Prairie in northern Indiana in 1834-1835 but did not find a suitable site combining timber and prairie there. They continued west to Lake County, where they located a desirable mixed area and founded the settlement of Pleasant Grove.[33] About the same year, in nearby Will County, Illinois, a New Hampshire settler wrote to his brother, advising him:

> Make a claim as I told you of More Timber and some prairie . . . If I had thousands [I would] invest it all in claims, for claims of from a quarter to a half section of prairies and 70 or 80 acres of Timber can be bought enough of them at from $400 to $1000. . . .[34]

The letter also explained that woodlots were not often adjacent to the prairie property.[35] This was the case even in unsurveyed lands, where, according to one account, squatters "meted & bounded every man's *wood land,* allowing each family 40 acres of timber & as much Prairie as he pleased to take up."[36] . . .

The 1830's also witnessed the beginning of Yankee settlement in southern Wisconsin. A native of New Hampshire described his land near South Port in the southeastern part of the state in 1837 as follows:

> The land is on Fox river—75 acres of it is high prairie and scarsely a tree on it—60 acres botom land contained in a bend of the river. . . . The most of the remainder is oak openings & groves of good timber.[37]

Twelve years later, a New Yorker settled near Aztalan, Wisconsin, encouraged his relatives to buy land near his, and described it as having "some 4 or 5 Acres of prairie on it and the rest of it is in timber—No water."[38] He testified to the advantages of having some prairie land to farm. . . .

It appears, then, that the majority of northerners felt most at home in the mixed vegetational areas. They settled on the fringes of the woodlands, as many of their southern predecessors had done, and they farmed the adjacent prairie. Almost without exception, they were not attracted by the forested areas, a sentiment well expressed by a New Yorker in Indiana in 1840 who wrote, "the timber is so heavy . . . it is a great deal of hard labor to clear a farm . . . I do not like this country."[39] . . .

English

One does not generally think of English immigration in connection with the Old Northwest, perhaps because the English were so quickly Americanized, but there were, nevertheless, several colonies. The most important of these was the English settlement in Edwards County, Illinois,

32. Earnest E. Calkins, *They Broke the Prairie* (New York, 1937), pp. 35, 45, 50, 62.
33. B. Bryant, "Reminiscences of Pleasant Grove," *Reports of the Historical Secretary of the Old Settlers' Association of Lake County, Indiana, from 1885 to 1890* (Crown Point, Ind., 1893), p. 33.
34. "Letters of Richard Emerson Ela," *Wisconsin Magazine of History* 19 (1935-1936):437, 443, 444.
35. Ibid., p. 447.
36. Alfred Brunson, "A Methodist Circuit Rider's Horseback Tour From Pennsylvania to Wisconsin, 1835," *Wisconsin Historical Collections* 15 (1900):277.
37. "Letters of Joseph V. Quarles," *Wisconsin Magazine of History* 16 (1932-1933):297.
38. "Silas J. Seymour Letters (I)," *Wisconsin Magazine of History* 32 (1948-1949):195.
39. "Pollock Correspondence," *Indiana Magazine of History* 31 (1935):51.

which was colonized in 1818. The two founders, M. Birkbeck and G. Flower, sought a mixed vegetational area, where the advantages of both forest and prairie could be enjoyed (Fig. 1). Flower wrote that he "shrank from the idea of settling in the midst of a wood of heavy timber, to hack and hew my way to a little farm, ever bounded by a wall of gloomy forest."[40] . . . Birkbeck and Flower finally decided to buy part of a small, dry prairie: ". . . rich natural meadow bounded by timbered lands, within reach of two navigable rivers, and [which] may be rendered immediately productive at a small expense. . . . Nothing but fencing and providing water for stock is wanted to reduce a prairie into the condition of useful grass land; . . . the transition to arable is . . . a simple process."[41] . . .

In 1842, near Rochester in Racine County, Wisconsin, an English settler wrote that he had bought an eighty-acre farm, which included ten acres of timber and seventy acres of openings and prairie, including some marshy land for pasture. He farmed on the prairie and obtained water by digging a well.[42]

These examples serve to indicate that the English, too, chose the areas of prairie-forest mixture in which to settle. Their choice of land was apparently no different from that of native Americans.

Germans and German-Swiss

. . . One of the earliest encounters between German-speaking immigrants and the mixed prairie-forest areas occurred in 1831 near Highland, Madison County, Illinois, when a group of Swiss settled on the fringe of small, dry Looking Glass Prairie. The "parklike" site was chosen only after a long search, and, in the words of an original settler, it was taken in preference to "the endless forests of Missouri" and the "monotonous, boundless prairies of Illinois."[43] Two years later, in 1833, a group of High German farmers settled on Loop Prairie in St. Clair County, Illinois, a short distance to the south of the Swiss (Fig. 2). The site was chosen after a lengthy search, and it consisted of a small, dry prairie watered by a creek and surrounded by wooded hills. Each settler obtained a farm which contained both prairie and woods, often in two or more non-adjacent plots, and most of the houses were built along the edge of the forest. The Germans recognized the fact that the best farmland lay in the grassland portion of their holdings.[44]

Of all the states of the Old Northwest, Wisconsin received the largest share of German-speaking immigrants. For the most part, they settled in the forested portions of the state, a phenomenon which led many to believe that the Germans were expressing an innate fondness for wooded areas. Schafer reached the conclusion that the reason for German avoidance of the prairies was that it cost more to buy and develop farms there.[45] What Schafer said in effect was that the Germans did not have a free choice of vege-

---

40. Flower, *History of the English Settlement,* p. 36.
41. Morris Birkbeck, as quoted in Milo Milton Quaife, ed., *Pictures of Illinois One Hundred Years Ago* (Chicago, 1918), pp. 14, 16.
42. Milo M. Quaife, ed., *An English Settler in Pioneer Wisconsin, The Letters of Edwin Bottomley 1842-1850* (Madison, 1918), pp. 34, 55.
43. Köpfli, "Die Schweizer-Kolonie Highland in Ilinois," Heft 1, pp. 58, 59.
44. G. Engelmann, "Zur Geschichte der ersten deutschen Ansiedlungen in Illinois, I, Die deutsche Niederlassung in Illinois, fünf Meilen östlich von Belleville," *Deutsch-Amerikanische Geschichtsblätter* 16 (1916):249, 250, 259, 264, 278, 279. This was reprinted from an article in the periodical *Das Westland,* Heidelberg, 1837.
45. Joseph Schafer, *A History of Agriculture in Wisconsin,* Vol. 1 of the Wisconsin Domesday Book (Madison, 1922), pp. 38, 39.

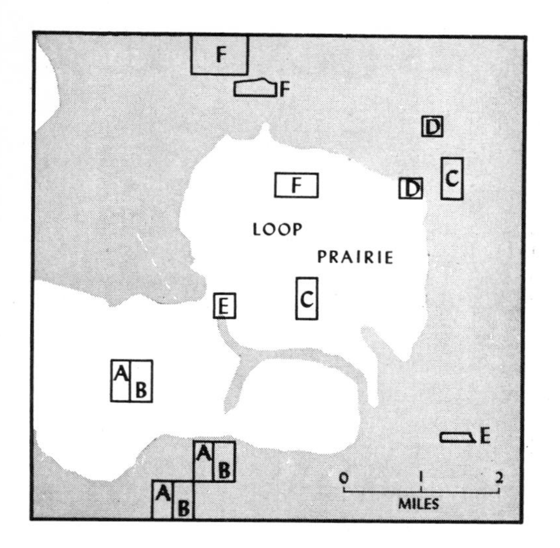

FIG. 2. Map of the German Settlement of Loop Prairie in St. Clair County, Illinois, in 1833. Unshaded areas represent prairie, shaded areas forest. The scattered holdings of various individuals are outlined and lettered for identification. For example, settler A owns three separate plots, settler E, two plots. Map taken from G. Engelmann, "Zur Geschichte der ersten deutschen Ansiedlungen in Illinois, I: Die deutsche Niederlassung in Illinois, fünf Meilen östlich von Belleville," "DeutschAmerikanische Geschichtsblätter," vol. 16, 1916, opp. p. 248. (This is a reprint of an article which appeared in "Das Westland," Heidelberg, 1837.).

tational sites due to the differential prices and expenses involved, and therefore it did not necessarily follow that they preferred the forested areas. Indeed, the following examples indicate that some Germans in Wisconsin recognized the advantages of settlement in the mixed prairie-forest areas and sought such sites when they were available and when the immigrant had adequate funds.

One of the best examples expressing German opinion on settlement sites was contained in the writings of W. Dames, who arrived in Wisconsin in the late 1840's. He advised prospective emigrants not to settle in the forests, "in which the settlers almost work themselves to death . . . ," suggesting instead the advantages of the mixed areas.[46] Dames believed that the ideal site would include timber for fuel and construction, dry prairie for farming, and wet prairie for grazing. . . .

The founders of the Swiss colony at New Glarus, Green County, Wisconsin searched over wide areas of the Midwest in 1845 for a suitable site before deciding on a mixed prairie-forest area. At first, the timbered land was held in common by the settlers, but after a year it was divided into two-and-one-half acre plots. Each farmer had, in addition, twenty acres of prairie to use for cropland.[47]

In the German colony of Frankenlust, Saginaw County, Michigan, founded in the late 1840's, the settlers were quick to realize the advantages of the wet prairies there for use as pastures (Fig. 3).[48] . . . Most of the landholdings in the colony reached from the forest out into the wet prairie, so as to include natural pasture, and the houses were built just within the shelter of the woods (Fig. 3).[49]

It may well be true that Germans, as a people, have an affinity for timbered areas, but certainly the virgin forests of America were far different from the cultivated, remnant woodlands of Germany. This sentiment was well expressed by a settler in Indiana, who wrote: "The road led us

46. William Dames, "Nordamerika: Der Staat Wiskonsin; Wie Sieht es in Wiskonsin Aus?," a pamphlet (Meurs, 1849), p. 18.

47. John Luchsinger, "The Planting of the Swiss Colony at New Glarus, Wisconsin," *Collections of the State Historical Society of Wisconsin* 12 (1892):347, 362. A map of the colony can be found in Dieter Brunnschweiler, *New Glarus (Wisconsin) Gründung, Entwicklung und heutiger Zustand einer Schweizerkolonie im amerikanischen Mittelwesten* (Zürich, 1954), p. 45.

48. Friedrich Carl Ludwig Koch, *Die Deutschen Colonien in der Nähe des Saginaw-Flusses* (Braunschweig and New York, 1851), p. 8.

49. Ibid., p. 11.

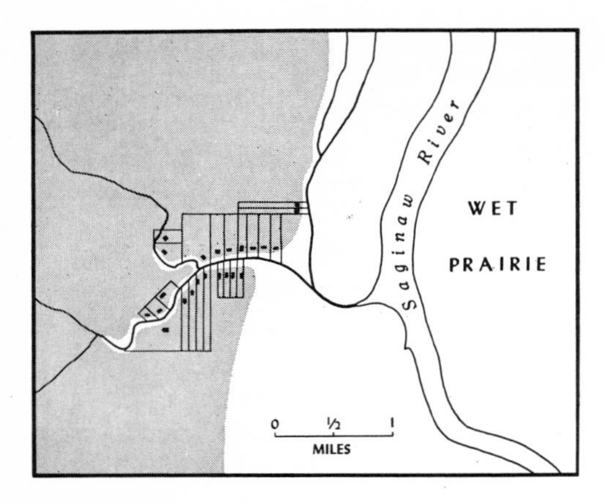

FIG. 3. Map of the German colony Frankenlust, in the vicinity of Saginaw, Michigan, 1851. Unshaded areas represent wet prairie, shaded areas forest. The property lines of each settler's holding and the location of each farmstead are shown. Map taken from F. C. L. Koch, "Die Deutschen Colonien in der Nahe des Saginaw-Flusses" (Braunschweig and New York, 1951), opp. p. 48.

through an endless virgin forest. . . . Although in Germany I loved the woodland solitudes, this was entirely too much for me. I no longer derived any pleasure from the woods because I realized that the whole vast region was covered with them, and that there was no beautiful landscape to be seen anywhere around."[50] Indeed, one might well argue that it was the mixed prairie-forest areas that most closely resembled the woodlands of Germany.

Conclusion

On the basis of examples cited in the preceding sections, some tentative conclusions can be made. First, the mixed vegetational areas would seem to have offered more advantages for settlement than either forest or prairie, and the generally accepted notion of a dichotomy between woodland and grassland needs to be revised to include this extensive land between the forest and the prairie. Second, the advantages were recognized by peoples of varied origins over a long period of time, and to judge from the scattered evidence, the mixed areas may well have been preferred as sites for settlement as long as they were available and accessible (Table 2). Any anti-grassland prejudice which might have existed was of minor importance in guiding the course of settlement. It was not the grassland as such that was avoided, rather, only the open prairies, for only there did the prairie problem really begin.

TABLE 2. Summary of Examples

Location	*Date*	*Vegetation type (see Table 1)*
Southerners		
White County, Ill.	1817	2
Edwards County, Ill.	1818	2
Madison County, Ill.	1831	2
Montgomery County, Ill.	1832	2
Peoria County, Ill.	1831	4
Lawrence County, Ill.	1816	2
Kalamazoo County, Mich.	1829	2
Northerners		
Kalamazoo County, Mich.	1830	2
St. Joseph County, Mich.	1827	2
Madison County, Ill.	1818	2
Lee County, Ill.	1834	4
Bureau County, Ill.	1829	4
Knox County, Ill.	1836	4
Lake County, Ind.	1835	4
Will County, Ill.	1835	4
Southeastern Wis.	1837	1, 2, 3
Jefferson County, Wis.	1849	2
English		
Edwards County, Ill.	1818	2
St. Joseph County, Mich.	1834	2
Racine County, Wis.	1842	1, 2, 3
Germans and German-Swiss		
Madison County, Ill.	1831	2
St. Claire County, Ill.	1833	2
Green County, Wis.	1845	4
Saginaw County, Mich.	1848	3

50. Jakob Schramm, *Letters of Jakob Schramm and Family from Indiana to Germany in 1836,* tr. Norma M. Stone (Hanover, N.H., 1951), pp. 51, 52.

B. *Migrants in a Plural Society*

The Immigrant and the Urban Melting Pot

Francis X. Femminella

The United States is one of those nations in the world which got a good deal more out of its immigrations than just people. No nation gets *only* people—that is, population statistics—but America received much more; it acquired an "immigrant culture." What this means and how it happened can be understood by exploring the fascinating interconnections between a number of ideas—ideas concerning immigration, concerning intergroup processes, and concerning cities.

The Social Uses of Theory

Certain salient ideas have a multiplicity of statuses and functions. To illustrate briefly what this implies, we can take the idea of the "melting pot" as an obvious example. In this country, the melting pot idea can be categorized in a number of ways. First, it represents a belief, a hope, and a symbol for allaying fears; it is thus a collective *ideology*. Next, it is a description and explanation of social events and processes, and serves as a kind of *social theory*. Finally, this idea can be seen as one of those historical fictions and myths whose function was to stabilize the social order, or what Karl Mannheim referred to as a "utopian wish image."

The very mention of the terms "immigrants" and "cities" stimulates in some people images which are ideologically colored and which have in the past generated feelings of strangeness and prejudice. Judgments were made regarding reasons for immigration, city life, and the "types" of people who moved to cities, largely apart from either empirical or historical reference. . . .

The most usual pattern in the United States was for immigrants to settle in cities; and one can hardly understand either immigration or cities in the United States without taking the developmental dynamics of both into account. These assertions are not enough, however, since they fail to provide adequate methodological or theoretical direction for finding important

Reproduced (with omissions) by permission from *Perspectives on Urban America,* edited by Melvin I. Urofsky (Garden City, N.Y.: Anchor Books, 1973), pp. 43-65.

distinctions in the various immigrations to the United States or migration within the states, or for understanding the implications of these differences. William Petersen's typology may help us out of this problem. He distinguishes between the 1) *Primitive* (Wandering, Ranging; and Flight from the Land) migrations which result from ecological necessity; 2) *Forced* (Displacement; and Slave Trade); 3) *Impelled* (Flight; and Coolie Trade) migrations resulting from the pressure of social institutions; 4) *Free* (Group; and Pioneer) migrations which result from social norms and man's higher aspiration; and 5) *Mass* (Settlement; and Urbanization) migrations resulting from social momentum and which are examples of collective behavior. In this classification scheme, the first parenthetical term of each class of migration represents what Petersen calls a *Conservative* type of migration, in that persons move geographically in order to retain as much else of their former life as possible; and the second term of the parenthesis represents an *Innovating* type of migration in that persons move in order to achieve something new. The immigrations to the United States during the nineteenth century changed in character from Free to Mass migrations and, toward the end of the century, at nearly the same time that our economy was shifting from an agrarian to an industrial base, the migrations shifted from a Conservative Settlement type of migration to an Innovating Urbanizing type of migration. Industrialism, urbanization, and immigration became tied to one another at the same time that the United States was becoming a very changed nation. Initially, the interconnection of economy, ecology, and demography was grossly misunderstood, and popular interpretations of the meaning of these social processes were largely ideological. In the mind of nativist and immigrant alike the problems generated by one process became confused with the problems generated by others. . . .

If we accept the anthropological truism that cultures are integrated, then there is an apparent contradiction in placing high value on both conformity with concern for the opinion of others, on the one hand, and nonconformity and individuality, on the other; between equality for all with racial heterogeneity (the "melting pot") and disdain and distrust of foreigners with feelings of superiority over them. These important paradoxes are supported by a kind of logic which emanates out of the ideologies of the group. Thus, there is no contradiction in a group's "strain for consistency" with its consequent imposition of uniformities, and its stress on personal competition for economic advantage. Immigrants residing in the cities were a locus where these contradictory forces came together. As foreigners, they had to learn the meaning and the manners of society, at first for sheer survival; then after some initial success they were impelled, seemingly by some inner human dynamic, to participate in the great American dream. In practice, this meant they entered into the life of the city–and especially the action of the market–learning to compete. Once this happened, the "race relations cycle" began. When an immigrant retained his foreign ways, the competition became racial and impersonal and conflict followed; but when he obliterated the external differences, personal competition ensued, and people attained positions they were "best fitted to fill," out of which developed friendships and ultimately assimilation.

In time it became a basic tenet of belief that cities served as the primary agency for the assimilation of foreign groups. Robert E. Park wrote: "Great cities have always been the melting pots of races and of cultures. Out of the vivid and subtle interactions of which they have been the centers, there have come the newer breeds and the newer social types." The inference that, to a very large extent, immigrant groups in the United States were not assimilating on the farms and the villages, would have to be denied, although there is some truth to it. First, however, a question must be raised about the meaning of "assimilation."

Park used the term "assimilation" to refer to that social process whereby people of different races and cultures are drawn into "the ever narrowing circle of a common life." This meant the erasing of external differences, the development of superficial uniformities particularly in manners and fashion but also in language, which enabled newcomers to participate in the new life, in a "practical working arrangement," so that likemindedness in individual opinions, sentiments, and beliefs could eventually accrue. H. P. Fairchild, on the other hand, wrote: "The process by which a nationality preserves its unity while admitting representatives of outside nationalities, is properly termed 'assimilation.' "

Two important points are raised by these definitions. First, the difference in the direction of change should be noted in those two conceptions. For Park, assimilation denoted change on the part of the alien, but it also implied change on the part of the host society, in compromises and accommodations. Accommodation always preceded assimilation; secondary relationships based on interests inevitably engendered personal intercourse and friendship, based on sentiment, which would break down social distance between people. [H. P.] Fairchild, on the other hand, placed the burden of change on the immigrant: "It is he who must undergo the entire transformation; the true member of the American nationality is not called upon to change in the least. . . . There is no 'give and take' in assimilation."

A second important point raised by these definitions is the distinction between "cultural" assimilation and "social" assimilation. While the newcomer may indeed acquire the behavioral patterns of the host society, that is, be acculturated, he may not as yet be admitted, as Milton M. Gordon points out, to the "cliques, clubs and institutions of the host society on a primary group level," that is, he may be *culturally* but not *structurally* assimilated. Structural assimilation precedes marital amalgamation, which is followed by the development of a unifying sense of peoplehood based exclusively on the host society. More interpenetrating aspects of unification follow wherein prejudice, discrimination, and value and power conflicts are all absent. While the melting pot refers to assimilation of peoples, we now see two areas of inquiry. First, which "direction of change"—change of immigrant, change of host society, or some combination of both—does the melting pot imply? Second, does this idea refer to cultural assimilation or to structural assimilation and deeper levels of unity?

A Nation of Immigrants

The melting pot idea, with its profound influence on United States history, is best analyzed in its socio-historical context as it related to the peopling of the country and the development of a culture. The union of the people of the United States has been legally defined, and it has been defended with bloodshed, but with all this the meaning of union is variegated. The early colonists distrusted governments, but were beginning to establish a sense of themselves as a united group whose elusive nature was yet to be determined. Were they to be a people, a nation, a civilization, or some combination of these? It must be remembered that the United States is a nation which originated among immigrants and had, for its first hundred years as a republic, a policy of open migration. In all, from the initial colonization of America by northern Europeans to the present, nearly fifty million immigrants have come to these shores. Although immigration statistics were not kept before 1820, it is estimated that during the first century of the republic, nine and a half million persons entered the country. While the numbers are significant in themselves, they do not tell the whole story. What is even more meaningful is the cultural diversity of these millions of people and the fact that they poured in over the nation like huge waves crashing over a sea wall. The influence this had on the nation was put poetically by Oscar Handlin in the introduction to his Pulitzer prize-winning *The Uprooted:* "Once I thought to write a history of the immigrants in America. Then I discovered that the immigrants *were* American history." Historians have vividly described the migration of foreigners from England, Scotland, Wales, Ireland, Germany, Scandinavia, The Netherlands, France, and Africa. Jews from all over Europe, but particularly from Germany and Poland, came to the United States, and by the middle of the nineteenth century, a small number of Italians had already arrived. In addition, a limited migration from the Orient is also recorded. This intermingling of cultural groups was early observed and extolled by Crèvecoeur, who wrote, "The Americans were once scattered all over Europe, here they are incorporated into one of the finest systems of population which has ever appeared." Crèvecoeur seems to have been one of the earliest writers, if not the first, to herald the melting pot idea, and it is worth recalling his classic description:

> . . . whence came all those people? They are a mixture of English, Scotch, Irish, French, Dutch, Germans, and Swedes. From this promiscuous breed, that race now called Americans has risen.
>
> . . . What then is the American, this new man? He is either a European, or the descendant of a European, hence that strange mixture of blood, which you will find in no other country. I could point out to you a family whose grandfather was an Englishman, whose wife was Dutch, whose son married a French woman, and whose present four sons have now four wives of different nations. *He* is an American who, leaving behind him all his ancient prejudices and manners, receives new ones from the new mode of life he has embraced, the new government he obeys and the new rank he holds. He becomes an American by being received in the broad lap of our great *Alma Mater*. Here individuals of all nations are melted into a new race of men, whose labours and posterity will one day cause great changes in the world.

The evidence, however, seems rather to indicate that this intermixing was not as general as Crèvecoeur made it out to be, and one can document the failure of assimilation among the Germans, the Dutch, the Irish, the Scots, and the French during the years 1789 to 1829. Indeed, in reviewing the literature of the period it seems clear that English immigrants arrived in sufficient numbers and exhibited sufficient aggressiveness and strength to impose their standards on all of their co-settlers and among the native inhabitants as well. By the close of the colonial period, white, Anglo-Saxon, Protestant standards dominated. Because the growth of the nation required more manpower, free immigration was allowed, regulated only by the states. Nevertheless, critical attitudes toward non-English immigrants developed early, with some states taxing non-English and non-Welsh immigrants, and abusive treatment was accorded the German and Scotch-Irish immigrants of that time. Their attempts at, or resistance to, becoming anglicized over the next three or four generations, and the success of some, particularly in Pennsylvania, at maintaining their own language and customs seemed to presage the ethnic struggles of our history. Far worse than this was the pernicious torment the colonists inflicted upon Indians and Africans in their midst, whom they used. That the melting pot idea was not understood, or rather was interpreted differently at different times according to prevailing ideologies, is seen in the arguments for and against free immigration which began early in our history and still go on today.

In some of these early arguments one can discern the distinctively bourgeois characteristics of the emerging middle class beginning to crystallize. The "Native American" and the "Know-Nothing" movements in the mid-nineteenth century developed out of antipathy for alien ways and what was taken to be a threat of "take over" by foreign kings, socialists, and papists. "America for the Americans" was the motto they proclaimed. White, Anglo-Saxon, middle-class, Protestant United-Statesians, and also those others who had shed all vestiges of their former heritage, exhibited fear and hostility equally toward immigrants and toward those fellow-citizens who refused or were unable to be anglicized. For these Anglo-Americans, whether consciously or not, the melting pot had a very distinct meaning: it meant the dissolution of all non-English ways. Pride in the product—a free, democratic, egalitarian, successful, non-urban people, the new superior "American"—prevented them from seeing either any inconsistencies in their beliefs or any good in cultural diversity. . . .

As the country expanded, the need for manpower both for the frontier and for industry continued, and so did free migration. But the xenophobic forces opposed to open migration kept at their work, too. In March 1875, the first restrictive federal legislation was passed, prohibiting the admittance of felons and prostitutes into the country. In May 1882, the first racial restriction was legislated—Chinese laborers were denied entry—and in August of that year "convicts," "idiots," "lunatics," and potential paupers were rejected. In subsequent acts, the list of restricted persons gradually lengthened, and eventually quotas for the admittance of selected immigrants were established in May 1921.

This and the even more prejudicial amended Quota Act of 1924 grew out of a race ideology synthesizing beliefs in 1) the superiority of Anglo-Saxon people; 2) the right of Anglo-Americans to set behavioral and cultural standards for all the citizens of the United States; and 3) the formation of an "American" race. . . . In June 1952 a completely revised law relating to immigration and naturalization was enacted; and the persistence of the Anglo-Saxon superiority myth was evident both in the congressional debate before enactment and in the law itself. In addition, the restrictive aspects of the law were made more stringent, under the guise of protecting the national interest against anarchy, communism, and other "foreign" political doctrines. In October 1965 a new Immigration Act was signed into law, whose purpose was to rid the law of race prejudice and discrimination. The quota system was abolished, although immigration reform continued. Still unresolved, however, is the meaning of the "melting pot."

The Melting Pot

The last decades of the nineteenth century have been called an era of upheaval. They were a time of tumultuous change in the economic history of the country—mass industrialization, paralyzing depressions, the organization of labor. As the new century began, cities bulged with newcomers from the farms of this country and from foreign lands. The immigrants themselves were different, coming not from Northern and Western Europe but from Southern and Eastern Europe. They were Italians, Greeks, Poles, Jews, Russians, and Slavs; and each year sufficient numbers of them came to populate a good-size city. And indeed, it was to the cities that they came rather than to the farms or the frontier. Nativists could now link their anti-newcomer, anti-Catholic, and anti-Semitic sentiments to their anti-urban sentiments. . . . Israel Zangwill's play *The Melting Pot* was produced at this time (1909) and served as oil poured on troubled waters. It projected a new image of the teeming-with-immigrants city, presenting it as a seething cauldron into which have been poured people from all the nations and all the races of mankind, and out of which comes a new unified super-being, the "American." The "melting pot" became, for a while, a popular symbol of hope for the future unity and homogeneity of the country and of its people.

The melting pot ideas of Crèvecoeur and Zangwill predicted change in the immigrants and change in the host society as well, leading to total assimilation. There are some differences, however, that should be noted. . . . The product which supposedly emerged from the melting pot of Crèvecoeur was the rural, Protestant, Anglo-American. But what could emerge from the pot of Zangwill? Certainly if we take the analogy seriously we can expect that a new "American," not an Anglo-American will emerge. And his destiny will be tied to an *urban,* not a rural way of life. Zangwill's view was that a superman would be produced. The Anglo-American view around the turn of the century was that if immigration were unchecked, the great American race would be diluted, its strength dissipated, its worth spent, its future one of decadence. The Quota Acts of 1921 and 1924, following this view, severely restricted non-Nordic peoples. . . .

Cultural Pluralism

The immigrants came to the cities of the United States; they made the cities; and the cities made them urban United-Statesians. As we review the recent studies of these groups, however, we find that they have not "melted." These Germans, Italians, Irish, Jews, Poles, Africans, Japanese, and others have in so many ways not become Anglo-Americans, and indeed, they seem not to *want* to be Anglo-Americans. They want to be German-Americans, Italian-Americans, Irish-Americans, Jewish-Americans, Polish-Americans, African-Americans, Japanese-Americans, and so on. In view of this, we must move along two avenues of inquiry. First, how is this hyphenated form of group adjustment and assimilation to be explained? Secondly, what does this signify about "American," that is, United States culture? . . .

Even after passage of the Quota Acts, new little worlds grew up in the cities. Migrations from rural areas to cities went on. In the next decade or so, the rural-urban trek was made by ever increasing numbers of persons. From the South, both whites and blacks moved into northern and western cities and they established colonies. Mexicans and Canadians, not restricted by the law, moved into the United States. Even casual observers of cities recognized that neither the "Anglo-conformity" nor the "melting pot" nor the "Americanization" concepts explained either the characteristics of the population or the processes that produced them. Real cities in this country were not monocultural fields. On the contrary, they reflected the "nation of nations" that the United States was becoming. Cultural pluralism, a concept first introduced by Horace Kallen in 1915, was revived in the late thirties and early forties both as an ideology and as an explanation of the observed behavior. Briefly, it implies that each ethnic group can, should, and does maintain itself as a "community" with its distinctive culture, even while its members become citizens and participate in the politics and economy of the wider society. We could call this kind of behavior "structural pluralism" with each group exhibiting some degree of cultural assimilation. A clear example of non-assimilation in this society is the adherence to various religious institutions found here. For the cultural pluralist, democracy guarantees the right of these groups to remain structurally separate, and it prohibits discrimination based on religious affiliation. That ethnic groups in the cities of the United States have shown some degree of assimilation is as obvious from what has been said as the fact that they have not been totally assimilated. They, as groups, have learned to communicate in English, become citizens, acquire the values of success and upward mobility, and so on. In a word, they have moved in the direction of the Anglo-American.

The Anglo-American cultural system was predominant at the time of the founding of the nation and it remains the core of our society. Anglo-American is essentially English, but English modified by the experience of crossing an ocean, of settling in a virgin territory, of clearing land, building homes, and of taming a frontier. The social experience of the colonists matched for novelty their ecological experience. The English engaged in social contact with peoples of different races and cultures. They united and led the insurrection against their English motherland, and they began a political and economic revolution based upon a non-English ideology leading to the creation of a new nation. To be Anglo-American is not to be English-American. But being Anglo-American does, more often than not, mean being white, Anglo-Saxon, and Protestant. Because Anglo-Americans placed such high value on their own ways and excessively low value on other cultures, and because they feared and even hated, without reason, those who looked or acted in ways unfamiliar to them, Anglo-Americans did what had to be done to keep people believing that they were the only "real" or "true" United-Statesians. White, Anglo-Saxon, Protestants, however, are now seen not as the model to which all other groups must necessarily conform but rather as the most successful fellow-United-Statesian group, with whom one must deal. What this means is that WASP-Americans are entering, consciously or unconsciously, willingly or unwillingly, into accommodation patterns with the ethnic communities around them; and particularly in the cities, they have recognized that structural pluralism is a salient aspect of United States culture. Assimilation, then, must be seen as having two directions—toward the core culture and then back to the ethnic sub-culture. In this sense, the culture of the United States may be described as a fluctuating "emerging culture." Change itself is the most salient characteristic of this life. Ethnic groups in this culture are not to be thought of as merely unassimilated holdouts left over from the earlier immigrations which will disappear in time. Rather they have become a fundamental part of United-Statesian social structure and they are most evident in the cities.

Impact-Integration

Finally, in discussing this form of group adjustment and assimilation, we may use the idea of "impact-integration." The more familiar term integration was taken over from mathematics and was apparently first used by Nathan Glazer as a neutral substitute for such words as assimilation and acculturation. For Glazer, immigrants are integrated with Americans when: 1) they no longer present any special social problem; 2) their old-nation political interests are subordinate to United States interests; and 3) when, in the United-Statesian culture which they have changed, they as well as old United-Statesians are at home. William S. Bernard, in using the term, wrote as follows: "Our immigrant stock and our so called 'native' stock have each integrated with the other. That is to say that each element has been changed by association with the other, without complete loss of its own cultural identity, and with a change in the resultant cultural amalgam, or civilization if you will, that is vital, vigorous, and an advance beyond its previous level. Without becoming metaphysical, let us say that the whole is greater than the sum of its parts, and the parts, while affected by interaction with each other, nevertheless, remain complementary but individual." "Integration" as used here is located in the tradition of cultural pluralism, and it describes a dimension of emerging culture. "Impact" refers to certain aspects of the *coming together* of ethnic groups. The term rings with a negative, destructive tone in that it suggests a *booming collision* resulting in a violent fusion, a forced entanglement. . . .

In the conflict that ensues the price demanded of the immigrant to legitimize his presence is social, economic, and cultural subordination and submission. . . . The empirical evidence seems to indicate that no ethnic group in the United States has ever totally submitted. Race and ethnic conflicts have been and are still a very real and important part of our history; for it is out of this impacting that new syntheses evolve. The conflict is resolved in a cultural integration that changes not only the persons involved, nor even also their groups, but the whole society itself. One sees this best in the cities, where, as Michael Parenti has shown, ethnic colonies persist. But it can be seen, too, in the suburbs where voluntary segregation along ethnic as well as social class lines has developed.

Impacting also changes the people in the society; the immigrants are changed most of all, but so are the earlier residents. Sociologists have provided us with general descriptions about these changes in the newcomers. They have described the confusion, the alienation, and the fears that the immigrant experiences when first settling and the comfort and security he derived from moving into close physical proximity to friends and relatives. These are the immigrant communities, the foreign colonies about which we have heard. Second-generation ethnics, the United States-born children of immigrants, ashamed of the foreign behavior of their parents, often rejected their ancestry; others, as a defense against the overt cruel acts of prejudice directed toward them, overidentified with the old culture of their parents. Many of this generation felt the pain of marginality, not knowing whether they were United-Statesians or foreigners. In the third generation and beyond, the immigrants' progeny have felt more secure in their belongingness, in their "United Statesness." As they become young adults, they are able, in assessing their own self-resources, to ask about their distinctive backgrounds and develop new interest in their ancestral heritage. The process of coming to feel at home in the United States has, for most ethnic groups, been a work of generations. . . .

References and Suggested Additional Readings

Alloway, David N., and Francesco Cordeasco, *Minorities and the American City* (New York: David McKay, 1970).

Bailey, Harry A., Jr., and Ellis Katz, eds., *Ethnic Group Politics* (Columbus, Ohio: Charles E. Merrill, 1969).

Banton, Michael, *Race Relations* (New York: Basic Books, 1967).

Bernard, William S., ed., *Americanization Studies: The Acculturation of Immigrant Groups into American Society* (Montclair, N.J.: Patterson Smith, 1971).

Crèvecoeur, Hector St. John de., *Letters from an American Farmer* (New York: E. P. Dutton, 1912).

Dinnerstein, Leonard, and Frederic C. Jaher, eds., *The Aliens* (New York: Meredith, 1970).

Fairchild, Henry P., *Immigration: A World Movement and Its American Significance* (New York: Macmillan, 1925).

Glazer, Nathan, and Daniel P. Moynihan, *Beyond the Melting Pot* (Cambridge, Mass.: M.I.T. and Harvard University Press, 1963).

Gordon, Milton M., *Assimilation in American Life* (New York: Oxford University Press, 1964).

Handlin, Oscar, *The Uprooted* (Boston: Little, Brown, 1951).

Hansen, Marcus L., *The Atlantic Migration 1607–1860* (New York: Harper and Row, 1961).

———, *The Immigrant in American History* (New York: Harper and Row, 1964).

Kallen, Horace M., *Culture and Democracy In the United States: Studies in the Group Psychology of the American Peoples* (New York: Boni and Liveright, 1924).

———, *Cultural Pluralism and the American Idea: An Essay in Social Philosophy* (Philadelphia: University of Pennsylvania Press, 1956).

Kennedy, John F., *A Nation of Immigrants* (New York: Anti-Defamation League of B'nai B'rith, 1963).

Lieberson, Stanley, *Ethnic Patterns in American Cities* (New York: The Free Press, 1963).

Mannheim, Karl, *Ideology and Utopia: An Introduction to the Sociology of Knowledge* (New York: Harcourt Brace, 1951).

Parenti, Michael, "Ethnic Politics and the Persistence of Ethnic Identification," *American Political Science Review* 61 (1967): 717–26.

Park, Robert, *The Growth of the City* (Chicago: University of Chicago Press, 1925).

Petersen, William, "A General Typology of Migration," pp. 271–90, in his *The Politics of Population* (New York: Anchor, 1965).

Zangwill, Israel, *The Melting Pot: Drama in Four Acts,* originally published ca. 1914 (New York: Arno Press, 1975).

The Indian and the Frontier in American History—A Need for Revision / *Wilbur R. Jacobs*

The proposition that I am setting forth here is that although much traditional Indian-white-frontier history is of great significance in illuminating our knowledge of the past, there is a need to focus more of our attention on what might be called the Indian point of view. In fact, I am suggesting that we revise certain of our traditional ideas about the frontier in American history with a hope of seeking a balance to offset some of the widely accepted interpretations that have repeatedly appeared in our textbooks and in many learned journals. If we are going to tell the whole story of Indian-white relations, we must make an all-out attempt to picture the clash of cultures so that there will be an understanding of both cultures, not just one. . . .

Let us begin by looking at the matter of population and population growth. Frederick Jackson Turner's whole concept of American frontier history is founded upon white census data. He based his famous essay of 1893, describing the significance of the frontier in American history, on the 1890 census count, which indicated that the white frontier of settlement had come to a halt. Likewise, in twentieth-century history, population pressures have been very important in recent world history. We might even say overpopulation was a direct cause for the outbreak of World War II because Germany, Italy, and Japan argued they needed more territory as a reserve for their oversupply of people.

What about Indians? Why are they a force in the history of human population? Until about ten years ago we generally accepted the data set forth by James Mooney and A. L. Kroeber, leading anthropologists of the last generation, that in 1492 there were approximately one million Indians in North America, give or take a few hundred thousand. In all of the Western Hemisphere Kroeber estimated a total of 8,400,000 Indians at the time of discovery. One of his later contemporaries concluded after careful evaluation of the evidence that there might be as many as 13,385,000.

But in the 1960s and early 1970s, as a result of the statistical findings of Henry Dobyns, Woodrow Borah, Shelburne Cook, Harold Driver, and other scholars, our whole concept of Indian population and methodology in computing estimates has changed. For instance, Dobyns, an anthropologist has set forth what is becoming a recognized projection of 90,043,000 Indians at the time of discovery for the Western Hemisphere and 9,800,000 for North America. Cook and Borah, combining their skills as physiologist and historian in a 1971 study on native populations of Mexico and the Caribbean, provide figures that are even higher than

Reproduced (with omissions) by permission from *Western Historical Quarterly* 4 (1973):43-56.

Dobyns's, for instance their estimate of 8,000,000 for the pre-Columbian island of Española (modern Haiti and Santo Domingo). Using the same exponential mathematical techniques as Borah and Cook, Dobyns estimates that the figure for the whole Western Hemisphere might be over one hundred million. . . .

We must now acknowledge that the discovery and settlement of the New World cannot ever be described as the movement of Europeans into areas sparsely occupied by native peoples. No longer can commencement speeches about the peaceful occupation of a largely vacant land be accepted with credibility. In fact, what we are dealing with here seems to be a genuine invasion of the New World by Europeans and the dispossession of a hundred million or more native indigenous peoples. The whole rationale of colonial and frontier history in the Western Hemisphere and the arguments explaining the origins of New World nationalities and nations must somehow cope with this new mass of evidence.

What happened to all those Indians? Cook and Dobyns, researchers in the spread of epidemic diseases among Indians, argue convincingly that millions of Indians were killed off by catastrophic disease frontiers in the form of epidemics of smallpox, bubonic plague, typhus, influenza, malaria, measles, yellow fever, and other diseases.[1] (Besides bringing Old World strains of virus and bacteria, Europeans brought weeds, plants, rats, insects, domestic animals, liquor, and a new technology to alter Indian life and the ecological balance wheel.) Smallpox, caused by an air-borne virus, was and is about the most deadly of the contagious diseases. Virulent strains, transmitted by air, by clothing, blankets, or by slight contact (even by an immune individual), snuffed out whole tribes, often leaving only a handful of survivors. Although some kinds of epidemic diseases might be reduced to a mild virulence among Indians (as among whites) after generations of exposure, smallpox was undoubtedly the Indians' worst killer because it returned time and again to attack surviving generations of Indians to kill them off too. Where did it all start?

Dobyns is convinced, and he has convinced me too (in conversations, correspondence, and articles), that the epidemic disease frontiers began with the first European contacts with the New World in the 1400s and 1500s by explorers, fishermen, and the first colonizers. There is evidence, for example, in Carl Sauer's book, *Sixteenth-Century North America, The Land and the People as Seen by the Europeans,* that De Soto's expedition of 1539-42 spread diseases over a wide area, greatly reducing Indian population. There were, then, disease epidemics after the discovery of America which swept like wildfire through the whole Indian world, swiftly moving over the entire continent before Jamestown and Plymouth were going concerns. Thus, in American frontier history we have a more significant frontier to discuss and think about, a virulent disease frontier that preceded the often destructive impacts of fur trading, mining, and agricultural frontiers, which also had much to do with the continued spread of epidemic diseases and the depopulation of the Indian. . . .

What actually happened in our frontier history of land occupation is perhaps best

1. Woodrow Borah and Shelburne Cook argue that the Spanish "disruption of native society and the introduction of new, unusual, and harsh systems of exploitation" also had "a severe effect" on native depopulation in Española. Cook and Borah, *Essays in Population History: Mexico and the Caribbean,* vol. 1 (Berkeley, 1971), pp. 407-9.

measured, not by a historian, but by the eminent geographer Carl O. Sauer in a chapter called "Plant and Animal Life Destruction in Economic History," in his book of essays called *Land and Life*. Sauer argues that "the modern world has been built on progressive using up of its real capital." Surprisingly, Sauer points out that one of the "worn out" parts of the world is the United States, an area of relatively recent settlement in world history. "The United States," he writes, actually "heads the list in exploited and dissipated land wealth. Physically, Latin America is in much better shape than our own country. The contrast in condition of surface, soil, and vegetation is apparent at the international border between the United States and Mexico." Sauer, after making this point that America, erroneously considered the wealthiest nation in the world, is actually a country impoverished because its land has been looted, goes on to give doubtful readers proof. If you really want to see what the land was like before it was depleted, go to Mexico, he says. Indeed, for Americans who want to see for themselves "a reconstruction of soil profiles, and normal vegetation of California," Sauer says, "we must go to lower California." And "Chihauhua," he argues, "shows us what New Mexico was like a generation ago." Think about that. Think of the enormous forces at work over hundreds of years which would bring about such a dissipation of the land and the frontiers of the fur traders, graziers, miners, farmers, and industry. . . .

. . . The Indian, who was basically a conservator, whose religious and totemic beliefs and tribal customs prevented him from following a policy of soil exhaustion or animal extermination, is all but ignored in our history except to account for various wars, uprisings, and conspiracies, which were put down by the gun and the sword. In all, the Indian seems to have been regarded only as a kind of geographical obstacle to the westward movement of white people, as a kind of difficult mountain range or pass through which swarms of whites had to pass on their way to the Midwest, to Utah, Oregon, and California. Turner dismissed the Indian in his lectures and writings as a mere "consolidating influence," a physical danger on the frontier which forced the settlers to consolidate for mutual defense and set up pioneer forms of government.

Despite the tendency to relegate the Indian to historical insignificance, he may have something to say of importance for all Americans, especially on the subject of ecology. Here, for example, are some facts about the Indian which show how completely different his attitude was toward the land and his natural surroundings. These illustrations are largely about the woodland Indians, those great tribes that once occupied all of America's forest lands east of the Mississippi River.

First. It is reasonably certain that the Iroquois, as well as many of the southern woodland tribes, had a form of birth control to prevent overpopulation and exhaustion of food supply. Both John Lawson and Benjamin Franklin wrote about the manner in which Indian families were able to practice what we now call a type of family planning.

Second. In regard to the soil, many of the woodland tribes, including the Shawnee of Tecumseh's tribe, believed that the soil of Mother Earth was so sacred that it should not be defiled by metal tools. Mother Earth's body could only be caressed with a hoe made from the shoulder blade of an animal or a pointed stick. In contrast, think of our gigantic earth-moving machines that rip whole mountains away for dams and freeways, few of which we really need anymore, but nevertheless continue to build. Frank Speck, eminent anthropologist of the woodland Indians, pointed out that some of these great farming people of the woodland tribes resisted the use of metal plows for farming in the nineteenth century when they lived on Oklahoma reservations. Even then they refused to disturb the soil with metal tools. Indeed, the Indian's religion in many respects almost precluded carrying on the kind of agriculture the white man associated with Christianity.

Third. The Hurons and Iroquois (as well as many other woodland farming tribes) were able to keep extensive cornfields productive for a dozen years or more without resorting to what modern farmers depend upon—metal tools, fertilizers, and pesticides. Their fields were burned in the fall and in the following spring were planted with both maize and beans. Burning released nutrients for the soil, but there is no question that the growing of beans and maize together increased the soil's yield. Today we know of nitrogen fixation by bacteria to roots of leguminous plants, but with the Iroquois it was a belief in the spiritual union of beans and corn that gave vitality to the soil.

Fourth. Many of the woodland Indian tribes maintained elaborately planned and well-marked family hunting territories where, for example, beaver population was carefully watched and nurtured to prevent the extermination of these valuable animals. However, it is not generally known that the later introduction of the fur trade, especially the fierce competition between the French and the Albany traders for colonial beaver, with enticements of rum, guns, hardware tools, and clothing, actually brought about an almost complete extermination of both beaver and otter in the Iroquois country by the year 1640, only thirty years after the coming of the white man to colonial New York. The impact of the trading frontier so shattered native concepts of conservation that the Iroquois pursued the beaver into the Great Lakes country in the middle of the seventeenth century. It was on the fringes of their territory that the Iroquois hunters fought off Ottawa, Illinois, Twightwee (Miami Indians of Ohio), and other Algonquian tribes. By the 1680s the Iroquois were fighting for their share of distant Great Lakes beaver-hunting territories. As the colonial historian Cadwallader Colden wrote: "The Five Nations have few or no Bever in their Country, and for that Reason are obliged to hunt at a great Distance, which often occasions Disputes with their Neighbours about the Property of Bever." Clearly, this beaver war actually developed into one of the great bloodlettings of American history by the 1680s, as the Iroquois attempted to destroy not only Canadian Indian rivals in the beaver trade, but also their French allies.

The significance of this saga about beaver hunting and colonial warfare is that it helps to silhouette forces that propelled the early frontier to the West. It also illustrates the fact that although the Indians were basically conservationist (and the Iroquois easily lived within the ecological balance of the northeastern forest before the decimation of forest wildlife), unfortunately they were partners in the destruction of beaver in their eager search for furs to obtain guns, liquor, and other articles the Albany traders had on supply. Another factor was of equal importance—the ecological catastrophe of the decimation of the beaver in the fur trade, a valuable animal which so easily provides a habitat in ponds for many other animals and birds as well as for fish and a variety of plants.

Surprisingly, the story of the extermination of beaver is almost always treated in our histories as fur-trade enterprise, a step in the progressive development of American society, and the taming of the West. Reflecting the frontiersman's viewpoint, white historians have generally equated frontier progress with fur-trade business because progress meant frontier expansion and implied elimination of the Indian frontier, a barrier to peaceful white occupation of the continent. What has seldom been pointed out is that the disappearance of the beaver closely followed the disappearance of the Indian as free-roaming tribesmen. By 1840, two hundred years after they had been cleaned out of the area of New York state, the beaver, according to Kit Carson, had been practically killed off in the Rocky Mountain area. It was in this decade according to a recent doctoral dissertation, that the Indian reservation system in the Far West had its beginning.[2] The beaver, along with the plains buffalo, the antelope, the California grizzly, and the free, independent Indian, all gave way to the white frontier of conquest about the same time. . . .

The whole story of the Indian-white confrontation in American history is tragic and full of violence and atrocities. The fact that the Indian and the white man are differing about approaches to our ecological problems is to be expected, for the Indian and the white man have for centuries been disagreeing about religion, government, and a host of other things. So they will continue to disagree, especially about history and the Indian's place in history. Yet at some future time it may be that even Old Posey, an intrepid, determined Ute and the leader of a local war in Utah, as well as Tecumseh, Pontiac, Blackhawk, Sitting Bull, and Chief Joseph, will be recognized as truly national figures in our history. As much as the heroic figure of the scout, the plainsman, the mountain man, and the cowboy himself, these courageous Indians deserve our respect and admiration. For they and all their Indian brethren may have made contributions to our life-style which may ultimately bring about a better America. As Vine Deloria says, the Indian's message is: "Man must learn to live with other forms of life and not destroy it."

2. Robert Trennert, "The Far Western Indian Frontier and the Beginning of the Reservation System, 1846-1851," Ph.D. dissertation, University of California, Santa Barbara, 1969.

Bibliographical Notes

Henry F. Dobyns's "Estimating Aboriginal American Population, An Appraisal of Techniques with a New Hemisphere Estimate," *Current Anthropology: A World Journal of Sciences and Man,* 7 (October 1966):395-449, contains an addendum with critiques by Bruce Trigger, Harold Driver, Shelburne F. Cook, and other experts, plus a reply by Dobyns. Harold Driver in *Indians of North America,* 2nd ed. (Chicago, 1969), pp. 63-65, cuts Dobyns's estimates by some 50 percent. Dobyns's theories on Indian depopulation resulting from epidemic diseases are also found in his "An Outline of Andean Epidemic History to 1720," *Bulletin of the History of Medicine* 37 (November-December 1963):493-515. Shelburne Cook's and Woodrow Borah's brilliant essays on Hispanic population history have appeared in a number of books and articles. Their latest work, *Essays in Population History: Mexico and the Caribbean* (Berkeley, 1971), has a perceptive essay on methodology (pp. 73-118) and a painstakingly thorough analysis of data (pp. 376-410) behind their estimate of eight million population for Española. The population of Indians in the United States, according to the 1970 census count, was 792,730, excluding Alaskan Eskimos. This figure, of course, does not include hundreds of thousands of Indian people who are blending into the mainstream of American society, many of whom still consider themselves native American Indians but are not counted as such. See U.S. Bureau of the Census, *Census of Population 1970: General Population Characteristics* (Washington, D.C., 1972), p. 293. One estimate is that there are some five million people of Indian descent in the United States. See William Meyer, *Native Americans, The New Indian Resistance* (New York, 1971), p. 82.

Duke Project tapes at the Western History Center, University of Utah, resulting from hundreds of oral history interviews with Indians of many tribes in various stations of life, some of them college students and others elderly Indians on reservations (whose replies must be translated into English), record Indian resentment about white encroachment on sacred places, white destruction of the land, white cruelty and duplicity in trade, treaties, and war. Many of the accounts reach back into the seventeenth century dealing with subjects as early as white contacts with Indians, Spanish slavery of Indians, Acoma Indians, and outrages committed by priests. See, for example, tapes numbered 36, 65, 73, 102, 148, 198. One of the most interesting tapes told by a white pioneer on last skirmishes with the Indians in Utah is that of Lynn Lyman, Blanding, Utah, interviewed by Charles Peterson, December 9, 1967, as recorded on Duke Tape No. 668, Western History Utah. Another interesting tape is Duke Tape No. 550, an interview with Jim Mike, on Old Posey's death, allegedly by poisoning.

Themes in Indian oral history tapes reappear in N. Scott Momaday's *House Made of Dawn,* which tells the authentic and powerful story of modern Indians, who often must live in two worlds, one of which becomes a cycle of dissipation and violence. Momaday's searching essay "The Morality of Indian Hating" in *Ramparts* 3 (Summer 1964): 29-40, echoes much of the pride and disillusionment of Indian oral history, as does Vine Deloria's *Custer Died for Your Sins* (New York, 1969).

The impact of the Judeo-Christian ethic upon the Indian and the wilderness is analyzed by Vine Deloria in a perceptive essay, "An Indian's Plea to Churches," *Los Angeles Times,* February 6, 1972. Similar concepts are in Lynn T. White's "The Historical Roots of Ecologic Crisis," *Science* 155 (March 10, 1967):1203-6. The white man's ruination of the American Southwest, resulting in the black blizzards of the plains, is dramatically portrayed in Pare Lorentz's great film of 1936, "The Plow That Broke the Plains," now available for purchase from the National Archives at an inexpensive price. According to Vernon Carstensen of the University of Washington, "The Plow," once considered an extremely controversial film, was withdrawn by the government from circulation. The case in which it was carried in the 1960s, after it was finally released for showing, bore this warning: "To Be Used for Study as an Art Form Only. Because Subject Matter Is Long Obsolete It Is Not to Be Used for Public Showing." Woody Guthrie's dust-bowl ballads, analyzed by John Opie of Duquesne University at the 1972 Washington meeting of the Organization of American Historians, combine to make a searching social-ecological commentary on the plight of dust-bowl refugees.

Much of this story of land dissipation is recorded in Carl O. Sauer, *Land and Life* (Berkeley, 1965), pp. 148 ff. Sauer's *Sixteenth-Century North America, The Land and the People as Seen by the Europeans* (Berkeley, 1971) details the ecological impact of European exploration frontiers. Donella H. Meadows et al., *The Limits of Growth, A Report of the Club of Rome's Project on the Predicament of Mankind* (New York, 1972), has a unique assessment of the ecological stage of global equilibrium on pages 156-84. This volume and the rigorous review it received in the *New York*

Times Book Review, April 2, 1972, by Peter Passell, Marc Roberts, and Leonard Ross, are eye-opening documentaries for anyone interested in controversies on resource exhaustion and pollution crises. The Indian's resistance to the white man's historic conquest of the land is discussed in W. R. Jacobs, *Dispossessing the American Indian: Indians and Whites on the Colonial Frontier* (New York, 1972), pp. 19-30, 126 ff. Modern Indian criticism of the way in which native Americans have been portrayed in secondary textbooks is succinctly set forth by the staff members of the American Indian Historical Society in Rupert Costo and Jeannette Henry, eds., *Textbooks and the American Indian* (San Francisco, 1970). Pages 33, 38, 51, 85, 153, 173, and 216 have critical appraisals of textbooks written by leading American historians. An important new book which provides a sweeping view of the Indian's losing battle with the white man through the courts is Wilcomb E. Washburn's *Red Man's Land–White Man's Law: A Study of the Past and Present Status of the American Indian* (New York, 1971). William Brandon's learned and fascinating volume, *The American Heritage Book of Indians* (New York, 1961), available in an inexpensive paperback edition (1969), is the best overall synthesis of the Indian in our past.

Geographical Perspectives on the History of Black America / *Richard L. Morrill and O. Fred Donaldson*

. . . The purpose of this paper is to examine a number of geographic aspects of black America as they have developed through time; these include: the changing distribution of the black population from the period of slavery on southern plantations, to the recent period of migration to the cities and concentration in the ghettos; regional variations in the conditions, treatment, and revolts of black people; and finally the development of ghettos and other forms of segregation.

The Colonial Period, 1500 to 1790

The Slave Trade

During the sixteenth century, many Portuguese, Spanish, and later British plantations in the New World became short of labor. Disease, enslavement, and overwork had so decimated the Amerindian population that the importing of slaves from Africa to the colonies came rather early (they had been imported earlier to Portugal and Spain) [*12,* p. 25]. From European trading posts in Senegal, Gold Coast, Ivory Coast, and Slave Coast (mainly Nigeria), Portuguese, and in the seventeenth century, British and Dutch companies began to purchase slaves from local rulers, generally in exchange for European manufactured goods (especially clothing, metal goods, spirits, and weapons). These slaves were sometimes criminals or debtors but usually captives taken during conflicts among the West African States. Most went to Cuba and Brazil, but some were taken to Florida in the late sixteenth century.

Under Portuguese and Spanish rule, slaves were treated according to Roman law, with the right to purchase their freedom, and to own property [*12,* p. 26]. Black men often were on the Portuguese and Spanish trips of exploration, and traveled to many areas on the North American continent before 1619 [*3,* p. 360]. The first non-Indian permanent settlers in America may have been blacks, slaves who revolted and fled from a Spanish colony near the Peedee River, South Carolina, in 1526. Blacks helped build the city of St. Augustine, in 1565, and Cortes brought 300 blacks with him to the California coast in 1737. In the sixteenth century, Estevanico, an African explorer with the Spanish expeditions, explored parts of Florida, New Mexico, and Arizona. The purpose of his last journey was to find "Cibola, or the Seven Cities of Gold."

Black Settlement

Continuous black settlement in America began with the landing of nineteen indentured black servants in Jamestown, Virginia in 1619. At first, restrictive laws were few, and some purchased their free-

Reproduced (with omissions) by permission from *Economic Geography* 48 (1972):1-23.

dom. By the end of the century, however, the traffic in slaves had increased. The number entering New York, New Jersey, and New England was small in comparison with the number entering Virginia to work on tobacco plantations, and the Carolinas to work on tobacco, indigo, and rice plantations [*12,* pp. 36-40]. Most of the plantations were very close to tidewater. Particularly productive were the Sea Islands along the Carolina coast. As more slaves were imported, the form of slavery soon became more restrictive. Under English law, slaves were mere property and had no human rights themselves.

After 1700, the demand for plantation products increased rapidly, as did the opening of new lands, and consequently the rate of slave importation. But the largest numbers of black slaves were still being taken to Brazil and Cuba and other islands of the Caribbean. In Senegal and particularly the Slave Coast and Guinea, the increasing demand for slaves soon led to cruel and destructive intertribal and interkingdom warfare, by which whole villages were sold into slavery and the countryside depopulated.

The British soon came to dominate the profitable slave trade. A kind of triangular pattern was common. British goods purchased the slaves; British ships transported them to New World plantations; and the plantation products, including sugar for the rum which became a major commodity in trading for slaves, moved back to Britain.

By 1750 there were at least 236,000 slaves in the American colonies (including French Louisiana), still predominantly in Virginia and Maryland. The proportion of blacks in the total population reached its apex (21 percent) during this period. Settlement and slavery were moving slowly westward from the coast, but slavery never gained a major foothold in the Piedmont or mountain areas, owing mainly to the small size of farms. The plantation system with its prodigious labor demands slowly spread down the coast into Carolina and Georgia.

Between 1750 and 1800 some 500,000 to 1,000,000 slaves came to this country. New England shippers began to share in the fortunes to be made from the slave trade. Still, in the North slaves were rarely more than 5 percent of the population. In the South, however, the slave proportion was increasing, owing to the predominantly large-scale plantation agriculture, orientation to growing commercial exports, and only moderate white immigration [*12,* pp. 39-40].

By 1770 exploitative agriculture in more accessible but marginal lands near the Virginia coast had already worn out the land; new slave shipments were now destined for the Carolinas and Georgia. About 1780, a new and valuable crop, cotton, was introduced, greatly increasing the demand both for land, especially in more southerly, warmer areas, and for slaves to clear the land and farm it. At first, because of its high humidity requirements, cotton was grown mainly along the coast, from Virginia to Georgia; plant disease, land erosion, demand for more cotton varieties, and the invention of the cotton gin in 1793, led to a fairly rapid shift south and west after 1800.

Black Resistance

From the beginning of slavery in the colonies, black resistance occurred. In fact, the first slave revolt took place in the Pedee River colony in South Carolina. Slave revolts were not the only forms of resistance to bondage. There was the day-to-day resistance of destroyed tools and crops, and work slowdowns. Attempts to kill masters and set fires also appear to have been common. In some slave states so many fires were set that some insurance companies refused to insure homes [*9*, p. 100]. Slaves pretended to be lame, sick, blind, or insane in order to interrupt the work of the plantation; running away was common. Thousands escaped to cities, the North, Canada, Mexico, Indian areas, and wilderness areas. Maroon colonies grew up in forested mountains or swampy areas of the Carolinas, Virginia, Louisiana, Florida, Georgia, Mississippi, and Alabama. Evidence of at least fifty such communities in various places and at various times from 1672 to 1864 have been found [*1*, p. 167].

The Antebellum Period: Plantation and Slavery, 1790 to 1865

The Slavery System

By 1790 the economy of the South was based firmly on export agriculture, which in turn depended on slave farm labor for its low cost. The majority of farmers may not have been slaveholders, but their farms usually were small, occupied less desirable land, and were essentially subsistent [*12*, p. 56]. Economic and political powers were a function of the amount of land owned, and rested in the hands of large plantation owners. In the North, however, plantations were never really successful, farming practices being transferred fairly directly from practices in the mother country. Many northern farmers, nevertheless, did employ immigrant indentured servants. Further white immigration was not encouraged by the plantation owners of the South.

In 1820 slavery was as much a part of the few urban places in the South as it was of rural farms and plantations. During the antebellum period the residences of blacks and whites in southern cities usually were not spatially segregated; this was, of course, not intended to promote integration but to prevent the growth of a cohesive black community. There were, however, segregated black residential areas; and by 1860 housing segregation was increasing. The segregated black areas were usually near markets, docks, alleys, and the peripheries of the cities and towns. Town slaves, while at times restricted to the owner's compound, tended to be much better off than slaves on the plantations. Many worked at building and other trades. Not much contact or aggregation of slaves was permitted; loyalty was aided by the terrible threat of being sold off to a plantation. . . .

Gradually, in the areas of early settlement, mainly coastal Virginia, Maryland, and North Carolina, the land deteriorated from misuse and overuse, and owners found it more and more costly to maintain large slaveholdings. Fortunately for these declining plantation areas, the rapid expansion of settlement into the richer lowlands of Georgia, Alabama, Mississippi, Louisiana, and Tennessee after 1800, and the emergence of cotton as the most profitable export crop created a huge demand for slaves, just as the slave trade was becoming more difficult.

Migration of Slaves

From 1790 to 1810 the slave trade continued high, with the origins shifting east and south to Nigeria, the Congo, and even Angola, where the Portuguese engaged in direct kidnapping raids. Some slaves were brought from Cuba to be sold in the United States. Meanwhile the American market for slaves shifted south and west to Alabama (Mobile) and the

Mississippi Delta (through New Orleans). The British Parliament outlawed the slave trade in 1808, and although American ships ran the British blockades, the volume of trade began to fall drastically.

In the older settled areas, especially in Virginia, the black population had grown rather in excess of local needs, simply through years of natural increase. Instead of being feared, the "surplus" was desired, for the owners in declining farming areas found it most profitable to specialize in the breeding and raising of slaves for sale and shipment to the expanding plantation areas of the Southwest [*3*, pp. 83-84; *12*, p. 51]. The local slave markets, such as Alexandria, blatantly advertised the fecundity of female slaves, and owners gave privileges to women who bore many children. Slaves were thought of as a capital investment, earning between 5 and 15 percent per year.

From 1810 to 1865, then, a large and profitable internal trade in slaves occurred from the "old" to the "new" South. In the early part of the century, before 1830, blacks went mainly from Virginia and Maryland to Kentucky, Tennessee, Georgia, and Alabama; after 1830, the Carolinas, and even Georgia and Kentucky, began to export slaves to Mississippi, Arkansas, Louisiana, and Texas. Table 1 summarizes the relation between the shifting black population and the expansion of cotton. The trade routes ran along the coast, down the Piedmont, along the Appalachian Corridor, and down the Mississippi and Ohio rivers. Since most slaves had to walk in chains, it is not surprising that many did not make it.

Population Redistribution

As a consequence of the decline of agriculture on the coastal plain, and the rapid

TABLE 1. Population* and Cotton, 1790 to 1910

	Black Population				*Slave Shift*	*Black Shift*	*Percent of Cotton Production*			
States	*1790*	*1820*	*1850*	*1910*	*1820 to 1860*	*1860 to 1910*	*1810*	*1830*	*1850*	*1910*
Virginia Maryland Delaware	430	636	727	1092	—230	—200	10	3		
North and South Carolina	214	485	710	1534	—160	—131	60	26	15	15
Georgia Florida Tennessee Kentucky	56	389	891	2221	0	—100	25	40	30	22
Alabama Louisiana Mississippi	30	154	918	2631	+180	—108	5	31	50	28
Arkansas Texas Oklahoma		22	107	1428	+150	+210			5	35

Sources: United States Census of Population and Agriculture. U.S. Department of Agriculture Cotton Statistics, various years.
* (000s).

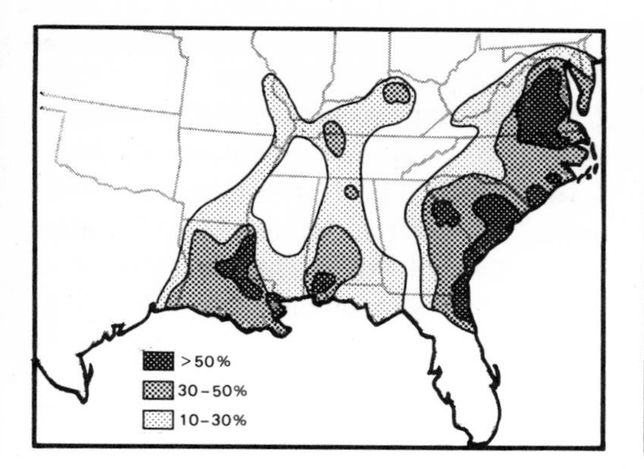

FIG. 1. Proportion of the population black in 1820.

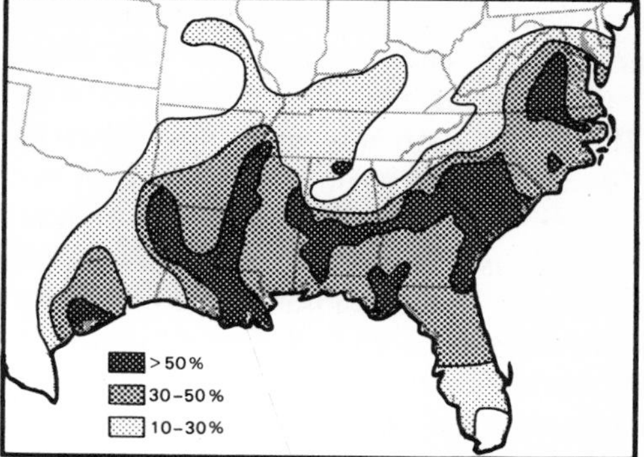

FIG. 2. Proportion of the population black in 1850.

expansion in the Southwest, the distribution of slaves changed radically between 1790 and 1860. Although Virginia remained the leading slave state, its slave population had increased rather slowly; Maryland dropped from second to tenth in number of slaves. The proportion of blacks had fallen in both. From 1790 to 1850, Tennessee, Alabama, Mississippi, and Louisiana grew the most. By 1850 South Carolina (59 percent), Mississippi, and Louisiana (each 51 percent) had slave majorities. By 1850 the center of the black population had shifted from Virginia to South Carolina, and by 1865 west into Georgia (Figs. 1, 2).

Health on the Plantation

The health care of blacks on the plantation must be understood in relation to the general environment, medical practices, and social climate of the time. The frontier conditions, inadequate medical facilities, isolated settlements, undrained lowlands and swamps, coupled with a mild climate, difficulty of preserving food, and ignorance of health practices all contributed to make the population, white and black, vulnerable to epidemic and endemic diseases. But the provision of health care was the responsibility of the dominant white society which, as it often continues to do, treated blacks as "outpatients" at best, or not at all. Under the conditions of plantation society, the food, shelter, clothing, and medical care of the slave was subject to the control and whim of the master.

Black Mortality

It was generally true throughout the South that slaves had higher death rates and shorter life expectancies than whites [*17,* p. 158; *14,* p. 318; *15,* p. 573]. There were two to three times as many black as white deaths in South Carolina from 1853 to 1859. The infant death rate differential between white and black was even greater than that of the general mortality rate. On a sugar plantation in Louisiana 21 percent of the black babies born from 1834 to 1857 died; on a North Carolina plantation during the 1850s, 67 percent of the black infants died; in an eleven-year span in Charleston 48 percent of the black babies died before they were four years old [*14,* p. 320].

The size, type, and location of the plantation seems to have made a difference in the quality of slave life. In general it seems that housing, food, clothing, and health care were better on small farms than on large plantations [*3,* p. 72]. The health problems were most acute in the swampy coastal areas of South Carolina and Georgia and in the river-bottom plantations of Alabama, Mississippi, Louisiana, and Arkansas. Most unhealthy of all were the rice plantations [*10,* p. 141; *14,* p. 297].

There was also an abnormally high death rate among blacks in the cities [*7,* p. 227]. Even though Wade [*17,* p. 134] has indicated that slaves were treated better in the city than in the countryside, black mortality rates in the antebellum city were at least twice those of whites [*7,* p. 42].

Black Rebellion

From the beginnings of slavery in America, the strategy of whites was to make the slave forget his African culture and accept the slave identity and permanent inferiority of his status as property.

Blacks from different tribes were mixed, so that communication was difficult; talk was often forbidden and learning to read and write English was proscribed, so that "ignorance" became self-fulfilling. Even "good" masters acted as though slaves had no rights, often selling members of families separately; "good" plantations offered incredibly bad living conditions, and only the economic value of slaves as workers kept the death and maiming rate from alarming levels.

As a result of injustice, cruelty, and inhuman conditions, the slave was naturally discontented, and often driven to rebellion. The layout and security measures taken within the plantation and the distance of one plantation from another made successful large-scale revolt impossible. Organization for revolt within the plantation was made difficult by a system of favoritism and informing.

But the difficulties imposed upon black communication and organization did not ensure peace for the whites. Guerrilla raids, carried out by bands of escaped slaves living in the extensive swamps or forests, were common from the seventeenth century until the Civil War. No one is certain how many "revolts" occurred, partly because the definitions of "revolt" do not coincide. Kilson [*11*], defining "revolt" as an attempt by a group of slaves to achieve freedom, has identified 65 cases. Aptheker [*2,* p. 16] has recorded approximately 250 revolts and conspiracies, not including those outbreaks and plots that occurred aboard slave traders; he requires a "revolt" to involve at least ten slaves, to have the aim of freedom, and to have contemporary references labeling the event in terms equivalent to revolt. If revolt was defined as it was in Texas in 1858, as a group of three or more slaves with arms who intend to obtain freedom by force, Aptheker asserts that several hundred slave insurrections could be counted.

Slave revolts were not evenly distributed among the states but were concentrated in Virginia, South Carolina, and Louisiana. Within these states, the revolts were clustered in only a few counties. In Virginia, for example, revolts tended to occur in the coastal, tobacco counties. In South Carolina most took place in Charleston County. And in Louisiana most revolts occurred along the Mississippi River north and west of Baton Rouge.

The more successful revolts tended to be where the slaves were better treated, especially near cities such as Richmond and Charleston where the chance to go to black churches made it easier for slaves to organize their revolts. (In the North, too, riots broke out in the cities–in Cincinnati in 1820, Providence in 1824 and 1834, Philadelphia in 1834, and in New York in 1834 and 1836 [*12,* pp. 71, 97].) In the Southwest, where plantations were larger, conditions for the slaves harsher, and discipline more severe, revolts were rarer, although discontent was undoubtedly greater.

The Underground Railroad

Escape of the individual slave to freedom in the North was a more practical alternative to armed rebellion, but his chances of success were not high, considering the great distances and his ignorance of the geography beyond his immediate area. Nevertheless, hundreds of thousands of attempts resulted in some many thousand successful escapes. The underground railroad was the clandestine network of antislavery individuals, including many escaped slaves, by which an escaped slave could be guided into a haven in the North [*4, 15*]. So perilous was the journey within the South that little is known about the routes or the mechanisms; within the North the "railway" was more organized but still secret, since the national Anti-Fugitive Slave Laws of 1850 required northern states to return escaped slaves and permitted owners' representatives to go north and capture them. There remains a controversy over whether or not the underground railroad was a systemized network or rather a restricted number of blacks and whites organized to move slaves in certain localities [*12,* p. 112].

Depending on time and place, the black slave had a number of options in terms of places to which to escape. These options included Mexico, Canada, free states, southern cities, maroon colonies, or Indian tribes such as Creeks, Cherokees, and Seminoles. In the early nineteenth century, a movement developed, among white abolitionists and some blacks, for emigration of blacks to colonies in Africa. The Liberian colony was established in 1821, but only about 15,000 emigrated over a fifty-year period [*3,* p. 131; *12,* pp. 121, 128]. At different times certain border cities were seen by blacks as entry points or gateways to freedom. During the 1700s Pittsburgh was used by slaves escaping to the Northwest Territory. By the turn of the century, Cleveland also served this function; it was touted as the "negroe's paradise" [*13*].

Many sought the relative security of the small, free black communities of northern cities, such as New York, Chicago, Rochester, Philadelphia, and Boston, where many joined the growing abolitionist forces in the North [*3,* chap. 6]. Their accounts of the hideousness of life in the South were hardly believed at first, and abolitionist white sentiment began largely on ethical and religious grounds among the Quakers and Congregationalists. By 1783 slavery had been abolished in Massachusetts, and by 1805 in most of the North. In the 1850s too, Massachusetts was not zealous in enforcing the Anti-Fugitive Slave Laws. On the other hand, after about 1815, New England industrialists entered the market for cheap cotton, and defended slavery–at a distance.

Escapes before the Civil War (about 90,000 went North on the underground railroad) and movement North during and just after the Civil War added up to a sizeable migration of blacks. Before 1850 most movement was to Baltimore, Philadelphia, Cincinnati, and other cities close to the South. After the Anti-Fugitive

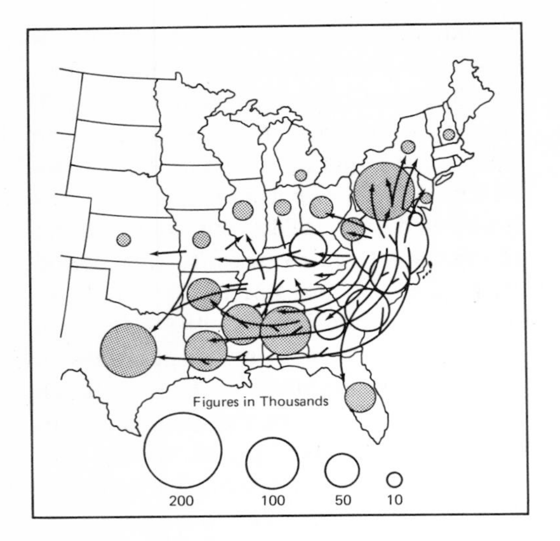

FIG. 3. Lifetime migration of blacks to 1870. Shaded circles represent net gains.

Slave Laws of 1850, migrants had to reach Canada to be safe (see Fig. 3). . . .

Betrayal, Lynching, and Migration, 1865 to 1940

The freeing of the slaves, the enfranchisement of the blacks, and in a few areas of more "radical" military administration, the allocation of some land to the former slaves, brought about a period of hope. For a few years after 1866, under military protection, many blacks were elected to Congress and to state legislatures and state offices in the South; they never in fact gained even temporary control of any state, but had enough influence at least to see a system of public education set up throughout most of the South. The blacks had little preparation for legal intrigue. As memories of the war receded, sentiment in the North ceased to support military intervention. Most people in the North, while opposed to slavery, also viewed blacks as inferiors, not to be given power. Thus, in the disputed election of 1876, Hayes became president on a promise to end Reconstruction and remove the northern "carpetbaggers." It took almost no time for southern whites to disenfranchise most blacks through the imposition of literacy tests and other devices, including sheer terror. In the early 1890s a hopeful alliance of poor whites and poor blacks under the banner of Populism emerged, but this alliance was short-lived.

Under slavery, social distance was automatic and institutionalized; spatial separation was needed less to maintain superiority of whites. After the Civil War, physical separation became legislated through a set of Jim Crow laws, forbidding miscegenation, providing for separate institutions and facilities, and depriving blacks of legal rights such as the right to be empaneled on a jury [*3*, chap. 9]. These laws became increasingly severe throughout the late nineteenth and early twentieth centuries.

Sharecropping Serfdom

Most former slaves remained on their former plantations. Even where they held title to the land, blacks depended on the plantation owners to market their cotton. In most cases, however, no ownership changed; black farmers were essentially landless peasants. A kind of serfdom emerged—the former slaves leased land, usually very little, from the plantation owner for a rent of from one-third to one-half of the crop. Very quickly, most sharecroppers became permanently indebted to the owner, and were then legally forbidden to move from the owner's holding. Not only was the sharecropper kept in abject poverty, but the system of agriculture was so inefficient (i.e., too many minute holdings, lack of uniform variety, inadequate care of land) that production fell, and landowners, too, were much worse off than before the war [*12*, p. 140].

The plantation was rearranged: the sharecroppers were now scattered about on small holdings throughout the former plantation. Gradually, too, many blacks drifted back into the direct employ of the plantation owner, a life materially not much better than slavery, but psychologically preferred, because the laborer was free to leave providing he was free of indebtedness.

Condition of Black People

Since the blacks were still overwhelmingly rural, perhaps even more scattered than before, scarcely educated or often illiterate, and extremely poor, organized resistance to the new forms of subjugation was difficult. The white community, both through grossly unfair local police power and through the terrifyingly effective tool of lynching, could keep the black man "in his place." Terrorist organizations like the Ku Klux Klan were effective in maintaining "correct" attitudes among whites as well as in terrorizing the black population. Lynchings, and other violent and arbitrary treatment of blacks, were most intense around 1905, especially in Mississippi and Georgia [*6*].

For evidence of the general condition of the black population in 1910, illiteracy statistics are useful. In the North and West, white illiteracy varied between 1 and 3 percent, black illiteracy from 12 percent (New England) to 25 percent (West North Central, mainly Missouri). In the South, thirty-five years after the Civil War, white illiteracy was 12 percent and black illiteracy was 48 percent—casting doubt on the adequacy of the rigidly segregated school system operated for blacks, and reflecting the difficulty of regular or long attendance.

The situation had improved by 1930, but was still extremely discriminatory. In the South, white illiteracy varied from 1 to 6 percent, and black from 11 to 27 percent. The low level of educational achievement of blacks, while being used to support the white view of innate black inferiority, was mainly a function of discrimination in school expenditures per pupil. Despite the alleged "separate but equal" facilities accepted by the Supreme Court in *Plessy* v. *Ferguson* in 1896, in the Deep South in 1931 expenditure for a black pupil was less than one-third that for a white pupil. In Mississippi and South Carolina, it was only one-sixth ($5 per pupil per year).

Naturally, the notion of leaving such a precarious life occurred to many. Proposals for a separate state were made, but to think that whites were going to make land available for such a venture was folly. Many blacks did attempt to establish colonies in the new territories of the West. In 1879, some 40,000 migrated to Kansas, in a partly successful venture [*4*, chap. 5]. In the South itself, some all-black communities were founded in isolated, marginal land not needed by whites. Other blacks revived the idea of migration to Africa, such as to the Liberian colony established originally in 1821. This proposal was encouraged by many whites, friendly and unfriendly; not many blacks, however, wanted to return to a continent whose culture they in fact no longer shared. Some blacks gradually drifted north, but they were unwelcome in the countryside, and were subjected to rough and discriminatory treatment by the city immigrants who feared the competition for jobs. Race riots were not uncommon. . . .

Population Redistribution (to 1910)

During the period from 1850 to 1910, although the blacks remained almost totally

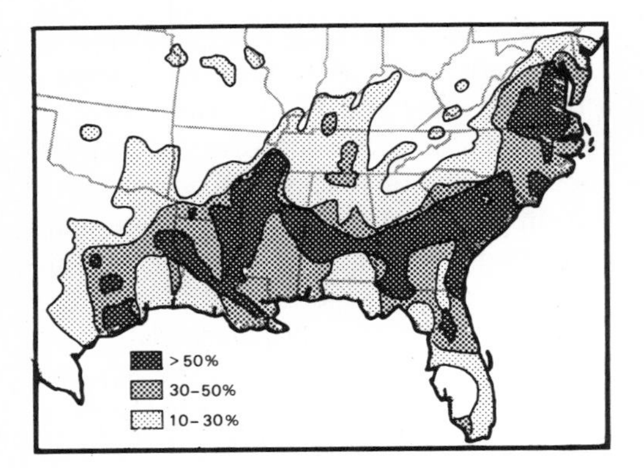

FIG. 4. Proportion of the population black in 1900.

rural and southern (Fig. 4), there was a continuous shift of black farmers and farm laborers toward the Southwest. The number of blacks continued to grow moderately, especially in North Carolina and Georgia, but expanded rapidly in Mississippi, Texas, and Louisiana. In 1880, the black population reached its maximum proportion of about 45 percent of the population of the South (but only 13 percent of the nation, owing to massive European immigration into the North).

Blacks were a majority in Louisiana (51 percent), Mississippi (57 percent), and South Carolina (60 percent), and closely approached half of the population in Alabama (47 percent), Georgia (47 percent), and Florida (47 percent). By 1910, although the proportion of blacks had fallen slightly, the absolute size of the black population reached a maximum in Georgia, Kentucky, and South Carolina. In 1850, Virginia and South Carolina had the largest black populations; by 1880, Virginia had the third-largest black population, below Georgia and Mississippi. By 1910 the dominance of the Deep South was clear: Georgia, Mississippi, Alabama, South Carolina, and Louisiana had the largest black populations, absolutely and relatively. The South still had 89 percent of the black population, and 80 percent of that was rural. In the North, where 11 percent of the blacks lived, only 5 percent of the population was black; these were already 80 percent urban in 1910.

Migration (to 1910)

Considering the large size of the black population in 1910 (10,000,000), the amount of lifetime migration revealed in Figure 5 does not show great mobility. Nevertheless, the out-migration from the South Atlantic states was large; the majority of people did not move too far to the northeast (especially to Baltimore, Philadelphia, and New York). There was a smaller net migration from the East South Central states, about half of whom went across the Mississippi to Texas and Louisiana and about half to the North and West, especially St. Louis, Chicago, Cincinnati, and Indianapolis.

A Slow Awakening, 1910 to 1950

The terrible conditions at the end of the century led on one hand to a prevailing black reaction of "accommodation," as enunciated by Booker T. Washington in 1895, and on the other to a strong current of bitterness and protest, led by W.E.B. Du Bois and others [*3, 23*]. Washington stressed gradual economic improvement through education and self-help; Du Bois stressed the denial of fundamental rights of blacks. After the NAACP was founded in 1910 and the Urban League in 1911, a more activist approach was accepted. The NAACP stressed legal challenges, and gains through the courts date from 1911. The Urban League worked to improve job opportunities and community relations—a difficult task.

As before, war led to an improvement

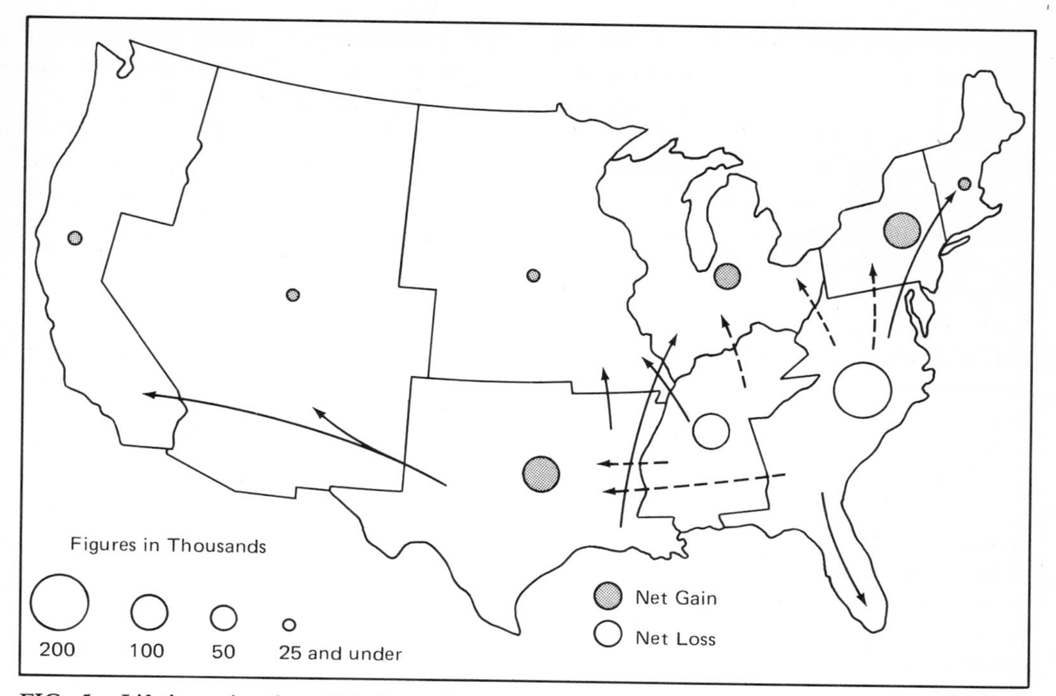

FIG. 5. Lifetime migration of blacks to 1910.

in the position of the blacks [*3,* pp. 289-95]. The slowing of European immigration, particularly after 1914, and the increased demand for labor in shipyards and other war industries, for the first time opened up better industrial jobs to blacks. Many were actively recruited from the rural South, and went North, especially to Chicago, Detroit, Philadelphia, and to other industrial cities. Not surprisingly, when the war bubble burst, blacks were first to be fired. Unemployment increased and a period of severe race riots ensued, becoming worst in the Red Summer of 1919, when there were severe riots in Washington, Chicago, East St. Louis, Omaha, and Knoxville.

During the early 1920s, Garvey revived the idea of colonization, but few were interested [*4,* chap. 13]. Conditions for blacks in the cities slowly improved in the prosperous 1920s. Blacks, concentrated in large ghettos such as New York and Chicago, had become so numerous that the idea of black separatism and black businesses became popular. Chicago elected the first black Congressman in 1928.

The Great Depression destroyed the hopes of equality gained within "Black Metropolis." Again blacks were first to be fired, but since most blacks were desperately poor already, some side effects of the Depression eventually proved beneficial.

New Deal legislation, such as the minimum wage, social security, unemployment insurance, and the various work and training programs, while perhaps instituted for the benefit of white workers, greatly aided blacks as well [*12,* pp. 212-13]. Perhaps the agricultural programs were most significant. Designed to modernize and mechanize agriculture, especially in the South, the programs forced hundreds of thousands of black sharecroppers off the land. The tiny shareholdings were hopelessly inefficient, the sharecroppers unbelievably poor, terrorized by white vigilantes, and weakened by dispersal. Forced to migrate to the northern cities, they found adjustment hard, and life in the slum ghetto far from pleasant; but a move to a northern city was the only realistic means of improving income, obtaining an education, and gaining political power.

World War II, like World War I, greatly aided blacks by opening up far more industrial jobs than ever before, for example in the steel and automobile industries. And the military itself provided valuable education and training for many blacks, although in World War II segregated units were still required. Indeed, as of 1945, in the North as well as the South, most institutions and accommodations were still segregated.

Migration and Urban Growth, 1910 to 1970

Population Redistribution and Migration, 1910 to 1940

The "Great Migration" of 1915 marked the beginning of a significant shift in the distribution of black people from the rural South to the urban North (Fig. 6) [*4, 16*]. In the North an increasing need for unskilled labor accompanied by a halt in European immigration opened the labor market. As a consequence, agents were sent south to recruit black labor for northern industry. In the South, the ravages of the boll weevil and floods reduced the income of the planters, thus cutting the income, supplies, and credit of the tenants. And many people wanted to escape the legal and educational systems and terrorism. From 1910 to 1940 the proportion of the black population in the South fell from 89 to 77 percent and the black proportion of the South fell from 30 to 24 percent, while it increased in the North from 2 to 4 percent. The proportion of black people in cities rose from 27 to 48 percent (35 percent in the South, 88 percent in the North). For the first time a northern state, New York, was a leader in total black population. After 1910, growth of the black population ceased in the East South Central states, and slowed markedly in the South Atlantic and West South Central, but increased greatly in the Northeast, exceeding 2 million by 1940. The rate and volume of black migration out of the South increased dramatically after 1910, so that by 1940 the Northeast had 1.3 million blacks (60 percent of its total black population) who had been born in the South. The some 1.5 million blacks who left the South represented 10-15 percent of its black population. States with largest inmigration were New York (308,000), Illinois (230,000), Pennsylvania (217,000), and Ohio (170,000); those with the largest net out-migration were Georgia (358,000), South Carolina (323,000), Mississippi (255,000), and Virginia (234,000). The pattern of migration followed the major rail corridors—up the Atlantic coast from the South Atlantic states, up the Mississippi and Ohio to the Great Lakes states, and from Arkansas, Louisiana, and Texas to the West Coast.

The Growth of Black Communities in Cities

By 1900 the black population in 14 cities, 10 of them in the South, had passed 25,000. The largest were those in or quite near the South: Washington (87,000), Baltimore (79,000), New Orleans (78,000), and Philadelphia (63,000). But in the next twenty years growth was rapid in

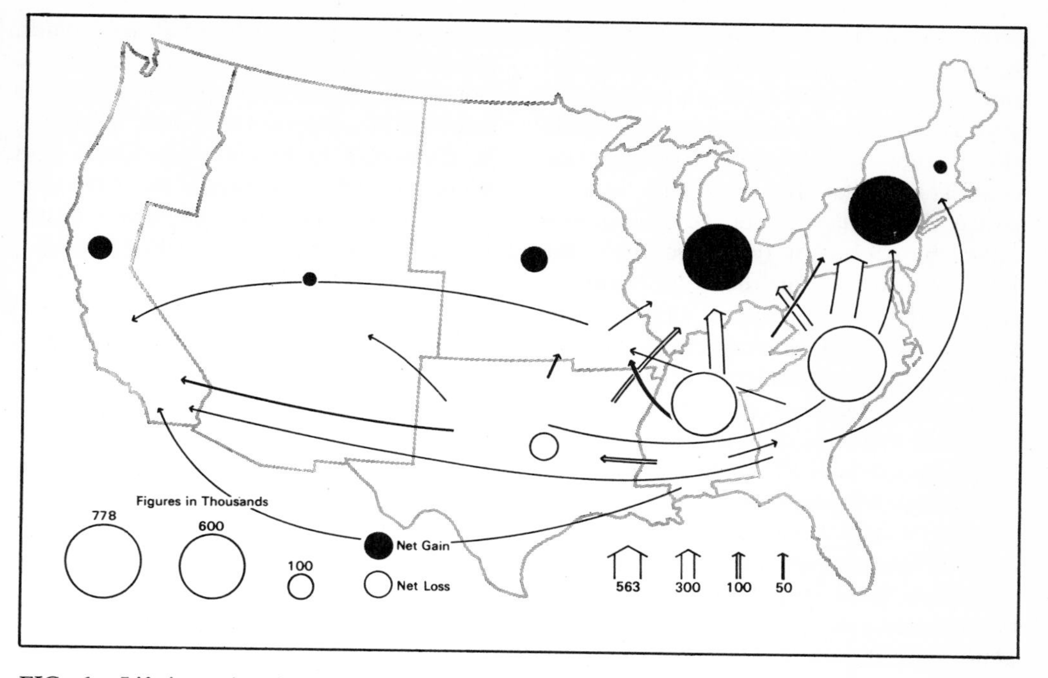

FIG. 6. Lifetime migration of blacks, 1910 to 1940.

the North and only moderate in the South; in 1920, of 24 cities having a black population over 25,000, 10 were in the North, although the largest populations, except for New York (169,000), were still in or near the South–Philadelphia (134,000), Washington (110,000), New Orleans and Baltimore (101,000).

From 1920 to 1940 growth was marked in the South, but more so in the North and especially rapid in Chicago, New York, Detroit, and Cleveland, indicating a shift of emphasis to longer moves, and in the direction of the Great Lakes. New York's black communities comprised more than half a million, and those of Chicago and Philadelphia 250,000; there were more than 100,000 in New Orleans, Memphis, Birmingham, Atlanta, and Washington. In the cities of the South, the proportion of blacks was often about 25 percent; in the North, it was more than 10 percent only in St. Louis, Philadelphia, and Detroit. . . .

Population Redistribution and Migration, 1940 to 1970

After 1940, the growth of the black population of the Northeast continued to accelerate, slowing only slightly in the Middle Atlantic states after 1960, and in the East North Central states after 1965. By 1960, the latter, with somewhat better job opportunities, had a larger black population than the Middle Atlantic states. By 1960 both regions passed the East South Central region, whose black population had been declining absolutely, and the West South Central, whose black population was growing only moderately. The black population of the Northeast passed six million by 1963, its proportion of the total black population rising from 22 percent in 1940 to 40 percent by

1968. After 1940 the black population of California grew rapidly, reaching one million by 1960. The West's proportion rose from 1 percent to 8 percent while that in the South fell from 77 to 53 percent. The South will probably be the residence of less than half of the black population by 1972. At the same time, the black proportion of the total southern population fell from 24 to 19 percent, while it increased in the Northeast from 4 to 8.5 percent and in the West from 1 to 5 percent. The proportion of the black population living in urban areas reached 95 percent outside of the South and even 60 percent in the South by 1968 (up from 35 percent in 1940).

In 1940, only one of the eleven states with high black populations was to be found outside of the South and that was ninth ranked New York. By 1960, New York had become the leading state. Illinois now ranked sixth, California ninth, and Pennsylvania eleventh. Within the South, a relative shift out of the Deep South (Mississippi, Alabama, Georgia, S. Carolina) to Florida, Louisiana, and especially Texas occurred. By 1970, the three highest states were all located outside of the South: New York, California, and Illinois.

The distribution of the black population in 1960. The black proportion of the population gives an initial impression that the black population is almost entirely southern (Fig. 7). As the less familiar map (Fig. 8) of the absolute black population shows, this is not so. Figure 7 illustrates that in the South the relative number of blacks remains moderately high in rural, small town, and city areas, from south Maryland through east Texas; and the proportion even exceeds 50 per-

FIG. 7. Proportion of the population black in 1960.

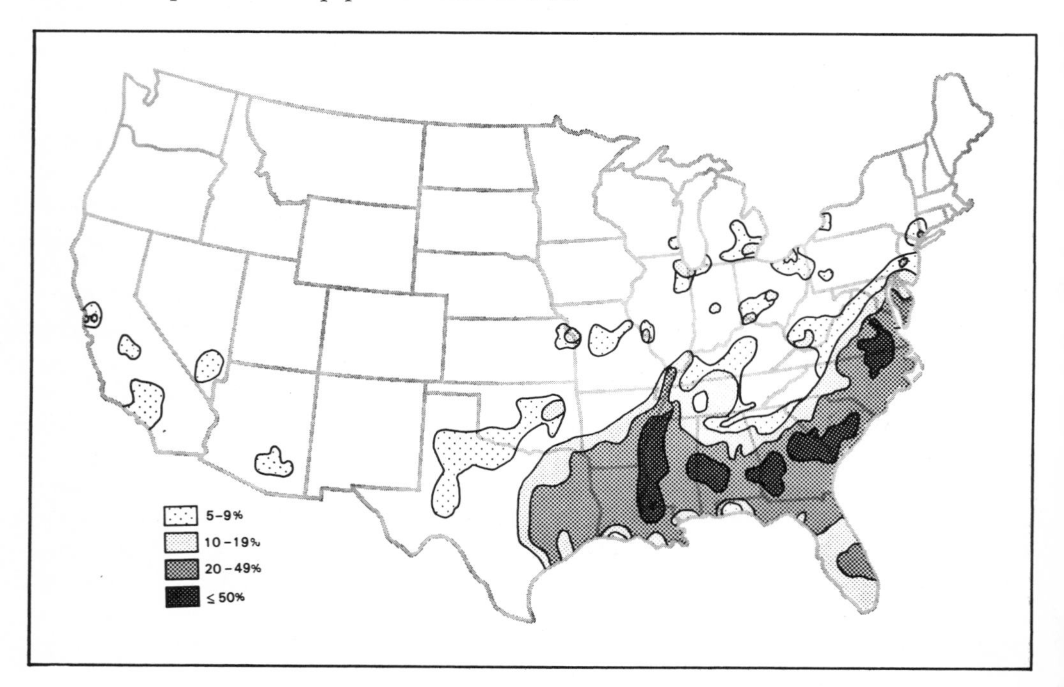

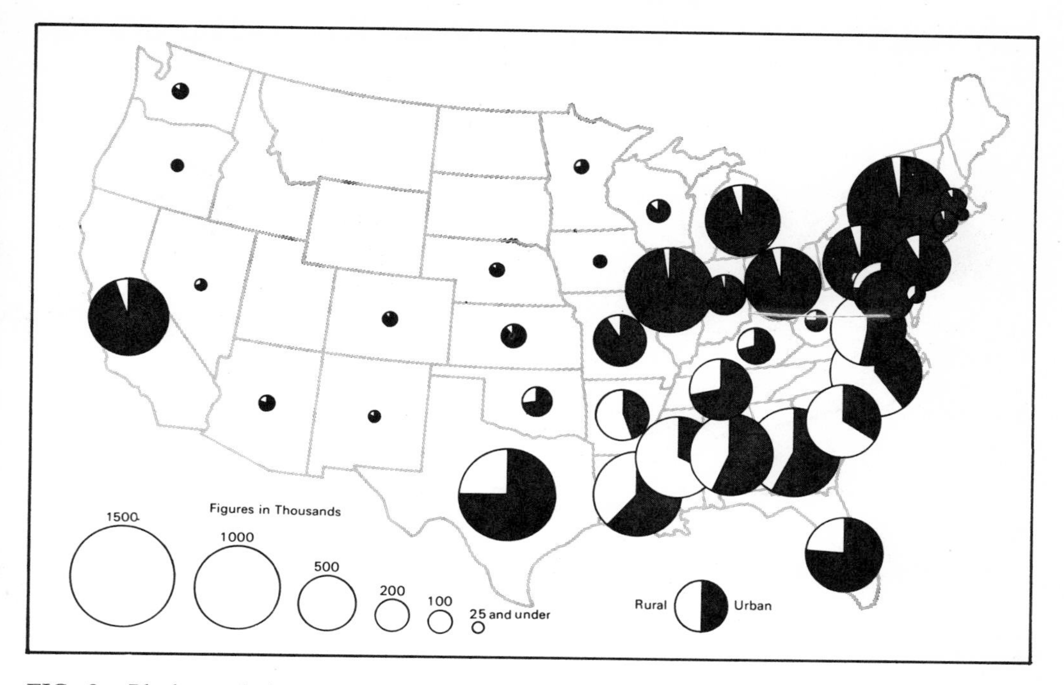

FIG. 8. Black population, urban and rural, 1960.

cent in some of the early settled areas of coastal Virginia and the Carolinas, and also in the rich cotton areas of the Mississippi delta and the "black belts" of Mississippi, Alabama, and Georgia. Figure 8 reveals that in absolute terms, the industrial states of the North and California are as important as the leading southern states, but the black population is concentrated in a few metropolitan areas. The rural black population was still a majority (in 1960) only in North and South Carolina, Mississippi, and Arkansas. Both maps reveal the virtual absence of black population in the northern plains, the mountain states, and the Pacific northwest.

Between 1940 and 1960 the black population at least tripled in most major northern cities and doubled in most southern cities. The gradual trend toward convergence, or similar proportions of blacks in the North and South, is revealed by Figure 9.

Migration, 1940 to 1970

Figure 10, lifetime migration of blacks to 1960, illustrates the great increase in

FIG. 9. Centers of the total population and the black population, 1790 to 1960.

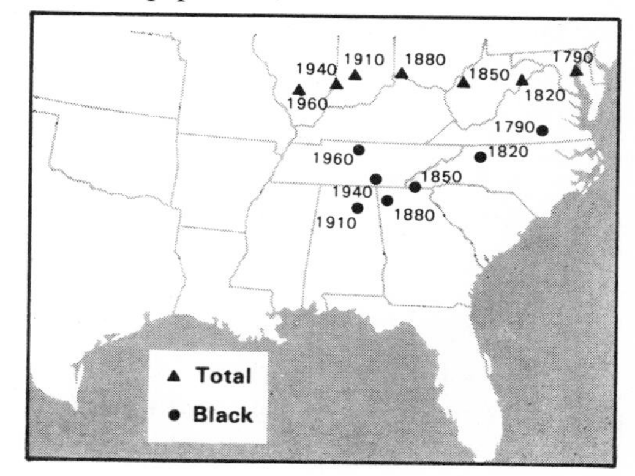

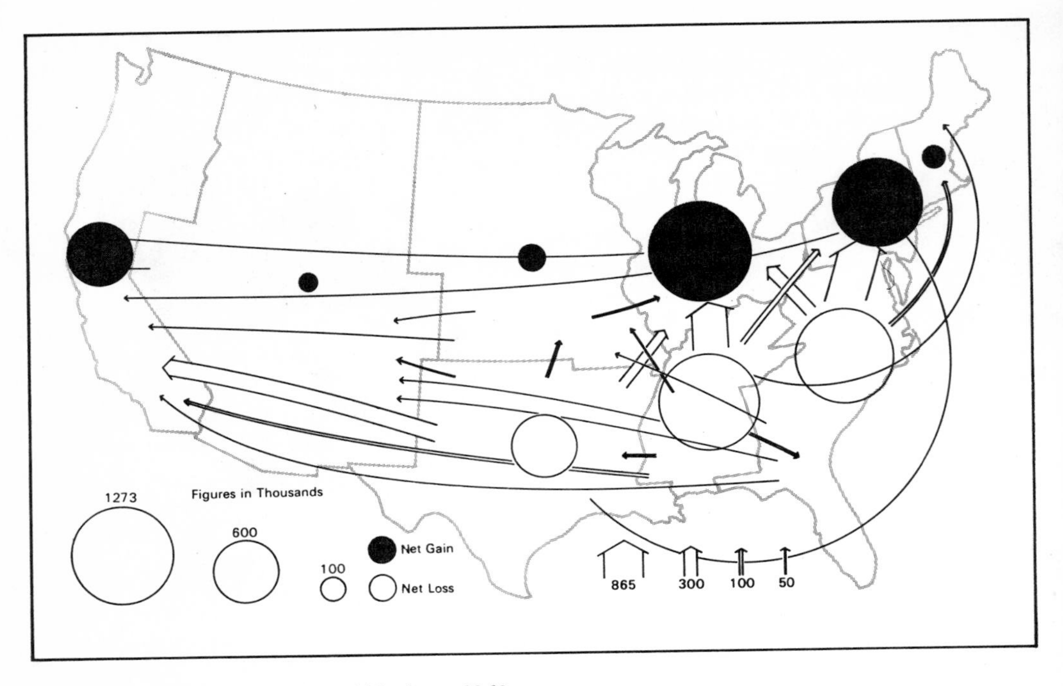

FIG. 10. Lifetime migration of blacks to 1960.

movement after 1940, and the relative shift to the Great Lakes region and California. About three-fourths of the 1.2 million blacks leaving the South Atlantic states moved north to the Middle Atlantic and New England states and about one-fourth to the East North Central states. From the East South Central states, about 70 percent of the 1.25 million moved up into the North Central states, 12 percent to other parts of the South, 10 percent to the northeast, and 8 percent to the West; 643,000 blacks moved from the West South Central states, 60 percent to the West and 40 percent into the North Central. These paths strongly reflect the perception of the nearest opportunities from the various regions as well as previous migrations of friends and relatives. By 1960 the leading destination had changed to the East North Central states. The rapid pace of northward migration continued to 1965. Since then, it has greatly slowed as: blacks are finding increasing opportunities in southern cities; the physical insecurity of northern ghettos now may exceed that of the South; and young blacks now wish to fight the battle for equality on their home ground. . . .

References

1. Aptheker, H. "Maroons Within the Present Limits of the United States," *Journal of Negro History* 24 (April 1939):167-84.
2. Aptheker, H. *American Negro Slave Revolts* (New York: International Publishers, 1963).
3. Bennett, L., Jr. *Before the Mayflower*, rev. ed. (Baltimore: Penguin, 1964).
4. Bontemps, A., and J. Conroy. *Anyplace But Here* (New York: Hill and Wang, 1966).

5. Brandt, L. "Negroes of St. Louis," *Journal of the American Statistical Association* 8 (March 1903):203-68.
6. Ginzburg, R. *100 Years of Lynchings* (New York: Lancer Books, 1969).
7. Green, C. M. *The Secret City* (Princeton: Princeton University Press, 1967).
8. Hart, J. F. "The Changing Distribution of the American Negro," *Annals of the Association of American Geographers* 50 (September 1960):242-66.
9. Katz, W. L. *Eyewitness: The Negro in American History* (New York: Pitman, 1967).
10. Kemble, F. A. *Journal of a Residence on a Georgia Plantation in 1838-1839,* ed. A. Scott (New York: Alfred A. Knopf, 1961).
11. Kilson, D. "Towards Freedom: An Analysis of Slave Revolts in the United States," *Phylon* 25 (Summer 1964): 175-87.
12. Meier, A., and E. M. Radwick. *From Plantation to Ghetto* (New York: Hill and Wang, 1966).
13. Peskin, A., ed. *North Into Freedom: The Autobiography of John Malvin, Free Negro, 1795-1880* (Cleveland: Western Reserve University Press, 1966).
14. Stampp, K. M. *The Peculiar Institution* (New York: Vintage Books, 1956).
15. Still, W. *The Underground Railroad* (Philadelphia: People's Publishing Co., 1871).
16. Sydnor, C. S. "Life Span of Mississippi Slaves," *American Historical Review* 35 (April 1930):566-74.
17. Taylor, O. W. *Negro Slavery in Arkansas* (Durham: Duke University Press, 1958).
18. Wade, R. C. *Slavery in the Cities; The South 1280-1860* (New York: Oxford University Press, 1964).

Migration to an American Frontier / *John C. Hudson*

In a recent book, George Wilson Pierson purports to find in the "M-factor" (for migration) a key to the American experience.[1] To Pierson, a critic of the frontier thesis, "Americanization by Motion" is a worthy replacement for Turner's ideas about American institutions. Recent historical studies have shown that massive population mobility is nothing new; Americans were a "restless, migratory people" well back into the nineteenth century.[2] The current situation, in which an average of one in four or five Americans moves each year, differs only in degree from that prevailing in earlier generations.

According to Stephan Thernstrom, late nineteenth century urban dwellers who did not find upward mobility "were tossed helplessly about from city to city, from state to state, alienated but invisible and impotent."[3] Discovery of this large population turnover, which ran from the frontier to the metropolis, has naturally stimulated thought on the effects of migration on social institutions, especially those of the working class for whom migration and upward mobility were often not synonymous. Since rural to urban migration began well before the frontier of population had completed its sweep across the continent, the processes shaping the nation's settlement pattern today have their origins in the earliest of these movements. . . .

Juxtaposition of these ideas against those of migration modelers, who seek rational motivation for population movements based on notions of expected satisfaction, the friction of distance, and other venerated concepts, makes it hard to believe that the same phenomenon is being described. Rootless individuals living in a constantly changing environment with little sense of community sounds more like particles in Brownian motion than like the pushes and pulls to overcome inertia and distance friction which are discussed in contemporary models of migration. At the very least it is clear that migration may be conceptualized in many different ways, that it is nearly as difficult to predict as to understand, and that its consequences go deeply into nearly all facets of human geography.[4] . . .

1. G. W. Pierson, *The Moving American* (New York: Alfred A. Knopf, 1972). A similar theme with a more contemporary focus is developed in V. Packard, *A Nation of Strangers* (New York: David McKay, 1972).
2. S. Thernstrom and P. R. Knights, "Men in Motion: Some Data and Speculations about Urban Population Mobility in Nineteenth Century America," in T. K. Hareven, ed., *Anonymous Americans: Explorations in Nineteenth-Century Social History* (Englewood Cliffs, N.J.: Prentice-Hall, Inc., 1971), pp. 17-47.
3. S. Thernstrom, "Urbanization, Migration, and Social Mobility in Late Nineteenth-Century America," in B. J. Bernstein, ed., *Towards a New Past: Dissenting Essays in American History* (New York: Pantheon Books, 1968), pp. 158-75.
4. An up-to-date review of migration literature is in R. P. Shaw, *Migration Theory and Fact* (Philadelphia: Regional Science Research Institute, 1975).

Reproduced (with omissions) by permission from the *Annals,* Association of American Geographers, 66 (1976):242-65.

Migration Studies

The study of past migrations has relied heavily on comparing manuscript censuses for various decades and computing population turnover rates. Studies of nineteenth century frontier populations by Malin in Kansas and Curti in Wisconsin established that the frontier was not a stable zone where agriculturalists moved once and for all to occupy the land; the frontier was, instead, a zone of considerable in and out movement.[5] Urban historians have documented similar high rates of population mobility for nineteenth century American cities.[6] . . .

Turnover studies reveal nothing about individuals after they leave a given study location, or before they arrive. Changing jobs is a prime reason for moving, so studies confined to a single place are essentially useless for a study of interregional migration and associated occupational mobility. The strong evidence for massive population turnover on the farm and in the city and the lack of any data connecting individual moves into life histories fosters the Brownian motion view of migration—a chaotic movement in which many individuals are "tossed helplessly about."

When other kinds of data, such as life histories, are available they are almost always seized upon by migration researchers looking for a more detailed view of the process. During 1938 and 1939 the State Historical Society of North Dakota and the Works Progress Administration undertook an ambitious "Historical Data Project," collecting questionnaires and autobiographies from several thousand pioneer settlers in the state. White occupance of the region was so comparatively recent that many people living in the late 1930s remembered the early days and were able to respond to the survey. This paper is an analysis of approximately one thousand of these completed records. It is an effort to place frontier migration in the broader perspective of interregional and international migration, to examine several hypotheses about migration and mobility in American life, and to examine some of the influences on the way of life in the northern plains, one of the remaining lacunae on the map of American culture areas.

Dakota Settlements

The first massive influx of settlers into Dakota Territory occurred in the 1880s. The westward push beyond the subhumid Middle West took place during an era of liberal land policy and coincided with the arrival of thousands of northern European immigrants. Dakota Territory became the new home of landless Middle Westerners, Norwegians, Germans, Swedes, Canadians, and other groups who came in smaller numbers. . . .

Since North Dakota was settled around the magic date of 1890, which supposedly marked the closing of the frontier, it offers a particularly valuable comparison with earlier frontiers and with the emerging urban society. Conditions for settlement during this brief period toward the end of westward expansion and during the rise of an urban-industrial economy are reflected in migration patterns. European immigrants, especially, were filtered through the Northeast and Mid-

5. J. C. Malin, "The Turnover of Farm Population in Kansas," *Kansas Historical Quarterly* 4 (1935):339-72; and M. Curti et al., *The Making of an American Community* (Stanford: Stanford University Press, 1959).

6. Thernstrom and Knights, "Men in Motion," A critical review of recent historical studies on mobility and migration is S. L. Engerman, "Up or Out: Social and Geographic Mobility in the United States," *Journal of Interdisciplinary History* 3 (1975):469-89.

dle West on their way to the plains frontier, a fact reflected in numerous shifts of occupation by the immigrants in their westward movement through the increasingly diverse regional economies.

. . . Much can be made of the perceived versus real opportunities open to those who moved toward the Great Plains —whether there was deception in the process of luring people to the west (there was), and whether many who joined in should have done so. A less pathological view is suggested by the data presented here. What is most striking is not the lack of information possessed by pioneers wandering into the unknown grasslands, but rather the apparently well-used information networks specific to ethnic groups which formed a bond between the widely scattered enclaves, and the usefulness of these informal networks in spreading information about economic opportunities when and where they arose. It is appropriate to begin the analysis of these migrations with a description of the various groups and to thus build up an overall picture of the process.

Ontario Settlers

Ontario natives were most numerous among the Canadian-born who settled northern Dakota. Their migration to the American west was often no more than one generation removed from a transatlantic crossing by their ancestors (Fig. 1). Three-fourths of the Ontario-born Dakota pioneers had foreign-born parents, with Scotch, Irish, and English ancestry predominating.

One or two generations before the migration to North Dakota, the Canada Company was vigorously promoting set-

FIG. 1. Birthplaces of Ontario migrants to North Dakota.

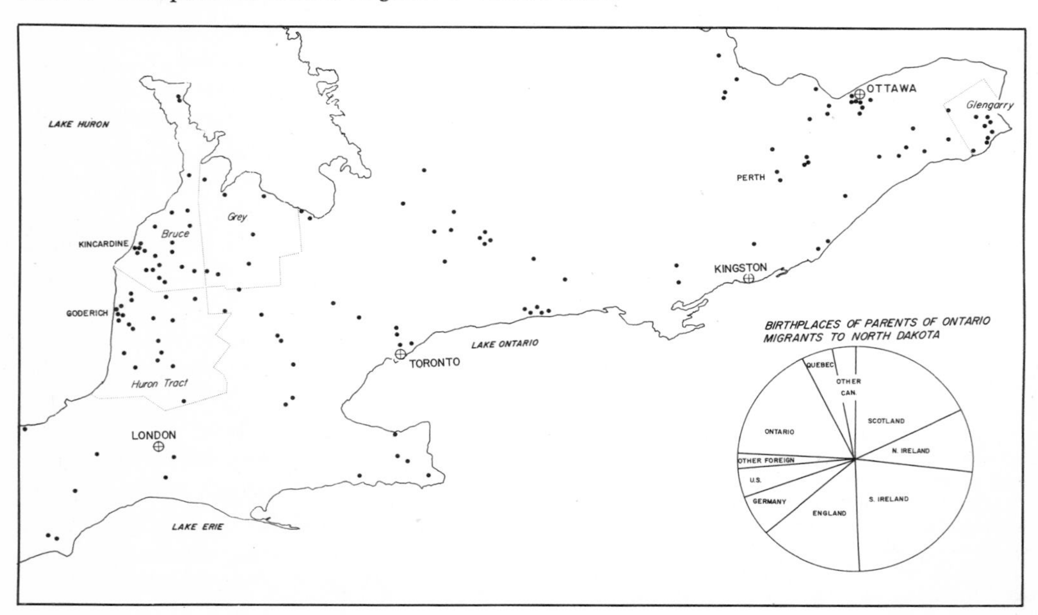

tlement by these groups in the Huron Tract north of London, Ontario.[7] Their offspring, in turn, moved to Dakota in large numbers between 1875 and 1880, as did several organized groups from Glengarry County, east of Ottawa. The Glengarry colony itself had resulted from the resettlement of a disbanded group of Scottish Highlanders early in the nineteenth century. Those from the Ontario Glengarry settled near Pembina, where the Red River of the North crosses the international boundary.

A third source area within Ontario illustrates the rapid turnover of population in the westward movement in North America. Bruce and Grey counties, between Lake Huron and Georgian Bay, had just begun to be settled in 1851; the population increased tenfold by 1861, and more than doubled again by 1881. The population of 65,000 in these two counties in 1881 represented a density as great or greater than that in the more agriculturally favorable counties to the south and east, making them likely source areas for subsequent frontiers.

Nearly all Ontarians who migrated to North Dakota did so directly, with no intervening place of residence. They generally moved by rail or water to the western end of the Great Lakes and then via St. Paul to Winnipeg, where settlement fanned out to the south and west. Most of them took land in Manitoba, but thousands were induced to cross the border between Pembina and the Turtle Mountains (Fig. 2).[8]

German Russians

In contrast to the Ontario natives, who traveled the least distance of any of the foreign-born groups, the German Russians who settled the Dakotas in large numbers during the late 1880s made a long and often difficult journey from their adopted homelands in south Russia. German Russians moved almost exclusively within a network of colonies established by their predecessors and by immigration agents who were eager to lure these sturdy farmers to the North American Great Plains.[9]

The movement of large colonies to America followed approximately one hundred years after Catherine the Great had attracted German peasants to southern Russia. There they had lived in agricultural villages of a few hundred inhabitants each, usually founded either as wholly Catholic or wholly Protestant communities. Most of those in this sample who eventually moved to North Dakota were living north of the Danube delta in Bessarabia and traced their an-

7. R. L. Gentilcore, "Settlement," in R. L. Gentilcore, ed., *Ontario: Studies in Canadian Geography* (Toronto: University of Toronto Press, 1972), pp. 23-44.

8. The Ross family from Bruce County, Ontario, came to the United States because "Canada gave reservations for Indians, half breeds and Mennonites. This was the best land and British subjects had to take what land was left. Uncle Sam said if they came to Dakota Territory they could have the best land available and he would take care of them." Some of those who came via Winnipeg had planned to settle in Manitoba. Mary McGinnis' family from Dungannon, Ontario, intended to settle near Brandon, but did not like the country. The Northern Pacific railroad had an advertising map for Dakota lands in the hotel lobby at Brandon where they stayed; another advertisement boomed the Okanagan valley of British Columbia, but they chose Dakota. A detailed study of southern and western Manitoba settlement is J. L. Tyman, *By Section, Township and Range* (Brandon, Manitoba: Assiniboine Historical Society, 1972).

9. They were not unaware that they were being sought and that immigration agents tended to exaggerate. Andrew and Valzurika Wentz from Rudolph, South Russia, recalled talking with other immigrants on the voyage to New York: "we were willing to discount the stories fifty percent and still be well-satisfied."

FIG. 2. First Dakota residences of Ontario group.

cestry to Baden, Bavaria, or Württemberg. Some emigrated via Odessa, but most chose to retrace their ancestors' steps and left for New York via Hamburg or Bremen. . . .

After the first group of settlers chose lands near Yankton, South Dakota, German Russian Catholics, Mennonites, and Hutterites established separate settlements around Tyndall, Menno, and Freeman, which served as a staging area for later expansion northward in the Dakotas and finally into Canada (Fig. 3). The peasant agricultural village from south Russia did not fit the American land system, though the Hutterites retained and even strengthened their communal settlement pattern. Small, agriculturally based towns did proliferate, however, and the spread of German Russians across Dakota saw the creation of dozens of village-centered rural communities; many hamlets were identified as either "Katholisch," "Evangelisch," or "Mennoniten." Noncolony Hutterites generally settled in Mennonite communities.[10]

. . . The channels of migration and social communication were well established but, like the communities themselves, they were practically closed to outsiders. The economic life of the German Russian settlements were not closed, however; these settlements established themselves early as major grain shipping points.[11]

Germans

German-born and German American pioneers in northern Dakota had language and often religion in common with the German Russians, but there were few other similarities. By 1880 the large German population in North America was widely scattered in urban and rural concentrations. Such enclaves often attracted newer immigrants, but their kinship bonds and information feedbacks were neither as strong nor as exclusive as those of the German Russians. Those calling themselves Germans in this sample came from several parts of the German Empire, with a majority from the northern provinces, especially Pomerania and Brandenburg, or from Alsace-Lorraine. Of all the immigrant groups who came to North Dakota they were the least likely to have had prior agricultural experience in North America. On the northern plains they did not gain a reputation for being the best farmers.

Most of the Germans entered through New York, but some came up the St. Lawrence, and some entered at Baltimore (Fig. 4). They moved westward in a succession of usually blue-collar, nonfarm jobs in or around major industrial cen-

10. J. A. Hostetler, *Hutterite Society* (Baltimore: Johns Hopkins University Press, 1974), pp. 121-22.

11. A promotional bulletin of the day described Eureka: "You must not return," Gertrude added, "without a visit to Eureka, the northern terminus of the 'Milwaukee,' in McPherson county. This county and those adjoining, is largely settled by German Russians, who came to the country from Russia but were originally from Württemberg, Germany, and are excellent farmers. This town has thirty-two elevators and warehouses in busy operation, and these will average loading during the season thirty-six cars every twenty-four hours, the largest amount of wheat received from first hands of any town in the world." S. H. Arnold, *South Dakota . . . The Sunshine State* (Chicago: Chicago, Milwaukee and St. Paul Railroad, 1897), p. 9.

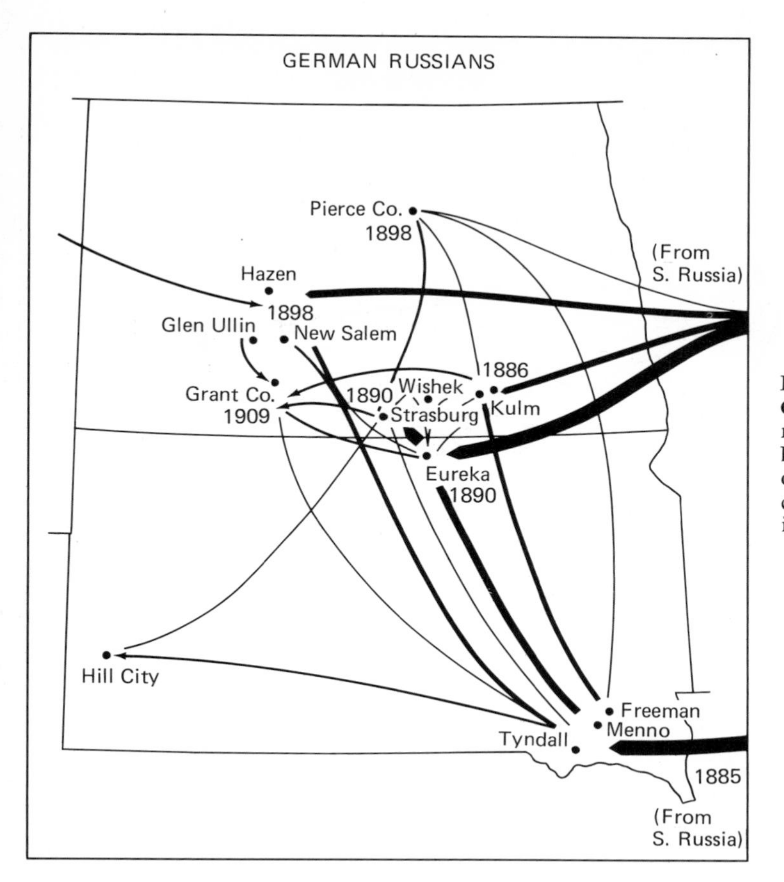

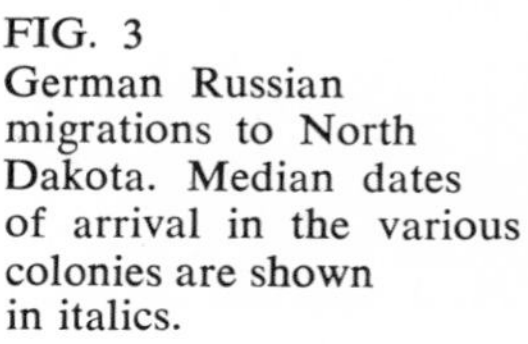
FIG. 3
German Russian migrations to North Dakota. Median dates of arrival in the various colonies are shown in italics.

ters. Buffalo, Cleveland, Detroit, Chicago, St. Louis, and Milwaukee were to those from Prussia what Tyndall, Menno, Freeman, and Eureka were for their German-speaking counterparts from Bessarabia. As they moved toward the frontier the German-born turned to agriculture, usually as tenant farmers; nearly all took homesteads when they reached free land. . . .

Scandinavians

The exodus of Norwegians and Swedes from overpopulated rural districts in those countries after 1850 was engineered in part by railroad and public immigration groups in the United States. Those who sought the Scandinavians more or less succeeded in getting them where they wanted them—on the homesteads and railroad quarter sections of the Middle West. This immigration probably would not have continued but for the volume of letters sent home by the early immigrants praising the new lands. These letters, in turn, would not have had such an impact if literacy had not been so widespread in the two countries.[12]

12. A recent collection of immigrant letters is H. A. Barton, ed., *Letters from the Promised Land: Swedes in America, 1840-1914* (Minneapolis: University of Minnesota Press, 1975).

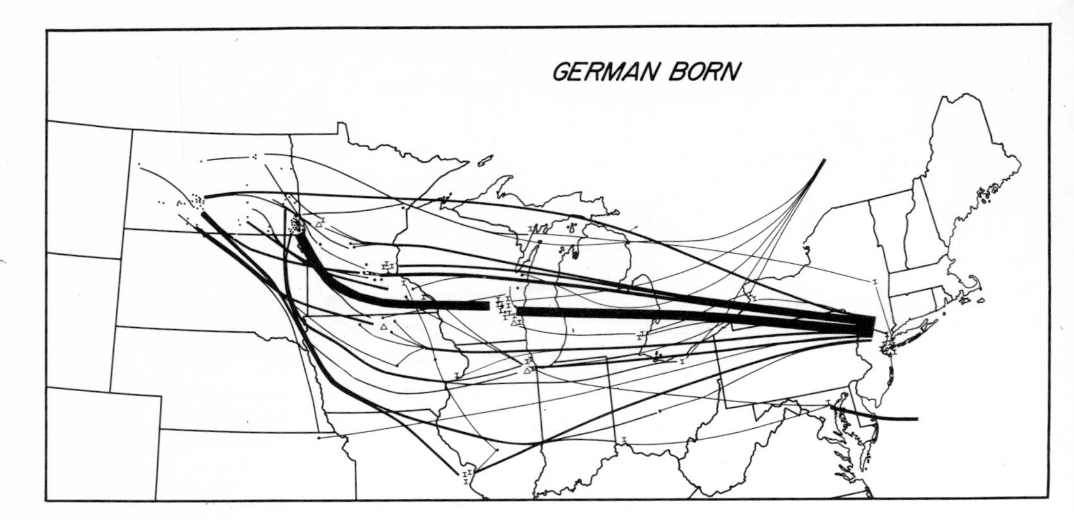

FIG. 4. Migration routes and previous occupations of German-born North Dakota settlers. "I" indicates work as a farm or nonfarm laborer; open triangle indicates employment as a skilled or clerical worker, merchant, or professional; a dot indicates farm owner or tenant. Occupations are not differentiated within North Dakota.

Swedes from Värmland, Dalsland, Småland, and other provinces settled northern Dakota in the 1880s. By 1910 there were nearly 30,000 Swedes in the state, and more than four times that many Norwegians. Before moving to the northern plains many Swedes worked in the lumber camps of northern Minnesota; others were farmers, especially in the heavily Swedish areas around Willmar and Alexandria in central Minnesota (Fig. 5). Later North Dakota settlers born to Swedish parents came from these enclaves and from Chicago and the Twin Cities. . . .

For Swedes and Norwegians in America, newspapers printed in their native languages served as information clearinghouses, carrying news from home and from their fellow countrymen who had moved west. A typical sequence of events began with an initial small group moving to a new location in response to advertising or traveler's accounts in a native-language newspaper; then a trickle of migrants came to the new location from several previously established enclaves in response to personal or published correspondence encouraging others to follow. This sequence occurred over and over again as small groups, many of only a few families each, took up land at progressively more distant locations.

Norwegian settlement of the northern Middle West was accomplished by this semipublic circulation of information.[13] Except for a few scattered communities within and around New York and several other small clusters around ports where Norwegian seamen were based, the Norwegians ignored the country east of Lake Michigan. Few of those who eventually settled North Dakota even sought work in the Northeast, unlike the Germans. Instead they moved directly to the Mid-

13. C. C. Qualey, *Norwegian Settlement in the United States* (Northfield, Minn.: Norwegian-American Historical Association, 1938).

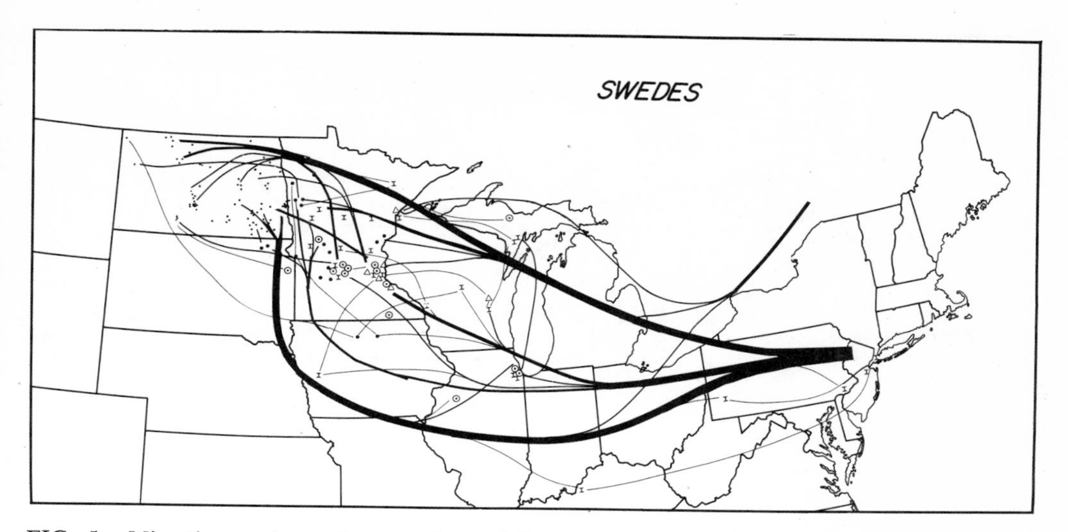

FIG. 5. Migration routes and occupations of Swedish and Swedish American pioneers in North Dakota. See caption for Figure 4.

dle West and settled on farms as owners, tenants, or laborers depending on their means and when and where they arrived. When Iowa and southern Minnesota had been taken, they turned west to Dakota (Fig. 6). . . .

The mosaic of rural communities was thus built up, with Norwegians either at hand or not far away over most of the state. Norwegian farmers took some of the best land, beginning in the Red River valley and then moving west to the spring wheat region of the glaciated Missouri plateau northwest of Williston. They were not agricultural innovators like the German Russians, but they were successful farmers, adapting quickly to grassland agriculture. Like the Germans and the Swedes, Norwegians supplemented their incomes from farm work or other sources. Many men were carpenters, teamsters, and railroad employees when work did not keep them on the homestead. Single women, especially, worked as maids, cooks, and laundresses for the more affluent landowners in town, though "home" was always on the quarter sections homesteaded, preempted, or otherwise held by the family.

Older American Stock

The geographic origins and backgrounds of the North Dakota pioneers with American-born parents were nearly as diverse as the degrees of success they enjoyed when they moved to the northern plains. . . .

"Land hunger," a term often used to describe the motivations of Europeans who took homesteads in North America, is seldom used in connection with the natives. Still, for thousands of Middle Western farmers, escaping tenancy must have been a prime reason for moving west to take a homestead. . . .

The birthplaces of second-or-later-generation American-born Dakota pioneers who were principally engaged in farming on the northern plains were scattered from Maine to the eastern edge of the Red River valley (Fig. 7). Few came

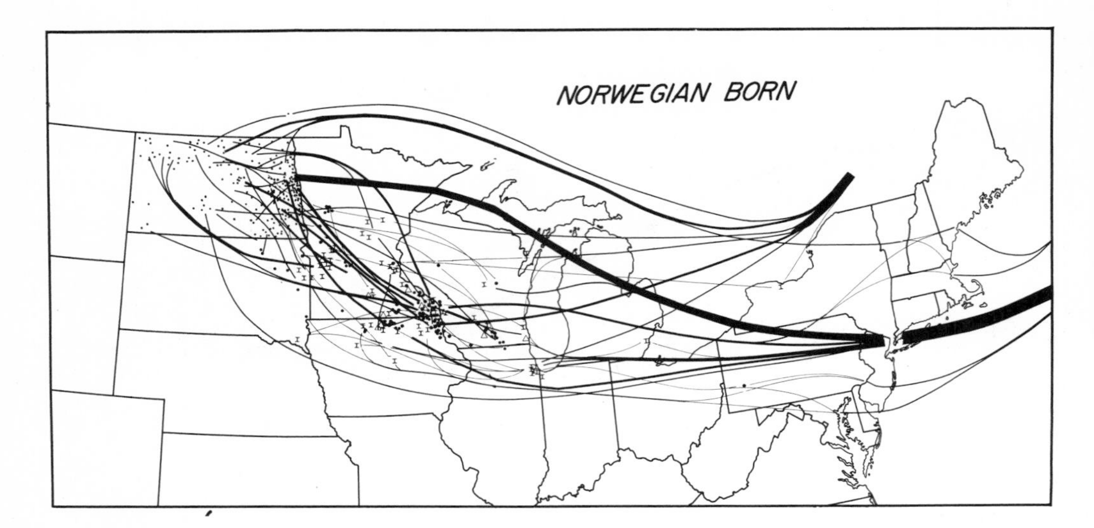

FIG. 6. Migration routes and previous occupations of Norwegian-born North Dakota pioneers. See caption for Figure 4.

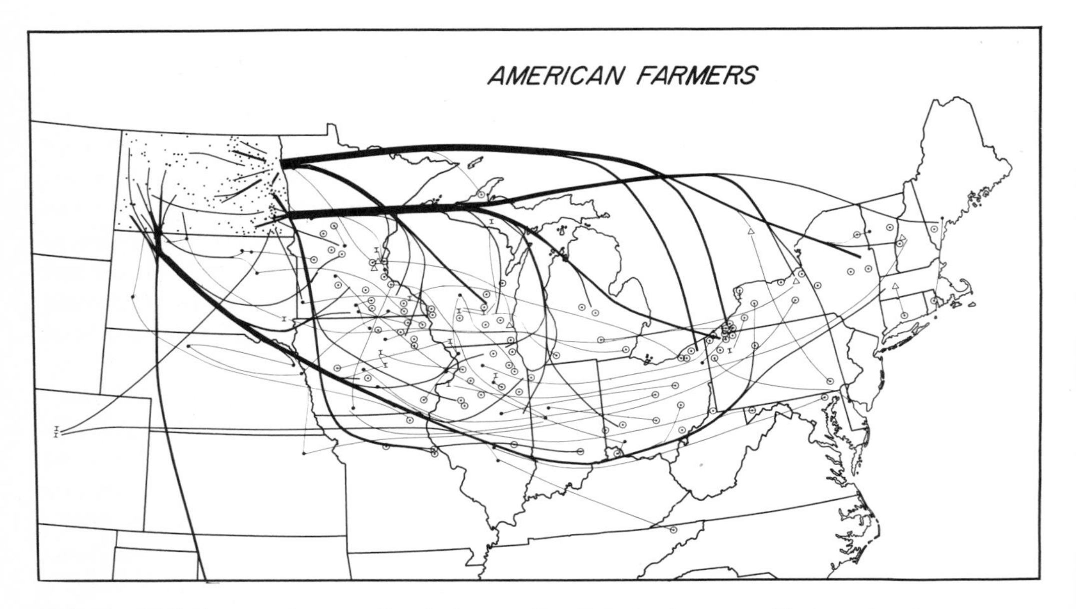

FIG. 7. Birthplaces and occupational changes for Dakota pioneers with American-born parents. Those who engaged mainly in farm work during their first five years in North Dakota are shown. See caption for Figure 4.

FIG. 8. Unloading an emigrant car at Richardton, North Dakota, 1910. The Middle Western family pictured took land thirty-five miles south in Hettinger County. William H. Brown collection; State Historical Society of North Dakota.

from the south, the one exception being Anglo Texans who came north with cattle and decided to stay.

Many of those who came from the Northeast were single young men (as was typical of all groups migrating to the frontier) who worked at a succession of jobs before taking a homestead in Dakota. They worked in the Pennsylvania oil fields, looked for gold at Eureka, Nevada, read law, joined the U.S. Cavalry, worked as lumberjacks, farmhands, millhands, and laid rails. Some were farmers, but they were less likely to have been so engaged than were their Middle Western-born counterparts who also moved west. Their migration extended the more or less east-west stratification of population movements through the upper Mississippi valley and into the plains.

The mode of transportation chosen depended on the length of the journey. Short moves were often by wagon; wagon trains were assembled for the longer migrations, but they were loaded into emigrant cars at a central location for the remainder of the trip (Fig. 8). . . . Not all who moved in emigrant cars were in large groups, nor did all such groups travel by rail, but it was the most common mode once a network of rail lines had been laid.

Many of the offspring of earlier generations of Americans sought a living in Dakota as farmers or ranchers, but the frontier also attracted merchants, craftsmen, and professional people who, although they often filed on a piece of land, clearly intended to make their living in town. The geographical origins of this group, as revealed in the sample, were widely scattered behind the frontier (Fig. 9). Some of the migrants were well connected back east; others were drifters who probably had no intention of settling in Dakota, but arrived there on a railroad

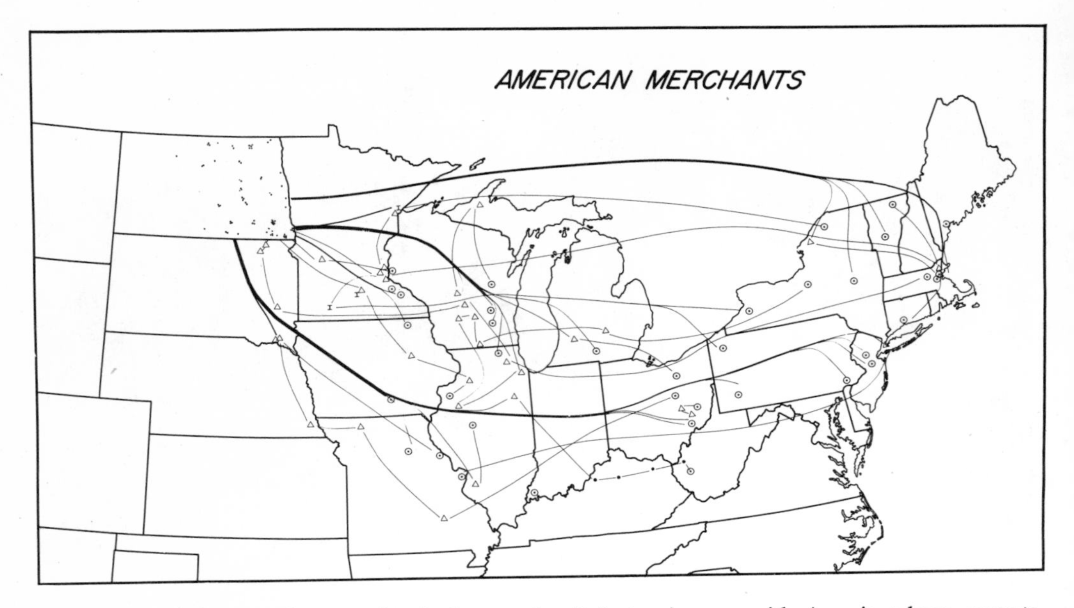

FIG. 9. Birthplaces and occupational changes for Dakota pioneers with American-born parents. Those who were principally self-employed in the trades during their first five years in North Dakota are shown. See caption for Figure 4.

labor gang or threshing crew and decided to remain. . . .

These men and women founded most of the central places in Dakota, opening up businesses on railroad townsites or, in many cases, erecting a shack in the middle of nowhere to which they affixed a sign proclaiming it a town. When one business failed, they tried another. When their self-proclaimed town attracted neither merchants nor railroad lines they simply moved the shack elsewhere or sold it to a homesteader and started again. There was no orderly collection of "places" performing central functions into which the aspiring merchant could move with any certainty that the town would continue. . . .

The Migration Process

. . . The people who settled the frontier were not passive; they were neither tugged out by the magnet of free land, pushed ahead by the glacially slow but sure advance of civilization into the wilderness, nor expelled like a cloud of steam by the labor safety valve of the great eastern cities, to mention a few more dubious analogies. The frontier population was recruited by those who knew their business, and the frontier was sought by those who had heard, even vaguely, about the opportunities it offered (Fig. 10). Uncertainty was reduced and dreams were translated into action when a few pioneers moved west and reported favorably, not to the general population, but to relatives and friends at home. The information feedbacks were private (letters) or semipublic (foreign-language newspapers) for the non–English-speaking groups. The migrations thus encouraged were not secret, of course.[14] Often-

14. The spread of migration-inducing information is discussed in John Hudson, "Two Dakota

FIG. 10. Publicity photo issued by the William H. Brown Company of Chicago which sold land near Flasher and Mott in southwestern North Dakota. The caption read "This is how they make the start on the prairie. There is a comfortable farm house now and a good big barn and it looks like an Eastern farm home after just three years of cultivation. The people are happy and contented. You can buy the same kind of land at $15.00 to $25.00 an acre." State Historical Society of North Dakota.

times others joined in a group migration as "Dakota fever" spread through a Middle Western community, but the long-distance information networks remained discrete—just as discrete as the population subgroups internally linked but effectively cut off from one another as a result.

Those who had an overview of what was happening were in the Minneapolis headquarters of the railroad land companies, in the territorial immigration bureau at Yankton, but in few other places. They were the ones who ran newspaper advertisements, sent agents to Christiania and Hamburg as well as to New York and Quebec City, and set up booths displaying bountiful harvests of grain at county fairs from New York practically to the Dakota border, all in hopes of luring new settlers. As in any market, there were sellers and buyers, both active, and with their own network of operations, formal or informal. Add to this the fact that Dakota was not the only territory or state with its salesmen so deployed, and the fact that those receiving information about frontiers heard about Texas, California, and dozens of other places as well, then an idea of the magnitude of information flow emerges.

The maps of migration suggest that

Homestead Frontiers," *Annals,* Association of American Geographers, 63 (1973):442-62.

westward movement of the frontier population was accomplished through successive concentrations and scatterings of the foreign-born and first-generation groups and through what appears to have been a haphazard series of trial and error approaches by the native-born. They came in contact with one another at various points and all eventually took up land, many times in the same county of a single state. Did this experience produce social contact between groups of the kinship variety?

TABLE 1. Proportion of Marriages within Ethnic or Residence Groups for North Dakota Pioneers Married in the United States or Canada

	Married outside North Dakota	*Married in North Dakota*	*Total*
Proportion of men marrying within group			
Foreign-born			
German Russian	1.000	.970	.975
German	.857	.750	.785
Swedish	.667	.600	.622
Norwegian	.943	.926	.932
Ontario[a]	.677	.456	.554
First generation			
German American	.600	.696	.658
Norwegian American	.714	.933	.863
American stock born in			
Northeast[b]	.800	.473	.641
Middle West	.686	.420	.554
Proportion of women marrying within group			
Foreign-born			
German Russian	1.000	.865	.889
German	.900	.843	.865
Swedish	.636	.933	.808
Norwegian	.857	.899	.885
Ontario[a]	.750	.465	.577
First generation			
German American	.692	.917	.838
Norwegian American	.923	.814	.855
American stock born in			
Northeast[b]	.640	.409	.532
Middle West	.660	.344	.491

[a] Marriages among those of Scots, Irish or English descent.
[b] States east of Ohio.

Marriage

One of the most often used and certainly one of the simplest surrogate measures of the amount of social contact between ethnic groups out of their homelands is their degree of intermarriage. . . .

Marriage data were computed only for the groups represented in largest numbers (Table 1). Of 790 marriages which could be classified by place of occurrence, 52 took place in Europe, 286 in the United States outside of North Dakota, and 452 occurred within the state, reflecting the young age of the pioneers. All but one of the European marriages involved partners in the same country. For the Ontario migrant group, marriages in Ontario are included, but no other foreign marriages are tabulated.

The proportion of within-group marriages shows no systematic difference between men and women. For most of the foreign-born, marriage outside the group became slightly more likely on the Dakota frontier than it was in their communities of residence farther south and east, but endogamy prevailed.[15] German Russians were the most endogamous, followed by Norwegians; their colonies were

15. The proportion of Norwegians marrying within the group was nearly the same in Dakota as it was on the Trempealeau County, Wisconsin frontier in 1880 (.938 for men, .831 for women in Trempealeau County); within-group marriage among Germans was slightly more common there (.885 for men, .955 for women) than in the Dakota sample; Curti, making, p. 105. Among the German-born in the North Central states in 1970, the proportions are .241 for men and .286 for women over age forty-five (*U.S. Census of Population,* 1970). Intermediate in this range are data collected in Clay County in the Red River valley of Minnesota in the early 1940s; the proportions with spouses of the same nationality (including first and second generation as well as foreign-born) were German, .387; Norwegian, .467; and Swedish, .190; L. Nelson, "Intermarriage Among Nationality Groups in a Rural Area of Minnesota," *American Journal of Sociology* 48 (1943):589.

the most internally structured and they preserved this through successive moves into Dakota. The slight tendency toward exogamy on the frontier was not apparent for the first generation of the foreign-born, however; German and Norwegian Americans were no less likely to move within their "own" circles when they moved to a frontier community than were the young men and women of the same age born to parents who had not emigrated. The one exception is Norwegian American women.

Whether this degree of endogamy was high or low can be determined by comparing marriage data for Americans with native-born parents. For the older American stock, previous locality groupings had little effect on choosing a marriage partner on the Dakota frontier. Ohioans often had affinities for other Buckeyes, as did Hoosiers for other Hoosiers, living in a strange land hundreds of miles from home, but it apparently did not affect the institution of marriage. Ontarians of Scotch, Irish, and English descent were also likely to marry outside their group when they reached Dakota, most often taking American-born wives or husbands.

Assuming marriage data represent a reliable surrogate for a larger set of social relationships, it appears that the frontier migration process consisted of a series of spatially overlapping but socially discrete patterns of movement. For the non–English-speaking population, migration fostered endogamy which in turn preserved the group itself through successive moves into and out of the Middle West to the Dakota frontier of the 1880s and later. The groups coming the shortest distances intermarried most freely; those coming from farthest away were the most endogamous. The frontier did not break up these patterns any more than the cities did; if there was a Dakota melting pot, New Englanders, Scotch-Irish Canadians, and Iowa farm boys were in it, not the others.

Migration and Mobility

This impression of pluralism should not be taken to the extreme, to envision a patchwork of tiny communities whose inhabitants spoke only to one another. There were such social neighborhoods, but there were also other locality groupings, such as trade areas and journeys to work, in which economic motives took precedence and out of which a much larger set of interesting relationships between people and place evolved. To understand the role of migration in the economic life of the frontier it is instructive to examine the sequence of occupations pursued by four types of migrants as they moved west: foreign-born pioneers moving directly to northern Dakota, foreign-born who first settled in the Northeast or Middle West, first-generation groups born outside Dakota, and native-born pioneers born to native parents (Fig. 11).

The proportion of farmers in each group increased dramatically when they reached the homestead frontier. Part of this increase was related to the youth of immigrants who had worked only on the family farm before coming to Dakota; the rest of the increase in the farmer category was caused largely by a decrease in the proportion employed as laborers, on farms and in other ways. Although farmer tenants and owners are not differentiated, it may be supposed that the transition to farming in Dakota, where free or cheap land abounded, at least initially, meant achieving owner status for those who had not been owners before.

Westward migration and mobility show a definite relationship for the foreign-born. For any pair of foreign-born

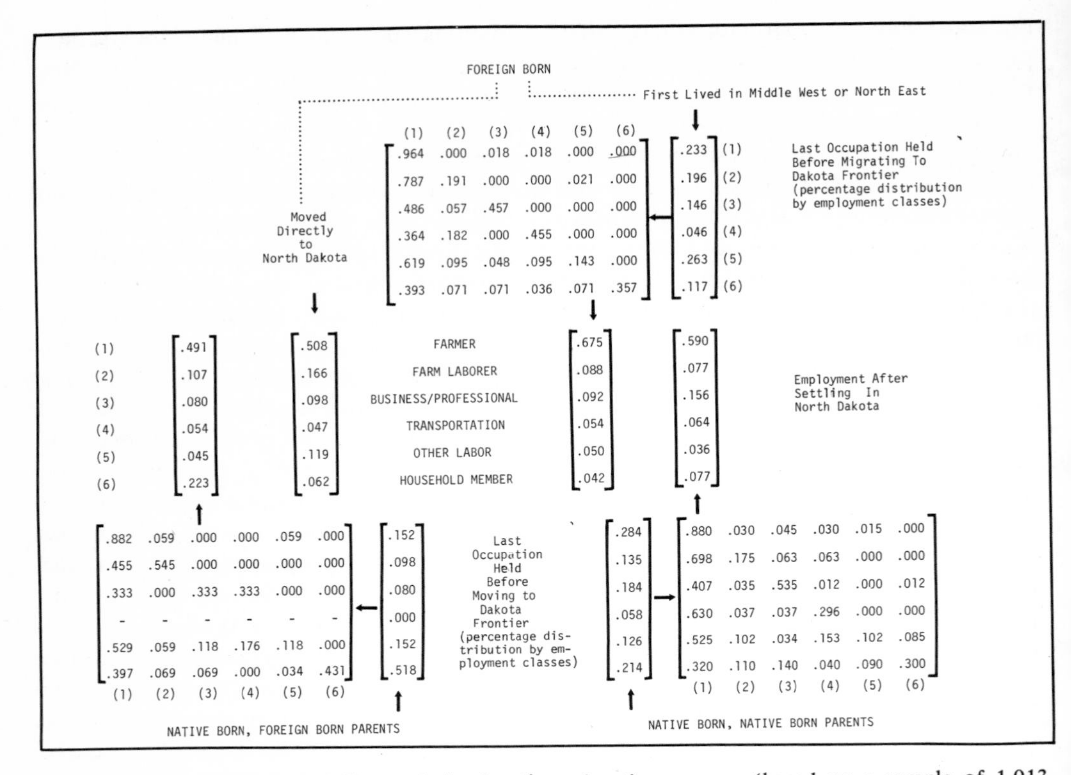

FIG. 11. Occupational mobility and the frontier migration process (based on a sample of 1,013 migrant records). The *i*th element ($i = 1, \ldots 6$) in each column represents the proportion employed in each category. The element a_{ij} in each transition matrix represents the proportion of individuals moving from category *i* to category *j*. Thus, 19.6 percent of the Dakota-bound foreign-born who settled in states to the east began as farm laborers; when they moved to North Dakota, 78.7 percent of the farm laborers became farmers; 67.5 percent of the foreign-born first settling outside North Dakota began as farmers when they reached the state.

pioneers who eventually settled in North Dakota, the one making a temporary home in the Northeast or Middle West was only half as likely to start farming immediately as was the one who settled on the Dakota frontier in the first place, but when the first of the pair finally moved to Dakota he was more likely to be a farmer than the immigrant who came directly. Nearly half of the Dakota-bound foreign-born worked as laborers initially, but when they arrived in Dakota two-thirds started as farmers. This change reflects the types of work available to an immigrant in the older part of the nation and the increased wealth of those who had worked first as laborers.

In comparison, the proportion in each group engaged in trade, or as craftsmen, managers, clerks, or professionals remained stable; it was highest for the native-born native-stock group and remained that way through migration. This proportion actually declined among the foreign-born who moved in stages; coopers, tinsmiths, and cobblers from the old country joined the rush into farming when they reached Dakota, though many returned to their trades when they saw the shortage of skilled labor on the frontier. . . .

The laborer category was more commonly occupied by the foreign-born than by the native-born, but movement to the frontier tended to eradicate these differences in the best Turnerian tradition of equality of opportunity. The foreign-born and first generation made the transition from blue to white collar much less frequently than the native stock in late-nineteenth-century American cities.[16] Assuming that farm and nonfarm laborers are blue collar, and applying the ridiculous label "white collar" to farmers (owners and/or operators), then the agricultural ladder seems to have been working better for the foreign-born on the Dakota frontier than whatever ladder was available to their urban counterparts. . . .

Seasonal Migration

It is well known that lumberjacks, millhands, and railroad laborers took up homesteads as the frontier moved west; it is not as well known that they worked at these occupations while they were farming. Men did not work off their farms because a 160-acre homestead was too small to support a family; in the early years, especially, even fewer acres were used effectively. Men worked off their farms because of the basic necessity for cash income in order to survive the transition to a more established economic life (Fig. 12).

Forty percent of the homesteaders in my sample had worked off their farms at some time during the early years. Most common was farm labor within thirty miles from home. The arrangements varied little from place to place: they worked for wages far more often than they shared work in a cooperative arrangement. From the very beginning there were "custom farmers" who derived their income from breaking the prairie sod, and others made much of their living during harvest season with a steam-powered threshing rig. Those for whom they worked derived their income, in turn, from other sources. Within Dakota, the bonanza farms of the Red River valley were large employers during the harvest. . . .

In addition to seasonal labor migration within Dakota, there was an annual winter exodus to the lumber camps in the Upper Lake states. Many waited until early spring when the sawmills opened. In summer it was either back to farm work or construction. Grading for hundreds of miles of railroad track and other labor took the Dakota farm population west with construction gangs, where some remained to work in lumber camps.

During their long absences, the women and children did the farm work, battled blizzards, and fought prairie fires. Some bachelor homesteaders returned to their claims infrequently. It was not uncommon for them to find their claim shacks missing because of fires or theft of that scarce commodity, lumber. Four or five years of seasonal labor was enough, one way or the other. Some settled down to full-time farming on their own lands, others turned to other occupations, and, of course, many decided their fortunes had best be sought elsewhere.

The territory supporting the frontier population was thus much larger than the individual's quarter-section. Movement to the frontier was followed by another kind of migration that involved the whole northern part of the country from the

16. Thernstrom, "Immigrants and WASPS: Ethnic Differences in Occupational Mobility in Boston, 1890-1940," in S. Thernstrom and R. Sennett, eds., *Nineteenth Century Cities, Essays in New Urban History* (New Haven: Yale University Press, 1969), pp. 125-64.

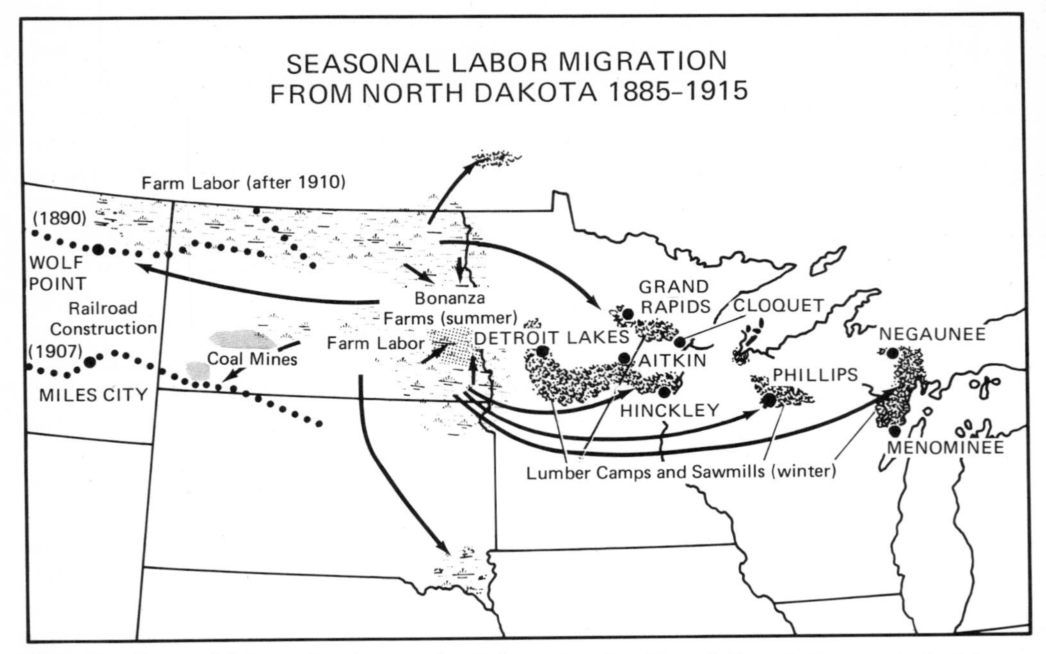

FIG. 12. Seasonal labor migration on the Dakota frontier. Dotted lines indicate principal transcontinental railroad activity. The general direction of seasonal movement was toward the east in winter and toward the west in summer. Coal mines in western North Dakota drew farmers from the southwestern corner of the state.

Great Lakes to the Pacific at one time or another. There was also a constant shifting of occupation from farm to town and from business to business as the regional economy began to take shape. This occupational mobility was of a very different sort than in the city.

Frontier Mobility

Two separate images of American frontier life have the population either as rugged and self-sufficient or as willing helpmates for one another in barn raisings, housing bees, and so forth. To these characterizations must be added a third which seems most relevant for the late nineteenth century—the frontiersman as multiply employed. On the Dakota frontier a relatively fine division of labor began to appear as soon as settlers arrived. Turner's waves of settlement and accompanying stages of economic complexity were plainly impossible in a region where settlement was so rapid.

All the major groups settling the northern plains, with perhaps the exception of the German Russians, came from highly structured societies where technological progress had created many specialized roles with a division of labor to match. Northwestern Europe and eastern North America were similar in this respect; when their people moved out to the Dakota grasslands they carried with them the common expectation that their individual skills would be marketable. There were no rules about who should perform what type of work, and many a person worked at a variety of specialized jobs simultaneously or in succession. With these relationships in a state of fluidity, shifting occupations did not indicate that the individual was searching for a stable niche in the system, but rather that there were many such niches, and many to fill them. . . .

At this point the information networks established in the migration process became relevant again. In the first years after taking a claim many individuals returned to their previous communities of residence for seasonal work. The German Russians settling in central Dakota thus were most apt to return to the southeastern Dakota colonies for farm work, especially in years when their own harvests were poor. Those who had worked in the woods before coming to Dakota similarly returned there in the winter, since they were aware of precisely the way in which they could get such jobs again. Migration routes were often retraced in the pattern of seasonal work trips, which tended to stimulate more migration. When a homesteader-farm laborer from Dakota came back to his old community to marry or get temporary work (or both), or when a Dakota homesteader-lumberjack told others about his prairie estate on a winter trip back to northern Minnesota, the established channels of communication were reactivated. The effect was to link farms and forests to the east with the western frontier, and to strengthen the bonds through inclusion of information about work opportunities.

A decade after initial settlement the population was still highly mobile, though longer-distance seasonal migrations had started to disappear. The railroads had been built, the "woods" became the "cutover," and centralized control of bonanza farms gradually broke up into share tenant parcels in a process resembling that which occurred on the southern plantation. The large frontier population lost those temporary individuals attracted by the boom as many moved west with the flurry of activity on successive frontiers.

The new migration patterns were internal (Fig. 13). Turnover on the farm drew in the offspring of the original settlers. Farm tenancy increased, especially in eastern North Dakota, because of mortgage foreclosures and because the original homesteaders retained their land when they moved to town; some returned briefly when World War I caused a shortage of farm labor, but the net movement was away from the farm, and it remained that way. A secondary occupational mobility caused by these new vacancies resembled the pattern in the Middle West a generation or two earlier. The frontier migration process thus ended by absorption into a more stabilized set of economic and social relationships whose course eventually saw the syndrome of rural depopulation and decline in the small towns.

Final Speculations

Migration accomplishes more than a mere rearrangement of population. Those thousands of people who managed to get to the Dakota frontier not only brought themselves and their possessions, but also their attitudes, habits, and their individual strategies for coping with new situations. These data, along with what else is known about northern plains life, offer grounds for some speculations about the emergent cultural geography of the region.

Had there been no foreign influences one might make a case for simple extension of a New England or Northern culture area northwestward across Minnesota into the Red River valley and then directly west. The experiences of most of

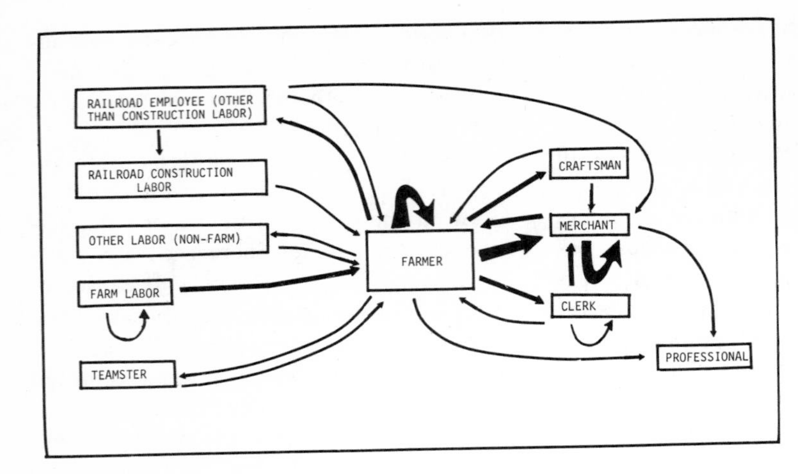

FIG. 13
Occupational mobility of the frontier population after settling in North Dakota (based on a sample of 856 job changes within the state, 1880-1910). Width of line is proportional to numbers making the transition. Farm to farm moves were most common, followed by farm to town moves as the early settlers shifted into nonagricultural occupations.

the older American stock settlers in North Dakota had been north of a line running from central Ohio through southeastern Iowa and thence northwest to the Missouri River at the boundary between the two Dakotas. Linguistic studies indicate the difficulty of drawing such a boundary, however, because mixing with Midland influences began in the central Middle West.[17]

Such an interpretation would not be useful for two other reasons. Culture area models are weakest where they involve multiple origins, clearly an essential for understanding the northern plains. Any attempt to overcome this difficulty through including foreign-born groups as subcultural units would miss the role of economic activity in bringing the various groups together. Although social patterns could remain discrete in rural ethnic neighborhoods, trade areas nearly always encompassed a variety of such neighborhoods, drawing diverse groups together in the marketplaces which, in turn, connected the population with the national economy. The grain buyers, the millers, the railroad tycoons, and the politicians whom they often owned were all represented symbolically, if not in fact, in the trade center. More than anything else, the way of earning a living was the way of life. . . .

The Dakota frontier was not a melting pot, nor did the cultural geography of this region emerge from the mosaic of rural ethnic enclaves because of an early and common orientation to the economic necessities of life controlled or mediated through the sphere of influence of the Twin Cities. The way of life on the northern plains was not the result, either, of the westward extension of a cultural complex from farther east, because the Northeast was only one of several important source areas. Labor mobility and a large turnover of population on the Dakota frontier was evidence of a wide rather than a narrow range of opportunities open to the population, contrasting this frontier with current interpretations of

17. H. B. Allen, *The Linguistic Atlas of the Upper Midwest,* vol. 1 (Minneapolis: University of Minnesota Press, 1973).

late nineteenth and early twentieth century American cities. The similarities and contrasts with previous frontiers and with simultaneous happenings in the city illustrate the unique circumstances of a particular time and place and at the same time highlight a familiar set of cultural geographic processes which interacted to produce such a unique result.

Suggested Additional Reading

In addition to the general works cited at the end of the Introduction, the following references elaborate many of the themes raised in this section.

A. Landscape and Identity

Allen, John L., *Passage through the Garden Lewis and Clark and the Image of the American Northwest* (Urbana: University of Illinois Press, 1975).

Blouet, Brian W., and Merlin P. Lawson eds., *Images of the Plains: The Role of Human Nature in Settlement* (Lincoln: University of Nebraska Press, 1975).

Bowden, Martyn J., "The Great American Desert and the American Frontier, 1800-1882: Popular Images of the Plains" in Tamara K. Harevan, ed., *Anonymous Americans: Explorations in Nineteenth-Century Social History* (Englewood Cliffs, N.J.: Prentice-Hall, 1971).

Johnson, Hildegard B., *Order Upon the Land: The U.S. Rectangular Land Survey and the Upper Mississippi Country* (New York: Oxford University Press, 1976).

Kniffen, Fred, "Folk Housing: A Key to Diffusion," *Annals of the Association of American Geographers* 55(1965): 549–77.

Lewis, Peirce F., "Small Town in Pennsylvania," *Annals of the Association of American Geographers* 62 (1972):323-51.

Marx, Leo, *The Machine in the Garden: Technology and the Pastoral Ideal in America* (New York: Oxford University Press, 1964).

McManis, Douglas R., *European Impressions of the New England Coast* (Chicago: University of Chicago, Department of Geography, Research Paper, No. 139, 1972).

———, *The Initial Evaluation and Utilization of the Illinois Prairies, 1815-1840* (Chicago: University of Chicago, Department of Geography, Research Paper, No. 94, 1964).

Merrens, H. Roy, "The Physical Environment of Early America: Images and Image Makers in Colonial South Carolina," *Geographical Review* 59 (1969): 530-56.

Nash, Roderick, *Wilderness and the American Mind* (New Haven: Yale University Press, 1967).

Pattison, William D., *Beginnings of the American Rectangular Land Survey System, 1784-1800* (Chicago: University of Chicago, Department of Geography, Research Paper, No. 50, 1957).

Rostlund, Gerhard, "The Myth of a Natural Prairie Belt in Alabama: An Interpretation of Historical Records," *Annals of the Association of American Geographers* 47 (1957):392-411.

Rothstein, Morton, "The Big Farm: Abundance and Scale in American Agriculture," *Agricultural History* 49 (1975): 583-97.

Sauer, Carl O., *Sixteenth Century North America: The Land and the People as Seen by the Europeans* (Berkeley and Los Angeles: University of California Press, 1971).

Schmitt, Peter J., *Back to Nature: The Arcadian Myth in Urban America* (New York: Oxford University Press, 1969).

Smith, Henry N., *Virgin Land, The American West as Symbol and Myth* (New York: Vintage, 1957).

Thrower, Norman J. W., *Original Survey and Land Subdivision: A Comparative Study of the Form and Effect of Contrasting Cadastral Surveys* (Chicago: Rand McNally and Company, 1966, Association of American Geographers, Monograph Series, No. 4).

Zelinsky, Wilbur, "The Pennsylvanian Town: An Overdue Geographical Account," *Geographical Review* 67 (1977):127-47.

B. Migrants in a Plural Society

Abramson, Harold J., *Ethnic Diversity in Catholic America* (New York: Wiley, 1973).

Allen, James P., "Migration Fields of French Canadian Immigrants to Southern Maine," *Geographical Review* 62 (1972):366-83.

Curtin, Philip D., *The Atlantic Slave Trade: A Census* (Madison: University of Wisconsin Press, 1969).

Fey, Harold E., and D'arcy McNickle, *Indians and Other Americans: Two Ways of Life Meet,* rev. ed. (New York: Harper and Row, 1970).

Gordon, Milton M., *Assimilation in American Life* (New York: Oxford University Press, 1968).

Hofstadter, Richard, "Population and Immigration," in his *America at 1750: A Social Portrait* (New York: Knopf, 1971).

Handlin, Oscar O., *The Uprooted: The Epic Story of the Great Migrations that Made the American People,* 2nd ed. (Boston: Little, Brown, 1973).

Hansen, Marcus L., *The Atlantic Migration, 1607-1860: A History of the Continuing Settlement of the United States* (Cambridge, Mass.: Harvard University Press, 1941).

Higgs, Robert, *Competition and Coercion: Blacks in the American Economy, 1865-1914* (Cambridge: Cambridge University Press, 1977).

Jacobs, Wilbur R., *Dispossessing the American Indian: Indians and Whites on the Colonial Frontier* (New York: Scribner's, 1972).

Jones, Maldwyn A., *American Immigration* (Chicago: University of Chicago Press, 1960).

Potter, John, "The Growth of Population in America, 1700-1860," pp. 631-88, in David V. Glass and D. E. C. Eversley, eds., *Population in History: Essays in Historical Demography* (London: Arnold, 1965).

Smith, Timothy, "Congregation, State, and Denomination: The Forming of the American Religious Structure," *William and Mary Quarterly* 25 (1968):155-76.

Thernstrom, Stephan, and Peter R. Knights, "Men in Motion: Some Data and Speculations about Urban Population Mobility in Nineteenth-Century America," *Journal of Interdisciplinary History* 1 (1970):7-35.

Thomas, Brinley, *Migration and Economic Growth: A Study of Great Britain and the Atlantic Economy,* 2nd ed. (Cambridge: Cambridge University Press, 1973).

Zelinsky, Wilbur, "Changes in the Geographic Patterns of Rural Population in the United States, 1790-1960," *The Geographical Review* 52 (1962):492-524.

Zelinsky, Wilbur, "An Approach to the Religious Geography of the United States: Patterns of Church Membership in 1952," *Annals of the Association of American Geographers* 51 (1961):139-93.

II The Regional Mosaic

Efforts to seek a synthetic overview of the changing and varied relationships between the American population and its environment have been complicated by the pluralism of the people and the diversity of environments. This complexity of people and environments is most graphically displayed at a regional rather than a national scale. In general, most geographically sensitive scholarship on the American past is based on findings derived from one of the major economic or sociocultural regions of the United States. Generalizations are modified and tailored to refer to a specific period and defined region. Frequently, the divergence of regional development from some national pattern is stressed. The articles by Jordan and Hudson in Section I relied on data derived from a limited region, but the regional effect was of less consequence than the demonstration of a general relationship. Many of the papers in this section similarly examine general relationships, but the regional effect is usually a dominant theme.

The papers are organized into two groups: the first set is devoted to the colonial period and the development of the three major specialized economies and the distinctive subcultures of that period; the second set is concerned with the westward movement of settlement and the differing specializations of the emerging regional economies. Three themes stand out in these papers irrespective of their period or place of reference. The first theme is the selective transfer of culture and economy by migration. The second involves the relationship between the social identities of different groups in different regions and their predominant economic commitments. The third concerns the scale of analysis to be applied in defining those groups and regions. Discussions of scale are critical to a geographic perspective not only because of a need to identify an appropriate universe for analysis but also because the internal complexity of a region must be considered along with the more general issue of the distinctiveness of the region as a whole.

The different movements of ethnic groups to selected destinations was a major factor in defining sociocultural regions within the United States. Although the movements were not mutually exclusive, some groups were so concentrated in a well-defined location that their identity became associated with that particular region. Sociocultural differences between regions are not simply a result of the transfer of inherited differences to new locations: migration involves the emergence of new patterns of life in new environments. Whenever several groups settled in close proximity, these adaptations tended to reduce their original cultural variability. Alternatively, whenever the same group settled in widely different parts of the United States, their separate adaptations tended to diversify their common heritage.

The papers in this section deal with the relationship between inherited cultural traits and modifications made in the new environment. They reveal how immigrant traits were intensified, diluted, or redefined in their new homes. Philip Greven, James Lemon, and Robert Mitchell examine the adjustments made by West European migrants in the colonial period, while John Rice provides evidence of the experiences of nineteenth-century European migrants who settled directly in the West. William Parker, Andrew Clark, Morton Rothstein, Terry Jordan, and Donald Meinig focus upon the internal movements of Americans from long settled to newly settled parts of the United States. Lemon, Mitchell, Clark, Parker, and Rice all stress that in spite of the cultural diversity of particular regional populations, in economic life and especially agricultural land use priorities, there was a strong tendency for all groups to respond to the comparative advantages of each region. Rothstein, Jordan, and Meinig explore the internal complexities of the South and West and question some of the assumptions about high levels of regional homogeneity.

A. The Colonial Inheritance

Philip Greven in "Old Patterns in the New World: The Distribution of Land in Seventeenth-Century Andover" reveals how English immigrants re-established familiar patterns of settlement and landholdings in the first generation of their occupation of New England. Nucleated villages or "towns"–formed by groupings of farmstead lots and common fields divided among the residents–characterized the initial settlement of Andover and other New England towns. Within thirty years, however, this pattern no longer prevailed. Land was granted in contiguous parcels, making town residence inconvenient for many farmers, who eventually moved to homesteads adjacent to their fields. The ready availability of land and the emergence of a second generation of settlers with their own needs for land quickly altered traditional patterns. These changes were also occurring in some parts of England, but at a much slower rate and with much greater resistance.

In "The Agricultural Practices of National Groups in Eighteenth-Century Southeastern Pennsylvania" James Lemon evaluates the farming strategies of a more diverse population. Some eighteenth-century travellers extolled the superiority of German over British farming practices. Lemon not only questions the validity of these statements but also argues for a more careful specification of cultural groups in terms of religious rather than national categories. References to German farming were usually generalized from the Mennonites, and comments on the British were often based on the Scotch Irish. He concludes that most groups made similar adaptations to the opportunities of southeastern Pennsylvania by growing wheat for the market economy and that their common values were those of petty proprietors. These same values were prevalent in parts of western Europe, where the older traditional agricultural regime had begun to dissolve and the source of many immigrants to Pennsylvania. There was indeed a group consciousness in church-focused communities, but in economic life, these differences were of minor consequence.

Robert Mitchell in "The Shenandoah Valley Frontier" discusses the settlement of the backcountry of Virginia in the late eighteenth century. The economies of the coastal South were dominated by large landholdings devoted to staple production, but the interior was settled in smaller farms primarily by people from the Middle Colonies. Consequently, the Virginia backcountry was marked by greater cultural and economic diversity than the coast. Like southeastern Pennsylvania, however, agricultural preferences were not strikingly different among groups. The broad regionalization of English America into the New England, the Middle and Southern colonies obscured smaller-scale differences such as those between the long settled coast and the frontier backcountry. Mitchell also stresses the early commercial development of the backcountry. Although household subsistence consumed much of the time of the pioneering settlers, almost all were involved in the market economy.

B. Westward Expansion

This theme of a commercial frontier is critical to much of the material in the papers by William Parker ("From Northwest to Midwest: Social Bases of a Regional History") and Andrew Clark ("Suggestions for the Geographical Study of Agricultural Change in the United States, 1790-1840"). The commercial aspirations of frontier pioneers resulted in similar efforts to take advantage of the opportunities afforded by the improving transportation links between East and West. Parker also explores the paradox of the individualism of economic life and the community consciousness of social life. Many settlers eventually were prepared to create and accept institutions which regulated their social life but often resisted the idea, if not the practice, of intervention in economic matters.

During the first half of the nineteenth century, few foreign-born immigrants contributed to the westward movement, but between 1850 and 1890, large numbers of Germans and Scandinavians moved directly from Europe to the agricultural frontier of the Midwest. John Rice follows the destinies of Swedish migrants from their home parish to Minnesota in "The Role of Culture and Community in Frontier Prairie Farming." Rice—like Lemon, Mitchell, Parker, and Clark—concludes that in agricultural specialization the identities of immigrant groups did not vary greatly from one another, nor were the foreign born strikingly different from Yankee and other native-born farmers. In social life, however, ethnic differences were critical; in particular, church affiliation was often the basis of community cohesion. In short, Rice documents the emergence of church-centered communities in Minnesota among settlers whose economic goals were founded on the market economy. In Minnesota, settlement and community were influenced more by provincial or parish origins than by national origins.

The diverse groups of eastern Americans and West European immigrants who settled the Midwest rarely ventured south of the Ohio River. The lower Mississippi Valley, or Gulf South, was settled almost exclusively by the descendants of whites and blacks from the coast or backcountry of the colonial south. The substitution of cotton for colonial southern staples reinforced the plantation system of production utilizing black slave labor of the coastal South. Thus economic institutions, identified with the distinctiveness or separateness of the coastal South, were transferred to the lower Mississippi Valley. Morton Rothstein in "The Cotton Frontier of the Antebellum South" describes the plantation system but also stresses that only a minority of southerners were large landowners with slave holdings. The majority of southerners were "yeoman" or small farmers with modest landholdings devoted mainly to food crops and dependent primarily on family labor or slaves rented on short terms from planters. He also reviews those arguments which conceive of the plantation system as a paternalistic "neo-feudal" or noncapitalist system, in which profit motives were softened by a sense of social responsibility to slaves and to poor whites. Rothstein emphasizes the entrepreneurial and capitalist bases of plantation production and concludes that however distinctive southern culture may have been in other ways, cotton was produced within a capitalist agrarian economy. In "The Imprint of the Upper and Lower South on Mid-Nineteenth-Century Texas," Terry Jordan examines the distinction between "yeoman" and "planter" in southern life and assesses how it was transferred to a newly settled section of Texas before and after the Civil War. He finds that the traits which distinguished the two groups were indeed reestablished in different parts of Texas; this process was facilitated by the adaptability of the dominant staple crops of the long settled South to some parts of Texas.

Donald Meinig in "American Wests: Preface to a Geographical Interpretation" proposes a developmental model for the settlement and development of those parts of the West where the frontier experience was somewhat different from those of the Midwest and the South. Quite apart from their adjustments to subhumid and highly variable climatic conditions, settlers in the far West encountered substantial numbers of Spanish-speaking Americans and aboriginal Indian Americans. The distinctiveness of western settlement was compounded by a pioneering experience involving a prolonged period of spatial isolation. The various isolated centers of settlement, therefore, retained their individual characteristics. Although they were always linked to the East, communication was often spasmodic and the various centers of initial settlement exhibited marked individualities. In the process of incorporation into the regional and national economy, however, these diverse centers of settlement experienced a common set of changes which Meinig presents as a developmental model: the emergence of each western region from a condition of initial distinctive settlement to relatively similar metropolitan regions. In the nineteenth century, at least, the term "West," like the term "South," fails to express the range of divergent patterns within each region.

Overall, these papers suggest that the regional mosaic–based upon the selectivity of migration by different groups and the specialized economic development–created large-scale regional differences, which today are the basis of popular perceptions of regional identities. In addition, however, there were many small-scale subregional variations which did not conform to each region's generalized identity.

A. The Colonial Inheritance

Old Patterns in the New World: The Distribution of Land in Seventeenth-Century Andover

Philip J. Greven, Jr.

The early colonists of Essex county were Englishmen transplanted into the wilderness. Those who had ventured across the ocean brought with them a complex set of experiences, traditions, and expectations shaped by their lives and the lives of generations of men before them in England. When faced with the necessity of establishing a new community for themselves in the wilderness, it was to be expected that attempts would be made to re-create as much as possible familiar patterns of life reminiscent of those left behind in England. For a while, the old patterns seemed adaptable to the strange new environment, but soon their experiences and the radically altered circumstances of life in New England began to transform the old patterns into something new and unanticipated. The history of the town of Andover during the mid-seventeenth century is illustrative of the ways in which the New World changed the patterns of the Old.

The initial settlement of the wilderness plantation of Andover was undertaken during the mid 1640s by a group of eighteen men, twelve from Newbury, one from Ipswich, two from Salisbury, one from Rowley, and two whose earlier residences are unknown. By 1660, at least forty-two men had come to Andover, with nearly 70 percent of them becoming permanent residents. As a group, the first settlers were relatively young, their average age in 1645 being about thirty-two years. About half of the initial group were married prior to their settlement in Andover, and the others married later. Six of the men in the initial group of settlers brought their children with them into the wilderness, but the oldest boy in the new settlement in 1645 was only fifteen years old. The youthfulness of the settlers, and the consequent lack of mature children in their families, placed the principal burden of clearing the land and carving out tillable fields from the wilder-

Reproduced (with omissions) by permission from *Essex Institute Historical Collections 101* (1965): 133-48. For elaboration see also the author's *Four Generations: Population, Land, and Family in Colonial Andover, Massachusetts* (Ithaca, N.Y.: Cornell University Press, 1970).

ness upon the men who settled. Few evidently could afford servants. Most of the settlers were men of limited means and humble social backgrounds (several had arrived as servants themselves). For these men, Andover promised gains in economic and personal terms which would have been difficult if not impossible to attain in their initial towns of residence along the coast.

. . . By English standards of the early seventeenth century, Andover was exceptionally large. Since in England a village of 6,000 acres was unusually large, with the average village containing perhaps between 1,500 and 2,000 acres, Andover was roughly six times the size of large English villages.[1] If these men had immigrated to the New World to obtain land, it was available to them in quantities unimaginable in the Old World.

Many of the early settlers of Andover, however, had been accustomed to life in small, compact villages in England, surrounded by a carefully defined area of open fields and commons, and had grown up in an environment in which available space was at a premium, having been portioned out and cultivated for generations. . . . The principal characteristics of open field villages in England were the nuclear structure of the towns, with all of the inhabitants living side by side on streets within a compact area, rather than being scattered about on their separate farms, and the use of large open fields in which all the inhabitants possessed parcels of land, rather than having consolidated and separate farms spread about the town.[2] Despite the radically different problems created by the possession of 38,000 acres of uncleared land, Andover's settlers set about re-creating this familiar pattern of community life and land distribution in the middle of the American wilderness.[3] . . .

The distribution of house lots in the new village was a matter of the utmost concern to every inhabitant, since it was to determine their allotment of land in the new community. No record remains for Andover to illuminate the decisions taken to limit the largest house lots to twenty acres, and the smallest to four acres, but the probability is that Andover was following the example set in 1643 by the neighboring town of Haverhill. At a town meeting held in Haverhill, November 6, 1643, it was voted "that there shall bee three hundred acres laid out for house lotts & no more, and that he that was worth two hundred pounds should have twenty acres for his house lott, and none to exceed that number, and so every one under that sum."[4] . . . The smallest house lots were given mostly to the young, landless settlers who joined the plantation. For these men, several of

1. See, for example, the acreages for Oxfordshire villages in Howard Levi Gray, *English Field Systems, Harvard Historical Studies,* vol. 22 (Cambridge, Mass., 1915), Appendix 4, pp. 536-42.

2. For further information on the open field system in England, see Gray, *English Field Systems,* and C. S. Orwin, *The Open Fields,* 2nd ed., (Oxford, 1954). See also the illuminating study of the open field village of Sudbury, Mass., and its English background in Sumner Chilton Powell, *Puritan Village: The Formation of a New England Town* (Middletown, Conn., 1963).

3. The distribution of land in early Andover has received little attention by earlier historians. Abiel Abbot's *History of Andover from its Settlement to 1829* (Andover, 1829), p. 12, is superficial and somewhat misleading. The best discussion of the original settlement is to be found in Sarrah Loring Bailey, *Historical Sketches of Andover (Comprising the Present Towns of North Andover and Andover)*, Massachusetts (Boston, 1880), pp. 27-33. See also Claude M. Fuess, *Andover, Symbol of New England: The Evolution of a Town* (Andover, 1959), pp. 33-35.

4. Haverhill, MS Town Book Number 3, p. 5 (located in the vault of the City Clerk's office, Haverhill, Mass.)

whom had once been servants, the possession of a four-acre house lot provided the basis for a notable improvement over their previous estates, and ultimately constituted the foundations for extensive holdings of land in Andover. As other men arrived to settle in the new plantation, they, too, were granted house lots in the village. By 1660, at least thirty-six house lots had been granted, seven of which were ten acres or more, eight were between six and eight acres, and twenty-one were between four and five and one-half.[5] For all of the inhabitants, the distribution of the house lots fixed their initial status within the new town and shaped their future prospects for economic prosperity and social standing.

The decision to begin by distributing house lots to the settlers of the new plantation was itself a reflection of their desire to create a compactly settled village similar in form to the ones left behind in England. . . . The long rectilinear house lots, ranging in size from four to twenty acres, were placed abutting one another along two roughly parallel streets separated by open land.[6] To the south lay the area which was to be set aside for the commons. From the top of one of the nearby hills, the settlers could survey the rest of their forests and open lands, stretching out to the south and west, extending far beyond the Shawshin River, and bordered on the north and west by the Merrimac River. For nearly twenty years to come, most of this land remained remote, unallotted wilderness. The reason for this lay in the decisions taken by the inhabitants of Andover to distribute their land in relatively small open fields, located outside the village.

The first grants of upland or ploughing ground made by the town to all of the early settlers were in a single large field, called the Shawshin field.[7] Evidently the field bordered upon the Shawshin River, the grants being made on the west or far side of the river. The rate decided upon was one acre of upland for each acre of a house lot. The least a man might have in the Shawshin field was four acres, the most was twenty acres, allowing for slight variations due to differences in the quality of the land each man received. . . . Some of the grants were broken up . . . into smaller parcels, while others were consolidated into single holdings corresponding to the acreages of their house lots.[8] The fragmentation of individual holdings in the Shawshin field was characteristic of open fields in England and remained a characteristic of farming in Andover for many decades and generations. Not only the fragmentation of holdings but also the size of the grants reflected the settlers' English backgrounds, since the total acreage granted for twenty-one house lots in the Shawshin field was only approximately 160 acres, comparable to a small English field. Not only was

5. For details, see the particular grants to the householders in Andover in the Record of Town Roads and Town Bounds, *passim*. At least nine of the early settlers later acquired additional land for their house lots, either as a gift from the town or by purchase, which entitled them to a proportionate increase in their accommodation lands.

6. I am indebted to Mr. Forbes Rockwell, of North Andover, Mass., for permitting me to see the meticulous maps which he has drawn, reconstructing in minute detail the nucleus of the village in the 17th century, and tracing each successive alteration in the ownership of this land through the 18th century.

7. The dates of this division as well as the second and third divisions of upland are unknown since the early records of the town have disappeared. Although the exact chronology is uncertain, the distribution of land in the two open fields can be reconstructed from the records of individual grants remaining in the Record of Town Roads and Town Bounds.

8. Andover, Record of Town Roads and Town Bounds, pp. 17, 21, 26, 32, 138.

the village itself designed to be small and compact, but the area of cultivation, too, was compact in size.

The second division of upland was located in another field equal in size to the first. It was called, appropriately, the Newfield. . . . In view of the fact that in England a "fundamental trait" of both two- and three-field systems was "that the arable acres of a holding were divided with approximate equality between the two or three fields," the inhabitants' decision to allot one acre in the Newfield for each acre of a house lot, as had been done previously with the first field, is indicative of their attempt to re-create in Andover patterns of farming which were similar to those familiar to many of them in England.[9]

The attempt on the part of the early settlers of Andover to re-create a traditional pattern of village life and farming, giving every freeholder land in large general fields, was successful, it seems, as long as traditional methods seemed effective in the new environment. At the outset, the wilderness had to be cleared and the land broken up for plowing and sowing crops. Few of the first settlers during the early years of settlement had children old enough to provide much help in the arduous labor of clearing the land and establishing their families in the new plantation. Few had servants to aid them. In terms of transforming the wilderness into arable land, the small grants distributed within the two large fields not only were manageable for individual settlers but also provided a clearly defined context for communal labor and farming. Every householder within the village possessed land in both the Shawshin field and the Newfield. Possession of a four-acre house lot in the village center gave an individual approximately eight acres of ploughing land divided equally between the two fields. An eight-acre house lot entitled a person to sixteen acres of land, and a twenty-acre lot had the right to forty acres. By virtue of the first two grants of upland in the two fields, few of the settlers actually possessed much land, but this must have seemed less important to them than the creation of a tightly knit and defensible community on the edge of the wilderness. For the time being, the two fields sufficed.

By the mid 1650s, however, the initial assumptions which had governed the creation of the two open fields in Andover evidently began to be questioned, and a new direction in the development of the community became apparent.[10] Instead of creating additional open fields as further divisions of land were desired by the town's inhabitants, as the men of Sudbury did,[11] the third division of upland, voted by the town sometime prior to 1658, was granted in parcels of land scattered about the town. No new field was created.[12] . . . The third division allotted four acres of upland for each acre

9. Gray, *Field Systems,* p. 40.

10. The evidence available for Haverhill suggests that a similar development was taking place there, too, at approximately the same pace and during the same period. Since the records of Haverhill are complete from 1643, it warants further study. For the successive divisions of the town's land, see the Haverhill, MS Town Book Number 3, *passim.* A useful but limited discussion of these early grants is found in George Wingate Chase *The History of Haverhill, Massachusetts, From Its First Settlement, in 1640, to the Year 1860* (Haverhill, 1861), pp. 74-92. The development of Andover, and perhaps of Haverhill are complete from 1643, it warrants bury, Mass., which split apart because of a controversy among the inhabitants over the retention of the open field system. See Powell, *Puritan Village,* pp. 118-38.

11. Powell, *Puritan Village,* p. 95.

12. For the allotment of the third division grants, see the individual holdings in the Andover, Record of Town Roads and Town Bounds.

of a houselot, which amounted to a considerable increment in the landholdings of every resident householder in the village. . . . The third division thus provided the first sizeable addition to the landholdings of the inhabitants of Andover. The significance of this third division, however, does not lie as much in the increase of an individual's acreage as in the fact that no new field had been created. With this division of upland, a decisive alteration had occurred in the policy of land distribution in the community. It was no longer to be shaped entirely according to the patterns of an English open field village.

The disintegration of the original field system in Andover, evident in the third division of upland, was reflected as well in the grants of land given out by the town to newcomers arriving during the 1650s. For those who acquired house lots, rights to equal accommodations with those of the earlier settlers were granted also, but the location of their land grants was different. Grants for the first two divisions of upland no longer were made in the Shawshin field and the Newfield. . . .

Although newcomers to Andover during the late 1650s were granted land on a different basis from that which had governed the initial grants during the 1640s, they nonetheless entered a community which still bore many of the physical characteristics of the open field village which the first settlers had created. The characteristically nuclear structure of the village was intact, since all of the inhabitants continued to live in houses constructed upon adjacent house lots in the village center. Their farming lands were located outside the village, sometimes at a considerable distance, but many of their parcels were placed close by those of their neighbors, just as in English open field villages. . . .

By the early 1660s, the signs of decay within the old structure of the open field village were pronounced. The third division of upland already had provided many of the townsmen with sizeable parcels of land outside the village, rendered inconvenient for daily farming by distance and the difficulties of travel. Some townsmen, in order to alleviate these difficulties, desired to build dwelling houses upon their division land.[13] The threat which such intentions posed for the closely knit community, with all of the inhabitants settled together upon adjacent house lots, met resistance and condemnation from the town as a whole. "Att a generall Towne meeting March 1660," the inhabitants took

> into consideration the great damage that may come to the Town by persons living remote from the Towne upon such lands as were given them for ploughing or planting and soe, by their hoggs & cattle destroy the meadows adjoyning thereunto.[14]

They accordingly ordered

> that whosoever, inhabitant or other shall build any dwelling-house in any part of the towne but upon such house lott or other place granted for that end without express leave from the Towne shall forfeit twenty shillings a month for the time he shall soe live in any such p'hibited place.

---

13. In Haverhill, a similar dispersal of the inhabitants from the original village center was occurring during this period. Chase, *Haverhill,* p. 92, noted that the town meeting votes of February 28, 1661, indicated "the change already taking place in the town. The settlers were fast approaching the present individuality in property." By 1661, he added, "The settlers had already begun to form their lands into farms, by 'laying down,' 'taking up,' buying, selling, and exchanging lots; many had built themselves houses, and removed their families on to their farms. . . ." The Andover town meeting records from 1660 are filled with similar transactions.

14. Andover, Ancient Town Records. Quoted in full in Bailey, *Andover,* p. 33.

. . . The stiff fine imposed by the town seemed to have little effect in halting the dispersal of the farming inhabitants, however. Within twenty years, nearly half of the inhabitants of Andover resided in the south end of the town, remote from the original village center.[15] By 1680, the new pattern of community life and farming, in which dispersed enclosed farms had been substituted for an open field village, had emerged fully.

Much of the impetus for the modifications in land policy in Andover during the 1650s and early 1660s probably resulted from the maturing of the second generation.[16] By 1662, the problem of the integration of the next generation into the community was an urgent one for most families, many of whom, at the time of settlement during the 1640s, had had only young children whose futures had not been taken into consideration at that time. In 1662, five families which had been among the first settlers in Andover had eleven sons over twenty years old. The children of seventeen of the original settlers included eight sons ranging in age from fifteen to nineteen years, nine sons ranging from ten to fourteen years, and twenty-two sons under ten years of age. . . . For settlers such as these who wished to keep their sons in the same community, established upon enough land of their own by means of inheritance to enable them to become husbandmen and independent farmers, the small grants allotted to them under the open field system of the early years of settlement could not suffice. More land and a new system of distribution were needed. The turning point came in 1662, with the fourth division of upland.

At a general town meeting, held in Andover, November 24th, 1662, the inhabitants "ordered and Granted That for every acre of houselott There shall be laid out to it Twentie acres of upland to be Taken up and chosen the same way and order that hath been used in the divisions of Land according to the Time of mens comming to the Town."[17] By a single vote, the house holders thereby gave themselves five times as much land as they had in their third division and twenty times as much as they had received in either of the first two divisions in the early years of the plantation. Nearly twenty years had passed, however, before a grant of this magnitude was voted. Since the smallest of the house lots in Andover were not less than four acres in size, the minimum grant given by the fourth division of 1662 was eighty acres. The largest grants, given to the holders of twenty acre house lots, were princely in comparison to earlier grants. . . . The fourth division alone thus would have provided each householder in Andover with a sizeable farm, but taken in conjunction with the three previous divisions of upland, two divisions of meadow, and the division of swamp land which the town voted in 1661, each of the resident householders in the village after 1662 owned no less than one hundred acres of land, and often far more, distributed about the town in parcels of varying size. . . . These extensive fourth division grants could be taken up "in any

15. See the town rate list for December 27, 1680, in the Andover, MS Old Tax & Record Book 1670-1716 (located in the Town Clerk's office, Andover, Mass.) The process of dispersal from the old village center eventually necessitated the division of the town into two parishes, which was accomplished in 1709 after a protracted quarrel. In 1855, the two parishes became two separate towns, Andover and North Andover.

16. The experience of Sudbury provides a sharp contrast with Andover. See Powell, *Puritan Village,* esp. pp. 118, 119, 126, 134, 135.

17. Andover, Ancient Town Records.

place beyond shawshin River" to the west or any place on the eastern (or village) side of the river, provided only that no part of the division land "be within four miles of the meeting house." No trace of the old field system thus remained. The old patterns of village life which had shaped the actions of the settlers as they began to create their new plantation in the American wilderness had been abandoned for a more loosely structured community of dispersed dwellings and privately cultivated farms based upon extensive private holdings of land.

The amount of land now possessed by those who had chosen to participate in the settlement of Andover was in most instances enough to permit the first generation not only to establish independent farms of their own but also to think in terms of being able to provide their second generation sons with farms of their own carved from the original family estate. As a result of the four division grant of 1662, for instance, Simon Bradstreet's land holdings in Andover amounted to at least 630 acres.[18] John Osgood's family also possessed at least 604 acres, which ranked them second only to the Bradstreets in wealth.[19] Other families also consolidated their economic positions as a result of the fourth division. Nicholas Holt received more than 510 acres from successive divisions of land.[20] Joseph Parker, the town miller and tanner, left an estate of more than 306 acres of land in Andover as well as a grist mill upon his death in 1678.[21] His brother, Nathan Parker, who arrived in 1638 as an indentured servant, left an estate of more than 225 acres in 1685.[22] Daniel Poor, also a servant originally, bequeathed at least 240 acres of upland and meadow to his wife and children in 1689, including 140 acres of "wildernesse land."[23] His estate evidently included more land than was needed by his family prior to that time. . . . The land which they or their heirs had accumulated by 1662 far exceeded anything which they had owned or might have anticipated owning previously.

The fourth division was the first and last of its magnitude in the history of Andover. It signified an important change in the assumptions of the town's inhabitants. The earlier desire to create a compact village surrounded by outlying fields had been replaced by a desire for large dispersed farms which could provide a means of livelihood for the next generation. It pertained only to those thirty-six families which had participated in the earliest years of settlement and must have been, in their minds, the final act in the establishment of the community according to the new pattern. This is suggested by the fact that by the late 1660s, in the place of the former house lot grants with accompanying divisions of upland and meadow which had been given to newcomers and several second-generation sons, the town began to offer twenty-acre plots of land for sale to those who wished to settle in the town.[24] The purchase of

18. Andover, Record of Town Roads and Town Bounds, pp. 1-4.
19. Ibid., pp. 7-9.
20. Andover, Record of Town Roads and Town Bounds, pp. 17-19.
21. Joseph Parker's particular grants, ibid., p. 21, included about 237 acres of upland, meadow, and swamp. For his will and inventory, see *Essex Quarterly Court,* vol. 7, pp. 142-44.
22. See Nathan Parker, MS inventory, July 17, 1685, Probate File #20536, Probate Record Office, Registry of Deeds and Probate Court, Salem.
23. See Daniel Poor's inventory, September 23, 1689, in Essex County Probate Record, 302, 198 (photostat copy); his will is found on pp. 196-97.
24. See the Andover town meeting, March 22, 1669, and subsequent meetings for the grants of 20 acre lots. Andover, Ancient Town Records.

these twenty-acre plots included the privilege of becoming a townsman and rights to the common land, but in no sense did it make one the economic or social equal of those who had received house lots and land in the first four divisions. All of these small parcels of land were located at a considerable distance from the original village center, reflecting the complete abandonment of the wish to keep all the inhabitants of the town together within a compact area. None of the sources for the history of Andover during this period explain the reason for this change of policy. One can only guess that it was the decision of the most influential inhabitants of the town to discontinue free land grants—a decision which in effect froze the social structure of the community and made Andover no more advantageous to settle in than any of the other well-established towns in Massachusetts Bay colony.

By 1670, a quarter-century after the initial settlement of the inland plantation, the formative period of Andover had come to an end. As the patterns of life and farming techniques brought from England were adapted to the needs of the settlers in the new plantation, the crude replica of an English village was transformed into a form of community which few of the settlers in 1645 could have anticipated. Instead of a closely knit community in which all of the inhabitants dwelt side by side and tilled their land in small plots adjacent to those of their neighbors in the general fields of the village, Andover had become a town in which more than half of the inhabitants lived outside the village center on their own farming lands, separated by considerable distances from their neighbors, and concerned principally with their own interests and their own farms. . . . The old patterns of English villages seldom could be made to fit communities created out of the enormous quantities of unsettled land in the New World.

The Agricultural Practices of National Groups in Eighteenth-Century Southeastern Pennsylvania

James T. Lemon

The farming practices of the "Pennsylvania Dutch" in the eighteenth century have often been described as superior to those of settlers from the British Isles. Governor George Thomas, Lewis Evans, Benjamin Franklin, and Benjamin Rush, among others, believed that agricultural traditions of national groups were quite distinct. Thomas[1] said the Germans were responsible for the high productivity of Pennsylvania. Franklin,[2] despite his dislike of these Palatine "boors," expressed admiration for their "habitual industry and frugality," which permitted them to "underlive others." Rush, whose "Account of the Manners of the German Inhabitants of Pennsylvania"[3] has been widely quoted, concluded that "a German farm may be distinguished from the farms of the other citizens . . . by . . . the fertility of their [*sic*] fields; the luxuriance of their meadows, and a general appearance of plenty and neatness in everything that belongs to them." Among modern commentators, Shryock[4] has drawn a sharp distinction between German and British farming traditions, and a new general history of the people of the United States by Handlin[5] has helped to nurture the belief. Dissenting voices have been few; recently Shoemaker,[6] in a discussion of Pennsylvania barns, expressed doubt whether the Germans differed greatly from their neighbors from the British Isles.

Within the whole range of agricultural activities it is not possible to distinguish the Germans, English, and Scotch-Irish as national groups with distinctive cul-

1. George Thomas to the Bishop of Exeter, April 23, 1748, William Stevens Perry, ed., *Historical Collections Relating to the American Colonial Church*, 5 vols. (Hartford, 1870-1878), vol. 2, p. 256.
2. Benjamin Franklin, *The Papers of Benjamin Franklin*, ed. Leonard W. Labaree and others, vol. 4 (New Haven, 1961), pp. 120 and 479-86, and vol. 5 (New Haven, 1962), pp. 158-60.
3. Benjamin Rush, "An Account of the Manners of the German Inhabitants of Pennsylvania," ed. Theodore E. Schmauk, *Pennsylvania-German Soc. Proc. and Addresses 1908*, vol. 19, 1910, pp. 1-128; reference on pp. 72-73. Rush's work first appeared in the *Columbian Magazine, or Monthly Miscellany*, vol. 3 (January 1789), pp. 22-30.
4. Richard H. Shryock, "British versus German Traditions in Colonial Agriculture," *Mississippi Valley Hist. Rev.* 26 (1939-1940):39-54.
5. Oscar Handlin, *The Americans: A New History of the People of the United States* (Boston and Toronto, 1963), pp. 92-93.
6. Alfred L. Shoemaker, "The Pennsylvania Barn," in *The Pennsylvania Barn*, ed. Alfred L. Shoemaker (Lancaster, Pa., 1955), pp. 4-11; especially p. 8.

Reprinted (with omissions) from the *Geographical Review 56* (1966):467-96. For elaboration see also the author's *The Best Poor Man's Country: A Geographical Study of Early Southeastern Pennsylvania* (Baltimore: Johns Hopkins University Press, 1972).

tural traits. The eighteenth-century record, including tax lists and estate inventories, makes it clear that most writers have been biased in characterizing the Germans as the best farmers. Conversely, on insufficient evidence the Scotch-Irish have been rated as inferior farmers but as typical "frontiersmen."

In an investigation of skill in selecting land, kinds of crops and livestock, techniques for improving yields, attitudes about work and saving, and degree of material success this lack of differentiation among groups becomes apparent. Many specific beliefs held by Rush[7] and others—that Germans seldom incurred debts, for example, and that they cleared their lands in a more orderly fashion than others—are assessed here and found untenable. The attitudes about the Germans and Scotch-Irish seem to be based on widespread agreement on stereotypes of "national character." Some speculations are offered to account for the existence of such biases in America, because a study of spatial patterns undertaken by a historical geographer must consider the values both of those who interpret and of those who act.

National Groups in Southeastern Pennsylvania

Of the major national groups in southeastern Pennsylvania in 1730 and 1760 (Figs. 1 and 2), the English predominated in the East, the Germans in the North, and the Scotch-Irish in the West, but there were several areas of overlap, and a large number of the Scotch-Irish had settled among the English, and between the English and the Germans, in the South. In 1790, of the some 325,000 people living in the counties south and east of Blue (North) Mountain, persons of German-speaking ancestry accounted for 40 to 45 percent, English and Welsh for slightly more than 30 percent, and the English-speaking Scotch-Irish, including some Scots and Irish, for nearly 20 percent. There were also a few Swedes, Dutch, and French.[8]

Chester and Lancaster counties provide a more precise view and warrant comparative treatment because of their mixed ethnic and religious populations[9] and their high agricultural productivity. The predominantly English character of Chester, the Germanness of Lancaster, and the strong representation of Scotch-

7. Rush, "An Account," pp. 54-73.

8. The populations of Philadelphia, Delaware, Chester, Montgomery, Bucks, Northampton, Berks, Dauphin, Lancaster, York, Cumberland, and Franklin Counties were added together to reach the figure of 325,000 (the population of Pennsylvania in 1790 was 434,373). Parts of Cumberland, Dauphin, Berks, and Northampton lay beyond Blue Mountain, but few people lived in those parts ("Heads of Families at the First Census of the United States, Taken 1790: Pennsylvania" [U.S. Bureau of the Census, Washington, D.C., 1908], especially pp. 9-11). Percentage estimates were adjusted in part from Howard F. Barker, "National Stocks in the Population of the United States As Indicated by Surnames in the Census of 1790," *Ann. Rept. Amer. Hist. Assn. for the Year 1931* (Washington, D.C., 1932) 3 vols., vol. 1, pp. 126-359; see especially p. 307. Higher percentages of English, Scotch-Irish, and Scots were found in western Pennsylvania, because of heavy immigration from the British Isles in the 1770s. This accounts for the discrepancy between Barker and the text figures. The estimated percentage of Germans in southeastern Pennsylvania may still be too low.

The distribution of groups on Figures 1 and 2 is based primarily on the location and founding dates of churches identified with national groups. Few Germans and Scotch-Irish had settled in 1700, but by 1755 the area was well covered with settlers; the pattern in 1790 closely resembled that in 1760.

9. The writer is particularly indebted to Miss Dorothy Lapp of West Chester, Miss Elizabeth Kieffer of Lancaster, and the Reverend Ira Landis of Manheim Township, Lancaster County, for their aid in the assessment of the national backgrounds and religious affiliations of early residents.

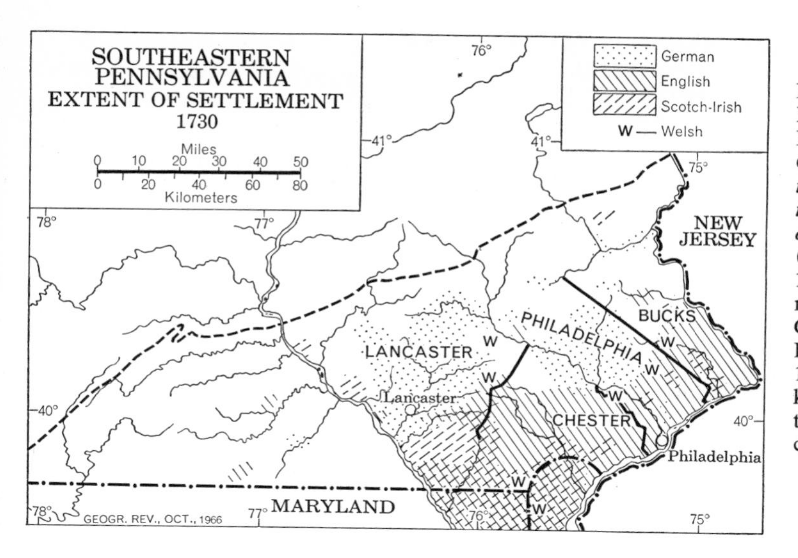

FIG. 1
Data were taken from Frederick L. Weis, *The Colonial Churches and the Colonial Clergy of the Middle and Southern Colonies, 1607-1776* (Lancaster, Mass., 1938); from Hunter Rineer, "A List of Churches Founded in Pennsylvania before 1800" (manuscript, kindly lent by the author); and from various county histories.

Irish in both are apparent in Table 1. So, too, is the declining numerical importance of the non-Germans in Lancaster between 1760 and 1782 and of the Welsh in Chester between 1730 and 1760. In 1782 the Germans were prominent in the central and northern parts of Lancaster and on the northern edge of Chester, and the Scotch-Irish were most numerous in southwestern and western Chester and eastern, southern, and west-central Lancaster. The English were dominant in eastern and central Chester and were found also in Scotch-Irish areas. These distributions will be analyzed in relation to some of the problems raised below.

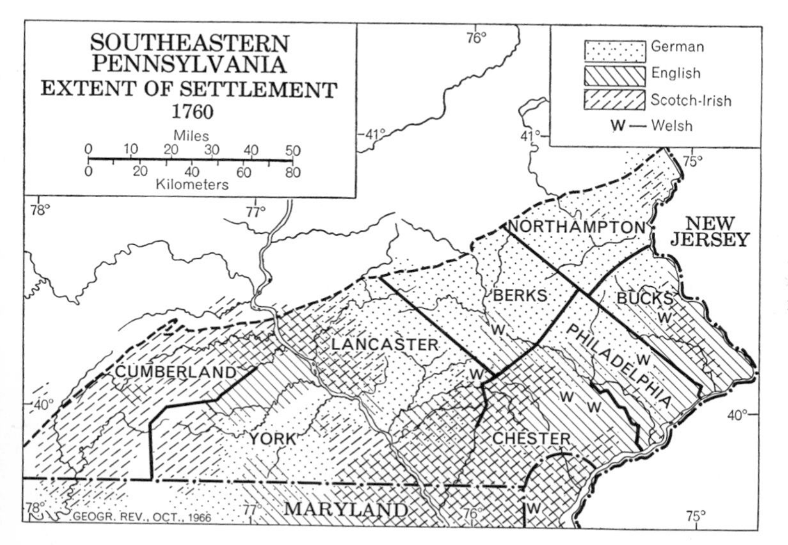

FIG. 2
Source of data same as in Figure 1.

TABLE 1. National Groups in Chester and Lancaster Counties* (*In percentages of population*)

	Chester			*Lancaster*		
	1730	1759	1782	1722	1759	1782
English	67	59	63	35	15	10
Welsh	17	8	7		1	1
Scotch-Irish, Scots, Irish	12	23	19		19	13
German-speaking	2	5	8	65	58	68
Other and unassigned	2	5	3	—	7	8
Approximate population	10,025	24,500	34,500	1,150	25,550	42,775

* Figures were derived from an analysis of surnames in tax lists: for 1722, from H. Frank Eshleman edit.: Assessment Lists and Other Documents of Lancaster Prior to 1729, *Papers Lancaster County Hist. Soc.*, vol. 20, 1916, pp. 155-94 (Lancaster County was part of Chester until 1729); for 1782, from the *Pennsylvania Archives,* ser. 3, vols. 11, 12, and 17, 1897; and for the other years, from manuscript lists of returns and assessments in the Chester County Historical Society library and the Lancaster County Historical Society library. The English category includes undifferentiated British; names, such as Smith and Brown, that often could not be distinguished as those of German- or English-speaking persons who relegated to the "Other and unassigned" group. Because the percentages in this group are higher for Lancaster than for Chester, probably more Germans than non-Germans were unassigned.

Initial Selection of Land

The selection of good-quality land accessible to markets is a mark of skillful farming. Greater perception of good land has been attributed to Germans. For example, some nineteenth-century writers believed that most Germans sought heavier limestone lowland soils covered with thick forests, and that the other national groups, especially the Scotch-Irish, desired lightly wooded but poorer-quality shale uplands. These choices were thought to have been a consequence of homeland experience.[10] Similarly, many writers have held that as a consequence of Celtic restlessness and Teutonic stability the Scotch-Irish were frontiersmen par excellence and the Germans usually bought their land from others, notably the Scotch-Irish.[11] These assumptions are unwarranted.

To assess the relationship of national groups to the land, the areal variations in its qualities must first be considered. The patterns of climate and vegetation were relatively uniform in southeastern Pennsylvania in the eighteenth century. The water supply was easily accessible only at streams and springs; indeed, some limestone areas had intermittent streams. But of greatest relevance to agricultural activity was the quality of the soil, a result of the kinds of parent materials and of the

10. Franklin Ellis and Samuel Evans, *History of Lancaster County, Pennsylvania* (Philadelphia, 1883), p. 345; Sylvanus Stall, "The Relation of the Lutheran Church in the United States to the Limestone Districts," *Lutheran Quarterly,* N.S., vol. 13 (1883), pp. 509-15, reference on p. 509; editorial note in Rush, "An Account," p. 57; Stevenson Whitcomb Fletcher, *Pennsylvania Agriculture and Country Life, 1640-1840* (Harrisburg, 1950), pp. 49-50 and 53. Fletcher's monumental work is useful, though, since it is an "institutional" rather than an analytical systematic study, it is replete with uncritical assertions.

11. Rush, "An Account," p. 57; Benjamin Rush, "Dr. Benjamin Rush's Journal of a Trip to Carlisle in 1784," *Pennsylvania Mag. of History and Biography* 74 (1950):443-56, reference on p. 451; Theophile Cazenove, *Cazenove Journal 1794: A Record of the Journey of Theophile Cazenove through New Jersey and Pennsylvania,* tr. and ed. Rayner Wickersham Kelsey (Haverford, 1922), p. 44, but see also p. 84; Samuel Vaughan, "Samuel Vaughan's Journal, or Minutes Made by S. V., from Stage to Stage, on a Tour to Fort Pitt," *Western Pennsylvania Hist. Mag.* 44 (1961):51-65, 159-73, and 261-85, reference on p. 62; Fletcher, *Penn. Agriculture,* pp. 52 and 54.

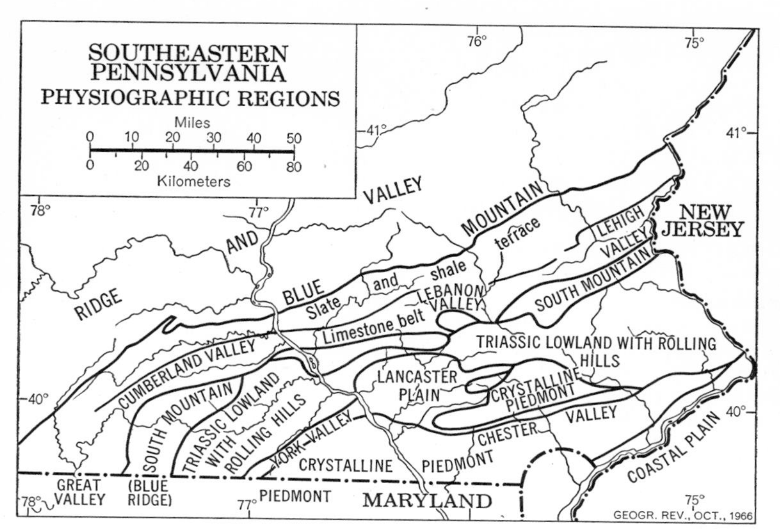

FIG. 3
Physiographic regions adapted from A. K. Lobeck, *Physiographic Diagram of Pennsylvania* (New York, 1951), and from Raymond E. Murphy and Marion Murphy, *Pennsylvania: A Regional Geography* (Harrisburg, 1937), p. 18.

topography, specifically the degree of slope. . . . The distribution of the three commonest kinds of parent materials—limestones, shales, and crystallines—and their relationship to the physiographic regions are shown in Figures 3 and 4. Gentle slopes (less than 3 percent) are much more frequent in limestone areas than in others; however, except in the hills, slopes are generally less than 8 percent. Gently sloping areas of limestone and crystalline soils are the most productive (Table 2). Where slopes are between 3 and 6 percent, deep limestone and crystalline soils are about equally productive. Shale soils of moderate slope have only 55 to 85 percent of the fertility of the others.

No clear relationship is apparent between soils and the position of national groups in 1730 and 1760 (Figs. 1, 2, and 4). By 1760 the English and Welsh had

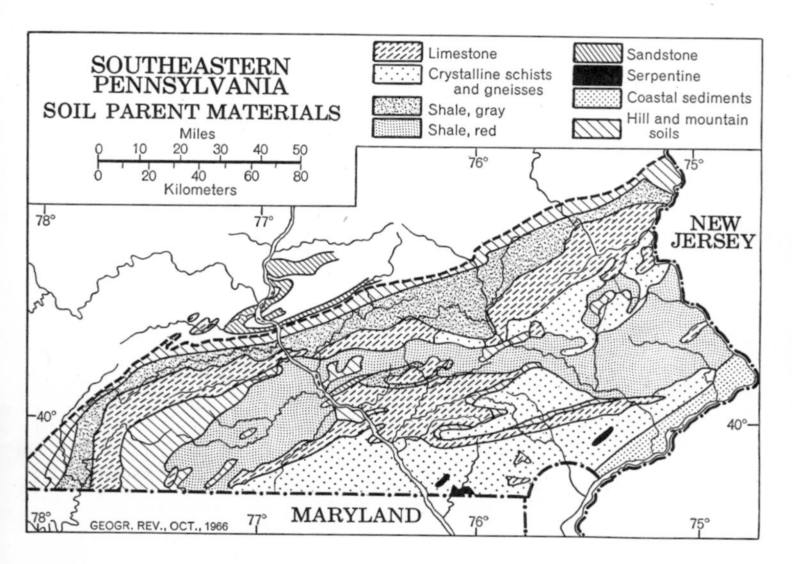

FIG. 4
Soil parent materials modified from Charles F. Shaw, "The Soils of Pennsylvania," *Pennsylvania Agric. Exper. Sta. Bull* 132(1915): 224-25.

TABLE 2. Soil Fertility in Present-Day Lancaster County*

Soil	% Slope	Condition	Productivity Index of Seven Kinds of Crops
Limestone loams	0-3	Little erosion	100
	3-6	Moderate erosion	90-100, mostly 98
Crystalline loams	0-3	Little erosion	97-100, mostly 100
	3-6	Moderate erosion	75-100, mostly 90 on deep soil, 85-87 on moderately deep
Shale loams	3-8	Moderate erosion	55-85, average 71

* Values for Lancaster only are given, as used by John B. Carey ("Soil Survey of Lancaster County, Pennsylvania," *U.S. Soil Conservation Service, Soil Survey,* ser. 1956, no. 4, 1939, pp. 8 and 85-98), because W. Merrill Kunkle ("Soil Survey of Chester and Delaware Counties, Pennsylvania," *Soil Survey,* ser. 1959, no. 19, 1963), especially p. 124, does not use quite the same categories for Chester. The indices of productivity are based on the Hagerstown-Duffield Series, 0-3 percent slope with little erosion being taken as 100 for all kinds of crops: corn, winter grain, clover, timothy, bluegrass cover, potatoes, and orchards.

settled on soils derived from crystalline bedrock (Chester and Lancaster counties), from red shales (Bucks and York counties), and from limestones (Chester Valley, Lancaster Plain, and Lebanon Valley). The Scotch-Irish had settled chiefly on crystalline soils (Chester, Lancaster, and York counties), on limestone and shale soils (in the Cumberland and Lehigh valleys and western York), and on limestones (eastern Lancaster County). Germans had settled on the limestone soils of Lancaster and York, and of the Lebanon and Lehigh valleys, where they also occupied gray shales. Germans were the most prominent group on the extensive area of red shales in Montgomery County. The heavy settlement of Germans on the shales clearly weakens the validity of the generalization that as a group they commonly sought lowland limestone soils. Furthermore, in 1759, after a generation of settlement, 49 percent of the 235 taxables in almost exclusively German Cocalico Township, Lancaster County, were on "poor" land, which constituted 33 percent of the 25,953 acres assessed.[12] In short, Germans settled on all qualities of land.

Many areas of good soils were selected by individuals or religious groups. Mennonites occupied some of the best limestone land in Lancaster County in 1710, though others later took up poorer land in the same county and another large group settled on the red shales of Montgomery. The limestone soils of the Lancaster Plain and the Chester Valley attracted not only land speculators but some of the more affluent Quakers, Scotch-Irish Presbyterians, Welsh Anglicans, German Lutherans, and German and Huguenot Reformed folk.[13]

Water supply was also a major consideration among the first settlers. Early survey drafts indicate that in newly opened areas the settlers took up land in stream bottoms or near springs, leaving the interfluves to those who followed. An example is found in a Scotch-Irish settlement in the Lebanon Valley.[14] This evi-

12. Lancaster County tax lists [see footnote to Table 1 above].

13. See, for example, Ellis and Evans, *History,* p. 989. In Rapho and Mount Joy Townships the Scotch-Irish took limestone soils and the Germans gravelly hill soils.

14. Drafts are numerous in the Taylor Papers and the Lightfoot Papers in the Historical Society of Pennsylvania. This particular draft, showing thirty-eight Scotch-Irish holdings strad-

dence denies that these people invariably sought uplands.

"Frontier" locations were not the monopoly of any one national group. Before 1680 the Swedes were on the edge of European settlement, though confined to the margins of the Delaware River; by 1700 the English and Welsh were clearly the most numerous frontiersmen; and later the Germans dominated the northern line and the Scotch-Irish the western (Fig. 2). The North was as much a frontier as the West, and during the conflicts of the 1750s Scotch-Irish and Germans suffered equally from Indian attacks in the Great Valley. There seems little doubt that all groups had numerous representatives willing to live beyond areas already settled.

A detailed analysis of the distribution of national groups is not appropriate here, but the factors should be recognized in distinguishing other aspects of cultural antecedency from so-called "national character." Familiarity in the guise of the same language, the same religious denomination, kinfolk, and old neighbors, exerted a pull in the establishment of initial nuclei of settlements and on subsequent settlers. These cultural factors operated in conjunction with the time and place of entry into the province, ability to pay for land, availability of land, and, in some instances, government policies.[15]

dling streams, was in Hanover Township, Lancaster County (later Dauphin and Lebanon Counties), Lightfoot Papers, Box 3, Lancaster Co. etc. See also Thomas Paschall, "Letter of Thomas Paschall, 1683 . . . to . . . J. J. of Chippenham," in *Narratives of Early Pennsylvania, West New Jersey, and Delaware, 1630-1707,* ed. Albert Cook Myers (New York, 1912), pp. 250-54.

15. See James Thomas Lemon, "A Rural Geography of Southeastern Pennsylvania in the Eighteenth Century: The Contributions of Cultural Inheritance, Social Structure, Economic Conditions and Physical Resources" (unpublished Ph.D. dissertation, University of Wisconsin, 1964), chap. 5.

Crops and Livestock

A superior approach to farming has been cited as a major reason for the supposed greater productivity of German farms. To check this hypothesis, the kinds of crops and livestock (though few writers made an issue of these), the types of farming, and techniques related to the use of land will be considered.

A large number of crops were produced in Pennsylvania in the eighteenth century. Most were of European origin; maize was the major addition from the Indians. . . . Wheat both for domestic consumption and for export was "the grand article of the province. They sow immense quantities," exclaimed the anonymous author of "American Husbandry" in 1775, footnoting a fact established by 1700.[16] Rye was also a major crop, amounting to one-fifth to one-third of the acreage of wheat.[17] Differences in the amounts of crops grown by national groups could not be established firmly because the assessment lists for the falls of 1759 and 1784, the only years for which these amounts are available, combine rye and wheat as "winter grain."

The locations of average acreages sown with winter grain do not correlate with the locations of national groups. In a list

16. "American Husbandry . . . By an American" (2 vols., London, 1775; ed. Harry J. Carman, New York, 1939), p. 113; James Logan to William Penn, March 14, 1703/4 (Penn-Logan Correspondence, vol. 1, p. 278, MSS, Historical Society of Pennsylvania).

17. See, for example, the claims of farmers in Chester County against the British troops who foraged there: 9,062 bushels of wheat; 2,324 bushels of rye; John S. Futhey and Gilbert Cope; *History of Chester County, Pennsylvania* (Philadelphia, 1881), p. 108. See also "A Geographical Dictionary of the United States of North America" (Philadelphia, 1805) by Joseph Scott, who noted that the average farm of 200 acres produced 500 bushels of wheat and 100 to 150 each of rye and Indian corn (article on Pennsylvania).

TABLE 3. Average Acreages Sown in Winter Grain, Lancaster County, Fall, 1759*

Sample Townships	*All Groups*	*German*	*English*	*Scotch-Irish*	*Welsh*	*Other and Unclassified*
Bart	7.8	8.9	6.9	7.8	—	8.1
Caernarvon	11.3	10.1	10.4	5.2	14.8	5.5
Donegal	10.5	8.8	11.6	11.5	—	11.3
Lampeter	11.9	12.2	17.0	11.0	8.8	10.0

* *Source:* Chester and Lancaster tax lists (see footnote to Table 1 above).

of sample townships (Table 3) averages for every group fall above or below the township averages. South-central Chester County and the Lancaster Plain had higher average acreages than elsewhere in the two counties (Fig. 5); the former area was identified chiefly with English Quakers, the latter with German-speaking Mennonites and a few persons of other national and religious groups (Fig. 6). Smaller acreages were found among Germans in the northern parts of the two counties and among Scotch-Irish and English in the southern parts. Generally it appears that this regional pattern was associated with affluence rather than with nationality (Fig. 7).[18] Chester and Lancaster counties had about the same average acreages (9½ in Chester, 10 in Lancaster), but Chester was mainly English-speaking and Lancaster about three-fifths German.

. . . It is impossible to identify particular crops with national groups. This is the case with livestock also, though with some qualifications about sheep. Oxen are noted only rarely in tax lists and estate inventories.[19] Horses were without question the chief suppliers of locomotive power, both for plowing and for hauling wagons.[20] Tradition has identified the Conestoga horses and wagon with the Germans of Lancaster County, but there is no justification for this association.[21] The name "Conestoga" was given by Philadelphians who in earlier years considered the Conestoga area (Lancaster County) synonymous with backcountry. However, there are also references to "Dutch," "English," and even "Irish" wagons, and, in the inventories of Lancaster farmers, to "Philadedphia" wagons.[22] There is little evidence from tax lists and inventories that any national group owned more horses than any other. This is also true for cattle, despite Rush's

18. Chester and Lancaster tax lists [see footnote to Table 1 above].

19. They were somewhat more common in Quaker areas, yet in the only tax list noted that specified oxen, for Upper Darby (now in Delaware County), 1782, only twenty were noted (manuscript lists, Chester County).

20. Travelers frequently commented on numbers. For example, Andrew Burnaby, "Travels through the Middle Settlements in North-America, in the Years 1759 and 1760; With Observations upon the State of the Colonies," (reprinted from the 2nd ed., 1775; Ithaca, N.Y., 1960), p. 62 noted 9,000 wagons, or one for every twenty persons; this would mean one horse for every five persons if we assume four horses to a wagon. See numbers of livestock listed in Stella H. Sutherland, *Population Distribution in Colonial America* (New York, 1936), p. 168.

21. Gary S. Dunbar, "Wagons West–and East!" *Geogr. Rev.* 55 (1965):282-83, reference on p. 282; Fletcher, *Penn. Agriculture,* pp. 198-200.

22. "Dutch" quoted in a petition for a road in 1728 in Futhey and Cope, *History,* p. 167; "English" noted in the *Pennsylvania Gazette,* June 5, 1760; "Irish" noted by William Logan to John Smith, November 30, 1762 (Smith MSS, Vol. 6, Library Company of Philadelphia); "Philadelphia" in, for example, the inventory of Peter Bricker, 1760 (MS, Lancaster County Register of Wills Office, Lancaster).

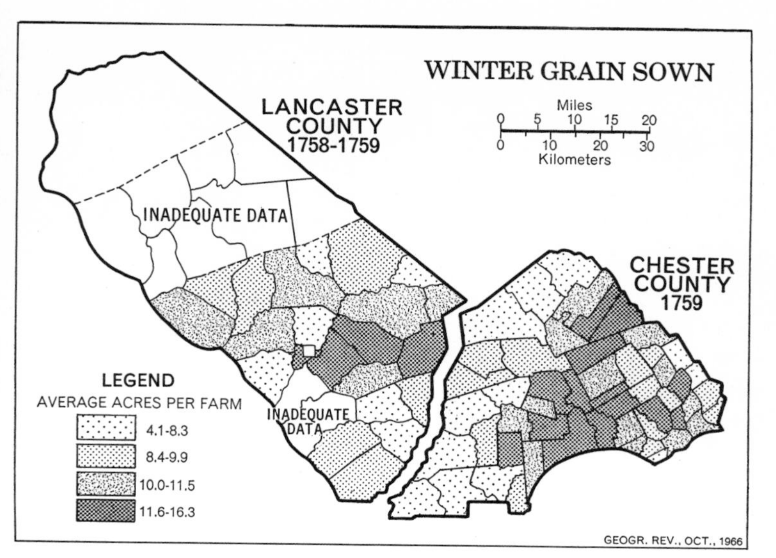

FIG. 5
Data from tax lists (see footnote to Table 1).

assertion that the Germans kept fewer.[23] More affluent areas, such as parts of the Lancaster Plain, had more of both per farm. Quantitative data for swine are limited to inventories; most farms had between five and ten hogs, but no distinction by national groups can be hazarded. Despite the lack of information, it is clear that pigs were important in the rural economy of all groups.

Although sheep were less prominent in Pennsylvania than in the British Isles, there was a slight tendency for the Scotch-Irish and English to raise more than the

23. Rush, "An Account," p. 59.

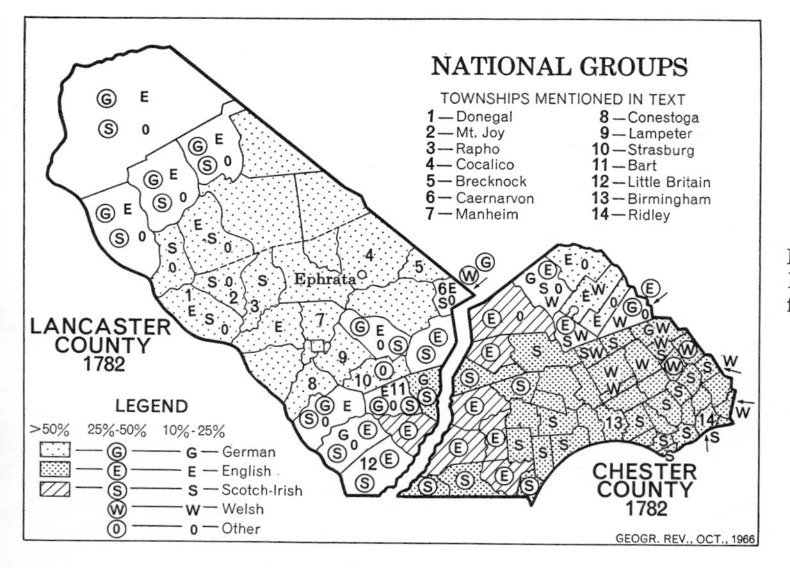

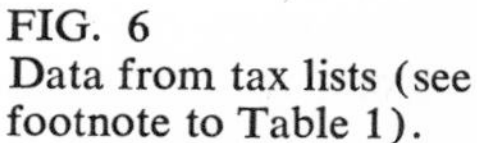
FIG. 6
Data from tax lists (see footnote to Table 1).

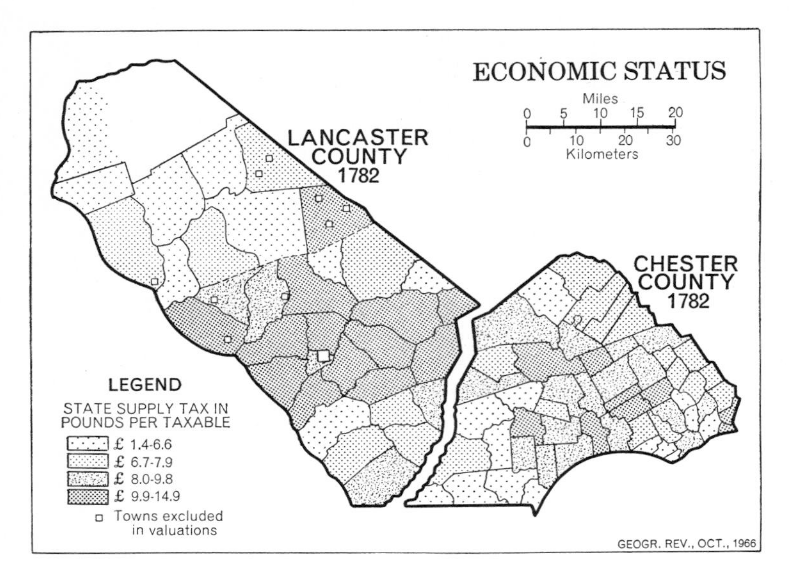

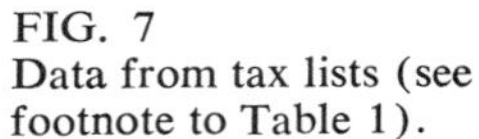
FIG. 7
Data from tax lists (see footnote to Table 1).

Germans. . . . The pattern related to ethnic groups is not nearly as apparent as the distinctions based on economic status. A breakdown of inventory data is by no means clear, though non-Germans held on the average slightly more sheep.

It should be apparent from this survey of a few crops and livestock that differences among national groups were slight or uncertain. Regional variations, noted for winter grain and sheep, were more clearly associated with affluence than with national groups.

Farming Techniques

Good techniques are necessary for high productivity. The Germans have been praised as having superior skills; they were allegedly more sophisticated on arrival and were responsible for several innovations in Pennsylvania. Specifically, they have been credited with the cutting rather than the girdling of trees, the best horticultural ideas, stall-feeding, large bank barns, the watering of meadows, the use of gypsum fertilizer, the "Dutch" fan, and the Conestoga horses and wagon.[24] Rush[25] suggested that the Scotch-Irish of Donegal had learned their good farming techniques from the Germans. But the historical record is by no means clear as to who were the greatest innovators or who possessed superior skills.

Sometimes it has been assumed that more German-speaking settlers than others had been farmers in Europe.[26] However, a review of all available data does not clearly indicate differences among Ulstermen, English, and Germans. Even if differences existed, it is debatable whether a farming background would have provided the skills necessary in the husbandry of Pennsylvania. Undoubtedly many immigrant craftsmen became farmers, and perhaps these might have been more flexible in adopting Pennsylvania practices than immigrant farmers.

In Pennsylvania there were signs that

24. See Fletcher, *Penn. Agriculture;* Rush, "An Account," pp. 54-73.
25. Journal of a Trip to Carlisle, p. 451.
26. For example, Shryock, "British vs. German," p. 46; Ralph Wood, ed. *The Pennsylvania Germans* (Princeton, 1942), p. vii.

innovations identified with the "Agricultural Revolution" in England in the century and a half following 1650 were recognized, if not consistently adopted. In England the key element was the introduction of forage crops—most notably red clover and, less widely, turnips—into rotation schemes. The increase in fodder production that was the direct effect resulted in more and fatter animals for human consumption. In addition, the soil was improved by the greater use of manure and by the more frequent cultivation of clover. German-speaking areas, including the Rhine, the area of origin of most immigrants into Pennsylvania, were not as inclined to change as England before 1750.[27]

The "revolution" did not strike Pennsylvania farmers with the same degree of necessity that many English farmers felt. Because of persistent and successful marketing patterns, grain, and especially wheat, was relatively more important than livestock in Pennsylvania throughout much of the century.[28] This resulted in a rather general pattern of extensive farming, which clearly did not call for the practices needed in more intensive use of the land, despite all the disparaging remarks about agriculture by travelers and the pleas of Philadelphia gentlemen farmers. Certain modifications were made, nevertheless, and certain practices did result in better land use by some farmers.

"The two principal links in good farming, are proper Rotation of Crops . . . and Manures," John Bordley asserted in 1792.[29] Some concern was expressed about rotations from the earliest days of the province, beginning with William Penn.[30] Mid-century tenant agreements specified that winter grain could be sown but once in every three or four years on any one field, and that one or two fields should be held for spring grain and one for fallow.[31] Although red clover may have been sown in meadows as early as 1740, there is no evidence of its presence in rotations until about 1790. Upland meadows with other grasses may have been taken into the pattern earlier.[32] In the 1790s records indicate that the number of fields in use had increased generally and that clover was being grown, possibly because the market patterns in the period 1775-1789 encouraged more meat production. . . . There does not seem to be any evidence that the Germans practiced rotations with clover or grass

27. The most recent summary of research on the situation in England is E. L. Jones, "Agriculture and Economic Growth in England, 1660-1750: Agricultural Change," *Journ. of Econ. History* 25 (1965):1-18. The most recent summaries of German agricultural history are Wilhelm Abel, *Geschichte der deutschen Landwirtschaft vom frühen Mittelalter bis zum 19. Jahrhundert* (Stuttgart, 1962); and F. Lutge, *Geschichte der deutschen Agrarverfassung vom frühen Mittelalter bis zum 19. Jahrhundert* (Stuttgart, 1963).

28. Although few cattle were held as compared with the dairying areas of Europe at the time or with dairy farms in this country in recent times, most farmers kept some cows, many were raised in certain parts of the backcountry, and near Philadelphia dairying and the fattening of beef cattle became prominent. Only in the 1740s and 1780s does there seem to have been a stronger trend toward livestock. In the nineties there was again a stronger market for grain in Europe ("American Husbandry," pp. 129 and 138-147; reports and other publications of the Philadelphia Society for Promoting Agriculture in the *Columbian Magazine* and the *American Museum;* Lemon, "Rural Geography," pp. 368-88).

29. John Beale Bordley, *Sketches on Rotations of Crops* (Philadelphia, 1792), p. 32.

30. Penn to J. Harrison, February 28, 1686/7 (Penn MSS, Letters Domestic & Miscellaneous, vol. 10, p. 52, Historical Society of Pennsylvania).

31. See, for example, the Taylor Papers (MSS, Historical Society of Pennsylvania), vol. 16, pp. 3402½ and 3445.

32. Benjamin Hawley, *Diary, 1761-1763* (MS, Chester County Historical Society), March 20, 1761.

earlier than others; indeed, in the Lehigh Valley, Cazenove said, clover was a recent acquisition.[33]

Among fertilizers animal manure was the most prominent, though lime and, eventually, gypsum were used. The lack of manure and the failure to use it when available are mentioned from the beginning of Penn's colony. In 1684 Pastorius said that the Swedes made no use of manure.[34] In 1733 Hassert, who had just arrived from Germany, asserted that farmers "know of no manuring."[35] Kalm in 1749,[36] Francis Alison in 1770,[37] and postrevolutionary travelers commented on the neglect. An assertion by Hummel, who founded a town in Dauphin County (part of Lancaster until 1785), that manure was unnecessary brought the German traveler Schoepf in 1783 to reply: "Such over-confident opinions regarding the inexhaustible goodness of his soil gradually puts the farmer's industry to sleep, and when, finally, betterment is necessary many of them had rather move on to take up fresh land than to be at the trouble of improving the old."[38] A correspondent to the *Germantauner Zeitung* on July 24, 1787, while praising Mennonites and other sectarians, indicated that farmers thought the use of manure unnecessary.

Despite these negative statements, manure was used by many farmers. Some rental agreements specified dunging.[39] Part of the problem was the lack of dung because of a low ratio of cattle to land area, and the lack of fencing to keep animals from the woods. Often the grainlands had to do without manure. From the evidence it seems clear that the Pennsylvania Dutch shared these problems with their neighbors.

By mid-century lime, and toward the end of the century gypsum, had come to be rather widely used as fertilizer. . . . The introduction of gypsum, or plaster of Paris, was specifically identified with the Germans of Lancaster County by William Strickland of the British Board of Agriculture. However, Richard Peters claimed to have introduced it to that country before the Revolution.[40] In any case, Schoepf in 1783 reported its use from Philadelphia to York.[41] There does not seem to be any correlation of gypsum use with Germans alone.

The irrigation of meadows Strickland also attributed to the Germans of Lancaster County,[42] perhaps because of Pownall's comment in 1754 that he had not seen irrigation with sluices in America (or England) until he reached a "Swisser's" farm in Lancaster County.[43] The

33. Cazenove, *Journal*, p. 24.
34. Francis Daniel Pastorius, "Circumstantial Geographical Description of Pennsylvania," in *Narratives of Early Pennsylvania*, pp. 353-448; reference on p. 397.
35. Arent Hassert, Jr., to Deputy van Ostade in the Netherlands, January 9, 1733 (from the Hague Archives 74.1.13), in *Letters and Documents Relating to the Reformed Church of Pennsylvania, 1699-1752*, tr. William J. Hinke (MMS, Reformed Church Library, Lancaster).
36. Peter Kalm, *The America of 1750; Peter Kalm's Travels in North America: The English Version of 1770*, revised from the original Swedish and edited by Adolph B. Benson, 2 vols. (New York, 1937), vol. 1, pp. 97-98 and 307.
37. Francis Alison to American Philosophical Society, April 2, 1773 (MSS Comm. to A.P.S. on Trade, &c., Vol. 6).
38. Johann David Schoepf, *Travels in the Confederation, 1783-1784*, tr. and ed. Alfred J. Morrison, 2 vols. (Philadelphia, 1911), vol. 1, p. 212.
39. David Schultze, *Journals and Papers of David Schultze*, tr. and ed. Andrew S. Berky, 2 vols. (Pennsburg, Pa., 1953-1955), vol. 1, p. 141.
40. Fletcher, *Penn. Agriculture*, pp. 132-36, discusses the issues.
41. Schoepf, *Travels*, vol. 1, p. 196.
42. William Strickland, *Observations on the Agriculture of the United States of America* (London, 1801), p. 68.
43. "Governor Thomas Pownall's Description

practice was widespread, however, and need not be identified with Germans. Strickland himself noted that it was common in Connecticut at an early date and also prevalent in the west of England,[44] and recent evidence for the latter area suggests that sophisticated methods were practiced by 1700.[45] A large number of English settlers in Pennsylvania and Connecticut came from this west country. . . .

If German farms were more productive than the farms of other groups, the reasons do not lie in the field of technology. The national origins of many techniques are obscure; and as for fertilizer, many Germans had a positive aversion to its use. Resistance to change, perhaps as much a consequence of market conditions as of conservatism, was widespread. On September 4, 1787, "Ein Bauer" in a letter to the *Germantauner Zeitung* complained about a columnist who on May 29 had suggested ways in which farmers might improve their land and production; farmers, he said, had always gotten along without this kind of help. That Germans were not then considered exemplary farmers is indicated by the absence of references to them in the agricultural writings of gentlemen farmers during the last two decades of the century. These experimenters strove constantly to emulate English farming practices.

Innovations did occur, however; the use of clover, lime, and gypsum, more fattening of livestock, and more-sophisticated rotations were apparent by the end of the century. Instead of being attributable to any particular national groups or even chiefly to the gentlemen experimenters, it would seem likely that permanent improvements were the work of better-than-average ordinary farmers who could afford to risk some of their capital.[46] Because the Mennonites and the Quakers were the most affluent farmers, they may well have been the chief innovators.[47]. . .

Habits and Customs

We have not been able to establish that German settlers were generally more perceptive in their initial selection of land or superior in the use of technical skills, but were they more industrious and frugal than others, as has been asserted? Work habits, food consumption, indebtedness, and locational stability need to be investigated.

Whether any national group worked harder than others cannot be answered with any degree of precision, though some comments can be made on land-clearance practices, labor-saving devices, and servants and slaves. Rush's suggestion that Germans were more diligent than the indolent English and Scotch-Irish because they cut rather than girdled trees can be neither denied nor confirmed.[48] Many travelers thought American farms lacked neatness—an indication, perhaps, that girdling was ubiquitous. In 1780 Timothy Matlack speculated that girdling

of the Streets and the Main Roads about Philadelphia, 1754," *Pennsylvania Mag. of History and Biography* 18 (1894):211-17; reference on p. 215.

44. Strickland, *Observations,* pp. 215 and 68 respectively.

45. Jones, "Agriculture," p. 4.

46. Fletcher, *Penn. Agriculture,* p. 126, although he often praised the Germans, said the gentlemen farmers, "not . . . the working farmers," made the first moves toward improvement. If they did, establishment of the practices depended on others. Among the gentlemen farmers toward the end of the century were Bordley, George Logan, George Morgan, Washington, and Jefferson.

47. Success and self-satisfaction may also inhibit change. An analysis of early-nineteenth-century economic life might help to determine whether Quakers and Mennonites became less interested in changes.

48. Rush, "An Account," p. 58.

was commonplace because the first settlers, "full of *English* ideas of farming [his italics]," cleared by felling only, but this "broke their hearts with the labor"; poorer settlers "urged by necessity" to practice girdling got better yields. Thus the idea spread.[49]. . . The development and use of other labor-saving devices are also unclear. Cradles were discussed, and advertisements in newspapers indicate that new kinds of scythes and sickles appeared, but there are no indications of other new means of harvesting. . . . There is no clear indication that Germans were either more or less inclined than non-Germans toward labor-saving improvements.

Whether Germans were less inclined to use hired and indentured servants and slaves is likewise open to question. The presence of more Negro slaves among the Scotch-Irish and English has been cited as an indication of greater German self-reliance. However, most Quakers eschewed the use of slaves, after mid-century at least, and even in Scotch-Irish townships the percentage of servants and slaves on tax lists was very low—less than 4 percent of the population.[50] Tax lists do not give the number of indentured servants, but German farmers used them.[51] The whole question of labor in relation to the kind of agriculture practiced needs clarification. Except during harvestime, possibly because of the greater emphasis on grain farming than on livestock, and because families averaged five or six members, hired labor was not needed continuously except on the largest farms. . . . As for the propensity for work, the Scotch-Irish women of Cumberland County were found to "do all the drugery [*sic*] of a family as well as any German woman you ever saw."[52]. . .

With respect to dietary habits, Rush asserted that the Germans were self-effacing in using cheaper grains rather than wheat for their own consumption, and that they were less inclined than others to imbibe liquor. The evidence does not support his view. . . . An analysis of widow's dowers specified in the wills of farmers, chiefly "plain folk" (Table 4),[53] indicated that generally wheat was the grain most preferred, echoing a German diarist who in 1728 noted that "wheat-bread is eaten in almost all places."[54] Muhlenberg suggested that less palatable buckwheat was only for the poor, and

49. Timothy Matlack, *An Oration Delivered March 16, 1780, before . . . the American Philosophical Society* . . . (Philadelphia, 1780), p. 13.

50. Scotch-Irish townships in Chester, Lancaster, York, and Cumberland counties tended to have close to 4 percent. Ridley Township, now in Delaware County, had 10 percent in 1759. Usually Negroes constituted about half of the servants and slaves listed.

51. See discussions in Otto Pollak, "German Immigrant Problems in Eighteenth Century Pennsylvania As Reflected in Trouble Advertisements," *Amer. Sociol. Rev.* 8 (1943):674-84; and Cheesman A. Herrick, *White Servitude in Pennsylvania* (Philadelphia, 1926). Advertisements for runaways appear in the *Germantauner Zeitung* and the *Wochentliche Philadelphische Staatsbote* and in English papers such as the *Pennsylvania Gazette*.

52. Mrs. Eleanor Campbell at Shippensburg to Mrs. Ewings and Mrs. Yeates in Lancaster, October 14, 1769. D. W. Thompson and others, *Two Hundred Years in Cumberland County* (Carlisle, 1951), pp. 48-49.

53. Of the 159 wills stipulating goods of some kind that were assessed, 109 were German, 30 English, 16 Scotch-Irish, and 4 others. The preponderance of "plain folk," mostly Mennonites, was established with reasonable assurance by whether the witnesses affirmed rather than swore before the probate judge. Quakers and non-"plain folk" were inclined to specify a cash allowance instead of goods.

54. "Diary of a Voyage from Rotterdam to Philadelphia in 1728," tr. Julius F. Sachse, *Pennsylvania-German Soc. Proc. and Addresses 1907*, vol. 18 (1909), pp. 1-25; reference on p. 23. See also Lawrence Henry Gipson, *Lewis Evans, To Which Is Added Evans' A Brief Account of Pennsylvania* (Philadelphia, 1939), p. 116.

TABLE 4. Proportions of Grains Cited in Widow's Dowers*

Crop	*Frequency*	*Average Allotment*	*Crop*	*Frequency*	*Average Allotment*
Wheat	116 wills	13.2 bushels	Oats	11 wills	9.0 bushels
Rye	58	5.4	Buckwheat	4	4.8
Barley	17	3.8	Indian corn	13	6.3

* Based on 159 wills from Chester and Lancaster counties in the offices of the Register of Wills, West Chester and Lancaster.

corn may have been used more by non-German poor.[55] However, Mennonites seem to have used corn as a breakfast food.[56]

. . . That the Germans were learning whiskey-making from the Scotch-Irish in 1784, as Rush said,[57] is without foundation; a cursory glance at tax lists and inventories indicates that reasonably affluent Germans had been distilling rye whiskey and brandy long before this. Therefore, to attribute to the Scotch-Irish the production of rye for whiskey, and to the Germans the use of rye for grain, has no empirical basis. In general, the dietary elements were similar among groups; all ate well, and the food included large amounts of meat.[58]

Rush's statement that the Germans were "afraid of debt, and seldom purchase anything without paying cash for it,"[59] does not hold up under scrutiny, especially in view of the widespread scarcity of cash.[60] Credit was the machinery of trade and the basis of capital. A glance at inventories listing debts, the mortgage deeds entered in deed books, and the mortgages held by the government loan office indicates widespread use of credit by Germans. In 1774, from a sample of 509 mortgages, half of whom were farmers, 116 had German names, 249 English names, and 101 Scotch-Irish names.[61] Bookkeeping was used as a major device to facilitate commerce.

Ownership and tenancy patterns do not show sharp differences among groups. From the tax lists it appears that tenancy was less common among English and Welsh than among Germans and Scotch-Irish (Table 5), presumably a reflection of the earlier arrival of more of the English and Welsh than of the Scotch-Irish and Germans.

55. Henry Melchior Muhlenberg, *The Journals of Henry Melchoir Muhlenberg*, tr. and ed. Theodore G. Tappert and John W. Doberstein, 3 vols. (Philadelphia, 1942-1958), vol. 3, p. 613. See also among others regarding corn, William Moraley: *The Unfortunate: or, The Voyage and Adventures of William Moraley, in the County of Northumberland, Gent . . . Containing Whatever is Curious and Remarkable in the Provinces of Pennsylvania and New Jersey . . .* (New Castle, England, 1743), p. 9.
56. Vaughan, "Journal," p. 61.
57. Rush, "Journal," p. 456. See also Strickland, *Observations,* p. 47.
58. From the wills assessed for Table 4, the average allotment of beef was 50 pounds and of pork 100 pounds.
59. Rush, "An Account," p. 64.

60. In 1684 Pastorius hoped for economic development because he felt that "William Penn will coin money and agriculture will be better managed" (see footnote 34 above); see also p. 376). See also Arent Hassert, Jr., to Deputy van Ostade (see footnote 35 above); and John Frederick Koffler, "A Letter from a Tradesman in Lancaster to the Merchants of the Cities of Philadelphia, New-York and Boston, Respecting the Loan of Money to the Government, With Some Remarks upon the Consequences of the Refusal" (Philadelphia, 1760). On credit see Arthur L. Jensen, *The Maritime Commerce of Colonial Philadelphia* (Madison, Wis., 1963), chaps. 2 and 3.
61. Compiled from General Loan Office, Accounts, 1773-1800 (MSS, Division of Public Records, Harrisburg).

TABLE 5. Nonlandowners in Chester and Lancaster Counties* (*In percentages of taxable persons*)

	German	*English*	*Scotch-Irish*	*Welsh*	*Other*	*County*
Chester 1758-1759	46	24	28	20	39	27
Chester 1782	35	26	31	20	30	27
Lancaster 1758-1759	36	27	39	14	37	36
Lancaster 1782 (present-day area)	31	36	34	18	37	32
Dauphin and Lebanon, part of Lancaster, 1782 (present-day area)	32	20	23	—	26	29

* Figures include those specified as tenants, sharecroppers, and "inmates," who generally did not work any land. In calculations the unmarried freeman was usually excluded. Based on tax lists (see footnote to Table 1 above).

The degree of locational stability needs to be considered also. Changing population distributions are shown in Table 1. In both Chester and Lancaster counties between 1760 and 1782 the majority group tended to gain at the expense of some minority groups. The tendency was most marked in the decrease of the Welsh in Chester and of the English-speaking people in Lancaster, particularly on the plain.

However, for several reasons the data in Table 1 cannot be used to support the contention that Germans as a national group were less mobile than others. First, the population densities in the two counties remained at about the same level between 1760 and 1790.[62] Also, the Quakers of Chester County, like the Mennonites of Lancaster, showed a strong degree of stability.[63] Moreover, instances of extreme German mobility can be cited. Henry Melchior Muhlenberg complained that only half of his congregation of 1742 in upper Philadelphia County (later Montgomery) were still there in 1747.[64] On Richard Penn's "Manor of Andolhea" in the German Tulpehocken settlement in the Lebanon Valley, only three of sixteen persons who had originally settled in 1723 had lands warranted and surveyed in 1741.[65] In Brecknock, a very poor German township in Lancaster County, less than 60 percent of the taxables of 1771 remained in 1782.[66] These figures would seem to indicate that some Germans were highly mobile. Geographical mobility was a consequence of the desire for social and economic improvements; Germans had to deal with the problem of economical-sized farms as much as others.

In habits and customs, then, Germans

62. Present-day Lancaster County's density was 24 persons per square mile in 1759 and 37 in 1790; Dauphin, separated from Lancaster in 1785, had a density of 22 in 1790. Present-day Chester's density was 23 in 1759 and 37 in 1790; Delaware, separated from Chester in 1789, had a density of 51 in 1790. Data from tax lists (see footnote to Table 1 above); "Heads of Families at the First Census" (see footnote 8 above); and "Areas of the United States: 1940" (Sixteenth Census of the United States: 1940 [Washington, 1942]), pp. 14, 234-35, 237.

63. This is based on the observation that few meetinghouses were established by Quakers and Mennonites between 1740 and 1780 beyond the limits of areas already settled by them. No decrease in the numbers of these peoples could be detected. Other groups were more expansive geographically. See footnote 8 above.

64. "Reports of the United German Evangelical Lutheran Congregations in North America, Especially in Pennsylvania," (tr. Jonathan Oswald, 2 vols. (Philadelphia, 1881), vol. 2, p. 52.

65. George Wheeler, "Richard Penn's Manor of Andolhea," *Pennsylvania Mag. of History and Biography* 58 (1934):193-212.

66. Tax lists in the *Pennsylvania Archives,* ser. 3, vol. 17, 1897.

do not seem to have been endowed with any more virtue than others. . . .

Success In Agricultural Activities

Because of a paucity of data covering the productivity of farms, the best information is the economic worth of individuals as indicated in inventories and amount of taxes paid. From Table 6 it appears that differences were insignificant, though a number of large inventories in the "Other and uncertain" category perhaps distort the picture. In average values of inventories English Chester and German Lancaster advanced at about the same rate between 1713 and 1790.

Corroboration can be found in tax lists. In 1758-1759 the average tax paid in Chester was 16*s*. 7*d*., as compared with 14*s*. 11*d*. in Lancaster; in 1782 the average tax was £7 18*s*. and £8 4*s*. respectively.[67] Figures for other counties show that some strongly German counties were similar to strongly non-German ones—Berks and Cumberland for example. Moreover, among the most affluent persons, only the Welsh seem to have been excessively out of line with population distributions (Table 7). Detailed calculations for all income levels in a number of townships with mixed populations in both Chester and Lancaster also support the view that economic status did not vary greatly among national groups. Likewise, distributions of national groups did not correlate with affluence (Figs. 5 and 7). Wealthy and poor townships were identified with each of the national groups.[68]

TABLE 6. Consolidated Statement of Values from a Sample of Inventories, 1713-1790*

	Inventories	*Average Value (£)*
German names	160	254
English names	130	281
Scotch-Irish names	83	254
Welsh names	23	261
Other and uncertain	51	325

* Data from Register of Wills offices, West Chester and Lancaster. Standard deviations were German 484, English 592, Scotch-Irish 661, Welsh 306, "Other and uncertain" 929. An analysis of variance disclosed that at the 5 percent significance level differences among German, English, and Scotch-Irish samples were not statistically significant.

The major distinction among religious groups should be noted: among the sixty wealthy Germans in Table 7 nearly 60 percent were Mennonites, yet Mennonites constituted only one-quarter of Lancaster's population. In Chester, Quakers headed list after list. Much of the explanation for the differential regional patterns of economic status (Fig. 7) lies in the presence of these two groups in the affluent areas. It is in part to them that credit for the productivity of Pennsylvania belongs, although some members of other groups became affluent. . . .

Persistent Stereotypes and Concepts

Reasonable doubt has been cast on the widespread belief that Germans were better farmers than others in eighteenth-century Pennsylvania. An obvious question that now arises is why the view was held in early Pennsylvania and why it has

67. From tax lists. See also provincial assessments for counties in James T. Mitchell and Henry Flanders, eds., *Statutes at Large of Pennsylvania,* 15 vols. (Harrisburg, 1896-1909), vol. 4, p. 231, and vol. 5, pp. 465-67.

68. Tax lists are the source of data. Although according to Figure 7 affluence is more highly concentrated on the Lancaster Plain than anywhere else in Chester County, a Kolmogorov-Smirnov test showed that the economic status of the populations of the two counties was homogeneous. See Sidney Siegel, *Nonparametric Statistics* (New York, 1956), pp. 127-36.

TABLE 7. Proportions of Persons Paying Taxes of £40 or More in Lancaster County, 1782*

	Number	*% of Group*	*% of Population*
German-speaking	60	67	67
English	6	7	10
Scotch-Irish	11	12	13
Welsh	6	7	1
Other and uncertain	7	8	9

* Data from tax lists, *Pennsylvania Archives,* ser. 3, vol. 17, 1897. Forge owners, who were heavily assessed, and unmarried freemen were excluded from the calculations.

persisted to the present time. Fundamentally, one can speculate that many persons in the modern period of Western history have tended to differentiate national cultural traits rather sharply. The power of national states in Europe and the identification of citizens with them seem to bear witness to this view of culture. Stereotyped images of, for example, Irishmen and Frenchmen are widespread. More specifically, early Pennsylvanians inherited, I believe, a set of attitudes from England by which they judged other people. This contention is supported by the general comments found in the literature. Rarely are there references to "English" Pennsylvanians or "English" farming practices in America. Writers certainly spoke of Germans, Scots, and Irish, but English Quaker farmers and other English settlers were, and still are, largely unnoticed by scholars and others. It seems reasonable to assume that historically we have tended to look through "English" eyes at our society and to distinguish minority groups of Germans, Scotch-Irish, and others in America more sharply than the "English." Given a set of stereotypes held by Englishmen about the German peasant and the Celtic peoples,[69] it is not surprising that these attitudes have been continued on this side of the Atlantic.

Perpetuation of these beliefs has depended on reasons that need to be considered briefly. Writers have generalized about a whole area from images derived from particular regions and have adopted ideas from other persons. Political circumstances have encouraged praise or denigration of what have been thought to be distinct national groups. Philosophical trends have also coincided with stereotypes of national groups and have reinforced ideas about them. First, there is the transference of impressions from one area to the whole. For example, late-eighteenth-century writers regarded the well-traveled Lancaster Plain, an area inhabited by German-speaking Mennonites, as the most productive agricultural region in the state. Identification of all Germans with them, as is done today with the Amish, was easy, given a stereotyped belief in German agricultural superiority.[70] Eighteenth-century writers were also prone to copy from others, frequently without credit. . . .

In the late nineteenth century ethnic societies began to foster myths about their ancestors. Although the Scotch-Irish could not praise their forefathers' skill in farming, they could point to their courage and Calvinism. Of course, in excess this has resulted in attitudes of "racial" superiority. In the 1930s the Pennsylvania Dutch were identified with the wider German culture.[71]

69. See Samuel Johnson's definition of oats: "A grain which in England is generally given to horses, but in Scotland supports the people," from his "Dictionary," quoted in John Barlett, *Familiar Quotations,* 13th ed. (Boston, 1955), p. 337.

70. See, for example, Thomas Cooper, *Some Information Respecting America,* 2nd ed. (London, 1795), pp. 95 and 137; Schoepf, *Travels,* vol. 1, p. 103, and vol. 2, p. 20.

71. The Scotch-Irish Congress initiated publications in 1889, and the Pennsylvania-German Society was begun in 1891. See Emil Meynen, "Das

Ethnic superiority seems less of a live issue today. Yet the concept of "national character" is still widely used. Margaret Mead and Geoffrey Gorer, for example, have been strong proponents of the concept in general.[72] Such an idea may be useful; in Pennsylvania certain architectural styles and food preparations had a traditional regional foundation in Europe, at least for a time. However, the concept has little validity for the comprehending of problems related to agriculture, or even to basic consumption habits. It seems more sensible to approach Pennsylvanians of the eighteenth century as Americans with a Western European background in which major differences in behavior and attitudes were the result of religious beliefs, social status, and economic circumstances, rather than attributable to a vague, elusive, and unchanging phenomenon called "national character." I agree with the writer in the *Pennsylvania Herald* of York in 1792, who, while referring specifically to the election of the sheriff of York County, perhaps had Rush in mind:[73]

> [I] offer some observations on a dangerous prejudice, which has been actually fomented by a few designing men—I mean the distinction of *Dutch* and *Irish*—a distinction calculated to convulse our County—to raise and perpetuate national reflections, and to separate in interests and sentiments the nearest neighbors.
>
> What is it to me, when I am about to vote, whether the great grandmother of the candidate came from Germany or from Ireland—from the banks of the Rhine, or the Lake of Calarney—whether he and his ancestors have dined oftenest on cabbage or potatoes? . . . I don't think one of those vegetables more calculated to make an honest man or a rogue than the other. All national prejudices are the growth of a contracted mind or a silly head—it raises a distinction which destroys all enquiry into the merit of a candidate.

---

pennsylvaniendeutsche Bauernland, *Deutsches Archiv für Landes- und Volksforchung*" 3 (1939):253-92, as an example of German interest in the Pennsylvania Dutch.

72. See Bernard C. Hennessy," Psycho-cultural Studies of National Character: Relevances for International Relations," *Background: Journ. Internatl. Studies Assn.* 6 (1962):27-49. See also "The Little Community" and "Peasant Society and Culture" by Robert Redfield (Chicago, 1956); in "Peasant Society" (pp. 63-66) Redfield discusses the rural values of French-Canadians, Bulgarians, English, and Irish often attributed to the Germans. Cf. Frederick B. Tolles, *Quakers and the Atlantic Culture* (New York, 1960), p. 128; Tolles uses Redfield's ideas to support German agricultural superiority in Pennsylvania.

73. October 3, 1792, quoted in part in Shoemaker, "Penn. Barn," pp. 8-9. The results given in the paper on October 17 were Lenhart 2399, McClellan 2345.

The Shenandoah Valley Frontier / *Robert D. Mitchell*

. . . This paper employs a developmental approach to early American frontier regions by examining the major elements of the earliest interior population thrusts of the eighteenth century, and their consequences. . . . The particular approach used here produced insights into frontier communities which are different from those of other geographers and historians, and some of the conclusions are thus also different.

The Shenandoah Valley

The Shenandoah Valley was chosen as a case study for three reasons. Forming the northern part of the Valley of Virginia, the Virginia component of the Great Valley of the Appalachians, the Shenandoah Valley provided a vital link in the major route complex for interior population migration prior to 1800. This complex originated in southwestern Pennsylvania and followed the Great Valley south and west through Maryland and Virginia into the southern backcountry (Fig. 1).

Secondly, the valley displayed considerable regional variations in its settlement and livelihood patterns, reflecting contributions from both the Middle and the Chesapeake Bay colonies. The upper (southern) half of the valley was initially more of a "frontier" area than the lower half in the sense that it was more remote, physically and socially, from eastern Virginia and southeastern Pennsylvania. . . . Despite the fact that most early valley settlers were German, English, or Scotch-Irish migrants who came from or through Pennsylvania, the patterns developed within the valley were not merely an extension of those characteristic of Pennsylvania. Land acquisitions by eastern Virginians of English origins played a very significant role in the development of the lower valley.

Thirdly, the three-quarters of a century of settlement from the pioneer years of the late 1720s until 1800 provide a substantial period, and sufficient primary source materials exist for most of this period to make a thorough study feasible. . . .

Environmental Issues

Although Europeans had made efforts to settle the Shenandoah Valley as early as 1704 or 1705, the first permanent settlements were not recorded until the late 1720s.[1] Frederick Jackson Turner, in at-

1. For the abortive attempts to establish Swiss and German colonies in the Valley of Virginia, see C. E. Kemper, "Documents Relating to Early Projected Swiss Colonies in the Valley of Virginia, 1706-1709," *Virginia Magazine of History and Biography* 29 (1921):1-17 and 180-82; idem, "Documents Relating to a Proposed Swiss and German Colony in the Western Part of Virginia," ibid., 29 (1921):183-90 and 287-91; and Great Britain, Board of Trade, *Journal of the Commissioners for Trade and Plantations* (London: H. M. Stationery Office,

Reproduced (with omissions) by permission from the *Annals, Association of American Geographers* 62 (1972):461-86. For elaboration see also the author's *Commercialism and Frontier: Perspectives on the Early Shenandoah Valley* (Charlottesville: University Press of Virginia, 1977).

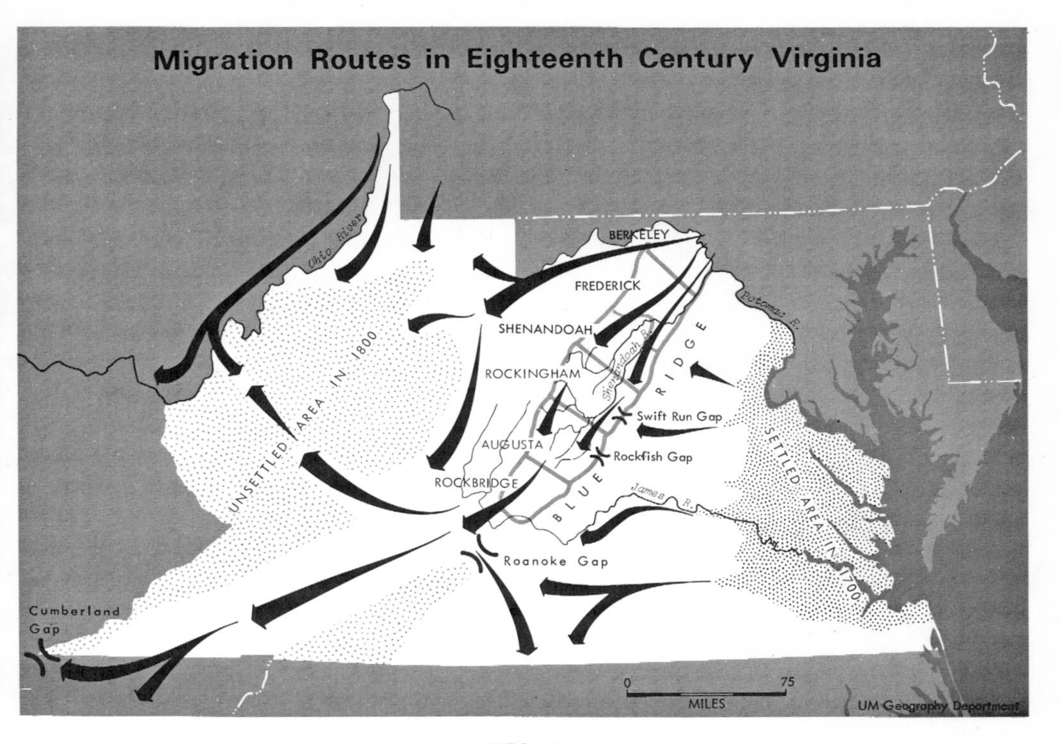

FIG. 1

tempting to explain the importance of the Great Valley for early westward expansion, emphasized accessibility from the north, cheap lands, and fertile limestone soils.[2] Other historians have mentioned the uncertain Indian situation in western Pennsylvania, which was so well exploited by the French, and the consequent desire by the governments of Pennsylvania, Maryland, and Virginia to establish settlements in the Great Valley as buffers against the French and their Indian allies; the confusion over the precise location of the Pennsylvania-Maryland boundary, which led settlers to move farther to the south; and, above all, the cheapness of land in the Great Valley of Maryland and Virginia relative to prices in southeastern Pennsylvania and adjacent areas after the mid-1720s[3] (Fig. 2).

1920-1938), vol. 6, pp. 188-89 and 232. Adam Müller (Miller) is generally regarded as the "first" settler in the Shenandoah Valley, about 1726, on the basis of his naturalization paper, reproduced in "First Settler in the Valley," *William and Mary College Quarterly Historical Magazine,* 1st ser., vol. 9 (1900-1901), pp. 132-33. See also H. M. Strickler, *Massanutten, Settled by the Pennsylvania Pilgrim, 1726: The First White Settlement in the Shenandoah Valley* (Strasburg, Va.: Shenandoah Publishing House, 1924).

2. F. J. Turner, *The Frontier in American History* (New York: Henry Holt, 1920), pp. 100-01.

3. R. A. Billington, *Westward Expansion: A History of the American Frontier* (New York: Macmillan, 3rd edition, 1967), pp. 90-92 and chap. 6; O. T. Barck and H. T. Lefler, *Colonial America* (New York: Macmillan, 2nd edition, 1968), pp. 268-72; and C. Bridenbaugh, *Myths and Realities: Societies of the Colonial South* (Baton Rouge: Louisiana State University Press, 1952), pp. 120-30.

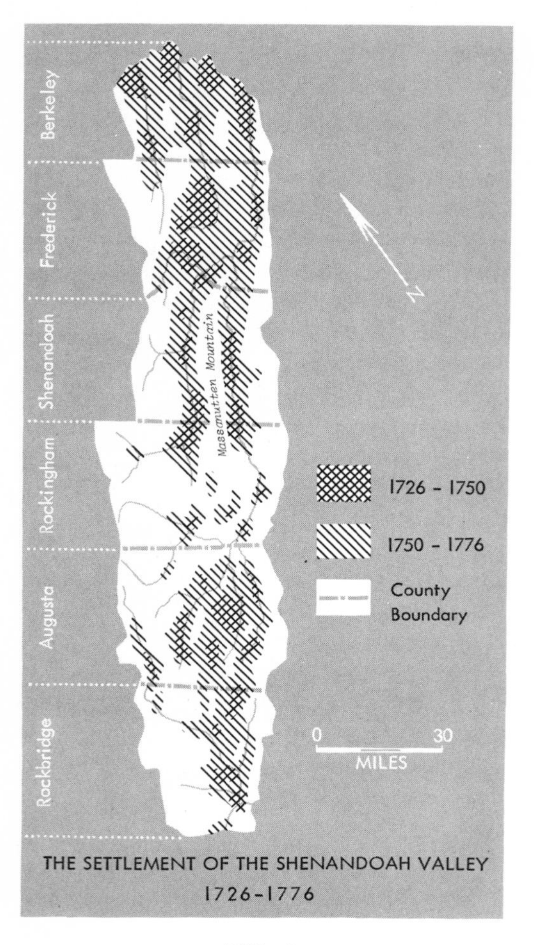

FIG. 2

. . . Two other factors of major significance were the nature of Indian settlement in the Appalachians and the availability of land for European settlement.

Unlike western Pennsylvania, which was occupied intermittently during the early eighteenth century by several Indian groups, the Valley of Virginia lacked permanent Indian settlements and, indeed, had not been effectively occupied for at least 100 years. The absence of Indian residents allowed for a more peaceful settlement of the area than on many other interior frontiers. On the other hand, prior Indian activity in the form of regular, systematic use of fire to drive and trap game had resulted in widespread vegetation change by favoring the selective growth of grasses and fire-resistant tree species. . . .

Political and Economic Factors

The prevalent notion that frontier areas evolved in a manner largely independent of existing governmental policies could not be farther from the truth in colonial Virginia. Frontier areas were of strategic importance in the struggles against the French and the Indian, and Virginia governments attempted to protect settled areas east of the Blue Ridge by developing buffer settlements to the west. Land grants were the principal devices used to encourage such settlements.

Land-grant policies. Beginning in 1710 with the administration of Governor Spotswood, Virginia began actively to encourage frontier expansion. Spotswood's cancellation of the traditional 1,000-acre limit per grantee for new land grants opened the way for a more generous land policy which was to provide land on a large scale for favored members of the moneyed class. This policy encouraged widespread land speculation, which was virtually unavoidable even if official policies had encouraged it. The Shenandoah Valley was first settled during the administration of Governor Gooch (1727-1749). As part of the Virginia Council's policy, all landowners who received large grants had to settle one family on their lands for every one thousand acres granted within two years of the date of the grant.[4] Although such rules were seldom applied stringently,

4. *Executive Journals of the Council of Colonial Virginia, 1680-1739,* ed H. R. McIlwaine (Richmond: 1925-1930), vol. 4, p. 223.

the desire of grantees to sell the bulk of their lands and be relieved of the quit rents (land taxes paid by owners in lieu of feudal obligations) helped to produce a rapid settlement of the Shenandoah Valley. As a further result of this policy, the Virginia government virtually "planned" the westward expansion of land ownership by tidewater gentry into areas which were often to be settled by migrants from the Middle colonies. A similar land policy was carried out by Lord Fairfax, whose ownership of the lower Shenandoah Valley was long disputed by the Virginia government. . . .

Land prices. The initial prices of potential farmland were low in Virginia frontier areas. During the 1740s William Beverley boasted that he could sell his Shenandoah Valley lands at a third of the price currently charged in southeastern Pennsylvania. Initial prices for land charged by the Virginia government, Fairfax, and such large grantors as Beverley were relatively similar: about £3 to £3 10s. 0d. (£2 2s. 0d. to £2 8s. 0d. sterling) per hundred acres, or 7½ to 8½ pence per acre. Payment could be deferred at the grantor's discretion if the incoming family did not have enough money to buy a hundred acres immediately. One good deer-hunting season might bring in the needed cash; six or seven elk hides or thirty deerskins could pay for a hundred acres.[5]

Prices for unpatented lands increased gradually after the mid-1740s and distinct variations emerged in the prices charged by the major grantors. By 1775, average prices for unimproved land were 2½ to 3 shillings per acre, about a fourfold increase, but generally commodity prices had increased tenfold over the same thirty-year period. . . .

There were few indications that the large grantors altered their prices significantly with variations in the location and estimated quality of their land, although lands set aside for future town sites were invariably poor quality farm land.[6] The greatest variations in land prices occurred in the resale of unimproved or partially improved land by the settlers themselves. . . .

. . . Many first-generation frontier settlers were risk takers, and moved on when they perceived that the degree of risk or opportunity had diminished. In the Shenandoah Valley they were able to do so as a result of the availability of land farther south or west, and the high level of population movement through the valley, which provided a regular supply of potential buyers.

The First Generation

The first generation of settlers consisted of two major groups. The majority migrated southward from southeastern Pennsylvania and adjacent areas of Maryland, Delaware, and New Jersey. Most of these settlers before 1760 came from Lancaster, Chester, Bucks, and Philadelphia Counties. They were primarily of German or Scotch-Irish origin, with smaller numbers of English and Welsh.[7]

5. R. E. and B. K. Brown, *Virginia 1705-1786: Democracy or Aristocracy?* (East Lansing: Michigan State University Press, 1964), p. 21.

6. See, for example, the reports on the site of Staunton in Augusta County Order Book 1, pp. 102-03, and Lexington in Rockbridge County Order Book, 1778-1783, p. 7.

7. This conclusion was reached after a detailed comparison of family names in W. H. Egle, ed., *Pennsylvania Archives,* 3rd ser., vol. 24 (Harrisburg, Pa.: 1897-1901), which contains abstracts of land warrantees in fifteen Pennsylvania counties for the period after 1733, with early deed books for Orange, Frederick, and Augusta Counties. See also the articles by C. E. Kemper, "Early Westward Movement of Virginia," *Virginia Magazine of History and Biography* 13 (1905):1-16 and 113-18; "Settlement of the

Migration was conducted on a family basis and, according to available records, the average stay in Pennsylvania before moving to Virginia was between seven and ten years. A few early German settlers seem to have migrated from the Germanna settlement founded on the Virginia piedmont in 1714.[8] All of these settlers had been farming in the American colonies prior to moving to the Shenandoah Valley, which might suggest that they were better prepared psychologically and economically than settlers who migrated directly from western Europe.

Were direct immigrants from Europe much less prepared economically than their more experienced neighbors? The historical literature suggests that most Scotch-Irish immigrants arrived in the colonies as indentured servants, but Shenandoah Valley county records indicate that the majority had financed their own passage across the Atlantic. . . .

Although settlers had occupied lands from the Potomac to the James River by 1750, there was no continuous line of settlements in the Shenandoah Valley. Areas of settlement were distributed discontinuously along the main stream courses (Fig. 2).[9] The most densely settled area in the lower valley was in the vicinity of Winchester, and a similar concentration was focused on the future site of Staunton in the upper valley.

Emigration and Through-Migration

Despite the spotty nature of the earliest county records, settlers were evidently moving out of the Shenandoah Valley on a second phase of their migration by the early 1740s. Emigration from the valley took on significant proportions after the mid-1750s. . . .

Through-migration is the most difficult to document of all phases of colonial migration. . . . Despite the unprotected frontiers south of Rockbridge County, white travelers moved southward through the upper Shenandoah Valley as early as the mid-1740s.[10] Moravian missionaries and peddlers from Pennsylvania were active throughout the valley after 1750, and cattle drives originating as far south as North Carolina passed northward to markets in Pennsylvania from the mid-1750s onward. Perhaps the most important indicator of all was the increasing number of ordinaries (private residences licensed as taverns) that were established, particularly after 1765.[11]

Change, 1760-1776

In 1745 the Shenandoah Valley had approximately 10,000 inhabitants, or about 8 percent of Virginia's total population. Slightly more than half resided in the lower valley.[12] Population grew steadily

Valley," ibid., 30 (1922):169-82; and "Early Settlers in the Valley of Virginia," *William and Mary College Quarterly,* 2nd ser., vol. 5 (1925), pp. 259-65.

8. H. R. McIlwaine, ed., *Executive Journals of the Council of Colonial Virginia,* vol. 4, p. 250; and W. J. Hinke, "The 1714 Colony of Germanna, Virginia," *Virginia Magazine of History and Biography* 40 (1932):317-27, and 41 (1933):41-49.

9. This map has been compiled from information on land acquisitions in the court order books and deed books for Orange County (1734/35-1745), Frederick County (1743-1776), and Augusta County (1745-1776), and from the Land Office Abstracts for colonial Virginia in the Virginia State Library, Richmond.

10. W. J. Hinke and C. E. Kemper, "Moravian Diaries of Travels Through Virginia," *Virginia Magazine of History and Biography* 11 (1903-1904):113-31, 225-42, and 370-93, and 12 (1904-1905):134-53 and 271-84.

11. Licenses for at least 220 separate ordinaries were granted by Frederick and Augusta county courts between 1746 and 1776. Almost 65 percent of these licenses were granted after 1765. Substantial numbers of ordinaries were in the vicinities of Winchester and Staunton and along the Great Wagon Road.

12. Frederick County Order Book 2, p. 45, and Orange County Order Book 4, p. 449. Compare

during the colonial period, but the upper valley clearly lagged behind the lower valley. The total population rose from 18,000 in 1760 to 35,000 by 1775, of whom almost two-thirds (about 23,000) were in the lower valley. The most rapid population growth occurred during the last quarter of the century, and by 1790 the lower valley had 50,000 settlers, two-thirds of the Shenandoah Valley's total population.[13]

Although more than half of the region's eighteenth-century population was added after the colonial period, the best agricultural land was patented and settled before 1776. The period from 1750 to 1776 was one of major settlement expansion and infilling, yet even by 1776 no continuous band of settlement extended the length of the valley. . . .

It is difficult to assess the impact of land costs on rates of settling before 1776. Incoming settlers rarely had a perspective from which to judge the best land in the valley. The differential rates of population growth after 1750 indicate that most new immigrants from the north settled the first areas where farms or unpatented lands were available, that is, Berkeley and Frederick counties, which also attracted planters from eastern Virginia after 1760.[14] . . .

Several other factors were as important as land prices in determining a settler's choice of site: soil fertility, water supply, vegetation cover, neighboring settlers, and road access to service centers. . . . Both geographers and historians have injected cultural factors into location preferences without thorough study of original land records.[15] A map of national-cultural groups in the valley in 1775 was compiled (Fig. 3).[16] The agriculturally useful soils of the region are predominantly of limestone or limestone-shale derivation.[17] Scotch-Irish settlers

---

E. B. Greene and V. D. Harrington, *American Population before the Federal Census of 1790* (New York: Columbia University Press, 1932), p. 140.

13. For the tithables for 1775, see especially Frederick County Order Book 16, p. 401, and Augusta County Order Book 16, pp. 29 and 440. For 1790, see U.S. Bureau of the Census, *Heads of Families at the First Census of the United States Taken in the Year 1790: Virginia* (Washington, D.C.: Government Printing Office, 1908), p. 9.

14. W. F. Bliss, "The Rise of Tenancy in Virginia," *Virginia Magazine of History and Biography* 58 (1950):427-41, and "The Tuckahoe in New Virginia," ibid., 59 (1951):387-96. Partly because of boundary changes during the second half of the eighteenth century, and partly because of incomplete tithable records, comparable growth figures are not available for the entire valley until 1790.

The 1790 census showed:

County	Whites	Blacks	Totals
Berkeley	16,781	2,932	19,713
Frederick	15,431	4,250	19,681
Shenandoah	9,998	512	10,510
Rockingham	6,677	772	7,449
Augusta	9,318	1,567	10,886
Rockbridge	5,846	682	6,528

15. Turner tried to show that pioneer farmers followed the fertile limestone soils all the way through the Appalachian back country, Turner, *Frontier*. Other historians and geographers have associated German settlements with low-lying, fertile, limestone soils, *Westward Expansion,* p. 92; Bridenbaugh, *Myths,* p. 133; R. H. Shryock, "British versus German Traditions in Colonial Agriculture," *Mississippi Valley Historical Review* 26 (1939):47; and E. E. Evans, "Culture and Land Use in the Old West of North America," *Heidelberger Studien zur Kulturgeographie,* Heft 15 (1966), p. 79.

16. This map was compiled from county court order books, deed books, and will books for the period 1775 to 1782. Extensive use was also made of the 1782 tax returns for both land and personal property. Earlier attempts at this kind of national-culture reconstruction are in M. S. Malone, "The Distribution of Population on the Virginia Frontier in 1775," unpublished doctoral dissertation, Princeton University, 1935, pp. 55, 64, 87, 92, 115, and 123; and in Freeman H. Hart, *The Valley of Virginia in the American Revolution, 1763-1789* (Chapel Hill: University of North Carolina Press, 1942), p. 6.

17. Commonwealth of Virginia, *Geologic Map of Virginia* (Charlottesville: Division of Mineral Resources, 1963); R. C. Jurney, *Soil Survey of Rockbridge County, Virginia* (Washing-

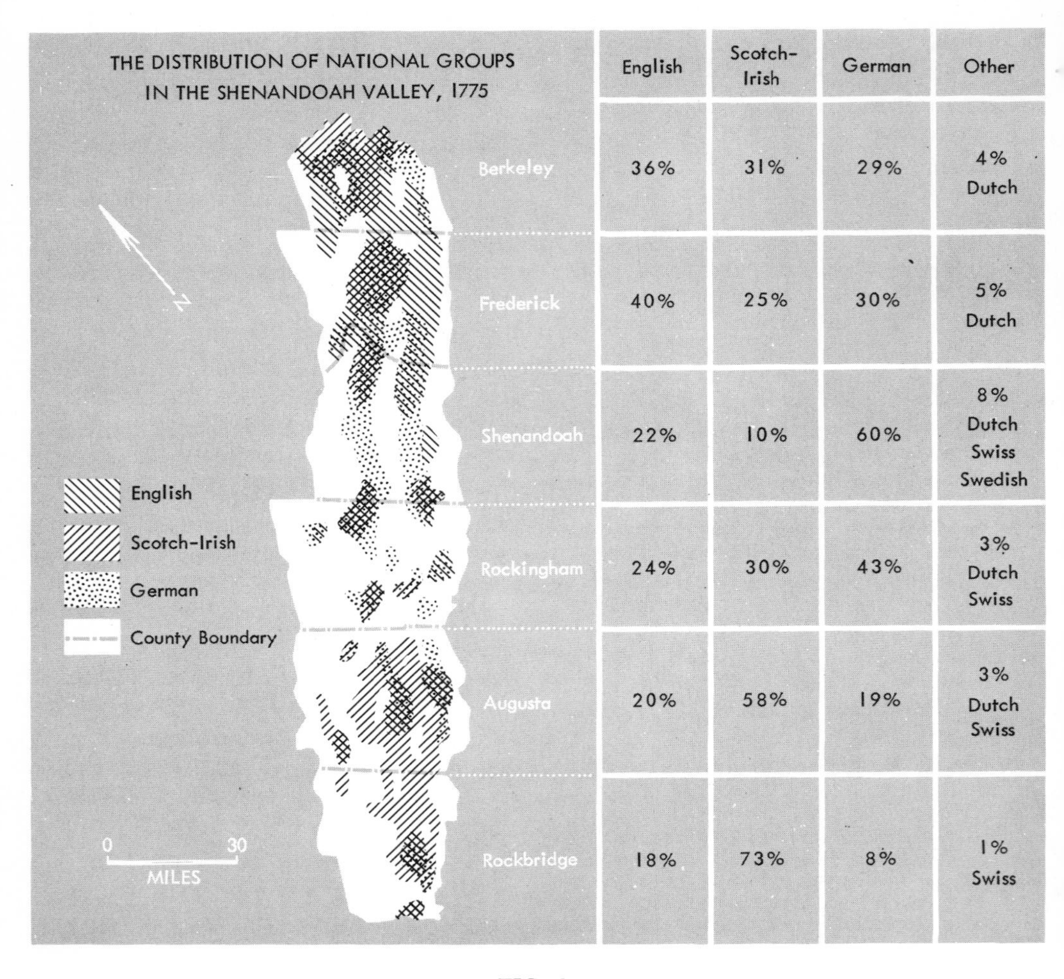

	English	Scotch-Irish	German	Other
Berkeley	36%	31%	29%	4% Dutch
Frederick	40%	25%	30%	5% Dutch
Shenandoah	22%	10%	60%	8% Dutch Swiss Swedish
Rockingham	24%	30%	43%	3% Dutch Swiss
Augusta	20%	58%	19%	3% Dutch Swiss
Rockbridge	18%	73%	8%	1% Swiss

FIG. 3

were prominent on the limestone-derived soils of Augusta and Rockbridge counties, but such soils were occupied mainly by German and English settlers in Berkeley, Shenandoah, and Rockingham counties. There is no evidence that early German settlers monopolized the "best" limestone soils, or that Scotch-Irish settlers consciously chose marginal, hillier areas more "suitable" for pasture.[18] . . . A traditional contention of Virginia historians is that the entire valley could be regionalized on a cultural basis.[19] English

ton, D.C.: U.S. Dept. of Agriculture, Series 1931, No. 4, 1934); and idem, *Soil Survey of Augusta County, Virginia* (Washington, D.C.: U.S. Dept. of Agriculture, Series 1932, No. 13, 1937).

18. J. T. Lemon came to a similar conclusion in *The Best Poor Man's Country: A Geographical Study of Early Southeastern Pennsylvania* (Baltimore: Johns Hopkins University Press, 1972).

19. Kemper (1922), pp. 181-82; W. Couper, *History of the Shenandoah Valley* (New York: Lewis Historical Publishing Co., 1952), vol. 1, p. 171; and J. W. Wayland, *Twenty-Five Chap-*

settlers were proportionately most numerous in Berkeley and Frederick counties, Germans in Shenandoah and Rockingham counties, and Scotch-Irish in Augusta and Rockbridge counties, yet only in the latter two counties, where the Scotch-Irish composed almost two-thirds of the entire white population, did any national group represent a substantial majority.

The concentration of Scotch-Irish in the three upper valley counties was one of the major elements of regional differentiation in the Shenandoah Valley during the eighteenth century. . . .

Cultural Change

The religious changes which swept through the American backcountry after 1740, referred to as the Great Awakening, remind us that cultural change was one of the most dynamic aspects of eighteenth-century frontier America. . . . To what extent was the identity of discrete national-cultural groups maintained?

The evangelical movement increased the popularity of Baptist, Methodist, and more fundamentalist affiliations at the expense of Presbyterian, Lutheran, and even Mennonite faiths, particularly after 1775.[20] Changing religious adherence appears to indicate a weakening of ethnic ties during the last quarter of the century.[21] Both English and German communities contained sectarian minorities (Quakers in the former; Moravians, Mennonites, and Dunkers in the latter), and their persistence throughout the eighteenth century provides some evidence of cultural continuity. Scotch-Irish communities did not contain any distinctive sectarian groups. Their familiarity with the English language, and the relative lack of social cohesion among many of their members, together with the elitist training and the paucity of Presbyterian ministers, may explain their relatively quick adoption of English social traits and their enthusiastic response to the evangelical movement.

Social customs and language characteristics changed much less rapidly among German settlers. Throughout the valley German remained a viable community language until the 1820s, when it was replaced by English in the church, but it survived much longer in the home.[22] Language appears to have had a significant impact on the occupations of Germans, most of whom were farmers and artisans. They were unfamiliar with English traditions of local government, and few played prominent roles in political, civic, or merchant affairs until after the Revolution.[23] Participation in these concerns was

---

ters on the Shenandoah Valley (Strasburg, Va.: Shenandoah Publishing House Inc., 1957), pp. 81-82.

20. Records, Smith Creek Baptist Church (Shenandoah County); Linville Creek Baptist Church (Rockingham County); Brock's Gap Baptist Church (Rockingham County), 1756-1844, No. 19984 (typewritten), Virginia State Library, Richmond; H. A. Brunk, *History of the Mennonites in Virginia, 1727-1900* (Staunton, Va.: McClure Printing Co., 1959), pp. 40-41; and K. Wust, *The Virginia Germans* (Charlottesville: University Press of Virginia, 1969), pp. 135-43.

21. Intermarriage could further break down cultural distinctions, but much more research is needed on this topic; see H. Moller, "Sex Composition and Correlated Culture Patterns of Colonial America," *William and Mary Quarterly,* 3rd ser., vol. 3 (1945), pp. 113-53.

22. Wust, *Virginia Germans;* E. L. Smith, et al., *The Pennsylvania Germans of the Shenandoah Valley,* vol. 26 (Allentown, Penn.: The Pennsylvania German Folklore Society, 1962), pp. 58-59; and J. Stewart and E. L. Smith, "The Survival of German Dialects and Customs in the Shenandoah Valley," *Society for the History of the Germans in Maryland,* Report 31 (1963), pp. 66-70.

23. With the exception of Shenandoah County, Germans do not appear as members of county legislatures until the 1780s. As late as 1792 Germans in Augusta County petitioned successfully to have the Virginia legislature print the

more typical of second-generation Germans.

By Virginia standards the Negro population of the Shenandoah Valley was never large. The relatively small percentage of Negro slaves west of the Blue Ridge was one of the most significant differences between eastern and western Virginia. Throughout the century, slavery was always more prominent in the lower valley. In 1755 the upper valley had fewer than 100 Negroes, compared with seven times that number in the lower valley. By 1790 the total slave population of the upper valley was estimated at 3,021 in contrast with 7,594 in the lower valley.[24] . . .

The eastern Virginia precedent lent respectability to slaveowning for a substantial minority of valley households, and evidence from the valley seems to support the view that Germans strongly opposed slavery.[25] In 1790 the most heavily German county, Shenandoah, had the lowest proportion of slaveowning households (ten percent as against thirty-eight percent in Frederick). All Germans did not oppose slavery, and perhaps the strongest opposition came from sectarian groups, as it did among English Quakers. Moreover, part of the explanation is economic. German farmers produced virtually no commercial tobacco and hemp, the two most labor-demanding crops cultivated in the region after 1760. This fact is probably as important as social aversion in explaining why so few German families owned slaves.[26]

Landholding

Eighty percent of all land patents during the colonial period were for 400 acres or less. On Crown lands settlers could buy individual treasury rights from county surveyors for up to 400 acres. The large grantors who received their lands from the Crown were not bound by this stipulation, and individual grants on their lands tended to be somewhat larger. In addition, about 20 percent of all settlers on Crown lands acquired more than one parcel, and more families owned over 400 acres than is evident from a first examination of land records. By the mid-1760s the great majority of settlers in the Shenandoah Valley owned between 100 and 400 acres of land (Table 1). . . .

The importance of tenancy in the valley during the eighteenth century is difficult to estimate. Prior to the early 1760s it seems to have been relatively insignificant. According to the tax records it was never of any consequence in the upper valley, although short-term leases made between neighbors were probably common. . . .

The latter part of the eighteenth cen-

laws of Virginia in German (Legislative Petitions, Augusta County, October 16, 1792, Virginia State Library, Richmond).

24. For estimates of the racial composition of Virginia's population during the 1750s on a county basis, see A list of Tithables in the Dominion of Virginia, 1755, transcripts of British Public Record Office, Colonial Office class 5, piece 1338, p. 364, in Research Department, Colonial Williamsburg; and Great Britain, Board of Trade, Report on His Majesty's (George II) Colonies and Plantations in America, Whitehall, May 11, 1756, in Loudoun Papers, Henry E. Huntington Library and Art Gallery, San Marino, California. The totals for 1790 are derived from the first U.S. census, footnote 13, p. 9. Maps showing the changing distribution of Negroes in Virginia between 1750 and 1790 are in R. D. Mitchell, "The Upper Shenandoah Valley of Virginia during the Eighteenth Century," unpublished doctoral dissertation, University of Wisconsin, 1969, pp. 226-28.

25. Shryock, "British vs. German," pp. 39-54, and J. W. Wayland, *The German Element of the Shenandoah Valley* (Charlottesville: privately printed, 1907), pp. 179-81. However, Germans were very prominent in the use of indentured servants.

26. It does not explain why so few Germans produced tobacco and hemp.

TABLE 1. Landholding in the Shenandoah Valley, 1762-64

	Number of Landholders		*Percentage of Landholders*		*Percentage of Acreage*	
Acres	*Frederick County*	*Augusta County*	*Frederick County*	*Augusta County*	*Frederick County*	*Augusta County*
over 1,000	70	40	7.5	3.3	22.5	23.5
901-1,000	15	13	1.6	1.0	3.2	2.7
801-900	23	13	2.5	1.0	4.6	2.5
701-800	28	23	3.0	1.9	5.0	3.7
601-700	44	34	4.7	2.9	6.9	5.0
501-600	61	65	6.4	5.5	9.8	7.8
401-500	183	96	20.0	8.1	19.0	9.6
301-400	155	250	16.5	21.0	12.6	19.2
201-300	208	288	22.2	24.3	12.0	15.7
101-200	120	288	12.8	24.3	4.1	9.4
1-100	31	78	3.3	6.6	0.5	1.0

Sources: Frederick County Rentals (1764), Fairfax Papers VII, Huntington Library, San Marino, Calif., and Augusta County Rent Rolls (1760-62), Preston Papers, Virginia Historical Society, Richmond.

tury witnessed four major trends in valley landholdings. Inequalities of size were reduced in the upper valley, and the average size decreased. In the lower valley landownership became increasingly concentrated because of the large acreages owned by absentee planters from eastern Virginia; in 1783 only seventeen owners held more than 2,500 acres in the valley, and twelve (almost all eastern Virginians) had their lands in Berkeley and Frederick counties.[27] Substantial tenancy began to emerge in the lower valley; by 1792 the former Fairfax manor lands alone had more than 200 tenants. The proportion of landless settlers increased; although difficult to estimate from tax records, they seem to account for 45 to 50 percent of all households in the upper valley and 60 to 65 percent of all households in the lower valley by 1800. . . .

The Pioneer Economy

In areas of eighteenth-century frontier settlement highly commercial economies were rarely if ever attained immediately. The limited market capacities of eastern seaboard centers, the lack of capital for investment, and the unsophisticated means of transportation and redistribution precluded large-scale export of primary products (Fig. 4). . . . The seeds of commercialization were present from the beginnings of permanent settlement, because the great majority of settlers were eager for any profit-making possibilities. Migration to and through frontier areas, together with the need for materials which were not always available locally, encouraged early trading activities.

Subsistence and Surplus

The basic patterns of pioneer economies seem to have varied little in the eighteenth-century interior. Agriculture was of a mixed, relatively unspecialized character utilizing crop and livestock combinations which had already proven successful along the Atlantic coast. The subsistence requirements of settlers in the Shenandoah Valley were based upon maize, wheat, and rye as the primary grains; cattle, horses, and swine as the major live-

27. 1783 Land Tax Books for Frederick County, Virginia State Library.

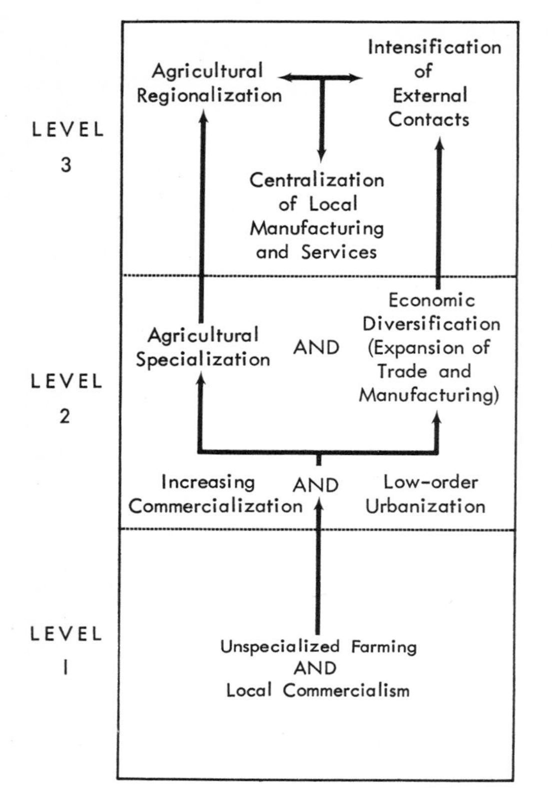

FIG. 4. Developmental change.

stock; flax as the principal fiber; and a small number of vegetables and deciduous fruits. Farms seem to have had no more than ten to twelve acres of cleared and cultivated land during the first generation of settlement. Maize has generally been regarded as the major pioneer crop, but wheat and rye seem to have been almost as widely used as maize. Crop yields were comparatively low, ten to twelve bushels per acre for wheat and rye, fifteen to seventeen for maize.[28] . . .

Before the late 1750s probably 90 percent of all farm products were used for subsistence, and the rest were sold locally to new settlers, through-migrants, or local militia.

Militia who were stationed in the region during the French and Indian War provided an important market. Their demands for flour, beef, and pork encouraged valley farmers to grow more wheat and slaughter more cattle and swine. Cattle, and to a lesser degree, horses and swine that might otherwise have been driven to Philadelphia were sold to frontier militia. By the early 1760s the average valley farmer had probably reduced the subsistence proportion of his total output to less than 75 percent, with farmers in Berkeley and Frederick counties probably achieving the highest commercial proportions.

External Contacts

There is no better evidence of the desire of frontier settlers for contact with eastern markets than in the petitions to the Virginia Assembly for roads during the first decades of permanent settlement. The backbone of the region's road network was the "Great Philadelphia Wagon Road." Prior to the mid-1740s much of this route within the valley remained nothing more than a trail along which wagon transport was extremely difficult. It was only after 1750 that a route began to be cleared between Staunton and Roanoke Gap (Figs. 1 and 5). The earliest efforts to establish external contacts actually focused on building roads from east to west rather than from north to south. . . .

Settlers depended on outside sources

28. Crop yields were estimated from information in county will books and court judgments. During the 1750s wheat was worth 2/6d. to 3 shillings per bushel in the valley, corn 1/6d. to 2 shillings, rye 1/6d. to 1/9d., and barley and oats 1 shilling to 1/3d. Thus a farmer's will inventory which included one acre of wheat evaluated at £1-10 shillings would suggest an anticipated yield of twelve bushels, if calculated at 2/6d. per bushel, or ten bushels, if a 3-shilling base is used.

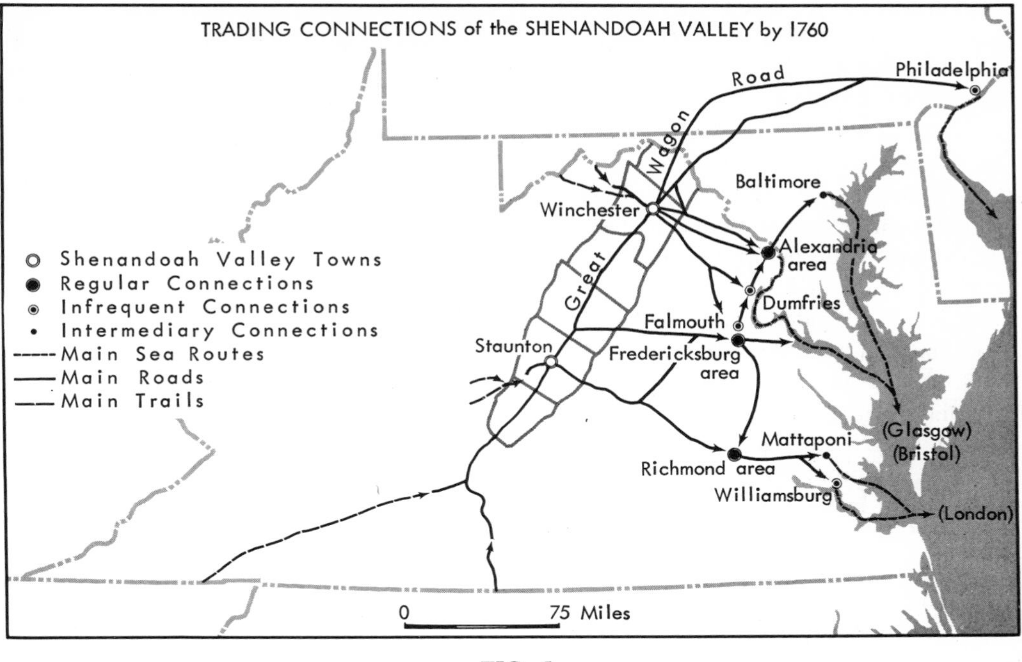

FIG. 5

for some foodstuffs and manufactured goods, such as salt, sugar, iron, nails, and a variety of cloths and sundries. Pioneer exports consisted predominantly of products from livestock-raising and hunting: cattle, horses, butter, hides, and deerskins. Whiskey was the only grain-based product which appeared frequently in trading accounts. . . .

Postpioneer Developments

The shift to a postpioneer phase of development during the early 1760s was characterized by four major processes: 1) more distinct agricultural specialization, especially in crops; 2) increasing diversification in manufacturing and service functions; 3) elaboration of low-order central-place tendencies; and 4) more frequent and sustained commercial contacts with eastern market centers (Fig. 4).

Agricultural Specialization

The valley's agricultural geography after 1760 was dominated by four commercial components, livestock (especially cattle), tobacco, hemp, and wheat, all of which had been present during the pioneer period. Consumption levels per head probably remained constant, and the growth of commercial proportions was the result of shifting crop emphases, increasing acreages under arable, and, in some instances, increasing yields. With the possible exception of tobacco plantations owned by absentee planters, few farms increased their commercial proportion of total farm output much above half by 1800.

The commercialization of agriculture took place within a mixed farming economy, with few areal patterns of crop or livestock specialization. Hemp and wheat were produced in successive phases of crop specialization, but farmers who grew them did not exclude other commercial activities. Almost all valley farms had livestock, which ensured widespread pasture and corn cultivation. The Shenandoah Valley experienced each phase of the diffusion of upper southern agriculture. Tobacco and hemp, which had been major commercial crops in eastern Virginia, were cultivated in the valley after 1760 and had moved on to Kentucky by 1780. Wheat moved from the northern Virginia piedmont in the late 1750s to the valley by 1776 and Kentucky during the 90s. The improved breeding of cattle, which began in the valley during the late 70s, also moved to Kentucky in the 90s.

Livestock. Livestock products were important sources of income for valley farmers in the last part of the eighteenth century. Beef cattle went to the markets of Philadelphia, and to a lesser extent, Alexandria, Richmond, and Baltimore. After the Revolutionary War Winchester became a distribution center for cattle from western Virginia and Kentucky moving to these eastern markets. . . .

The Shenandoah Valley also made substantial contributions to the improvement of quality and breeding in backcountry livestock, particularly cattle. Livestock yields seem to have increased significantly during the second half of the century.[29] Butter was the most frequent livestock product traded. . . .

Tobacco. Tobacco was a major export crop of colonial Virginia, a currency, and a tax payment, so early attempts were made to grow it in the Shenandoah Valley. Eastern Virginians introduced the plant into the lower valley during the 1740s, but production was irregular until the late 1750s.[30] Planters employed overseers to supervise slave production of tobacco, corn, and sometimes hemp and wheat on the cultivated parts of their valley estates. . . . Several Tidewater planters had their most profitable acreages in the Shenandoah Valley by 1775, yet valley producers had to market their crop at Alexandria or Falmouth until after the Revolution, despite numerous petitions for local inspection stations.[31] Tobacco farming continued to expand after the war because settlers could pay their taxes with it, and farmers in the lower valley requested construction of more conveniently located warehouses, but tobacco was not able to fill the void left by the decline in hemp.

29. Beef yields from steers slaughtered for the army averaged 500 to 600 pounds, compared with only 350 to 375 pounds during the French and Indian War. By the late 70s a few farmers, such as Matthew Patton of Rockingham County, made efforts to improve the quality of beef cattle by importing English bulls. Patton emigrated to Kentucky about 1790 and helped to establish improved cattle breeding in the Bluegrass region; N. F. Cabell, "Some Fragments of an Intended Report on the Post-Revolutionary History of Agriculture in Virginia," *William and Mary College Quarterly Historical Magazine* 26 (1918):168; and P. C. Henlein, *Cattle Kingdom in the Ohio Valley, 1783-1860* (Lexington: University of Kentucky Press, 1959), pp. 25-29.

30. George Washington mentioned the plant during his surveying activities for Lord Fairfax in Frederick County in 1748; see his *Journal of my Journey over the Mountains . . . 1747-48* (Albany, N.Y.: Joel Munsell Sons, 1892), p. 24. Hart, footnote 16, p. 5 argued that tobacco was not significant in the valley during the early periods because the soils were not suitable.

31. For example, in 1775 Nathaniel Burwell received most of his profit from tobacco produced on two estates in Frederick County, and most of his expenses there were overseers' wages or pork and corn sent over the Blue Ridge to feed his slaves; Burwell-Millwood Records, Store and Farm Accounts, 1789-1870, microfilm, Alderman Library, University of Virginia, Charlottesville, especially pp. 21-52. In 1774 and 1775 Landon Carter's two estates in the lower valley provided more than one-third of his total plantation income.

Hemp. Tobacco was the specialty of planters in the lower valley, but hemp was more typical of small farmers throughout the area. Some tobacco planters produced hemp as a second commercial crop when tobacco prices were low, which was a common practice in eastern Virginia. Valley farmers did not begin to produce substantial amounts of hemp for sale until 1760. . . . Two-thirds came from Scotch-Irish producers in the upper valley. Large-scale hemp production in Augusta County created the first demand for Negro slaves in the upper valley, because hemp is a labor-intensive crop. The Revolution radically altered backcountry hemp production and marketing. . . . Hemp production doubled in the valley, which supplied as much as a quarter of Virginia's total output. The upper valley, which dominated western production, had 9,000 acres under hemp during this time. Commercial hemp production continued in the upper valley on a small scale despite the drastic postwar drop in hemp prices, but valley hemp could not compete in quality with the Kentucky product or imports from Russia, and cotton had begun to replace hemp in clothing manufacture by 1790.[32]

Wheat. Although tobacco and hemp overshadowed wheat as an export crop in the colonial period, the shift from tobacco to wheat, which began in the northern Virginia Piedmont around 1760, had reached the lower valley by 1776. Wheat and flour were exported from the lower valley before the Revolution.[33] . . . After the war the decline of tobacco and hemp, and the growing demand for wheat and flour, made wheat the commercial staple of the region. . . .

Manufacturing

Economic diversification took the form of expanding local manufactures. Manufacturing was small and highly localized during the first thirty years, and after 1760 the main function of the region's manufacturing was not so much to add to its range of exports as to reduce its dependence on outside areas. Manufacturing was highly dispersed within the valley, reflecting the processing of agricultural commodities and the exploitation of local forest and mineral resources. Basic industries, such as ironworking, which might have attracted other industries, do not seem to have done so. Small metal-using plants were located in the small towns where skilled labor was available. . . .

Despite the widespread availability of most agricultural and forest products, some regionalization of manufacturing was apparent by 1775. Manufacturing in the lower valley was more substantial and diversified. Tanning and leather was the leading craft industry, with the Winchester area specializing in leather clothing and saddles, and Shenandoah and Rockingham counties producing footwear and shoe thread. The making of furniture and metal and wooden craft goods was also more typical of the lower valley. Although the linen trade was widespread, the upper valley dominated production, and the Staunton area became known for its

32. Legislative Petitions, Augusta County, June 8, 1784, Virginia State Library; and James McDowell Papers and Andrew Reid Account Books, McCormick Collection, Wisconsin State Historical Society, Madison.

33. William Allason Papers, Virginia State Library: Shenandoah Store Account Books, 1761-1765 and Ledgers, 1757-1801; Adam Stephen Papers, Library of Congress, Washington, D.C.; and Hart, op. cit., footnote 16, pp. 11n and 149-50. Given the small costs of milling, it was more profitable to export flour than wheat. A settler would have received ten shillings for 2.5 bushels of wheat in 1776, but fourteen shillings from the hundredweight of flour that could be made from 2.5 bushels of wheat.

oznaburg clothing. Distilling was also important in the upper valley, which had become the leading whiskey-producing area in Virginia by 1783.[34]

Urban Trends and Trade

What were the relationships between the valley's expanding economy, its urban characteristics, and its external trading contacts? One might have expected an increasing concentration of service and trading functions in urban centers and a noticeable increase in the urban proportion of the population, yet the emergence of such a pattern was slow. Winchester and Staunton dominated the developing low-order urban system, but internal trade remained decentralized.[35] After 1775, as the valley became less of a frontier area, it was incorporated into the expanding hinterlands of Virginia's coastal and fall-zone towns, which enhanced the importance of Winchester and Staunton.

Basic services for local settlers were supplied from scattered country stores. Local accounts seldom reached more than £10 annually, and helped to keep a large number of farmer-shopkeepers in operation. Wealthier individuals tended to conduct their external purchases independently of local merchants in Berkeley, Frederick, and eastern Shenandoah counties. Eastern Virginia merchants often acted as no more than freight agents for goods imported from Britain.[36]

Nevertheless, a hierarchy of small towns had begun to appear in the lower valley by 1775, and spread throughout the region by 1790. Its definition was more a function of local population than of external trade. . . . The more densely settled lower valley was earlier to support a central-place structure (Fig. 6). . . .

By 1790 Winchester, with 1,650 inhabitants, was the largest town in western Virginia, and the sixth largest in the state; Staunton, the second largest town, had just over 800 residents.[37] In addition to their county administrative and other local service functions they became district court centers. By 1800, in addition to Winchester and Staunton, seven towns in the lower valley and two in the upper valley had more than 200 inhabitants.

34. Comparative figures for the valley do not appear until 1810. The contribution of Berkeley and Rockbridge counties was small, but the other four counties made the Shenandoah Valley a leading industrial area which dominated Virginia's output of cloth and clothing, leather goods, lumber, furniture and wood products, and distilled products; it was also a leading area for iron products, boots and shoes, and small crafts; T. Coxe, *A Statement of the Arts and Manufactures of the United States of America for the Year 1810* (Philadelphia: A. Cornman, Jr., 1814), pp. 88-114.

35. This reemphasizes points made in H. R. Merrens, *Colonial North Carolina in the Eighteenth Century* (Chapel Hill: University of North Carolina Press, 1964), pp. 142-72. Winchester and Staunton would have been towns of the fourth order; J. T. Lemon, "Urbanization and the Development of Eighteenth-Century Southeastern Pennsylvania and Adjacent Delaware," *William and Mary Quarterly* 24 (1967): 501-42. Urban settlements in colonies that lacked primate cities were often more sophisticated, especially as transactional centers, than their mere size might indicate; J. H. Soltow, *The Economic Role of Williamsburg* (Charlottesville: University Press of Virginia, 1965).

36. The Fairfax family dealt mainly with William Allason in Falmouth, who merely arranged for direct, periodic shipments of British and local goods from Falmouth to the Fairfax residences in Frederick County; Allason Papers, Ledgers, Account Books, and Letter Books; and Wykeham-Martin Papers, 1672-1820, microfilm, Virginia Historical Society, Richmond, especially correspondence of 1790 to 1792. The independent transactions of such prominent settlers as the Fairfaxes, Samuel Washington, and Horatio Gates, and the proclivity of absentee planters to supply their valley quarters with many basic necessities, may have retarded centralized marketing after 1775 in the lower valley.

37. U.S. Bureau of the Census, p. 10; one of every twelve persons in Frederick County lived in Winchester, and two of every twenty-seven persons in Augusta County lived in Staunton.

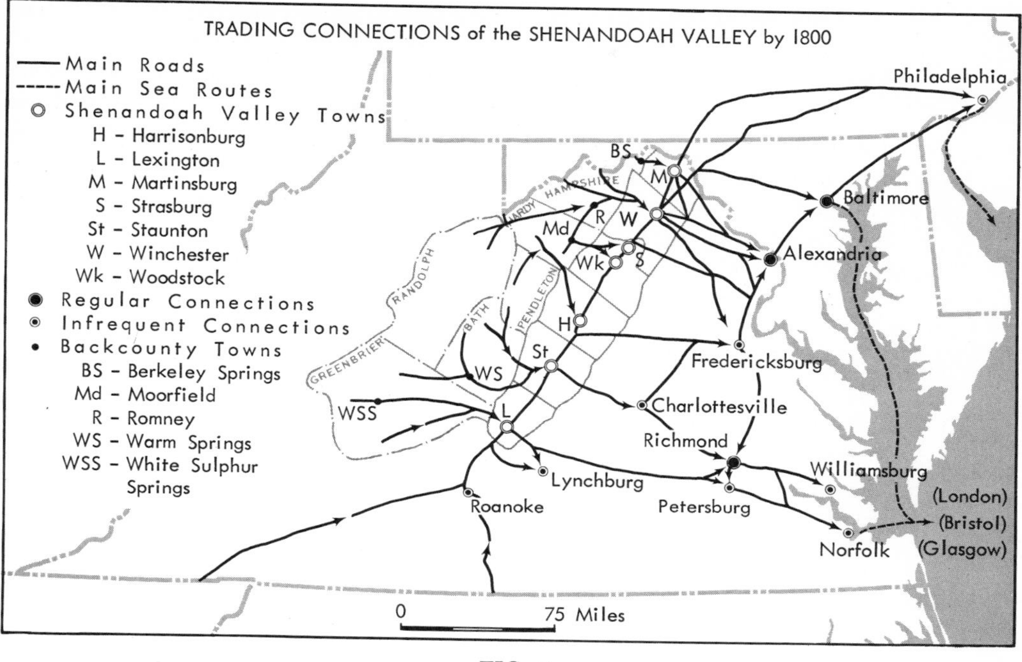

FIG. 6

About a dozen small hamlets laid out by local landowners formed a third level in the hierarchy, with a few local services on only a slightly larger scale than the country store or wayside tavern.

Winchester and Staunton, the major entrepôts of western Virginia, dominated the import trade and increased their share of the export trade despite competition from other urban settlements within the valley.[38] Their twice-weekly markets received small quantities of wheat, corn, rye, hemp, linseed, butter, wax, honey, hides, and skins. In these towns the region's most active merchants engaged in trade, provided commercial ties with eastern merchants and, through them, connections with British firms. Those who had served as hemp agents during the Revolution had been able to strengthen their contacts in Richmond and Alexandria, and they shifted the valley's trading relationships to these towns from Falmouth and Fredericksburg, a process which had begun during the 1760s.[39]

External Relationships

The expansion in the valley's external contacts resulted in the improvement and expansion of the major east–west high-

38. Winchester served a wealthier clientele than Staunton, and this was reflected in its social characteristics. It catered to the Anglican, planter-dominated part of the valley; its weekly newspaper had the most extensive subscription list in western Virginia; and it supported a number of artists and highly specialized craftsmen, a variety of formal social gatherings and theater entertainment and, during the summer, horse racing. The town was the main staging point for Berkeley Springs, which had been developed as a spa for both local and piedmont planters (Fig. 6); Bliss, "Rise of Tenancy," pp. 387-96.

39. Andrew White in Winchester was able to solidify trading connections in Alexandria and Philadelphia, and Sampson Mathews in Staunton strengthened his ties with Richmond; Mitchell, "Upper Shenandoah Valley," pp. 435-38.

ways. By 1800 five main wagon roads, four of which had been designated as turnpikes by 1787, connected the lower valley with eastern Virginia (Fig. 6). The construction of the road between Lexington and Richmond during the Revolution gave the upper valley three roads. . . .

The amount of postwar indebtedness reveals the degree to which the Atlantic economy had affected the valley by 1790. At least thirty prominent settlers in the lower valley, and probably half that number in the upper valley, were heavily in debt. The creditors ranged from Philadelphia and Baltimore, through Alexandria, Falmouth, Fredericksburg, Richmond, Williamsburg, and Norfolk, to London, Bristol, and Glasgow. . . .

Eastern Trading Patterns

The shift in the focus of the region's trade to Richmond and Alexandria was clearly consolidated by 1780 (Figs. 5 and 6). Richmond and Alexandria were founded ten to fifteen years after Fredericksburg and Falmouth. Both quickly outstripped potential rivals as the other two towns had failed to do.[40] After 1760 their merchants began trading westward into the Shenandoah Valley. Alexandria merchants had begun trading in the lower valley even before 1750; partly through sustained merchant contacts, and partly through planter connections between the two areas, the town had become the leading fall-zone market for lower valley goods by 1775. Richmond merchants were a decade later in tapping the upper valley, and that town's valley hinterland was only really consolidated after 1775 as a result of Virginia's control of the hemp trade, which made Richmond a major hemp marketing center. . . .

Philadelphia's connections with the valley, except for the cattle trade, were most obvious during the Revolutionary War when several city merchants sent agents into the lower valley to purchase hemp. Baltimore merchants seem to have made little penetration into the valley until after 1783, but they replaced Philadelphia as the valley's main trading center outside of Virginia, particularly through the merchants of Winchester.[41] At no time did either of these cities seriously challenge the commercial connections between the valley and the Virginia fall-zone towns.

Socioeconomic Change

What effects had these economic changes on the valley's social patterns? . . .

Early American frontier populations had great economic equality, considerable social fluidity, and low differentiation of wealth. The keys to this socioeconomic homogeneity lay in the easy acquisition of land, the relatively similar economic backgrounds of the pioneer settlers, and the ubiquitous pattern of mixed agriculture. . . . The rent rolls for the early 1760s provide evidence of a relatively middle-class socioeconomic structure (Table 1). The valley's population was composed mainly of small farmers; only 30 percent owned more than 400 acres of land, fewer than 10 percent

40. R. E. Grim, "The Origins and Early Development of the Virginia Fall-Line Towns," unpublished master's thesis, University of Maryland, 1971.

41. Frederick County Order Books 19 through 23; Frederick County Superior Court Order Book, 1789-1793; Augusta County Order Books 23 and 24; and Augusta County District Court Order Book, 1789-1793. Hart, pp. 20 and 150n, was correct in stating that Philadelphia was much more significant in valley trade than Baltimore during the Revolutionary War, but was erroneous in his belief that Philadelphia disappeared completely as a market for valley produce after the war.

owned less than 100 acres, and fewer than 10 percent owned slaves, yet regional and structural variations were already apparent. A higher proportion of residents owned slaves and more than 400 acres of land in Frederick County than in Augusta County, and it appears that at least 35 percent of all valley taxables owned no land at all.[42]

By 1783 the valley's property-ownership structure clearly had become more restricted, especially in the lower valley, where the top 10 percent of the landholders controlled 45 percent of all land granted, and 38 percent of all households in Frederick County held slaves.[43] Socioeconomic differentiation increased in the upper valley in the last two decades of the century; 30 percent of the taxables owned no land in 1782, but by 1800 the figure had risen to 48 percent.[44] Twenty-two percent of all households in the upper valley owned slaves in 1782, but eighteen years later only 17 percent did so. The proportion of taxables who owned neither slaves nor livestock increased from just under 3 percent in 1782 to 17 percent in 1800. At the end of the century the richest tenth of the resident population of the upper valley owned 35 percent of total landed and 46 percent of total personal property.

These changing proportions indicate two tentative conclusions. First, the concentration of wealth was increasing slowly but not unexpectedly in the valley during the colonial period. Second, the gap between rich and poor widened perceptibly in the last two decades of the century, probably most distinctly in Berkeley and Frederick counties.[45] . . .

Conclusions

. . . The Shenandoah Valley might be termed a frontier area until the late 1770s. There was no clearly identifiable settlement zone west of the valley until this time; overall population density was only five persons per square mile; and urban population was less than one-tenth of total population. However, economically, the valley's farm population was strongly commercialized by the late 1770s; culturally, a pluralistic pattern was still dominant; socially, differences in distribution of wealth were evident but not comparatively great; and politically, participation

42. The number of landholders recorded in the rentals and rent rolls was compared with the total number of tithables for the early 60s. There appear to have been over 2,000 landless tithables in the valley at this time. Even if one allows for the generous possibility that one-quarter were young sons living at home or indentured servants, this would still leave at least 35 percent of all tithables holding no land. A substantial proportion of these settlers must have been tenants.

43. Although these ratios are not particularly impressive when compared with eastern Virginia counties (Hart, p. 162), they still more than qualify the lower valley as a "commercial area"; J. T. Main, *The Social Structure of Revolutionary America* (Princeton: Princeton University Press, 1965), pp. 62-63 and 276-78; the ratios for the upper valley place it in the same bracket.

44. An increasing number of landless settlers was in urban centers; equally revealing is the indication that in 1800 the twelve nonresidents who each owned more than 10,000 acres controlled almost 40 percent of the taxable acreage. The richest tenth of the resident population owned another 35 percent of the land, leaving only 25 percent of the total taxable land to 89 percent of the landowners.

45. Cultural differences do not appear to have been very significant, although English and Welsh Quakers seem to have been prominent among the region's wealthy settlers; J. T. Lemon and G. B. Nash, "The Distribution of Wealth in Eighteenth Century America: A Century of Change in Chester County, Pennsylvania, 1693-1802," *Journal of Social History* 2 (1968): 22-23.

in local decision-making was quite broad. . . . The settling of the entire Appalachian province seems to have been distinctive; it occurred in intermittently rather than continuously occupied areas, largely during a period of colonial dependency, and had overwhelmingly rural, agrarian populations. There were few towns to act as alternative opportunities for settlers who might otherwise have moved off their lands. How applicable might generalizations derived from the study of Appalachian areas be to other settlement zones?

Several hypotheses derived from the study of the Shenandoah Valley need to be tested in other frontier areas. First, government decision-making, particularly in terms of land settlement policies and military strategies, was of major significance, whether consciously or inadvertently, in molding the character of newly settled areas. Second, the initial identity of cultural groups was replaced by socioeconomic factors which produced communities of increasingly more complex and differentiated social structures. Third, there was no clear-cut division in newly settled areas between subsistence and commercially oriented economies, but gradual change toward greater agricultural specialization and commercialization accompanied by some elaboration of secondary and tertiary functions. Fourth, the changing nature of an area's external relations was critical to its socioeconomic development. The emergence of specialized mercantile functions and urban settlements was dependent upon the size of the population, upon its transportation links with outside market centers, and upon its export and import trade. Fifth, as frontier populations increased in size and capacity to utilize available resources, patterns of regionalism emerged. Formal regions frequently appeared as a result of different settlement histories and economic activities; frontier areas could also become parts of larger functional regions as the expansion of economic specializations and urban-based trading hinterlands affected them. . . .

B. Westward Expansion

From Northwest to Midwest: Social Bases of a Regional History / *William N. Parker*

I

History books tell us that the United States in 1860 was divided into three parts: South, Northeast, and West. The South had in turn three subregions: the border states, the southeast and the "old southwest"; the Northeast included New England and what had been the Middle Colonies. The Far West had hardly entered into American economic history, except as a land of mining excitements. A new and arid Southwest lay beyond Texas. A new Northwest on the Pacific was replacing the "old Northwest." The latter had hardly become "old"; its settlement and culture patterns were still vigorously penetrating across into Kansas and Iowa heading into the Great Plains. In each of these three sections–South, Northeast, and Northwest–the population had developed a characteristic social organization and with it a characteristic culture, which the subregions exemplified with minor variations.

At a century's distance, and with the record of the War in retrospect, the South appears indeed as a nation, a monolith whose economy, politics, society, and morality were dominated by the class of slave-owning planters. Slave owners made up only 3½ percent of the South's population (5½ percent of the population excluding slaves), and the "planters" with ten or more slaves, whose holdings accounted for three-quarters of the slaves and at least three-quarters of the cotton grown, numbered only about 100,000 individuals out of a southern population of about four million slaves and 7,200,000 free persons.[1] One hardly knows whether

1. Census of 1860, *Agriculture,* p. 247. G. Wright calculates that on the basis of a Census sample the top 20 percent of slaveholders (i.e., about 75,000 individuals) held 77.7 percent of the slaves and that the top 20

Reproduced (with omissions) by permission from *Essays in Nineteenth Century Economic History: The Old Northwest* (Athens, Oh.: Ohio University Press, 1975), pp. 3-34.

to marvel more at the politics or at the economics of this vast region. Among other peoples and soils, a small aristocracy had ruled over a large area, restricting its economy along lines compatible with its social dominance. One thinks of the eighteenth-century English aristocracy, or more aptly, of the Prussian Junkers and other East European landed groups. But those noble classes ordinarily possessed a degree of local sovereignty, legal control of local justice, and even force, and they dominated the values of a population committed deeply to the principle of social organization through subordination. The achievement of the southern planters was the more remarkable in that it was carried off in a nineteenth-century nation-state, where democracy and free markets had received their supreme expression. To understand the planters' power, one must no doubt look to a system and traditions of local government founded on seventeenth- and eighteenth-century English landed precedent.[2]

The free North presents no such clear picture of class organization and dominance.[3] Along the eastern seaboard from Baltimore to Boston and on to the shipping towns of Maine, the mercantile activity of colonial times, after its crisis from 1808 to 1818, had restored itself by the 1830s. It drew on the cotton trade, whaling, and the speed of clipper ships, and increasingly on the connections with the interior by the canals and railroad, the growing exchange of western grain and meat against European manufactures, and the growing manufactures in southern New England and around New York and Philadelphia. The location, wealth, working population, and financial institutions of the seaboard cities had gathered to them not only shipping, transshipping, warehousing, and packaging of the stream of goods, but also the activities of selling, financing and promoting the trade, and with that the job of modifying through manufacture the form and qualities of the goods in transit.[4] . . .

By 1860, then, the North was like a long animal whose head rested in the eastern urban region; its body, including factories, shops, and commercial farms, stretched from fifty to one hundred miles inland and a little like the Cheshire cat, faded back into the woods, hills, and flatlands of the West, half dissolved and uncertain in outline. Despite home gardens and domestic livestock in the cities, the seaboard's food needs, including hay for workstock, were mainly supplied from a

percent of cotton growers grew 77.4 percent of cotton produced in 1860. These are almost certainly nearly wholly overlapping classifications. G. Wright, "The Economics of Cotton in the Antebellum South," unpublished dissertation, Yale University, 1969, p. 102.

2. Concerning the "oligarchical principle" and influence of the property qualification on English local government, see Sidney and Beatrice Webb, *The Development of English Local Government 1689-1835* (London: Oxford University Press, 1963), Part 1. (First published as Chapter V of Volume IV of *English Local Government,* London, 1922.)

The extensions of these principles in Virginia are alluded to by Wertenbaker. T. J. Wertenbaker, *Patrician and Plebian in Virginia* (Charlottesville: Michie Co., 1910), pp. 33-34, 39, 57-58.

3. William B. Weeden, *Economic and Social History of New England 1620-1789,* Volume 2 (Boston: Houghton, 1891), pp. 786-815, 840-76. Kenneth Lockridge, "Land, Population and the Evolution of New England Society 1630-1790," *Past and Present* 39 (April 1968):62-80. See also Robert E. and B. Katherine Brown, *Virginia 1705-1786: Democracy or Aristocracy?* (East Lansing: Michigan State University Press, 1964).

4. G. R. Taylor, *The Transportation Revolution 1815-1860* (New York: Rhinehart & Co., 1951), pp. 207-49 describes the transition from household to factory organization in manufactures. See also R. M. Tryon, *Household Manufactures in the United States, 1640-1860* (Chicago: University of Chicago Press, 1917), pp. 242-303.

vast farming area which had begun organizing itself for two decades into cropping regions on a continental scale. The rural out-migration from upper New England and central Pennsylvania and New York had been in two directions: toward the coastal cities and to the West. Much of the westward migration was in part the transfer of a commercial farming activity to a more suitable region—the movement of grain and meat producers into the Ohio Valley and thence across to the Mississippi, the spread of New York dairying to Wisconsin.[5] These market-directed movements were guided by the prices for land in various locations and strongly affected by the opening of new land and the availability of credit. The degree of spread of a single commercial economy is indicated by the repercussions of the banking crisis of 1819, 1837, 1842, and 1857 producing bursts of bankruptcies and unemployment even in young western towns.[6]

The lands between the Ohio and the Mississippi were connected then in 1860 to the seaboard through the market for their farm products—that "surplus" to which the transport improvements had given vent.[7] In this respect their position did not differ from that of the South, except that their product was a bit more varied and their position in foreign markets much less prominent or secure. Like the South, the West received back from the East manufactures—textiles and iron ware and a thousand miscellaneous items. Both West and South were collections of local economies, of semi–self-sufficient families or neighborhoods which formed economic and political regions not because of an internal interdependence, but because of a common link to eastern and European markets and suppliers. But the West's connection to the East had grown far closer than the cotton South's in more vital and intimate ways—in the movement of loans for landholding, railroad and minerals development, and in the movement of men from the same farms and stock as those from which men had moved into seaboard cities.[8] Westward movement both regions had enjoyed, but the Old Southwest was settled from *its* East, where the procession of planters, slaves, and yeomen farmers moved out to reproduce the same social and economic system on new and more fertile soil. The old Northwest received free small farmers from the border South and the Northeast, and placed them in a social structure looser than the South's and an economic structure more varied and more complex. In 1860 this broad and populous farming region stood on the eve of an industrial development whose end is even today not yet in sight. . . .

5. Lewis D. Stillwell, "Migration from Vermont (1766-1860)," in *Proceedings of the Vermont Historical Society* V2 (1937):135, 185-96, 214, 215.

6. Richard C. Wade, *The Urban Frontier: The Rise of Western Cities, 1790-1830* (Cambridge, Mass.: Harvard University Press, 1959), pp. 161-202. See also the extended discussion of western cycles in Thomas S. Berry, *Western Prices before 1861* (Cambridge, Mass.: Harvard University Press, 1943), chaps. 12-16.

7. This development is recognized by G. S. Callender in his discussion of western settlement in *Selections from the Economic History of the United States 1765-1860* (Boston: Ginn and Co., 1909), pp. 600-601.

For a discussion of the "surplus" concept in the South and West, see R. A. Billington, *Westward Expansion, A History of the American Frontier* (New York: Macmillan, 1949).

8. Douglass C. North, "Interregional Capital Flows and the Development of the American West," and Douglas F. Dowd, "A Comparative Analysis of Economic Development in the American West and South," *Journal of Economic History* XVI 4 (1956):493-505, 558-74; James S. Duesenberry, "Some Aspects of the Theory of Economic Development," *Explorations in Entrepreneurial History* III 2 (December 1950):97-102.

II

The rural society of the old Northwest was peculiarly well adapted, it might be argued, to what a Marxist would call its "historic role" in the mid-nineteenth century. Taken across the whole area from central New York and Pennsylvania to the Plains, conditions were remarkably homogeneous. The land, cut up by the rectangular survey and offered at auction sales, had undergone settlement between 1800 and 1860 under rather steady or regularly recurrent conditions of population growth and credit availability. Land auctions, the knowledge of insiders, the pressure of squatters, the homemade banking institutions, the presence of eastern speculators—all of these had left each tier of counties settled in turn in a pattern of free farms, clustering in size between 80 and 160 acres, enough to occupy a family labor force, with some help at harvest, and perhaps some surplus land for speculative sale. Unlike the European or early New England pattern, settlement was not in villages, but in the isolated farmstead, set in the middle of a large, consolidated holding, with no common lands and very little fragmentation. Except for mortgaging, landownership was absolute; speculators, early ranchers, states, and railroads who had large holdings held them to sell, not to farm with tenants. Within this monotonously repetitive pattern of rural settlement supplementing and drawing on the versatility of the settlers, a marked specialization of economic function early appeared. Speculators, ranchers, mixed farmers, dairymen, even frontier bankers on occasion, moved West as the comparative advantage of a county shifted with growing density of settlement. . . .

The homogeneity of the population and of its fortunes was of course not absolute. In the scramble for settlement, families were sucked in from the South as well as the East—from Kentucky and western Virginia, as well as central Pennsylvania, New York and the backcountries of New England. The Ohio River, geographical boundary between slavery and freedom, was overlapped by a zone of southern border settlement extending into the southern half of Illinois, far up into Indiana and cutting off the southeastern hill country of Ohio. The outlawry of slavery by the Ordinance of 1787 was an absolutely decisive fact in the social development of this region: it meant that the southern stock of settlers—whatever habits of mind and sympathy they evinced—was formed of the non-slave-owning class, the yeomen farmers of Owsley's history[9]—or the drifters and footloose population of the backcountry and hills. . . .

New Englanders came early into the territory from the settlements of Connecticut veterans on the so-called Western Reserve, and a steady stream moved from Massachusetts and Vermont after 1830 as those farming regions shifted cropping patterns under the joint pressure of the pull of labor to the mills and the market competition of western grain and meat. Spreading across northern Ohio,[10] eastern Michigan, where Boston money had always been involved, and down from the lake into central Illinois, Yankee farmers and villagers settled quickly into all the money-making activities that were to be

9. Frank Lawrence Owsley, *Plain Folk in the Old South* (Baton Rouge: Louisiana State University Press, 1949), chap. 2.

10. A. L. Kohlmeier, *The Old Northwest as the Keystone in the Arch of American Federal Union* (Bloomington, Ind.: Principia Press, 1938), pp. 209-11; Carl Wittke, ed., *History of the State of Ohio,* vol. 2 (by F. P. Weisenburger), (Columbus, Oh.: Ohio State Archaeological Society, 1941), p. 47.

found—activities which included farming but were by no means limited to it.

Between southerners and Yankees, the migrants from Pennsylvania and New York shared with the German and the later Scandinavian migrants to Wisconsin and beyond a certain peasantlike competence in the agricultural arts. Their origins did not lie in the uplands of Appalachia but generally in flat and fertile farming areas, where careful tillage and husbandry had long been rewarded by good yields, where stable family and village structures had made for a solid, conservative, and dependable style of farming and of living—a style which could take root quickly and flourish abundantly on good soils under good market opportunities.[11]

Any reconstruction of a regional character must be partly imaginary, particularly at a hundred years' distance, and a tracing of its origins must involve a degree of plausible myth. Yet it is hard to feel that the Midwestern character as it shows itself in farming, business, and politics after the Civil War does not owe something to this mix of rural backgrounds of the region's native population. The three groups shifted West initially in rather fixed geographical strata: the Yankees moved into the belt of ultimately greater financial opportunity around and below the lower lakes; settlers from the Middle Colonies and rural immigrants from Europe moved in above and below them; New Yorkers, Germans, and Swedes into Wisconsin after the 1850s; and Pennsylvanians and Germans across the middle counties of Ohio and down the Miami River. The southern hill people settling at the bottom of the area occupied a great southern belt across to the Mississippi.[12] As transportation improved and markets shifted, these groups mixed and mingled, facing a rather uniform natural environment, similar economic experiences, and enjoying easy mobility within a loose and democratic social structure. As they did so, a middle-western character was formed. Is it too fanciful to see in its upper reaches the drives, acuity, shrewdness, and hardness of the Yankee combined with the animal energy, competence, and sturdiness of the German peasant, and among its common people an emotionality, tempered by a sophistication about human suffering, that must have belonged to a people that grew up among the moral and human ambiguities of southern slavery?

These distinctions among the population, nebulous as they are, based on its points of ancestral origin, were accompanied by, and not completely correlated with, distinctions based on wealth. How these arose and were reinforced by economic activity is an interesting matter for speculation. It would indeed have been surprising if, despite the rather considerable uniformity in land distribution—at least among the large share of the population that got land—the distribution of wealth or income had been exactly equal. There were some differences in the resources that settlers brought in with them, and considerable difference in their luck at the land sale and in their access to credit. Whatever their source, differences were to a degree reinforced by early ventures in farming or business. Now the shape of wealth distribution in a rural area has important consequences for the area's later industrial development. A very skewed distribution favors saving and capital accumulation but provides only restricted markets particularly for

11. Wittke, ed., *History of the State of Ohio*, vol. 2, pp. 48-52.

12. Ibid., p. 47.

factory products; an equal distribution has the reverse effect. Obviously, as in most economic problems, there is an optimum level of spending and accumulation which combines these two contradictory effects to an optimal degree for rapid economic growth. Our concern here, however, is with the relation of wealth distribution to the structure of society. Quite obviously, too, as many observers of American manners have pointed out, in a society so new, so democratic and homogeneous in most respects, such differences in wealth stood out, as almost the only mark of individual or familial distinction and prestige. The worship of wealth appeared where so little else existed on which men could exercise the impulse to make distinctions or establish a standard by which to define and imitate success.

Beneath the surface of homogeneity and equality in 1860 in the Northwest lay elements of social differentiation based on family origin and especially on wealth. In social organization too, one sees a similar blending of opposites: the opposition of a family-centered individualism and a community-centered corporate spirit. . . . Midwestern individualism, as it showed itself in farming and in business achievement, was rooted in the family organization brought into the region and reinforced by the conditions of rural settlement on isolated farmsteads, growing crops initially only for themselves, then for sale in anonymous competition with neighbors for distant markets. A direct physical sharing of crops—the dominant mode of distribution in tribal and village societies from time immemorial in the world's agriculture, the basis on which Egyptian, Oriental, and Medieval lords, dynasties, and ecclesiastical organizations were supported and their populations tied to the soil—was wholly unknown, undreamed of by the original rural population of the Middle West. Some exceptions to this stark, small-family individualism appeared among immigrant groups and among southerners or among adherents to a sectarian religion like the Mennonites[13] where settlement in larger family or community groups occurred. But these are notable as exceptions, and their cohesiveness was often short-lived under the corrosive influence of the markets for crops and land and the ready mobility of a second or third generation.

And yet—and yet, that is surely not quite the whole story. If it had been, midwestern society could never have survived. In European villages, the peasant household had been incorporated within a village structure. The European peasant of the nineteenth century may have revealed a narrow selfishness when village and feudal organization was dissolved. Then unrelated households were nakedly exposed in all their anarchy, like worms under a suddenly lifted rock. But the earlier agrarian culture of northern Europe added to its nuclear families a certain organization of public cooperation and responsibility. This was evident particularly in the German and Scandinavian groups, but it existed also among native Americans whose culture derived from the England or Scotland of the seventeenth or early eighteenth century.

To this basis for cooperation were added also the effects of common dangers, common tasks, and common abundance in the early western environment.

13. For accounts of Mennonite religious and community life in Illinois see Harry Franklin Weber, *Centennial History of the Mennonites of Illinois 1829-1929* (Goshen, Ind.: Mennonite Historical Society, 1931); in Indiana and Michigan, see John Christian Wenger, *The Mennonites of Indiana and Michigan* (Scottdale, Penn.: Herald Press, 1961); and in Ohio, see William I. Schreiber, *Our Amish Neighbours* (Chicago: University of Chicago Press, 1962).

Perhaps loneliness and the desire to escape it is an innate characteristic of the human mind, an inextricable element in the human condition. But the premium on news must have been high in the darkness and uncertainties of a frontier, and settlers longed not only for the sound of a voice, but for what a voice might say—about Indians, neighbors, politicians, and other potential intruders on their lives. Together with information gained through social contact, community projects—for defense and later for the creation of public goods—yielded high returns to community self-help. The federal government was remote, and, through constitutional theory and the strength of southerners in Congress, it remained weak. State governments financed and organized canals and railroad projects and established a basic framework of control and law. But they were large, and much of their sovereign powers devolved on the locality—the county, the township, the school district. Taxes, roads, fire, police, and schools were all largely local matters; the division of the land into regular townships with surveys contemplated a close local organization of those who purchased their land at a single land office. The abundance of land in new areas, the prodigality of nature in crude necessities—food and lumber—made it easy to welcome the stranger and to incorporate his strength in community tasks. The rural neighborhood with schools, churches, and politics added then to the family life an indispensable element of social organization. Midwesterners were individualistic on their farms and in their productive activities, but they were generous to neighbors and combined readily in community projects. Clubs, churches, circles, lodges, societies flourished in the Midwest soil—the more so because their members felt themselves to be free and equal individuals. And certainly there were some who found in such association the means to respect and status that seemed so hard to achieve in a near egalitarian society, except, as we have noted, through lucky and successful economic activity. Of all the puzzles in the frontier character, the paradox of individualistic neighborliness is the most striking and potently pregnant with promise of strength for the industrial culture that was to come.

The society of the old Northwest in 1860 is to be viewed, in short, as a variant of the peasant society of Protestant Europe from which it derived all those intimate values and ethical norms expressed in religion and family structure, and much even of what was expressed in community life. But the conditions of formation of this society differed from those in Europe in two respects—each obvious when taken by itself, but producing together an interaction that might not have been predicted. On the one hand, these farmers and villagers were placed in an economic framework of pure market capitalism and given the means of maintaining independent fortunes and positions. No titles, no feudal dues, no tenancies, no village obligations existed in law or memory to restrain their utter economic freedom. On the other hand, the settlers were placed, as the colonists had been in the first coastal settlements, in a new, unknown, and often menacing natural environment, whose rich returns would be yielded only to individual effort sustained and helped by considerable community organization. The counterpart of individual freedom was the danger of social isolation—no established church, no landlord, no clustered village, and hardly a state. These could be compensated for by hard work only up to a point; beyond that, the performance of their functions required organization.

To what extent did this transforming experience differ from that of the New Englanders or the Virginians two centuries before? The Puritan, more often a townman than a peasant, brought to the wilderness a firm corporate spirit and a strict hierarchy; he was to see both dissolve under the corrosive influence of free land, money, markets, and trade. The Virginian brought a venturesome individualism, which was transformed along the seaboard, under the opportunities of profit and power, into the caste system. The westerners in both regions from the eighteenth century on, form the prototypes of the midwestern spirit and society. A hundred years of semi–self-sufficiency in farmsteads and rude settlements across the Appalachians was the immediate forerunner of midwestern settlement, mixed after 1830 with movement from the already commercialized farms of up-country New England and the middle states. What was truly new to the nineteenth century was the growing commercial opportunity for "western" crops—an opportunity which was apparent with the first shipments on rafts down the Ohio and the Mississippi and the driving of animals through the Cumberland Gap, which built up to the intense demand for internal improvements in the 1820s and 1830s, and reached a climax in the opening up of European markets after 1850. It was in response to these opportunities before 1860, and for several decades thereafter, that the western character and rural society was to achieve its fixed and final form. . . .

III

A huge net of opportunity then unfolded over the Northwest as one tier of counties after another was opened up. But land values could rise with settlement only as farming grew more productive of value; that in turn depended both on the growth of a local economy, with trade and specialized production, and on the possibility of export. . . .

The period before 1830 was also one of a decided southern orientation of the Northwest's economy—toward the Ohio and Mississippi valleys. Exact figures on the trade must be viewed with suspicion, but Kohlmeier's search in state and federal documents showed that nearly all the corn and corn products (hogs and whiskey) and over 70 percent of the wheaten flour exported from the Northwest in 1835 went downriver either for consumption or for transshipment from New Orleans, and that nearly half the region's imports, by weight, came up that route.[14] This trade was great enough to create Cincinnati as a city of four thousand by 1814 and six thousand by 1816. It was confirmed and intensified by the steamboat in the 1820s.[15] The canals into the Ohio marked the route even plainer, and as settlement extended to the southern counties of Indiana and Illinois, the advantage of trade over this route was even more marked. Until the 1840s, the lower Northwest settlement was an extension of the upper South, without slaves, but with mostly southern and border people, with crop mix and farming patterns characteristic of Kentucky and Tennessee. . . .

. . . Two sorts of events before 1850 —one immediate and major, the other, less prominent at first, but later quite decisive—began to cause the region around the lower edge of the Lakes to grow and to be linked within itself and to the East. They were events that were to be repeated with increasing strength over the nineteenth century.

First, of course, were the transport im-

14. Kohlmeier, *The Old Northwest,* pp. 20-21.
15. Wade, *The Urban Frontier,* p. 54.

provements: the National Road opened in 1818 to Wheeling and by 1833 to Columbus, the Erie and Ohio canals, the clumsy Pennsylvania canal and road system. These for the first time gave shippers in eastern Ohio the chance to play rival routes off against one another, and against the great natural route to the South. The timing of these and their economic effects have been often described, or assumed, but never thoroughly analyzed and measured. We may cite several such effects, some directly observed in the record of settlement and shipment, others coming under the head of effects which economic theory tells us must have taken place. First, there was an undeniable speed-up in the rate of immigration from the Northeast, the more rapid because it could move into a region where northerners already predominated. But much of the economic efficiency of a new agricultural region depends on the mass of settlement; even without external trade a large enough population can generate its own industrial civilization. Second, the existing farm population—in particular the wheat growers who had already entered from Pennsylvania—enjoyed a market advantage, and the development of eastern Ohio in wheat soon followed. Third, the impact of eastern manufactures must have had the same effect as that observed along the Erie Canal itself: the disappearance of home industry and a shift of farm labor to farming tasks, notably dairying, or to village manufactures where the small-scale shop still had a place. Finally, it should be emphasized that the East-West improvements were not confined to northeastern and central Ohio. The whole southern short of Lake Erie was affected by the canal links at Cleveland and Toledo to western Ohio and Indiana. The Illinois-Michigan canal joined Chicago to the Mississippi; and the Soo Canal, opened in 1855, linked Lake Superior to Lakes Michigan and Huron which already carried surpluses from northern Illinois and eastern Wisconsin. By the late 1840s, the lake trade was a flourishing, mercantile enterprise, developing all the institutions of markets, credit, and competition with which Boston, New York, and Cincinnati had long been familiar.

Apart from the water transportation improvements, a second stimulus to wealth accumulation and commercial enterprise with an eastern orientation appeared in the 1840s: the minerals rush into Michigan copper. The rush, coming in the wake of the geological reports of Houghton in 1843, reached a climax in May, 1846, when about one thousand permits for exploration were issued in a single month. By 1847 the bubble had burst, but the beginnings of an orderly exploitation and of continued disorderly exploration into the mineral resources of the upper Lakes had been laid.[16] The form of the episode was followed closely in the rush into Pennsylvania oil in 1856. The impetus both for the rush and for the continued exploitation in these two cases came partly from the surrounding areas—from lower Michigan and from western Pennsylvania—and partly from New England. In Michigan in particular, Boston financial control of the major mines was established as regular exploitation began in the early 1860s. More important than the ore discovered and the dividends paid out was the stimulus given to further exploration in the upper peninsula of Michigan and to the improvement of navigation of Sault Ste. Marie. The south shore of Lake Superior—the farthest reach of the Great Lakes system—was joined to

16. W. B. Gates, Jr., *Michigan Copper and Boston Dollars* (Cambridge, Mass.: Harvard University Press, 1951), pp. 12-22.

the developing agricultural and industrial region of northern Ohio. The way was prepared for the movement into Minnesota wheat and more significantly into Menominee and Mesabi iron.

IV

By the late 1840s, the lines of connection of Northwest and Northeast were well laid. Two great forces in that decade and the one following were to rivet the two regions together: the railroad and the struggle over slavery.

. . . The Baltimore and Ohio stretched toward the West in the 1830s, the rivalry of the three mid-Atlantic ports pushed the whole system west, and by the early 1850s local lines in Ohio could be joined to the east at three points with only small extensions of track.[17] In choice of terrain, in mode of finance, in the assembly of construction gangs, in leading settlement and agriculture along lines into which rail traffic could flow—the canals were a test run of the railroads along many of the main routes. And the rails, with their wider choice of terrain, their all-year operation, and their speed, and with the technical and engineering skills they used and diffused, were decisive instruments of industrial development—no matter how arithemeticians may calculate, under restrictive assumptions and with self-corroborating data, their exact contribution to the national product in a given year.

The 1850s saw railroad development in the Midwest at two levels: (1) a penetration from the East of lines joining to the great and new trunk systems: the Baltimore and Ohio, the Pennsylvania, the Erie, and the New York Central, and with this (2) a great thickening of the connections in the interior, especially from North to South. The development of the 1840s had connected only a few obvious points, in such a way as to leave the region's orientation still ambiguous. A rail line across southern Michigan effectively gave access from Lake Michigan to Detroit. Indianapolis was joined to the Ohio River, and the Ohio lines followed the Miami valley from Cincinnati north, meeting Lake Erie at Sandusky and at Cleveland. Obviously traffic on such lines could move both ways—to the Ohio-Mississippi valley or to the Great Lakes water system. But the movement of the trunk lines from the East across to Chicago and St. Louis effectively settled the outcome. Then local lines became feeders to the North and East, and the days of the downstream river-oriented economy, even in the southern Midwest, were virtually over. . . .

The second source of the connection with the Northeast—the joint struggle against slavery and for the Union—was a more complex affair. . . . The breakup of a political union is chiefly important for the opportunity it gives the constituent regions to conduct their own economic policies. In the mid-nineteenth century, this meant mainly tariffs. But a tariff between Northeast and Northwest in 1860 was unthinkable; all the economic policies and development of six decades had been directed to stimulating trade, lowering transport costs, increasing interdependence. Industrial growth in neither the Midwest nor the South had been sufficient to make the economies of those two regions complementary. The South, indeed, was itself more closely bound to New York, Philadelphia, and

---

17. R. A. Billington, *Westward Expansion*, p. 294; G. R. Taylor, *The Transportation Revolution*, pp. 45-48, and recent fine study by Harry N. Scheiber, *Ohio Canal Era: A Case Study of Government and the Economy, 1820-1861* (Athens, Oh.: Ohio University Press, 1969).

the New England mills than to Ohio or the upper Mississippi Valley.

But why then should not the North—east and west—simply have let the South secede? Such a question draws the economist far, far from home. Certainly the "mind" of the Northwest—if one may permit one's self such a construct—as late as the mid-1850s was still divided. Economically, the southern orientation of the region's lower half was far from extinguished. The boom in the Southwest continued to pull trade down the Mississippi; Kohlmeier's figures, shaky but indispensable, show that the transport watershed for the traditional staples—corn and hogs—still ran straight along the line of the National Road from Wheeling and Columbus on west to the Mississippi.[18] What had happened in the previous decade was that the settlement, farming, and light manufactures in the area north of that line, tributary to the Great Lakes, had sprung into life. Paradoxically, then it was the interest most involved in the Southern route that was most intent that New Orleans should not be controlled by a foreign power. If southern Ohio, Indiana, and Illinois could not secede with the South, then the South should remain in the Union with them. The American system was a living fact in most minds, and its definitions encompassed the vision of the backcountry along the whole length of the Mississippi, as well as the East-West connections.[19] Yet the Northeast could probably have taken over the surplus produce of this lower region directly at very slight increase in transport cost. Most of the produce found its way back up the Atlantic Coast anyway, and the Mississippi route was clearly heading for obsolescence. So one must move to more intangible fears and passions to explain the war.

. . . Across the Northwest from the start had grown up a substantial stratum of local industry. This is not surprising, yet it is often forgotten in focusing on the area's huge agricultural expansion and the central place of construction and transportation projects. Many industrial skills had come in from the Northeast or middle South with the settlers—iron working, leather working, and a wood working that encompassed carpentry and the making of wooden machinery. Rural neighborhoods had organized themselves readily to produce jobs for specialized craftsmen—a blacksmith, a miller, a harness maker, a teacher—quite soon. The rapid growth of small towns—and of central market cities—with good supply of urban services is a testimony to this. The respect for schooling and a real interest in the practical arts is everywhere present in the rather thick layer of middle-class "culture" that lay on top of the canal men, laborers, and roughnecks. Wherever an industrial opportunity appeared, the skills, enterprise, and institutions needed to utilize it were present. The differences in this respect from the civilization of the middle South are very sharp indeed.

So around Pittsburgh, as early as 1800, around Cincinnati and the Miami and Scioto Valley by the 1830s, along the

18. Kohlmeier, *The Old Northwest,* pp. 202-5.

19. Douglas as late as October, 1860, was defining the role and interests of the Northwest as mediate between Northeast and South. At a speech in Dubuque on October 11, 1860, he said, "Bordering upon the Mississippi and upon the Great Lakes; with commerce floating Southward and Eastward, we have an equal interest in the North and in the South. ("That's so" and applause.) We can never consent to any arrangement that would deprive us of our Eastern trade. Nor can we ever permit a toll gate to be established on the Miss. R., that would prevent our free navigation to the gulf and upon the ocean." Text from R. Carey, *The First Campaigner: Stephen A. Douglass* (New York: Vantage Press, 1964), p. 86.

Lakes, at Cleveland, Chicago, and Detroit after 1840, and in a great grid across the whole area where farmers could get out produce for sale, small-scale commercial manufactures arose. The growth was helped by the very lack of water power which encouraged not only canal building but the making of steam engines. It utilized native materials—flax, wool, wood—to produce for local or regional markets on a large enough scale to maintain competition against imported goods.

The importance of such a grid, and of the business and political institutions accompanying it, for the industry of the upper Midwest after 1860 is obvious. No doubt in retrospect the South, as part of the Federal Union, was not essential either as a market or as a materials source for the industry of the Midwest. But the instinct of the small business civilization of the Northwest in 1860 was profound and passionate. A national union, protecting free labor, the free ownership of property, and the integrity and expansion of its own territorial markets, was an economic ideal for American society under which the Republican class of the Northwest could dominate and prosper.[20] . . .

20. An abundant historical literature examines these questions. See, for example, the very interesting treatment by Eric Fonor, *Free Soil, Free Labor, Free Men: The Ideology of the Republican Party before the Civil War* (New York: Oxford University Press, 1970).

Suggestions for the Geographical Study of Agricultural Change in the United States, 1790-1840 / *Andrew Hill Clark*

. . . There are many kinds of geographical change to which we might direct our attention, although the period has been described as a relatively static one in the development of American agriculture. In terms of crops, there were new varieties[1] and there was some new blood in the various kinds of livestock. There were some late advances in tillage and threshing. But, except for the explosive diffusion of upland cotton, spurred by the development of the gin, and the ephemeral merino sheep craze, we are not for the most part dealing with new crops or kinds of livestock, with the impact of new implements, or with new forms of organization for the producing units. Indeed, although the point is moot and will be discussed later, it is often argued that per capita agricultural productivity changed little in the half-century.[2] Others have seen the spurt in urbanization toward the end of the period as implying a substantial increase in productivity since a smaller proportion of the total population was supplying food for all of it. But if, as has been suggested, an urban market was largely replacing a foreign export market in 1840, this argument is much blunted.[3] It has been said that there was a marked shift toward a more commercial bias but this is a little dubious and will be discussed below. On the whole it is probably safe to say that, if representative farmers of 1790 from Connecticut, tidewater Virginia, or piedmont South Carolina could have been set down, in 1840, on representative farms, with similar crop-livestock emphases, in the Western Reserve, the Bluegrass, or the Black Belt, they would have felt quite at home.

But if fundamental changes in either the raw materials, the methods, or the purposes of American agriculture may have been minor, the sheer exposition of the vast spread of the population and ex-

1. Clarence H. Danhof, *Change in Agriculture in the Northern United States, 1820-1870* (Cambridge, Mass.: Harvard University Press, 1969) discusses the constant experiment with new varieties. By 1839 some forty-one varieties of wheat were listed for New York State alone.

2. See especially Marvin Towne and Wayne E. Rasmussen, "Farm Gross Product and Gross Investment During the Nineteenth Century," in *Trends in the American Economy in the Nineteenth Century,* National Bureau of Economic Research, Studies in Income and Wealth, vol. 24 (Princeton, N.J.: Princeton University Press, 1960); George Rogers Taylor, "American Economic Growth Before 1840: An Exploratory Essay," *Journal of Economic History* 24 (December 1964):427-44; and William N. Parker, "Sources of Agricultural Productivity in the Nineteenth Century," *Journal of Farm Economics* 49 (1967):1455-68.

3. George Rogers Taylor, "American Urban Growth Preceding the Railway Age," *Journal of Economic History* 27 (September 1967):328.

Reproduced (with omissions) by permission from *Agricultural History* 46 (1972):155-72.

pansion of the settled area—the much celebrated march of the frontier across the Lake Plains and the Gulf South—is a historical-geographical epic in itself. That population was in process of rapid growth in 1790, despite a marked slump in immigration, and since it was overwhelmingly agricultural it was admirably suited for the colonization of the lands across the mountains. From the small nuclei that existed west of the Allegheny Front in 1790, at the Forks of the Ohio, in Kentucky, and in Tennessee, Americans flooded to the northwest and southwest with unparalleled rapidity and established important bridgeheads across the Mississippi from Iowa to the Gulf.[4]

As full of geographical interest as the spread of settlement itself, was the establishment of a circulatory system. The migrants moved, in the great surges through which this occupation was accomplished, along many well-defined routes and along these, or others, which they rapidly developed or improved, they shipped surplus regional production and imported the things they wanted or needed. This was the era of roads, rivers, lakes, and canals (and coastwide shipping routes) rather than of railroads. Despite the existence of more than 3,000 miles of railroads in the northern states in 1840, their significant agricultural impact was still confined to limited areas of the northeast. Yet through the period the outlines of a changing geography of circulation appeared as the Erie, Pennsylvania, and Ohio canals opened, as a sailing fleet was built up on the lakes and as steam vessels joined, and to some extent replaced, arks, other flatboats, and keelboats on the Ohio, Mississippi, and tributary rivers.[5] Roads were multiplied and extended, if not much improved, in both north and south, although the new Gulf South depended more on rivers leading to tidewater. Across the Appalachians scattered "service-station" depots marked the droving routes over which so much surplus trans-Appalachian production walked its way to seaboard markets.[6] Most of the population was still agricultural in 1840—as it was overwhelmingly so in 1790—but was keenly interested in the nonsubsistent elements of its economy which, in turn, often were closely tied to the circulatory system.

It is perhaps worth stressing that, when the Indians had been pushed back and the personnel to make the trans-Appalachian push were available, the Appalachian roughlands did *not* prove to be a significant barrier. . . . Nor was

4. Especially useful for conditions at the beginning of the period are Merrill Jensen, "The American Revolution and American Agriculture." *Agricultural History* 43 (January 1969): 107-24, and Justin Winsor, *The Westward Movement: The Colonies and the Republic West of the Alleghenies, 1763-1798* (Boston and New York: Houghton Mifflin Co., 1897), chap. 18. Two excellent later cross-sectional views are Henry Adams. *History of the United States of America, 1801-1817,* 9 vols. (1880-91: reprint ed., New York: Antiquarian Press, 1962), 2:1-134, and Ralph H. Brown, *Mirror for Americans: Likeness of the Eastern Seaboard, 1810* (New York: American Geographical Society, 1943). Parts 2 and 3 of Ralph H. Brown, *Historical Geography of the United States* (New York: Harcourt, Brace and Co., 1948) are most useful for a geographer's look at the changing scene.

5. The literature of geographical interest on transport is immense. Much of it is discussed in the bibliographical notes of Brown, *Historical Geography*. New light on the Canal era in Ohio is found in John G. Clark, *The Grain Trade in the Old Northwest* (Urbana: University of Illinois Press, 1966) and Harry N. Scheiber, *The Ohio Canal Era: A Case Study of Government and the Economy, 1820-1861* (Athens: Ohio University Press, 1969).

6. Paul C. Henlein, "Cattle Driving from the Ohio Country, 1800-1850," *Agricultural History* 28 (April 1954):83-95; and Paul C. Henlein, *Cattle Kingdom in the Ohio Valley, 1783-1860* (Lexington: University of Kentucky Press, 1959).

the forest as nearly impenetrable a barrier as often has been suggested. . . . The eastern forest in the seventeenth, eighteenth, and early nineteenth centuries was honeycombed with extensive patches of grass and brush.

The Regional and Ethnic Origins of the People

I have argued at length, elsewhere,[7] that differences among people, in terms of their cultural baggage of preference and prejudice as exhibited in geographies of cultural and national origins, may be expected to be reflected in geographies of settlement and land use. . . . On the whole I found Old World origin differences to be of far less significance than I had expected, although this tentative negative conclusion may be useful in itself. In fact, the period 1790-1840 well may be the era when the regional impact of varied European origins in the white population was less than at any other time. . . .

The first twenty-five to thirty years of the half-century represented a notably slack period of immigration. Some stray groups like the Dominican Frenchmen who fled the slave revolts and a few thousand Irish or Germans were the major white accretions before 1820. In the twenties and thirties, there were two striking features of the immigration of two million or so Europeans (chiefly from Ireland, Great Britain, and the German-speaking states).[8] First, despite Irish and German colonies in New Orleans and other southern cities, this influx tended to avoid the South and, second, it showed a much greater tendency to concentrate in towns and cities than did the general population.

The shutting off of immigration for so long apparently allowed the American melting pot to boil along merrily. We may have run across one example of it in one of my seminars which attempted to follow the Scotch-Irish in migration from Pennsylvania through the Great Valley to Kentucky and Tennessee.[9] In terms of characteristics that differentiate them from tidewater Marylanders and Virginians of English origin, the Scotch-Irish blend into the populace toward the end of the century and, in effect, we lose track of them before they pass through the Cumberland Gap. Clearly we can identify many by name, or infer origins from Presbyterian credal affiliation, but there seems to be no evidence that, after 1800, their Scotch-Irish origin, in itself, made the slightest difference to where or how they settled or how they farmed. . . . Even those new immigrants from northwestern Europe who did go farming in the Middle West in the twenties and thirties, even if farmers by background, were handling generally familiar crops and animals with generally familiar equipment—if, also generally, in much more extensive and slovenly ways. Their avoidance of the South, indeed, has often been interpreted as the avoidance of the unfamiliar in crops as well as in social context.

There are vitally important changing ethnic geographies of this period, of course, reflecting the displacement of the Indians and the spread of Negro slaves thickly and broadly over the trans-Appa-

7. Andrew H. Clark, "Old World Origins and Religious Adherence in Nova Scotia," *Geographical Review* 50 (July 1960):317-44.

8. U.S. Bureau of the Census, *Historical Statistics of the United States, Colonial Times to 1957* (Washington: U.S. Department of Commerce, 1960).

9. Robert D. Mitchell, "The Presbyterian Church as an Indicator of Westward Expansion in Eighteenth Century America," *Professional Geographer* 18 (September 1966):293-99.

lachian and Gulf South.[10] The correlation of greater density with concentrations of cotton growing and better soils was close if not perfect. The lagging of immigration of Europeans may not have applied to the African-origin population. Philip Curtin, in his census of the Atlantic slave trade, has accepted a figure of some 100,000 Negroes imported as slaves for the period to reinforce the natural increase of the black population.[11] . . .

Just as the black population of the newly settled western lands had ascertainable local seaboard origins and is believed to have been closely associated with the westward movement of cotton, so there well may have been closer associations than we have hitherto discerned between the seaboard localities of origin of the white population of the border South and the Northwest and the crop and livestock biases their agriculture exhibited.[12] The pronounced latitudinal trends are very evident from any study of westward movement. New England and New York dominated the settlement of the northern sectors of the Old Northwest; Kentucky and Tennessee basically were extensions of Virginia and North Carolina; and South Carolina and eastern Georgia spearheaded the settlement invasion of Mississippi and Alabama. The implications about crop and livestock specializations are apparent. The locational pattern of crop-livestock systems established in the trans-Appalachian region may have owed more to this latitudinal bias of westward migration than to geographical locations of markets and trade channels or questions of ecological suitability.

. . . One suspects that, ultimately, we shall conclude that locality of origin of population in Europe was not very important to the shape of geographical change during this period but that the locality of origin of the westward migrants on the eastern seaboard well may have been.

Crop-Livestock Systems

. . . Unhappily, it is only at the end of this period that we have our first agricultural census that allows us to map distributions. We can do a great deal for that year (1839 in the case of crops) in the mapping of absolute quantities, ratios, densities (for the few states for which we have accurate county areas), carrying out regression analyses, and the like. But for the previous half-century . . . we must depend on merchant and transport records, travel accounts, inferences from newspaper information, and so forth.

Still it is most useful to look at 1840 patterns . . . to see them as the culmination of fifty years of geographical change. In Ohio the concentration of dairy cattle and wheat toward the North and East, and of corn and hogs toward the West and South, invites all manner of questions about environmental suitability and market demands, the prejudices, habits, and prior farming practices of the

10. See especially Alfred H. Conrad and John R. Meyer, *The Economics of Slavery and Other Studies in Econometric History* (Chicago: Aldine Publishing Co., 1961).

11. Philip D. Curtin, *The Atlantic Slave Trade: A Census* (Madison: University of Wisconsin Press, 1969), pp. 72-73, does not provide figures for precisely this period, but he does accept a figure of 70,000 for the 1791-1807 period when the legal trade ended and of roughly 1,000 per year from then until 1861. This would give 103,000 for the period 1791 to 1840.

12. Russell H. Anderson, "Advancing Across the Eastern Mississippi Valley," *Agricultural History* 17 (April 1943):97-104; John D. Barnhart, "Sources of Southern Migration into the Old Northwest," *Mississippi Valley Historical Review* 22 (June 1935):48-62; and Richard L. Power, *Planting Corn Belt Culture: The Impress of the Upland Southerner and Yankee in the Old Northwest* (Indianapolis: Indiana Historical Society, 1953).

people, and so on. Did the New Englanders and New Yorkers of the Western Reserve have a predilection for wheat and hay? Did they have a special fondness for dairying? How strongly were they reacting to markets opened by the northern part of the Ohio Canal and the Erie Canal, markets which preferred flour, wheat, and cheese to the salt pork, whiskey, and grain corn of the Cincinnati hinterland? Indeed, we may ask how old was the division of Ohio into northeast-facing and southwest-facing areas of commercial export and how much of the difference in product emphasis was attributable to the population's regional eastern origin, to environmental suitability, or to the distance-friction to different markets?

A thoroughgoing attempt to hypothesize the course of diffusion of either or both wheat and cotton, of shorthorn-type improved cattle, and a variety of other things certainly would be helpful. . . . The maps of diffusion would serve as the locational base for much broader discussions of socioeconomic implications of the crops themselves or the agricultural-commercial systems associated with them.[13]

As a footnote here I should like to emphasize the importance to a geographer of fineness of grain in establishing patterns. Information by states may be of extremely limited value whereas information by counties or smaller areas may enable us to develop good explanatory hypotheses. . . .

Thus the South, like all of our other areas, is intriguing geographically in this period as much or more by its internal variety as by the way its general characteristics stand out in regional contrasts. The South was the cotton area, yet scores of its counties had little or no cotton: slaves, mules, and corn were ubiquitous but the variations of density were profound. The patterns revealed by a finer-grained analysis are fundamental for our retrospective views of geographical agricultural change.

Agricultural Productivity

Some analysts have concluded that there was little increase in per capita productivity during this period.[14] But however small, or great, the change during the half-century in mean productivity, the regional variation may have been substantial. Overall national estimates will have their own utility, but even information about the *range* of productivity within the country would be of limited use if we could not locate different values within the range. With such location we can incorporate information as to climate, soils, and drainage, the background of the farmers, marketing opportunities or facilities, the diffusion of technological improvements or of better seed and stock—indeed about any relevant material which can be located and correlated. . . .

Any geography of agricultural productivity clearly would be associated with changing patterns of labor needs and supplies. . . . We would be able to test such

13. Morton Rothstein, "Antebellum Wheat and Cotton Exports: Contrast in Marketing Organization and Economic Development," *Agricltural History* 40 (April 1966):91-100; and Sam B. Hilliard, "Pork in the Antebellum South: The Geography of Self-Sufficiency," *Annals, Association of American Geographers* 59 (1969): 461-80.

14. Danhof, *Change in Agriculture,* 1, quotes David M. Potter, *People of Plenty: Economic Abundance and the American Character* (Chicago: University of Chicago Press, 1954) about agricultural production in the early nineteenth century: "An infinite supply of free land would never, by itself, have raised our standard of living very far, for it would never have freed us from the condition in which more than 70 percent of our labor force was required to produce food for our population."

common assumptions as that much of upland New England's enthusiasm for sheep was an effort to compensate for decreased labor supply as rural youth headed westward, millward, or cityward. And perhaps from the many and elaborate studies developed to support the pro and con arguments on the profitability of slavery[15] we might be able to speculate more confidently on the dependence of the dominant role of cotton in many southern areas on the kind and amount of labor that slavery made possible. We might ask if the kind of labor contemporaneously available in the Old Northwest could have supported a cotton economy—or might it thus have been even more profitable and securely based? After all, a surprisingly large amount of white labor, in total, did go into early nineteenth-century cotton production in the South. . . .

Agricultural Subsistence and "Commercial" Farming

. . . Self-sufficiency of the individual farm unit is virtually unknown in the history of European expansion to this continent. It was a common experience for a farm to be self-sufficient in many individual categories of needs or wants, that is, for the subsistent element in the individual farm economy to be high. But, like Robinson Crusoe or the Swiss Family Robinson, our earliest colonists and the frontiersmen of later days always started with an indispensable initial capital equipment of implements, arms, clothing (and often) domestic animals and seeds. Even if some operations then seemed to continue for years with no discernible commercial enterprise this is not self-sufficiency. They did not do without metal goods and most of them even if they were adequate amateur smiths, could not and did not smelt iron, nor when iron gave out did they revert to a neolithic stage. The ever-present need for certain kinds of supplies which could not be grown, cut down, dug up, gathered, caught, or shot, drove them all into various kinds of nonsubsistent activity. . . .

Clearly what is meant when "self-sufficient" farming enterprises are described is that the subsistent sector of the whole operation is very large and that a great many categories of needs are supplied entirely from the farm itself. Such a farm is clearly highly subsistent, and from that class of enterprise to a highly, or even completely, commercial operation where little or nothing of the farming effort contributes directly to subsistence one can trace a continuum in the broad total spectrum of American agricultural experience. I have not seen any convincing arguments for cutting that continuum at any particular point—say 25 percent, 50 percent, or 75 percent subsistent, if such could be measured—and then describing the whole operation as either commercial or subsistent. And yet we constantly encounter the phraseology that a farming area has "ceased to be self-sufficient" (or "subsistent") and become "commercial," thus presumably having passed some such (unspecified) point on the continuum. . . .

It may not be in the interests of clarity to think of the efforts of agriculturists as falling entirely into the two categories, "subsistent" or "commercial." In fact, the nonsubsistent sector of any individual

15. Conrad and Meyer, *Economics of Slavery;* James D. Foust and Dale E. Swan, "Productivity and Profitability of Antebellum Slave Labor: A Micro-Approach," *Agricultural History* 44 (January 1970): 39-62; Kenneth M. Stampp, *The Peculiar Institution: Slavery in the Antebellum South* (New York: Alfred A. Knopf, 1956); and Harold D. Woodman, "The Profitability of Slavery: A Historical Perennial," *Journal of Southern History* 29 (August 1963): 303-25.

farmer's economy was usually quite varied. He could work for wages for longer or shorter periods off the farm. He could supply services as a minister or teacher, in medicine, law, surveying, blacksmithing, shoemaking, or whatever, in exchange for money, kind, or other services. A surprisingly large number of settlers involved in the westward expansion of the period had some nonagricultural skill or knowledge on which to rely. . . .

In most discussions of the commercial element in farming I find the assumption (implicit or explicit) that commercialization is signaled by, and largely measured by, the extent of regional exports of goods, and where this is demonstrably (or presumptively) low, the subsistence proportion of the whole farm economy is assumed to be high for the area or situation—and thus for the individual farm operations therein. At least I would judge this to be a general assumption for the period until regional cities began to replace extraregional markets as major absorbers of commercial agricultural production. This latter process begins midway in this period but rises to significance only toward its end.[16] Yet in the course of this half-century there were countless examples, especially west of the Allegheny Front, in which commercial export was negligible and yet the *non*subsistent element was still substantial. The latter, of course, included the significant increments to individual wealth involved in amelioration of land, buildings, and fences, and accretions to flocks and herds, but rather especially the supplying of new immigrants during a settling stage that might last for two or three decades.[17]

. . . The precise number of migrants to any area, in any year, is hard to establish but in qualitative terms we often know that it was large, widespread in location, and persistent until all but the poorest qualities of agricultural lands were taken up. As the migrants arrived they had to be fed almost totally for the first year and often partially for many years thereafter. What they consumed they largely purchased locally. They also purchased land, livestock, machinery, and buildings, or their own capital equipment. . . .

All of this discussion of subsistence is prologue to the suggestion that one of the most revealing studies of the geography of agricultural change during this half-century would be that of changing patterns of the subsistence ratio in the agricultural enterprise. That ratio we might define as that proportion of the total productive effort of the farmer, his family, and his hired or owned labor which was devoted to producing commodities or providing services enjoyed or consumed by themselves. The rest of the 100 percent, of course, consisted of off-the-farm sales of commodities or services (for cash, kind, and other services) and investments in terms of improvements and livestock increase.

One caveat is essential: the basis for our discussion is the economy of the individual farms. In any agricultural village the internal interchange of goods and services might substantially increase the subsistence ratio; thus it would usually be greater for a township than for a village, for a county than a township, and so, in general, the larger the unit considered the larger the ratio. Thus if we designate any substantial area as being lower or higher in the ratio we refer, for that area, to hypothesized means of conditions on individual farms.

16. Taylor, "Urban Growth Preceding the Railway Age."
17. Parker, "Agricultural Productivity in the Nineteenth Century"; and Taylor, "Economic Growth Before 1840."

Imagine, if you will, a statistical surface which, at any time, rises and falls over the outline of the country as the subsistence ratio rises and falls. The traditional interpretation would postulate a surface of rather strong relief. It would be low near major cities and particularly near ports and always lower wherever opportunities for exchange of goods were greatest. It would be low along major routes of communication and trade. But, as for example, in Bidwell's view of southern New England, the surface would rise sharply away from the sea, the cities, the roads, rivers, and canals, to reach a rather high plateau no great distance off (in 1790 at least). From the traditional interpretations we would expect that the surface would, at all times, average much lower in the staple-product areas of the South (tobacco, cotton, rice, and sugar) than with the more varied crop–livestock mixtures, with their built-in advantages in terms of subsistence for food, as in much of New England, the Middle Atlantic, and the East North Central areas. . . .

None of this has been tested statistically and it won't be easy to do, but I would judge that the convolutions of the statistical surface represented by the subsistence ratio would be much less deep at any time than I have supposed that the traditional interpretations would have shown. I think the slope of the surface toward the interior and away from trade arteries and cities would be less and that changes in the surface over the half-century would be on a rather modest scale. Nor am I satisfied that the Cotton South, even in its large plantation phase, would have shown so much lower a subsistence ratio (in terms of food at least) than would most of the Old Northwest.

Geographers of change are, understandably, fascinated by the growth and development of central places (cities and towns) and of the arteries of communication between them. The increases of size and volume of trade along the latter are seen as reliable indicators of commercial advance. There is no doubt that this kind of evidence of circulatory activity arising from the disposal of surplus farm commodities was especially strong as this period drew to a close. But the evidence from the South is mixed; certainly central places were developing less rapidly than in the North despite the snowballing trend of cotton exports. Yet there is more talk of "commercial" agriculture in the South than in the North. I conclude that a study of the changing geography of the subsistent element in the farming economy in this period cannot infer too much from presumed derivative indicators but will have to be based as much as possible on reconstructions of the economies of individual farming operations. . . .

There is abundant evidence of a substantial increase of regional exports and imports and increased flows of agricultural commodities along the major arteries during this period. Coincidentally, however, as the western lands became settled and as the rapidity of farms changing hands diminished, many of the important early nonsubsistent elements of their farming economies declined. On balance, the subsistence ratio may have tended to become lower but, clearly, not as much or as rapidly as historiographic tradition would have it; certainly there is nothing in a geographical view of the records to suggest that a rapid change from a highly subsistent agricultural economy to a markedly commercial one was characteristic either of the older seaboard areas or of the more recently settled western lands in these years. A more accurate picture is that of men who had always emphasized the nonsubsistent aspects of their activities to the greatest degree possible and were delighted, when possible, to move farther in the same direction.

As in so many other aspects of the interpretation of American settlement history in these years I think we may have been led up the garden path in our thinking about subsistent and commercial elements of farming by the "frontier" model. That model generally hypothesized a series of relatively well-defined stages through which the settlement of a frontier area moved—a sort of sequent occupance experience with rather sharp and rapid changes during often (putatively) brief periods of transition. A rapid shift from subsistent to nonsubsistent emphasis was a natural inference. But the evidence to support this position has not been adduced.

Most interesting geographically are those areas which, in frontier theory, did not advance beyond one of the early stages of development. The hill country of present West Virginia, eastern Kentucky, southeastern Ohio, and western Pennsylvania is an excellent example. Frontier settlers were scattered through much of these lands south and east of the Ohio River before the start of this period. They lived partly by hunting, partly by patch farming and rough livestock husbandry. But they sold supplies to new settlers and travellers, they enjoyed increases in their livestock, and they steadily, if slowly, improved the value of their holdings. Many soon engaged in the strongly commercial act of selling out and moving on. Those who stayed probably achieved a minimum of the subsistent ratio for their individual enterprises fairly early and then over many decades saw that ratio remain stationary or even increase. These folk became the neglected, forgotten, bypassed hillbillies of Appalachia. But although these stand out, there were many other areas like them. For a host of pedologic, hydrographic, or geomorphologic reasons there always were difficult, lightly settled—even relatively empty—areas scattered over all of the American lands east of the Great Plains, including the Atlantic slope.[18] To the degree that they remained on their farms those rural New Englanders whom Bidwell describes at the start of the period[19] (although I would maintain that he exaggerates the size of their subsistence ratio) may also have enjoyed little contraction of that ratio through the period and perhaps they too experienced its slow growth through the rest of the half-century. These examples may suggest something of the intricacy of the geography of change in this ratio during the period. . . .

---

18. See especially Herman R. Friis, *A Series of Population Maps of the Colonies and the United States, 1625-1790* (New York: American Geographical Society, 1940); and Fulmer Mood, "Studies in the History of American Settled Areas and Frontier Lines: Settled Areas and Frontier Lines, 1625-1790," *Agricultural History* 26 (January 1952): 16-34.

19. Percy W. Bidwell, "Rural Economy in New England at the Beginning of the Nineteenth Century," *Transactions of the Connecticut Academy of Arts and Sciences* 20 (1916): 241-399.

The Role of Culture and Community in Frontier Prairie Farming / *John G. Rice*

Rural settlement in the Upper Middle West during the nineteenth century was distinguished by a great number of different immigrant groups. Nowhere else in the United States was there such a variety of cultural backgrounds among the farming population. Many of the first settlers came directly from Europe. Others had spent short periods of time in places farther to the east.[1] Almost all had been farmers before they came, and each settler brought a set of values, attitudes, and habits from his European homeland. For most of these immigrant farmers the land they came to was quite different from the land they left behind. There were woods and parklands, which might have recalled a little of home, but most of the land which lay waiting, especially beyond the Mississippi River, was prairie. This was an environment with which they had no experience. To the problems of adjusting to a strange society were added the difficulties of developing new strategies to cope with an unfamiliar and what often seemed even to be a hostile environment.[2]

The extent to which the varying cultural backgrounds of these settlers affected their farming practices . . . may be found in accounts of midwestern agriculture.[3] One is that certain culture groups are responsible for introducing specific crops and farming techniques into American agriculture. The other is that some groups maintained over a considerable period of time distinctive farming practices which differed significantly from those being followed by others around them. . . . In his study of settlement in a Wisconsin county, Merle Curti examined settlers who had come from the east as well as a number of immigrant groups and found that, although the groups start out with roughly the same amount of farmland per household, measures of property value and value of implements, livestock and produce show the Americans and English-speaking foreign-born well ahead initially.[4] As time passes, however, the poorer groups gain steadily and the differences are reduced. In the matter of economic status then, Curti finds Turner's ideas confirmed. . . .

. . . Curti dealt exclusively with *national* groups. In working with large populations it would be unreasonable to ex-

1. The source areas and migration routes of some one thousand North Dakota pioneers of different cultural backgrounds are discussed and mapped in J. C. Hudson, Migration to an American frontier, *Annals of the Association of American Geographers* 66 (1976):242-65.
2. The reactions of Norwegian settlers to the prairie environment are well depicted by Ole Rolvaag in his novel *Giants in the Earth* (New York and London, 1927).

3. A. G. Bogue, *From Prairie to Corn Belt* (Chicago and London, 1963), p. 237.
4. M. Curti, *The Making of an American Community* (Stanford, Cal., 1959), pp. 176-221.

Reproduced (with omissions) by permission from the *Journal of Historical Geography* 3 (1977):155-75. For elaboration see also the author's *"Patterns of Ethnicity in a Minnesota County"* Geographical Reports, 4. Department of Geography, University of Umeå, Sweden, 1978.

pect the researcher to go beyond the census identification of country of birth. Yet we know that in rural areas of Europe during the nineteenth century culture varied considerably over short distances. Language, food, dress, building style, and farming practices could be very different in two provinces of the same country, or even in two parishes of the same province. Second, the role of the local church-centered community in the development of rural society has not been fully appreciated. It commonly happened that immigrants settled in clusters and created church-centered communities that served to preserve cultural identity and even language through a number of generations. Where these communities were formed by people who had had close ties in the old country the stability of the population was especially strong.[5] In this situation one might reasonably expect the cultural background of the group to have more of an impact on the farming experience than in a situation where people came from disparate parts of the same country. . . .

In this study frontier farming will be examined within a six-township area on the prairie of Kandiyohi County, Minnesota. It is part of a larger project in which a group of emigrants from a single parish in Sweden is being followed to North America in an effort to document fully the process of transplantation. Most of the settlers in the area were Swedes, though a large number of Norwegians and some families from Eastern North America and the British Isles also made their homes there. The Swedes came mainly from three provinces–Skåne, Småland, and Dalarna–and almost all the people from Dalarna had left the parish of Gagnef or its chapelry of Mockfjärd. The Norwegians were more diverse in their origins, though the very early settlers tended to come from a few restricted districts. The area thus offers the possibility of comparing culture groups defined at the national, provincial and parochial levels. The three subnational Swedish culture groups were given further cohesion by the fact that each dominated one of the three major church communities. . . .

Early Settlement

The study area is located about eighty-five miles due west of the Twin Cities (Fig. 1). The land is level to rolling prairie and contains a chain of lakes which are a source of the sluggish, eastward-flowing Crow River.[6] In addition to these lakes there were before settlement a great number of prairie sloughs scattered over much of the area, and drainage was one of the major problems the early settlers had to face. Another was the scarcity of wood, the only trees being found in the groves of elm, ash and burr oak which fringed some of the lakes.

The land was surveyed in 1856 and placed on sale shortly afterward. The first settler to take land in the area filed a preemption claim in August of 1857, and within two years eighteen such claims had been entered.[7] . . .

5. R. C. Ostergren, "Cultural Homogeneity and Population Stability among Swedish Immigrants in Chicago County," *Minnesota History* 43 (1973):255-69, and J. G. Rice, *Patterns of Ethnicity in a Minnesota County, 1880-1905* (Umeå, Sweden, 1973), pp. 64-91.

6. The map of the environment was compiled from information extracted from the surveyors' field notes, plat maps in the county atlas of 1886, and a general soils map in the county atlas of 1972.

7. This study owes much to the wealth of information available in the Kandiyohi County history. Certainly one of the best of its kind ever published, this history contains, *inter alia,* lists of county, township and church officers, school board members, children who attended

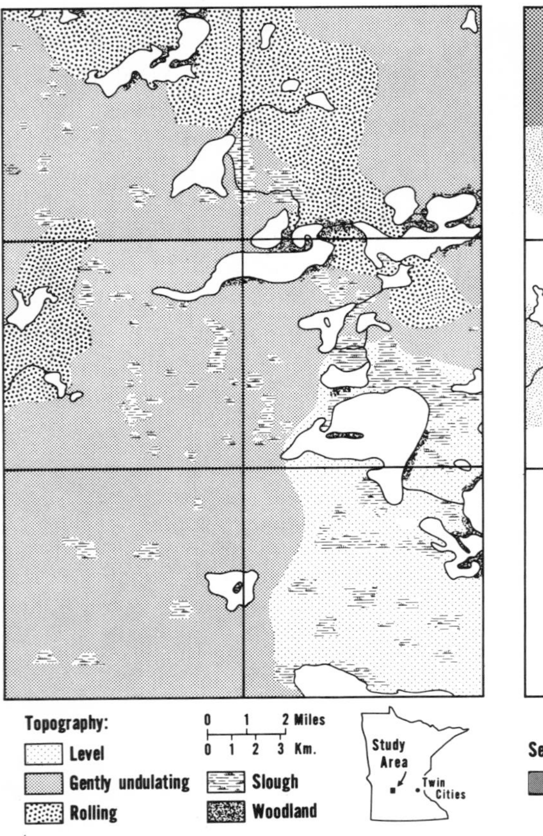

FIG. 1. The environment.

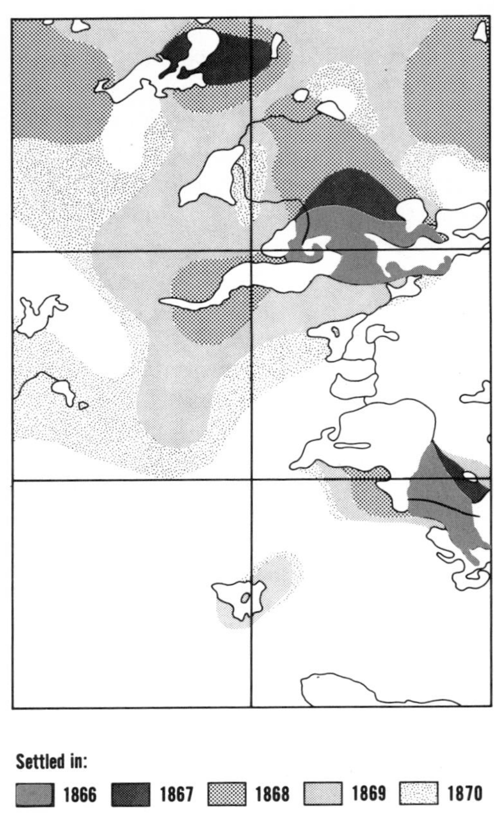

FIG. 2. The spread of settlement.

Claim taking went slowly in the late 1850s. Certainly the economic depression must have slowed activity, but more importantly the railroad had not reached Minnesota, and the trip by horse and wagon from St. Paul took five or six days. Most settlers spent only brief periods of time in the summer on their claims–long enough to plough a small patch of land in the spring, sow some grain and harvest a crop in the fall. Winters were spent in the more established settlements to the east, the men taking work in the lumber camps of the Rum and St Croix valleys. . . .

In 1866 the pace of settlement picked up, and within two years the area was being inundated by a flood of new settlers. The great attraction was the free land now being offered under the Homestead Act passed in 1862. Virtually all of the land taken by settlers in the late 1860s was claimed under this act. . . . The sites closest to the lakes were the first to be taken. From these early cores settlement spread quickly across the surrounding prairie (Fig. 2). By 1870 homestead-

school in different years, as well as numerous biographies rich in detail. V. E. Lawson, *Illustrated History and Descriptive and Biographical Review of Kandiyohi County, Minnesota* (Willmar, Minn., 1905).

ers had claimed almost 23,000 acres and most of the federal land was gone. What had not been granted to the state for railroads, education, internal improvements, and the building of the state capitol was in the hands of nonresidents.

The availability of homestead land was not the only factor that promoted the rapid settlement of the area in the late 1860s. In 1864 the St. Paul and Pacific Railroad Company had been granted a right-of-way through this area for its main line to the west. The line was surveyed in the summer of 1868 and the station villages of Willmar and Kandiyohi were platted. Merchants were already setting up businesses in these places in 1869 although the tracks did not actually reach Willmar until the following year. By this time Kandiyohi, Willmar and Lake Lillian townships had been organized, the principal churches had been established and four schools were functioning. The federal census of 1870 returned a population of 1,150 in the study area, of whom 160 resided in Willmar and 13 at Kandiyohi Station. A total of 276 families had now established themselves here—over one-third of all who would come during the first forty years (Fig. 3).

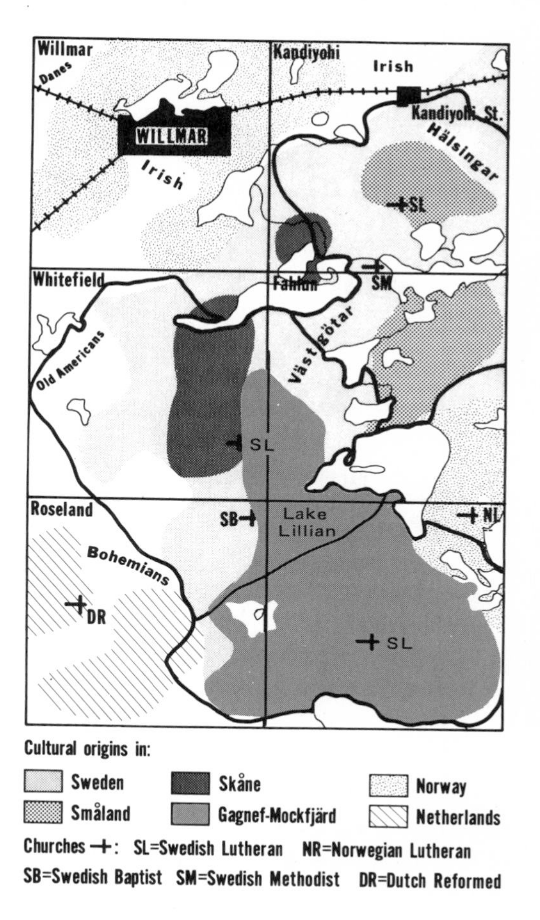

FIG. 3. Settlement areas of main culture groups in the late nineteenth century.

The Settlers

. . . In the early days of settlement the great majority of all households in this area held land. Tenancy was rare, and most of the landless people were young farm and railroad laborers, most of them single, a few with small families. Seldom do any of this group appear in two successive census rolls.[8] Their names are almost never inscribed in the church registers, and one searches in vain for mention of them in the county history. In only a few instances did laborers eventually acquire land and settle down as members of the community. Though few at first, their numbers increased with time and by 1905 probably 20 percent of the area's rural population belonged to this restless group. It is an important and fascinating feature of frontier society, but a shortage of source material makes it difficult to study.

This study will deal exclusively with

8. For nineteenth-century Minnesota manuscripts of the federal census are available for 1860, 1870, and 1880. The 1890 census was destroyed in a fire and use of the one taken in 1900 is highly restricted. A census was also taken by the state at ten-year intervals from 1865 to 1905. All are open to public inspection.

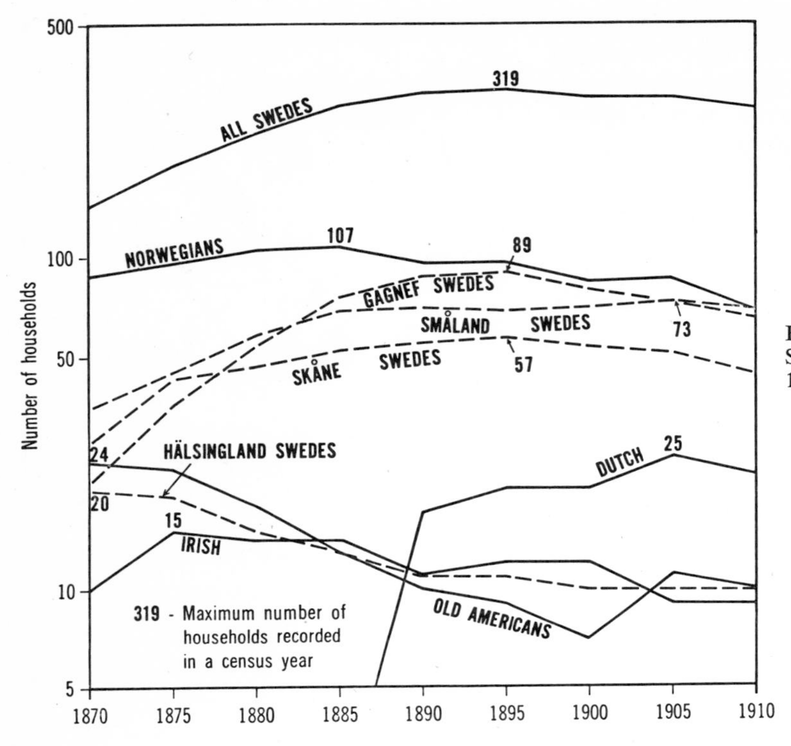

FIG. 4
Size of culture groups, 1870-1910.

those households that held land. Figure 4 shows the relative sizes of the major culture groups over time, expressed in numbers of landholding households. . . . The census has been used to establish the nationality of each household head. Church registers and material from the county history have permitted the identification of provincial and even parish origins for most of the Swedish population.

The total number of households in the area rose steadily to 1895 and then declined as farm size began to increase. Although the Old Americans, Irish, and Norwegians were on the scene early, their relative importance diminished as time went by. As this happened the dominance of the Swedes increased until a large-scale colonization by Dutch settlers began in the Southwest during the late 1880s. The distribution of these groups by the end of the nineteenth century can be seen in Figure 3. Spatial clustering, not only of national but also provincial groups, was pronounced.[9]

The groups varied in their farming

9. The map provides a generalized picture of the distribution of the culture groups. In fact, of course, some intermixture was present. In an earlier study the author devised a measure of ethnic "segregation" based on ownership of the forty acre parcels of land (see Rice, *Patterns of Ethnicity,* pp. 49-56). The measure produces an index which varies from 1.000, representing complete segregation, to 0.000, representing complete integration. When this measure is applied to the entire county of Kandiyohi in 1905, the following results are obtained: Swedes 0.387, Norwegains, 0.375, Dutch 0.525, Bohemians 0.285, Old Americans and Irish 0.288, Swedes from Gagnef–Mockfjärd 0.456, Småland 0.272, Skåne 0.327. Three random distributions of farm families and their land failed to produce an index higher than 0.081, indicating that the groups were segregatetd to a significant degree.

backgrounds and in the paths they traveled on their way to the Kandiyohi prairie. Most of the Old Americans were Yankees with roots in New England. Many had been in Minnesota fifteen or twenty years before they arrived here. They were part of that vanguard of Yankee settlers who in the 1850s had dreamed of making Minnesota the New England of the West. The Irish also had been in Minnesota for some time. Most had been born in the Maritime Provinces of Canada; only the most elderly had come to America from Ireland. . . .

The first Norwegians in the area settled around Lake Lillian in the southeast. They came from the Balsfjorden district south of Tromsø in North Norway and formed a spatially distinct settlement around the lake (much of it outside the study area to the east). By far the largest number of Norwegians, however, settled in the north around Willmar. Among the earliest was a small group from Vinje in Telemark and another from the western fjord district of Hardanger. No strong regionally based communities developed, however, as many of the first settlers moved away and other Norwegians with diverse origins took their place. Most of the Norwegians came from communities in western Wisconsin and had already gained ten or fifteen years of American farming experience before they arrived in Kandiyohi. They were, however, closer to their European past than the Old Americans or Irish. The farming system everywhere in Norway in the nineteenth century was based on the production of hay and livestock. Milk products from cows and goats dominated the diet, and the only bread grain of any importance was barley. . . .

Unlike the Norwegians the Swedes developed several strong regionally based communities. The areas from which these

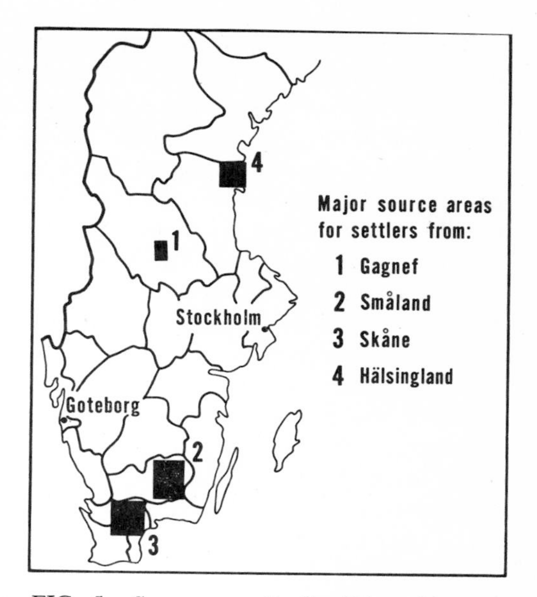

FIG. 5. Source areas for Swedish settlers.

groups came may be seen in Figure 5. The most tightly knit community was the one formed by the people from the Dalarna parish of Gagnef and its chapelry of Mockfjärd. The first families left this forest region in the spring of 1867, and by 1869 a large emigration was underway from the valley of Mockfjärd to the prairies of Kandiyohi. Of major importance in stimulating this movement were the crop failures of 1867–1868, which brought distress to all of northern Europe, but the effect of the "American letters" cannot be overlooked. A note in the county history records that these letters were read and reread, passed from hand to hand until they themselves fell apart, whereupon several copies were often made to be circulated more widely. . . .

While the movement from Gagnef to Kandiyohi was direct, the other three groups considered here came via earlier established Swedish settlements in Illinois and eastern Minnesota. Most of the Småland settlers came from the region of Värend, one of the earliest parts of Sweden to experience "America fever," and therefore they often formed the largest element in the early settlements. These settlements continued to supply settlers for Kandiyohi, but many others arrived directly from Småland in response to letters sent home by friends and relatives. Though people from Värend remained most numerous many Småland families came from other parts of the province.

Skåne, the province to the south of Småland, also provided many of the first emigrants from Sweden. They came mainly from the plain of Kristianstad and forest region of Göinge to the north. Large numbers of these people had settled in Illinois in the 1850s, and it is from these communities that the first Skåne settlers in Kandiyohi seem to have come.

Although located in the north, the province of Hälsingland also experienced an early emigration, largely because of the strength of the nonconformist movement there. Those who came to Kandiyohi had left the valleys of the northeast and made their way first to Illinois. Initially they were well represented among the settlers in the study area, but they failed to develop a major community here. They are included in the following analysis to provide a second northern group for comparative purposes.

Table 1 provides a rough comparison of the farming systems with which these four Swedish groups had been familiar.[10] Like the Norwegians the Gagnef settlers came from an area where arable land was confined to narrow valley bottoms and agriculture was based on livestock, especially cattle, and the use of the summer farm (*fäbod*). Here, too, the marginal nature of the environment forced the farmer to turn to part-time work, frequently the making and hauling of charcoal for the nearby iron industry. In contrast to much of the rest of Sweden the crofter (*torpare*) was absent in Gagnef. Much of Dalarna was traditionally a land of smallholders, although by the middle of the nineteenth century the cottager (*backstugusittare*) was a familiar figure. The emigration tended to be led by the landholding families, however, and more than 80 percent of the Gagnef settlers in Kandiyohi had owned their own farms. These farms were very small as the low grain and milk yields per inhabitant suggest. The effect of the short northern growing season is reflected in the low milk yield per cow.

In most ways the farming system in Hälsingland was similar to that in Ga-

TABLE 1. Some Comparative Aspects of the Farming Systems in Swedish Source Areas

	*Skåne**	*Småland**	*Hälsingland**	*Gagnef**
Crofters per 100 farm units	66.6	71.6	60.6	0.0
Hectares cultivated per 100 inhabitants	98.7	57.4	66.2	42.6
Grain yields per inhabitant (kg)	706	549	274	271
Milk yield per inhabitant (kg)	696	635	524	480
Milk yield per cow (kg)	2,069	1,790	1,516	1,545

* The following districts (*härader*) have been used for each provincial group: Skåne-Villands, Östra and Västra Göinge; Småland-Konga, Norrviddinge, Uppviddinge, Kinnevalds; Hälsing-Forsa, Bergsjö, Delsbo; Gagnef and Mockfjärd together comprised a single district.

10. The figures are based on information in G. Sundbärg, *Emigrationsutredningen* (Stockholm, 1910). They describe the situation at the beginning of the twentieth century, but the regional differences they point up were of long standing.

gnef. The main difference was that crofting was widespread there, and a number of the settlers in Kandiyohi came from this background. Crofters were also present among the immigrants from Skåne and Småland. The milk yield per cow suggests that Småland enjoyed a somewhat better environment than the northern areas. However, farming was unquestionably best in Skåne, especially on the plain of Kristianstad. Even the crofter here could be expected to have had a richer and more varied farming experience than the smallholder from Gagnef.

The Farming System

. . . The census rolls of both 1870 and 1880 show the grip which King wheat had on prairie agriculture in Minnesota at this time. In spite of the fact that the railroad did not reach Willmar until the summer of 1870 and no wheat was shipped out until the following spring, the 1870 census (reporting the situation in 1869) showed that the bulk of the sown area was devoted to this crop. In 1869 the St. Paul and Pacific Railroad Company built grain elevators in both Willmar and Kandiyohi Station. By 1880 three additional elevators and a flour mill had been built in Willmar, and a second elevator had been added in Kandiyohi Station. In spite of the grasshopper plagues which had devastated the county in 1876–1877, wheat was more dominant than ever, occupying 75 percent of the total area tilled. The only other grain of any importance was oats. This was the most widely grown cereal crop in nineteenth-century Scandinavia, but an analysis of the wheat–oat ratio by culture group revealed that the Swedes and Norwegians were growing no more of it than the Old Americans and Irish. It mattered little that the Norwegian or the Swede from Gagnef or Hälsingland had had no experience with wheat at home. Faced with the realities of the market everybody grew it.

The raising of livestock was secondary to wheat farming. Animals were kept largely to supply needs of the family. A little butter, a few eggs, and a fleece or two might be marketed each year, but most of the animal products were consumed at home. In this activity, without a market to dictate terms, people could afford to express their cultural preferences. Table 2 gives a comparative picture of the stock raising practices of the major culture groups in 1870 and 1880. It also shows what was happening in the home areas of the four Swedish groups in 1905.

Draught animals (columns 1 and 2) had more to do with the commercial than with the subsistence side of production, but even here there was opportunity to exercise choice. Both horses and oxen were used for draught in 1870, but oxen were far more numerous. Only among the Old American–Irish and Hälsingland groups were horses relatively important, yet all of the Swedish groups except the one from Småland had strong horse traditions. Between 1870 and 1880 the use of oxen declined dramatically. Cost appears to be the overriding determinant here. In the short run it was cheaper for the new settler to buy a pair of oxen to use while he got his farm started and accumulated a little capital. After a while he could afford to purchase a horse or two which, although individually more expensive, were more suited to the mowing and reaping machinery used at the time. All the groups were making the switch to horses in the 1870s. Oxen remained most important to the settlers from Gagnef, even though they were virtually unknown there, because a steady

TABLE 2. Livestock Raising

	Draught			Non-draught		
	(1) No. of animals/ 100 acres cultivated	(2) % Oxen	(3) No. of animal units/100 acres cultivated*	(4) % Cattle	(5) % Sheep	(6) % Swine
			Kandiyohi: 1870			
Old Americans and Irish	9.7	56.7	11.8	93.2	1.6	5.2
Norwegians	9.6	78.1	26.6	94.1	4.1	1.8
Swedes from:						
Skåne	11.4	78.9	13.3	89.6	3.9	6.5
Småland	8.2	91.5	10.9	90.2	6.1	3.7
Hälsingland	13.0	46.9	20.7	88.5	6.8	4.7
Gagnef	10.4	83.7	21.1	95.0	4.9	3.1
			Kandiyohi: 1880			
Old Americans and Irish	4.9	6.1	10.3	91.0	2.6	6.4
Norwegians	6.4	23.4	18.0	90.7	6.8	2.5
Swedes from:						
Skåne	5.1	2.0	16.2	89.0	8.1	2.9
Småland	6.4	25.0	18.6	88.1	7.4	4.5
Hälsingland	9.7	6.2	23.0	89.0	6.1	3.9
Gagnef	9.3	39.8	21.8	90.0	7.2	3.9
			Sweden: 1905†			
Swedes in:						
Skåne	8.4	5.4	32.4	69.7	2.9	27.4
Småland	14.5	68.1	50.4	87.0	5.6	7.4
Hälsingland	7.1	0.9	37.3	89.4	6.2	4.4
Gagnef	7.2	0.0	39.0	90.9	3.0	6.1

* Animal units have been calculated in the way used by the Swedish Bureau of Statistics (Statistika Centralbyrån) 1 cow = 10 sheep = 4 swine

† Data are from G. Sundbärg, *Emigrationsutredningen* (Stockholm, 1910). The districts used for each provincial group are listed in the footnote to Table 1.

flow of new immigrants continued to arrive directly from that parish throughout the decade.

Column 3 in the table relates the number of nondraught animals to the total area cultivated and thus provides a measure of the relative importance of cropping and livestock raising. The three different kinds of animals have been reduced to a common "animal unit" through the use of a standard formula (see footnote to table). The greater emphasis placed on livestock by the three North Scandinavian groups in 1870 agrees well with the farming backgrounds of these people. On the other hand the settlers from Småland have not preserved this trait. By 1880 the overall importance of animals has risen slightly and all the Scandinavian groups stand out strongly as livestock raisers in contrast to the Old Americans and Irish.

Columns 4–6 show the relative importance of cattle, sheep and swine for each group. Cattle were of overwhelming importance for all groups in both years. It is in the relative emphasis on sheep versus swine that one must look for cultural preferences to surface. Of all the groups the Swedes from Skåne had the greatest experience with swine. That experience is reflected, albeit weakly, in the 1870 pattern, but it has vanished in 1880. The groups from Hälsingland and Småland came from traditions in which sheep had been important, and again that shows up in the 1870 figures. The Norwegian preference for sheep over swine can also be linked easily to their previous experience. By 1880 all the Scandinavians once again stand together—this time as sheep raisers—in contrast to the Old Americans and Irish for whom swine were clearly more important.

The reasons why farmers chose particular activities may, of course, also be sought in the environment. . . . The southeastern part of the area is especially flat and until the turn of the century remained poorly drained (cf. Figs. 1 and 6). Land suitable for cultivation was therefore limited while meadow and rough pasture were in abundance. The high concentration of sheep here fits particularly well the picture of a marginal environment. Grain growing was more intensively practiced on the better drained lands of the north and west, the greatest specialization in wheat occurring where these lands approached the rail line.[11] . . .

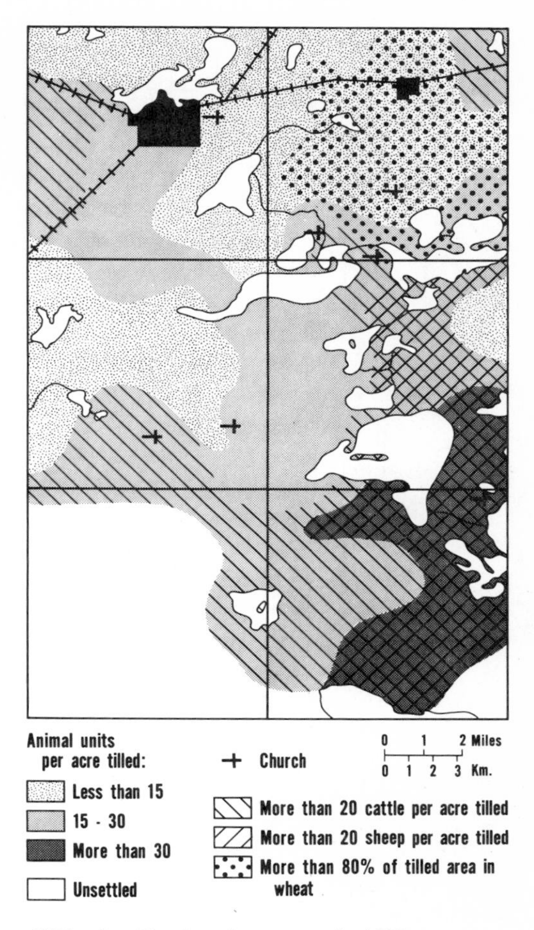

FIG. 6. The farming system in 1879.

Between 1880 and 1900 the farming system in Kandiyohi County began to change. The dominance of wheat slackened as farmers experimented with other crops and turned increasingly to livestock raising. In the first decade of the twentieth century the pace of change was dramatic. Wheat acreage fell from 71 percent of the total area cultivated in 1900 to 37 percent in 1910. Substantial gains were made by corn, oats, and barley. By 1910 there were twice as many cattle per farm as there had been in 1880. Butter production had increased by 70 percent and most was now being marketed. With the expanding urban market in the Twin Cities area and the consequent increase in land values, the zone of

11. Around Willmar wheat did not occupy a very high percentage of the total area tilled because much of this area seems to have remained unsown in 1879. This was a time in which the town was expanding rapidly, and the lack of cropping calls to mind Sinclair's argument that anticipation of urban encroachment reduces the intensity of agricultural land use. R. Sinclair, "Von Thünen and urban sprawl," *Annals of the Association of American Geographers* 57 (1967): 72-87. Conzen made the same observation on the urban fringe of nineteenth-century Madison. M. P. Conzen, *Frontier Farming in an Urban Shadow* (Madison, Wis., 1971), p. 96.

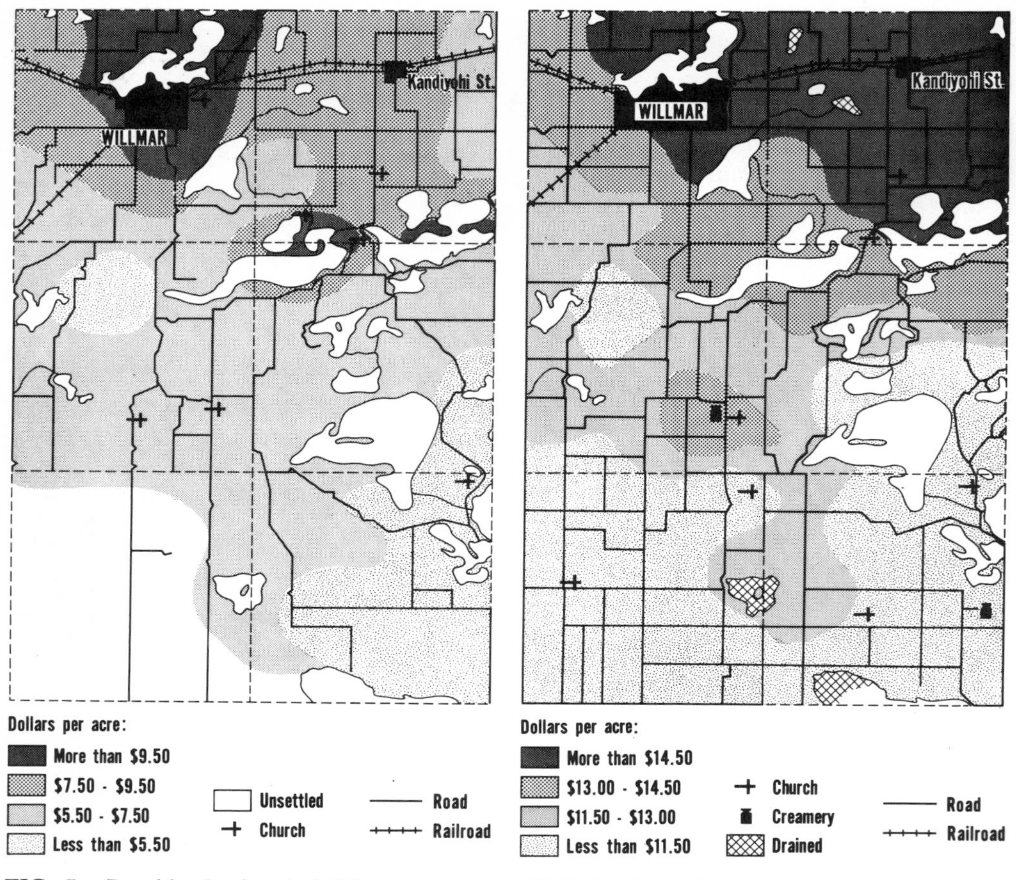

FIG. 7. Rural land values in 1880.

FIG. 8. Rural land values in 1910.

extensive wheat production was moving quickly out of Minnesota and diversified farming was taking its place. The trend in the study area was similar to that in the county as a whole. . . . We do not have the data to trace our culture groups through this agricultural revolution, but it seems fair to assume that they differed little in their responses to it.

Economic Status

In this study economic status has been measured in terms of wealth in real property. The source materials used are the real estate tax lists compiled each year and kept in the county courthouse. . . .

The tax assessors seemed to have had three criteria in mind as they made their judgments. One was certainly distance from Willmar and the rail line. Figures 7 and 8 show clearly the tendency for land values to decrease with increasing distance to market. The second was the quality of the land. A comparison with the map of the environment in Figure 1 shows, for example, that the poorly drained level land in the southeast was still given a low value in 1910 even though it had been farmed thirty or forty years. The third criterion seems to have been intensity of land use. This is not readily apparent from the maps because of the way in which they have been constructed, but to test for it the value of homesteaded land was compared with the value of railroad land in Kandiyohi Township for both 1880 and 1910.[12] Since homestead land was found in even-numbered sections and railroad land in odd-numbered sections there could be no systematic difference between the two in either quality or distance from market. The only difference is that, since homestead land was taken first, it had been cultivated for a longer period of time and was normally the site of the farm buildings. Railroad land was purchased later and added to the farm cores developed on the homestead land. The difference in land use intensity is reflected in the per acre values—$7.75 versus $7.20 in 1880, $16.55 versus $15.33 in 1910. In each case the value of railroad land is just under 93 percent of homestead land. . . .

Others who have looked at the question of economic status have found it to be closely linked to persistence.[13] The longer a family stays in an area the wealthier it becomes, so that in a given year those who have been resident for the longest time should, *ceteris paribus,* be among the best off. Tables 3 and 4 show that this was the case here. In Table 3, for each of the years studied, "newcomers," those who arrived during the previous decade, are compared with "old residents," those who had been in the area for more than ten years.

12. The maps were prepared by calculating the average value for moving four-square-mile cells. This technique was employed to smooth out the irregularities introduced by the checkerboard pattern of land alienation.
13. See, for example, Curti, *Making of an American Community,* pp. 65-77, and Conzen, *Frontier Farming,* pp. 125-41.

TABLE 3. Median Value of Taxable Real Estate ($)

	1880	1890	1900	1910
Old residents	910	1,118	1,228	2,518
Newcomers	733	620	911	1,969

TABLE 4. Median Value of Taxable Real Estate ($)

	1880*-90	1890*-1900	1900*-10
Stayers	881	963	1,167
Leavers	688	660	996

* Wealth at the beginning of the period.

The higher property values of the established households are evident. Table 4 compares the real wealth of those households which persisted through each of the three decades between 1880 and 1910 with that of the ones which did not. Not only did one do better by staying longer, one also elected to stay longer if one was doing better.

Other studies have also pointed out that persistence may be related to community cohesion.[14] The social atmosphere produced in a rural church-centered community, particularly where the population derives largely from the same province in Europe, is conducive to putting down roots and inhibits rapid population turnover. This kind of "rural neighborhood" is thus viewed as a community of a quasi "Gemeinschaft" type. To try to separate this effect on persistence from the effect of wealth the following analysis was performed. For each of the four observation years all landholding households were ranked by property value and then divided into five equal groups (quintiles). The persistence rates for the households in each quintile were then calculated for

14. Rice, *Patterns of Ethnicity,* and Ostergren, "Cultural homogeneity."

TABLE 5. Decennial Rates of Persistence by Quintile* (percentage of households remaining)

	1	2	3	4	5
1880-1890	84.0	74.0	75.3	66.7	60.6
1890-1900	83.1	87.5	77.5	73.0	60.2
1900-1910	80.7	76.4	80.7	70.8	64.8

* Quintiles are numbered in descending order of wealth.

TABLE 6. Decennial Persistence Indices for Selected Groups 1880-1910

	1880-1890	1890-1900	1900-1910
Old American and Irish	0.65	0.89	1.12
Norwegians	0.83	0.84	0.87
Swedes from:			
Gagnef	1.36	1.21	1.04
Småland	1.23	1.17	1.14
Skåne	1.07	1.09	1.01
Other Provinces	1.00	1.00	1.04

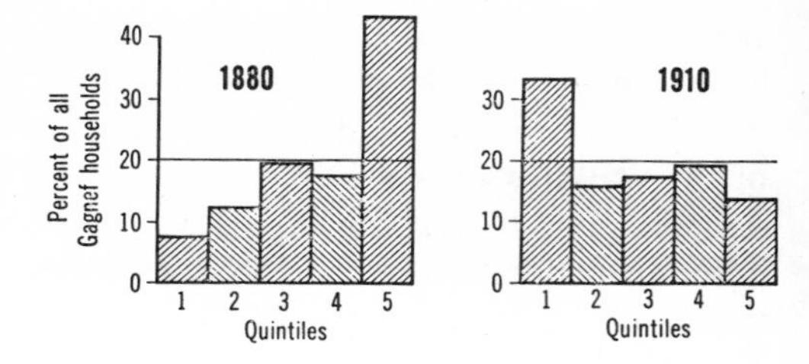

FIG. 9. Economic betterment of Gagnef households, 1880-1910.

each of the three decades.[15] The results are shown in Table 5.

For each of the culture groups these rates were applied to the number of households in each quintile and an expected persistence was calculated. The expected persistence was then related to the observed persistence to produce the indices shown in Table 6. A ratio of more than one indicates a greater persistence than expected. The three Swedish regional groups stand in strong contrast to the Norwegians and the Old Americans and Irish, especially during the first two decades. The indices for the Gagnef group are especially high. Among the Swedes, those from "other provinces," i.e. a group known to have diverse origins, demonstrate the lowest indices.

These findings seem to lend support to the hypothesis that community cohesion promotes persistence. They also suggest that, since persistence promotes the accumulation of wealth, community cohesion may be an important factor in determining economic status. The improvement made by the Gagnef households between 1880 and 1910 is striking (Fig. 9). From a situation in which over 40 percent of the households were in the fifth quintile they moved to one in which 35 percent were in the first quintile. No other group improved so dramatically. Strong persistence in spite of initially low economic status is probably an important reason.

Economic advancement might, however, be related to factors other than length of residence. To eliminate the effect of different persistence rates two Gagnef cohorts were compared with similar cohorts from Småland and Skåne. The cohorts consist of households which persisted to the end of the study period, in one case from 1870, in the other from 1880. . . . Initially both Gagnef cohorts ranked quite low. This group came directly from Sweden to Kandiyohi County and had had no intervening time in North America during which to accumulate some capital as had many of the settlers from Småland and Skåne. Their rate of economic progress is remarkable, however, especially that of the 1880-1910 cohort. This was a tightly knit, much interrelated population. It may be that once the community was established its mem-

15. A household is regarded as continuing after the death of its head if ownership of the farm passes to another related household member.

bers gained benefit from the mutual aid and support it fostered and were thus able to overtake the less cohesive groups from Småland and Skåne. . . .

The question of whether people were better off for having emigrated to America is an especially difficult one to answer. This kind of an appraisal is complex and economic status is but one factor. Nevertheless, if we accept the premise that economic advancement was the prime motivation of most emigrants, it seems reasonable to measure their success in these economic terms. For the Gagnef settlers on the Kandiyohi prairie there can be little question about absolute betterment. The 1910 tax records reveal that on the average they had 257 acres (104 ha) of farm property. If the portion cultivated was the same as for the county as a whole (79.8 percent) they would have had 205 acres (83 ha) in that category compared with only 6.5 acres (2.6 ha) for their friends and relatives who stayed behind.

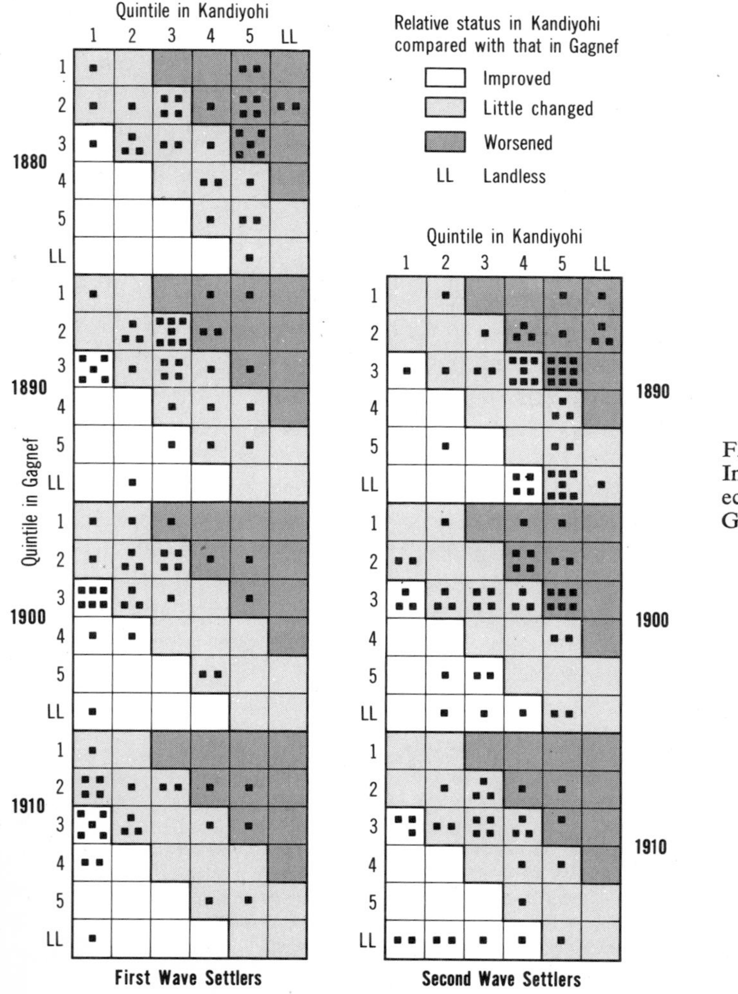

FIG. 10
Improvement in relative economic status of Gagnef households.

Nor could the alluvial soils of the Dal River valley compare with the rich black earth of the Kandiyohi prairie, a few dry years and grasshoppers notwithstanding. . . .

Another way to view economic status is in relation to other members of the same society. To be on top of the pile in Gagnef was probably a different experience from being somewhere in the middle in Kandiyohi. A picture of the changes in the economic status of Gagnef settlers which took place over time is given in Figure 10. The rows locate each settler in the economic order he left behind. The columns give the position he achieved in his new home. The progress the settlers made may be followed from decade to decade. Of the thirty-five first-wave settlers, fourteen were relatively worse off in 1880 than they had been before they left while one had improved his position. By 1910 of the twenty-five settlers remaining just three were not as well off, while eight had bettered their lot substantially. The same trend is apparent for the second-wave settlers. In economic terms, at least, the move to Minnesota brought positive results, both absolutely and relatively, to most of the Gagnef settlers.

The farming frontier in nineteenth-century America was a more complex place than Frederick Jackson Turner made it out to be. Certainly the opportunity to succeed was there for anyone who wished to seize it. But the settlers did bring their cultural heritage with them and, especially where people from the same district built strong church-centered communities, it could have an effect on the decisions people made. It is hard to find evidence that cultural biases led people to make decisions which did not make sense from an economic point of view. One did not choose to grow oats when wheat was what the market demanded. Perhaps it was not cultural identity so much as the community which grew out of that identity which had an impact on economic behavior. The frontier experience of the Gagnef settler in his close-knit community transplanted from the valleys of Dalarna certainly seems to have been different from that of his neighbor from New England, or Norway, or even Skåne.

The Cotton Frontier of the Antebellum South: A Methodological Battleground / *Morton Rothstein*

. . . The American cotton frontier had its roots in a long-standing commitment among the southern mainland colonies to staple production, plantation organization, and a slave labor force. Insofar as these colonies concentrated on the large-scale production of tobacco, rice, indigo, and sugar, they shared in a major form of economic development in the Western Hemisphere. From the sixteenth through the eighteenth centuries, that development depended on the utilization of European capital and organizing energy and the forced mobility of an African labor force for the commercial exploitation of untapped land resources. Philip Curtin systematically examined the slave trade, and his evidence drastically revises our knowledge of its extent. He places the cumulative total of African slaves brought to the New World within an upper limit of nine million. Another recent study, by Kenneth W. Stetson, shows that the importation of slaves to the British colonies, both in the Caribbean and on the mainland, was less than 1,500,000 between 1700 and 1773, and that the mainland's share was less than 20 percent of the British total. Moreover, there is no evidence of an increase in the share of the North American mainland in the slave trade after the colonies won their independence.[1]

These findings suggest that the colonies which established themselves as the United States were relatively marginal participants in the overarching economic relationships between Europe and all the plantation systems that flourished throughout the tropical and semitropical regions of the Americas. From the outset, there were sharp differences between staple production in the North American colonies and those in the rest of the hemisphere, differences that persisted and were elemental in shaping the later cotton frontier. On the British North American mainland, the indigenous Indian population was pushed aside rather than incorporated into the main societal body, even at the fringes. The majority of white settlers were individual landowners who did not own slaves, the barriers to entry into agriculture apparently remained low, and there was a relatively high natural increase in the slave population compared with rates in other plantation economies. Staple production was no less oriented toward the European market, but it was conducted on a frontier which was an amalgam of numerous small farmsteads, a few large slave plantations, and many gradations in between.[2]

1. Curtin has published results of one aspect of his study in "Epidemiology and the Slave Trade," *Political Science Quarterly* 83 (June 1968):190-216. On the British slave trade, see Kenneth W. Stetson, "A Quantitative Approach to Britain's American Slave Trade, 1700-1773" (Master's thesis, University of Wisconsin, 1967).

2. For a systematic treatment of a southern re-

Reproduced (with omissions) by permission from *Agricultural History* 44 (1970):149-65.

However, there are some astonishing gaps in our knowledge about the colonial South. We do not have enough reliable information on the extent of staple output or how it compared quantitatively and qualitatively with the output of the same commodities in the rest of the Western Hemisphere. The colonial South had a later start as a commercial frontier than the Caribbean or Brazil, but was it really gaining ground as we assume? If so, at what approximate rate? We do not yet know enough about the differences between plantations in the colonial South and those in the rest of the hemisphere to explain fully the striking contrasts in slave mortality. Nor do we have enough intensive studies of land distribution–including such matters as the price of land and its relationship to the pace of settlement or to changes in European demand for commodities. Data do exist in wills, tax reports, and other documents in county and state archives that would help us fill these gaps.

An outstanding characteristic of the eighteenth-, as well as the nineteenth-century plantation frontier, was its expansionist tendency–the increasing proclivity of settlers to move their slaves and their capital into new, contiguous areas of the continental land mass in the quest for better opportunities for commercial production. Reinforcing that trend, which had carried the occupation of new lands across the southern piedmont to the Appalachian valleys by the time of the Revolution, was the succession of changes that took place in the last quarter of the century. Political independence thrust staple growers outside the shelter of a formal colonial relationship into the different and perhaps more hazardous economic environment of an informal colonial status. Gone were the advantages of direct subsidies and indirect protection that had encouraged production of hemp, rice, indigo, and other items. Marked geographic shifts in tobacco production were already underway, and more of it may have been moving into the hands of individual proprietorships. These are impressions. As yet we have no systematic treatment of the impact of the Revolution on agriculture in any of the older districts of the South that furnishes empirical support for them.[3]

On the other hand, there is no doubt about the striking growth of cotton production. It expanded with remarkable speed until it became the predominant fact of economic life across much of the broad southern prairies and alluvial districts from the Carolinas to Texas. Within a dozen years after the cotton gin removed the major constraint on feasible commercial output of short-staple varieties, the United States was producing almost a tenth of the world's cotton supply. By the 1820s, it was the world's largest producer and also surpassed all other Western Hemisphere nations in the number of slaves.[4] Nowhere else was there

---

gion in the colonial period, see Aubrey C. Land, "Economic Base and Social Structure: The Northern Chesapeake in the Eighteenth Century," *Journal of Economic History* 25 (December 1965):639-54.

3. For an example of what might be done in measuring the response of a single frontier subregion to the changes brought by the Revolution, see Robert D. Mitchell, *Commercialism and Frontier: Perspectives on the Early Shenandoah Valley* (Charlottesville: University Press of Virginia, 1977).

4. Stuart Bruchey has assembled a useful series of tables on the cotton trade, along with a good, representative collection of materials related to the North thesis, in his *Cotton and the Growth of the American Economy, 1790-1860: Sources and Readings* (Baltimore: Johns Hopkins University Press, 1967). For comparative data on the demography of races, and mixtures thereof, in the Western Hemisphere, see the authoritative work by Angel Rosenblatt, *La poblacion*

such a strong and resilient response to European demand for raw cotton, and the expansion continued until the United States accounted for more than two-thirds of total world output. In terms of size of crop, number of producing units, number of forced laborers, the American Southland achieved the dubious distinction of being the preeminent plantation economy of its time. The general outlines of this development are reasonably clear and familiar. The complex and interacting factors by which the response was established are less firmly connected. . . .

. . . Did the nonslaveholding majority of southern farmers confront more restricted economic opportunities than their northern counterparts because of the presence and growth of slave plantations? The more heavily capitalized sugar and rice plantations that made up about a quarter of the slaveholdings in the United States were located on the coastal fringes of the region, in areas where most other forms of crop cultivation presumably had little comparative advantage, and thus were less in conflict with a system of nonslaveholding pioneer families. Cotton was different. Though production may have been less efficient on small individual units than on plantations, it did yield a cash crop and required comparatively small capital inputs. The small cotton grower who did not own a gin or press could usually have his crop prepared for market in the facilities of a wealthier neighbor. But did these small producers participate in the market economy in a meaningful sense? How large a proportion of their income did they derive from cotton crops? How large was their share of total output? We now know, for example, that plantation units with fifty slaves or more in Georgia, Alabama, Mississippi, and Louisiana produced more than one-third of the 1859 crop in the four states on less than one-fourth of the improved acreage.[5]

James Foust, using the data from the Parker-Gallman sample, provides us with a much more intensive analysis of production and wealth as functions of unit size and slaveholdings for 1849 and 1859. His work demonstrates that the number of farms on which there were no slaves was much larger in the upland regions of the newly settled South (the states west of Georgia) in 1849 and that they increased their proportion during the next decade, accounting for about half the total number of farms. This is a strong support for the point that the large slaveholders were not pushing the yeomen farmers out of the southern agricultural economy. Yet his evidence also indicates that the units containing twenty or more slaves in the older states of the South and in the alluvial districts of the cotton frontier account for an increasing proportion of total cotton output. More than half the cotton crop in the sample came from these units; in the case of the alluvial areas they accounted for virtually 85 percent by 1859. Such intensive studies, pursued with greater caution and rigor than was possible for either Owsley or Linden, will give us more of the specific answers we need before we can tell whether the large plantations crowded out the small farmer.[6]

Although there is an impressive litera-

indigena y el mestizaje en America (Buenos Aires: S. A. Nova, 1954).

5. Joseph K. Menn, "The Large Slaveholders of the Deep South, 1860" (Ph.D. diss., University of Texas, 1964), pp. 35-38.

6. Frank L. Owsley, *Plain Folk of the Old South* (Baton Rouge: Louisiana University Press, 1949); Fabian Linden, "Economic Democracy in the Slave South: An Appraisal of Some Recent Views," *Journal of Negro History* 31 (1946) 140-89; James D. Foust, *The Yeoman Farmer and Westward Expansion of United States Cotton Production* (New York: Arno Press, 1975).

ture on the elite minority of very large slaveholders, there is still uncertainty as to whether they dominated the cotton frontier in any sense: political, economic, or social. Genovese has revitalized Phillips's contention that they did in fact so dominate and has placed the interpretation of the South as a neofeudal, precapitalist society within a sophisticated neo-Marxist framework.[7] Yet the relatively cohesive social groups of the largest planters in the Louisiana-Mississippi delta region and the Black Belt of Alabama seem to have lost much of their political influence by the 1830s. There is even less support for the notion that planters had frozen themselves into an anticapitalist stance and were lacking in entrepreneurial drive. The most successful slaveholders engaged in a broad range of economic activity in addition to raising staple crops. They were also mining magnates, builders and promoters of transportation facilities, bankers, factory owners, speculators in urban real estate, and merchants.

Many of the planters who were not successful enough to do more than run plantations nevertheless undertook their endeavors in the expectation of quick profits. No one who has read the plantation correspondence of individuals who started anew on the frontier to undertake cotton growing can fail to be impressed by the importance in their thinking of the chance for large, short-run returns. The very South Carolina elite who participated in the expansion of the cotton frontier viewed settlers farther west as "grasping" and "money-mad." As in almost all economic analysis, motivation is an imponderable that must remain subsumed under assumptions about rational self-interest. If the southern frontier environment warped that self-interest in any way, it was probably in the direction of shortening the time horizons of slaveholders. Pervading much of the private discussion about future expectations was a fear that death and natural disasters would wipe away all long-run considerations. Mortality rates among both whites and blacks may have compared very favorably with those in tropical plantation economies, but still seem impressively higher than those of the rest of the United States. By far the most common query in southern correspondence was, "Is your district healthy?" i.e., free from cholera and yellow fever.[8]

Rather than pursuing the feudal or precapitalist analogue, it might be fruitful to reexamine the ways in which the cotton frontier resembled or differed from the structure of plantation economies in the rest of the world. If there was a marked dualism on that frontier between diffused small family farms and a plantation system based on large-scale use of slave

7. Eugene D. Genovese, *The Political Economy of Slavery: Studies in the Economy and Society of the Slave South* (New York: Pantheon, 1966); Ulrich B. Phillips, *Life and Labor in the Old South* (New York: Grosset and Dunlap, 1929).

8. The fear of death, combined with strong kinship ties, often induced planters to transfer title to part of their holdings long before they actually relinquished the management of the property. Nor did they forego the profits. The result is another distortion, among many, in the manuscript census data so basic to studies of the cotton frontier. For example, Stephen Duncan, one of the wealthiest planters in the South during the 1850s, was in the process of transferring $500,000 in various assets to the estates of each of his six children when the Civil War broke out. Compare, too, the inventory of holdings by Edward McGehee, another Mississippi plantation magnate, with his listings in the 1850 and 1860 census schedules. (See the Stephen Duncan Papers and McGehee Collection, Louisiana State University.) For a further discussion of problems in the census data, see Barnes F. Lathrop, *Migration into East Texas, 1835-1860* (Austin: University of Texas Press, 1949); and my article, "The Antebellum South as a Dual Economy: A Tentative Hypothesis, *Agricultural History* 41 (October 1967):373-82.

labor, was it not somewhat akin in functional terms to the "dual economies" observed elsewhere? To be sure, the dichotomy in the South was primarily between competing forms of commercialized agriculture rather than an antagonism between "new" and "traditional" forms of economic activity. But a modified version of the concept can provide a useful starting point from which to analyze manageable parts of the cotton economy in greater depth.

Some of the issues raised thus far about the production side of the cotton frontier may be beyond our power to resolve, but to the degree that we do find answers we will come closer to sound judgments about the vitality of the southern economy. According to Richard Easterlin's estimates, and the modifications by Stanley Engerman, the South's share of the nation's income in 1840 and 1860, measured in per capita terms, was impressively higher than was that of the northern frontier during the same period.[9] Moreover, there is no good reason to believe that, because the vanguard of cotton planters had reached the apparent geographic limits for cultivating the crop, the system was in jeopardy. Yet even if we are persuaded by recent discussions that the cotton frontier was profitable for planters, viable for the region, and produced wealth in amounts that compared favorably with other regions in the United States, the record of other plantation areas in modern times must leave many of us unconvinced that, apart from the question of slavery, the commitment to staple commodity production for export could lead anywhere but to disaster. The Easterlin figures, as he has warned us, are but crude approximations based on frail evidence. Further tests of these estimates and, perhaps more meaningful, some calculations about the extent to which the distribution of southern income may or may not have been unusually skewed might be more convincing and would assuredly offer a fruitful challenge to the ingenuity of the quantifiers.

The methods used to investigate the various aspects of production on the cotton frontier have sometimes been unsatisfactory, unimaginative, and neglectful of available materials. If this is not so much the case with matters related to demand, especially the external relationships linking the producer to the overseas market, it is primarily because there have been fewer investigations into these matters. One can search the general literature in vain for adequate discussions of transportation, marketing, or banking as they were related to the spread of cotton culture. Only a few southern towns and ports have been favored with anything more than loose, antiquarian descriptions for the period when they were serving the commercial needs of the Cotton Kingdom. Not surprisingly, therefore, some of the more interesting work in progress or published within the last five years, employing either institutional or quantitative methods, lies in these areas.

To the extent that the cotton frontier was oriented toward external markets the occupation and utilization of land in the region was largely a function of existing or anticipated transportation facilities. The early settlers in any region almost invariably located themselves near navigable waterways and later turned to overland transportation to reinforce their initial advantages in access to markets. These facilities were less subject to seasonal constraints than in the North, though floods and dry spells often inter-

9. Stanley L. Engerman, "The Effects of Slavery upon the Southern Economy: A Review of the Recent Debate," *Explorations in Entrepreneurial History*, Ser. 2, 4 (Winter 1967):71-97.

rupted service at the height of the shipping season. Louis Hunter's classic account provides much descriptive information about the impact of steamboats on shipping cotton, and historical geographers have given us several interesting attempts to map the region's antebellum transportation and trading routes. But no economic historian has yet surpassed the insights derived from traditional methods and sources that Ulrich B. Phillips offered in his work on the eastern cotton belt of more than fifty years ago.[10] The need for further work along these lines for the Gulf states is obvious.

Insofar as the majority of historians have handled the commercial relationships of cotton planters at all, they have tended to emphasize the complaints of the producers and have looked at those relationships primarily from an agrarian slant. To be sure, the detailed institutional and business histories, such as Robert G. Albion's work on the shipping trade, Ralph Hidy's study of the Barings, and Thomas P. Govan's pieces on banking, have contained useful corrective elements.[11] New and detailed studies of banking in Louisiana and Mississippi now underway by George Green, Irene Neu, Julius Bentley, and Robert Roeder promise to enlighten us further.[12] Woodman's recent study of cotton factorage, the first full-length treatment of the institutional features of the cotton trade, tells us more about the organization and functions of merchants in the interior towns than was previously available, but skims the surface on the complexities of business at the seaports.[13]

Further patient sifting through the voluminous mercantile records can tell us more about the mechanisms by which the frontier regions were drawn into the commercial nexus. From the beginning, merchant shipping houses established direct connections with the most remote parts of the cotton frontier. Members of several British importing firms were making annual visits to the Charleston and Natchez hinterlands from the first decade of the nineteenth century.[14] When the district around Huntsville, Alabama, was thrown open to settlement during the boom that ended in 1819, Alexander Brown & Sons provided funds to an agent there for the purchase of cotton. Indeed, by the late

10. Louis C. Hunter, *Steamboats on the Western Rivers* (Cambridge, Mass.: Harvard University Press, 1949); F. V. Emerson, "Geographic Influences in American Slavery," *American Geographical Society Bulletin* 43 (January-March 1911); Joseph A. Hazel, "The Geography of Negro Agricultural Slavery in Alabama, Florida, and Mississippi" (Ph.D. diss., Columbia University, 1963); Sam B. Hilliard, *Hog Meat and Hoecake: Food Supply in the Old South, 1840-1860* (Carbondale: Southern Illinois University Press, 1972); Ulrich B. Phillips, *A History of Transportation in the Eastern Cotton Belt to 1860* (New York: Columbia University Press, 1908).

11. Robert G. Albion, *The Rise of New York Port* (New York: Scribner's, 1939) and *Square Riggers on Schedule* (Princeton: Princeton University Press, 1938); Ralph Hidy, *The House of Baring in American Trade and Finance* (Cambridge, Mass.: Harvard University Press, 1949); Thomas P. Govan, "Banking and the Credit System in Georgia, 1810-1860," *Journal of Southern History* 4 (May 1938):164-84.

12. George D. Green, *Finance and Economic Development in the Old South: Louisiana Banking, 1804-1861* (Stanford: Stanford University Press, 1972); Irene D. Neu, "Edmond Jean Forstall and Louisiana Banking," *Explorations in Economic History* 7 (1970) 383-98; Julius M. Bentley, Jr., "Financial Institutions and Economic Development in Mississippi: 1809-1860" (Ph.D. diss.; Tulane University, 1969); Robert E. Roeder, "Merchants of Antebellum New Orleans" *Explorations in Entrepreneurial History* 10 (1958) 113-22.

13. Harold D. Woodman, *King Cotton and His Retainers* (Lexington: University of Kentucky Press, 1968).

14. See the Minor Family and Mary Ker Papers, Southern Historical Collection, University of North Carolina; Butler and Farrar Family Papers, Louisiana State University.

1820s and early 1830s, that firm was reputedly financing about half of the South's cotton trade, though it gradually withdrew from direct involvement after the mid-1840s.[15] Bolton, Ogden & Co. of Liverpool, the largest British importers of cotton during the early 1830s, had a partnership with a long-established New York firm and extensive correspondence with all the major southern ports.[16] The relationships of these firms with the cotton economy remain largely unexplored.

A critical element in the profits of these firms, for example, lay in their ability to obtain favorable rates of currency exchange for themselves and the large planters with whom they dealt directly. Since the firms held credits at southern ports, in New York or Philadelphia, and in western Europe, they could take advantage of the constant fluctuations in exchange rates by converting those credits, or transferring them, at the most promising time and place. With premiums for exchange sometimes ranging as high as 10 percent on gross amounts, the planter who was able to maintain credits in several markets could obtain far greater returns on his cotton sales than the planter with debits or minimal balances on the merchant's books. Letters between planters and merchants contain few matters that received greater and more constant attention than exchange rates and the transfer of funds to optimal advantage.[17] Yet if this was a crucial feature of the monetary system within which the cotton frontier expanded, it remained virtually *terra incognita* among students of southern economic institutions.

There has been more of a critique of existing literature and an agenda for future research in this discussion than a detailed examination of methodology. In part, this is because the previous work on the cotton frontier has, more than almost any other feature of American economic history, suffered grievously from distortions and misconceptions. Too often, the sweeping generalizations of the scholars who used traditional methods have covered a flimsy empirical base, but we would lose too much sensitivity to the complexity of change and its institutional framework by abandoning those methods. The new methods of quantitative research have proved devastating critical weapons but in only a few cases thus far have they added much substantive knowledge. It is, of course, better to be ignorant than to know something that is not so, but the new techniques can be put to better use in handling the increasing amounts of data being dredged from the sources. If I am right in the contention that the current generation of traditional economic historians is emerging from some of the blind alleys into which a repellent intellectual climate led them, why use the new methods to prove that those alleys were blind? Too much basic work remains to be done before we can reach a better understanding of the subject. The value of that work will depend less on differences in methodology than on the relevance and analytical power of the questions we ask.

15. Thanks to the efforts of Bennett Wall, the Alexander Brown & Sons Papers are preserved in the Library of Congress, but few scholars have consulted them. Stuart Bruchey includes examples of their correspondence in *Cotton and the Growth of the American Economy*.

16. The papers of the New York branch, an extremely voluminous collection, are housed in the New York Historical Society as the major part of the Ogden, Day & Successors Collection.

17. For especially illuminating discussions of this subject between planters and merchants, see the business correspondence in the Leverich Family Collection, New York Historical Society, and the Charles P. Leverich Papers, Mississippi Department of Archives, Jackson, Mississippi.

The Imprint of the Upper and Lower South on Mid-Nineteenth-Century Texas / *Terry G. Jordan*

Yeoman and Planter Within the Antebellum South

It has long been recognized that a fundamental twofold social and economic division existed within the pre–Civil War South, a dichotomy that has commonly found expression in the terms "Upper South" and "Lower South." As the southern economy was dominated by agriculture, it is to be expected that the major differences between the Lower and Upper South pertained to farming.

The Lower South, which by 1860 encompassed almost the entirety of the Gulf and Atlantic Coastal Plains (Fig. 1), was a land of cotton and slavery, a land dominated economically by the plantation type of agriculture. . . . Not until after the American Revolution did the economy of the Lower South become linked to cotton. Largely under the impetus provided by this single crop, the areal extent of the Lower South was rapidly expanded, involving a great surge westward out of the colonial Tidewater bases, across the Gulf Plains, and beyond the Mississippi River. Only a little over half a century was required to complete the spread from the Atlantic seaboard states to the pine forests of eastern Texas.

In contrast, the Upper South was primarily the domain of the slaveless yeoman farmer, an area largely devoid of cotton and the other subtropical cash crops. Grains, especially corn and wheat, formed the backbone of the rural economy, supplemented in certain areas by tobacco and hemp. The cultural-economic origins of the Upper South were quite different from those of the adjacent Lower South. It was, above all, a child of southeastern Pennsylvania, the single most important colonial core area in America, from which the agricultural traits that were to shape much of the nation were diffused. . . . The westward expansion of the Upper South began earlier than that of the Lower South, with yeomen penetrating Tennessee and Kentucky even before the Revolution. . . . In the nineteenth century, much of Missouri and Arkansas was added to the domain of the Upper South (Fig. 1).

. . . There were . . . numerous slaveless yeomen to be found in the antebellum Lower South, just as there were select areas within the Upper South where the slave plantation had taken root, most notably the Nashville and Bluegrass basins.[1] Nevertheless, the generalization of a slave-cotton Lower South and a yeo-

1. See, for example, F. L. Owsley, *Plain Folk of the Old South* (Baton Rouge: Louisiana State University Press, 1949).

Reproduced (with omissions) by permission from the *Annals,* Association of American Geographers, 57 (1967):667-90. For elaboration see also the author's *German Seed in Texas Soil: Immigrant Farmers in Nineteenth Century Texas* (Austin: University of Texas Press, 1966).

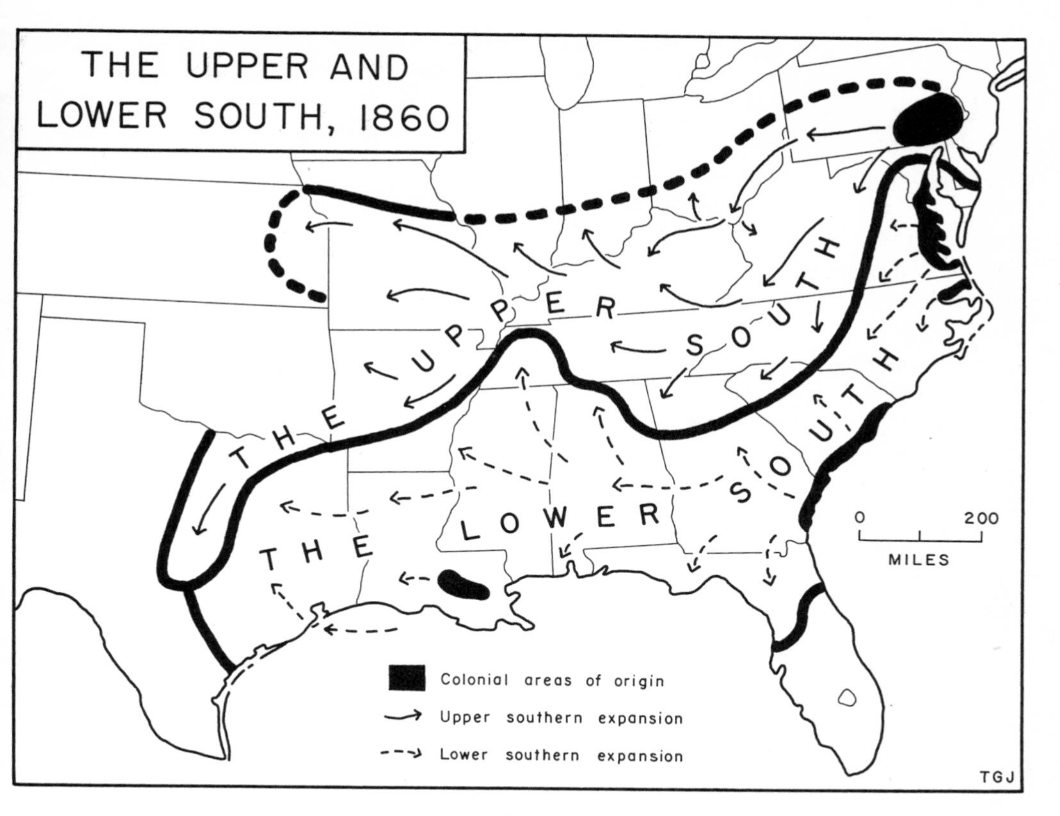

FIG. 1

man-non-cotton Upper South is a valid one which few would dispute. . . .

The Position of Texas in the Southern Dichotomy

. . . The place occupied by Texas in the dichotomy of Upper and Lower South has received little attention from historical geographers or historians. Perhaps most generally, Texas has been assumed to have fallen wholly within the realm of the Gulf or Lower South. It is, however, the thesis of the present paper that there existed within nineteenth-century Texas two clearly defined areas, one of which was, indeed, typically lower southern, but the other of which bore the unmistakable imprint of the Upper South; that the dichotomy which existed within the South as a whole also existed within Texas (Fig. 1). . . .

Origins of the Texas Population

Perhaps the most obvious index to use in delimiting the areas of upper and lower southern influence in Texas is a study of the birthplaces of the settlers who peopled the state in the nineteenth century. Anglo-American colonization in Texas began in earnest in the early 1820s, at which time the area was still a part of Mexico. The Mexican government, aware that Texas was largely an empty land, instituted a policy designed to attract settlers to the province. Contracts were made under which vast tracts of land were turned over to certain selected individuals called *empresarios,* who were responsible for introducing specified numbers of settlers into their grants. The first such contract was made with a certain Moses Austin, an American who had acquired Spanish citizenship during an earlier residence in Missouri. . . . A second *empresario* who had some measure of success was Green DeWitt, whose colony lay adjacent to Austin's on the West, in the valley of the Guadalupe River some distance inland from the coast (Fig. 2).[2]

In both the Austin and DeWitt colonies, the majority of the settlers were from the Upper South, notably the transmontane states of Tennessee and Missouri. A census of the DeWitt Colony in 1828 revealed that nearly 60 percent of the population was of upper southern origin, and Missouri was the leading contributing state in the early years in Austin's Colony.[3]

To the east, beyond the area of *empresario* colonization, in the vicinity of the old Spanish town of Nacogdoches (Fig. 2), unorganized and often illegal immigration occurred in the 1820s and 1830s. These settlers, too, were dominantly yeomen from the Upper South.

Under Mexican rule, then, Texas appeared destined to become in its entirety a part of the Upper South. . . . In Mexican Texas, lower southerners gained only a small foothold in the bottomlands of various rivers and creeks near the Gulf Coast in the Austin Colony, where some fine plantations were established (Fig. 2).

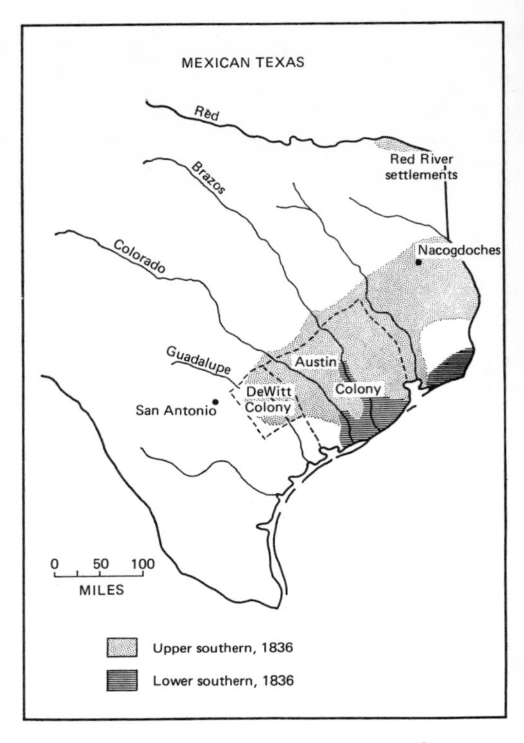

FIG. 2

One of the major factors which retarded lower southern immigration in the pre-1836 period was the official opposition of the Mexican government to Negro slavery. Though the antislavery policy was never rigorously enforced, any southerner who brought Negroes to Texas ran the risk of forfeiting them.

The Texas Revolution resulted in the creation of an independent republic, and with the separation from Mexico, all restrictions on slavery were removed. The response was the first large-scale influx of lower southerners into Texas, mainly from the Gulf Coastal Plain states of Alabama, Georgia, Mississippi, and Louisiana. By the time of the first Federal census in 1850, it was obvious that Texas was no longer exclusively within the domain of the Upper South (Table 1). To be sure, natives of Tennessee still constituted the

2. The only satisfactory work on DeWitt is E. Z. Rather, "DeWitt's Colony," *Texas State Historical Association Quarterly* 8 (1904): 95-192.

3. Ibid., pp. 189-91; E. C. Barker, *The Life of Stephen F. Austin* (Nashville and Dallas: Cokesbury Press, 1925), p. 149.

TABLE 1. Origins of the Free Population in Antebellum Texas

	1850		1860	
Place of birth	*Number*	*As a percentage of the immigrant Anglo-American population**	*Number*	*As a percentage of the immigrant Anglo-American population**
Transmontane Upper South	33,002	37	80,616	36
Tennessee	17,692	20	42,265	19
Kentucky	5,478	6	14,545	7
Missouri	5,139	6	12,487	5
Arkansas	4,693	5	11,319	5
Gulf South	30,696	35	87,392	39
Alabama	12,040	14	34,193	15
Georgia	7,639	9	23,637	11
Mississippi	6,545	7	19,902	9
Louisiana	4,472	5	9,660	4

Sources: *Seventh Census of the United States, 1850,* p. xxxvi; *Eighth Census of the United States, 1860,* volume on population, p. 490.
* Excludes foreign-born and all persons born in Texas.

largest single nativity group, but Alabamians ranked a not-too-distant second, and natives of Georgia and Mississippi ranked third and fourth. By the eve of the Civil War in 1860, Gulf southerners had become the largest group in the state (Table 1). Still more significant was the fact that the upper southerners were localized in one part of Texas and the Gulf southerners in another. . . . By 1880 there was a large contiguous area of Gulf southern dominance in eastern and southeastern Texas, adjacent to a comparable area of upper southern majority in interior north-central Texas (Fig. 3). In addition, there were numerous counties in which Mexicans and Europeans were the largest groups present. Evidence provided by scholars who have dealt with the manuscript census of population schedules for 1850 and 1860, unpublished returns which list the place of birth for each inhabitant of the state, suggests that the pattern observed for 1880 is essentially correct for the antebellum period as well.[4]

. . . From 1836 to the Civil War, the area dominated by Gulf southerners had been expanded from the small foothold in the coastal bottomlands, and the upper southerners had been forced to seek land in the interior of Texas, primarily in the fertile Blackland Prairie. . . .

Phenomena Related to the Pattern of Origins

Although interesting and suggestive, the pattern of population origins taken alone does not constitute adequate evidence to support the thesis that Texas was characterized by an economic, political, and social dichotomy. Rather, it is necessary to discover correlations between the pattern of origins and various other cultural patterns, and this will be the concern of the remainder of the present paper.

4. B. F. Lathrop, *Migration into East Texas 1835-1860* (Austin: Texas State Historical Association, 1949); and W. W. White, "Migration into West Texas, 1845-1860" (Master of Arts thesis, Department of History, University of Texas, Austin, 1948).

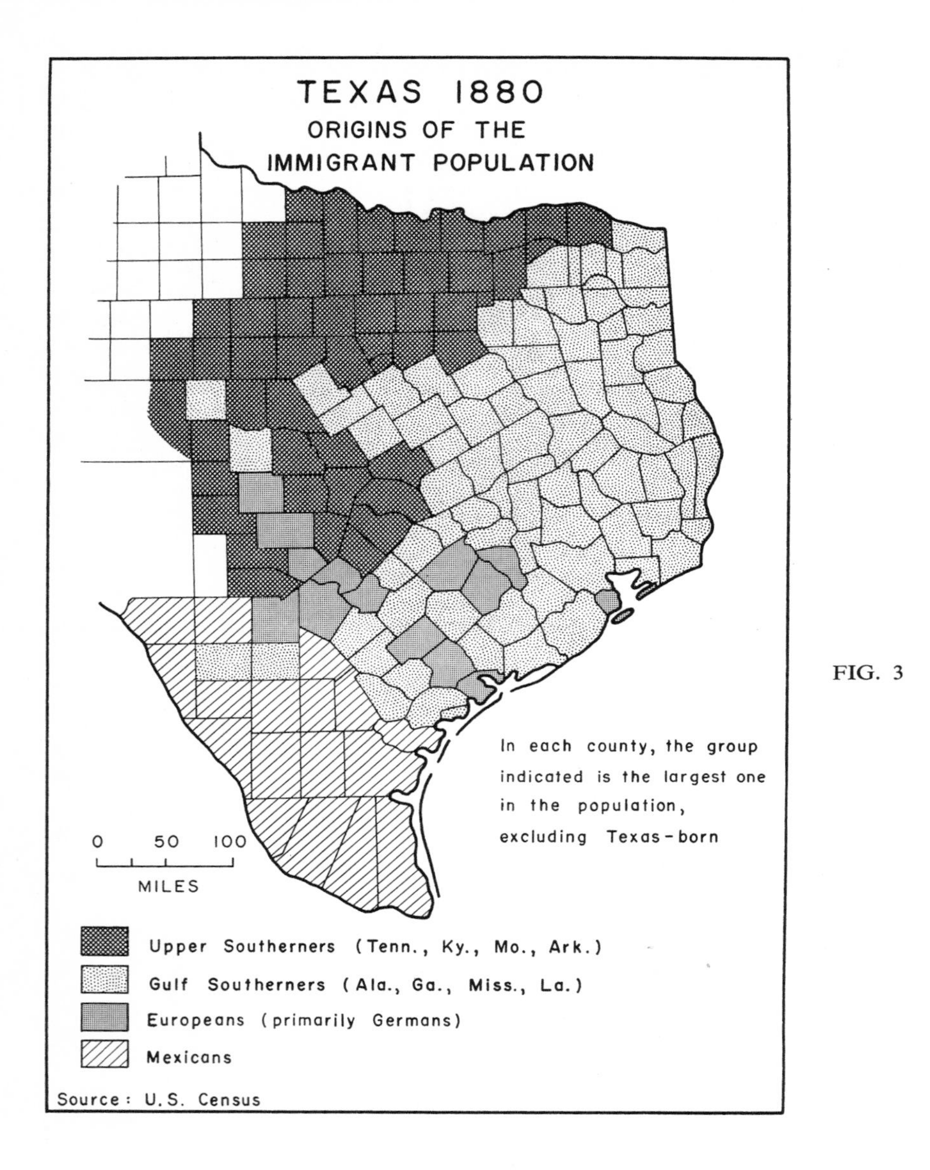

FIG. 3

Negro Slavery

One of the most obvious areal correlations to be expected concerns the presence or absence of large numbers of Negro slaves. It would be anticipated that areas dominated by Gulf southerners have a fairly high proportion of slaves in the total population, whereas the converse would be true of upper southern counties. This expectation proved to be true. . . . Only in the plantation areas near the mouths of the Brazos and Colorado rivers were Negroes common in Mexican Texas. The immigration of large numbers of Gulf southerners after 1836 caused a

TABLE 2. A Comparison of Upper and Gulf Southern Texas in the Antebellum Period

	*Upper southern counties in Texas***	*Gulf southern counties in Texas***
Negro slaves as a percentage of the total population, 1860	17	37
Cotton, bales per 100 inhabitants, 1859	17*	94
as a percentage of total cultivated area, 1858	5	35
Wheat, bushels per 100 inhabitants, 1859	783*	126
as a percentage of total cultivated area, 1858	31	7
Oats, bushels per 100 inhabitants, 1859	519*	84
Corn, bushels per 100 inhabitants, 1859	1680*	3232
as a percentage of total cultivated area, 1858	51	48
Mule + Ass : Horse ratio, 1860	1 : 10	1 : 4
Percentage of electorate voting *against* secession, 1861	46	12

* The crops in upper southern Texas were badly cut back by drought in 1859, especially corn.

** The counties included in each area are based on the population birthplace figures of the 1870 and 1880 censuses and are as follows:

Gulf southern counties: Anderson, Angelina, Bastrop, Bee, Bosque, Bowie, Brazoria, Brazos, Burleson, Caldwell, Cass, Chambers, Cherokee, Comanche, Coryell, Falls, Fort Bend, Freestone, Goliad, Gonzales, Grimes, Hamilton, Hardin, Harris, Harrison, Henderson, Hill, Hopkins, Houston, Jackson, Jasper, Jefferson, Karnes, Kaufman, Lavaca, Leon, Liberty, Limestone, McLennan, Madison, Marion, Matagorda, Milam, Montgomery, Nacogdoches, Navarro, Newton, Orange, Panola, Polk, Refugio, Robertson, Rusk, Sabine, San Augustine, Shelby, Smith, Titus, Trinity, Tyler, Upshur, Van Zandt, Walker, Washington, Wharton, Wilson, Wood.

Upper southern counties: Bandera, Bell, Blanco, Brown, Buchanan (Stephens), Burnet, Clay, Collin, Cooke, Dallas, Denton, Eastland, Ellis, Erath, Fannin, Grayson, Hays, Hunt, Jack, Johnson, Kerr, Lamar, Lampasas, Llano, Montague, Palo Pinto, Parker, Red River, San Saba, Shackelford, Tarrant, Throckmorton, Travis, Williamson, Wise, Young.

Sources: *Eighth Census of the United States,*

sharp rise in the percentage of slaves in the Texas population. The state census taken in 1848 revealed that 26 percent of all Texans were Negro, and by 1860 the proportion had risen to 30 percent.[5] Even more significant to the thesis of the present paper was the concentration of slaves in the areas of Texas peopled by Gulf southerners, and the relative absence of slaves in the counties settled by upper southerners (Fig. 4, Table 2). To this day the upper southern areas have only a small number of rural Negroes. . . .

The Cultivation of Cotton

The agricultural characteristic most closely identified with the Gulf South was the presence of cotton as the dominant cash crop. Accordingly, one would expect to find cotton in those parts of Texas settled by natives of the Gulf South. In colonial Texas, under the Mexican regime, cotton was not a crop of major consequence. . . . Cotton production rose sharply after the revolution, and the Gulf southern parts of Texas became the western extremity of the great Cotton Belt which stretched across the Lower South. By 1860, the state production had risen to 431,000 bales, and once again the areal contrast between upper and Gulf southern Texas was evident (Fig. 5, Table 2). The total cotton production of counties dominated by Gulf southerners was seventeen times as great as that of the upper southern counties. Nor can the ex-

1860; "Census of the State of Texas for 1858," in *Texas Almanac for 1859* (Galveston, Texas: Richardson, 1858), pp. 208-11; E. Winkler, ed., *Journal of the Secession Convention of Texas 1861* (Austin: State Library, 1912), pp. 88-90.

5. *Journals of the House of Representatives of the State of Texas,* Third Session (Austin: William H. Cushney, 1849), pp. 33-35, 136-37; *Eighth Census of the United States, 1860,* volume on population, p. 486.

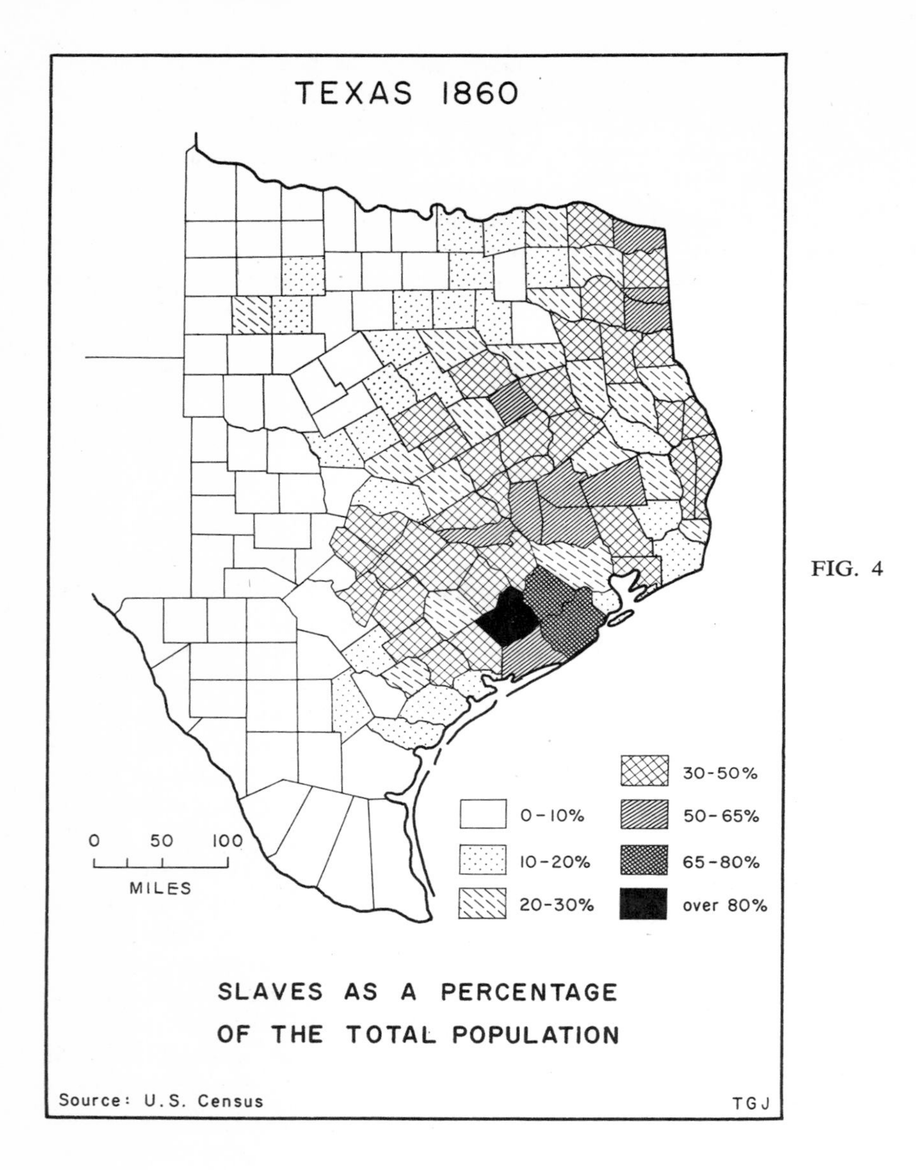

FIG. 4

planation for this divergence be found in environmental factors, for virtually all of the settled portion of Texas in 1860 was well suited to cotton. By no means had the crop reached its environmental limits by the Civil War, because in the fertile Blackland Prairie, which held as much promise for cotton as had the Black Belt of Alabama, only very small amounts were produced by 1860. Instead, as mentioned previously, the Blackland was the domain of yeoman farmers from the Upper South, who had little experience in raising cotton. The failure of the slave-cotton economy to penetrate this fertile area in antebellum times is perhaps par-

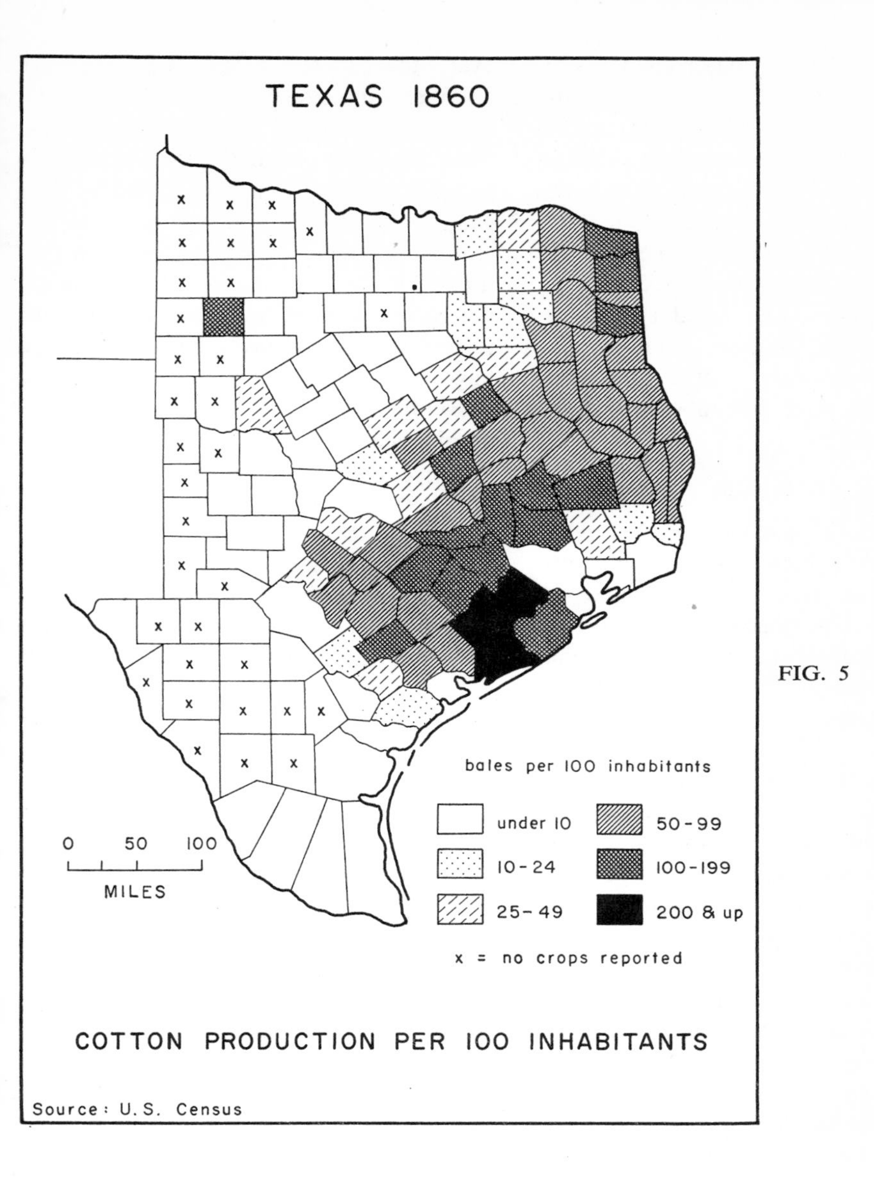

FIG. 5

tially explained by problems of transportation. The Blackland had no navigable rivers or railroads, with the result that the cotton would necessarily have been moved overland by expensive wagon transport to markets that lay hundreds of miles away. Almost everywhere in the antebellum South, cotton raising was closely tied to water transport, and the Blackland Prairie lacked such facilities.

Eventually cotton did come to the Blackland, in the decades after the Civil War, when railroads were built. In fact the Blackland became one of the major parts of the Cotton Belt in the early twentieth century. The result was the disappearance of one of the major elements in the dichotomy within Texas, a disappearance which should be viewed as part of an assimilation of upper southern population into the Gulf southern economy. Still, cotton farming in the postbellum Blackland had a certain uniqueness about it owing to the relative absence of Negro sharecroppers. The rapid spread of cotton into upper southern counties was facilitated by the demise of competition from the large slave plantations of preabolition times.

The Cultivation of Wheat

Wheat had been closely identified with the Upper South since the eighteenth century expansion from Pennsylvania. It attained great importance in the Valley of East Tennessee in the first half of the nineteenth century and was found in significant amounts through much of the Upper South. It was, in short, part of the agricultural heritage of the yeoman farmers who settled in Texas. In contrast, wheat had little place in the crop economy of the Lower South, perhaps more because it did not thrive in the hot, humid climate of the Gulf states rather than for any reasons of cultural preference.

Upper southerners introduced wheat into Texas in the valley of the Red River in the far northeastern part of the province as early as the Spanish period. . . .

As the upper southern pioneers pushed southward from the bottoms of the Red River, they encountered for the first time the fertile lands of the Blackland Prairie. . . . Wheat grew so well in the Blackland that in the decade before the Civil War it became the principal cash crop in the upper southern prairie counties in north-central Texas, an area centered on the thriving river-ford town of Dallas (Fig. 6). . . . It should be noted, however, that most of the Gulf southern counties were not well suited climatically for small grains. Efforts to raise wheat were made by some German settlers in counties similar to those occupied by Gulf southerners, but in spite of persistent attempts, the result was repeated crop failure.[6] This environmental factor should not be overlooked, however important the respective agricultural heritages might have been.

By the year 1860, wheat enjoyed a dominance in the northern Blackland Prairie far greater than any upper southern precedent. By way of comparison, the wheat production in the Valley of East Tennessee in 1850 was about 300 bushels per 100 inhabitants,[7] whereas in the upper southern counties of Texas a decade later the figure was nearly 800 bushels (Table 2). With its large acreage in wheat, the Blackland took on more the appearance of the midwestern frontier states. Midwestern, too, was the increasing reliance on agricultural machinery. . . . The use of machinery was related to the scarcity of Negro labor in the Blackland, and it was probably encouraged further by the farm labor shortage resulting from the Civil War. . . .

It should be noted in passing that the cultivation of another small grain, oats, corresponded very well to the pattern observed for wheat. The upper southern counties of Texas reported over six times as much oats per capita as the Gulf southern counties in the census of 1860 (Table 2), in spite of the fact that the year 1859, on which the crop census was based, was

6. T. G. Jordan, *German Seed in Texas Soil: Immigrant Farmers in Nineteenth Century Texas* (Austin: University of Texas Press, 1966), pp. 79-81.

7. L. C. Gray, *History of Agriculture in the Southern United States to 1860* (New York: Peter Smith, 1941), vol. 2, p. 876.

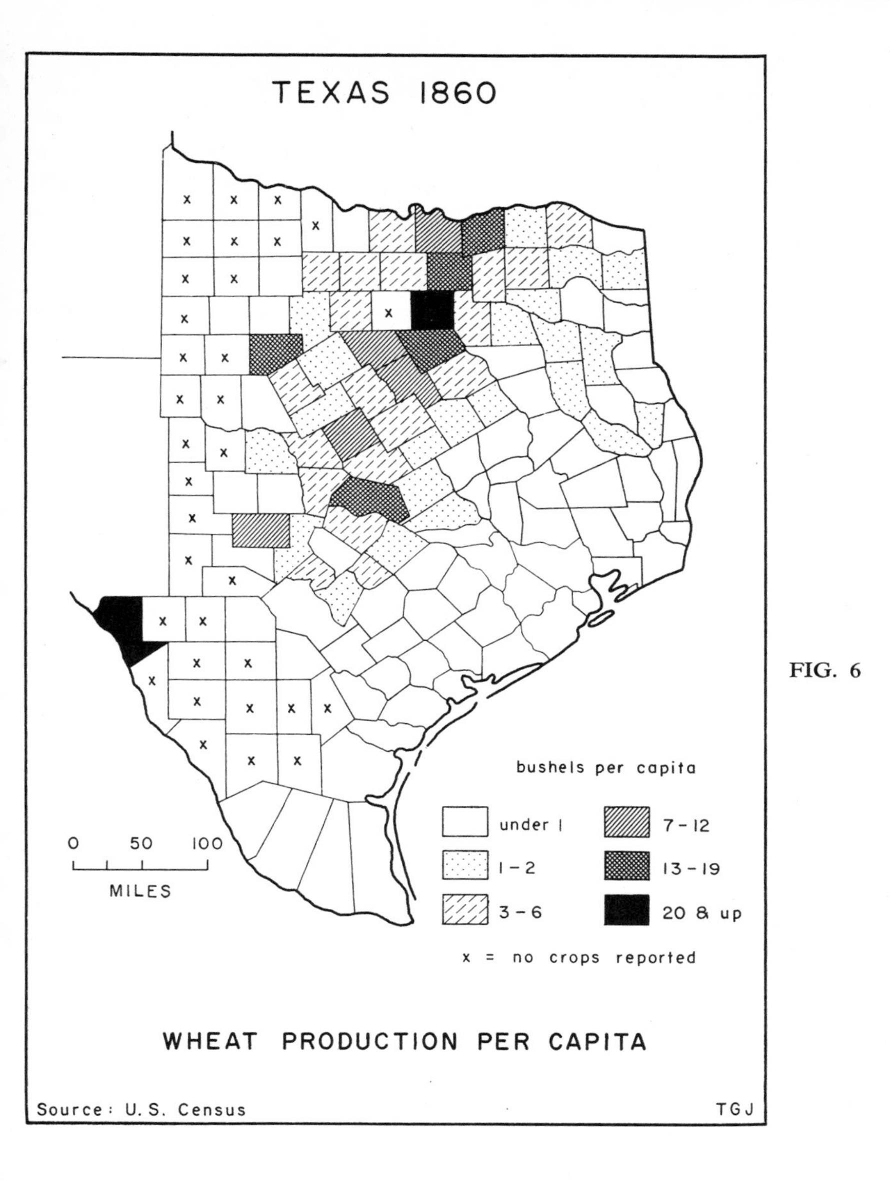

FIG. 6

one of severe drought in the upper southern parts of Texas. The concentration of oats production among the yeomen of the interior of Texas was in keeping with a pattern well established in more eastern portions of the South. In 1850, for example, the per capita production of oats in the upper southern Valley of East Tennessee was over three times as great as in adjacent Alabama, in the Gulf South.[8]

8. *Seventh Census of the United States, 1850,* pp. 421, 429-33, 573-74, 584-90. The counties chosen to represent the Valley of East Tennessee were Greene, Hamilton, Hawkins, Jefferson,

The Cultivation of Corn

Throughout the South, the almost universal staff of life was corn. . . . The Upper South traditionally produced more corn per capita and devoted a larger proportion of the total cultivated acreage to corn than was the case in the Lower South, with the result that one area produced a corn surplus whereas the other had a deficiency. In short, corn in the Upper South was to a degree a cash crop, marketed as grain, whiskey, or fattened livestock, in contrast to the Lower South, where non-food cash crops were dominant. . . .

Within Texas, the production of corn bore some of the same characteristics of the more eastern states of the South. The upper southern counties in Texas constituted a corn surplus area, as is evidenced by the fact that over one-half of the total cultivated acreage was planted to corn in 1858 (Table 2).[9] Still, the very great importance of wheat in interior Texas caused the corn acreage and production per capita to be less than might be expected of a typical upper southern area. In fact, the concentration on wheat cut back the corn acreage to the point that the proportion of land in corn was not greatly different in the two parts of Texas (Table 2). . . .

Rice and Sugar Cane

Both rice and sugar cane were crops closely identified with portions of the Lower South, and in antebellum times, both were tied to the slave-plantation system as well. Rice, some of it the nonirrigated upland variety, was raised only in very modest amounts in antebellum Texas. The entire production of the state reported in the census of 1860 was only 26,000 pounds, of which all but 175 pounds came from Gulf southern-populated counties.[10] Sugar cane enjoyed somewhat greater commercial importance than rice during the pre–Civil War period in Texas, but the total production of the state was only slightly over 5,000 hogsheads by 1860.[11] Not only the agricultural heritage of the settlers, but also climatic requirements caused sugar cane to be limited almost entirely to areas peopled by lower southerners, primarily certain counties fronting on the Gulf of Mexico.

Tobacco and Hemp

In several respects, the crop economy of the interior portions of Texas failed to fit the generalized concept of the Upper South. Tobacco, which was a major crop in parts of Tennessee and Kentucky, was never raised to any notable extent by upper southerners in Texas. Instead, the larger part of the modest tobacco production of the state was in the hands of German immigrant farmers who settled among Gulf southerners in several counties of south-central Texas.[12] The cultivation of hemp, which was of major consequence in portions of the Upper South, was never of importance in any part of Texas.

Draft Animals

Within the antebellum South, there were distinct regional differences concerning the choice of draft animals. In the yeoman-dominated Upper South, the horse

---

Knox, McMinn, and Roane; following the example of Gray, *History of Agriculture,* vol. 2, p. 876.

9. "Census of the State of Texas for 1858," in *Texas Almanac for 1859* (Galveston: Richardson, 1858), pp. 208-11.

10. *Eighth Census of the United States, 1860,* volume on agriculture, pp. 141, 145, 149.

11. Ibid., volume on agriculture, pp. 143, 147, 151.

12. Jordan, *German Seed,* pp. 67, 69-70.

was the almost universal work animal, giving way only in frontier areas to the ox; but in the Lower South, the mule attained considerable importance. Prior to 1860 the use of mules was very largely confined to areas where Negro slaves did the field work. . . . Even though mules were confined as far as usage was concerned to the Lower South, they were bred in the Upper South, primarily in the Nashville Basin and the Missouri River Valley, and they served as still another item of intraregional trade within the South.

The usage of draft animals in Texas very closely followed the pattern suggested above. In the upper southern counties, mules were most uncommon and were usually outnumbered 10 : 1 or more by horses, but in Gulf southern Texas they definitely rivalled horses as draft animals (Fig. 7). The ratio of mules and asses to horses in these counties often approached 1 : 1, and in one East Texas county, mules actually outnumbered horses. In fact, there was only one way in which the yeoman-dominated interior of Texas failed to fit the upper southern stereotype regarding draft animals, and that was the absence of mule-breeding.

Food Surpluses, Food Deficiencies, and Trade

. . . It was the Upper South, in addition to the Midwest, that supplied not only the additional food needs of the Lower South, but also sent large amounts into international trade. The West Indies plantations of the British and French were major consumers of this surplus food.

Within pre–Civil War Texas, this same contrast of food-surplus and food-deficient areas was observable. In the period shortly after the Texan war of independence, when a lower southern society and economy was taking firm root in the southeastern part of the Republic, food imports began to attain major importance. As an example, during the first half of the year 1838 nearly 10,000 sacks of corn were imported from New Orleans to Texas,[13] and the trade increased in the years that followed as the lower southern foothold expanded to include much of the settled portion of Texas. By the 1850s, wheat flour was being imported to Gulf southern Texas from sources as distant as Ohio.[14]

In the interior counties dominated by upper southerners, on the other hand, large food surpluses were characteristic. Fully 82 percent of the cultivated acreage in this area was planted to corn and wheat in 1858, as compared to 55 percent in the Gulf southern counties.[15] However, in one very important respect, the interior of Texas differed from the more eastern states of the Upper South, a divergence involving the markets for the food surplus. . . . The upper southern counties apparently engaged in very little exchange of goods with the Gulf southern areas, and the two parts of Texas functioned independently of one another. The cotton-slave counties did not serve as a market for the surplus grain produced by the yeomen of the interior, nor did the Gulf ports handle any notable volume of grain destined for ocean trade. The primary barrier was a lack of adequate transportation facilities. Texas lacked the fine river connections which characterized the more eastern areas of the South, and prior to the Civil War there were no railroads

13. J. E. Winston, "Notes on Commercial Relations Between New Orleans and Texan Ports, 1838-1839," *Southwestern Historical Quarterly* 34 (1930):103.

14. F. L. Olmsted, *A Journey Through Texas; or, a Saddle-Trip on the Southwestern Frontier* (New York: Dix, Edwards and Co., 1857), p. 170.

15. "Census of the State of Texas for 1858," pp. 208-11.

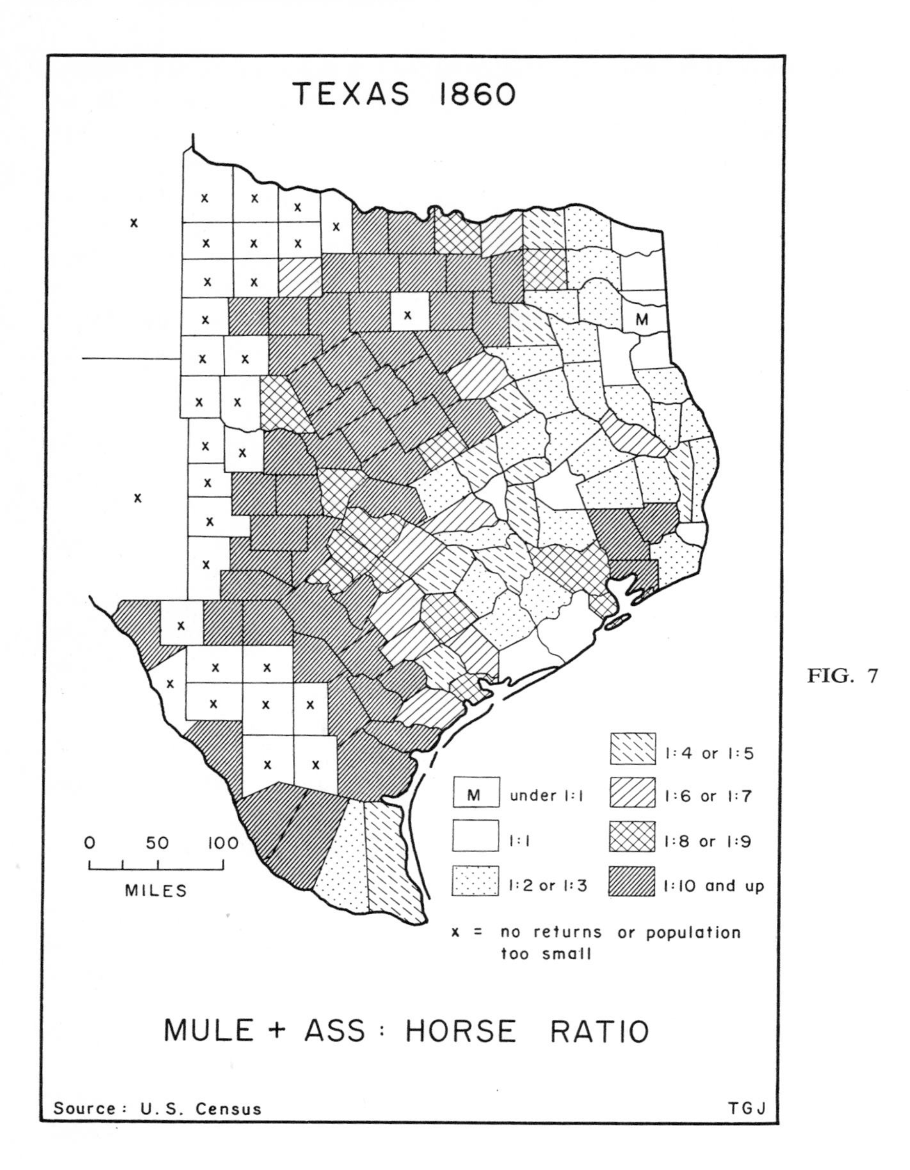

FIG. 7

linking the two parts of the state. The only alternative was overland transport by ox-wagon, which was apparently too expensive. Contemporary observers estimated that flour from the northern Blackland Prairie could bear ox-wagon transport for only 100 to 150 miles, not far enough to reach the markets of lower southern Texas.[16] Accordingly, the yeomen of the interior of the state sought other markets for their surplus produce.

16. J. W. Latimer, "The Wheat Region and Wheat Culture in Texas," *Texas Almanac for 1859* (Galveston: Richardson, 1858), p. 69; J.H.S. (only initials given), "The Wheat Region of Texas," *Texas Almanac for 1867* (Galveston: Richardson, 1866), p. 224.

Fortunately, such trade outlets were available. The principal customer was the United States government, which was obliged to purchase large quantities of food and livestock feed, including corn, wheat, and oats in order to provide supplies for the federal troops stationed at the numerous forts along the Comanche-infested Texas frontier.[17] The government also bought foodstuffs in upper southern Texas for use in various agencies within the Indian territory to the north.[18] Even with these outlets, many of the yeomen had difficulty disposing of their surplus crops. . . .

Following the Civil War, the rail lines were extended even farther into the Texas interior, and it became a regular practice to transport produce to the head of construction of the Houston & Texas Central.[19] Finally, in the early 1870s, several railroads linking upper and lower southern Texas were completed, but the result was not what contemporary observers had expected. For instead of serving as outlets for the surplus wheat and corn of the interior, the railroads facilitated the spread of cotton into the upper southern counties. Within a very few years following the construction of the railroads, cotton had largely displaced wheat, reduced the per capita level of corn production, and eliminated the food surplus.

The Issue of Secession

As the United States drifted toward civil war in the months following Lincoln's election in 1860, the socioeconomic dichotomy within the South attained a notable political importance. More specifically, it was the issue of secession which lent a distinct political tone to the contrast between Lower and Upper South. The movement toward secession had its origins in the Lower South, and by the end of January, 1861, the only states that had severed ties with the Union–South Carolina, Georgia, Florida, Alabama, Mississippi, and Louisiana–lay in that area.[20] . . .

In the Upper South, on the other hand, popular sentiment was about evenly divided on the secession issue. This lack of a consensus in the upper southern states had several results. Of the four transmontane states of the Upper South, only two left the Union, Tennessee and Arkansas, and even these delayed action until May and June of 1861. Within the state of Virginia, the mountainous western portion, which belonged unmistakably to the Upper South, refused to accept the decision to secede and entered the Union as West Virginia during the war.

The secession controversy, then, revealed two different Souths: the strongly secessionist Lower South and the politically divided Upper South, where unionists and secessionists were of approximately equal strength. Significantly, this same contrast was observable within the state of Texas. . . . After a detailed study of voting returns for a five-year period preceding the Civil War, Smyrl was able to list the counties in which notable and persistent unionist activity occurred.[21] Of the sixty-six counties in Texas populated dominantly by Gulf southerners, only eight experienced any significant resistance to secession, but in the thirty-four upper southern counties, unionist sentiment was noted in fully twenty-one. That is to say, there was never any nota-

17. Latimer, "Wheat Region and Wheat Culture," p. 69.
18. J.H.S., "Wheat Region," p. 224.
19. Ibid.

20. R. A. Wooster, *The Secession Conventions of the South* (Princeton, New Jersey: Princeton University Press, 1962), pp. 11-120.
21. F. H. Smyrl, "Unionism in Texas, 1850-1861," *Southwestern Historical Quarterly,* 68 (1964):194-95.

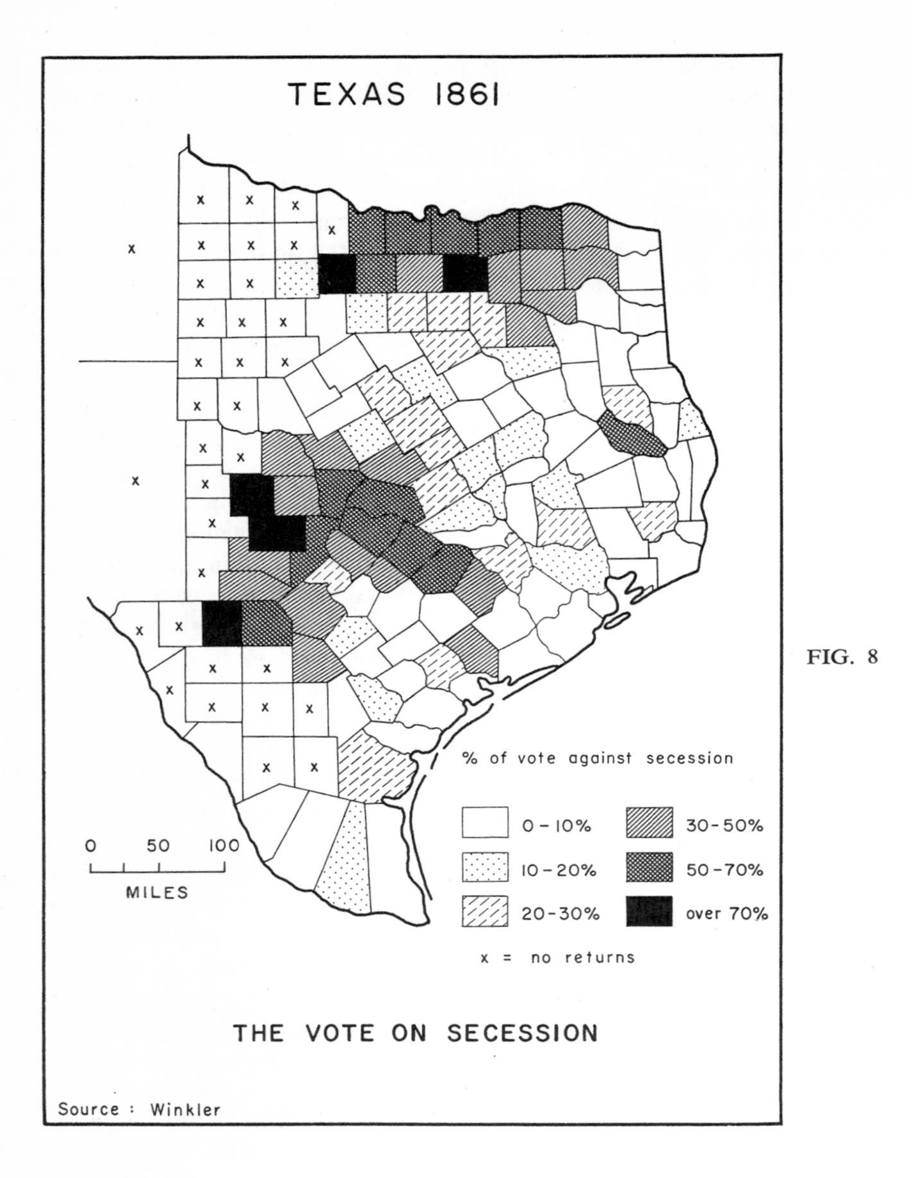

FIG. 8

ble degree of opposition to secession in Gulf southern Texas, in keeping with the mood of the Lower South as a whole, whereas the upper southern counties were racked by dissention and the populace was unable to achieve a consensus on the issue.[22] The clearest possible expression of this political cleavage within Texas was provided by the vote of the people of Texas in a referendum held in February of 1861 in which the electorate had the opportunity to voice support for or opposition to secession (Fig. 8).[23] The results

22. F. F. Ewing, Jr., "Origins of Unionist Sentiment on the West Texas Frontier," *West Texas Historical Association Year Book* 32 (1956):23.

23. The election returns by counties are pre-

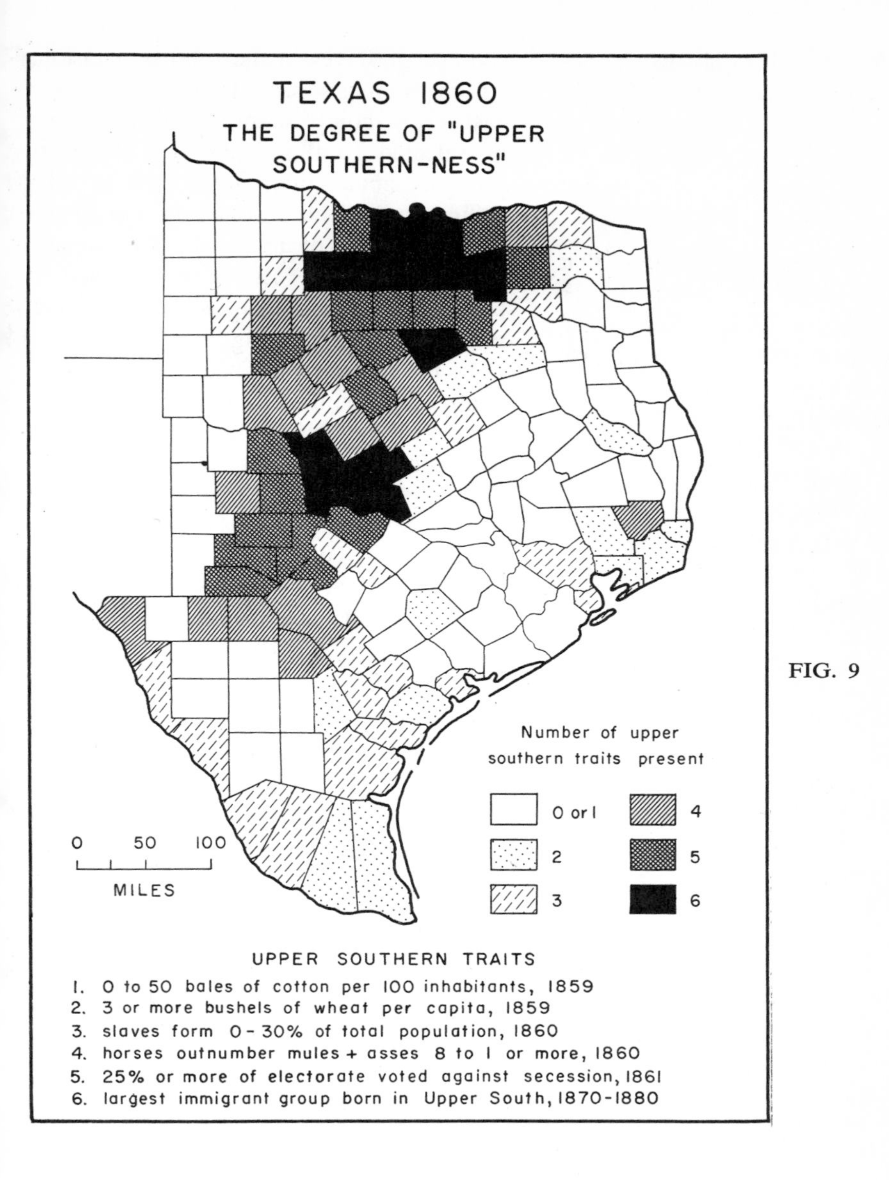

FIG. 9

revealed that Gulf southern counties voted very heavily for secession whereas the electorate in upper southern Texas was about evenly divided (Table 2). . . .

Prior to the statewide vote on secession, there was one other action taken within the upper southern counties which served to reveal how far the two parts of Texas had drifted apart politically. A written document demanding the separation of the upper southern stronghold in northern Texas from the state as a whole and its entry into the union as a separate

sented in E. W. Winkler, ed., *Journal of the Secession Convention of Texas 1861* (Austin: State Library, 1912), pp. 88-90.

state was widely circulated in two counties immediately to the north of Dallas.[24] . . .

Conclusion

The evidence presented indicates that within the portion of antebellum Texas settled by southern Anglo-Americans, there were two distinct socioeconomic regions. The eastern and southeastern parts of Texas were occupied mainly by lower southerners or, more specifically, natives of the Gulf Coastal Plain states of Alabama, Georgia, Mississippi, and Louisiana. These settlers transplanted the characteristics of the Lower South in the area they occupied, including 1) a high percentage of slaves in the total population, 2) an emphasis on cotton as the major cash crop, complemented by sugar cane in selected localities, 3) the unimportance of small grains, 4) a lack of self-sufficiency in food production, and 5) the widespread use of mules as draft animals. On the issue of secession, they proved to be strongly secessionist, as the remainder of the Lower South (Fig. 9).

In the interior of Texas, in a block of contiguous counties in and to the west of the Blackland Prairie, upper southerners were dominant in the population, and they too left a distinctive mark on the land they settled. In the economy of upper southern Texas was found 1) an emphasis on wheat as a cash crop, 2) a food surplus in corn and small grains, 3) an unimportance of cotton, 4) a scarcity of Negro slaves, and 5) a dominance of the horse as a draft animal. . . .

24. C. Elliott, "Union Sentiment in Texas, 1861-1865," *Southwestern Historical Quarterly* 50 (1947):449-77.

American Wests: Preface to a Geographical Interpretation / *D. W. Meinig*

. . . The American West, a world-famous area which has fostered a huge volume of interpretive literature, has been of little concern as a region, as a single unit in a two- or threefold national set, to American geographers. In the main body of that literature this famous West is generally synonymous with the Frontier and thus is less a place than a process, the realm of a great influential recurring American experience. It is a powerful symbol within the national mythology, but as soon as we attempt to connect symbol with substance, to assess the relationships between the West as a place in the imagination and the West as a piece of the American continent, we are confronted with great variation from place to place. Thus geographers have said little about the West as *a* region, but a good deal about the West as a *set* of regions. The purpose of this paper is to suggest that they could yet say a great deal more, and do so in a way that might involve them much more effectively in the larger, persistent, and important task of national interpretation. . . .

It is important at the outset to distinguish between two possible views of the West as a set of dynamic regions. On the one hand is the West as the Frontier, shifting in specific area in conjunction with the sequential expansion of the nation. . . . In such a usage "West" is a generic term referring to a specific *type* of area within a dynamic national context. On the other hand, there is the concept of the West as a specific "half" of the nation in apposition to the East, a huge area displaying some persisting basis of identity.

This paper is concerned only with this latter view. That means that we are dealing with the area which emerged as the "New West" or the "Far West" in the 1870s and 1880s. . . .

Scheme

Some basic differences between East and West were readily apparent during the emergence of the West as a distinct realm: the marked contrasts in physical environments; the differences in peoples, the West being the country of Indians, Mexicans, Mormons, and of gold rush, cowboy, and other tumultuous frontier societies; and the differences in the overall settlement pattern, western settlement having a clear insular character, each of the several main areas being isolated by great distances and inhospitable country from its nearest neighbors. These features

Reproduced (with omissions) by permission from the *Annals,* Association of American Geographers, 62 (1972):159-84. The reader is alerted to the fact that the abridgement of this article included one entire section entitled "Political Areas" in the original publication. For elaboration see also the author's *Southwest: Three Peoples in Geographical Change, 1600-1970* (New York: Oxford University Press, 1971).

were very generally perceived and emphasized even if only vaguely or confusedly understood at the time. Such characteristics offer clues for the formulation of a systematic comprehensive view of the West as a set of dynamic regions. Contrary to the popular emphasis of the time and to a later strong tradition in American geography, this proposed view emphasizes the insular pattern of colonizations more than the strong physical contrasts. For a retrospective look at the spatial character of American development does reveal a noticeable contrast in evolving patterns between East and West. Although folk colonization is always selective and uneven in area, in the East the general tide of settlement was relatively comprehensive and local nuclei and salients in the vanguard were soon engulfed and integrated into a generally contiguous pattern. Obviously such a description rests upon a particular scale of observation, but holding to the same scale, the pattern in the West is a marked contrast: several distinct major nuclei so widely separated from one another and so far removed from the advancing front of the East that each expands as a kind of discrete unit for several decades, only gradually becoming linked together and more closely integrated into the main functional systems of the nation. If we then add important dimensions of culture and environment to these nuclei we have the basis for a hypothetical scheme (Fig. 1), in which each western area is viewed as passing through four general phases of development as expressed in three general categories: population (numbers and areal distribution), circulation (traffic patterns within and between regions), and culture (selected features characteristic of the local society and its imprint upon the area).

The remainder of this paper is a sketch of the principal specific features in the American West associated with this model of historical geographical change.

Major Nuclei (Stages I and II)

Hispano New Mexico

The first nucleus of European settlement in the American West was established by the Spanish in the upper Rio Grande Valley at the end of the sixteenth century. . . .

The Spanish superimposed themselves upon the entire Rio Grande Pueblo area of village agriculturists. Santa Fé was founded as a capital pivotal to important populations and security areas, and a number of other formal towns were laid out. The introduction of sheep, cattle, horses, burros, and mules enlarged the resource possibilities of this semiarid region and provided the main basis for settlement expansion carried out by the mestizo population, which emerged as much the largest of the several peoples in the area. These "Hispanos" were a Spanish-speaking, Roman Catholic, peasant, and pastoral people living in closeknit communities structured on strong kinship and patronal relationships. The Pueblo Indians survived the heavy impact of this long imperial experience greatly reduced in numbers and area but basically intact as a general culture and as locally autonomous societies. Some of the peripheral Indian groups were significantly altered. The Navajo were transformed from a minor Apache band into a vigorous pastoral society with a strong sense of identity as a distinct people. Some other Apache bands were invigorated by the greatly enlarged social and economic returns from plundering the imperial frontiers.

For two and a half centuries New Mexico was one of the most isolated regions of European culture. Annual or less fre-

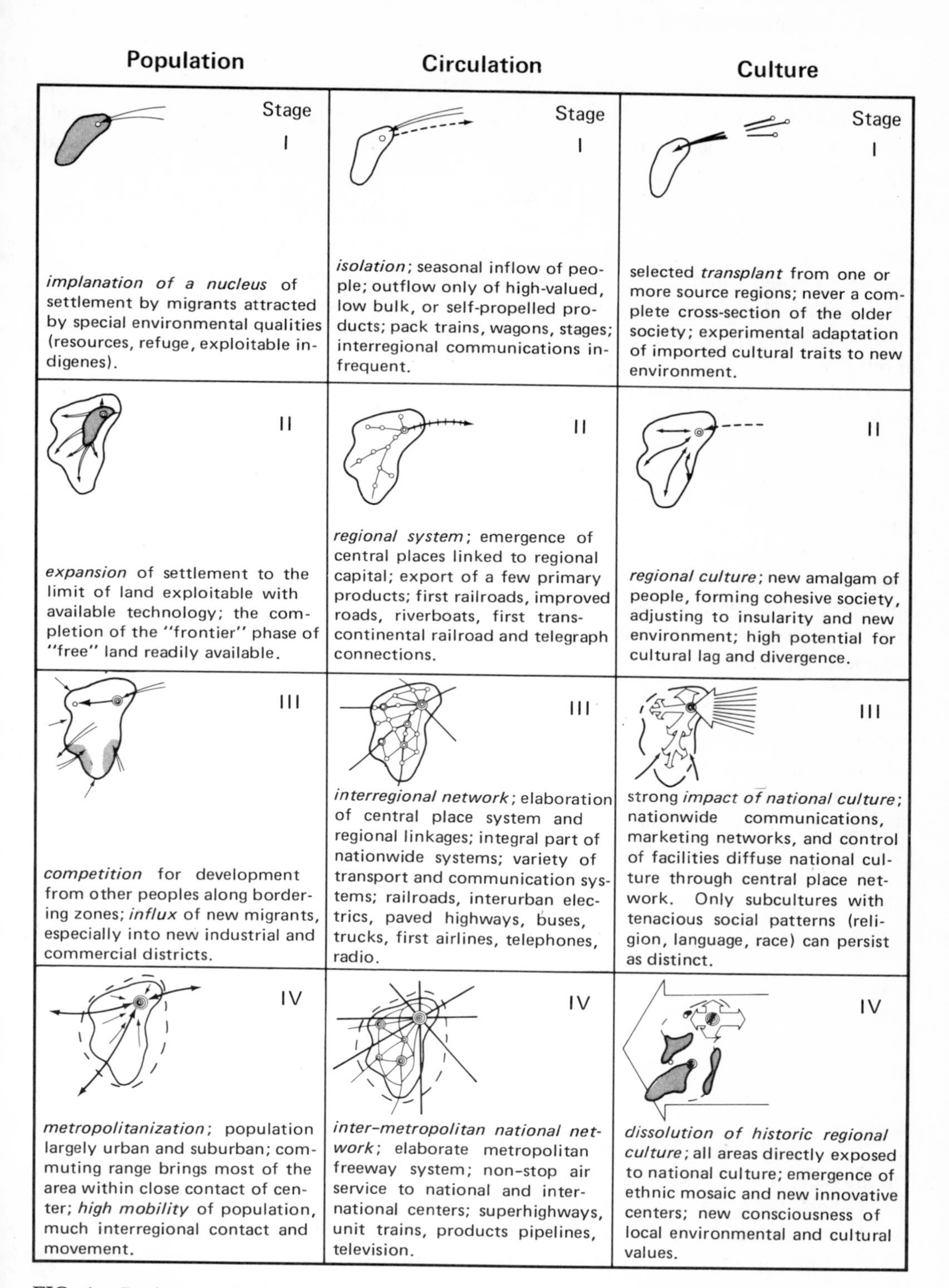

FIG. 1. Regional development within a national context through four stages; population, circulation, and culture.

quent caravans to Chihuahua long provided the only link with the civilized world. Under Mexican rule two new routes, the Santa Fe wagon road to Missouri and the droving trail from Los Angeles, somewhat mitigated the isolation but did not alter the insular character of the region. Such isolation over so long a time favored divergence from the mother culture, a feature most notably expressed in religion (i.e., the Penitentes).

American conquest initiated a new imperialism. The "Anglos" superimposed their polity and began to intrude into every important sector. Santa Fe was retained as the capital, but new Anglo facilities and at times whole new towns were established alongside those of the Hispanos. In the 1880s the railroads opened up greater economic possibilities and a considerably elaborated regional commercial system emerged, focused upon Las Vegas, Santa Fe, and Albuquerque and gathering from all but southernmost New Mexico. Wool and minerals were the principal regional exports exchanged for the manufactures ordered through the wholesale houses of Kansas City, St. Louis, and Chicago.

The strong outward extension of the Hispano domain, initiated in late Spanish times, continued to about 1880 when it was halted by competitive expansions of Anglos from surrounding regions. Within that domain the Hispanos were numerically dominant, but were steadily declining in proportion to the number of Anglos. The Pueblo Indians were a relatively stable population and each town and its immediately adjacent lands were enclosed within federal reserves. The nomadic Indians had been ruthlessly reduced to small remnants and confined to large reserves of unwanted lands on the periphery of the region.

Thus by the late nineteenth century, New Mexico was a functionally coherent provincial system in a complex plural culture area, with only limited commercial and cultural bonds to the national system.

The Mormon Region

In 1847 the nucleus of a highly distinctive western region was implanted in the Wasatch Oasis. The Mormons were a refugee population of unusual cohesion, originally formed by adult conversion to a common faith, unified under charismatic leadership, hardened by persecution, selected by the harsh experiences of expulsion and migration, sustained by the continuous addition of new converts, and powered by a strong faith in themselves as God's elected people.

Brigham Young, a powerful leader of great practical vision, undertook to create a vast Mormon commonwealth embracing a large part of the Far West. Although unable to sustain the original frame of this Deseret, the Mormons did spread north and south of their Salt Lake Valley nucleus until they had settled most of the habitable valleys from the upper Snake River to the Colorado and far east and west into the deserts and mountains. Most of that colonization was accomplished under some degree of formal direction by the church hierarchy and was in the form of village settlements surrounded by privately owned fields with some communal use of scarce resources. Agriculture was by irrigation, to these people a wholly new, empirical development. The church fostered numerous economic activities aimed at maximizing the self-sufficiency of the Mormon region.

In the 1880s the momentum of that great colonization program waned as along every front Mormons encountered colonists from bordering regions and the church leadership came under severe federal harassment. The Mormons were long a suspect people, widely regarded in America as politically and socially dangerous. In the late 1850s the federal government sent an army to occupy Utah to quell a supposedly recalcitrant people and to protect the interest of the non-Mormon minority ("Gentiles" in Mormon parlance) which had entered Utah in the wake of the early Mormon colonization. The military posts overlooking the valley oases were thus typical landscape symbols of an imperial relationship. Furthermore, the Mormon practice of polygamy was regarded as a shocking departure from accepted American mores and produced wide popular support for its absolute suppression by the national government. The capitulation of the Mormon Church on that issue in 1890 after severe persecution by federal authorities was not untypical of the cultural conformity forced upon occupied peoples by imperial powers.

The mineral wealth in the Wasatch region and the strategic location of Salt Lake City and Ogden with reference to the whole Far West sustained a growing Gentile population, concentrated in these main commercial centers, the mining and smelting districts, and the railroad towns. The rural areas remained almost entirely Mormon. The two peoples were latently antagonistic, ever conscious of their differences, and thus a plural society developed which was peculiar to the region and little understood beyond. . . .

The Oregon Country

The Oregon Country, a huge chunk of northwestern America, was under joint claim by Great Britain and the United States for several decades. Momentarily in the early 1840s competitive colonizations were juxtaposed in the lower Columbia district, with the British focus at Fort Vancouver, a major fur-trade center with flourishing farms and mills, and American farmer-migrants settling in the lower Willamette Valley. But the British nucleus disintegrated after the compromise division of Oregon along the 49th Parallel and subsequent colonization was by a relatively homogeneous body of American migrants. Local Indian societies had already been virtually destroyed by disease and economic and social disruptions.

The Willamette nucleus was a long-distant transplant from the Missouri-Ohio Valley region with a strong reinfusion of Yankee influences. Migration in the 1840s and 1850s drew about equally from the free states and from the slave states of the Border South. The general settlement pattern, architecture, and agricultural system were similar to that broad source region, modified by the failure of corn and tobacco to thrive in the cooler, summer-dry environment. The New England influence was markedly apparent in church, school, and civic organizations, and in commercial and manufacturing activities.

Portland, below the falls on the Willamette and accessible to ocean vessels, became the principal focus with the upsurge of exports to California in the 1850s. In the 1860s it became the regional gateway and supply center for an array of new mining districts deep in the interior, competing for trade as far away as the Kootenay, western Montana, and southern Idaho. Walla Walla, the principal interior trade center, became the nucleus of an expanding ranching and farming region which was settled primarily from the Willamette and served by Portland firms. By the early 1880s Portland was the focus of an extensive system of waterways, roads, and railroads tapping much of the old Oregon Country. Puget Sound, directly accessible by sea with an economy based upon a scattering of large tidewater lumber mills, was in some degree separate. Its incipient geography was obscured by the nervous rivalries among aspiring ports and its first railroad line led south to the Columbia to tie in with the more substantial Oregon nucleus. This Northwest system as a whole was bound into commercial networks focused on San Francisco. Californian capital was prominent in the lumbering and mining activities of the Northwest, and in the Willamette and especially in the drier Columbia Plain the grain farming system was strongly shaped by Californian innovations. . . .

Colorado

Although nearest to the main body of national population, Colorado was the last of the major western nuclei to be initiated, and that relative location and timing were important to the character of its beginnings. The discovery of gold along the base of the southern Rockies came a decade after similar electrifying news from California, and the nation responded eagerly to another possibility of such wealth, business opportunity, and adventure. . . .

Early mineral discoveries could not sustain the full initial influx and there was considerable instability in population for many years. The first railroad connections to the East, made in 1870, encouraged more substantial and diversified developments. Eastern and European capital invested heavily in livestock ranching on the Colorado Piedmont. Irrigation agriculture was strongly promoted, and benefited from a few highly publicized and successful colonies (e.g., Greeley and Longmont). Vigorous promotion of the scenic wonders and health-restoring qualities of this "American Switzerland" so conveniently accessible by railway car brought an ever greater number of tourists, summer sojourners, health-seekers, and those attracted by elegant towns of social pretension (i.e., Colorado Springs). Furthermore the mining industry itself underwent steady elaboration from placers to lode mining, and from gold to silver and lead. Location, timing, and special difficulties made Colorado an innovative center of scientific study, tools, and techniques in the American mining industry. . . .

Denver emerged successful from the town-site rivalries at the first ephemeral diggings, was well located to serve the first substantial district (Central City area), and was thereafter never seriously rivaled as the commercial, financial, political, and social center of Colorado. For thirty years its tributary region was rapidly expanded and enriched by significant new mineral discoveries in the southern Rockies, each the basis for new railroads and ancillary industries and the opening of new ranching, farming, and resort districts.

Denver became the focus of a remarkable railroad network which tapped every important mineral district. Much of it was narrow-gauge, a special adaption to the formidable terrain. No train service ran through Denver; it was a true node, the point of interchange between its tributary system and the trunklines across the Plains. Pueblo provided gateway connections between lines from the East and a route across the Rockies, but the actual services were geared to the patterns of the regional traffic focused upon Denver, and Pueblo was not a significant commercial competitor. . . .

This Colorado area had much clearer definition as a commercial region than as a culture area. Its population was drawn very largely but very broadly from the northern states. The development of an industrial labor class with large numbers of foreign-born (and Hispanos from New Mexico) was very like that of the mining and industrial districts of the East but quite unlike most regions in the West. What set Colorado apart was its particular combination of important activities—mining, heavy industry, ranching, irrigation agriculture, commerce, tourism, and recreation—which together formed a rather concentrated, integrated complex sustaining a relatively diverse and cosmopolitan society. . . .

Northern California

On the eve of the Gold Rush Northern California had only a few thousand mestizo and white settlers. There was no clear and substantial nucleus, only a scattering of points and small districts (e.g., Monterey, the Santa Clara, the Bay littoral, Sonoma, New Helvetia). However, so great and creative was the power of that event that a major urban focus, a regional axis, and several distinctive production districts were almost instantly apparent.

The general axis connected San Francisco with the north-central Sierras, in detail a water route bifurcating to the Valley centers of Sacramento and Stockton from which wagon roads and pack trails fanned into the mountain mineral districts. . . . Readily made tributary to that axis was a series of rapidly developing subregions—the Sierra valleys, the Sacramento and San Joaquin, the Coastal valleys, and the Redwood and Monterey coasts—tapped by an ever expanding system of coastal vessels, river boats, railroads, wagon and stage roads.

Beyond this undisputed hinterland, San Francisco was the principal metropolitan center for the rest of California and all of Nevada, and reached out to compete for trade over the entire Pacific Slope from interior British Columbia to central Arizona. Indeed, a good portion of the people and much of the money to develop this broad realm came from California. A critical feature in western regionalism is the amount of locally generated wealth concentrated in San Francisco which made it a financial center of considerable magnitude and independence rather than merely an outpost of Wall Street, as were most other cities in the nation. The building of the first transcontinental railroad, a feat of great practical and symbolic importance, is an effective illustration of this Californian autonomy, for the Central Pacific represented Californian capitalists reaching inland clear to the Great Salt Lake to meet on equal terms the Eastern-financed Union Pacific.

. . . Regional development was so dynamic as to make the geography of ethnic groups more a kaleidoscope than a mosaic. In sharp contrast with nearly all western regions, this Californian population was as variegated and cosmopolitan as that of the East, but differed in specific elements and proportions, and the size and character of development fostered a much more open and broadly integrated society with generally less tension than was apparent among the large ethnic blocs in the urbanized and industrialized East. Most important was the strong self-consciousness of Californians as constituting a dynamic and creative new society, a closer realization of the American dream.

Southern California

The country lying south of San Luis Obispo and the Tehachapi Range was so remote from the mother lode as to escape the heavy impact of the gold rush. Many Anglos passed through the area and some stayed, especially in the Los Angeles Basin, but they had to share the region with the Californios, the Mexican population dominated by the big ranching families. Although the Anglos continually increased in numbers and power, for thirty years southern California developed in considerable degree as a relatively balanced bicultural society. The extension of irrigation and subtropical crops provided a basis for growth, but the costs of development and difficulties of marketing impeded rapid expansion.

The great "Boom of the 80s" was southern California's equivalent of the gold rush, a sudden transformation which set a new pattern and scale of development. The boom was generated by an enormous speculative real estate promotion campaign which followed hard upon the completion of competitive direct railroad lines to the East. Tens of thousands of people came in, lured by the widely advertised virtues of life in America's subtropical paradise. Ranches were subdivided into thousands of suburban lots and scores of new towns. . . .

Such a land proved a powerful attraction to persons of moderate capital resources in the Middle West, who could sell farm, home, small business, or professional practice and move to a land of greater comfort and interest. Thus the main body of population was a relatively mature, conservative, property-minded bourgeois, but yet a society loosened by migration, the lack of firm roots, the instability of local communities, and the attractive possibilities for changing styles of life in a new physical and social environment. . . .

Los Angeles was from the first the main nucleus but it was the focus of a small region, hedged in by mountains and deserts. Irrigation projects provided an expanding agricultural base, but the main function of Los Angeles was to serve the ever-growing suburban population within its own immediate basin. By 1900 this last of the major western nuclei to emerge was famous across the nation as a very distinctive place.

Summary

To class these six regions as the major ones apparent toward the end of the nineteenth century is not to suggest that together they encompass the whole of the American West (Fig. 2). Several cities and districts lay beyond the bounds of clear dominance by any one of these major centers, most notably El Paso and its riverine oases and mining hinterland, central Arizona focused upon Phoenix, the Black Hills mining and ranching area, the Boise Basin and its extensive but thinly populated surroundings, and the Montana mining and ranching complex around Butte and Helena. Each had some degree of regional autonomy because of distance from large western cities and location on a railroad with direct service to the East, but each was very considerably smaller in population and commercial significance than the average of the major regions.

Nor does this nomination of six regions as major within the West mean that they were equal in all basic features. San Francisco was at a higher level than any of the other cities, the regional metropolis of the entire Pacific Slope, analogous to the role shared by Kansas City, Chicago, and Minneapolis–St. Paul for the Rocky Mountain half of the Far West. Denver, Salt Lake City, and Los Angeles were unchallenged regional capitals; Portland also, but within a contracting region for the quick rise of Seattle near the end of the century firmly detached Puget Sound from any significant Portland influence and also threatened its dominance of the Columbia Interior. New Mexico was the chief variant among the six. Its total population was relatively small and it had no large city, but its special multicultural,

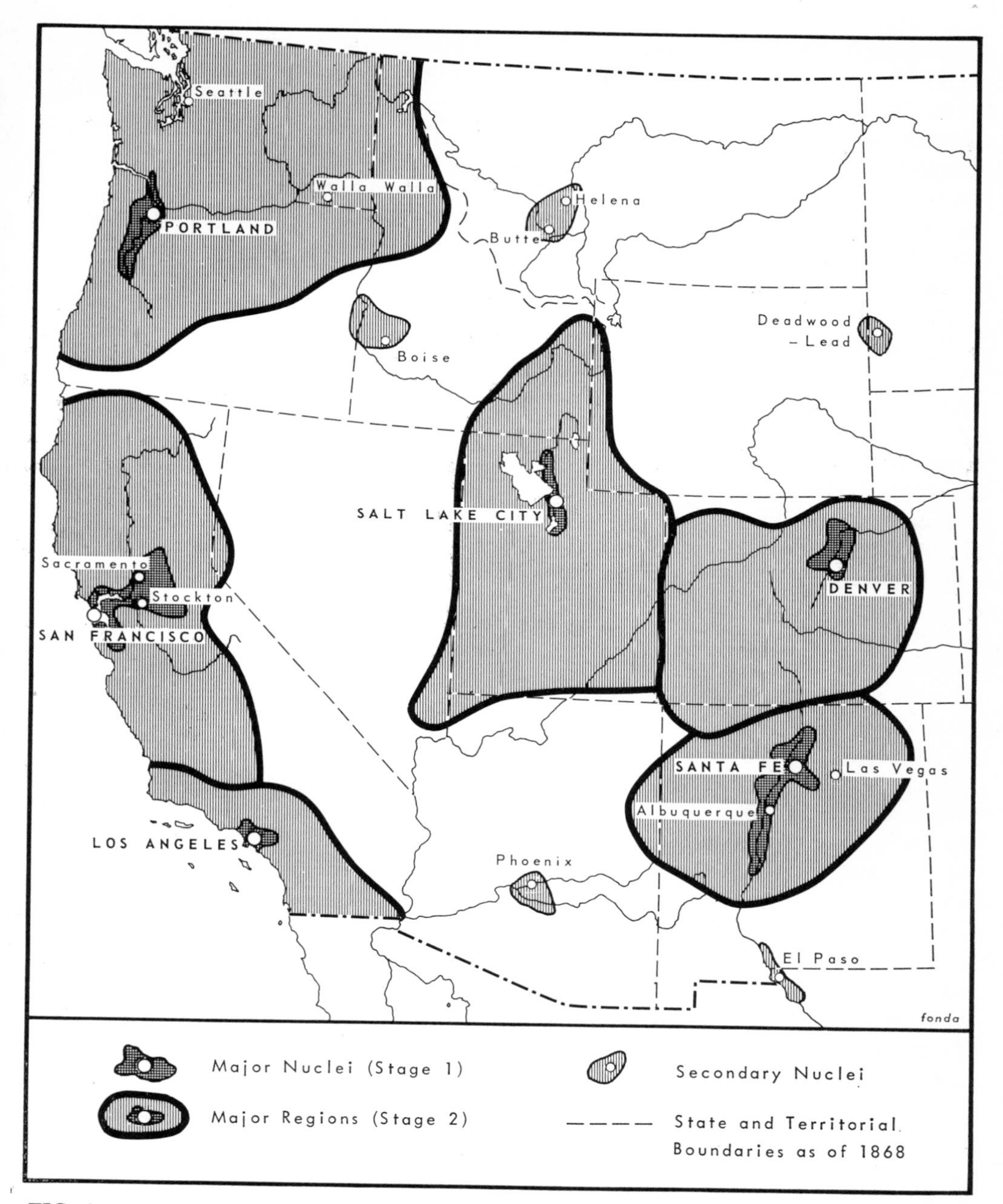

FIG. 2. Major nuclei and regions of the West in Stages I and II.

"imperial" character made it a very distinctive region wherein the relationships among its peoples had implications for a much broader Southwest. Santa Fe, though small in size and unable to dominate commercially even its own historic region, was nevertheless culturally a focal point of distinctly major significance. . . .

Circulation (Stages 1 and II)

Most of the famous western trails were primarily emigrant roads, serving as a means of getting people across the wilderness to new areas of settlement but by the very nature of the vehicles inadequate for effective communication and profitable commerce spanning such distances. Even the relatively large systems of wagon freighting and scheduled stage and mail service of the late 1850s did not effectively alter the isolation of these western nuclei. Much of the wagon freighting was in support of military posts and operations, heavily dependent upon government contracts. In the Oregon Country and California steamboats on the Columbia, Willamette, and Sacramento rivers aided the development of a commercial export agricultural economy, but elsewhere only goods of very high value, such as bullion or highly concentrated ores, or self-propelled, such as mules from New Mexico, could meet the costs of shipment.

The construction of a railroad to the Pacific became a major national issue almost from the moment that the United States acquired its Pacific frontage. The selection of the route for such a line was widely understood to be a momentous geographical decision. Northern California was so much the most important of the several western nuclei that San Francisco Bay was unquestioned as the Pacific terminus. But there were various possible routes for linking California with the East and it was generally assumed that the first railroad would become and long remain the principal transcontinental axis, the trunk line of the nation, with enormous consequences for subsequent patterns of development.

Because of the insular character of western settlement within such a vast area it was also generally accepted that, contrary to the situation in the East, the Pacific railroad would require heavy federal subsidy. The decision as to the route rested with Congress and thus was enmeshed in sectional politics. To appease competing areas the initial feasibility study authorized reconnaissance of five general routes between the Mississippi and the Pacific: one northern, two central, and two southern (Fig. 3). The War Department agency which carried out these surveys reported four of these routes as possible for a railroad, but recommended the southernmost as the most advantageous. Sectional rivalries blocked any decision until after southern secession, when Congress selected the central route which had been advocated by most northern interests. The Overland Telegraph, another federally subsidized service, was opened along the same general route in late 1861.

The central route was the shortest extending directly west from the most aggressive salients of the vigorously developing railroad system of the East. It had the added advantage of passing near Denver and Salt Lake City, thus linking three of these western regional systems with the nation. Land grant subsidies were later allocated to railroads building along all or major parts of the other five Pacific routes of the initial survey, and within

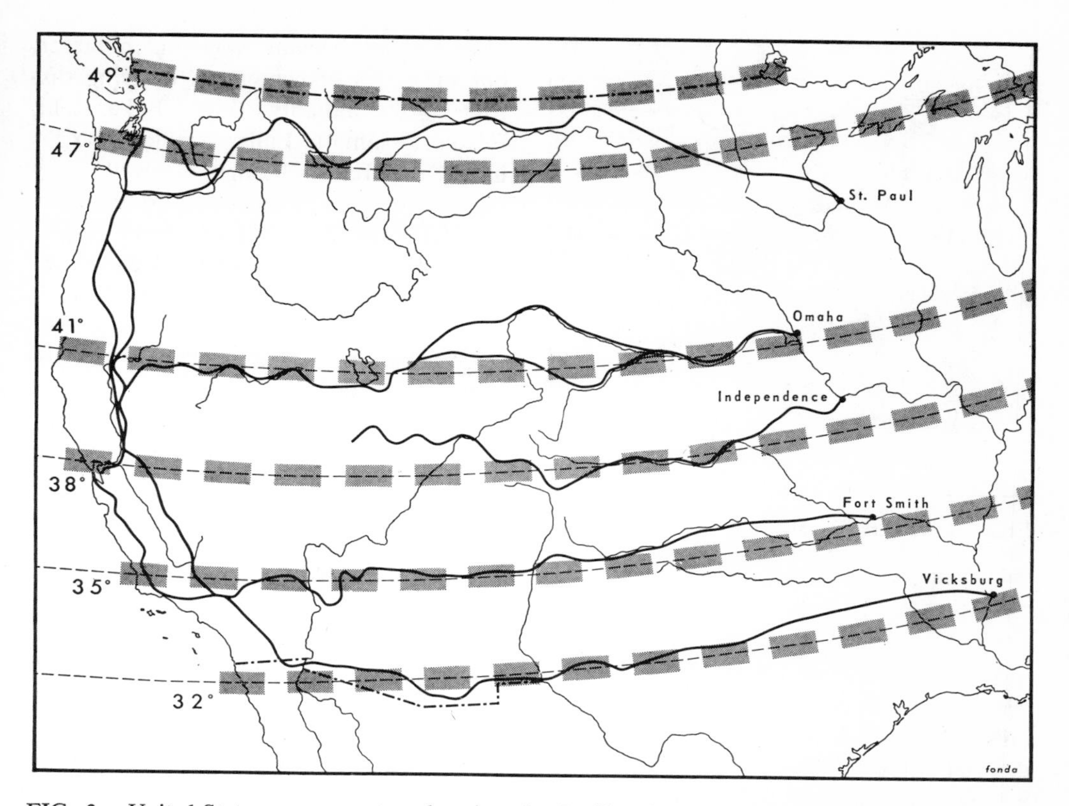

FIG. 3. United States government explorations for Pacific railroad routes, 1853-58. The routes were designated by reference to a particular parallel or parallels. The exploration of the 38th Parallel route ended when the leader of the exploration party was killed by Indians in Utah. All other routes were designated as practicable.

twenty years after the first golden spike all of the western regions were similarly linked by direct trunk lines to the East. That these several Western areas were more effectively linked to the East than to one another, except incidentally along transcontinental routes, was characteristic of this stage of development. Indeed, the insular pattern was so marked and regional interdependence so limited among certain areas that a complete network of direct railroad connections among the six major nuclei was never completed (Fig. 4). . . .

Population (Stages III and IV)

The end of the Turnerian frontier, when no large blocks of land suitable for traditional family farm colonization remained, marked the end of Stage II in the population pattern. Major expansions of agricultural colonization thereafter were dependent upon irrigation, and many of these were in large government projects such as in the Columbia Basin, the Snake River Plain, the San Joaquin, the Imperial Valley, and Central Arizona. Together with new mineral and forestry

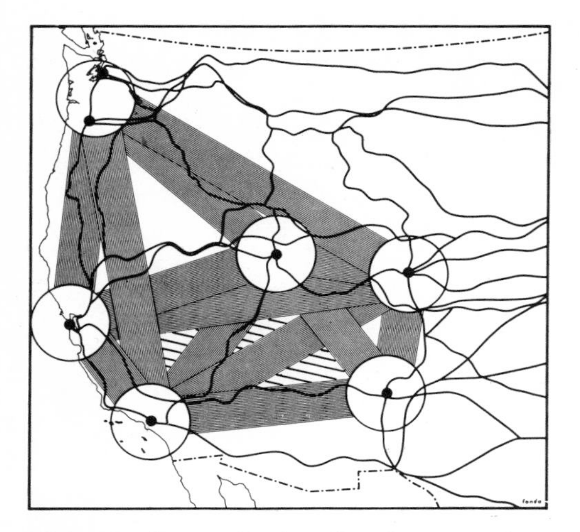

FIG. 4. Interregional railroad connections compared with a schematic pattern of direct links among all six regions of the West.

districts such developments altered western settlement patterns in numerous details. The growth of a more complex industrial base in the West, something beyond the elemental processing of local primary products, was critically dependent on activities fostered by the federal government, chiefly during the several wars of the twentieth century: shipyards, aircraft, ordinance, steel, and aluminum plants, as well as military installations. But migrants have also poured into certain areas for other reasons. "Westering" has continued to be a major feature of American life. In depressions as well as booms the image of the West as new country where one might embark upon a new life in more congenial circumstances has persisted as a powerful attraction. To a very considerable degree, industry has followed the population as well as lured it.

The total of such movements over a span of four or five decades did much to alter the shape and insularity of western regions. Major nuclei persisted and the largest cities became very much larger, but many lesser centers in outlying districts grew notably (e.g., Bakersfield, Fresno, Klamath Falls, Richland, Yakima, Great Falls, Billings, Roswell), giving a more even incidence of urbanization and blurring the earlier regional border zones. Migration patterns became increasingly complex. Inflows from the East were predominantly channeled to the large urban areas, but affected every district. Two new immigrations of distinct peoples became significant: the northward influx of large numbers of Mexicans who spread widely though selectively over the West as an industrial and agricultural proletariat; and, more recently, the westward influx of blacks, chiefly from Texas, Arkansas, and Louisiana, especially into urban California. There was also much interregional movement within the West, primarily to California, Portland, and Puget Sound. Most of this migration is obscure, but some of the most important streams are readily identifiable, such as that of New Mexican Hispanos spreading into the industrial and farm-labor districts of Colorado, Mormons colonizing alongside other settlers in the new irrigation districts and moving in large numbers to Pacific Coast urban areas, and the influx early in the century of Japanese and the more recent upsurge in Chinese immigration to California.

In the 1970s the West seems to be entering a fourth stage characterized by the emergence of huge metropolitan clusters of population. The Los Angeles Basin, San Francisco Bay, and the eastern shore of Puget Sound now appear to be truly megalopolitan in character. The older metropolitan centers of Portland, Denver, Salt Lake City, and Spokane have been suddenly joined by San Diego, Phoenix, Tucson, Albuquerque, and Las Vegas, Nevada. The rapid growth of cities is a common feature of the West through several stages, but the scale, character, and impact of recent urbanization is quite unprecedented. The efficiencies of transportation and communication and the relative affluence of a growing number of people combine to spread persons who are an integral part of urban culture far beyond the obvious bounds of continuously built-up urban areas. The seemingly rural countrysides of many western districts are actually dominated by essentially urban people scattered about in satellite towns, housing tracts, resorts, and homesteads, all in close functional and cultural connection with metropolitan areas by high-speed highways and individual or commuter air services.

Circulation (Stages III and IV)

Stage III saw the development of a far more elaborate and efficient combination of transportation facilities than the early railroad-stage and wagon road-sporadic riverboat combination of Stage II. The electric interurban railroad was a temporary addition; paved highways, local air service, pipelines, and a barge system on the Columbia were successive additions to the earlier railroad network, which was itself completed and greatly increased in efficiency during this period.

There were important similarities in the developmental phases of these spatial networks. Electric railroads began as urban-suburban lines and were later extended to connect neighboring cities. In areas of relatively dense agricultural and urban settlement (such as the Los Angeles Basin, Sacramento Valley, Willamette Valley, and Puget Sound Lowlands) fairly extensive systems were built. The network of paved highways began in similar fashion but went much further: first radiating out from urban centers, then connecting adjacent cities, expanding into regional systems, gradually linking adjacent regions, and ultimately forming a complete interregional network of relatively uniform quality. The superior efficiency of such government-financed trafficways soon drove the electric railroads out of business. Similarly, most of the local service airlines began as essentially regional companies connecting smaller cities with the regional metropolis. . . .

The transition to Stage IV is marked most significantly by the initiation of transcontinental nonstop air service, which was rapidly extended during the early jet age of the 1960s. The critical differentiating feature is the very rapid uninterrupted direct connection between major western urban centers and the national metropolises of New York and Washington and other cities in the national core, overflying intervening regions (Fig. 5). Such service forms a national and international network of nodal links which obliterates surface regions. This network, like all others, has its own peculiar pattern of sequential development: first from the two largest western metropolises, Los Angeles and San Francisco, to New York, then similar service from Seattle, then such service to other major eastern cities, then service between lesser western cities and the largest eastern cities. Such a sequence could be projected to the point where every major city has direct nonstop air service with every other major city. An analogous sequence is also underway in international service, beginning with scheduled nonstop flights connecting San Francisco and Los Angeles with major European cities.

Meanwhile local feeder airlines continue to amalgamate to form ever-larger systems. Today one company (Air West) dominates the entire Pacific Slope and

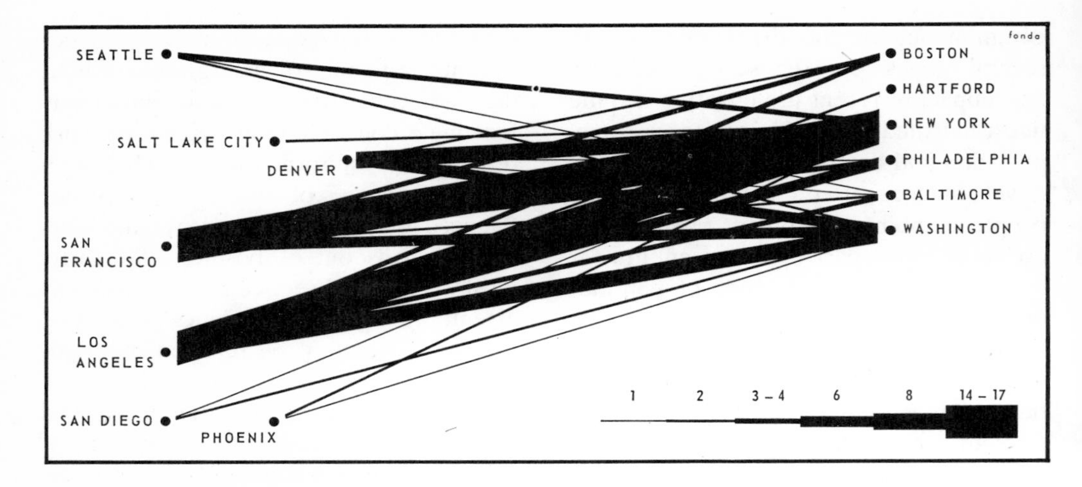

FIG. 5. Nonstop air service between cities of the West and the Northeastern Seaboard.

another (Frontier) the entire Rocky Mountain and High Plains country; the two systems interlock at Tucson, Phoenix, Salt Lake City, and Great Falls.

Complementing these developments are elaborate metropolitan freeway networks and the beginnings of a modern mass-transit system in the most congested megalopolis, and other forms of efficient long-distance transportation, such as pipelines, unit-trains, and the nationwide interstate superhighway system of uniform quality. . . .

Culture (Stages III and IV)

Stage III marks the end of insularity and a sharp increase in the power of forces working toward national cultural uniformity. Since most westerners and easterners have always shared a common basic "American" culture, it is important to define rather carefully the nature of this change.

The West was largely populated by migrants from the East who not only routinely brought their culture with them but sought to stay in touch with and to emulate the East in almost every way. Contrary to some of the more extreme and simple versions of the "frontier thesis," the West was always far more imitative than innovative. For example, in such basic institutions as churches, fraternal organizations, political parties, and educational systems westerners were mostly part of essentially national networks. Nevertheless, the insular conditions of Stage II allowed the preservation of conscious desired differences, as in the case of the Mormons and Hispanos; fostered divergences based upon isolation and environmental differences, as in diet, dialect, religious schism, and local economic and political issues; and caused a marked lag in the adoption of new features originating in the East because of the inefficiencies of diffusion processes. . . .

The triumph of the national over the regional is perhaps most readily illustrated in commercial activity. In Stage II retailing was dominated by local firms. The rise of the great mail-order houses with the development of a nationwide railroad network provided the first direct link between the western consumer and the eastern distributor, but time, cost, and physical separation left it a tenuous relationship of low intensity which did not greatly modify the general insularity of western regions. The development of national chain-stores and franchised service facilities, branch plants, and the acquisition of regional companies by national firms are the critical changes. Nationwide advertising combined with a nationwide network of distribution centers allowed new items to be introduced simultaneously into every region, and reduced the lag in adoption between center and periphery to relative insignificance.

Furthermore, "center" and "periphery" were no longer obvious characterizations for East and West. The national culture was being markedly influenced by Hollywood and other agencies which displayed a southern Californian style of life as the most modern and glamorous and thus implicitly worthy of emulation. From the 1920s to the 1960s American patterns of living were profoundly shaped by innovations spreading out from this world-famed western corner of the nation: the general style of informal, pleasure-centered living; the patio, barbecue, swimming pool, and stylish sports clothes; the architecture of houses and the design of interiors, as attested by the successive diffusion of the California "bungalow," "Spanish" stucco, "ranchhouse," and "contemporary" housetypes over all American suburbia. Above all, southern California set the national style in the use of the automobile and in the design of automobile-centered facilities and environments—carports, freeways, strip-cities, shopping centers, motels, drive-ins of all kinds. Detroit manufactured the cars but California showed how to live with them, and this critical influential link between the historic core and a burgeoning western region was a telling indication of a significant stage in national integration. But the very fact that southern California could play such a role was itself evidence that regionalism had not been completely eroded in the West. . . .

And despite the massive impact of national culture, other western regions retained a considerable degree of identity during Stage III. Colorado, never an obvious, self-conscious culture area, continued as a nodal region encompassing a very distinctive physical environment and combination of economic activities. The Pacific Northwest was rather more complex, with its three major urban centers and sharply contrasting environments of coast and interior. Though it had little sense of cultural cohesion, a loose sense of regionalism was based upon economy and environment, location in a far corner, Alaskan and Oriental trade connections, and a feeling of being sharply separate from and very much overshadowed in the national mind by California.

The Mormons illustrate very well the combined national-regional character of Stage III. Although still vigorously nurturing a strong sense of cohesion and identity as a distinct religious society, Mormon leaders worked toward an amicable accommodation with the nation. Indeed one can detect a gradual shift in corporate self-image from a "peculiar people" to "model Americans," the latter not in the sense of typical, but of the ideal godly, familial, puritanical, industrious people prominent in our national mythology. And while a strong sense of Utah as hallowed historic ground remained, the continual influx of Gentiles into the Mormon coreland, and the continual exodus of Mormons into neighboring regions and especially into California metropolitan areas, inevitably modified the strength of such Mormon regionalism. The building of a Mormon temple in Los Angeles in the 1950s was an overt acknowledgment of an important change in regional character and consciousness.

So, too, even though the Hispano culture of New Mexico remained strongly resistant of many facets of national culture, the continual influx of Anglos, reducing the earlier people to a minority in their own homeland, and the dispersal of Hispanos into Colorado and elsewhere, tended to blur regional identities. . . .

Transition to the next stage seems clearly underway but far from complete. The characteristics of that stage are as yet more a projection than a reality, but the direction of change seems so boldly evident to so many people and the pace of change so increasingly rapid that the future looms portentously. Briefly, current trends seem to suggest that the West will simply be the western half of a nation of many millions more people, of broadly uniform culture, living some form of urban life within a vast, intimately interconnected, nationwide, multimetropolitan system. Such a population will be fluid, highly mobile in work, impermanent in residence, capable of almost instant dispersal in recreation; the great western mountain and desert landscapes will become mere parks, as accessible and intensely used as city parks of today. . . .

Despite such developments, the historic regionalism in the West is by no means wholly dissolved, and these common projections are not necessarily immutable. While the West has grown rapidly during the last thirty years it (the eleven westernmost states) still contains only 16 percent of the nation's population in 38 percent of the area of the coterminous forty-eight. Large areas of the West are growing very slowly if at all; Montana and Wyoming were stagnant during the last decade, and Idaho and New Mexico grew by less than 5 percent, as did large sections of several other states. However, much the most remarkable demographic statistic is that net migration into California was only 26,000 in 1970 and may be transformed into a net exodus in 1971. Among the most remarkable recent events was the bold pronouncement by the governor of Oregon that his state had enough people and he would be pleased if no more moved in. . . . An end to westering would seem at least as important a change as was the end of the Turnerian frontier.

Such a shift can hardly be predicted with confidence at this point. Migrational changes are unlikely to be abrupt or uniform in effect, many other western areas are still relatively uncrowded and attractive, and the emergence of new attitudes about "growth" and "progress" and "development" will be slow and complex. But the very fact that trends of the recent past do loom in the minds of many westerners as a threat to their own future may have in itself halted the decline in regional consciousness. A heightened environmental awareness cannot but reinforce in some degree an appreciation of physical and cultural variations from place to place.

These very changes in attitudes have a geography of origin and diffusion, the outlines of which are recognizable in general if inscrutable in detail. Just as southern California exerted a massive impact upon American society in Stage III, so northern California seems destined to do so in Stage IV. Here seems to be the most concentrated awareness of many national problems and concern for solutions or alternatives. From here has come the main impetus of the new environmental consciousness, as epitomized by the Sierra Club. Here, certainly, is the major hearth of the "counterculture" which has mounted a comprehensive critique of American society and markedly influenced national patterns of fashion, behavior, and attitudes. . . .

Furthermore, some long-standing cultural differences within the West have lately been reinforced and seem certain to become even more prominent. Through all the decades, while national culture was eroding regional differences, a few resistant peaks remained above the broadening plain. A recent series of upheavals makes them loom much larger, and continuing tremors suggest more changes are incipient. American Indians, New Mexican Hispanos, Mexican Americans, and black Americans, never accorded full social integration and long resistant to cultural assimilation, now demand full rights and recognition as Americans even while they accentuate their own distinct culture patterns. Thereby many areas take on a new significance in the social landscape of America: areas such as the Central Valley, the Mexican border country, and the Indian reservations in various states. No one of these constitutes a new region on the scale and with the kind of functional integrity of the old. They are subregions of special distinction, and together with Hutterite colonies on the High Plains, conservative Mormon back valleys, the Hispano stronghold in the mountains, and, perhaps eventually, districts of Basques, Portuguese, Italians, Finnish, and other white groups of heightened ethnic consciousness, they form pieces in a complex American mosaic. That mosaic, which is becoming ever more visible, and which represents another reversal of long-projected trends, would seem to be a particularly important pattern for the future.

Thus, while the historic regions have markedly faded as discrete entities, the West is far from even an incipient uniform or united area. And the real test lies beyond academic evidence in what daily life is really like in the actual communities of the West. To any sensitive soul, surely, it does make a difference whether one lives in Provo, Pueblo, Pasadena, Pendleton, or Puyallup; such differences are rooted in historical legacies as well as environmental settings, in what kinds of people came and in what they have created and experienced in particular places.

Conclusion

. . . An approach which focuses upon the American West can be no more than a partial view of American development, yet this regional scheme has significance for national interpretation in two ways. First, as presented in this paper, in each topic at every stage the West is explicitly linked with the East, and the series of stages describes a cycle of divergence and convergence as between western regions and the national core and culture. Secondly, if this is indeed a useful generic model for the study of colonization and nation-building, the entire scheme could well be applied to the entire nation. For example, the initial European footholds on the American Atlantic shore as clearly fit the characteristics of Stage I as do the nuclear areas of the Far West. Carried forward, it would help define the regional complexities which existed underneath the broad sectional concepts of North, South, and West. With certain modifications the scheme could accommodate the emergence and unique position of a national core to which all other areas have been in some degree subordinate. Although profiting from the rich lode of Turnerian studies, the results would be very different from the old sectional interpretation.

But whether applied to the West or to

the nation, such an approach invites American geographers to address themselves directly to a task that they have never seriously undertaken as a field: a really comprehensive look at the full course of their nation's development with the object of contributing to a general assessment of its character. If, . . . in the wake of disillusion with a sequence of once widely espoused and now discredited theories, American historians now recognize Alexis de Tocqueville's *Democracy in America* as "the most respected of all interpretations of the United States," it would seem an especially opportune time for the geographers to join in the common quest for significant generalizations. For Tocqueville's interpretation rests upon a view of the United States as an "organic whole" with a recognizable "national character" which encompasses, under great tension, "oppressive conformity" and "kaleidoscopic variety," unmistakable "continuity" and "endless flux," regional diversity held together by multitudinous bonds of heritage and advantage. . . .

Suggested Additional Reading

In addition to the general works cited at the end of the Introduction, the following references elaborate many of the themes used in this section.

A. Colonial Period

Bumsted, John, and James T. Lemon, "New Approaches in Early American Studies: The Local Community in New England," *Histoire Sociale* 2 (1968):98-112.

Dunbar, Gary S., *Historical Geography of North Carolina Outer Banks* (Baton Rouge: Louisiana State University Press, 1958).

Earle, Carville, *The Evolution of a Tidewater Settlement System: All Hallow's Parish, Maryland, 1650-1783* (Chicago: Department of Geography, Research Paper No. 170, 1975).

Farnie, D. A., "The Commercial Empire of the Atlantic, 1607-1783," *Economic History Review* 15 (1962):205-18.

Friis, Herman A., "A Series of Population Maps of the Colonies and the United States, 1625-1790," rev. ed. (New York: American Geographical Society, 1968). Originally published, 1940. Condensed version, *Geographical Review* 30 (1940): 463-70.

Grant, Charles S., *Democracy in the Connecticut Frontier Town of Kent* (New York: Columbia University Press, 1961).

Greven, Philip J., Jr., *Four Generations: Population, Land, and Family in Colonial Andover, Massachusetts* (Ithaca, N.Y.: Cornell University Press, 1970).

Harris, R. Cole, "The Simplification of Europe Overseas" *Annals of the Association of American Geographers* 67 (1977): 469-83.

Henretta, James A., "Families and Farms: Mentalité in Pre-Industrial America" *William and Mary Quarterly* 35 (1978):3-32.

Lemon, James T., *The Best Poor Man's Country: A Geographical Study of Early Southeastern Pennsylvania* (Baltimore: Johns Hopkins University Press, 1972).

Lockridge, Kenneth A., "Land, Population and the Evolution of New England Society, 1630-1790," *Past and Present* 39 (April 1968):62-80.

McManis, Douglas R., *Colonial New England: A Historical Geography* (New York: Oxford University Press, 1975).

Meinig, Donald W., "The American Colonial Era: A Geographical Commentary," *Proceedings, South Australian Branch, Royal Geographical Society* 59 (1958): 1-22.

Merrens, H. Roy, *Colonial North Carolina in the Eighteenth Century: A Study in Historical Geography* (Chapel Hill: University of North Carolina Press, 1964).

Merrens, H. Roy, "Historical Geography

and Early American History," *William and Mary Quarterly,* Ser. 3, 22 (1965): 529-48.

Mitchell, Robert D., *Commercialism and Frontier: Perspectives on the Early Shenandoah Valley* (Charlottesville: University of Virginia Press, 1977).

Wacker, Peter O., *Land and People: A Cultural Geography of Pre-Industrial New Jersey* (New Brunswick, N.J.: Rutgers University Press, 1975).

B. Nineteenth Century

Andreano, Ralph L. (ed.), *New Views on American Economic Development* (Cambridge, Mass.: Schenkman Publishing Co., 1965).

Billington, Monroe L. (ed.), *The South, A Central Theme* (New York: Holt, Rinehart & Winston, 1969).

Billington, Ray A., *Westward Expansion: A History of the American Frontier,* 4th ed. (New York: Macmillan, 1974).

Bogue, Allan G., *From Prairie to Corn Belt: Farming on the Illinois and Iowa Prairies in the Nineteenth Century* (Chicago: University of Chicago Press, 1963).

Bowden, Martyn J., "Desert Wheat Belt, Plains Corn Belt: Environmental Cognition and Behavior of Settlers in the Plains Margin, 1850-99," in Brian W. Blouet and Merlin P. Lawson (eds.), *Images of the Plains: The Role of Human Nature in Settlement* (Lincoln: University of Nebraska Press, 1975).

Conzen, Michael P., *Frontier Farming in an Urban Shadow: The Influence of Madison's Proximity on the Agricultural Development of Blooming Grove, Wisconsin* (Madison: State Historical Society of Wisconsin, Logmark Editions 1971).

———, "Local Migration Systems in Nineteenth-Century Iowa," *Geographical Review* 64 (1974):339-61.

Clark, John G., *The Grain Trade in the Old Northwest* (Urbana: University of Illinois Press, 1966).

Curti, Merle E., *The Making of an American Community: A Case Study of Democracy in a Frontier County* (Stanford, Cal.: Stanford University Press, 1959).

Danhof, Clarence H., *Change in Agriculture: The Northern United States, 1820-1870* (Cambridge, Mass.: Harvard University Press, 1969).

Dykstra, Robert R., *The Cattle Towns* (New York: Knopf, 1968).

Easterlin, Richard A., "Population Change and Farm Settlement in the Northern States," *Journal of Economic History* 36 (1976):45-83, with comment by Allan G. Bogue and reply by Easterlin.

Fishlow, Albert, *American Railroads and the Transformation of the Antebellum Economy,* Harvard Economic Studies, vol. 127 (Cambridge, Mass.: Harvard University Press, 1965).

Gates, Paul W., *Landlords and Tenants on the Prairie Frontier: Studies in American Land Policy* (Ithaca, N.Y.: Cornell University Press, 1973).

Gibson, James R., *Imperial Russia in Frontier America: The Changing Geography of Supply of Russian America, 1784-1867* (New York: Oxford University Press, 1976).

Haites, Erik, James Mak, and Gary Walton, *Western River Transportation: The Era of Early Internal Development, 1810-1860* (Baltimore: Johns Hopkins University Press, 1975).

Hilliard, Sam B., *Hog Meat and Hoecake: Food Supply in the Old South, 1840-1860* (Carbondale: Southern Illinois University Press, 1972).

———, "The Tidewater Rice Plantation: An Ingenious Adaptation to Nature," *Geoscience and Man* 12 (1975):57-66.

———, "Pork in the Ante-Bellum South: The Geography of Self-Sufficiency," *Annals,* Association of American Geog--raphers 59 (1969) 461–80.

Jordan, Terry G., *German Seed in Texas Soil: Immigrant Farmers in Nineteenth-Century Texas* (Austin: University of Texas Press, 1966).

———, "Early Northeast Texas and the Evolution of Western Ranching," *Annals of the Association of American Geographers* 67 (1977):66-87.

Kollmorgen, William M., "The Woodsman's Assaults on the Domain of the Cattleman," *Annals of the Association of American Geographers* 59 (1969):215-39.

Lindstrom, Diane, "Southern Dependence upon Interregional Grain Supplies: A Review of the Trade Flows, 1840-1860," *Agricultural History* 44 (1970):101–13.

Malin, James C., "The Grassland of North America: Its Occupance and the Challenge of Continuous Reappraisals," in W. L. Thomas (ed.), *Man's Role in Changing the Face of the Earth* (Chicago: University of Chicago Press, 1956), pp. 350-66.

McIlwraith, Thomas F., "Freight Capacity and Utilization of the Erie and Great Lakes Canals before 1850," *Journal of Economic History* 36 (1976):852-77.

Meinig, Donald W., *The Great Columbia Plain: A Historical Geography, 1805-1910* (Seattle: University of Washington Press, 1968).

———, *Imperial Texas: An Interpretive Essay in Cultural Geography* (Austin: University of Texas Press, 1968).

———, "The Mormon Culture Region: Strategies and Patterns in the Geography of the American West, 1847-1964," *Annals of the Association of American Geographers* 55 (1965):191-220.

———, *Southwest: Three Peoples in Geographical Change, 1600-1970* (New York: Oxford University Press, 1971).

Peet, Richard, "Von Thünen Theory and the Dynamics of Agricultural Expansion," *Explorations in Economic History* 8 (1970-71):181-201.

Ransom, Roger L., and Richard Sutch, *One Kind of Freedom: The Economic Consequences of Emancipation* (Cambridge: Cambridge University Press, 1977).

Rothstein, Morton, "Antebellum Wheat and Cotton Exports: Contrast in Marketing Organization and Economic Development," *Agricultural History* 40 (1966): 91-100.

———, "The Antebellum South as a Dual Economy: A Tentative Hypothesis," *Agricultural History* 41 (1967):373-82.

———, "West Coast Farmers and the Tyranny of Distance: Agriculture on the Fringes of the World Market," *Agricultural History* 49 (1975):272-80.

Rubin, Julius, "The Limits of Agricultural Progress in the Nineteenth-Century South," *Agricultural History* 49 (1975): 362-73.

Shannon, Fred A., *Appraisal of Walter Prescott Webb's The Great Plains: A Study in Institutions and Environment* (New York: Social Science Research Council, Critique of Research in the Social Sciences, vol. 3, 1940).

Vance, James E., Jr., "California and the Search for the Ideal," *Annals of the Association of American Geographers* 62 (1972):185-210.

Walsh, Margaret, *The Manufacturing Frontier: Pioneer Industry in Antebellum Wisconsin, 1830-1860* (Madison, State Historical Society of Wisconsin, 1972).

Walsh, Margaret, "Pork Packing as a Leading Edge of Midwestern Industry, 1835-1875," *Agricultural History* 51 (1977): 702-17.

Webb, Walter P., *The Great Plains* (Boston: Ginn & Co., 1931).

III *Urbanization*

Although economic development and selective migration create and maintain striking regional differences in livelihood patterns and population composition within the United States, there were also parallel developments that diminish regional differences. Of these converging processes, urbanization is the most obvious. The same processes of economic development and migration which produced regional differentiation also stimulated the cityward movement of people and activities within each region. Although the rate of urbanization varied from region to region in response to local economic specializations, most regions had common needs for services and administration and for links with other regions which were met by urban centers. The parameters of the size, spacing, and functional complexity of regional urban systems certainly varied but the organization of local production and consumption through a system of service centers and the articulation of the national economy by means of metropolitan cities exerted a pronounced convergent effect on regional development. In providing these functions, urban settlements themselves also developed internal spatial arrangements of people and activities which were common to cities in all regions. The functional structure and population compositions of some settlements clearly recorded the distinctive employment and migration patterns of each region. But in almost all cities, there were common elements in their land use patterns and in the circulation of their activities and people. Accordingly, this section is divided into two parts: the first is devoted to the emergence of regional urban systems and the second to the internal spatial organization of urban life within cities.

A. Regional Urban Systems

Donald Meinig, in the final article in Section II, proposed a model of the sequence of development of western regions in which the final stage was defined by the emergence of metropolitan regions. These western regions were not only connected to each other by their metropolitan centers, but also to major cities elsewhere in the nation. This hierarchy of metropolitan regions is the topic of Michael Conzen's paper, "The Maturing Urban System: Changing Financial Networks in the United States, 1840-1910." Conzen documents the development of the metropolitan organization of the United States during the second half of the nineteenth century on the basis of the financial functions and networks of major cities. During the mid-1800s, the dominance of New York in banking was almost monopolistic and the pattern of banking networks reflected this primacy. By 1910 the nation had been subdivided into well-defined banking hinterlands, among which a four-level hierarchy could be detected and between which there were both hierarchical and lateral relationships. Although banking represented only one major metropolitan function, financial activities are sensitive to regional service functions. The regional patterns of financial activity clearly revealed the tendency for most specialized manufacturing cities, especially within the economic core region, to have much smaller hinterlands than those metropolitan centers with high levels of employment in regional services.

These relationships between industrialization and urbanization are confronted by Allan Pred in "Industrialization, Initial Advantage, and American Metropolitan Growth." Pred discusses the parallelism of industrialization and urbanization and emphasizes the fact that industrial innovations in specific urban centers produced initial advantages which then sustained its cumulative growth. He also explores factors contributing to the selective growth of cities, especially the greater comparative advantages some cities derived when transportation improvements made them more accessible to national markets. Conzen and Pred both focus on the growth patterns and hinterlands of the most populous cities, but regional urbanization also involved complex changes in the size, spacing, and functional role of smaller-order centers. Moreover, the relative contributions of different factors accounting for the variable growth of both metropolitan centers and smaller towns changed as settlement became more dense and the regional economy more developed.

Edward Muller addresses changes in these factors which determine the variable growth of settlements in the developing hinterland of Cincinnati, Ohio in "Selective Urban Growth in the Middle Ohio Valley, 1800-1860." He proposes a three-stage developmental model of regional urbanization in a newly settled region. The first stage was characterized by the primacy of a large entrepôt over many smaller and weakly differentiated settlements; during the second stage, this primacy was maintained but improvements in local accessibility, as canals and railroads supplemented rivers and roads, stimulated the selective growth of smaller centers. The third stage was defined by the effective competition of subregional centers in regional service functions and the growth of other settlements on the basis of dominance in local manufacturing. Consequently, the primacy of the regional entrepôt was greatly diminished. This model has general implications and may be applied to other newly settled and developing regions. Although the time span of the phases may vary from region to region, the processes of variable urban growth resulted in markedly similar regional urban systems within most metropolitan hinterlands.

If there is a region of the United States for which generalizations about urbanization are most hazardous, it is the South. Throughout its history, low levels of urbanization in the South have been attributed to the peculiarities of the regional economy. Plantations were assumed to be relatively self-sufficient in local supplies but dependent on one major entrepôt city or even cities outside of the region for most of their credit and for many manufactured goods. Plantations dominated only limited parts of the South. The remainder of the region was only partly commercial and had very limited needs for urban services. Low real income provided only weak bases for the kind of consumption which supported the growth of service centers. In short, neither component of the "dual" economy of the South required a dense network of service centers. H. Roy Merrens and Joseph Ernst in "'Camden's Turrets Pierce the Skies!' The Urban Process in the Southern Colonies during the Eighteenth Century" modify this view of the colonial South and their findings may have implications for the antebellum South too. Towns were fewer and smaller in the hinterlands of Charleston, Baltimore, and New Orleans than elsewhere in the nation, but the commercial life of the South was conducted by way of a network of centers whose small populations did not suggest their functions. Only further work on the South will reveal the full extent of the functional complexity of diminutive nucleated settlements providing for regional commerce and local services.

B. The City from Within

The concentration of activities in cities resulted in the emergence of well-defined districts devoted to urban employment and clearly separated from residential quarters. By far the most conspicuous concentration of urban employment in nineteenth-century cities was the central business district (CBD). Martyn Bowden's article, "Persistence, Failure, and Mobility in the Inner City," reveals the need to break down the CBD into several complex use categories. Different functions made claims on central land at different rates and different times; at certain critical periods, entire specialized districts relocated in other sections of the inner city. Individual business moved frequently and often did not last long, but in spite of this turnover, most major land use changes were determined by firms of substantial longevity adjusting to new locational needs and advantages.

Contemporary studies of residential patterns within the nineteenth-century city focused on the old, congested housing near the expanding CBD. This area was referred to as a slum and later, when foreign immigrants predominated, as a ghetto. These locations provided the largest supply of cheap housing and the largest pool of unskilled jobs in the city. Although this model of a blighted zone of slums housing newly arrived and poverty-stricken immigrants was attractively simple, it requires careful modification. David Ward in "The Internal Spatial Differentiation of Immigrant Residential Districts" suggests two modifications. First, the period of urban development must be specified. Before 1875, neither employment nor housing was necessarily most abundant in central urban locations and impoverished immigrants were scattered in many sections of the city and even in peripheral shanty-towns. After 1875 the inner city did provide the largest supply of cheap housing and unskilled jobs and most immigrants concentrated on the margins of the CBD. Second, the social and living conditions of the inner city varied considerably. Most of the inner city was characterized by overcrowding, but the high death rates and pathological social conditions, associated with the term slum, affected only a segment of the immigrant population. The immigrant ghetto was often highly organized politically and was the focus of ethnic institutions which assisted newcomers in their adjustment to an unfamiliar environment. Slums were areas where the adverse material environment resulted in pathological social conditions whereas ghettos were neighborhoods where people of a common ancestry had created their own distinctive institutions.

Although these ethnic residential concentrations were often voluntary, prejudice also contributed to segregated housing patterns. Before World War I, the movements of blacks to northeastern and midwestern cities was overshadowed by the massive immigration from Europe. During the nineteenth century, most urban blacks lived in southern or border cities. John Radford examines black residential patterns in "Race, Residence, and Ideology: Charleston, South Carolina in the Mid-Nineteenth Century." The racial pluralism of southern cities was reflected in distinctive residential patterns both before and after slave emancipation. Before the Civil War black slaves were generally accommodated on the rear sections of the residential lots of their owners, while free blacks were relegated to the periphery of the city. Indeed, free blacks were gradually pushed to the edge of the city by contrived planning ventures justified in the interests of urban improvement. These antebellum residential patterns persisted during

Reconstruction, revealing the continued role of a racist ideology rather than market processes in the urban locations of blacks.

The supply of cheap housing in the inner city was created by the abandonment of these areas by upwardly mobile households seeking new suburban homes. Suburbs are almost as old as cities themselves but, during the course of the nineteenth century, the proportion of urban residents moving to suburban locations increased so rapidly that their populations began to approach those of the central city. This growth was in part a consequence of a series of innovations in local transportation which progressively opened up suburban residence to the middle class. Peter Muller in "The Historical Evolution of American Suburbs: A Geographical Interpretation" reviews concepts of suburbs and then relates the successive innovations in transportation technology to changes in the rate and type of residential expansion. Finally, he discusses the rapid decentralization of employment during the early decades of the twentieth century and the alteration of patterns established in the nineteenth century.

The settlement of the United States has involved adaptations to a wide range of environments and each of these environments has been occupied by different combinations of ethnic groups. Within each regional environment, however, the form of urban growth has differed only in detail. Large cities eventually became the leading destinations of most population movements to and within the United States. This cityward movement has perhaps as great a claim to express a dominant American experience as has the more celebrated frontier movement of pioneers. The American city, which might have symbolized a distinctive common element in a country with striking regional differences in economy and sub-culture, has rarely aroused popular or literary enthusiasm. In the nineteenth century, conflicts between rural and urban interests divided most regions, and today these antagonisms remain in the conflicts between central cities and their suburbs.

A. *Regional Urban Systems*

The Maturing Urban System in the United States, 1840-1910 / *Michael P. Conzen*

Urban growth in North America has often been approached from two extremes. On the one hand, the process can be studied in the context of individual towns and cities with an emphasis on the particular factors that lead them to grow or stagnate.[1] Often this viewpoint is extended to include several settlements, either as a group of proximal places or as dispersed cities drawn together for specific comparison or contrast.[2] . . . At the other extreme, cities are viewed as components of an internally connected system in which individual cities have specific functional roles.[3] Such urban systems

1. Representative of the enormous literature in this vein are Robert G. Albion, *The Rise of New York Port: 1815-1860* (New York: Charles Scribner's Sons, 1939); Bessie L. Pierce, *A History of Chicago,* 3 vols. (New York: 1937-57); Catherine E. Reiser, *Pittsburgh's Commercial Development: 1800-1850* (Harrisburg: Pennsylvania Historical and Museum Commission, 1951); and Vera Shlakman, *Economic History of a Factory Town: A Study of Chicopee, Massachusetts,* Smith College Studies in History No. 20 (Northampton, Mass.: Smith College, 1936).
2. For example, Carl Bridenbaugh, *Cities in the Wilderness: The First Century of Urban Life in America, 1625-1742* (New York: The Ronald Press, 1938); and *Cities in Revolt: Urban Life in America, 1743-1776* (New York: Alfred A. Knopf, 1955); Richard C. Wade, *The Urban Frontier: Pioneer Life in Early Pittsburgh, Cincinnati, Lexington, Louisville, and St. Louis* (Chicago: University of Chicago Press, 1964); Kenneth Wheeler, *To Wear a City's Crown: The Beginnings of Urban Growth in Texas, 1836-1865* (Cambridge, Mass.: Harvard University Press, 1968). Two classic studies of specific rivalry between cities are Wyatt W. Belcher, *The Economic Rivalry Between St. Louis and Chicago, 1850-1880* (New York: Columbia University Press, 1947); and Julius Rubin, *Canal or Railroad: Imitation and Innovation in the Response to the Erie Canal in Philadelphia, Baltimore, and Boston,* Transactions of the American Philosophical Society (Philadelphia, 1961).
3. Eric E. Lampard, "The Evolving System of Cities in the United States: Urbanization and Economic Development," in Harvey S. Perloff and Lowden Wingo, Jr., eds., *Issues in Urban Economics* (Baltimore: Johns Hopkins University Press, 1968), pp. 81-138; Jeffrey G. Williamson and Joseph A. Swanson, "The Growth of Cities in the American Northeast, 1820-

Reproduced (with omissions) by permission from the *Annals,* Association of American Geographers, 67 (1977):88-108.

are ordered in terms of size and functional specialization.[4] Here, the emphasis lies on rank-size relationships or central place hierarchies and explanations seek to account for basic structure largely in terms of social physics.

The dangers of under- and overgeneralization in these extremes are readily apparent. Several recent studies have stressed the selective nature of growth among towns viewed as a loose system in which local aspirations can boost a settlement to the ceiling of tolerance imposed by the regional economy, relative location, technology, and other variables.[5] Conceptual advances in this area range from Pred's chain-reaction models of the seemingly perpetual dominance of large regions by their functionally elite cities, to Vance's mercantile model of large-scale settlement patterns, and to more constrained models of regional urban growth.[6] Implicit in such work is the fundamental relationship between cities and the hinterlands which provide the export surpluses and service demands that give them purpose. . . .

For all their importance, however, urban hinterlands have been assumed but not specified as factors in urban growth. As a result, much current wisdom rests upon unsubstantiated generalizations about the economic and territorial reach of cities.[7] Part of the explanation for this neglect undoubtedly lies in the paucity of data suitable for determining city-hinterland relations during the middle to late nineteenth century when the modern urban system took shape.[8] During this period a vast network of bank correspondent accounts evolved to link banks throughout the country with each other, forming a system whose outlines can be reconstructed from compilations of contemporary bankers' directories.[9] This article will analyze such bank correspondent activity as a simple index of urban connectivity over time in order to explore changing patterns of interdepend-

1870," *Explorations in Entrepreneurial History*, 2nd ser., vol. 4, Supplement (1966); Beverly Duncan and Stanley Lieberson, *Metropolis and Region in Transition* (Beverly Hills: Sage Publications, 1970).

4. For discussions of the "steady state" rank size distribution of American cities, see Carl H. Madden, "On Some Indicators of Stability in the Growth of Cities in the United States," *Economic Development and Cultural Change*, vol. 4 (1956), pp. 236-52; Brian J. L. Berry, *Geography of Market Centers and Retail Distribution* (Englewood Cliffs, N.J.: Prentice-Hall, 1967), pp. 76-78; Fred Lukermann, "Empirical Expressions of Nodality and Hierarchy in a Circulation Manifold," *East Lakes Geographer* 2 (1966):17-44.

5. John R. Borchert, "American Metropolitan Evolution," *Geographical Review* 57 (1967): 301-32; David Ward, *Cities and Immigrants: A Geography of Change in the Nineteenth Century* (New York: Oxford University Press, 1971); and Peter G. Goheen, "Industrialization and the Growth of Cities in Nineteenth-Century America," *American Studies* 14 (1973):49-65.

6. Allan R. Pred, *Urban Growth and the Circulation of Information: The United States System of Cities 1790-1840* (Cambridge, Mass.: Harvard University Press, 1973); James E. Vance, Jr., *The Merchant's World: The Geography of Wholesaling* (Englewood Cliffs, N.J.: Prentice-Hall, 1970); Michael P. Conzen, "Capital Flows and the Developing Urban Hierarchy: State Bank Capital in Wisconsin, 1854-1895," *Economic Geography* 51 (1975):321-38; and Edward K. Muller, "Selective Urban Growth in the Middle Ohio Valley, 1800-1860," *Geographical Review* 66 (1976):178-99.

7. One attempt to delineate developing urban spheres of influence is Michael P. Conzen, "A Transport Interpretation of the Growth of Urban Regions: An American Example," *Journal of Historical Geography* 1 (1975):361-82.

8. The urban system is understood in terms of a set of interdependent cities in which economic and demographic change in one city will directly or indirectly affect the economic and demographic structure of one or more other cities in the set. Pred, *Urban Growth*, p. 187.

9. Metropolitan centers in this historical period cannot be defined in modern census terms. For convenience, metropolitan centers are defined here as the twenty-three cities over 75,000 in 1880 and the twenty-eight cities over 200,000 in 1910.

ence among cities and the extent, configuration, and internal structure of urban hinterlands at all levels of the urban system.[10]

The Context

The later nineteenth century in America was an era of enormous growth in economic output, scale of production, division of labor, and interdependency through innovations in technology and management.[11] To the decline of traditional formulae for social and business intercourse that accompanied the continental expansion of settlement were added the politico-economic dislocation of Civil War and Reconstruction. These stresses fostered experimentation in government and finance that in turn generated pressure for stability and organization, in fact, a general "search for order."[12] In no sector of the economy was this transformation more apparent than in the financial community. Fragmented and disjointed before the Civil War, financiers and their institutions later faced immense pressures to unite in unlocking the capital flows that would stabilize prices and increase productive capacity. New forms of production and new locales for enterprise demanded a new efficiency in the transfer of funds across economic and geographical boundaries. Business partnerships and personal connections continued to be important but they did not furnish an adequate basis for long-distance business negotiation.[13] The Civil War inaugurated a national banking and currency system that remained substantially intact until the end of the century. Between 1870 and 1914 the outlines of a national investment market emerged that paralleled the rise of the limited-liability corporation.[14] In this same period the nation's cities emerged on a new scale. Some of the largest cities benefitted from an increasing urbanization of manufacturing as scale economies multiplied and market orientation intensified.[15]

This nationalizing of business occurred within a geographically expanding domain. The breakdown of "island communities" produced new vertical linkages with far-flung communities of interest, and a massive replication of settlement patterns spread this heightened interaction across the remaining thinly settled areas of the continent.[16] . . . Whatever degree of partial autonomy local communities enjoyed through cycling funds internally, the growing volume and complexity of commercial and industrial connections soon demanded a more elaborate hierarchy of banking channels.

Framework for Correspondent Analysis

Interregional and local capital mobility generally has been organized by the met-

10. An urban hinterland is considered to be the broad territory adjacent to an urban center "within which economic and some cultural activities are focused largely on the primary center." Eugene van Cleef, "Hinterland and Umland," *Geographical Review* 31 (1941):308-11.
11. Eric E. Lampard, "The History of Cities in the Economically Advanced Areas," *Economic Development and Cultural Change* 3 (1955): 81-136.
12. Robert H. Wiebe, *The Search for Order, 1877-1920* (New York: Hill and Wang, 1967), pp. 11-44.
13. Ida M. Tarbell, *The Nationalizing of Business, 1878-1898* (New York: Macmillan, 1936), p. 269.
14. Lance E. Davis, "The Investment Market, 1870-1914: The Evolution of a National Market," *Journal of Economic History* 25 (1965): 355-93.
15. Allan R. Pred, *The Spatial Dynamics of U.S. Urban-Industrial Growth, 1800-1914: Interpretive and Theoretical Essays* (Cambridge, Mass.: M.I.T. Press, 1966), pp. 13-14.
16. Wiebe, *Search for Order,* pp. xiii and 3-4.

ropolitan network.[17] . . . A necessary condition for the growth of banking in large cities was the organization of a financial tributary area that looked to the regional metropolis as its prime clearinghouse. Metropolitan centers had to increase their monetary linkages with surrounding areas to the point that entrepreneurs in the hinterland would look first to that particular metropolis rather than outside the region for loans and investment opportunities. The stronger this bond, the more the social and economic life of the hinterland was drawn within the organizational sphere of the metropolis.

The American system of bank correspondents arose from the need to channel business smoothly between the thousands of individual bank establishments around the country. The pattern of correspondent accounts represents the accumulated structure of tens of thousands of channels voluntarily set up between banks in large commercial centers and those dispersed across the country, and provides a first approximation of the flow of capital through the financial system. A correspondent relationship in the nineteenth century involved a bank in a small community maintaining a deposit account with a bank in a large city. The funds never fell below an agreed minimum and the city bank could use them to yield interest. In return, the city bank supplied the country bank with a variety of services such as specie redemption of out-of-town banknotes (in the period before national currency), clearing out-of-town checks, making large loans or bringing the country bank in on a profitable loan, counting the deposit account balance as part of the country bank's reserves, referral of new customers, and investment advice.[18]

The spatial structure of these correspondent accounts for the country as a whole has been reconstructed between 1840 and 1910, with detailed emphasis on the period 1881-1910.[19] The year 1840 marks a convenient point at which the correspondent system was first recognizably national in that it extended over the then solidly settled portions of the continent. The correspondent system had evolved to its maximum efficiency by 1910, with over 40,000 accounts linking banks around the country and it was regularized by the Federal Reserve System instituted three years later.[20] The period from 1881 to 1910 witnessed the major readjustments in the system and fortunately bequeaths the most systematic information.[21]

Banking hinterlands for selected dates, based on the principal correspondents of

17. Richard Sylla, "Federal Policy, Banking Structure, and Capital Mobilization in the United States, 1863-1913," *Journal of Economic History* 29 (1969):657-86.

18. A comprehensive list is in Gerald C. Fischer, *American Banking Structure* (New York: Columbia University Press, 1968), pp. 110-13.

19. *The Banker's Directory of the United States and Canada* (Chicago: Rand McNally and Company, 1876 onward). The data for 1881 are the first available that indicate any significant number of linkages not invovling New York, and they should reflect the prolonged competition of New York and the first reserve cities created in 1864.

20. Correspondent data have been studied before, but not in a nineteenth-century geographical context. An early call for the systematic use of correspondent data in studies of the urban system was made in Stanley Lieberson and Kent P. Schwirian, "Banking Functions as an Index of Inter-City Relations," *Journal of Regional Science* 4 (1962):69-81. Developing patterns in selected states have been analyzed in Duncan and Lieberson, *Metropolis,* pp. 99-111.

21. The actual use of each correspondent account is impossible to reconstruct. Only aggregate statistics of these accounts were required in individual bank reports to the Comptroller of the Currency under the headings of "due to banks" and "due from banks" without individual specification.

every commercial bank in the United States, show the orientation of cities and counties toward a metropolis on the basis of the correspondent affiliations of a plurality of their banks.[22] The size, shape, and regional associations of such hinterlands suggest the general structure of flows within the correspondent system. A city or county oriented to New York, for example, may be expected to have had most of its financial dealings (channeled through its banks) with New York directly rather than through intermediate centers; it is assumed that more capital flowed between New York and that city or county than between it and another metropolis.[23] . . .

Development of the Correspondent System

Correspondent banking began in 1818 in Boston with the Suffolk Bank.[24] By 1840, New York State law required all country banks to keep funds in New York City, mainly for note redemption. Many banks in other states followed suit in order to benefit from New York City's preeminence in the national money market. . . . New York's trade with the interior early required an almost continuous movement of funds to the city to pay for the goods.[25] Banks in Ohio, then Indiana and Illinois, followed banks in upstate New York in corresponding with New York City, followed by New England and Middle Atlantic banks. The South began to orient toward New York during the 1850s, concurrent with the next ring of Middle Western states. By the Civil War, most of the territory east of the Mississippi had established strong financial ties to New York.[26]

The 1863 National Bank Act established eight "reserve" cities to aid New York in the geographical management of a new national currency. New York was elevated to "central reserve" city status, thus conserving its national preeminence. The new reserve cities were Boston, Philadelphia, Baltimore, Cincinnati, New Orleans, Providence, Chicago, and St. Louis. An amendment in 1864 added Washington, Albany, Pittsburgh, Cleveland, Detroit, Milwaukee, Louisville, Leavenworth, and San Francisco.[27] The act gave large regional cities formal sanction to channel banking business in their hinterlands through their own institutions. . . . By 1912, the leading banks of New York and Chicago numbered their correspondents in the thousands.

New York was the only central reserve city in the nation until the National Bank Act of 1887 permitted cities of over

22. The term "principal correspondent" came into use in bank directories to denote those banks regarded by the client banks with which the latter did most business of this type. There was a practical limitation of directory space that limited the number of entries, and most client banks listed between one and four correspondents, with the vast majority listing two principal correspondents. See also "Correspondence about Correspondents" in Duncan and Lieberson, *Metropolis,* pp. 281-86.

23. This practical assumption is necessary since no comprehensive records exist on precise capital flows through individual accounts. While great differences doubtless existed between accounts, the sheer number of accounts involved, their geographical diversity, and the likely cancelling effect of many biases, combine to justify analysis of the correspondent system in terms of its simple network characteristics.

24. Paul Studenski and Herman E. Kroos, *Financial History of the United States* (New York: McGraw-Hill, 1952), pp. 88-89.

25. Margaret G. Meyers, *Origins and Development,* vol. 1 of Benjamin H. Beckhart, ed., *The New York Money Market* (New York: Columbia University Press, 1931), p. 103; and Duncan and Lieberson, *Metropolis,* p. 103.

26. Myers, *Origins and Development,* pp. 108-12.

27. Reserve city status in relation to the geographical aspects of intermetropolitan rivalry between 1864 and 1900 is thoroughly discussed in Duncan and Lieberson, *Metropolis,* pp. 101-7.

200,000 population to qualify for that status upon application by three-quarters of their banks. The act also liberalized the requirements for reserve status. In part, this act resulted from anti-New York pressure to distribute banking profits more widely. The increasing sophistication of the national money market encouraged expansion to accommodate its dispersed elements. . . . The fivefold growth of correspondent balances in Chicago between 1890 and 1910, and the eightfold growth of business in St. Louis, which achieved central reserve status in the same period, were not enough to challenge New York's primacy.[28] In 1907 it was still in firm control.[29] . . . Referring to the period following the law of 1887, Margaret Myers has written:[30]

> The national banking system was often discussed as if it were a complete hierarchy, with the country banks depositing their reserve balances in the banks of the reserve cities, while the banks of those cities in turn kept their balances in New York. The National Bank Act made such an organization permissive, but the actual operation of the system was by no means as simple as this would indicate. Many of the country banks skipped entirely over the reserve cities and took their balances directly to the central reserve banks.

The Growth of Financial Centers

. . . In banking . . . the nation's cities developed clearly identifiable hierarchical groupings (Fig. 1). A four-level hierarchy emerged by the early 1870s. Boston and Philadelphia were secondary to New York but clearly superior to all other cities. A third level distinguished cities with annual bank clearings above $200 million from other major cities with significantly lower banking activity. Some cities improved rank rapidly over time, in several cases far outstripping their improvement in population ranking. Chicago joined the second level by the 1880s, while Cleveland and Kansas City joined the third level. By 1910 Chicago was pulling away from Boston and Philadelphia and keeping pace with New York's proportional growth, while Kansas City and Pittsburgh had increased their rank swiftly within the third level.

New York's share of the national volume of clearings fell from 63.3 percent in 1875 to 46.8 percent in 1900 as more cities became established financial centers, whereas Chicago increased from 5.0 percent to 10.8 percent.[31] Boston and Philadelphia fell behind somewhat, and the stagnation of Cincinnati, New Orleans, Baltimore, and Milwaukee among third-level cities was balanced by the growth of Kansas City and Pittsburgh.

Banking functions gained more importance for Boston, Kansas City, and Omaha than their population size would suggest, and gained less importance for Buffalo, Cleveland, and Detroit. Boston's case rests on historical grounds since its long tradition of worldwide commerce led to early banking sophistication which then kept pace with competing centers through local industrialization and devel-

28. Myers, *Origins and Development,* p. 240.
29. F. Cyril James, *The Growth of Chicago Banks: Volume I, The Formative Years* (New York: Harper and Row, 1938), p. 733. New York was relatively less dependent on correspondent business in relation to individual depositors than either Chicago or St. Louis.
30. Myers, *Origins and Development,* pp. 240-41.

31. Calculated from data on clearings in *The Public* and its successor *The Commercial and Financial Chronicle;* the New York figures were adjusted for speculation by subtracting 2.5 times the value of stock exchange sales from the total New York clearings in order to approximate the estimated "legitimate business" activity of the city. This procedure is discussed in *The Public,* Vol. 21, No. 1 (January 5, 1882), p. 5.

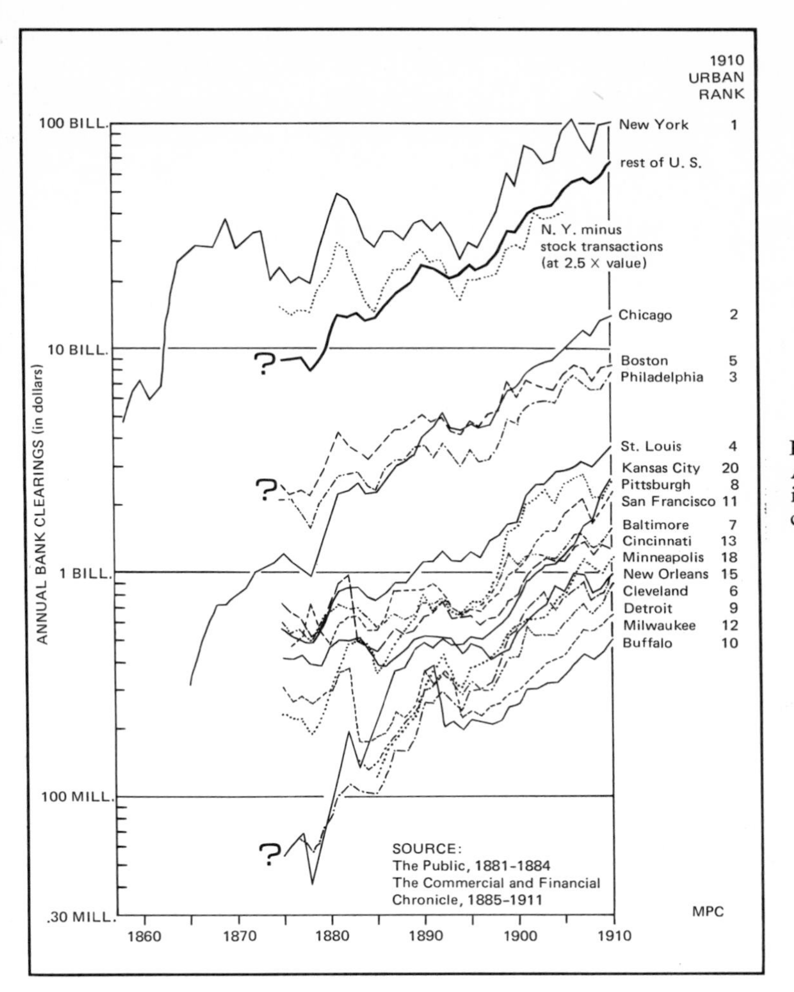

FIG. 1
Annual bank clearings in selected United States cities, 1858-1910.

oping western commercial connections.[32] More generally, however, the structure of urban employment in the later nineteenth century affected banking relations (Fig. 2). Before 1850, banking was distinguished sharply between well-established Atlantic or Gulf cities and frontier cities such as Cincinnati and St. Louis.[33] Functional specialization among cities in 1850 had little influence on ratios of population to bank capital, but by 1880 an economic bias was emerging to replace the previous geographical bias. By 1910, cities heavily dependent on manufacturing had low ratios of population to banking activity, and cities specializing in trade and services, especially wholesaling, had high ra-

32. Justin Winsor, *Memorial History of Boston* (Boston: James R. Osgood and Company, 1881-1883), vol. 4, pp. 151-78; Robert G. LeBlanc, *Location of Manufacturing in New England in the 19th Century,* Geography Publications at Dartmouth No. 7 (Hanover, N.H.: Dartmouth College, 1969), pp. 46-47; and Arthur M. Johnson and Barry E. Supple, *Boston Capitalists and Western Railroads: A Study in the Nineteenth Century Railroad Investment Process* (Cambridge, Mass.: Harvard University Press, 1967).

33. Wade, *Urban Frontier,* pp. 69 and 164-65.

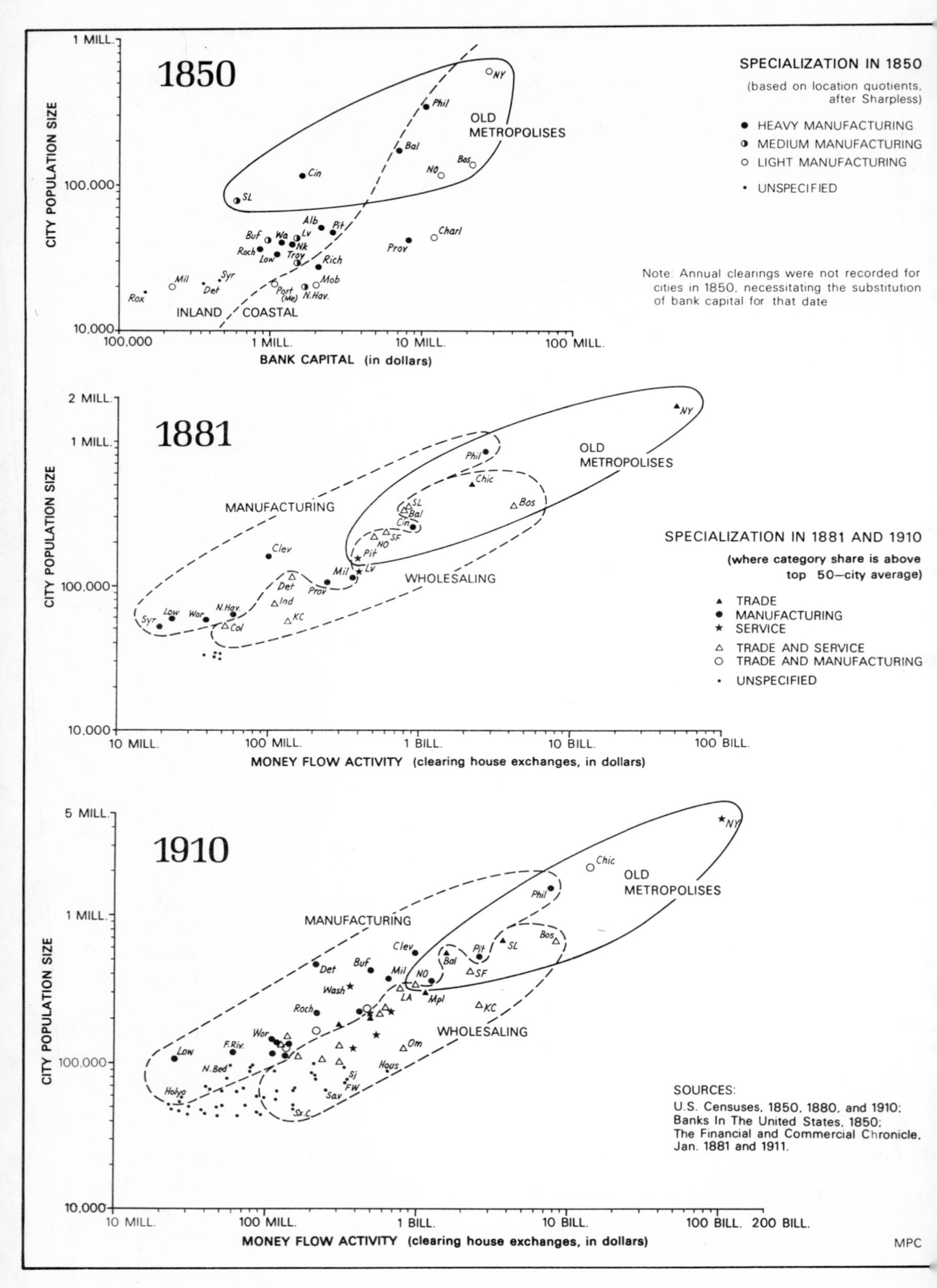

FIG. 2. The urban hierarchy according to banking measures, 1850-1910.

tios.[34] The low banking activity of industrial centers may have resulted from manufacturing enterprises bypassing local banks in favor of New York, or from a more national distribution of banks linked to broad industrial markets.

Organizing the Urban System, 1881-1910

Specialization in commerce or manufacturing was not a sufficient reason to account for major differences in banking among cities because most cities provided these and other functions at some level. Equally important is the historical stage of development which particular cities reached at particular times in generating "fields" of tributary relations with other settlements that would channel the business which ensured a regional and national basis for a city's individual growth. Large cities have rarely monopolized such ties, and a complex of banking fields overlapped, eclipsed, and nested within one another. The overall banking pattern included hinterlands at several stages of formation and modification as new cities were added to the urban system. The interaction patterns are mirrored in the correspondent linkages. . . .

Large City Interaction

. . . Horizontal links between the top twenty-four cities became extensive between 1881 and 1910 (Fig. 3). Boston, Philadelphia, St. Louis, and San Francisco all forged strong connections with many cities among the top twenty-four, and the strength of their bonds showed some association with city size and distance. Cincinnati alone among important early banking centers failed to develop di-

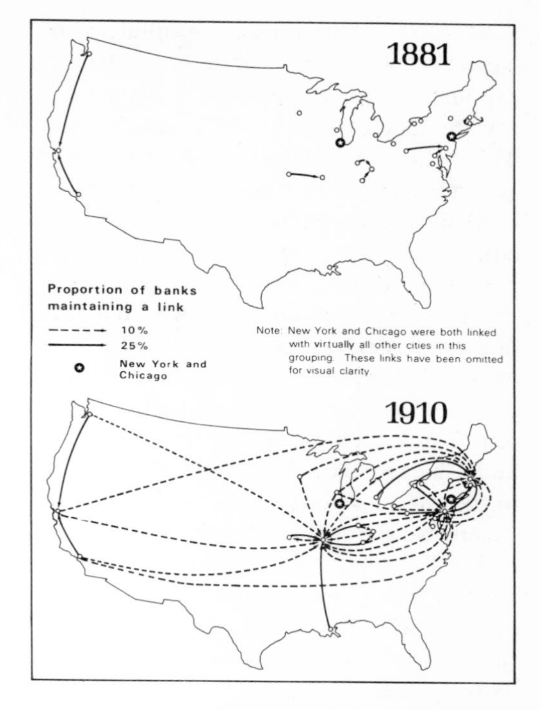

FIG. 3. Large-city interaction based on banking linkages, 1881 and 1910.

verse horizontal links.[35] These lateral connections within the upper levels of the urban system dispel any notion of a rigid hierarchy of flows based on the hierarchy of size among large cities. Proliferating lateral channels signal the integration of both the banking world and the urban system during this period.

Secondary Center Hinterlands

Large cities other than New York succeeded not only in creating lateral linkages but also in orienting smaller cities into regional hinterland clusters. For this stage of the analysis the top nine cities in 1881 and 1910 (including New York) are considered at a "secondary level," and a total of twenty-three cities in 1881 (twenty-eight in 1910) at a "tertiary

34. The latter correspond well with the wholesale centers discussed in Vance, *Merchant's World,* pp. 121-28.

35. Duncan and Lieberson, *Metropolis,* p. 108.

level."[36] If the overpowering influence of New York is offset by appropriate handicapping, the influence patterns of secondary centers can be approximated (Fig. 4).[37] These hinterland zones are rather general since the only data points used in their demarcation are the subsidiary cities. The changing structure of metropolitan influence, however, is striking at this level of generalization. All nine second-order centers except Baltimore and New Orleans influenced at least several of the fourteen third-order and thirty-eight fourth-order cities in 1881. New York and Chicago attracted most of the cities in the well-developed parts of the country except New England (Boston) and some cities close to Philadelphia, Cincinnati, and St. Louis. Thirty years later Chicago had spread its superior connections across the western United States except for some Texas cities. . . .

Tertiary Center Hinterlands

Changes at the tertiary level were associated with greater instability of urban rank in population and banking at this lower level. . . .

The main contrast between third-order and second-order patterns in 1881 was that several third-order cities competed vigorously enough to create their own hinterlands (Figs. 4 and 5). The strength of second-order centers was sufficiently strong that not all third-order places could do this. Even so, New Orleans and Baltimore, unable to generate second-order hinterlands, managed only feeble ones at the tertiary level. Most major centers which had secondary hinterlands had much larger tertiary hinterlands, indicating a clear dominance by large cities far down the national urban hierarchy.

Dramatic changes by 1910 resulted in bank hinterlands for nearly half the third-order centers. Such Middle Western wholesaling cities as Minneapolis, Kansas City, and Omaha challenged the old order, with consequent localized decline of the influence of New York, Chicago, and St. Louis. San Francisco made major gains in the Southwest. Milwaukee, Pittsburgh, and Buffalo exemplified the emerging tertiary hinterlands in the more densely populated portions of the country. Whereas Detroit and Cleveland rose between 1880 and 1910 from third-order to second-order status in population, this was accompanied neither by enlarged bank hinterlands nor improved general banking business. Albany retained a small hinterland in New York state, although the city declined in rank from eighteenth to fiftieth in the urban hierarchy. Boston stood fast, Philadelphia and Cincinnati improved somewhat, and New Orleans proved competitive as a reduced third-order center. New York and Chicago relinquished influence widely in the face of second- and third-order banking competition, although such retreat was both orderly in space and only relative. Their territorial dominance may have narrowed, but their absolute business in correspondent accounts still expanded.

36. Borchert's methodology based on natural breaks in the rank-size distribution was adopted here to secure similar numbers of cities in each category, although obviously some cities belonged to different categories at different dates; Borchert, "American Metropolitan Evolution," pp. 308-11. In this study the number of cities for categories I-V are 1, 8, 14, 38, and 164 for 1880-81 (226 cities above a threshold population of 10,000), and 1, 8, 19, 37, and 164 for 1910 (229 cities above a threshold population of 25,000).

37. New York is defined as the dominant second-order center for a given lower order city only if it had more than twice as many correspondent banking links as any other second order center. This assumes, following Borchert's methodology, that half of that city's links to New York resulted from New York's first-order function; John R. Borchert, "America's Changing Metropolitan Regions," *Annals*, Association of American Geographers, 62 (1972):352-73.

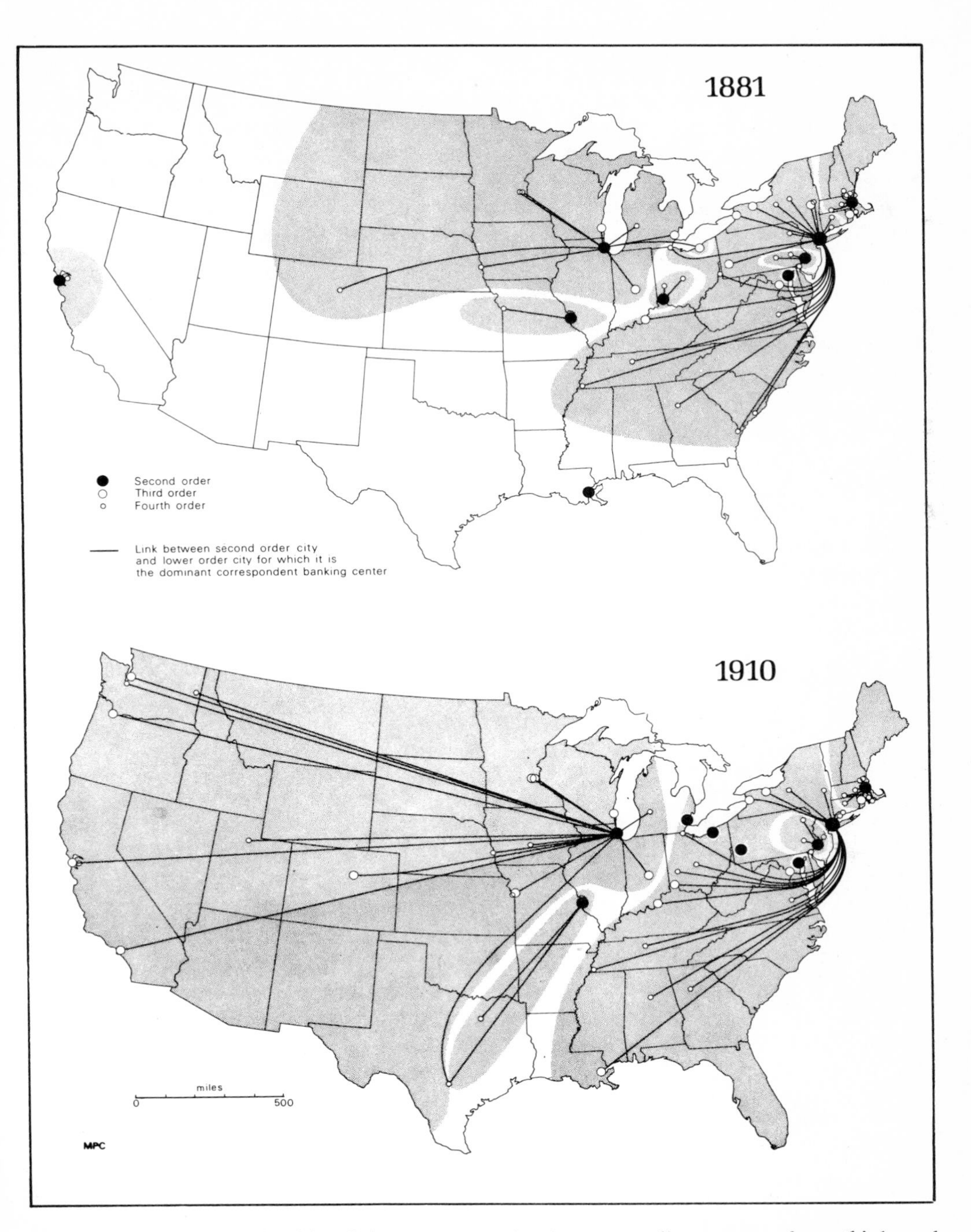

FIG. 4. Correspondent banking linkages to second-order metropolitan centers from third- and fourth-order centers, 1881 and 1910.

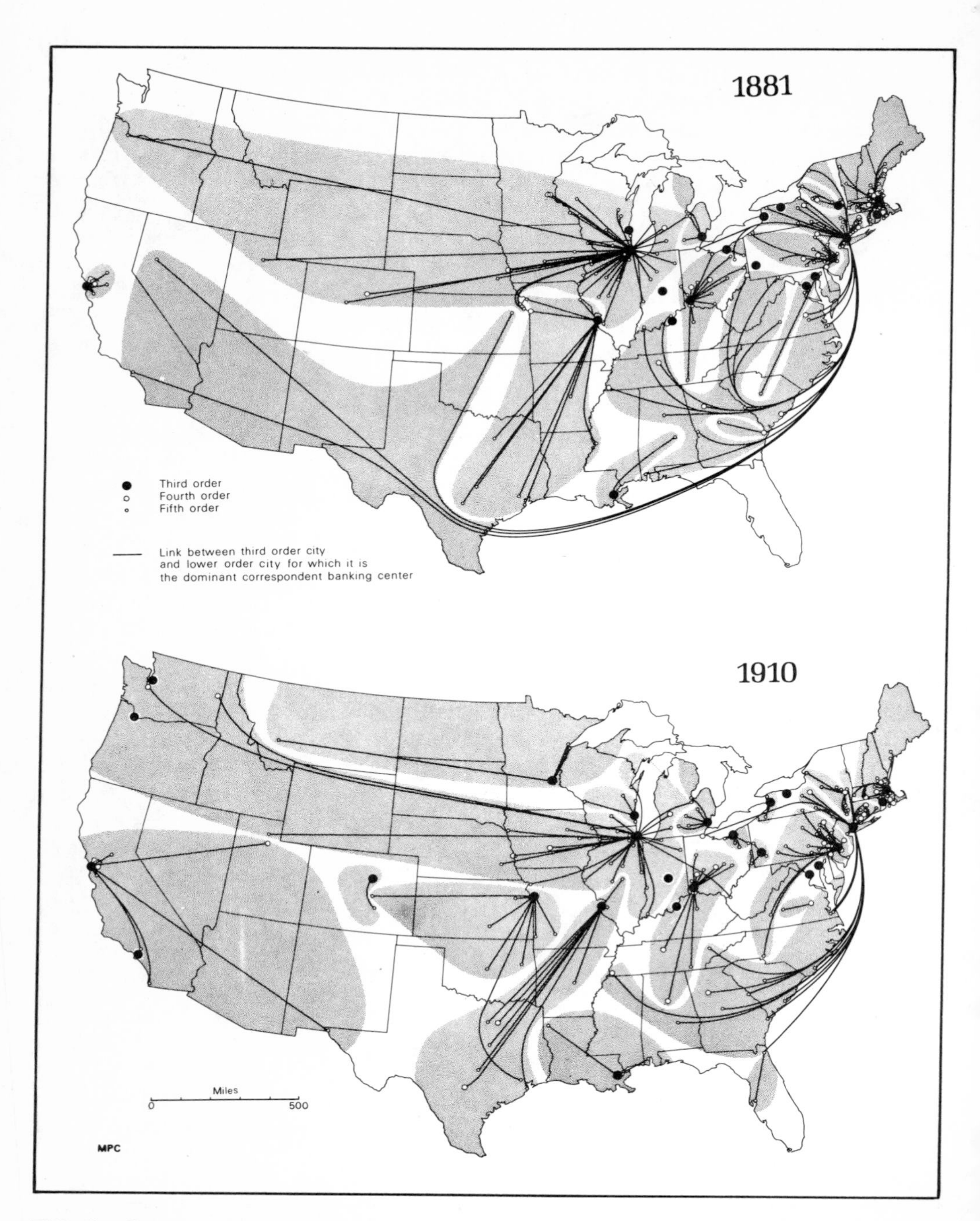

FIG. 5. Correspondent banking linkages to third-order metropolitan centers from lower-order centers, 1881 and 1910.

"Country" Correspondents[38]

If the structure of banking linkages between cities over 25,000 was also representative of the more widespread pattern of rural bank connections, the latter should likewise display a shift from direct links with New York toward multilevel interdependencies that included local metropolises. In order to cope with the strong New York and Chicago influence which permeated rural bank linkages as well as the upper-level urban system, a distinction will be made between overt and latent hinterlands. Overt hinterlands imply equal competition for rural correspondents from all possible cities; latent hinterlands exclude New York and Chicago competition.

Overt Banking Hinterlands

New York enjoyed a plurality of correspondent accounts in all counties, whether urbanized or rural, that had banks in 1876.[39] Only five years later, however, three other metropolises were competing successfully for exclusive banking territory in the northeastern United States, which can be taken as representative of trends across the country (Fig. 6). Boston, Philadelphia, and Chicago had established enough "country bank" correspondent accounts to orient a considerable number of counties toward them. . . .

Banking hinterlands that were quite well delineated in the East in 1881 had become more so by 1910, and few empty or shared areas remained. The boundary between Boston and New York control had barely changed and Philadelphia and Baltimore had consolidated their earlier dominance. At lower levels, Pittsburgh and Richmond followed suit. Chicago controlled Iowa, most of Wisconsin and Illinois, Michigan's Upper Peninsula, and northern and western Indiana. New York's recession, notwithstanding Chicago's expansion, had allowed subsidiary banking centers (e.g., Indianapolis, Cincinnati, and Louisville) to acquire exclusive territory. This decline was substantially complete by 1910, except in the transition zone between the East coast and Middle Western hinterlands—a temporary survival in the banking "watersheds" between the major cities of the area. . . .

Latent Banking Fields

New York and Chicago so clearly dominated the banking orientation of large sections of the Northeast that they may obscure more localized competition. The crude hierarchy of county-based bank hinterlands was analogous to the city-based ones. The influence of the largest centers has to be "peeled away," in order to understand the lower levels of regional organization. Setting aside the widespread influence of New York and Chicago, it is possible to reconstruct latent fields of banking orientation toward cities that may have been establishing hinterlands beneath the "umbrella" influence of the largest cities.

Latent banking hinterlands were reconstructed for a portion of the Middle West for 1881, 1891, and 1910 (Fig. 7). Two characteristics stand out. Banking fields of regional centers outside Chicago were

38. "Country" correspondents refer to banks located in any place not designated as a reserve city.

39. *Banker's Directory . . . for 1876,* see footnote 19. New York was so dominant that the only space for listing correspondent banks was headed "New York Correspondent." By 1881, however, the directory had one column for New York links and one for links with banks in other cities. Concentrations of counties that had no banks in 1881 were almost exclusively in northern Maine, Michigan, Wisconsin, and Minnesota, and in the Appalachians and Ozarks.

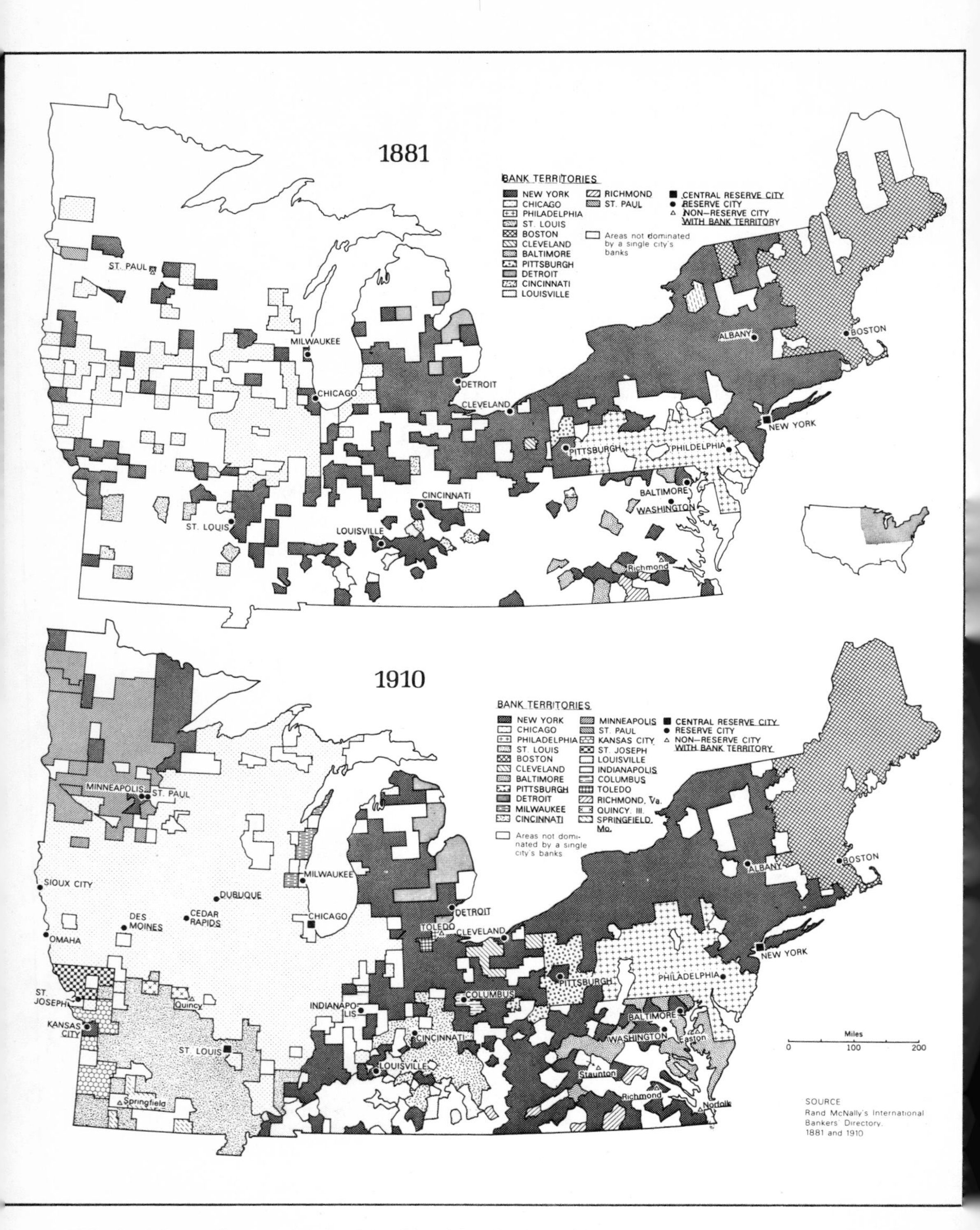

FIG. 6. Metropolitan county-level banking hinterlands in the urban-industrial core of the United States, 1881 and 1910.

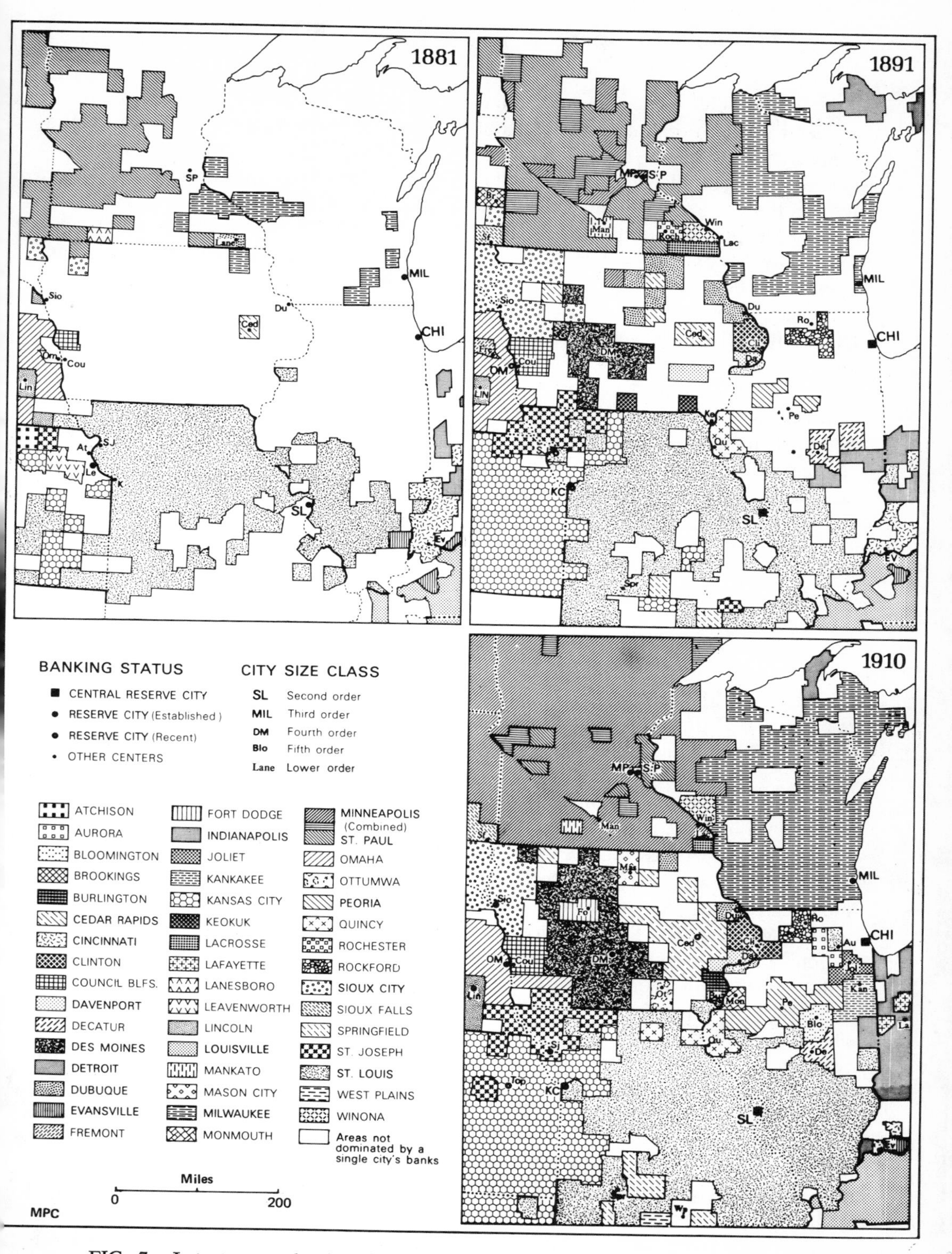

FIG. 7. Latent county-level banking fields in the Midwest, 1881, 1891, and 1910.

more plainly visible as discrete spatial entities, and smaller urban centers created a plethora of microfields. In 1881 much of the region showed allegiance only to Chicago, and thus does not appear on the map. The fields of St. Louis and St. Paul were relatively compact, but Milwaukee's fragmentary field reflected its proximity to Chicago. Some fledgling fields in Kentucky, Missouri, Iowa, and Kansas were quite scattered.

A decade later, changes were evident. Nearly all the nascent hinterlands of 1881 had grown by 1891, and the larger ones had consolidated their gains. At some distance from Chicago, significant zones emerged around Kansas City, St. Joseph, and Sioux City. Small cities such as Des Moines, Dubuque, Decatur, and Peoria within the more direct orbit of Chicago developed new hinterlands. Strong competition from Kansas City succeeded in diminishing St. Louis' influence in Kansas and northwest Missouri, while the rising importance of Minneapolis was reflected in some changing allegiance in Minnesota.

By 1910, little room remained for further expansion. Most counties had correspondent links with regional centers or local cities as well as New York and Chicago. Regional centers such as Milwaukee, Minneapolis, Kansas City, and St. Louis enlarged their fields far enough to be partly coterminous with state boundaries. Equilibrium had been achieved: most of Wisconsin and Upper Michigan was oriented to Milwaukee; Minnesota counties looked to the Twin Cities; Kansas to Kansas City; Indiana to Indianapolis; western Kentucky to Louisville; and St. Louis ruled the correspondent business of southern Illinois and most of Missouri. In Iowa, Des Moines' latent hinterland was twice that of Cedar Rapids and four times that of Sioux City, and St. Joseph had oriented adjacent parts of Missouri to its own banks. A large number of one-, two-, or three-county zones were oriented toward local places throughout the region.

. . . Two trends favored budding metropolises. The concentration of manufacturing in urban areas reduced the availability of many small manufactures in rural areas, thus necessitating the movement of funds to small cities to pay for their purchase. As the Middle West matured economically, some types of light manufacturing not only moved west into the large cities of the region, but also moved lower down the urban ranking, thus diverting toward the smaller metropolises funds formerly sent east or to the big cities.

The Emerging Geographical Structure

This analysis has documented the evolution of a multilevel, regionally organized, and nationally integrated banking system during the last quarter of the nineteenth century. Horizontal and hierarchical correspondent linkages between settlements were forged to channel the increasing financial flows. Collecting nodes multiplied in a decentralized pattern but were kept within the financial hierarchy. Between 1881 and 1910 seven metropolises joined twelve predecessors in dominating the linkages of fourth- and fifth-order cities, and the number of cities controlling rural banking territory rose from twenty-four to fifty-two (Table 1). As a partial consequence, New York's third-order control of smaller cities declined from forty-six to twenty-five and Chicago's from forty-five to twenty-nine. Similarly, the pattern of high-level influence narrowed somewhat as third-order cities, formerly oriented toward seven major cities, became

TABLE 1. Profiles of Metropolitan Banking Hinterlands, 1881-1910

Urban Rank 1881	Urban Rank 1910	City*	1881 Second Order Links	1881 Third Order Links	1881 Links to Counties	1910 Second Order Links	1910 Third Order Links	1910 Links to Counties
1	1	New York (CC)**	21	46	486	20	25	943
		Second Order Cities in 1910						
3	2	Chicago (RC)	9	45	90	17	29	339
2	3	Philadelphia (RR)	4	16	37	5	20	47
5	4	St. Louis (RC)	1	10	12	2	10	151
4	5	Boston (RR)	8	35	41	9	23	37
10	6	Cleveland (RR)	...	1	1	—	4	6
6	7	Baltimore (RR)	—	1	9	—	—	29
11	8	Pittsburgh (RR)	...	—	2	—	4	14
17	9	Detroit (RR)	...	3	5	—	6	14
		Third Order Cities in 1910						
12	10	Buffalo (NN)	...	—	—	...	2	—
8	11	San Francisco (RR)	1	4	21	...	6	29
18	12	Milwaukee (RR)	...	—	—	...	4	4
7	13	Cincinnati (RR)	2	14	5	...	12	44
9	15	New Orleans (RR)	—	1	1	...	2	17
	17	Los Angeles (NR)	...	...	—	...	1	1
37	18	Minneapolis (NR)	...	...	—	...	3	75
29	20	Kansas City (NR)	...	...	—	...	8	154
	21	Seattle (NR)	...	...	—	...	—	7
		Fourth Order Cities in 1910						
23	22	Indianapolis (NR)	...	—	—	...	—	10
15	24	Louisville (RR)	...	—	5	...	—	47
44	26	St. Paul (NR)	...	...	1	...	—	4
49	27	Denver (NR)	...	...	1	...	1	31
	28	Portland, Ore. (NR)	...	...	1	...	—	12
32	29	Columbus, O. (NR)	...	...	—	...	...	2
34	30	Toledo (NN)	...	...	—	...	...	2
48	31	Atlanta (NN)	...	...	3	...	...	3
53	37	Memphis (NN)	...	...	—	...	...	2
24	39	Richmond, Va. (NN)	...	...	3	...	...	9
62	41	Omaha (NR)	...	...	2	...	1	54
39	45	Nashville (NN)	...	...	—	...	...	30
20	50	Albany (RR)	...	—	1	...	6	—
		Other centers (comb.)	—	1	4	—	3	75
Total					692			2192
Number of cities acting as foci at each linkage level			7	12	24	5	19	52

Source: Author's calculations, based on Rand McNally's *International Bankers Directory, 1881* and 1910.
* Cities without banking hinterlands are excluded.
** Banking status of city (first letter denotes status in 1881, second letter denotes status in 1910; C = central reserve status, R = reserve status, N = nonreserve status).
. . . No linkages possible (e. g., in 1910 there were only nine second order cities, hence no second order links possible for cities ranked tenth or lower).
— No linkages.

focused by 1910 around only five major centers. . . . City age and population size accounted for some of the gradations in banking influence, but more impressive was reserve and central reserve city status. Reserve city status aided in producing the hinterlands, but it was not in itself sufficient to guarantee strong banking fields, as the latent hinterlands of four Iowa reserve cities as late as 1910 exemplify. The maturing of the urban system is to be seen, however, not in the widespread acquisition of reserve status or the establishment of vast networks of correspondent links by cities, but in the progressive integration of cities at all levels into an ordered system based on hierarchy and large-city interdependence.

This integration progressed with speed between the Civil War and the end of the century. Correspondent evidence shows the growth of interlocking relationships between cities in the upper levels of the urban system (Fig. 8). Where two or three dense links were a maximum in 1881, cities had developed generally four or five by 1910. At the earlier date, only New York and Chicago had dense links with a majority of the other major cities, whereas by 1910 they had been joined by Boston, Philadelphia, and St. Louis (Figs. 8 and 9).

The extent to which the largest cities strengthened their own interdependence increased noticeably during this period. The growth of tributary relations and interdependence was not, however, a routine function of a city's position in the upper echelon of the urban hierarchy. Cities rose and fell from national prominence in the urban system in part through their location at a particular time, given the general context of urban growth.

In the early nineteenth century, the United States urban system was fragmented (Fig. 10). There were only three

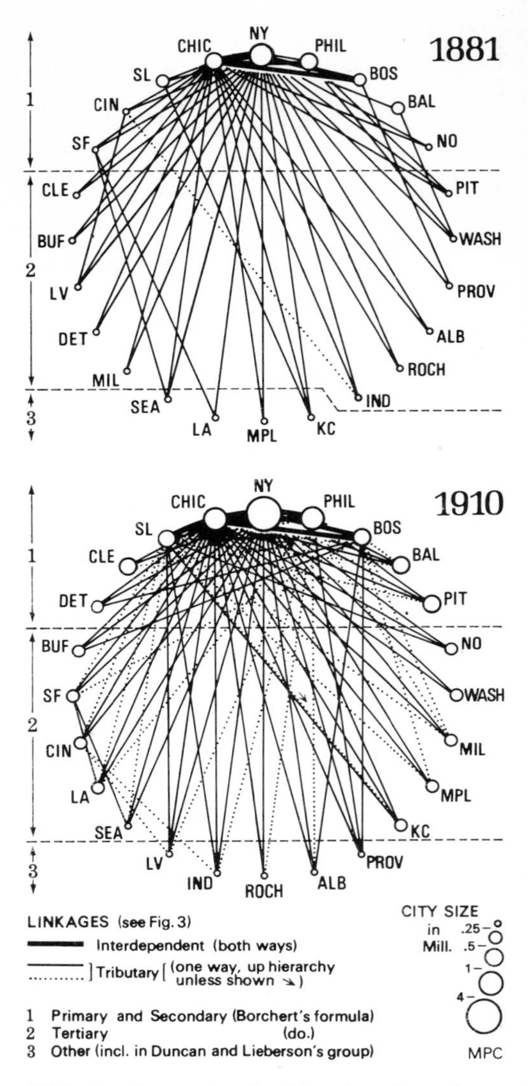

FIG. 8. Large-city banking interdependence, 1881 and 1910.

significant subsystems, and urban hinterlands were diverse and unrelated. By the 1880s, a three-level structure of urban regions existed. Under the primary influence of New York, with its national hinterland, there had formed a secondary level of regional organization in which the country was oriented toward seven major

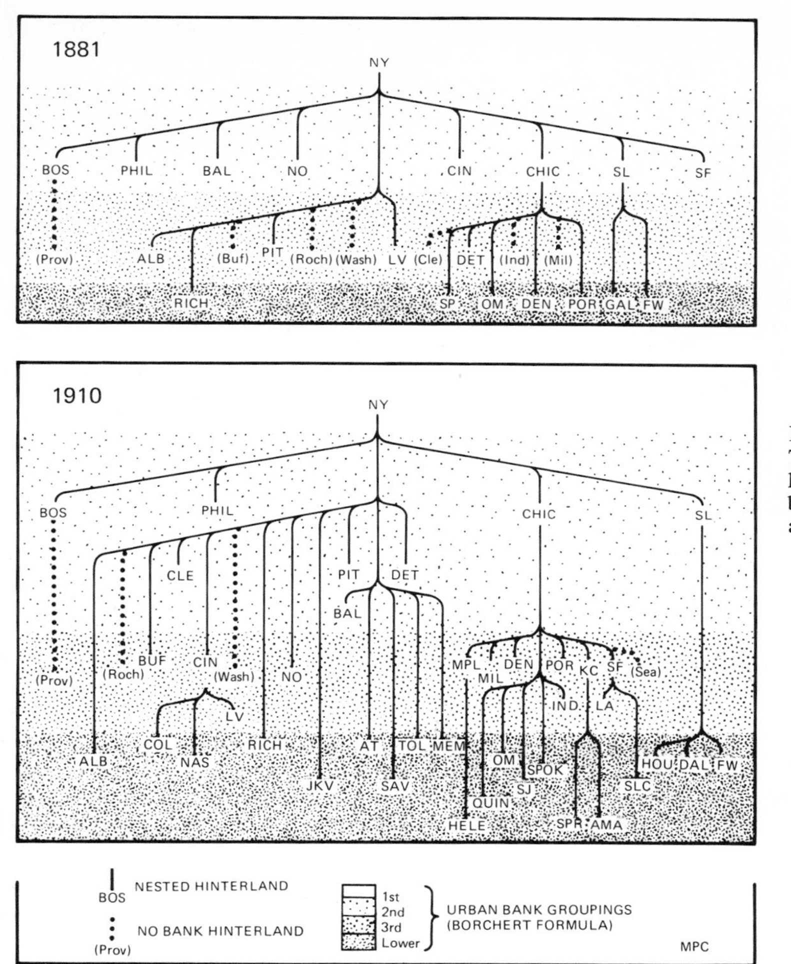

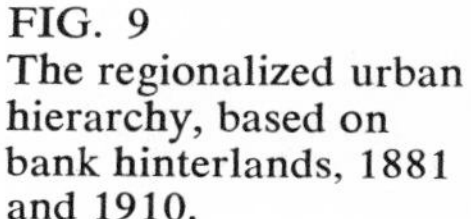
FIG. 9
The regionalized urban hierarchy, based on bank hinterlands, 1881 and 1910.

metropolises (Fig. 11). Chicago and New York (functioning now at the secondary level) divided the country with their influence, except for five small regions. The third level comprised urban hinterlands wholly within New York's zone of secondary influence.

Four urban banking regions rose from insignificance to major prominence in the thirty years after 1880. These hinterlands belonged to Kansas City, Denver, Omaha, and Minneapolis, and between them they succeeded in virtually filling the Plains and Eastern Rocky Mountain territory. They were part of a substantial redefinition of urban hinterlands in the United States before World War I that would in outline last to the present, with fairly predictable modifications. Atlanta, Dallas, and Los Angeles were the only significant banking centers in 1967 which did not have major banking hinterlands in 1910.[40]

40. Borchert, "America's Changing Metropolitan Regions," pp. 362-65.

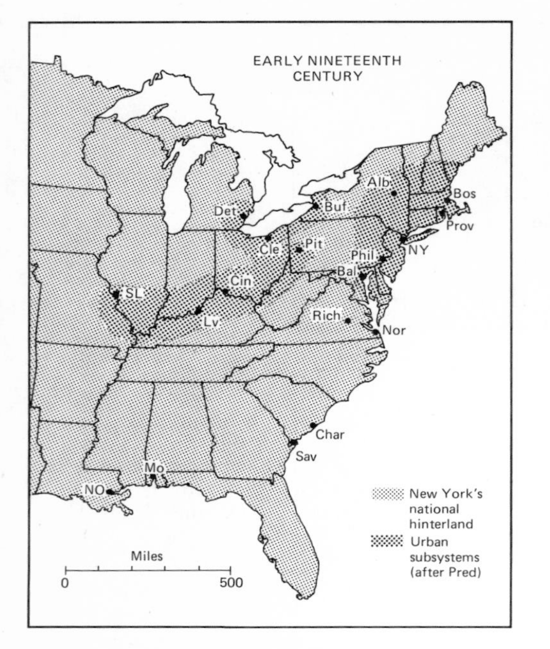

FIG. 10. Generalized urban regions in the United States, c. 1840.

Conclusion

Evidence of urban connectivity in the later nineteenth century drawn from bank correspondent data can provide only a small insight into the geographical linkages between cities. Other measures might possibly reveal different patterns of spatial structure. The growth of banking hinterlands between 1881 and 1910 does, however, correlate closely with general business turnover as measured by the aggregate annual clearing house activity of major cities. This correlation suggests that the geography of the evolution of banking hinterlands helps account for the general long-term prosperity of those cities—a claim often made but rarely demonstrated. The skewness of many larger banking hinterlands in 1881 and 1910 reflected both metropolitan "shadow" of neighboring large cities and the pull of western commodity belts beyond the fringe of the nation's urban-industrial core.[41]

Functional specialization among cities gave rise to and also resulted from differential hinterland-forming processes. On the one hand, large industrial cities such as Cleveland, Pittsburgh, and Milwaukee had small specific bank hinterlands. This was attributable in part to the national rather than regional scale of their markets, and partly also to the concentration of industrial cities within the nation's historical core region that reduced individual cities' share of locally available bank correspondent linkages.[42] On the other hand, the bulking functions of wholesaling centers emphasized tributary business at a regional scale, and large bank hinterlands could consolidate preeminence in this function.

Between 1840 and 1910 the urban system as a whole evolved from a primate order to a modified hierarchical one with high-level interdependencies.[43] At the outset New York was the only effective "clearing house." By the end of the century, linkages had become more attenuated and localized with the westward expansion of business and consequent dispersion of reserve cities. New York retained national influence at the primary level and considerable influence at other levels as other major cities took over responsibility for regional subsystems. Central place concepts are applicable only to selected characteristics of the evolving metropolitan system of the United States in this period, but emerging patterns of nested hinterlands suggest a partial con-

41. Ward, *Cities and Immigrants,* p. 19.
42. Pred, *Spatial Dynamics,* p. 32.
43. Pred finds a similar pattern of change in the urban system prior to 1840. Pred, *Urban Growth,* pp. 186-238. Since the indices of structure are not comparable and the historical contexts rather different, the issue of developing integration of the national system of cities awaits further elucidation.

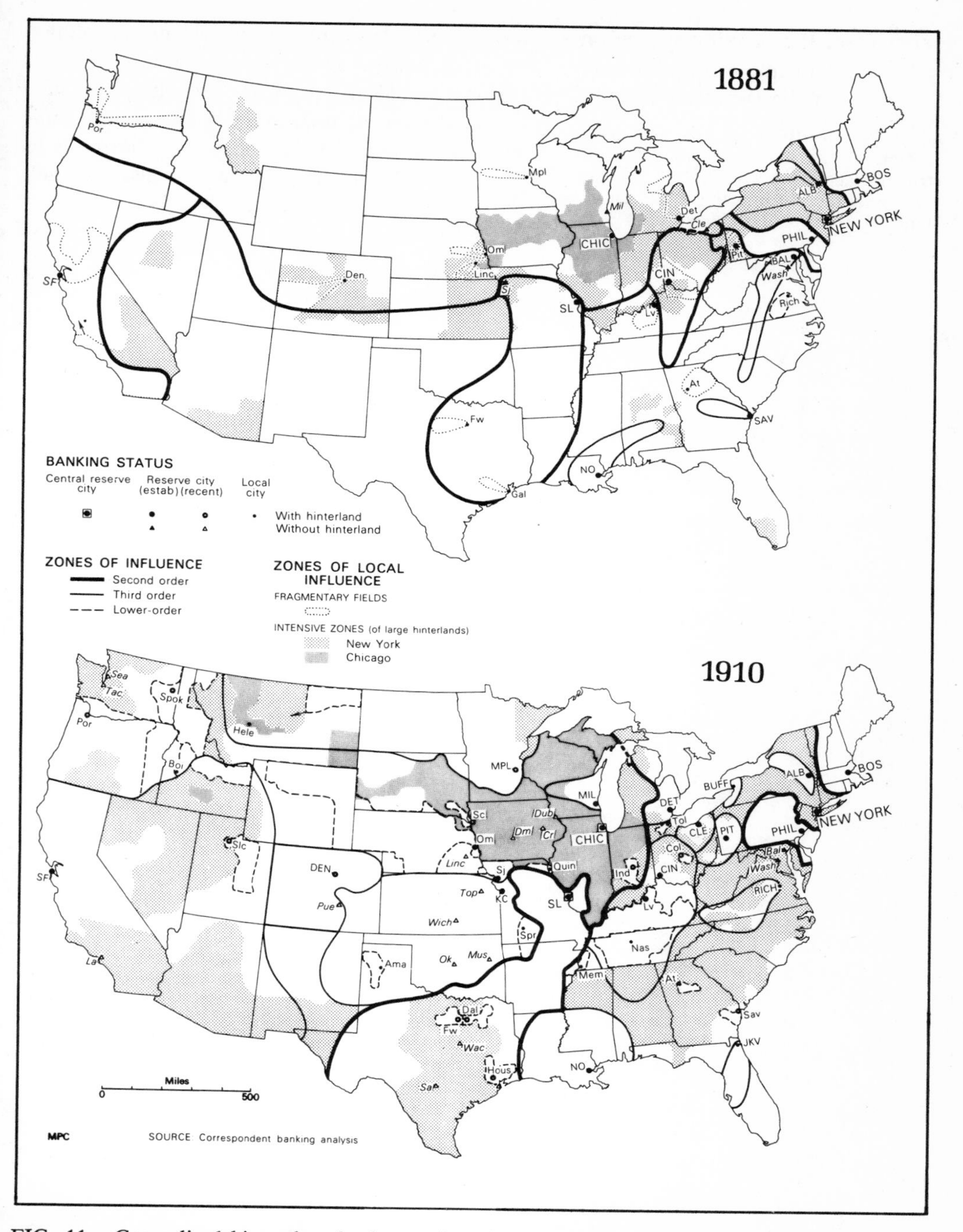

FIG. 11. Generalized hierarchy of urban regions in the United States, 1881 and 1910, based on nested banking hinterlands. This is a consolidation of Figs. 4, 5, and 6. Boundaries at each level of analysis were superimposed and modified to present a composite classification.

vergence of the banking system on a central place principle of organization by the beginning of the twentieth century.[44] The hierarchical urban subsystems developed increasing interdependence among their regional metropolises, resulting in substantial nonhierarchical horizontal linkages that tied the subsystems not only to New York or Chicago but also to each other. . . .

44. This conclusion accords with Vance's conception of the mercantile model of settlement structure acquiring a partial central place overlay sometime during the nineteenth century. Vance, *Merchant's World*, p. 165.

Industrialization, Initial Advantage, and American Metropolitan Growth / *Allan Pred*

The spatial, as well as the economic and social, processes of nineteenth- and twentieth-century urbanization and industrialization are not independent. The phenomena that led to the concurrent emergence of the modern American metropolis and large-scale manufacturing are dynamically involuted and nearly always inseparable.[1] Urbanization, as in the case of Washington, D.C., is not inexorably associated with industrial growth;[2] yet, conversely, the multiplication of factories, product output, and markets since 1860 is virtually synonymous with city development. . . . How and why do cities expand precipitately during periods of rapid industrialization? Why do some cities grow more rapidly than, and at the expense of, other cities? No fewer than three traditional frameworks of locational thinking provide theoretical ammunition with which to assault these two questions.

Underlying Theoretical Themes

Superficially, intellectual derivations from Weber's and Marshall's agglomeration and scale economies provide the most potentially fruitful source of theoretical concepts. The unique array of scale, localization, and urbanization economies available at urban industrial sites is frequently employed to explain the industrial growth and specialization of metropolitan centers. The city's internal and external manufacturing economies were presumably of particular importance during the nineteenth century. At that time individual firms were in a position both to minimize the internalization or absorption of external diseconomies and to maximize the reduction of per unit input costs "through acquisitions, combinations, or mergers with closely interdependent economic ac-

1. Some of the more cogent statements concerning the interrelationships between urbanization and industrialization in the United States are contained in Eric E. Lampard, "The History of Cities in the Economically Advanced Areas," *Economic Development and Cultural Change* 3 (1954-1955):81-136; and in R. D. McKenzie, "The Rise of Metropolitan Communities," in *Recent Social Trends in the United States: Report of the President's Research Committee on Social Trends,* 2 vols. (New York and London, 1933), vol. 1, pp. 443-96.

2. The bonds between urban and manufacturing expansion are obviously less pronounced in non-Western societies. For statistical comparisons see Thomas O. Wilkinson, "Urban Structure and Industrialization," *American Sociology Review* 25 (1960):356-63.

Reprinted (with omissions) from the *Geographical Review* 55 (1965):158-85.
The materials contained in this article were initially presented in much more detailed form in the author's *The Spatial Dynamics of U.S. Urban-Industrial Growth, 1800-1914* (Cambridge, Mass.: M.I.T. Press, 1966). The basic ideas have since been elaborated in *Urban Growth and the Circulation of Information: The United States System of Cities, 1790-1840* (Cambridge, Mass.: Harvard University Press, 1973), and in *City-Systems in Advanced Economies: Past Growth, Present Processes, and Future Development Options* (London: Hutchinson University Library, 1977).

tivities."[3] While these observations contribute to an understanding of why manufacturing grows in cities, they are inadequate for a comprehension of the precise dynamics of city-size growth, though agglomeration economies imply that manufacturing on a grand scale must be limited to a few cities. Even if these observations were of more definite assistance, "the concept of external economies is at best only one among a number of possible keys to the understanding of modern city development."[4]

The possible interrelationships between central-place theory and the urbanization-industrialization syndrome are somewhat less obvious, especially in view of the criticism that has been leveled at Christaller's theory for its failure to deal with the location of manufacturing activities. Attempts to apply central-place theory to the problem of urban growth have admittedly exaggerated the role of business and service activities and have generally emphasized small urban places at the expense of the multimillion metropolis.[5] However, these shortcomings aside, central-place theory may be combined with Löschian market-area hypotheses to provide two basic avenues of approach. One is the threshold concept, from which it can be inferred that industries "oriented" toward local or regional markets will not appear in cities until their local or regional thresholds are attained. Secondly, if the schema of a hierarchy of market areas is extended to include manufacturing activities, the largest or most nodal cities will logically have the greatest variety of manufacturing functions. . . .

Of the several other ingredients to be added to this theoretical amalgamation, the concept of initial advantage is probably most important. Initial advantage is here employed as an umbrella to cover three overlapping ideas: that existing locations are usually characterized by tremendous inertia and a temporal compounding of advantages; that existing locations often exert considerable influence on plant-location decisions; and that once concentration is initiated it is self-perpetuating.[6] These ideas contribute substantially to one of the major themes of this paper, namely that some urban centers, through rapid industrialization, generate their own conditions for growth into multimillion metropolises, and that such centers are usually those possessing relative initial advantages. A rationale for viewing urban and industrial growth as an interrelated process, with each stage of development a function of previous stages, is contained in Myrdal's "principle of circular and cumulative causation." He contends that "in the normal case a change does not call forth contradicting forces but, instead, supporting changes, which move the system in the same direction but much further. Because of such circular causation a social process tends to become cumulative and often to gather speed at an accelerated rate."[7] Of course,

3. Albert O. Hirschman, *The Strategy of Economic Development,* Yale Studies in Economics, no. 10 (New Haven, 1958), p. 58.
4. Alexander Gerschenkron, "City Economies—Then and Now," in *The Historian and the City,* Oscar Handlin and John Burchard, eds. (Cambridge, Mass., 1963), pp. 56-62; reference on p. 58.
5. See, for example, Richard L. Morrill, "The Development of Spatial Distributions of Towns in Sweden: An Historical-Predictive Approach," *Annals,* Association of American Geographers, 53 (1963):1-14.

6. See Edward L. Ullman, "Regional Development and the Geography of Concentration," *Papers and Proceedings Regional Science Association* 4, Fourth Annual Meeting, 1957 (Philadelphia, 1958), pp. 179-98.
7. Gunnar Myrdal, *Rich Lands and Poor,* in *World Perspectives,* vol. 16 (New York, 1957), p. 13. For related statements on cumulative

all cities would grow indefinitely if urban-industrial growth were merely a process of circular and cumulative causation. Therefore it is imperative to elaborate explicitly the means by which initial advantages favor some cities at the expense of others.

American Urbanization and Industrialization, 1860-1910

If it is contended that the emergence of inordinately large concentrations of manufacturing in the United States' greatest metropolises is a function of agglomeration economies, the fulfillment of successive market thresholds, and initial advantage, then the period when these forces were most operative should be identified and outlined; for there comes a time when tertiary activities supplant manufacturing as the principal determinant of urban-size growth.

The early 1860s are generally regarded as a turning point in American urban and manufacturing growth (Table 1). In the decades after 1860 the economy completed its transition from a commercial-mercantilistic base to an industrial-capitalistic one. Concomitantly, the top of the urban hierarchy became characterized more and more by industrial, multifunctional cities, and less and less by cities dominated by mercantilistic wholesaling and trading functions. . . . By 1910 evolving systems of mass production had been made economical by the development of mass domestic markets, despite

growth and initial advantage see Bertil Ohlin, *Interregional and International Trade,* Harvard Economic Studies, vol. 39 (Cambridge, Mass., 1933), pp. 235-36; Harvey S. Perloff and others, *Regions, Resources, and Economic Growth* (Baltimore, 1960), p. 82; and Joseph A. Schumpeter, *The Theory of Economic Development,* tr. Redvers Opie (New York, 1961), pp. 9, 64).

TABLE 1. Urbanization and Industrialization in the United States, 1860-1910*

	1860	1870	1880	1890	1900	1910	*% Increase*
1. Total U.S. population (*1000's*)	31,513	39,905	50,262	63,056	76,094	92,407	193.2
2. Total urban population (*1000's*)	6,217	9,902	14,130	22,106	30,160	41,999	575.6
3. Population in cities >100,000 (*1000's*)	2,639	4,130	6,211	9,698	14,208	20,302	669.3
2 as % of 1	19.7	24.8	28.1	35.1	39.6	45.5	. . . .
3 as % of 1	8.4	10.3	12.4	15.4	18.7	22.0	. . . .
Miles of railroad operated[a]	30,626	52,922	93,262	166,703	206,631	266,185	769.1
Rails produced (*1000's of long tons*)	183	554	1,305	1,885	2,386	3,636	. . . .
Pig-iron production (*1000's of long tons*)	821	1,665	3,835	9,203	13,789	27,304	. . . .
Steel ingots and castings produced (*1000's of long tons*)	11.8	68.8	1,247	4,277	10,188	26,095	. . . .
Index of Manufacturing production (1899 = 100)	16	25	42	71	100	172	975.0

* Compiled from "Historical Statistics of the United States" [see text footnote 31 below], pp. 7, 14, 427, and 429; and Edwin Frickey, *Production in the United States, 1860-1914,* Harvard Economic Studies, vol. 82 (Cambridge, Mass, 1947), pp. 10-11, 54.
[a] Not including yard tracks and sidings.

periodic interruptions by inflation, protracted deflation, and depression. Within a span of fifty years, much of which Rostow might term "the drive to maturity,"[8] the United States rose from its position as one of the world's secondary industrial nations to manufactural preeminence. . . .

Table 1 reveals that manufacturing output between 1860 and 1910 increased at a pace exceeding the growth rates of national population, urban population, and population in large cities. Manufacturing also outstripped the railroad development vital to its raw-material assembly and finished-product distribution. However, the extension of markets and the alterations in average scale of production, which were the outward expressions of rapid industrial growth, can be seen in their proper perspective only in relation to certain railroad developments: intensification of trunk lines, spread of feeder lines, and integration of fragmented operating units; technical improvement of freight-car carrying capacity, motive power, rails, roadbeds, and terminal facilities; financing innovations adopted by industrial enterprises; precipitation of an enormous demand for steel rails, steam engines, and rolling stock; and elaboration of consumer demand through wages paid to line employees and construction workers.[9]

TABLE 2. Population Growth in Ten United States Cities, 1860-1910*

	Population 1860	*Population* 1910[a]
New York	1,174,799[b]	4,766,883
Chicago	112,172	2,185,283
Philadelphia	565,529	1,549,008
St. Iouis	160,773	687,029
Boston	177,840	670,585
Cleveland	43,417	560,663
Pittsburgh	49,221	533,905
Detroit	45,619	465,766
San Francisco	56,802	416,912
Los Angeles	4,385	319,198

* Derived from the "Census of Population: 1960" [see text footnote 3 above], p. 1-66.
[a] This column understates metropolitan growth, since it includes only the population within the municipal boundaries. In 1860 transport facilities permitted a negligible degree of development beyond the central city; but by 1910, although suburbanization was still in its initial stages, there was considerable integration between these cities and the areas contiguous to their boundaries. The figures do particular injustice to Boston and Pittsburgh, both of which had long possessed a number of factories in their essentially rural surroundings.
[b] "New York and its boroughs as constituted under the act of consolidation in 1898" ("Census of Population: 1960," pp. 1-67).

A generous part of post–Civil War urban growth occurred in those cities which are now the country's ten most important industrial metropolises (Table 2). Except for Los Angeles, these cities were, to one degree or another, established commercial centers, and in the capacity of financial and transport nodes they served as logical foci for industrial development. However, commercial supremacy in 1860 was obviously not prophetic of future industrial significance: Baltimore, New Orleans, Cincinnati, and Buffalo, among the ten largest cities of 1860, are not among

8. W. W. Rostow, *The Stages of Economic Growth* (Cambridge, 1960), p. 59.
9. Although the role of the railroad as an initiator of economic growth has recently been a subject of contention, even the skeptics are willing to grant that the part it played was most dramatic in the era immediately following the Civil War. See Paul H. Cootner, "The Role of the Railroads in United States Economic Growth," *Journal of Economic History* 23 (1963):477-521; Leland H. Jenks, "Railroads as an Economic Force in American Development," *Journal of Economic History,* 4 (1944): 1-20; and George Rogers Taylor and Irene D. Neu, *The American Railroad Network 1861-1890* (Cambridge, Mass., 1956), p. 1.

today's ten most important urban-industrial concentrations.

A Model of Urban-Size Growth in Periods of Rapid Industrialization

It is commonly acknowledged that "there are close relations between urban growth and changes in the structure of urban activities."[10] Through the use of a simple descriptive model, such relationships for major American cities from 1860 to 1910 can be tersely expressed.

Imagine a mercantile city, with some minor industrial functions, which is indiscriminately located in space and unengaged in market-area competition with other cities (though it does import some goods that are not locally produced). Assumption of these isolated aspatial and monopolistic conditions permits concentration on the growth process itself and defers inquiry into the interplay of initial advantages and the growth of some cities at the expense of others.

10. Brian J. L. Berry and William L. Garrison, "A Note on Central Place Theory and the Range of a Good," *Economic Geography* 34 (1958):304-11; reference on p. 311.

Further imagine the introduction into this city of one or more large-scale factories, whose location may have been determined either rationally or randomly. Sooner or later this event evokes two circular chains of reaction (Fig. 1).

New manufacturing functions, whether or not they primarily served local markets, will have an initial multiplier effect; that is, new local demands created both by the factories themselves and by the purchasing power of their labor force will call into being a host of new business, service, trade, construction, transportation, professional, and miscellaneous white-collar jobs. The combined effect of new industrial employment and an initial multiplier effect will be an increase in population, or growth in urban size, and the probable attainment of one or more new local or regional industrial thresholds. These higher thresholds will support new manufacturing functions as well as additional plants in existing industrial categories. Once production facilities have been constructed in accordance with the new thresholds, a second round of growth is initiated, and eventually still higher thresholds are achieved. Plant con-

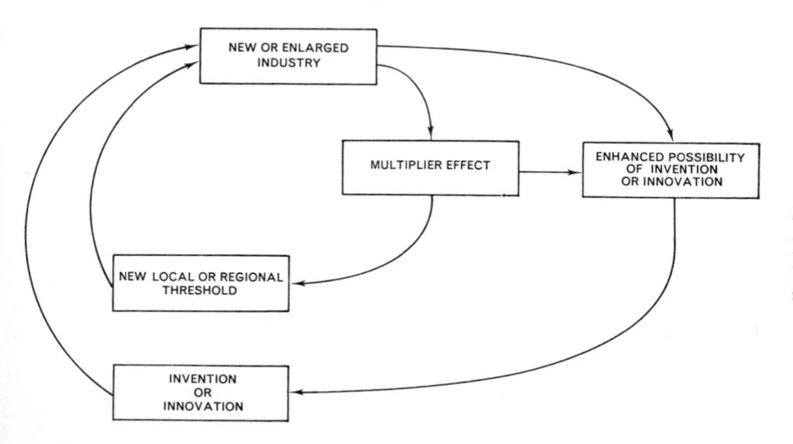

FIG. 1
The circular and cumulative process of industrialization and urban-size growth.

struction in response to these thresholds again generates a multiplier effect and higher thresholds, and the process continues in a circular and cumulative manner until interrupted or impeded.[11]

A second circular sequence of reactions occurs at the same time and compounds and reinforces the effects of the first. This chain stems from the continually more complex network of interpersonal communications and confrontations that derives from an expanding population. The multiplication of interactions among the growing number of individuals engaged in the manufacturing and tertiary sectors enhances the possibilities of technological improvements and inventions, enlarges the likelihood of the adoption of more efficient managerial and financial institutions, increases the speed with which locally originating ideas are disseminated, and eases the diffusion of skills and knowledge brought in by migrants from other areas.[12] Although, as Schumpeter[13] would have it, inventions and ideas are not immediately implemented but await an imaginative entrepreneur to exploit them, once implementation has occurred—that is, once new factories have been erected or old ones enlarged—employment and population increase, the web of interpersonal communications is again extended and densened, the chances for invention and innovation are further enhanced, and the circular process continues, perhaps even at an accelerated pace, until diverted or hindered.

Components of the Model

The Multiplier Effect

. . . The original expositions on the multiplier emphasized solely the effect of investment in the capital-goods industries on employment in other sectors of the economy.[14] Later, others independently developed a modified and broadened version, the basic/nonbasic ratio, and maintained that export (basic or city-forming) industries were the primary determinants of regional and urban growth.[15] If this is the case, how can the association of a multiplier effect with all new manufacturing be rationalized? For one thing: "There is no reason to believe that exports are the sole or even the most important autonomous variable determining regional [or urban] income."[16] In fact, it has been empirically demonstrated that local-market industries, by perpetuating income flow within the city, further gen-

11. For specific related statements on the cumulative effect of new manufacturing on regional rather than urban growth see Myrdal, *Rich Lands and Poor,* pp. 23-26; and Perloff and others, *Regions,* pp. 94-96. Note also H[ans] Carol, "Die Entwicklung der Stadt Zürich zur Metropole der Schweiz," *Geogr. Rundschau* 5 (1953):304-7, and observations on the effect of industrial growth "on the size of local industrial populations" in E. A. Wrigley, *Industrial Growth and Population Change* (Cambridge, 1961).

12. For a discussion of urban growth and the flow of ideas see Richard L. Meier, *A Communications Theory of Urban Growth* (Cambridge, Mass., 1962). See also Torsten Hägerstrand, "The Propagation of Innovation Waves," *Lund Studies in Geography,* ser. B, *Human Geoography,* no. 4 (1952), and the review of the diffusion literature in Everett M. Rogers, *Diffusion of Innovations* (New York, 1962).

13. Schumpeter, *Theory of Economic Development.*

14. John M. Keynes, *The General Theory of Employment, Interest and Money* (New York, 1936), pp. 113-31; and Richard F. Kahn, "The Relation of Home Investment to Unemployment," *Economic Journal* 41 (1931):173-98.

15. See, for example, Douglass C. North, "Location Theory and Regional Economic Growth," *Journal of Political Economy* 63 (1955):243-58; and Gunnar Alexandersson, *The Industrial Structure of American Cities* (Lincoln, Nebr., and Stockholm, 1956), pp. 15-17.

16. Charles M. Tiebout, "Exports and Regional Economic Growth," *Journal of Political Economy* 64 (1956):160-64, 169; reference on p. 161.

erate income and hence development.[17] Secondly, a multiplier effect restricted to export industries would often suppress the development-instigating qualities of local industries that provide inputs for the exporters. Or factories might shift from producing exclusively for local consumption to serving a more extensive area. Further support for dispensing with the basic/nonbasic distinction, and for conceding some multiplier effect to virtually all new manufacturing, may be gained from the common argument that the importance of exports dwindles as the economic unit (metropolis) grows in area and population. Finally, one may point to the somewhat mercantilistic observation that "a city may also grow by purchasing something locally that it has previously imported."[18]

Invention and Innovation

. . . Since the model implies that a multiplication of personal contacts and the importation of nonlocal skills and knowledge were fundamental to urban-size growth from 1860 to 1910 was the consequence of a great influx of European migrants and an "urban implosion" of the domestic rural population (brought about by agricultural surpluses, the downfall of rural manufactures, and "the lure of the city"), it is critical to emphasize that *knowledge of the labor market and destinations of previous migrants are two of the most important determinants of individual migration decisions.*[19] It follows logically that new industries and their multiplier effects created the employment opportunities which attracted migrants to the infant metropolises, and eventually led to additional manufacturing growth through the enhanced possibility of invention and innovation and the attainment of new market thresholds. Migrants, such as Pittsburgh's British and Dutch glassmakers and St. Louis' German brewers, often introduced new industries to the larger cities; and not infrequently "the larger and better established industrial centers" proved to be the most fertile "germinating grounds for new industries."[20]

The increasing complexity of the network of interpersonal communications does more than merely induce innovation within specialized industrial activities, because innovations usually constitute an addition to the existing repertory of know-how in a city. Put in slightly different terms, the communication-invention cycle of the model is validated by the fact that industrialization during the period under discussion "was characterized by the introduction of a relatively small number of broadly similar productive processes to a large number of indus-

17. Ralph W. Pfouts, "An Empirical Testing of the Economic Base Theory," *Journal American Institute of Planners* 23 (1957):64-69. As a case in point, Los Angeles' manufacturing growth before World War I was almost wholly confined to industries producing for a virtually local market.

18. Robert L. Steiner, "Urban and Inter-Urban Economic Equilibrium," *Papers and Proceedings Regional Science Association,* 1, First Annual Meeting, 1954 (1955), pp. C1-C10; reference on p. C8.

19. See Esse Lövgren, "The Geographical Mobility of Labour," *Geografiska Annaler* 38 (1956):344-94, reference on p. 352; Morrill, "Spatial Distribution," p. 13; and Torsten Hägerstrand, "Migration and Area," in *Migration in Sweden, Lund Studies in Geography,* Ser. B, Human Geography, no. 13 (1957):27-158, reference on p. 130. For an analysis of the voluminous literature relating industrialization, cityward migration, and migration theory see Allan Pred, "The External Relations of Cities during Industrial Revolution'" (University of Chicago, Dept. of Geogr., Research Paper No. 76, 1962), pp. 57-68.

20. Edgar M. Hoover, *The Location of Economic Activity* (New York, Toronto, London, 1948), p. 176.

tries."[21] Many production techniques could be converted with little or no adjustment from the manufacture of one commodity to that of another. . . .

This last point also casts light on the anchoring of so-called "footloose" industries in existing manufacturing complexes, and the further reinforcement of the hypothesized circular process of urban-size growth. Theoretically, the cost structure of footloose manufactures permits them to locate as economically in one area or city as in another. Since such industries generally serve a market area of vast or national dimensions, the fulfillment of local or regional thresholds is immaterial to economical operation. Therefore, the manufacture of special machinery, machine tools, and other products of high value per unit weight is likely to flourish at the place of invention, regardless of its size, though an already industrialized city is the most likely location of new technological conceptions. This line of reasoning regarding the adaptability of techniques and footloose industries is consistent with the traditional argument that additional opportunities for industrial specialization are associated with every increment in manufactural differentiation.[22] It should be added that the random inception of footloose manufactures is a major cause of dissimilar industrial structures among metropolises of similar size. . . .

Additional Stimulants to Urban-Size Growth

. . . Although it is generally conceded that migration dominated metropolitan population growth in the late nineteenth century, it is undeniable that natural increase also contributed to the aggregate demand of the metropolis and the realization of higher thresholds. Barring emigration from the city, natural increase of itself would have generated some enlargement of food processing and other essential local industries.

Average wages per manufacturing employee in the United States rose from $378 in 1869 to $512 in 1909 (data in current dollars).[23] The absolute increase of wages and real buying power meant that with the passage of time the multiplier effect of most manufacturing increments became more extensive, and thereby the speed of urban-size growth was accelerated. Higher average levels of per capita consumption were particularly stimulating to the expansion of industries whose products had a high income elasticity of demand. The ramifications of higher average earnings were compounded by the fact that total family incomes were also being increased through the more widespread employment of women; that is, the female working force was increasing more rapidly than total employment.

21. Nathan Rosenberg, "Technological Change in the Machine Tool Industry, 1840-1910," *Journal of Economic History* 23 (1963):414-43; reference on p. 422. Rosenberg also cites the recent literature that stresses the importance of technological change, as opposed to capital accumulation, in American economic growth.

22. See Allyn Young, "Increasing Returns and Economic Progress," *Economic Journal* 38 (1928):527-42, reference on pp. 529-39; and Lampard, "History of Cities," p. 99. See also subsequent comments in the present paper on vertical disintegration and linkages, and Simon Kuznets, "Retardation of Industrial Growth," *Journal of Economy and Business History* 1 (1929):534-60, especially p. 548.

23. Simon Kuznets, Ann Ratner Miller, and Richard A. Easterlin, "Analyses of Economic Change" ("Population Redistribution and Economic Growth: United States, 1870-1950," vol. 2), *Memoirs American Philosophy Society* 51 (1960):129. For a detailed breakdown of wage increases by industry and state see Clarence D. Long, *Wages and Earnings in the United States, 1860-1890* (National Bureau of Economic Research Publs., General Ser. No. 67; New York, 1960).

The growth process may also be accelerated because all "urban qualities which can be construed as providing external economies would seem in some measure to increase with size."[24] In other words, the locational attraction exerted by external agglomeration economies (or localization and urbanization economies) increases functionally rather than arithmetically. Furthermore, since agglomeration diseconomies also mount and eventually become oppressive, external economies were of "unique importance" in the period 1860–1910 to the urban concentration of manufacturing.[25] The multiplication of external economies at that time amounted to more than the benefits usually associated with more efficient interfirm communication and the sharing of facilities and urban "social overhead capital." Urban linkages and concentration were also the consequence of an increasing vertical disintegration of production and concomitant decreases in the locational influence of primary raw materials. As technology progressed there was a greater specialization of manufacturing functions, which often dictated locational proximity of successive stages of production.[26] . . .

Finally, acceptance of an adaptive-adoptive dichotomy of locational processes provides additional insight into the size growth of cities. Two polar viewpoints exist: one affirms that economic activities rationally adapt themselves to the conditions of the society in which they exist (firms rationally locate in cities because of the size of the local market or the availability of localization and urbanization economies); the other asserts that activities react to their environment in ignorance, with the "lucky ones" being adopted by the system.[27] In other words, the adaptive-adoptive dichotomy represents a conflict between purely random and economically rational forces. Acknowledgment of the concurrent operation of these two processes permits the addition of new productive capacity, with attendant multiplier effects and perpetuation of the circular and cumulative growth process, even before higher thresholds are attained or new innovations become economically sound. The long-term adoption or survival of some firms that have thus located purely by chance or in an effort to minimize their uncertainty (risk of input shortages is minimized in large metropolitan areas) is also a key to disparate industrial structures in metropolises of nearly equal size.

24. Aaron Fleisher, "The Economics of Urbanization," in *The Historian and the City*, pp. 70-73; reference on p. 72. This contention is supported by Lösch's logic regarding the coincidence of market networks in regional metropolises. August Lösch, *The Economics of Location*, translated from the 2nd rev. edit. by William H. Woglom with the assistance of Wolfgang F. Stolper (New Haven and London, 1954), p. 77.

25. Shigeto Tsuru, "The Economic Significance of Cities," in *The Historian and the City*, pp. 44-55, especially p. 49.

26. See Lampard, "History of Cities," pp. 90-91; and George J. Stigler, "The Division of Labor Is Limited by the Extent of the Market," *Journal of Political Economy* 59 (1951):185-93, reference on p. 192.

27. See Charles M. Tiebout, "Location Theory, Empirical Evidence, and Economic Evolution," *Papers and Proceedings Regional Science Association*, 3, Third Annual Meeting, 1956 (Philadelphia, 1957):74-86; and Armen A. Alchian, "Uncertainty, Evolution, and Economic Theory," *Journal of Political Economy* 58 (1950): 211-21.

Selective Growth of Cities in Periods of Rapid Industrialization

If the circular and cumulative process of urban growth during rapid industrialization functioned flawlessly, and if all cities were isolated units not in market-area competition with one another, then every city would expand indefinitely, or at least as long as available natural resources permitted. However, between 1860 and 1910 some cities in the United States grew more rapidly and at the expense of others. Only a few attained supremacy in the urban hierarchy, others grew moderately, some became stultified and declined. Today's ten leading industrial centers had already been singled out by 1910 (Table 2), and although their individual importance has varied, as a group they continue to dominate the urban hierarchy.[28] Clearly then, within an interacting system of cities in an expanding space economy, the circular and cumulative growth process does not persist indefinitely for all places. A number of ambivalent forces simultaneously break the circuit of cumulative growth in some instances and precipitate the emergence of multi-million metropolises in others. The most conspicuous of these forces may be construed as geographical expressions of initial advantages.

Transport Improvements

Railroad developments probably had the most profound influence on the growth of some centers at the expense of others. Reductions in the price of transport inputs, and expansion and intensification of the railroad net, both brought many repercussions for the relative importance of American cities.

On a representative railroad, innovations in motive power, carrying capacity, and operating procedure reduced average freight charges per ton-mile from 3.31 cents in 1865 to 0.70 cent in 1892.[29] Cheaper transport inputs "meant a spreading out of critical isodapanes, and an opportunity to realize previously untapped scale economies—even in the absence of advances in production technology."[30] This extension and enlargement of the firm's market area increased the feasibility of agglomeration and large-scale production (a tendency compounded by concurrent innovations in production technology), created the possibility of still further divisions of labor and mass-production economies, and increased the practicability of satisfying national and regional demands from a limited number of cities. Theoretically, then, *the spatial lengthening of production raised the threshold of some industries by increasing their minimum optimal scales of operation, and this, by extension, favored the growth of already efficiently producing centers over inefficient and nonproducing cities*. The occurrence of this phenomenon is crudely mirrored by an increase in the average length of railroad hauls from less than 110 miles per ton in 1882 to about 250 miles per ton in 1910,[31] and by the fact that some industries have historically not responded as quickly as others to regional redistributions of population and income; inertia,

28. See related remarks by Carl H. Madden in his "On Some Indications of Stability in the Growth of Cities in the United States," *Economic Development and Cultural Change* 4 (1955-56):236-52, and "Some Spatial Aspects of Urban Growth in the United States," ibid., pp. 371-87.

29. Figures refer to the New York Central and Hudson River Railroad. See Edward Atkinson, "Productive Industry," in *The United States of America,* ed. Nathaniel Southgate Shaler, 2 vols. (New York, 1894), vol. 2, pp. 671-734; reference on p. 712.

30. Pred, "External Relations," p. 31. "Critical isodapanes" for a production site, or agglomeration point, refer to the locus encompassing all alternative production points at which the transport advantages, in terms of inputs and costs, are equal to, or less than, agglomeration or labor economies at the production site (or city).

31. Atkinson, "Productive Industry," p. 708; "Historical Statistics of the United States, Colonial Times to 1957" (U.S. Bureau of the Census, 1960), p. 431.

partly in the form of rising thresholds, reduced the locational mobility of some industries.[32]

Cheaper transport inputs presumably also worked to the advantage of cities with plants having large market areas. Diminished transport rates normally favor growth—with attendant multiplier effects—of the firm "which already has a larger market area because of its lower marginal cost of production," since "the firm with a larger market area, and therefore more transport inputs, has its total costs reduced more by a lowering of transport rates than any of its competitors."[33]. . .

Large-scale production and specialized manufacturing agglomerations, and hence the growth of some cities at the expense of others, also gained impetus as it became apparent that railroad terminal and transshipment costs could be spread out by dividing them over increased distances. Realization of this cost relationship normally tended to promote a decrease in freight rates "for long hauls in comparison with short hauls" and encouraged the "movement of materials and products over longer distances."[34] Terminal and transfer costs also contributed to the polarization of manufacturing activity around trunk-line terminals and major rail intersections by inspiring both the elimination of multiple transshipments of product mixes and the locational adjacency of successive stages of fabrication. The paramount importance of initial rail and terminal-facility advantages to urban-industrial growth is best exemplified by Chicago. In 1860 Chicago was a city of moderate size (Table 2), with about 5,500 workers employed in industries that catered primarily to local markets. Within fifty years the industrial working force in the physically expanded metropolis had grown to more than 325,000, many of them in firms serving distant markets.[35] Chicago's phenomenal rise was foreshown by 1860, when the city had emerged as the nation's most important railroad center, a terminus for eleven trunk roads and twenty branch and feeder lines.

An expanded railroad net, decreasing freight tariffs, and lower volume rates also strengthened the initial advantages of efficient producers and added to their scale and external economies, by broadening possible supply areas and providing access to superior raw materials or semifinished goods. In effect, transport improvements permitted large producers, or agglomerations with low marginal outlays per unit of product, to usurp the potential raw-material consumption of nonproducing cities and firms with higher production costs. In general, this ultimately resulted in a still larger scale of output, some multiplier effect, and additional growth of the favored city. . . .

Agglomeration Economies and Reduction of Production Costs

Production innovations, like transport improvements, conferred advantages on a few cities rather than on all. Advances in American industrial technology during

32. Kuznets et al., "Analyses of Economic Change," pp. 110-15.
33. Pred, "External Relations," p. 38.
34. William Henry Dean, Jr., *The Theory of the Geographic Location of Economic Activities* (Cambridge, Mass., 1938), p. 32.
35. Eighth Census of the United States, 1860: Book 3, *Manufactures* (Washington, D.C., 1865), p. 87; Thirteenth Census of the United States, 1910: Vol. 10, *Manufactures*, 1909 (U.S. Bureau of the Census, Washington, D.C., 1913), p. 917. For a discussion of the impact of the railroads in the earlier decades of this expansion see Wyatt Winton Belcher, *The Economic Rivalry between St. Louis and Chicago, 1850-1880*, Columbia University Studies in History, Economics and Public Law, No. 529 (New York, 1947).

the period under discussion almost inevitably conduced diminished production outlays per unit. New machinery and new techniques also required large capital investment and an increase in the optimal size of operation. Thus the avalanche of innovations brought a tremendous impetus toward shifts in manufacturing scale and an attendant urban concentration of production, involving both the expansion of existing plants and the establishment of new facilities. The pronounced scale shifts in American manufacturing between 1860 and the outbreak of World War I were partly reflected by size of establishment. For example, the average establishment in 1860 had about nine employees and a product value of $13,420, as compared with more than twenty-five employees and nearly $88,000 product value in 1914. More revealing and imposing is the fact that, in 1914, 3,819 out of 275,791 establishments accounted for 35.2 percent of the nation's industrial wage earners and 48.6 percent of the product.[36]

In Weberian terminology, the reduction or "compression" of per unit production costs permitted a substitution of transport outlays for labor and other production outlays, and therefore prompted a greater extension of market areas than would have occurred if only transportation improvements had been present. Augmentation of market areas again promised the division of fixed costs over an increasing volume of production, which induced still larger optimal scales of production and higher thresholds.

Consequently, *technical innovations that yielded lower per unit production costs tended to favor growth and industrial agglomeration in those few cities which had originally initiated efficient production, and at the same time arrested the development of nonproducing and inefficient centers.* As thresholds reached higher and higher levels, the possibilities of entry into the market or expansion of existing facilities became confined to a smaller and smaller number of cities, and many functions shifted from lower-order to higher-order urban places. . . .

It must be repeated that urban diseconomies also accumulated and eventually became oppressive to some types of industries. Nothing that has been said should be interpreted as meaning that advantages accrued indefinitely to the major metropolises. In the half-century following 1860 urban diseconomies mounted—"diseconomies engendered by rises in the cost of living and money wages, in the costs of local materials produced under conditions of diminishing returns, in time-cost and other costs of transportation, and in land values and rents."[37] If it had not been for the continued accumulation of these diseconomies, and for the maturing of automotive transportation, new raw-material requirements, and regional population growth leading to the more widespread attainment of specific thresholds, it is probable that the ten largest industrial metropolises would account for even more than their present 37.5 percent of national value added by manufacturing.

Relative Accessibility

Relative accessibility, here defined as the accessibility of a city to the population or market of the country as a whole,[38] also

36. Isaac Lippincott, *Economic Development of the United States* (New York and London, 1922), pp. 476-77.

37. Walter Isard, *Location and Space Economy* (Cambridge, Mass., 1956), p. 183.

38. Relative accessibility is measured in terms of population potential or market potential. See John Q. Stewart, "Empirical Mathematical Rules Concerning the Distribution and Equilibrium of Population," *Geography Review* 37 (1947):

influences the selective growth of cities. In general, *transportation improvements and lower unit production costs work to the advantage of points with high accessibility as opposed to points with low accessibility.*[39] This is partly because, by definition, low-accessibility areas have relatively small aggregate populations and incomes and consequently encounter difficulties in meeting scale thresholds for other than essential consumer goods. In addition, in serving a regional market of given sales volume, manufacturers in low-accessibility cities would have longer average shipments, and greater allocations for transport, than their counterparts in high-accessibility cities. The late-nineteenth-century low-accessibility firm, being in a comparatively undeveloped area, was probably further hampered by a small-mileage railroad network with few connections and intersections.[40]

Despite these handicaps, some large metropolises should eventually arise in low-accessibility areas, even in the absence of the mass population shifts that have been characteristic of the United States in the twentieth century. Large metropolises are not totally alien to low-accessibility areas, but their potential numbers are limited. Growth of urban centers in such areas is possible partly because transportation economies may be substituted for production diseconomies; that is, for some goods lower scales of production, and consequently higher unit costs, are compensated by avoidance of the transcontinental freight costs that would be incurred if the product were imported from high-accessibility cities. Expressed somewhat differently, a small number of low-accessibility cities can achieve metropolitan proportions because they are beyond the critical isodapanes of many market-oriented industries in high-accessibility centers, or, alternatively, because they are at great distances from cities with equal rank in the urban hierarchy. Regardless of these circumstances, the low-accessibility centers that do grow quickly during periods of rapid industrialization, like the corresponding cities in older high-accessibility areas, almost invariably possess some pertinent initial advantages.

The influence of relative accessibility on American urban development in the late nineteenth century is roughly indicated by Figures 2 and 3. In 1860 the four largest cities in the country, New York (including Brooklyn), Philadelphia, Baltimore, and Boston, were in the highest-accessibility area. By 1900 centers such as Chicago, St. Louis, Cleveland, and Detroit had achieved large populations, though they were not in the area of highest accessibility. Agricultural development of the Midwest and the Great Plains, as well as urban-industrial growth itself, had created levels of accessibility between the Mississippi and the northern Appalachians that far exceeded those of any of the Atlantic Coast cities in 1860. The steady growth of the older eastern metropolises (Table 2) is understandable in the light of the more than doubling of their accessibility during the forty years. By the same token, no city on the low-accessibility Pacific Coast, including San Francisco and Los Angeles, had grown to the size of the largest midwestern and

461-85; and Chauncy D. Harris, "The Market as a Factor in the Localization of Industry in the United States," *Annals, Association of American Geographers,* 44 (1954):315-48.

39. It has been demonstrated that similar-sized cities "with high accessibility tend to have higher levels of manufacturing activity than those with low accessibility" (Duncan and others, *op. cit.* [see footnote 35 above], p. 128).

40. Cf. K. J. Kansky, "Structure of Transportation Networks" (University of Chicago, Dept. of Geogr., Research Paper No. 84, 1963), pp. 93-104.

eastern cities, though the rise of the two had been impressive (Figs. 2 and 3).

Combination and Competition

The growth of trusts and mammoth corporations, the vertical and horizontal integration of previously independent firms, and the consolidation of small railroads into vast systems also had ramifications that confirmed the ascendancy of a few cities at the expense of others. The previously cited size-of-establishment statistics provide only an inkling of the combination activity that gathered momentum after business recovered from the panic and depression of the seventies. The proliferation of limited-dividend manufacturing corporations, almost nonexistent in manufacturing in 1860 and numbering more than forty thousand in

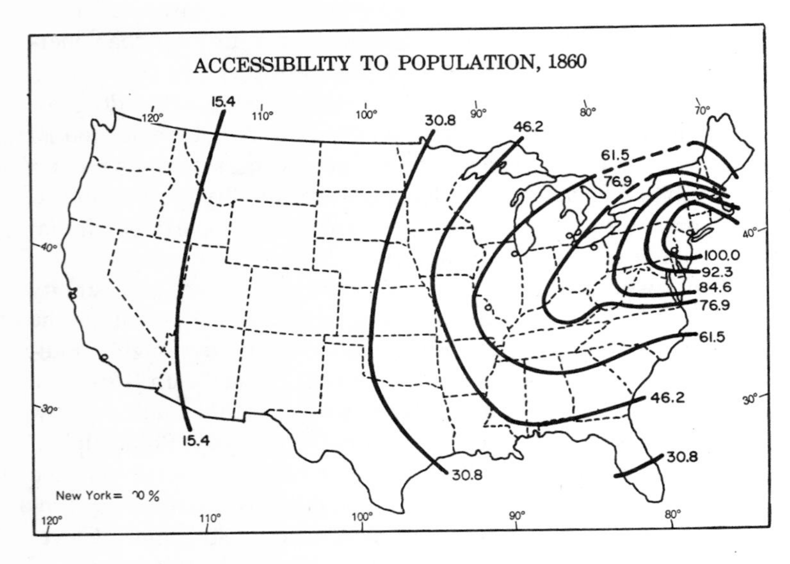

FIG. 2
Accessibility to population, 1860. Adapted from John Q. Stewart and William Warntz, "Macrogeography and Social Science," *Geographical Review* 48 (1958): 167-84, Fig. 7.

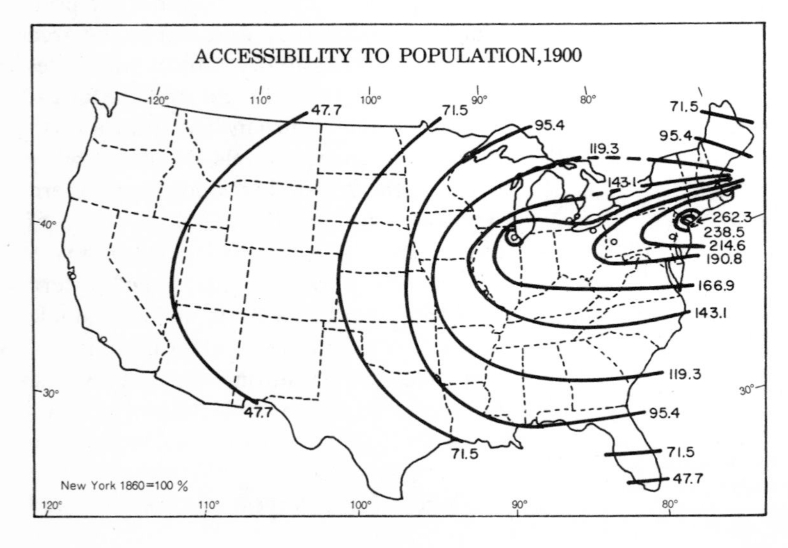

FIG. 3
Accessibility to population, 1900. Adapted from Stewart, "Empirical Mathematical Rules Concerning the Distribution . . . Population (see text footnote 38), Fig. 11.

1900, was another manifestation of the increasing concentration of industrial capital. Limited-dividend corporations "comprised barely a tenth of all establishments, [but] they produced 60 percent of the value, and almost completely dominated the metal and technical branches."[41]. . .

Preferential and discriminatory freight rates were an important byproduct of railroad combination and competition, and they too had repercussions on the selective growth of cities. In spite of the formation of the Interstate Commerce Commission in 1887, it was some decades before discriminatory rates began to be abolished on a wide scale. Throughout the period under discussion, below-average unit cost and below-operating-cost freight rates were not uncommon. Deficits were recouped on noncompetitive commodities and in areas where rivalry was lacking.

In general, rates were most propitious for terminal cities within "Official Territory" (a rate zone that included the first eight cities in Table 2). Rates were low for raw materials coming into the territory and high for goods manufactured outside it, and this arrangement "undoubtedly discouraged and retarded the diffusion of manufactures into outlying regions."[42]. . .

Availability of Labor and Capital

The external economies of labor and capital availability also operated as initial advantages favoring the growth of existing commercial foci over smaller places.

Many new or expanding industries may be viewed as having minimum labor as well as market thresholds. Therefore, older commercial and manufacturing centers were often the most probable places in which the undecided entrepreneur, making a marginal locational decision, would seek skills and manpower. Although semiskilled and unskilled labor might have been duplicated fairly easily from place to place, significance of the size of the local labor pool became magnified as the average size of establishment increased. The singular advantages of established industrial cities were even more pronounced with respect to skilled labor; for location or expansion elsewhere put the firm in the dilemma of finding "a labor market big enough to provide an adequate number of workers with the necessary aptitudes" or resigning itself "to a prolonged training period for a major segment of its labor force."[43]

Capital availability (a province of the economist and only cursorily treated here) and knowledge of capital outlets were crucial to industrial entrepreneurs. Capital was more readily available to innovators in traditional banking capitals such as New York, Philadelphia, and Boston, and in Chicago and St. Louis, the new central reserve cities created by law in 1887. The diffusion of knowledge regarding investment opportunities was most efficient in these and other centers, such as Cleveland, Detroit, and San Francisco, where the lines of commercial communication were of comparatively long standing. It follows that these few cities exerted a strong attraction on the undecided marginal locator, and that the chances for a new round of growth in smaller places were correspondingly diminished. As the size of the capital-goods sector became more important vis-à-vis the consumer-goods sector, capital availability also became more important, since, on the whole, "the food and clothing in-

---

41. Blake McKelvey, *The Urbanization of America (1860-1915)* (New Brunswick, N.J., 1963), p. 41.
42. Perloff and others, *Regions,* p. 219.
43. Martin Segal, *Wages in the Metropolis* (Cambridge, Mass., 1960), p. 20.

dustries need less capital to build and equip their factories . . . than such industries as iron, steel and engineering."[44] According to the logic of the circular and cumulative growth model, investment in new or expanded capital-goods factories created additional local capital outlets, since the multiplier effects of these new facilities called forth a greater demand for ubiquitous industries and tertiary activities.[45]

Other Considerations

. . . The achievement of a given threshold, and the consequent establishment or expansion of equal scales of production in different geographical locales, are not normally followed by exactly equivalent patterns of growth. All cities and firms are unique, and the manner in which their singularities interact in the circular and cumulative growth process cannot be duplicated like prints from a lithographic plate. Some plants expand more rapidly than others in the same industry, either because of entrepreneurial aggressiveness and ingenuity or because of some permutation of the factors discussed above. Because variable rates of establishment growth imply variable multiplier effects, the selective growth of plants is logically both an instigator and a corollary of the selective growth of cities. Not uncommonly, faster-growing plants obtain economies of scale that allow them to usurp the market area of slowly expanding factories. Such a sequence of events likewise tends to favor some cities at the expense of others. Different rates of plant growth also contribute to the dissimilar industrial structures of multimillion metropolises.

The circular and cumulative growth of smaller cities with limited initial advantages is often, but not always, impeded and short-circuited because their new or enlarged manufacturing does not have a multiplier effect capable of drawing a train of higher thresholds and new innovations. When such stagnancy occurs, many local demands must be satisfied with goods produced in regional and national metropolises whose growth is unobstructed.

Finally, no inquiry into the growth of some cities at the expense of others would be complete without passing mention of the part played by factor immobility. Because management is more prone to augment existing facilities than to relocate where large initial capital expenditures would be necessary, "the ability of a locality to hold an industry greatly exceeds its original ability to attract."[46] On a grander scale, large cities themselves "are much less subject to relocation than are individual units of production." This is because "the accumulated fixed investments of an urban mass in conjunction with its vested social institutions entail major geographic immobilities and rigidities."[47] These immobilities, as much as any other factor, lie at the crux of initial advantage. . . .

---

44. W. G. Hoffmann, *The Growth of Industrial Economies,* translated from the German by W. O. Henderson and W. H. Chaloner (Manchester, England, 1958), p. 38.

45. Obviously, investment in ubiquitous industries and tertiary activities "has to be located where the demand is." James S. Duesenberry, "Some Aspects of the Theory of Economic Development," *Explorations in Entrepreneurial History* 3 (1950-51):63-102; reference on p. 97.

46. Ohlin, *Interregional and International Trade,* p. 236.

47. Isard, *Location and Space-Economy,* p. 183.

Selective Urban Growth in the Middle Ohio Valley, 1800-1860 / *Edward K. Muller*

One of the most popular themes in the history of North America urbanization has been the success or failure of cities to amass population faster than their rivals. Although much scholarly attention has been given to the experience of the continent's largest metropolitan centers, the processes of selective growth among smaller, lower-order cities and towns within regions has remained relatively neglected. Theories of urban growth and of the spatial patterning of cities offer oversimplified explanations for the differential performances of these smaller urban centers because few of them take into account the interaction of specific functions of smaller cities with the conditions and timing of regional development. In the transformation of a frontier region to a fully integrated part of the national economy, there were well-defined changes in regional accessibility and economic activity to which the towns and cities within the region had to adjust. A changing locational and hierarchical pattern of nodality within the transportation network can be related to three phases of regional development, during each of which there were distinct patterns of selective urban growth. This argument is specifically evaluated in the middle Ohio Valley but offers general findings appropriate to most newly settling regions of North America. . . .

Periodization of Selective Growth

The evolution of export production and circulation (both intraregional and interregional) can be generalized into three periods of regional development that facilitate the positing of changing relationships among nodality, hinterland service, manufacturing, and urban growth.[1] The first period, the Pioneer Periphery, involved establishing permanent settlements, clearing the land for agricultural production, searching for viable crops, and experimenting with export commodities in a context of remoteness from external markets. Although regional trade and purchasing power remained relatively limited and rural settlement was confined to the vicinity of natural routes, the outlines of a commercial hierarchy emerged as a few towns undertook the provisioning of migrants and gained control of interregional contacts.[2] Most new towns,

1. The periodization is based on the staple theory to regional economic development in North America represented by (among others) Douglas C. North, *The Economic Growth of the United States, 1790-1860* (New York: W. W. Norton, 1961), pp. 1-14. Spatial characteristics of development reflect the propositions in Edward J. Taaffe, Richard L. Morrill, and Peter R. Gould, "Transport Expansion in Underdeveloped Countries: A Comparative Analysis," *Geography Review* 53 (1963):503-29.
2. James E. Vance, Jr.: *The Merchant's World: The Geography of Wholesaling* (Englewood

Reprinted (with omissions) from the *Geographical Review* 66 (1976):178-99.

however, primarily offered elemental goods and services for local areas. Urban growth was greatest at the few nodal points of contact between the intraregional and interregional circulation networks, frequently because of site and situational advantages, and also at the trade centers within the local areas of most rapid rural settlement.[3]

Expansion and intensification of rural settlement accompanied the vastly improved interregional connections and specialized staple productions that characterized the second period of regional development—the Specialized Periphery. The dominant regional entrepôt concentrated much of the increased interregional commerce, but the pattern of growth among other towns still depended on nodality with respect to the servicing of local and subregional hinterlands. The frequent internal improvements of a developing region sometimes caused dramatic shifts in the location of such nodality. Moreover, if processing of the staple products was required before exportation, the emerging processing industries at the nodal centers along the new transportation facilities enhanced their population growth at the expense of trade centers without such access.

The eventual integration of the region with the national transportation and marketing systems often resulted in a third phase—the Transitional Periphery of diversification in agricultural production and emergence of substantial secondary manufacturing activities. The few subregional nodal centers within the region initially benefited from the decentralization of some interregional functions and from the concentration of some formerly local activities. Although such locational changes maintained the fundamental outlines of the regional urban hierarchy as based on the regional commercial system, the development of exported secondary manufactures altered the bases of growth. With superior access to regional and external markets as well as to raw materials, the centers of greatest nodality in this third regional transportation network developed the largest amount and greatest variety of manufactures (their growth reflecting considerable locational inertia or advantages from earlier periods). In addition, a few towns near the regional entrepôt developed some specialized manufactures that were linked to the emerging industrial market of the entrepôt.

Thus, during the course of regional settlement and economic development the factors of selective urban growth shifted from accessibility to local hinterlands for providing commercial services and agricultural processing industries to accessibility to wider regional and external markets for the support of secondary manufactures. The locational impact of these shifting bases of urban growth depended on the distribution of nodality within the evolving transportation network. . . .

The Middle Ohio Valley, 1800-1860

A middle Ohio Valley region was selected for analysis because it exemplified the three hypothesized periods of regional development. A study area of forty-one counties in southwestern Ohio and southeastern Indiana was delineated on the basis of its dependence on Cincinnati and on the Ohio River for most external con-

---

Cliffs, N.J.: Prentice-Hall, 1970), pp. 96-98 and 161; and Julius Rubin, "Urban Growth and Regional Development," in *The Growth of the Seaport Cities, 1790-1825,* edited by David T. Gilchrist (Charlottesville: University of Virginia Press, 1967), pp. 10-13.

3. Taaffe et al., "Transport Expansion," pp. 503-5.

tacts during the initial periods of settlement (Fig. 1). . . .

The successive adoption of major transportation innovations facilitated the transition of the region from a remote frontier to a vigorous, integrated section of the national economy. The early river and road network spatially limited settlement and supported the production of small amounts of whiskey, flour, salt pork, and livestock which could withstand the arduous downriver journey to external markets. The construction of turnpikes and canals after 1830 stimulated rural settlement and commercial specialization in wheat, corn, and livestock. With the rapid adoption of railroads around 1850, the middle Ohio Valley began to diversify into secondary manufacturing while continuing to produce agricultural staples. . . .

Access to Local Hinterlands in the Pioneer Periphery, 1800-1830

In 1830, after three and a half decades of permanent American settlement, more than half a million people inhabited the middle Ohio Valley region. Settlement was concentrated along the Ohio River and in the four major tributary river valleys, where flatboats and crude country roads provided sporadic and seasonal

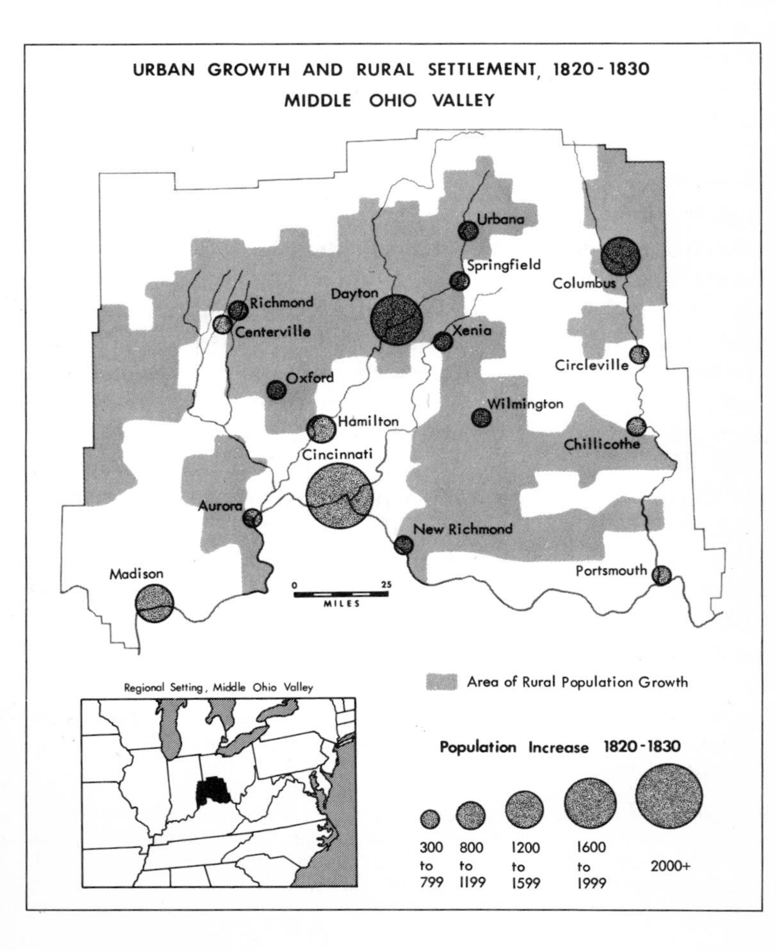

FIG. 1
Urban growth and rural settlement in the middle Ohio Valley, 1820-1830. Rural population growth is based on townships and is derived from data in published volumes and manuscript schedules of the United States censuses of population, 1820 and 1830. See also Muller, "Town Populations in Early Censuses" (see text footnote 5).

access to the Ohio River. In addition to a variety of crops grown for local consumption, farmers produced small surpluses of grains for conversion to forms feasible for movement by wagon and boat.[4] Although incoming settlers and passing migrants periodically provided markets for local produce, sustained economic development depended on the increased flow of goods down the Ohio and Mississippi rivers to external markets and on the driving of livestock eastward over the Appalachian Mountains.

A network of approximately 148 urban centers with populations of more than 100 gradually emerged to service this frontier economy.[5] At least three orders of centers can be identified by the end of the initial period. The concentration of interregional contacts and commerce, migrant influx, and local administration at the junctions of regional and interregional routes resulted in the growth of entrepôt towns, particularly along the Ohio River. While several smaller towns, such as Portsmouth, Ripley, and Lawrenceburg, provided these entrepôt functions for limited settlement areas, a few with substantial access to the interior of the region developed sizable commercial complexes and commensurate populations. . . .

The spread of settlement northward up the various river valleys led to the establishment of merchant and milling activities at the interior junctions of smaller streams and local roads with the major tributary rivers, and small towns frequently emerged at these sites as service centers for the immediate environs.[6] Most of these new communities remained local in orientation and quite small in population; some (hereafter called district trade centers) gained local prominence as market centers, county seats, or highway junctions. A few subregional towns with access to larger areas of the interior became intermediate trading points for the collection and distribution of goods and services between their extended hinterlands, including smaller centers, and the focuses of interregional commerce. For example, Dayton concentrated commercial activity at the junction of movement in the Mad River and upper Miami River valleys. . . . Thus by 1830 there had emerged a few interregional entrepôt towns, a dozen or more district trade centers and interior subregional nodal points, and many small, local service centers. The urban network corresponded closely with the spread and intensification of rural settlement and commercial agriculture.

The general impression of steady, almost inevitable growth in rural and urban settlement during this first period obscures evidence of selective growth among the larger towns. A regression analysis of the absolute increase in the towns' populations between 1820 and 1830 and the towns' populations at the beginning of the decade (1820) identified several towns that grew more or less than expected on the basis of their size in 1820 and of the general growth performance of all other towns in the region.[7] As antici-

4. Robert L. Jones, "Ohio Agriculture in History," *Ohio Historical Quarterly* 65 (1956): 229-58, reference on p. 234; and Fred Kuhnes, "History and Review of the Condition of Agriculture in Ohio" (Board of Agriculture, Ohio, 14th Annual Report, 1859), p. 468.

5. Edward K. Muller, "Town Populations in the Early Censuses: An Aid to Research," *History Methods Newsletter* 3 (1970):2-8.

6. R. C. Downes, *Frontier Ohio* (Ohio State Archaeological and Historical Society, Columbus, 1935), pp. 117-20.

7. The residuals of the regression analysis for each decade indicate exceptional growth performances. Estimated and interpolated population figures were excluded from the regressions; and, consequently, analyses for any given decade omit important towns. The analysis of the 1820-

pated, the differential growth performances of these larger towns was primarily related to the nodality of their locations on the developing transportation network with respect to the pace of rural settlement and expansion of agriculture in the local hinterlands. Because trade moved along the river and road network in much the same direction throughout this period, the few earliest nodal centers for large areas of the region benefited the most from proliferating regional commerce. Along with Cincinnati and Madison as regional entrepôts, the subregional nodal towns of Hamilton, Dayton, and Columbus attracted by far the largest numbers of new residents during the 1820s (Table 1). The other most rapidly growing towns in relation to their sizes were the district trade centers in areas of recent rapid rural expansion. Access to newly settling areas was important to and differentiated the growth of both the subregional nodal towns and the district trade centers (Fig. 1). Thus the northernmost subregional nodes of Dayton and Columbus more than doubled the decennial population increments of the two older subregional centers of Hamilton and Chillicothe in longer settled and less rapidly growing areas closer to the Ohio River. . . . Except for Cincinnati, the growth of the numerous small Ohio River ports also varied in relation to the timing of the development of their local hinterlands.

TABLE 1. Population Increase in Cities of the Middle Ohio Valley, 1820-1830*

City	*Absolute Increase,* 1820-1830	*Population Size Rank,* 1830
Dayton	1,882	1
Madison[a]	1,420	4
Columbus	1,335	3
Hamilton	835	5
Circleville	601	7
Portsmouth	536	10
Oxford	525	15
Centerville[a]	500	20
Richmond[a]	500	12
Springfield	463	9
Urbana	458	8
Chillicothe	420	2

Sources: Published volumes and manuscript schedules of the various United States censuses of population, 1800-1870. See also Muller, text footnote.
* Towns not listed here increased by fewer than 400 inhabitants.
[a] Partially estimated.

30 period was particularly incomplete; and no analyses could be run for earlier decades.

Manufacturing activities contributed little to the pattern of selective growth among these towns. Most trade centers contained sawmills and flour mills, distilleries, small meat-packing operations, and artisan productions of leather, wood, and hardware articles for the local market. . . . The few largest towns such as Dayton, however, contained a greater number and variety of these activities, reflecting their access to larger hinterlands within the region. In short, selective growth of towns during the pioneer period of settlement depended on access to and the growth of local hinterlands and, consequently, on the timing of settlement expansion within the region.

The Emergence of Urban Manufacturing in the Specialized Periphery, 1830-1850

The dramatic rise of the Old Northwest to national prominence in the production of corn and wheat by mid-century depended in part on the significant contribution of the middle Ohio Valley region. Vital to this development was the adoption of the latest transportation advancements, which extended improved accessibility to several areas within the region and provided greater internal interconnectivity (Fig.

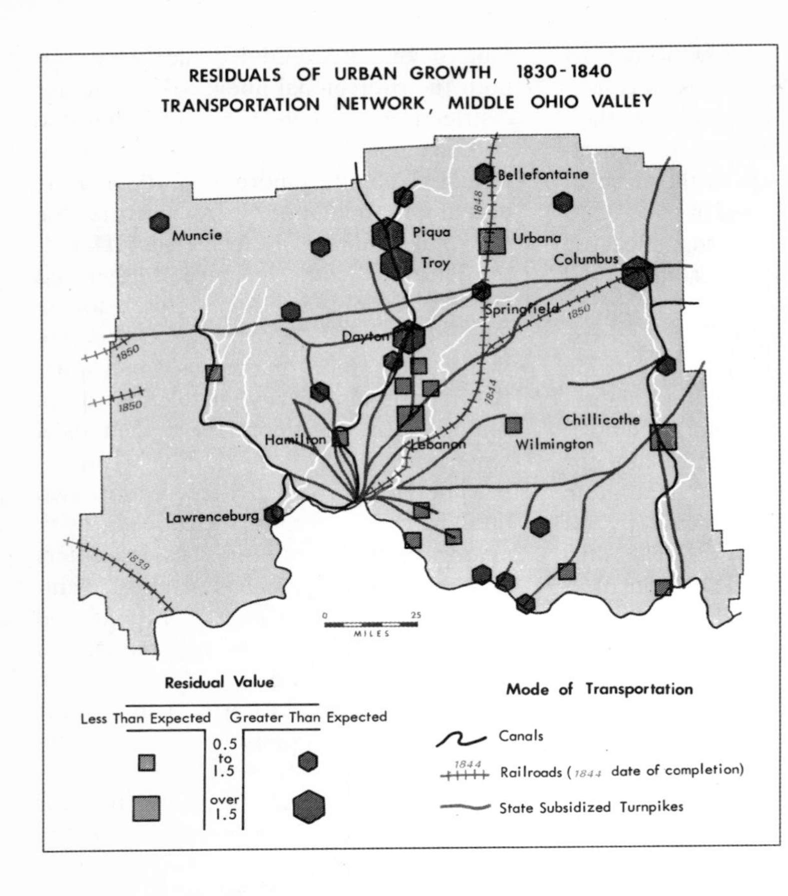

FIG. 2
Transportation network of the Specialized Periphery and residuals of urban growth in the middle Ohio Valley, 1830-1840. Sources of the data are discussed in Muller, see text footnote 5.

2). The Ohio, Miami, and Whitewater canals eliminated many of the navigational problems on the tributary rivers that had limited settlement and commercial agriculture before 1830. Moreover, three railroads and several turnpikes were built in areas that did not obtain the advantages of canals. . . .

The lower transport costs and greater bulk capacity of the canals and railroads stimulated specialization in wheat and corn-hog production in most of the region. Although measurement of regional production is impossible until 1840, the almost doubled output of wheat and corn crops during the 1840s and the dramatic rises in the clearances of these products and their derivatives at canal ports demonstrate the dimensions of commercial agricultural expansion.[8] Not surprisingly, the rural population increased by approximately 200,000 during the twenty-year period.

Urban settlement in the middle Ohio Valley increased at an even faster rate. By 1850, one-fifth of the region's inhabitants resided in the twelve cities with

8. "Compendium of the Sixth Census of the United States, 1840" (U.S. Dept. of State, Washington, D.C., 1841), pp. 275-77 and 287-89; "Seventh Census of the United States: 1850" (U.S. Bureau of the Census, Washington, D.C., 1853), pp. 790-97 and 868; "Ohio State Auditor, Annual Report," *Ohio Executive Documents,* 1853, Part 1, pp. 376-83; and "Board of Canal Commissioners and Board of Public Works, Annual Reports," *Ohio Executive Documents,* 1833-50.

populations in excess of 2,500. Similar to the earlier pioneer period, the expansion of settlement and agriculture that accompanied the spread of transportation facilities into unsettled areas supported the growth of new district trade centers, and these newer towns were again among the region's most rapidly growing ones, as indicated by the high positive residuals of the regressions of town size and absolute population increase for both decades. . . .

Most of the established towns were also well aware of the importance of these new transportation facilities and worked frantically to obtain their services. Access to growing local hinterlands remained a primary determinant of the towns' performances. The reduced transport costs enhanced their nodality by extending accessibility to larger areas within the region. Construction of waterpower sites along the canals augmented this position, as large-scale agricultural processing industries developed at most major canal ports.[9] Because the southern direction of movement prevailed until the late 1840s and because most large towns eventually acquired some form of improved access, the general distribution of nodality did not markedly change by the end of the period; and only two new towns–Piqua and Delaware, both of which were trade centers in the rapidly growing northern counties–broke into the region's list of fifteen largest. However, the considerable variation in growth rates between 1830 and 1850 (Table 2) indicates the efforts of towns to adjust during the evolution of the transportation network.

The canals' advantages for movement and waterpower had an immediate impact on the urban system. The opening of the Miami Canal in the late 1820s immediately shifted the focus of commercial activity to Middletown and Dayton on the

9. "Special Report of the Auditor of the State," *Ohio Executive Documents,* 1850-51, Part 1, pp. 827-29.

TABLE 2. Population Increase in Cities of the Middle Ohio Valley, 1830-1840 and 1840-1850

1830-1840		1840-1850	
City	*Absolute increase*	*City*	*Absolute increase*
Columbus	3,613	Columbus	11,834
Dayton	3,102	Dayton	4,910
Madison	1,398[a]	Madison	4,214
Richmond	1,170[a]	Chillicothe	3,123
Chillicothe	1,131	Springfield	3,046
Circleville	1,082	Portsmouth	2,373
Piqua	993	Hamilton	2,105
Springfield	982	Piqua	1,796
Troy	847	Xenia	1,617
Hamilton	844	Lawrenceburg	1,207
Cambridge City	827[a]	Circleville	1,193
Ripley	673	Delaware	1,176
Aurora	606	Urbana	950
Portsmouth	575	New Richmond	896
Miamisburg	565	Aurora	858

Sources: Published volumes and manuscript schedules of the various United States censuses of population, 1800-1870.
[a] Partially estimated.

canal. This concentration of commerce occurred at the expense of the trade centers of Lebanon and Xenia in the nearby valley of the Little Miami River. The residuals of the regression of urban growth for both the 1820s and 1830s clearly reflect this pattern (Fig. 2). . . . On the eastern branch of the upper Whitewater River, Richmond became the focus for the movement of goods by turnpike from rapidly settling east central Indiana to Dayton or Cincinnati and was one of the region's fastest growing towns, becoming the eighth largest in population. Like Dayton and Richmond, Columbus became the major nodal point for a large portion of rapidly settling central Ohio. Columbus obtained access to the Ohio Canal through an eleven-mile extension canal and was the hub of several turnpikes, including the National Road. Of course, its selection as the state capital further enhanced local business opportunities and, consequently, population growth.

As it became clear that no additional canals were to be constructed, many areas without such access turned to the railroads. The completion of several railroads and the remaining canal projects in the 1840s altered the pattern of nodality that had been evolving in the preceding decade. The opening of the Mad River and Little Miami railroads in the 1840s reversed the previously dismal growth performances of district trade centers in these valleys. Urbana halted its population loss and increased by 950 residents in 1840. Both Springfield and Xenia tripled their population increments over those of the preceding decade. The new Whitewater Canal on the western branch of the Whitewater River immediately shifted trade to the canal ports (particularly Cambridge City) away from Richmond. Richmond's growth declined by more than 50 percent, and the city dropped back to its lower position of 1830 in the ranking of regional cities.

Down the Ohio River from Cincinnati, the port of Madison constructed a railroad into south central Indiana, eventually connecting with Indianapolis. Within a few years the flow of agricultural commodities to Madison and the northward return of merchandise made it the second most active Ohio River port in the region.[10] Only Columbus and Dayton grew more than Madison during the 1840s. . . . Other river ports near but not at the terminals of the new intraregional transportation facilities faded into strictly local centers for their immediate environs. Similarly, many interior trade centers, such as Lebanon, Oxford, Wilmington, and Washington Courthouse, in already settled areas lost nodality to canal and rail towns when they did not get the service of a new mode of transportation.

The provision of commercial services for changing hinterlands only partially explains the pattern of urban growth in this second period. In 1830 Dayton, Chillicothe, Columbus, Madison, and Hamilton were similar in size and function. By 1850, population size and growth trends clearly differentiated these towns (Table 3). This sorting corresponded closely with variations in nodality on the circulation system and with the attendant amount and kinds of manufacturing activities. Manufacturing had become an important component of the assortment of functions in the larger towns, and urban population was positively related to the total value of manufacturing production. With the regional specialization in grains and livestock, agricultural processing industries predominated, providing 62

10. *Madison and Indianapolis Railroad, Annual Reports, 1843-1844 and 1848-1853,* Indiana State Library and Cincinnati Historical Society.

TABLE 3. Population Trends in the Leading Cities of the Middle Ohio Valley, 1830-1850, Ranked by Amount of Increase

City	*Population in* 1830	*Population in* 1850	*Absolute Population Increase*
Columbus	2,435	17,882	15,447
Dayton	2,965	10,977	8,012
Madison[a]	2,400	8,012	5,612
Chillicothe	2,846	7,100	4,254
Springfield	1,080	5,108	4,028
Hamilton	1,708	4,657	2,949
Portsmouth	1,063	4,011	2,948
Piqua	..[b]	3,277	2,789
Circleville	1,136	3,411	2,275
Xenia	..[b]	3,024	2,107
Lebanon	1,165	..[b]	923
Urbana	1,102	..[b]	918

Sources: Published volumes and manuscript schedules of the various United States censuses of population, 1800-1870.
[a] Partially estimated.
[b] Not ranked.

percent of the total value of production.[11] Large processing activities developed at canal waterpower sites and at the major junctions of other new transportation facilities. Correspondingly, urban populations also exhibited a positive relationship to the total value of output of processing industries. However, although the concentration of processing at specific nodal points stimulated urban growth, significant variations in this relationship obtained at those few places in which populations were larger than indicated by the value of processing manufactures (Fig. 3). In these instances, the greater nodal-

11. "United States Census of Manufactures, 1850," manuscript schedules for Ohio and Indiana (Ohio State Library, Columbus; and Indiana State Library, Indianapolis).

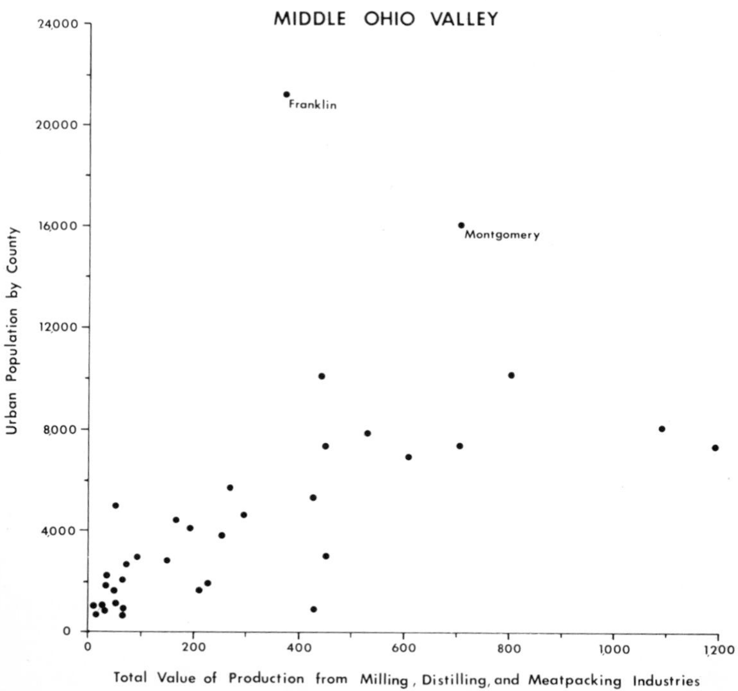

FIG. 3
Urban population and the total value of production from processing industries, by county, in the middle Ohio Valley, 1850. Sources: "United States Census of Manufactures, 1850," manuscript schedules for Ohio and Indiana (Ohio State Library, Columbus; and Indiana State Library, Indianapolis); and Muller, see text footnote 5.

ity with respect to regional markets seems to have supported the development of relatively large and diverse nonprocessing manufactures. In short, not only the amount but also the kind of manufacturing can be related to the pattern of selective growth.

By 1850 Dayton and Columbus had clearly become the two points of greatest nodality within the region. Both cities enjoyed access to extensive regional subareas through elaborate turnpike networks that focused on them as canal ports. Moreover, with the connection of both the Miami and Ohio canals to Lake Erie, these two cities increasingly handled northward interregional movements of wheat and flour from the central parts of the region. Except for the two Ohio River entrepôts of Cincinnati and Madison, Dayton and Columbus had by far the largest total values of manufacturing production in 1850; and with the exception of Cincinnati, they also had the most diverse array of manufactures. Although there were large grain mills in the immediate environs, agricultural processing industries contributed only a small portion of the total value of industrial production and of the work force in these cities (Table 4). Instead, they each produced large total values of fabricated goods such as hardwares, building supplies, wagons, railroad cars, finished leather and wood products, clothing, farm implements, machinery, and other foundry items.[12] With net changes of 8,012 and 15,447, respectively, Dayton and Columbus recorded the greatest population increments during the twenty-year period, nearly double that of any other interior town.

Madison and Chillicothe experienced the next largest increases in population, but their bases of growth were quite different from those of Dayton and Columbus. As with a few other smaller Ohio River and interior canal ports, these two cities were primarily commercial outlets

12. "United States Census of Manufactures, 1850," manuscript schedules for Franklin and Montgomery counties, Ohio (Ohio State Library, Columbus).

TABLE 4. Composition of Manufacturing in Cities and Towns of the Middle Ohio Valley, 1850

	Percentage of Total Value of Production			
City or Town	*Primary processing industries*	*Nonprocessing industries*	*Miscellaneous industries*	*Total value of production*
Dayton	21	77	2	$1,239,632
Columbus	10	76	14	1,022,151
Portsmouth	11	86	3	434,135
Springfield	37	59	4	320,975
Hamilton	31	67	2	293,866
Madison	64	34	2	1,675,052
Chillicothe	68	28	4	493,089
Lawrenceburg	85	15	0	648,685
Aurora	92	8	0	669,359
Rising Sun	70	30	0	161,550
Urbana	7	89	4	104,703
Eaton	34	66	0	96,820
Oxford	47	53	0	40,394
Middletown	53	37	10	72,827
New Carlisle	49	51	0	64,462

Source: "Seventh Census of the United States, Manufacturing," manuscript schedules for Ohio and Indiana (Ohio State Library, Columbus; and Indiana State Library, Indianapolis).

and processing points for vigorous agricultural areas. Processing industries dominated their total values of production, providing from 64 to 92 percent of the total values. Not one of these cities commanded a nodal position that offered substantial access to regional markets outside its agricultural hinterland. Compared with Dayton and Columbus, fewer and smaller nonprocessing manufactures developed. . . .

The two remaining most rapidly growing towns, Springfield and Hamilton, were most similar to Dayton and Columbus in the nonprocessing composition of their manufacturing, although they had considerably smaller total values of production. The growth of Springfield and Hamilton exemplifies the relationship between nodality within the region and the diversity of industrial activity. . . . Although the total value of Springfield's output was only a quarter of Dayton's total, diverse fabricating activities comprised almost 60 percent of the city's production. The net addition of a little more than 3,000 inhabitants during the 1840s represented a growth of almost 150 percent for Springfield.

The early commercial nodality of Hamilton, which was much closer to Cincinnati than was either Dayton or Springfield, was eroded with the improvement of transportation facilities leading to the "Queen City." Although Hamilton remained the Miami Canal terminal for turnpikes of the central Whitewater River Valley, as a depot on the canal and a recently completed railroad it had access throughout the densely settled Miami River Valley and to the emerging urban-industrial market at Cincinnati. The town developed clothing, wood, and iron manufactures that comprised 46 percent of its total value of production. Another 21 percent of its output came from paper mills, which probably depended on the large Cincinnati printing and publishing industry for their market.

The remaining trade centers within the region, represented in Table 4 by Urbana, Eaton, Oxford, Middletown, and New Carlisle, had considerably smaller productions of manufactures. These towns catered almost exclusively to their local rural markets. . . .

In summary, selective growth among the region's towns reflected reinforcement and shifts of nodality in the evolving transportation network. Maintenance of nodality was imperative for continued service to rural hinterlands during this second period of sustained settlement expansion and agricultural specialization. Moreover, the superior facilities of the canals (and later railroads) not only enhanced the commercial position of a few towns but also added to their growth with the attraction of large processing industries. Finally, through greater employment opportunities the expanding secondary manufactures of the few subregional nodal centers encouraged rapid city growth, particularly at Columbus and Dayton.

The Primacy of Nonprocessing Industries in the Transitional Periphery, 1850-1860

. . . Railroads quickly replaced the canals as the primary means of commerce. The tonnage and earnings of the canal system declined so sharply that both Indiana and Ohio state officials publicly admitted the vulnerability of the canals.[13] Although the southern river outlet remained surprisingly vigorous in the 1850s,

13. "Auditor of the State, Annual Report," *Ohio Executive Documents,* 1850, Part 2, p. 28; and "Trustees of the Wabash and Erie Canal, Annual Report," *Indiana Doc. Journal,* 1856, Part 2, p. 129.

the integration of the regional railroads with the eastern trunk systems increasingly attracted trade that had formerly moved to eastern markets by way of New Orleans. This shift in the mode and direction of movement enhanced the commercial position of railroad junctions in the interior of the region, while most Ohio River and canal ports in the southern portion drew on severely diminished, localized agricultural hinterlands (Fig. 4).

The dramatic alteration of movement in the middle Ohio Valley did not immediately produce major changes in economic activity, but signs of diversification in agriculture and manufacturing were evident by 1860. The traditional cash grain crops expanded as the few remaining underdeveloped areas moved into commercial production. At the same time high-value, locally oriented farm specialties such as dairying began to displace grain crops in some counties.[14] With expanded grain production, agricultural processing industries similarly increased throughout the region and still dominated the total value of manufacturing production in 1860. . . . In terms of employment, however, the nonprocessing industries generated the greatest growth, a

14. "Eighth Census of the United States, 1860: Agriculture" (U.S. Bureau of the Census, Washington, D.C., 1864), pp. 38-45 and 112-19.

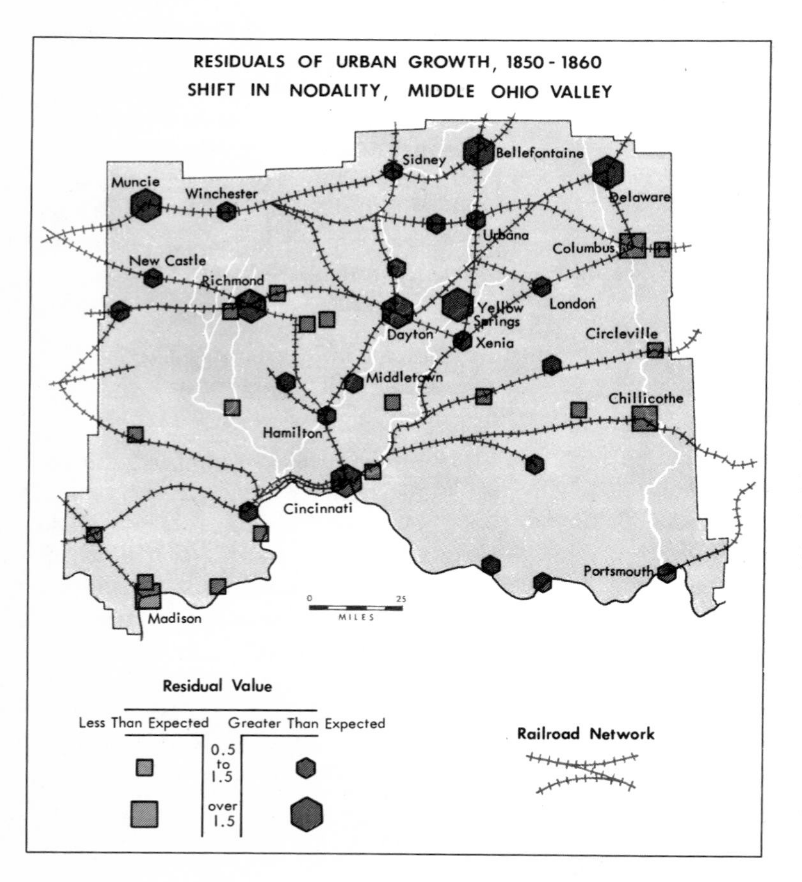

FIG. 4
Residuals of urban growth and shift of nodality in the middle Ohio Valley, 1850-1860. The railroad network was reconstructed from data in the annual reports of the railroad companies. These reports are scattered among several libraries, but the best collection for this region is held by the Cincinnati Historical Society. See also Muller, text footnote 5.

relevant consideration for urban growth.[15]

At first glance, the typical railroad explanation of selective urban growth seems to have validity. As a group, the towns that failed to obtain rail service performed poorly; and, furthermore, railroad junction towns outgrew mere way stations along the rail lines. However, variations in population growth within the groups of railroad towns indicate that the differential acquisition of rail service alone does not account for the pattern of growth.

The conversion of rail movement tended to shift the performance of some functions within the urban hierarchy, generally to the disadvantage of district trade centers. Before the railroad, district trade centers had functioned as intermediate collection, distribution, and processing points between local areas and canal ports or interregional shipping points. The creation of closely spaced rail depots (at lower-order places) decentralized the collection of farm products by bringing improved access directly to the small towns within the traditional hinterlands of the trade centers.[16] Concurrently, the reduction of overland transfer costs continued the earlier trend of concentrating many commercial and manufacturing activities at major nodal towns. For example, grains or livestock, loaded at local depots, frequently bypassed processors in the district trade centers and went instead to those at the new interregional junctions.[17] The moderately disproportionate growth of agricultural processing in the counties of major nodal cities indicated such a shift. Moreover, competition in consumer goods from eastern and regional manufacturers strongly challenged the traditional artisan basis of the trade centers.

The upward shift of these manufacturing functions in the urban hierarchy, combined with the diminution of the commercial role, left many trade centers in precarious positions. . . . Reflecting the locational shift of functions, the new railroad junctions in the northern counties and the few interior subregional nodal towns were the beneficiaries of the concentration of activity. The reorientation of trade to eastern railroad routes challenged the traditional importance of the Ohio River ports for interregional movement, even though several of them also obtained rail service. The most severe reversal occurred at Madison, where four east–west railroads sliced through its hinterland and diverted trade eastward. . . . The regional railroad junctions with the east–west trunk lines in the northern counties became the new focuses of interregional movement. Although many agricultural commodities merely passed through, these junction towns (including Union City, Yellow Springs, Xenia, and Urbana) experienced a relatively rapid growth from the new transport, trade, and processing activities. The contrast of their positive residuals in the regression analysis of population growth with the negative residuals of the river and canal ports in the southern portions of the region illustrates the locational shift of commercial nodality (Fig. 4).

The greatest population increases occurred in those cities that maintained

15. "Eighth Census of the United States, 1860: Manufactures" (U.S. Bureau of the Census, Washington, D.C., 1865), pp. 117-41 and 441-80. The manuscript, schedules of the 1860 Census of Manufactures for Ohio counties beginning with letters A through M have been lost. Thus it is impossible to compare systematically the manufacturing activities of many regional cities for 1850 and 1860.

16. "Ohio State Board of Agriculture, Annual Reports," *Ohio Executive Documents,* 1849-60.

17. See, for example, "Ohio State Board of Agriculture, Fourth Annual Report," *Ohio Executive Documents,* 1849-50, Part 2, p. 67.

or enhanced their superior accessibility within the region or within the emerging Miami Valley urban-industrial market, for by far the largest and most diverse array of nonprocessing manufactures developed at these centers. The importance of these industries for urban growth had been evident by 1850, but they became decisive when the region was linked with the national rail network. Although eastern manufacturers also obtained better access to the region, improved connections with regional and western markets and greater ease of assembling raw materials at specific centers of the regional circulation network gave those manufacturers augmented thresholds for potential sales and advantages in the transportation of bulky products. The relationship of nodality, nonprocessing industries, and urban growth is particularly clear in the differential experiences during the 1850s of those cities which had been the region's fastest growing ones in the preceding period (Fig. 5 and Table 5). . . .

. . . Although the rail network undoubtedly decentralized some former commercial functions to other railroad junctions, Dayton obtained accessibility to nearly all parts of the region as well as to other western markets. The city's county led the region in the growth of both processing and nonprocessing industries.[18] Assuming that the nonprocessing

18. Eighth Census of the United States, 1860, *Manufactures,* pp. 450-51, 467-68, and 140-41.

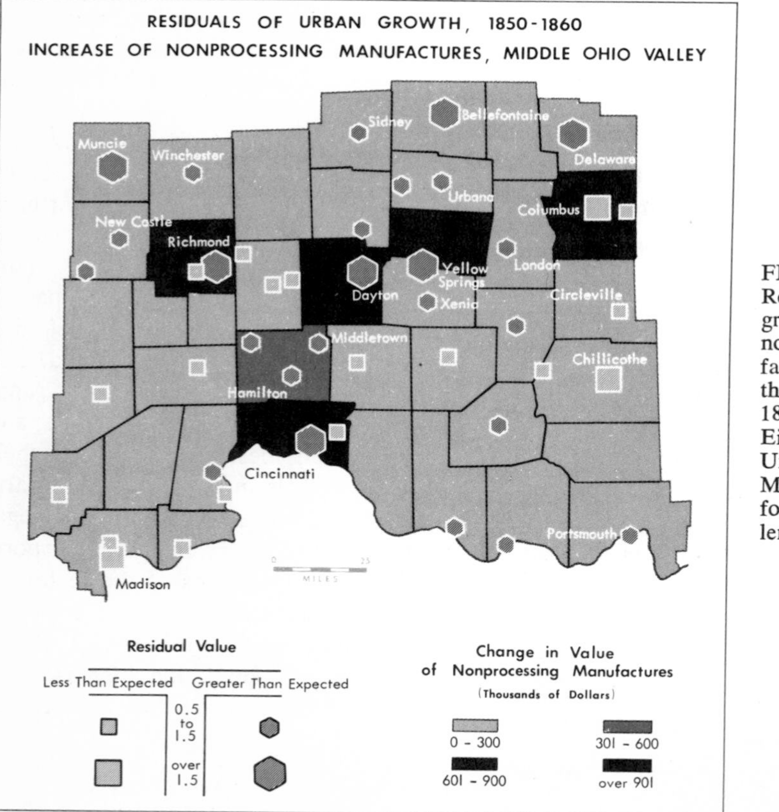

FIG. 5
Residuals of urban growth and increase of nonprocessing manufactures, by county, in the middle Ohio Valley, 1850-1860. Sources: Eighth Census of the United States, 1860: Manufactures (see text footnote 15); and Muller, see text footnote 5.

TABLE 5. Urban Growth in the Middle Ohio Valley, 1850-1860

City or Town	*Rank of Population Increase,* 1850-1860	*Rank of Increase in Total Value of Manufacturing in the County*	*Rank of Increase in Value of Nonprocessing Manufactures in the County*	*Value of Increase in Nonprocessing Manufactures in the County* (in thousands of dollars)	*Percentage of Total Value of County Manufactures from Processing Manufactures*	*Growth Relationship*
Dayton	9,104	1	1	1,039	47	Subregional nodality, urban-industrial market
Richmond	4,035	2	3	778	58	Subregional nodality
Hamilton[a]	2,566	6	5	563	51	Urban-industrial market
Portsmouth	2,257	5	10	191	47	Specialized manufacture, raw material
Springfield	1,894	4	4	609	50	Subregional nodality, urban-industrial market
Delaware	1,815	..	12	147	40	Railroad junction
Xenia[b]	1,634	12	..	19	79	Railroad junction
Urbana	1,409	..	..	5	79	Railroad junction
Bellefontaine	1,377	..	8	202	55	Railroad junction
Piqua	1,339	7	6	258	68	Urban-industrial market, railroad junction
Yellow Springs[b]	1,181	12	..	19	79	Railroad junction
Muncie	1,116	..	..	80	78	Railroad junction
Union City[c]	1,038	..	..	..	..	Railroad junction
Aurora	1,036	13	..	53	87	Agricultural processing specialization
Middletown[a]	983	6	5	563	51	Urban-industrial market
Circleville	972	15	..	60	68	Agricultural processing specialization
Columbus	958	3	2	847	29	Subregional nodality
Lawrenceburg	948	10	7	218	79	Agricultural processing specialization
Chillicothe	526	14	11	168	72	Agricultural processing specialization
Madison	118	9	9	201	65	Agricultural processing specialization

Sources: "United States Census of Manufacturing, 1850"; and Eighth Census of the United States: Manufactures [see text footnote 15].

[a] Hamilton and Middletown are both in Butler County.

[b] Xenia and Yellow Springs are both in Greene County.

[c] Union City lies in both Darke and Randolph counties.

activities were overwhelmingly concentrated in the city, as they had been in 1850, Dayton's population growth increasingly reflected the expansion of employment in its transport-oriented and consumer-goods industries.

The relatively rapid population growth of Hamilton, Portsmouth, and Springfield, third, fourth, and fifth in net population change after Dayton and Richmond, further reflected the importance of nonprocessing industries, as they prospered in marked contrast to the agricultural processing centers that had been their equals in size at the beginning of the decade. Nonprocessing industries contributed 47 percent or more of the total value of manufacturing in the counties of each of these cities in 1860 (Table 5). . . .

During the previous period of regional development, Madison, Chillicothe, Circleville, and Lawrenceburg had been among the leading cities in population growth, with specialized agricultural processing industries. As river and canal ports with reduced accessibility to localized areas, these cities not only suffered diminished commercial roles but also experienced relatively slower rates of industrial growth than those of the main interior nodal centers. Significantly, they continued their specialization in agricultural processing.[19] With the loss of nodality and failure to diversify manufacturing, these four cities experienced relatively little population growth during the 1850s.

Nodality and Selective Urban Growth

Selective urban growth in the middle Ohio Valley before 1860 corresponded rather well with the anticipated pattern. During the first two periods of initial settlement and agricultural specialization, nodality on the evolving transportation network and the associated access to local hinterlands primarily influenced urban growth. As a result, newer centers in recently settled areas and towns with the greatest subregional nodality tended to grow most rapidly. The construction of new modes of movement in the region concentrated some commercial and agricultural processing functions to the advantage of towns along these facilities. In a few instances, the new lines of circulation caused dramatic shifts in nodality and growth, although generally they reinforced the extant pattern of movement. As late as 1840, the populations of larger towns still related closely to the value of agricultural processing production, reflecting the primacy of the hinterland service functions. However, with the continued improvement of regional transportation during the 1840s, the few towns with the greatest access to regional markets began to develop diverse nonprocessing industries and experienced some of the largest population increments.

With the integration of the middle Ohio Valley into the emerging national transportation network after 1850, manufacturing assumed the decisive role in urban growth. Hierarchical and locational shifts in commercial and manufacturing functions that resulted from the construction of railroads undermined the position of district trade centers in general and benefited northern junctions on the regional rail network. Formerly important subregional and district centers that lost their nodal positions on the new rail net experienced atrophied commercial relations, failed to diversify their manufactures, and suffered through a disap-

19. "United States Census of Manufactures, 1860," manuscript schedules for Ohio and Indiana (Ohio State Library, Columbus; and Indiana State Library, Indianapolis).

pointing decade, never regaining their momentum during the remainder of the nineteenth century. In contrast, the few cities that maintained or acquired subregional nodality on the railroad network, as well as those of the industrializing Miami River Valley, grew rapidly with the concentration of commerce and nonprocessing industries. Moreover, these cities maintained their rankings among all regional centers throughout the century. Indicating the diminishing role of local hinterlands, the type more than just the amount of manufacturing clearly exercised the determining influence on urban growth. . . .

"Camden's Turrets Pierce the Skies!": The Urban Process in the Southern Colonies During the Eighteenth Century / *Joseph A. Ernst and H. Roy Merrens*

Students of early America have long held that urbanization in the southern colonies was of little consequence. The large and renowned towns have been accorded some attention, of course.[1] And in addition a few historians have recognized the emergence of a number of smaller centers in the Chesapeake Bay region by the middle eighteenth century.[2] Nonetheless the fact remains that scholars have largely ignored the urban process in the colonial South and emphasized only the rural qualities of the region.

The reasons ordinarily given for the presumed lack of significant urban development in the South are by now traditional and are familiar to all students of the period, although they tend to vary somewhat from region to region. Thus in the case of the Chesapeake Bay area, an

1. See, e.g., Oscar H. Darter, *Colonial Fredericksburg and Neighborhood in Perspective* (New York, 1957); Clarence P. Gould, "The Economic Causes of the Rise of Baltimore," *Essays in Colonial History Presented to Charles McLean Andrews . . .* (New Haven, Conn., 1931), pp. 225-51; Leila Sellers, *Charleston Business on the Eve of the American Revolution* (Chapel Hill, N.C., 1934); Thomas J. Wertenbaker, *Norfolk: Historic Southern Port* (Durham, N.C., 1931), and *The Golden Age of Colonial Culture* (New York, 1942). The Virginia capital of Williamsburg has also received some attention from historians; see especially James H. Soltow, *The Economic Role of Williamsburg* (Williamsburg, Va., 1965), and Carl Bridenbaugh, *Seat of Empire: The Political Role of Eighteenth-Century Williamsburg* (Williamsburg, Va., 1950). Bridenbaugh also has material on the larger urban centers of the South scattered throughout *Cities in the Wilderness: The First Century of Urban Life in America, 1625-1742* (New York, 1938), and *Cities in Revolt: Urban Life in America, 1743-1776* (New York, 1955).

2. See especially Carl Bridenbaugh, *Myths and Realities: Societies of the Colonial South* (New York, 1963), pp. 147-52; Robert W. Coakley, "Virginia Commerce during the American Revolution" (Ph.D. diss., University of Virginia, 1949), pp. 26-34; Calvin B. Coulter, "The Virginia Merchant" (Ph.D. diss., Princeton University, 1944), chap. 2; Arthur Pierce Middleton, *Tobacco Coast: A Maritime History of Chesapeake Bay in the Colonial Era* (Newport News, Va., 1953), pp. 40-42; and Ronald Hoffman, "Economics, Politics, and Revolution in Maryland" (Ph.D. diss., University of Wisconsin, 1969), chap 1. In a recent study of part of colonial Virginia, a geographer touches upon this kind of urbanization: Robert D. Mitchell, "The Shenandoah Valley Frontier," Association of American Geographers, *Annals* 62 (1972): 481-82.

A useful bibliographical guide to some of the studies of individual smaller towns is to be found in John W. Reps, *Tidewater Towns: City Planning in Colonial Virginia and Maryland* (Williamsburg, Va., 1972). Reps's work is also a source of information about the form of these smaller urban centers.

Reproduced (with omissions) by permission from *The William and Mary Quarterly,* ser. 3, vol. 30 (1973):549-74.

extensive riverine system is said to have offered ocean-going trading vessels easy access to the interior parts of the tobacco colonies. Consequently there was no cause to break bulk or to unload cargoes at port cities along the coast. In addition to this alleged topographical constraint upon urban growth, historians have noted several economic limitations. In the first place, they have generally held that the predominance in the Chesapeake area of a slave plantation system, whose staple export—tobacco—commanded a market in Britain, encouraged British ships to sail up-river. Such vessels could then disgorge their wares at a planter's dock in a direct barter exchange for local commodities.[3] Secondly, historians have blamed this system of direct trade between the tobacco colonies and the mother country for restricting the emergence of an extensive pattern of intercolonial and interregional exchange with an associated supporting network of urban places, both large and small; this was a pattern that seemed typical of the Middle and New England colonies. There is as well the suggestion that the creation of an extensive warehouse inspection system for tobacco lessened the need for those interior towns that served so effectively as collection and distribution centers for local commodities in the North.[4]

In the case of South Carolina and Georgia, where rice and indigo were the chief staples, and of the Cape Fear region of North Carolina, where naval stores predominated, historians have advanced a somewhat different set of explanations. Here Charleston is seen to have played a role which more nearly resembled that of Philadelphia, New York, and Boston. But Charleston is usually presented as an island of urbanization in a rural sea.[5] Once more scholars have detected a lack of the kind of interior service towns that characterized the North. And the reasons given are the familiar ones: the vast river system of the Carolinas and Georgia permitted small coastal and river boats to carry goods cheaply and efficiently to and from the interior parts to Charleston, while the economic pull of the Charleston market drew waggoners into the city from backcountry areas as far away as three hundred miles.[6]

Finally and more generally, in the case of all the staple colonies students of the period have asserted that the cheapness of land—or a more favorable man-to-land ratio—only reinforced a natural tendency toward the creation of a rural as distinct from an urban economy. Only when the South became more thickly settled, they

3. See, e.g., Middleton, *Tobacco Coast,* pp. 31-34, 353; Coakley, "Virginia Revolutionary Commerce," pp. 23-25; Lawrence H. Gipson, *The British Isles and the American Colonies: The Southern Plantations, 1748-1754* (New York, 1960), pp. 13-14; and the interpretation of an eminent historian of Virginia in Hugh Jones, *The Present State of Virginia from whence is inferred a Short View of Maryland and North Carolina,* ed. Richard L. Morton (Chapel Hill, N.C., 1956), p. 193.

4. See, e.g., Bridenbaugh, *Myths and Realities,* p. 5, and Middleton, *Tobacco Coast,* pp. 120-24, 353-54. A recent monograph by a geographer has paid incisive attention to urbanization in one of the Middle colonies: James T. Lemon, *The Best Poor Man's Country: A Geographical Study of Early Southeastern Pennsylvania* (Baltimore, 1972), esp. pp. 118-49.

5. See Sellers, *Charleston Business,* chaps. 1, 2. While Sellers's general view of the role of Charleston in the South Carolina economy was that of a "sort of city-state, drawing unto itself all the wealth of the surrounding country," she was nonetheless aware of the subordinate economic role of the port cities of Beaufort and Georgetown, and of the existence of a few "straggling" backcountry villages such as Camden. Ibid., pp. 4-7, 13, 25, 31, 34, 62, 88-91, 133-56, 181. In George C. Rogers, Jr., *Charleston in the Age of the Pinckneys* (Norman, Okla., 1969), p. 12, there is an intriguing line about "Charleston's satellite communities."

6. Sellers, *Charleston Business,* chap. 2.

have argued, and land became more expensive, would people need to follow trade and manufactures and to come together in towns and cities.[7] Similarly, the existence of a widespread system of plantation agriculture and, in the tobacco colonies at least, soil exhaustion is also said to have discouraged urbanization because of the accompanying practice of land engrossment. Lastly, some scholars have implied that a general commitment among the Southern colonists to Arcadian and rural values actually deterred local governments from doing anything in an effort to offset these various and substantial "natural" constraints upon urban growth.[8] On the face of it, it is difficult not to accept the truth in the assertion that in the colonial South urbanization was indeed of little importance. Certainly, European travelers frequently remarked on the sparseness and insignificance of cities, towns, and villages in the South. It was only to be expected, then, that historians, particularly those who have depended largely on travelers' accounts for their understanding of the urban process, should also adopt this view of the matter.

But despite its widespread acceptance and plausibility, the traditional theory is seriously flawed. The realities of the situation, especially by the eighteenth century, were far more intricate than the references to the lack of urbanization, and the reasons advanced for it, would allow. To begin with, there is the simple fact that the observer is always a part of the observation. In their comments about urbanization visitors to America were reflecting the wisdom of the day and their own crude and unsophisticated idea of what constituted urban life in Europe at the time. Consequently, eighteenth-century travelers typically conceived of villages, towns, and cities as substantial-looking places where a relatively large number of people and houses were clustered together in a relatively small area, and where certain significant functions were normally carried out.

Within this hierarchical ordering of villages, towns, and cities, villages, of course, appeared less substantial than towns and had fewer people and houses, while towns seemed inferior in the same way to cities. This view of an urban hierarchy was by the eighteenth century already an ancient one, and the categories that expressed it were built into the very structure of the English language. To the visitor to the colonies the size of population offered the most important criterion of urban significance. As a matter of course, these travelers from the Old World registered in their accounts of the places they visited in the South the numbers of people and houses to be found there—always providing the places were not too small. In his comments on Virginia at mid-century, for instance, Andrew Burnaby noted that "by Act of Assembly there ought to be 44 towns; but one half of these have not more than 5 houses; and the other half are little better than inconsiderable villages."[9] . . .

7. See, e.g., Bridenbaugh, *Myths and Realities*, pp. 3, 5.

8. See, e.g., Avery Odell Craven, *Soil Exhaustion as a Factor in the Agricultural History of Virginia and Maryland, 1606-1860,* University of Illinois Studies in the Social Sciences, XIII (Urbana, Ill., 1925), chap. 2, esp. pp. 58-60, and Bridenbaugh, *Myths and Realities,* p. 5.

9. Andrew Burnaby, *Travels Through the Middle Settlements in North-America, in the Years 1759 and 1760; With Observations Upon the State of the Colonies . . . ,* 2nd ed. (Ithaca, N.Y., 1960 [orig. publ. London, 1775]), p. 45.

The general remarks in this and the preceding two paragraphs concerning the views of European travelers about the urban process in the southern colonies are based upon extensive reading of eighteenth-century travelers' accounts. In addition to Burnaby, see especially Abel Doysié, ed., "Journal of a French Traveller in the Colonies, 1765," *American Historical Review* 26

Another contemporary criterion of urban significance was function. But it must be stressed that only rarely did visitors to America reveal any degree of sophistication in their remarks about function and that they always subordinated function to size. Consequently, smaller urban places, however vital their economic role to their rural surroundings or to a regional economy, were often simply mentioned by name but otherwise ignored. Larger towns, by contrast, might be expected to have been classified according to traditional urban functions, namely, the retailing of imported manufactured goods, the gathering, warehousing, grading, and distributing of commodities from local agricultural areas, and the administering of justice and of government generally. Moreover, larger urban places might have been regarded as centers of craft industries, as limited markets for neighboring produce, and as service centers. In the main, however, eighteenth-century travelers chose to associate urbanization with the advancement of trade and commerce, and only to a lesser extent with the conduct of government.[10] To the travelers, then, of the two criteria of urban importance, size and function, the former remained the primary concern. . . .

Given their experience and their interests, these observations of contemporary travelers on urbanization in the colonies were valid enough—as far as they went. Still one can argue that they did not go far enough, at least with respect to major developments taking place in the South during the mid-eighteenth century. In the first place, size is not the only or even the best guide to urban significance at any time in the past. Under certain circumstances a small settlement may be called upon to perform major economic functions. Secondly, in their remarks about towns and cities, European travelers ordinarily assumed that there was a natural congruence between size and urban forms, on the one hand, and urban functions, on the other. Or, to put it somewhat differently, they believed a direct relationship existed between size and place and the functions ordinarily performed in that place.

In the colonial South, the striking fact is that the usual urban functions of exchange, collection, storage, and distribution of commodities and manufactures were commonly performed in the smallest urban centers. Even more interesting, urban form and urban function often diverged. Traditional urban functions were sometimes performed outside, not inside, the traditional forms. To cite but a single example of these two points, in remote areas of Virginia, Maryland, and North Carolina dispersed, small Scottish "stores" appear to have operated in much the same fashion as did the "crossroad" service towns which were so familiar a part of the nineteenth-century American scene. Nor were these solitary stores always permanent: they opened and closed as market conditions required. In terms of size and form, therefore, the Scots' stores

(1920-21):726-47, 27 (1921-22):70-89; Nicholas Cresswell, *The Journal of Nicholas Cresswell, 1774-1777* (New York, 1924); "Journal of an Officer's [Lord Adam Gordon's] Travels in America and the West Indies, 1764-1765," in Newton D. Mereness, ed., *Travels in the American Colonies* (New York, 1916), pp. 367-453. Three accounts at the end of the period are J. F. D. Smyth, *A Tour in the United States of America* (London, 1784); Johann David Schoepf, *Travels in the Confederacy [1783-1784]* (New York, 1911); and Marquis de Chastellux, *Travels in North-America, in the Years 1780, 1781, and 1782* (Chapel Hill, N.C., 1963 [orig. publ. London, 1787]). In addition see the account of the traveler-resident William Eddis, *Letters from America,* ed. Aubrey C. Land (Cambridge, Mass., 1969).

10. Burnaby's comments in *Travels,* pp. 63, 64, 65, 66, 74-75, 80-82, and Cresswell's in *Cresswell Journal,* pp. 16, 17, 19, 20, 27, 56, provide typical examples of this point of view.

were insignificant and often fly-by-night. Their function nonetheless remained central to the life of the local economy.[11]

The traditional view of the urban process in the staple colonies fails to make it explicit that urbanization can be discussed only in relation to the structure and function of the several regional economies that defined the area. Urbanization in the South cannot be isolated from the context that explains it. European travelers missed this point altogether, and recent scholars seem to be only vaguely aware of it.[12] But we would insist that the southern urban experience cannot adequately be measured against models derived from eighteenth-century English and European developments. Rather, that experience has to be seen in relation to those underlying structures that characterized the regional economies of the staple colonies. . . .

A case study of Camden, South Carolina, is now offered as a prototype of the kind of detailed examination that appears to be in order. This case study will be followed by an interpretation of the urban process in North Carolina, Virginia, and Maryland. The use of a few special studies of these colonies by scholars who relied upon merchants' letterbooks rather than travel accounts and who focused upon trade and commerce will enable us by a process of extrapolation to go on from the case study to elaborate a view of the urban process in the southern colonies in general.

Colonial Camden was located some 125 miles northwest of Charleston. It was not actually on a river, although it lay close to and a little above the confluence of Pine Tree Creek and the Wateree River, about a mile from the latter. The town grew up on one of the main trading paths to the Catawba Indians and seems always to have been oriented toward land transportation rather than river movement.[13] It is worth emphasizing that a road rather than a river thus provided the earliest transportation access of significance.[14]

---

11. See especially Coulter, "Virginia Merchant," chap. 2. Although he does not address himself to the urban functions of the Scottish "stores" as Coulter clearly does, J. H. Soltow in his article, "Scottish Traders in Virginia, 1750-1775," *Economic History Review,* 2d Ser., 12 (1959): 83-98, nonetheless provides much useful information about the role of these "stores."

12. Important exceptions to this generalization are Coakley, "Virginia Revolutionary Commerce," chap. 1, and Coulter, "Virginia Merchant," chap. 2.

13. These and other roads and rivers are shown on the 1780 Stuart-Faden version of the 1757 *A Map of South Carolina and a Part of Georgia . . .* by William G. De Brahm. For instances of the subsequent importance of road transportation, even between Charleston and Camden, see Richard J. Hooker, ed., *The Carolina Backcountry on the Eve of the Revolution: The Journal and Other Writings of Charles Woodmason, Anglican Itinerant* (Chapel Hill, N.C., 1953), p. 16, and the letter from John Wyly to [Joseph Kershaw], Jan. 28, 1772, as well as the letter from William Bull to Mr. Kershaw, Mar. 1, 1766. The name Camden will be used throughout this article although the settlement was not so named until the late 1760s. Before then the settlement was known as Pine Tree Hill, or the Waterees, or even Fredericksburg.

14. There are two more or less detailed published accounts of early settlement in the vicinity of Camden, and the author of one of them makes much of the proximity of the so-called "fall-line" to Camden: Robert L. Meriwether, *The Expansion of South Carolina, 1729-1765* (Kingsport, Tenn., 1940), p. 99. There are other references in Meriwether's account to both the falls and the fall-line, but nowhere does the author actually demonstrate a functional relationship between either the falls or the fall-line and the settlement at Camden. One of the present authors has commented upon this pseudoissue elsewhere, both in general terms and with specific reference to conditions in another colony (North Carolina): see e.g., H. Roy Merrens, "Historical Geography and Early American History," *William and Mary Quarterly,* 3d Ser., 22 (1965):533-38, and *Colonial North Carolina in the Eighteenth Century: A Study in Historical Geography* (Chapel Hill, N.C., 1964), pp. 40-

The importance of overland transportation reflects the widespread priority of road transportation outside the Lowcountry.

During the first half of the eighteenth century, settlement in and around what later became Camden was entirely agricultural in nature, and nothing seems to have modified the complete "rural-ness" of settlement in the area prior to 1750. It remained an ordinary and unremarkable region of scattered farms, farms which doubtless gradually increased in number and became more and more imposing, durable, and expansive testimonies of man's secure occupance. But even at the end of the colonial period, despite the general northward and westward advance of settlement during the eighteenth century, Camden was still much closer to the fringes of the settled area than to the Lowcountry. . . .

A simple, crude, although fairly effective method of appraising the functional elaboration of the settlement is to identify the emergence of key structures in and around the early site, focusing upon their function rather than their form. The structures that matter in this context are not those that are exclusively residences but are rather buildings devoted to special purposes. Key structures would be buildings used for functions that symbolize the role played by the settlement in serving an area much more extensive than the town itself. Examples of such buildings would be an inn, a sawmill, a gristmill, a courthouse, a jail, a store, and a church. In all such buildings, services are performed that are indicative of the role of a settlement as a regional or local service center, and the presence of these buildings implies that a settlement was more than just a simple cluster of farmers' residences. But we should also concede that an exclusive and blinkered concern with buildings as indices of function would be simplistic: the Publick Times in Williamsburg provides a striking illustration of how crucial urban functions may be more or less unrelated to buildings and may have no tangible expression in terms of structures.[15] References to such buildings in the account that follows, and the lack of references to numbers of people and to the shape of the settlement, should be understood in the context of our intention of emphasizing the functions of Camden, and of the belief that the analysis of function reveals more than does the study of either population size or settlement morphology.

Several events of the 1750s foreshadowed the emergence of Camden. A number of Irish Quakers moved into the area, beginning in 1750 or 1751, in a more or less concerted attempt to settle as a group.[16] Their efforts flourished and the

41, 171-72, 177-79, 258-59. There is no point in raising the issue again here, and we will simply emphasize that we have found not one iota of evidence that relates either the origins or the growth of colonial Camden to falls in the Wateree or in any other river.

The other detailed published account of Camden is a local history: Thomas J. Kirkland and Robert M. Kennedy, *Historic Camden,* Part I: *Colonial and Revolutionary* (Columbia, S.C., 1905). The most informative study of early Camden's changing geography is unpublished: Judith J. Schulz, "The Rise and Decline of Camden as South Carolina's Major Inland Trading Center, 1751-1829: A Historical Geographic Study" (M.A. thesis, University of South Carolina, 1972). The maps in this thesis are particularly helpful, and both the maps and the text should provide the interested reader with a useful antidote to the more or less exclusively functional approach we are following here.

15. The nature and significance of the Publick Times in Williamsburg are described in Soltow, *Economic Role of Williamsburg,* pp. 6-19, *et passim.*

16. The Quakers can be identified in the records of the South Carolina Council sessions,

viability of settlement in this locale was securely established. One of the Quakers, Robert Millhouse, built a gristmill, and another, Samuel Wyly, seems to have set up a store.[17] A non-Quaker, Moses Kirkland, was also apparently operating both a store and a tavern in the early 1750s, tapping the custom provided by traders and travelers passing through the area as well as local needs.[18]

A petition of inhabitants to the Assembly in 1752 proclaimed great hopes for commercial growth if a few crucial transportation improvements could be made.[19] The petition, which specified the improvements needed and named Wyly, Millhouse, and a few others to serve as road commissioners, was granted in an act passed the following year.[20] The economic role that was envisaged was essentially a matter of trade: locally produced surplus, together with export items from places to the north and west, such as flour, butter, cheese, hemp, flax, and flax seed, could be collected and forwarded to the Charleston market. Such a trade would promote the development of South Carolina's interior at the same time that it would diminish the colony's traditional dependence on Pennsylvania and New York. Clearly, in looking for lucrative prospects the petitioners were viewing their settlement in the context of the commercial development of the colony as a whole, and were identifying the role they could play in larger trade patterns and linkages.

Just how far these hopes were realized in the 1750s is not entirely clear. The existence of a tavern, stores, and a mill indicates that rudimentary physical expressions of such a trade were indeed present. This is rather meager evidence, however. In the 1760s, by contrast, it is obvious that Camden had assumed essentially this kind of commercial role, and that a process of functional elaboration was by then well underway. In 1760, partly at least because of the need to satisfy the military market during the Cherokee War, imports of bread and flour had come from Philadelphia via Charleston and an overland haul through Camden to the interior.[21] But wheat growing had been rapidly expanding in the region, and Camden was becoming increasingly significant as a milling center and collection point for South Carolina wheat. By 1763 imports of wheat products were almost no longer needed.[22] Five years later a report from South Carolina carried in a Boston newspaper noted that "the produce of good wheat has been so great this year that we may soon expect, from Camden alone, 2000 barrels of flour and 1500 of ship bread."[23]

---

where they are named when they petitioned for land. For examples of such petitions by Quakers see the South Carolina Council Journals, Oct. 25, 1751, South Carolina Department of Archives and History, Columbis, S.C. A careful review of the Quaker phase of settlement appears in Kirkland and Kennedy, *Historic Camden,* pp. 73-77.

17. Milhouse's mill is mentioned in S.C. Council Jours., May 5, 1752, and Jan. 7, 1755. We have not yet been able to substantiate conclusively the early presence of Wyly's store, but it is described in Kirkland and Kennedy, *Historic Camden,* pp. 75-76, as the settlement's "chief center and nucleus, until the coming of Joseph Kershaw."

18. Nov. 15, Dec. 6, 1752, and June 5, 1753, S.C. Council Jours.

19. May 9, 1752, South Carolina Commons House Journals, South Carolina Department of Archives and History, Columbia, S.C., hereafter cited as S.C. House Jours.

20. Thomas Cooper and David J. McCord, eds., *The Statutes At Large of South Carolina* (Columbia, S.C., 1836-42), vol. 7, pp. 504-6.

21. June 20, 1760, S.C. House Jours. The accounts that were submitted on this day also seem to indicate that locally produced wheat and flour were of some significance.

22. *South Carolina Gazette* (Charleston), Sept. 10-17, 1763.

23. *Boston Chronicle,* Dec. 5-12, 1768.

Flour milling and the wheat trade are revealing facets of Camden's function because they point to its role in promoting the commercialization of the region in which the town was located, and because they express the diversification of the economy of the colony. But they were by no means the sole functions of the center. Stores and merchants handled many other items, both agricultural products for export and imported manufactured goods. The town contained a sawmill as well as a gristmill. Late in the 1760s it was named as a circuit court center, and this led eventually to the erection of a courthouse and jail. When tobacco inspection warehouses were set up in the colony early in the next decade, two of them were placed in or near Camden.[24] There seem also to have been at least two church meeting houses in Camden by the 1760s, one for the Quakers and the other much used by Reverend Charles Woodmason, an itinerant Anglican minister, when he established Camden as his base of operations during his backcountry sojourn.[25]

A major figure in Camden's commerce during this period was Joseph Kershaw. Although no one has yet pieced together a coherent picture of Kershaw's political and economic activities, assorted scraps of evidence suggest he was one of the leading members of a trading partnership that had its headquarters in Charleston, relied upon Kershaw to provide it with a crucial interior base of operations through his diverse trading ventures in Camden, and sought to enlarge its operation by promoting trade at two or three other focal points in the interior.[26] . . .

By the mid-1770s, the town contained at least one of each of the key structures that symbolize important urban functions, and more than one of some of them. The first phase of functional elaboration was over. Camden was well established as a multifunctional center. Its economic viability was assured by its flourishing regional base, and the town served as an integral component in the economic structure of the region in which it was located. As an inland urban center, its development reflected the increasing population density and commercialization of the interior: its trading role was intimately related to an increasing emphasis upon wheat growing and the development of overland transportation ties that gave backcountry farmers access to coastal markets via Camden. Even this brief scrutiny of Camden's development in functional terms has revealed, inevitably, more than just a few details about the birth of a particular town. Because all colonial urban centers were similarly part and parcel of the economies of the colonies in which they emerged, studies of their origins, development, and changing roles must reveal much of the changing economies of the colonies in which they functioned.

There is another kind of detail concerning early Camden that demands attention. At a different scale and at a

24. Cooper and McCord, eds., *S.C. Statutes,* vol. 4, pp. 327-31.

25. Hooker, *Carolina Backcountry,* p. 6.

26. The most revealing item is a memorandum of agreement made between the Kershaw brothers, Chestnut, Ancrum, and Loocock, which was to take effect on Jan. 1, 1764; this manuscript appears among the Chestnut-Miller-Manning Papers, 1744-1900, South Carolina Historical Society, Charleston, S.C. A little more information pertaining to Kershaw's activities can be gathered from a few of the early items in the Joseph Brevard Kershaw Papers, 1766-1888, in the South Caroliniana Collection of the University of South Carolina, Columbia, S.C. A detailed but fragmentary glimpse of the operations of Kershaw's stores is provided by the Account Book of Joseph Kershaw, 1774-1775, in the Draper Manuscripts of the Wisconsin State Historical Society, Madison, Wis.

higher level of generalization, Camden needs to be viewed in its entire Atlantic seaboard context, as a place with ties and linkages reaching far outside the surrounding local areas for which it functioned as a center, and beyond the bounds of the colony in which it was located. As an interior stopover town, for example, Camden was really on an axis, the southern end of which terminated in Charleston and included many points to the north, from North Carolina to Philadelphia. . . . This same axis was also used by a very different kind of traveler: it was the route followed by immigrants coming overland into this part of South Carolina from colonies to the north, and for this purpose, too, the axis extended all the way to Pennsylvania and New York.[27]

There was much more to these linkages with other colonies than the simple movements of migrants and travelers. Camden's trade ties, in a transactional and credit sense, were primarily with Charleston, and from Charleston, of course, the ties led in coastwise and overseas directions to a number of places. The partnership of the Kershaw brothers, Chestnut, Ancrum, and Loocock illustrates these ties with Charleston; and the Charleston firm of Ancrum, Lance, and Loocock did business with Philadelphia merchant John Reynell,[28] so that seemingly there were ties between Camden by means of Charleston merchants to the Philadelphia Quaker trading community. Joseph Kershaw's wife was a member of a particularly prominent family of Philadelphia Quaker merchants, and this kind of family connection was probably of consequence, even if its precise relevance cannot be proven. . . .

In taking a close look at the origin, growth, and functions of Camden, we hope to have exemplified a fruitful approach to the investigation of other urban centers in the southern colonies. It is not possible to present similarly detailed accounts of other places here, and to draw too many conclusions from this one case study would be fairly reckless. Fortunately, there are a few examinations of developments in colonial North Carolina, Virginia, and Maryland that tell us something, albeit sometimes incidentally, about urban functions. A cursory glance at these other colonies, viewed in the context of what has been presented on Camden, offers at least the opportunity to make some instructive comparisons and to draw some tentative conclusions.

In North Carolina, even at the end of the colonial period, the number of people living in urban places was small. It amounted to fewer than five thousand, less than the total population of Charleston. But the small urban places in which they lived played a key role in North Carolina's development, and their growth and function have been analyzed elsewhere by one of the present authors. One of the North Carolina urban centers, Cross Creek,[29] is of special interest because it bears a remarkable functional resemblance to Camden. Both Cross Creek and Camden operated as inland trading towns, and both developed in the third quarter of the eighteenth century. Both served as collecting and forwarding centers for wheat and flour of backcountry origin, and, a little later, as tobacco in-

27. For an example of an immigrant from New York see Feb. 6, 1748/9, S.C. Council Jours.

28. Letter from John Reynell to Ancrum, Lance, and Loocock, Nov. 29, 1763, in John Reynell Letter Books, 1729-1774, Pa. Hist. Soc., Philadelphia. Also pertinent is the reference in this letter to Elias Bland, who was a Quaker merchant in London serving as an agent for Philadelphia merchants.

29. The origins and functions of Cross Creek (later Fayetteville) are discussed in Merrens, *Colonial North Carolina,* pp. 116-17, 157-60.

spection centers, and both were closely tied to a much larger coastal port (the one to Wilmington, the other to Charleston).

Cross Creek testifies that Camden was not unique. As we learn more about colonial inland urban centers, as we cease to allow a past preoccupation with population size to mislead us into believing that these centers were inconsequential, and as we begin to identify and analyze their functions and spheres of influence, we will also begin to recognize the existence of distinct types of towns in the Southern colonies. Cross Creek and Camden were doubtless comparable to other urban places whose roles have yet to be identified and spotlighted, but all of which may have been fundamentally similar in that they began their urban existences serving as interior commercial centers associated with a particular kind of trade and growing on that base into urban places performing a variety of functions.

Another town to play a significant role in the urban process in North Carolina is New Bern. Site of the provincial capital, New Bern is best known to historians as the home of Governor William Tryon's "Palace," a symbol of western protest and an object of propaganda during the Regulator Movement. Less familiar is the fact that the location of the capital as well as the building of the governor's residence at New Bern figured prominently in a larger and far-ranging campaign for spurring economic growth in the colony.

From the beginning of his administration, Tryon had initiated with active Assembly support an ambitious program of internal improvements, including the building and repairing of roads, ferries, and bridges, and the clearing of streams and rivers. Also scheduled for improvement in this general effort to advance agriculture and commerce were harbor and port facilities. The specific object was to prevent backcountry trade from being siphoned off to Charleston where commodity markets and prices were generally better and transportation easier and cheaper. . . . The function of urban places in colonial Virginia has been almost totally ignored. But suggestive comments about urbanization that appeared some time ago in a study by Robert W. Coakley of Virginia commerce during the Revolution, and the findings of James Soltow's analysis of the role of Virginia's capital, are especially instructive.

In his as yet unpublished study of Revolutionary Virginia, Coakley argues that, however small and widely dispersed, urban centers in Virginia played an increasingly significant role in the operation of the local economy.[30] In effect Coakley makes two related observations. The first is that the rapid diversification of the tobacco economy in the decade after the middle eighteenth century, the increase of population in the more recently settled areas of the colony, the growing spread of the Scottish store system, and an expansion of trade with the West Indies produced substantial changes in the regional economic structure and, as a consequence of these, changes as well in urban patterns and developments.

Coakley's second point concerns the growing functional importance of local urban places. Most dramatic in this connection was the emergence of Norfolk on the eve of the Revolution as the "emporium" of trade with the West Indies. Less familiar, although unquestionably more important, was the growth and evolution of urban centers elsewhere in the province, a development that, as Coakley notes, did not escape contemporary ob-

30. The following account is based largely on Coakley, "Virginia Revolutionary Commerce," chap. 1.

servers: "Norfolk is by no means in such a state of increase and improvement as the more inland towns," J. F. D. Smyth commented in 1774. These "inland" towns, he continued, served as the major loci of "trade and commerce for the large, populous, and extensive back country, west and south of them. These having all the advantages of navigation, intercept the inland trade from Norfolk, which renders it, though flourishing, yet only so in an inferior degree."[31]

Smyth's remarks are not unknown to historians of colonial Virginia, and several scholars have noted the development of backcountry towns after mid-century. But Coakley recognizes the existence of a whole host of towns in the province and went on to show, however briefly, the important functions of many of these in the structure and operation of the Virginia economy at the beginning of the Revolution. On the Potomac, for instance, he finds that Alexandria, which began as a tobacco inspection site, had by the 1770s extended a complex of roadways west to the Great Valley to tap the burgeoning trade in grain.[32] By 1775 some twenty major mercantile establishments were operating out of the town, fourteen of which purchased wheat for export principally to the West Indies. This did not mean that Alexandria had simply become a northern competitor of Norfolk, operating in the same Caribbean marketplace while drawing on different sources of supply. Unlike Norfolk, Alexandria sent out vessels to the West Indies that either returned empty or did not return at all to Alexandria. In contrast to her rival to the southeast, Alexandria did not handle the distribution of West Indian commodities to other ports of the province. Down river from Alexandria were the smaller towns of Colchester and Dumfries. Controlled by Scottish storekeepers and factors, these two centers continued to concentrate on the tobacco raised in their area while also serving a gathering and warehousing function in the funnelling of local grain supplies to Alexandria.

Similar examples of functionalism are provided in Coakley's discussion of areas further south. On the Rappahannock, for example, the neighboring towns of Fredericksburg[33] and Falmouth dominated the local trade in tobacco and grains. Once again Coakley notes that the important connections of these two places with the surrounding countryside were all by road. Further down the Rappahannock were Leedstown and Hobbes Hole, small agricultural service towns whose role and importance closely resembled those of Dumfries and Colchester. Lastly, on the Appomattox Petersburg functioned as the largest tobacco trading center in North America and the hub of a regional trade area that encompassed large parts of southwestern Virginia as well as the tobacco counties of the Albemarle region in neighboring North Carolina. Intermediate between Petersburg and the mouth of the Appomattox were Broadways and City Point where larger vessels lay by to pick up cargoes shipped down from Petersburg.

The other instructive study of urbanization in Virginia is Soltow's analysis of

31. Smyth, *Tour in the United States,* vol. 1, pp. 10-11.

32. For a discussion of the connection between the development of towns in Virginia and Maryland and the rise of wheat growing, see Merrens, *Colonial North Carolina,* pp. 116-17.

33. Darter, *Colonial Fredericksburg,* is a deliberately provocative and sometimes exaggerated assertion of the cosmopolitanism of Fredericksburg, but it is also incidentally a most useful source for information on the functions of the town.

the role of Williamsburg in the Virginia economy. Soltow has ably demonstrated that Williamsburg was not simply a small, provincial Southern capital whose only significant function was an administrative one. Despite the absence of any significant movement of goods through the town, four times a year during the meeting of the General Court Williamsburg became filled with merchants and others who busily performed such vital commercial tasks as settling obligations, suing for debt, buying and selling sterling bills of exchange, and making contracts for delivery of goods and services. At such moments, Williamsburg served the same vital commercial functions as the far larger port cities of the North.[34]

In Maryland, as in Virginia, scholars have conventionally insisted that the multitude of rivers and streams that interlace the province deterred the growth of any sizable urban center, so that by the Revolution only a very few large towns had emerged. Despite this conventional wisdom, which has gone unchallenged, one scholar, Ronald Hoffman, has recognized the functional importance of the smaller urban places that did exist.[35]

Among the shore and river towns to which Hoffman has drawn attention is the entry port of Oxford in Talbot County on the eastern shore. Ships bound for this part of Maryland typically reported in at Oxford to pay their customs fees and either unloaded there or proceeded on to such other eastern-shore towns as Pocomoke and Chester Town. Of these, only Pocomoke—whose chief activity appears to have been the gathering and shipping of lumber—could boast a naval office by mid-eighteenth century. Pocomoke served as an entrepôt for a variety of local goods and commodities that were subsequently shipped to such larger places as Oxford and Annapolis for reloading on bigger vessels. Chester Town, by contrast, operated as the locus of the wheat trade from the Eastern Shore both in overseas commerce and with Philadelphia and later with Baltimore.

At the head of Chesapeake Bay, several smaller towns were by 1750 already beginning to compete as warehouse and distributing centers in the growing corn and wheat trade to Philadelphia—both from the eastern and western shores of Maryland and from the central counties of Pennsylvania. Chief among these rival towns were Elkton, Charlestown, and Havre de Grace. Their connections with their hinterlands were mostly by water, although to some extent, especially in the case of Havre de Grace on the Susquehanna, they were by road as well. By the time of the Revolution Baltimore had largely eclipsed the function of these places and had come to dominate the trade of the region.

On the western shore the major urban center (before the emergence of Baltimore at the very end of the colonial period) was Annapolis. Trade at Annapolis remained relatively small, however, because of the difficulty and expense of bringing goods to the town and the existence in neighboring waters of the dreaded *Toredo navalis*. But as the colonial capital and the site of the colony's

34. James H. Soltow, "The Role of Williamsburg in the Virginia Economy, 1750-1775," *WMQ*, 3d ser., 15 (1958):467-82.

35. The following discussion is based on Hoffman, "Economics, Politics, and Revolution in Maryland," chap. I, and "East Side, West Side, All Around the Towns, Ties and Variations in Colonial Maryland," a paper presented at the South Carolina Tricentennial Symposium at the University of South Carolina, Mar. 21, 1970; this paper was drawn largely from chap. I. Also of use is Reps, *Tidewater Towns*, chap. 10, although the author is chiefly concerned with the question of town planning and form rather than with the matter of the functional role of towns.

largest naval office, Annapolis nevertheless performed major administrative and commercial functions. All ships leaving the Upper Chesapeake Bay region, for instance, were required to register at Annapolis to pay export fees. In addition, the area around Annapolis seems to have functioned as the center of shipbuilding activities in the province.

Most of the other major urban places on the western shore of Maryland, according to Hoffman, were river towns. Thus on the Patuxent such small settlements as Queen Anne, Upper Marlboro, and Benedict operated chiefly as centers of the tobacco industry and had come under the domination of English and Scottish factors who were busily engaged in tapping the growing trade with the Piedmont. Similar developments on the Potomac and its branches gave rise to several other similar urban places such as Bladensburg, Georgetown, Piscataway, and further downstream Port Tobacco. Finally, there were the western communities like Frederickstown and Hagerstown that helped tie the local economy to the Atlantic world through the export of tobacco, wheat, lumber, and a variety of less important commodities. . . .

Whatever their function and significance, southern towns and cities did not exist alone. Rather they formed part of some urban system, a system that in turn fitted into some regional economy. But precisely what these regional economic structures were like and what roles the urban system played within these structures are questions that have rarely been asked and that require careful investigation. . . . That there was such an urban system operating in the colonial South, however much neglect it has suffered at the hands of historians, did not go unnoticed at the time. Thus, James Robinson, chief factor for William Cunninghame and Company of London, was very much aware of the operation of a major component in that system when he advised John Turner, who ran a central store for the Company at Rocky Ridge just below Richmond, that in selecting a proper place for a branch, or "Back store," farther up the James River in an area recently opened to settlement, "much regard should be paid to the Soil of Land in the Neighbourhood and the Circumstances of the People in a Circle of 12 or 14 miles as the Influence of such a Store seldom reaches farther."[36] . . .

---

36. Oct. 6, 1771, in William Cunninghame and Company Letterbooks, 1767-1773, National Library of Scotland, Edinburgh (microfilm, Colonial Williamsburg Research Library, Williamsburg, Va.). For evidence that a system of branch stores also operated in areas other than those penetrated by the Scots, see the Account Book of Joseph Kershaw, 1774-1775.

B. *The City From Within*

Persistence, Failure, and Mobility in the Inner City: Preliminary Notes / *Martyn J. Bowden*

The levels of geographic mobility in America in the nineteenth century are barely credible. Frontier county studies disclose that only a quarter of the farm operators enumerated at the beginning of a decade were there at the end.[1] A lower persistence rate for the urban population was found in Rochester for the period 1849-1859 (20 percent) and a slightly higher one in Poughkeepsie for 1850-1860.[2] Higher levels of persistence were found in Northampton, Massachusetts, for 1850-1860 and among the white population of Atlanta for 1870-1880 (53 and 43 percent, respectively).[3] But persistence, as used in these urban contexts, fails to differentiate between stable (place persistent) establishments and establishments that move within the region, e.g., town or central district (regional persistent). In all four towns decennial rates of place peristence (residential stability) must have been less than 30 percent and in some cases beow 20 percent.

1. James C. Malin, "The Turnover of Farm Population in Kansas," *Kansas Historical Quarterly* 4 (1935):339-72; Merle Curti et al., *The Making of an American Community* (Stanford: Stanford University Press, 1959), p. 68; Mildred Throne, "A Population Study of an Iowa County in 1850," *Iowa Journal of History* 57 (1959):305-30; Peter J. Coleman, "Restless Grant County: Americans on the Move," *Wisconsin Magazine of History* 46 (1962):16-20.
2. Blake McKelvey, *Rochester: The Flower City, 1855-1880* (Cambridge, Mass.: Harvard University Press, 1949), p. 3; and a computation made by Stephan Thernstrom and Peter R. Knights, "Men in Motion: Some Data and Speculations about Urban Population Mobility in Nineteenth-Century America," *Anonymous Americans,* ed. T. K. Hareven (Englewood Cliffs, N.J.: Prentice-Hall, 1971), pp. 20-21, from data in Clyde Griffen, "Workers Divided: Social Mobility in Poughkeepsie, 1850-1880," *Nineteenth-Century Cities,* ed. Stephan Thernstrom and Richard Sennett (New Haven: Yale University Press, 1969), pp. 49-97.
3. Data computed by Thernstrom and Knights, "Men in Motion," from Richard J. Hopkins, "Occupational and Geographic Mobility in Atlanta, 1870-1890," *Journal of Southern History* 34 (1968):200-213; and Robert Doherty, "Industrialization and Social Change: Northampton, Massachusetts, 1800-1860" (Paper prepared for Yale Conference on Nineteenth Century Cities, November 1968), cited in Thernstrom and Knights, "Men in Motion."

Analysis of population mobility in metropolises has just begun. But the initial city directory studies of Thernstrom and Knights in Boston indicate "the incredible fluidity of the urban . . . population."[4] They find that in a city with a population of 448,000 in 1890, 789,000 individuals moved into the city between 1880 and 1890 and 693,000 moved out. Each year between 1880 and 1890 only 40 to 53 percent of the populace remained in the same residence and each year 27 to 39 percent changed locations within the city.[5] As in the frontier counties and the smaller towns, the decennial rate of place persistence in Boston must have been far below 30 percent.

The findings of Thernstrom and Knights, and certain of their assumptions about business mortality in the nineteenth century, prompted me to go back to the San Francisco directories that occupied me between 1961 and 1967. My objectives were to establish the rates of persistence, failure, and mobility of business establishments in the central district of a fast-growing metropolis (San Francisco) and to examine the effects of the inflow of newcomers and the relocation of established activities upon the expansion and locational shifts of the districts of the Inner City and, ultimately, upon the Central District as a whole.

In San Francisco the growth (expansion and locational change) of the Central District during 1846-1936 took place in five "bursts" of activity, focused on twenty-four years: 1850, 1851-1854, 1866-1872, 1907-1911, and 1919-1925, inclusive.[6] In each of the five stages there occurred among the nuclei of the Central District a sequence of locational shifts, beginning in the financial and apparel-shopping nuclei—the *core districts*—and spreading to the garment, medical services, household furnishing, civic, theater (live and moving picture), hotel, and other nuclei—the *peripheral districts.*

During the years 1854-1865, 1872-1907, 1911-1918, and 1925-1936, limited peripheral accretion and relative stability in location for the Central District and its constituent nuclei were the rule. Thus, for the eight decades for which I was able to collect data on the persistence, failure, mobility, and entry of establishments, three decades were characterized by "bursts" of growth—1865-1875, 1905-1915, and 1915-1925—and five decades were characterized by locational stability of the Central District and its nuclei. Were the proportions of persistent and new establishments significantly different in the three decades of change compared to the five decades of stability? Which establishments initiated the locational changes of the nuclei within the Central District, the new entrants or the old establishments that relocated within the Central District? This paper presents some preliminary findings concerning the agents of locational change within the Central District.

Persistence is defined here as the survival establishments in a delimited region (Central District) for ten years or more, and the *persistence rate* is a measure made in a particular year of the number of persistent activities present in the district during the preceding decade as a percentage of all establishments in the activity group. *Place-persistent* establishments are those that are locationally stable in the region during the preceding decade, and *regional-persistent* establish-

4. Thernstrom and Knights, "Men in Motion," p. 31.
5. Ibid., pp. 27-31.
6. Martyn J. Bowden, *The Dynamics of City Growth: An Historical Geography of the San Francisco Central District, 1850-1931* (Ph.D. diss., University of California, Berkeley, 1967), pp. 266-69, 448-53, 478, 705-11.

ments are those that relocate within the region in the preceding decade.

Place-persistent establishments were few in most activity groups before 1875. Thereafter, in the periods of limited locational change of districts, until 1906, place-persistence rates were remarkably stable. This was true of activity groups experiencing marked increases in numbers as well as those that were not. The rates varied according to the mix of constituent establishments, being highest in activity groups composed exclusively of large establishments (e.g., theaters, 50-67 percent) and lowest in those composed exclusively of small establishments (e.g., medical services, 15 percent). Abrupt changes in place-persistence rates occurred in 1906-1915 as a direct result of the total destruction of the Inner City. In this decade, most activities returning to the Inner City took advantage of the opportunity to relocate. By 1915-1925, however, stable place-persistence rates were established at slightly higher levels than those current before the earthquake and fire.

Regional-persistent establishments were few before 1865, but in the next decade (one of marked locational change in the Central District) numbers and proportions of these establishments rose to a high peak. Thereafter, regional-persistence rates gradually declined to low points in 1896-1906. A high peak was recorded during the decade of marked locational change, 1906-1915, and again rates fell off rapidly for most nuclei in the next two decades.

In the relatively fluid nuclei composed of small- to medium-sized establishments, regional-persistence rates were higher than place-persistence rates, even during stable periods (Tables 1 and 2). Differences between the two rates were particularly marked in 1865-1875 and 1906-1915 (decades of major locational change in the Inner City as a whole). By contrast, it was only in these two decades that regional-persistence rates were higher than place-persistence rates in the more rigid nuclei composed of medium-sized and large establishments (Table 3), and in some of these nuclei the regional-persistent establishments were absent or rare.

Failure is taken here to be the disappearance of establishments from the city (as indicated by the city directory). It includes both business mortality and the seemingly insignificant movement of former Inner City activities to locations beyond the city's borders. The *failure rate* is the proportion of these establishments present in the Inner City at the beginning of a decade that had disappeared from the city by the end of it.

In the early decades, less than half of the establishments in most activity groups survived a decade in the Inner City. Thereafter, in the districts made up of small- and medium-sized establishments, the decennial failure rate appears to have been between 40 and 50 percent, rising on occasion to 67 percent in decades that included severe depressions (1855-96 and 1926-36). The rate was more variable in nuclei composed of large establishments and in those with establishments of various sizes. In the theater district, for example, the decennial failure rate was between 50 and 75 percent in five decades and between 25 and 33 percent in three decades, whereas in the banking nucleus failure rates varied between 12 and 38 percent after the disastrous banking decade of 1875-1885. The failure rate in the Inner City therefore, appears to have been between 40 and 50 percent, with low rates in 1875-1885 and 1915-1925 and high rates in the early and depression decades.

TABLE 1. Persistence, Mobility, Failure, and Entry in the Garment Activity Group by Decade, 1854-1936

	1854-65	1865-75	1875-85	1885-96	1896-1905	1905-15	1915-26	1926-36
A. Total Number of Establishments Beginning of Decade	17*	122	125	142	130	164	214	291
B. Total Number of Establishments End of Decade	122	125(+1)	142(+4)	130(+2)	164(+1)	214	291(+2)	216
Place Persistence (% of B)	0	2	20†	22†	25	4	13†	23
Regional Persistence (% of B)	2	36†	31§	23†	21†	35	23†	22
Persistence (Subtotal)	2	37‡	49‡	43‡	45‡	39	35‡	45
Centripetal Mobility (% of B)	0	0	0	1	1	0	0	0
Emergence (% of B)	98	63	51	56	54	61	65	55
Entry (Subtotal)	98	63	51	57	55	61	65	55
Centrifugal Mobility (% of A)	0	0	0	0	0	1	2	0
Failure (% of A)	90	61	42	59	42	50	48	67
Entry: Persistence	98:2	63:37	51:49	57:43	55:45	61:39	65:35	55:45
Mobility: Stability	100:0	98:2	80:20	78:22	75:25	96:4	87:13	77:23

* The count of establishments is incomplete for 1854.
† One establishment had changed category by the end of the decade, i.e., became an establishment in a different activity group.
‡ In the calculation of "persistence," establishments that changed category are not considered as part of the district at the end of the decade. The esablishments are considered part of the district in the calculations of place and regional persistence.
§ Three establishments changed category.

TABLE 2. Persistence, Failure, and Entry in the Medical Services Activity Groups, Percentages by Decade, 1885-1936

	1885-96	1896-1905	1905-15	1915-26	1926-36
Place Persistence	12	13	4	15	24
Regional Persistence	16	16	25	24	20
Persistence	28	29	29	40	44
Centripetal Mobility	6	4	24	8	3
Emergence	66	67	47	52	53
Entry	72	71	71	60	56
Centrifugal Mobility	12	10	15	2	5
Failure	40	51	48	38	42
Entry: Persistence	72:28	71:29	71:29	60:40	56:44
Mobility: Stability	88:12	87:13	96:4	85:15	76:24

TABLE 3. Persistence, Mobility, Failure, and Entry in the Banking Activity Group by Decade, 1854-1936

	1854-65	1865-75	1875-85	1885-96	1896-1905	1905-15	1915-26	1926-31
A. Total Number of Establishments Beginning of Decade	18	29	41	32	38	48	31	31
B. Total Number of Establishments at End of Decade	29	41	32	38	48	38†	31	19
Place Persistence	14	15	47	39	37	34	52	74
Regional Persistence	3	32	25	35	27	50	29	21
Persistence	17	47	72	74	64	84	81	95
Emergence (Entry)	83	53	28	26	36	16‡	19	5
Failure	73	35*	45	12	18	33*	19*	39*
Mobility: Stability	86:14	85:15	53:47	61:39	63:37	66:34	48:52	26:74

* Includes one or more mergers.
† Seven category changes were made at this point in time.
‡ Includes one centripetally mobile establishment.

Of the six types of mobility affecting the Inner City, one is considered above—regional persistence, and two others—shifts of Inner City establishments to locations outside the city and the reverse movement—appear to be of limited significance for central-district growth. Two additional types are *centripetal mobility* (movement of establishments located in the Outer City at the beginning of a decade to an Inner City location ten years later) and *centrifugal mobility* (the movement in reverse). Both types were of some significance for nuclei on the edge of the Inner City, particularly between 1906 and 1915 (see Tables 1 and 2).[7] Nevertheless, one of the surprising findings of the study is the limited scale of centrifugal and centripetal mobility detected so far.[8]

The sixth type of mobility is termed *emergence*—the creation of new establishments in the Inner City. Most establishments entering the Inner City are newly created, but it is practically impossible in directory studies to distinguish these true emergents from the few establishments that enter the Inner City from outside the city's boundaries. Thus, both types of establishments are called here *emergents*. Emergents taken together with establishments moving into the Inner City from the Outer City are called *newcomers*. And the *entry rate* is the proportion of newcomers in an activity group in the Inner City. In general, the entry rate, like that of regional persistence, rose during

7. In this decade, the total destruction of the Inner City scattered many Inner City establishments to the Outer City, where some remained, and later presented the opportunity for many activities located in the Outer City before the fire to move into new buildings constructed before 1915 in the Inner City.

8. Changes in the index of central tendency (the relative proportions of activities in the Inner and Outer cities) were primarily the result of changing numbers of failures and newcomers in the various activity groups.

periods of locational change of districts in the Inner City (Tables 1 and 2).[9]

Comparing entry and persistence rates by decade, we find that in activity groups composed of small establishments, and, presumably in the Inner City as a whole, entry: place-persistence ratios and, in most cases, entry: regional-persistence ratios were higher than 3 : 1 in the first decade and, generally, more than 2 : 1 thereafter. By contrast, after 1875, in activity groups composed of large establishments and of establishments of various sizes, the ratios were far more variable, with newcomers frequently being outnumbered by both place-persistent and regional-persistent establishments.[10]

An indicator of the fluidity of the Central District is the decennial ratio comparing mobility (including emergence and regional persistence) and stability (place persistence). In activity groups composed of small establishments, the ratio of mobile to stable establishments was at least 4 : 1 in each decade between 1854 and 1936 and frequently much higher. And, in the early decades, the same was true of activity groups composed of large or variously sized establishments. Thereafter in these activity groups, however, the mobility component was generally much lower and more variable, the ratio ranging from 2 : 1 to 1 : 4. It seems probable, nevertheless, that in every decade, mobile establishments outnumbered stable ones by at least 3 : 1 in the Inner City.

In establishing the importance of newcomers as against persistent establishments in effecting locational changes, the garment district provides a fine case. Newcomers consistently outnumbered persistent establishments, and most of the establishments were small to medium-sized, particularly in the early decades. Furthermore, the locational shifts of the district were clear-cut in space and time: a marked lateral shift in the early 1850s, a leapfrogging in 1869-1872 (Fig. 1), a lateral expansion, 1902-1911 (Fig. 2), and a leapfrogging and dismemberment in the 1920s (Fig. 3).[11]

Patchy directory coverage in the early fifties made it difficult to establish the detailed sequence of entry of establishments into the focal area of the new nucleus. However, the few relocatees discovered there were overwhelmingly outnumbered by newcomers who were presumably responsible in the main for the displacement. . . .

The second major locational change, the leapfrogging of the district (1869-1872), was started by the relocation of persistent establishments displaced by the rapidly expanding financial district (Fig. 1). And the locational shift of some well-established wholesalers from the section of the old garment district, threatened by the expanding financial district, consolidated the locational shift. Newcomers simply followed and filled out the frame of a new district established by regional-persistent establishments.

A similar sequence of events occurred after the turn of the century. Almost two-thirds of the garment establishments (132) in the Inner City in 1915 were

9. The only major difference between the rates detected so far is in the medical services activity group (Table 2).

10. It should be remembered that these decennial rates underestimate the total number of failures and entrants in each decade, simply because many establishments emerge and quickly fail without being caught at the cross-sectional dates, for example, 1865 and 1875. An underestimation of a smaller scale results from the fact that persistent establishments may survive eighteen years and yet be "caught" at the cross-sectional dates only once. In such a case, the establishment would appear as a newcomer and fail before being counted as a persistent establishment.

11. Bowden, *Dynamics of City Growth,* pp. 229-40, 405-15, 662-90.

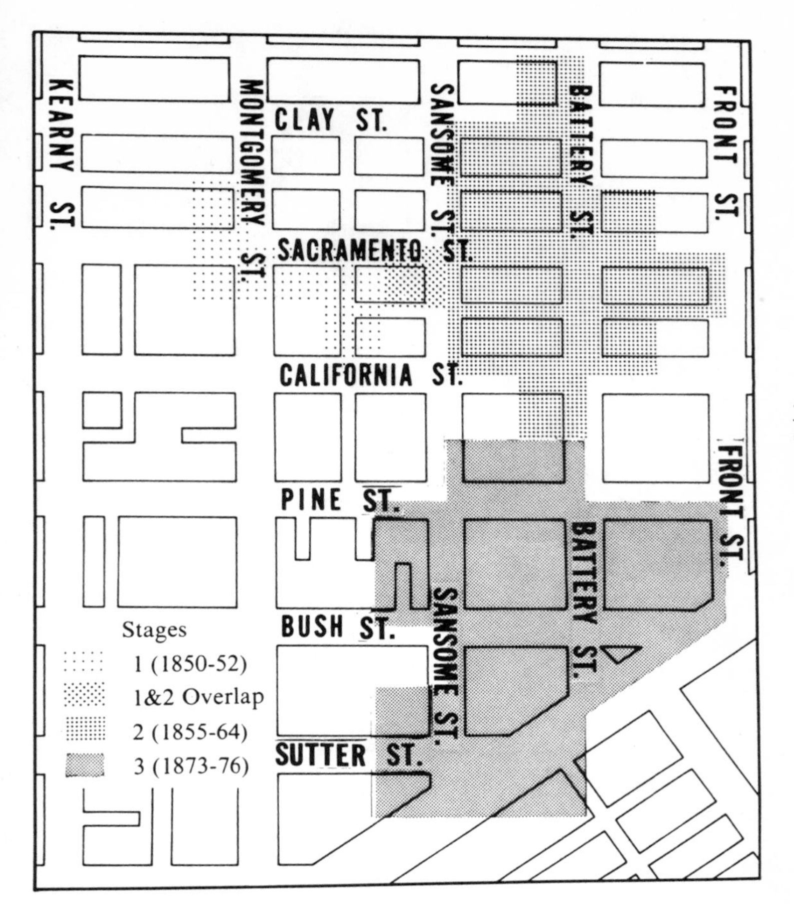

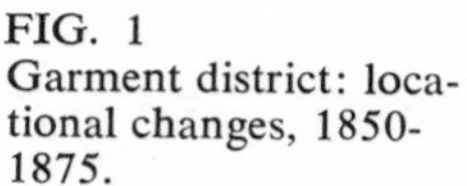
FIG. 1
Garment district: locational changes, 1850-1875.

FIG. 2
Garment district: locational changes, 1906-1915.

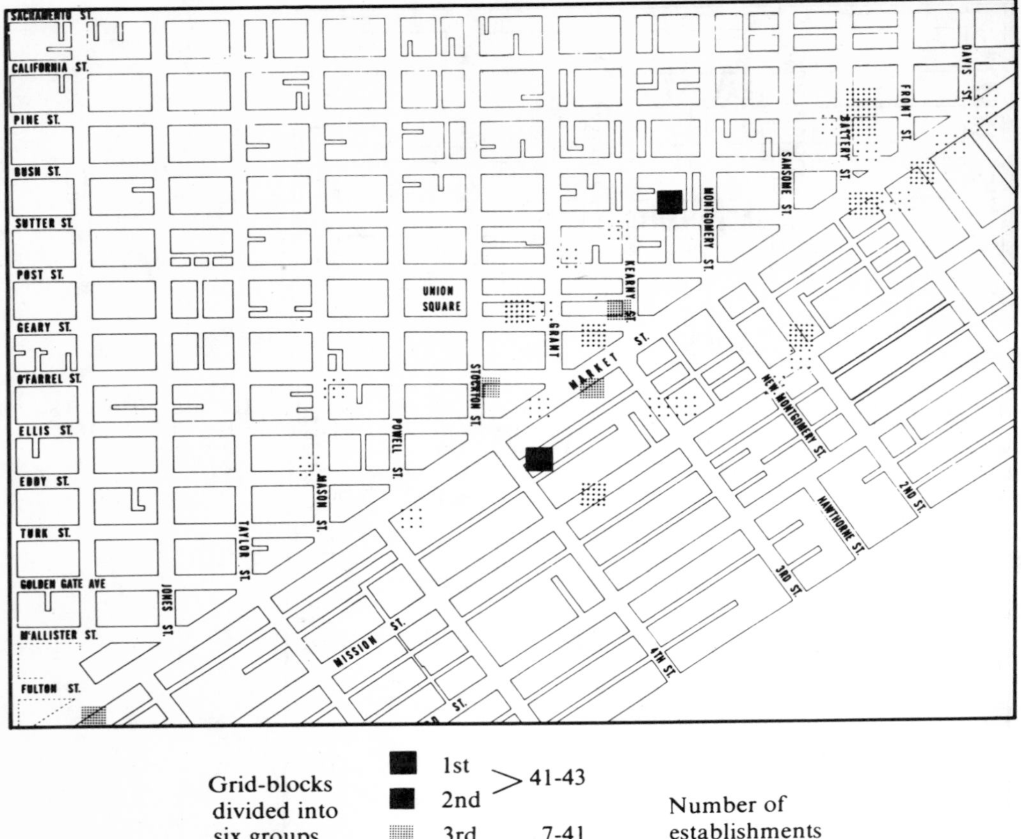

FIG. 3. Garment nuclei, 1931.

newcomers, yet this analysis shows that the new district and the three nuclei to the west (Fig. 2) were essentially formed and re-formed by persistent establishments that returned quickly after the fire. Eighty-two of these establishments persisted from 1905-1915.

In the next decade another surge of newcomers entered the Inner City (187 of 291 establishments present in 1926), and, at the same time, the garment district was dismembered (Fig. 3). But, as in the two previous phases of growth and locational change, it was the displacement of a large number of medium-sized activities by the expanding office and financial districts that precipitated the break-up. Analysis of the sequent occupance of four key buildings in the new nuclei revealed that persistent activities both laid the groundwork for and effected the early occupance of these buildings. The pro-

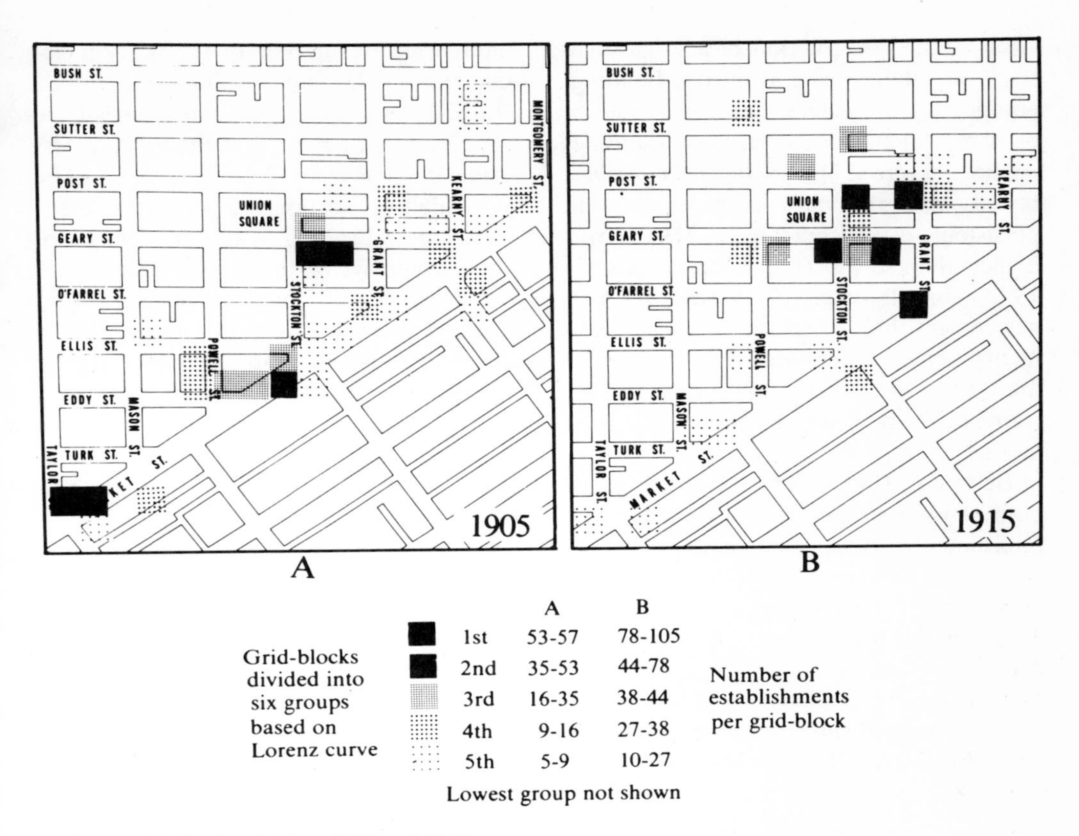

FIG. 4. Medical activities, 1905 and 1915.

portion of newcomers to persistent establishments in these key buildings was very low in the early years of occupance and then began to rise rapidly. This suggests that the high proportion of newcomers in decades of locational change of districts in the Inner City were a consequence of the special opportunities created in such times.

To establish the representativeness of the recurrent sequence of events in the garment district, analysis was carried out for an activity group in which circumstances pointed to maximum instability and optimal conditions for the creation of new nuclei by the flood of newcomers to the Inner City.[12] This was the medical services activity group (1915-1936). In this group, of which all establishments were small, there were three times as many newcomers as regional-persistent establishments in each decade between 1885 and 1936, and establishments that persisted in the same locale within the Inner City were very few (Table 2).

After the complete exodus of medical service establishments from the Inner City after 1906, there were, by 1915, 1,100 medical service establishments in the Inner City, of which 800 were newcomers and 300 persistent. The medical nucleus, horizontally adjacent to the apparel-shopping district before the fire (1906), was relocated above it after the fire (Fig. 4), a locational shift made pos-

12. Ibid., pp. 612-27.

sible by the construction of a large number of tall, steel-framed buildings equipped with modern elevators. Analysis of the sequent occupance of buildings opened before 1911 in the new nucleus reveals that the ratio of newcomers to persistent establishments in 1911 was higher than 8 : 3 (the district ratio in 1915) in all cases. This suggests that newcomers, half of which were establishments located in the Outer City before the fire, were instrumental in outlining the frame of the new nucleus and in establishing it.

Between 1915 and 1926, although both newcomers (940) and persistent establishments (620) were more numerous than in the previous decade, the entry-persistence ratio dropped from 8 : 3 to 3 : 2. In these circumstances, it was the persistent establishments that effected the marked lateral displacement and expansion of the medical nucleus in the twenties (Fig. 5). This conclusion is not equivocal, for analysis of the sequent occupance of the major buildings occupied in this move reveals an entry-persistence ratio of less than 1 : 3 in the early years, gradually rising to 2 : 3 and 3 : 3. The very high proportions of persistent establishments relocating in the first phases of the change were, to a large extent, the consequence of mass displacement of medical establishments by the expanding department stores and apparel-shopping district (see Table 4, which shows the succession of establishments in buildings that formed the core of the postfire medical nucleus). The sequence of events and the conditions existing before and after the locational shift were essentially the same as those in the garment district in 1865-1936. . . .

On one occasion each in the early years of growth of the apparel-shopping and financial districts, newcomers greatly outnumbered persistent establishments and, as a consequence, were critical in both

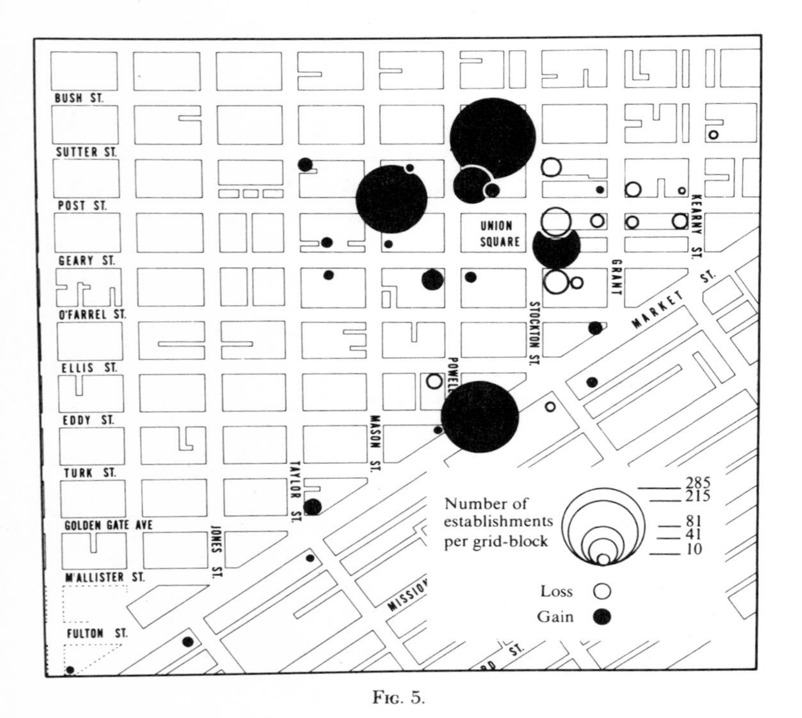

FIG. 5.

FIG. 5
Changes in number of medical activities, 1916-1931.

TABLE 4. Changes in the Functional Structure of Three Buildings East of Union Square, 1921 and 1931

	Number of Establishments							
	Howard Building (209 Post)		*Whitney Building (133 Geary)*		*Schroth Building (240 Stockton)*		*Totals*	
Type of Establishments	1921	1931	1921	1931	1921	1931	1921	1931
Jewelry	5	13	14	30	0	1	19	44
Beauty Shops, etc.	0	4	4	23	0	14	4	41
Women's Apparel	4	11	6	9	0	1	10	21
Other Apparel	0	2	3	9	0	1	3	12
Others	1	2	2	4	0	2	3	8
Christian Science Practitioners	0	0	49	32	0	0	49	32
Medical	92	59	40	21	63	29	195	109
Breakdown of Medical Services								
Physicians and Surgeons	43	15	13	5	46	5	102	25
Dentists	39	32	17	6	17	15	73	53
Other Medical	10	12	10	10	0	9	20	31

laying the groundwork and effecting the expansion and locational changes of both districts. For example, in the marked leapfrogging of the financial district,[13] well-established activities were responsible for the lateral expansion of the banking nucleus (and financial district) in the early fifties, but the marked leapfrogging of the financial district in the mid-sixties was effected largely by establishments new to the central district (Table 3). Two rival financial centers (California Street and the Northeast, see Table 5) comprised of new entrants grew up as discrete nuclei to the northeast and southeast of the existing financial district between 1854 and 1860. In the early sixties a further concentration of newcomers (see Table 5 under California Street), particularly San Francisco's first sizable (commercial) banks, determined that the southeastern rival would become the new financial district. Of the banks in 1865, 85 percent had been created since 1854.

After 1870, however, as the range in

TABLE 5. Number of Banks in Three Sectors of San Francisco, 1854-75

Year	*California St.**	*Upper Montgomery St.†*	*Northeast‡*
1854	4	11	3
1858	3	4	4
1860	3	7	6
1865	9	9	5
1869	9	7	2
1875	13	8	0

* California Street between Battery and Kearny streets.
† Montgomery Street between Sacramento and Washington streets and including all four corners of both the Montgomery-Washington streets intersection and the Montgomery-Sacramento streets intersection.
‡ The area northeast of upper Montgomery Street and north of California Street. It is bounded on the north by Pacific Street and on the east by Front Street.
Source: City directories.

13. Bowden, *Dynamics of City Growth,* pp. 145-53, 179-203, 335-58, 479-94, 648-62.

size of the constituent establishments broadened, it was the decisions of the persistent medium-to-large and, later, large establishments (dominants) that became critical. In terms of expansion and locational change, the financial and apparel-shopping districts became, in effect, districts composed of large establishments, like the theater district. Only the dominants mattered. Large numbers of newcomers surged into the financial district throughout the nineteenth and early twentieth centuries, but they were almost exclusively small establishments that tended to cling to the district framed by the dominants.

The apparel-shopping activity group[14] is the most complex in the Inner City in terms of structure, growth, and locational change. In rapidly growing cities in the nineteenth century, there were in the Inner City at any point in time a main district, numerous rival nuclei (interceptors), and numerous nuclei that had been bypassed or discarded (incubators). . . .

Between 1854 and 1865 a number of rival apparel-shopping centers developed as interceptors to the north and south of the established district, and in the middle and late sixties, the southern interceptor became the new apparel-shopping district. The effect of this was a leapfrogging of the district far to the south. Analysis has shown that the women's apparel shopping nucleus made the first locational change, followed by the men's clothing nucleus, and the jewelry cluster. The establishments instrumental in bringing about the first locational shift were small stores new to the Central District in the sixties, and medium-sized stores established before 1860 (Fig. 6). The former were very numerous and made it possible for a locational shift to take place to either the northern or the southern interceptor. The latter (medium-sized stores) were few in number, but by their selection of sites in the southern interceptor during the mid-sixties, they appeared to ensure that it would become the new women's apparel shopping district. These medium-sized stores were the embryonic department stores that would dominate the growth and locational shifts of the apparel-shopping district after 1870. In the sixties, however, some newcomers grew so rapidly to the status of embryonic department stores in the southern interceptor that it was becoming the new apparel-shopping nucleus without the embryonic department stores of the old nucleus. Hence, the entry of new establishments was perhaps more important than relocation of old ones in bringing about the leapfrogging of the apparel-shopping district in the late sixties.

By contrast, in the mid-seventies the rate of increase of new establishments dropped; well-established embryonic department stores were larger and more numerous than they had been in the sixties, and it was less likely that newcomers would grow rapidly enough to challenge these dominants. These large establishments effected the locational shift of the women's apparel shopping district in 1874-1877 and in all subsequent phases of growth. In sum, in districts composed of establishments ranging in size from very small to very large, the only potentially critical newcomers were dominants. And as these were uncommon, the locational shifts of districts of this type were effected almost exclusively by large establishments that relocated within the Inner City (regionally persistent establishments).[15]

14. Ibid., pp. 122-29, 204-29, 359-403, 494-528, 592-612.

15. Further support for this conclusion is provided in Susan H. Kelly and Bruce L. LaRose, "The Growth and Movement of Manhattan's

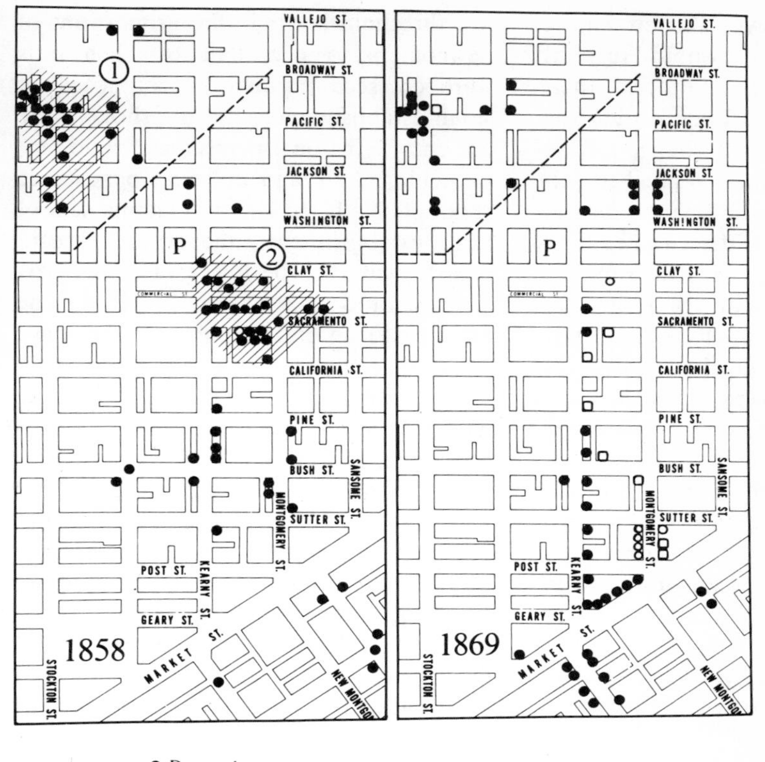

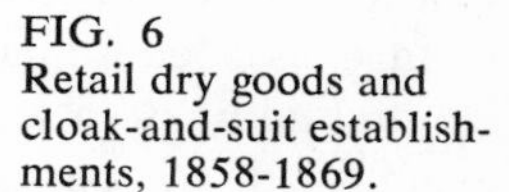
FIG. 6
Retail dry goods and cloak-and-suit establishments, 1858-1869.

In conclusion, throughout the nineteenth century the decennial rates of place persistence of establishments in most districts in the San Francisco Central District were similar to the very low decennial rates of residential stability found by historians in both frontier counties and growing towns and cities. In every decade there were at least three times as many mobile as stable establishments in the Inner City. Between 1850 and 1936, in every year in the Central District's history, there were probably more *newcomers* than *persistent activities*. And in many activity groups, the ratio of newcomers to persistent activities was greater than two to one. This entry-persistence ratio was particularly high during periods of marked locational change of nuclei[16] in the Central District as a whole.

The locational effects of this flood of

Central Business District as Indicated by Department Stores, 1860-1930," (Paper prepared for the Eighth Conference of the Eastern Historical Geography Association held at Briarcliff, N.Y., April 1974).

16. Martyn J. Bowden, "Downtown through Time: Delimitation, Expansion, and Internal Growth," *Economic Geography* 47 (1971): 130-31.

newcomers were, however, far fewer than their absolute numbers would suggest. Most newcomers were small and their chances of failure high. Even during the major bursts of locational change within the Inner City, newcomers tended to follow rather than lead locational shifts and to fill out the existing district rather than establish a rival center. The sharp upturn in the numbers of newcomers during periods of major locational change in many districts was not so much a cause of change as a consequence of the opening up of buildings in a new district already established by persistent activities that had shifted from the old district. This was particularly true in peripheral districts.[17]

Thus, in San Francisco newcomers effected major locational changes only in unusual circumstances, when certain critical threshold levels in the proportions of newcomers to persistent establishments were crossed. In districts composed of small establishments, the thresholds were an entry: regional-persistence ratio approaching 3 : 1 and an entry-persistence ratio of 2 : 1. In districts composed of large establishments, the critical thresholds appeared to be lower: an entry-persistence ratio of 3 : 2 and (based on one clear case) an entry: regional-persistence ratio approaching 2 : 1. In districts in which the range in size of establishments widened through time the critical thresholds were, at first, those of districts composed of small establishments and, later (after 1870 in San Francisco), presumably those of districts composed of large establishments. (In this latter situation, however, only the entry-persistence ratios of the dominants in the district would be significant.) When these critical thresholds were crossed, a new nucleus (nuclei) emerged and leapfrogging generally resulted, primarily because of the physical-morphological constraints placed upon the main (old) nucleus by contiguous districts. . . .

17. In these districts locational changes are frequently precipitated by external pressures, i.e., a large number of established activities, with competitive and complementary linkages, are forced to relocate in a short period of two or three years. These establishments tend to move together (leapfrogging) and in so doing create a new district or change the focus of the old one.

The Internal Spatial Differentiation of Immigrant Residential Districts / *David Ward*

Introduction

The term ghetto has frequently been applied to the concentrations of foreign immigrants who settled in many large American cities between about 1840 and 1920. By the last decade of the nineteenth century foreign immigrants and their children accounted for a large if not a dominant proportion of the populations of most large cities and, consequently, the concentration of an ethnic group in a particular district separated them from other ethnic groups rather than from some homogeneous majority population. Indeed, only a minority of the total population of a given ethnic group actually lived in the relatively small areas exclusively occupied by people of the same ethnic origin, while the boundaries of the different ethnic ghettos were seldom clearly defined, for there was a considerable mixing of groups in the intervening areas. Certainly almost all the ethnic institutions of a particular group were concentrated in the ghetto but these facilities presumably served the needs of the substantial proportion of the group who lived beyond the limits of the ghetto. Partly for these reasons, most contemporary observers tended to emphasize the common material deficiencies of immigrant living conditions and, in particular, the mortal and socially pathological repercussions of congested housing. Throughout the entire period of mass immigration, however, the areal coincidence of large immigrant populations, congested housing, excessive mortality, and manifestations of social disorganization occurred in decidedly limited sections of the immigrant quarters of most large cities. . . .

The Location of Immigrant Residential Districts

Since dwelling units which provided for the minimum housing needs of a family rented at rates far beyond the means of most immigrants, relatively few new low rent structures were built. The supply of low-rent accommodation was, therefore, largely dependent upon the abandonment of existing dwellings by high- and middle-income people in areas threatened by the invasion of an undesirable nonresidential land use or rendered obsolete by the development of new housing standards. Generally the largest number of abandoned older dwellings were located in districts adjacent to the expanding edge of the central business district, where the potential threat of commercial expansion into nearby residential areas prompted many occupants to seek new dwellings further removed from undesirable land uses. During the period between the de-

Reproduced (with omissions) by permission from Northwestern University, Department of Geography, *Special Publication Number 3* (1970), pp. 24-42.

parture of the original residents and the demolition of the dwellings, the single-family houses were usually converted into multifamily tenements and their rear yards or surrounding grounds were filled with cheap new structures. Although these converted single-family residences rented at rates appropriate to the low incomes of most immigrants, the congested, dilapidated, and unsanitary living conditions made even low rents exorbitant.

The central business district also provided the largest and most diverse source of unskilled employment opportunities, and although the facilities for local transportation were improved and enlarged during the second half of the nineteenth century, many immigrants were employed in occupations with long and awkward hours and preferred a short pedestrian journey to work. The domestic economy of most immigrant families was dependent upon the wages of all adult members of the family and consequently the multiplication of relatively low individual commuter fares inflated transportation costs beyond the means of most low-income families.[1] The tenure of most unskilled occupations was also characteristically uncertain, while daily hiring was the common procedure in general laboring. Immigrants thus faced not only frequent spells of unemployment but also constant changes in the location of their work. Under these circumstances, a pedestrian accessibility to the central business district facilitated the discovery of alternative employment whenever regular work was abruptly terminated. Indeed, the tendency of different ethnic groups to embrace and dominate particular occupations within the city may have encouraged their concentration in areas adjacent to that part of the central business district which housed their leading source of employment.

For example, Irish immigrants first helped to build and later found employment in the warehouses and terminal facilities of the business district while German immigrants found employment in the sewing machine and consumer supply trades which were housed in the upper stories of warehouse premises.[2] Italian immigrants in part replaced the Irish as general laborers but the distribution of fresh food from the central wholesale markets attracted Italian immigrants in large numbers.[3] Jewish immigrants, equipped with long experience in the handicraft industries and local commercial life of their East European homelands, rapidly developed many branches of merchandising at a time when the retail and wholesale segments of marketing were first firmly separated and established as distinct specialized areas within the central business district.[4] Jewish immigrants also rapidly engrossed the ready-made clothing industry and although they diverted production from the warehouses to residential premises, the credit and informational needs of the industry demanded locations with ready access to the central business district. Certainly many immigrant business enterprises which originally provided for the distinctive material or dietary needs of the immigrant

1. Cf. F. H. Streightoff, *Standard of Living among the Industrial People of America* (Boston and New York, 1911); and Robert C. Chapin, *The Standard of Living Amongst Workingmen's Families in New York City* (New York, 1909).

2. R. Ernst, *Immigrant Life in New York City: 1825-1863* (New York, 1949), pp. 17, 61-77; O. Handlin, *Boston's Immigrants: A Study in Acculturation* (Cambridge, Mass., 1959), pp. 54-87.

3. R. F. Foerster, *The Italian Emigration of Our Times* (Cambridge, Mass., 1919), pp. 332-44.

4. S. Joseph, *Jewish Immigration to the United States from 1881-1910* (New York, 1914), pp. 42-46.

community, eventually expanded to serve a far wider market.

Mid-Nineteenth-Century Patterns

This type of reasoning is, however, dependent upon two assumptions. Firstly, that the supply of abandoned housing adjacent to the central business district was sufficient to fulfill, even inadequately, the housing demand of large numbers of immigrants and secondly, that throughout the period of mass immigration the central business district was the dominant source of immigrant employment. . . . However, it is clear from the ward data for both Boston and New York that, before the Civil War, a substantial proportion of the Irish and German newcomers had to seek accommodation far beyond the immediate limits of the central immigrant concentrations. In New York City these central concentrations housed only about 30 percent of the total Irish- and German-born populations. Data compiled for the ninety-three enumeration districts of Manhattan for 1860 suggests that although a limited number of districts housed proportionately large numbers of the two major foreign born groups, the vast majority of divisions housed proportions within one standard deviation of the mean proportions of Irish- and German-born people for all divisions. The central German concentrations did, however, house a greater proportion of the total German community than did the central Irish districts of the total Irish population (see Table 1).

During the two decades before the Civil War, the supply of abandoned housing near to the central business district was inadequate to house the large influx of Irish and German immigrants. Many newly arrived immigrants found accommodation in "shanty-towns" constructed beyond the continuous built-up area of the city or in areas within the physical limits of the city neglected because of their undesirable site characteristics. Until the improvement and expansion of streetcar services in the sixties and seventies, middle-income Americans had few locational alternatives to continued residence near to their own places of employment.

TABLE 1. Distribution of Relative Proportions of Selected Ethnic Groups In Manhattan

	1860[1]		1890[2]	
	Irish Birth	*German Birth*	*Russian Parentage*	*Italian Parentage*
Mean:	24.32	15.75	3.89	4.94
Standard Deviation	10.79	12.49	10.22	10.97
+2	2	6	5	9
+1 to +2	14	9	4	1
$\bar{X}$ to +1	29	17	9	7
$\bar{X}$ to −1	33	60	96	97
−1 to −2	15	1	0	0
% of pop. in obs +1	26.7	36.1	70.7	62.7
correlation with total population:	0.81	0.39	0.35	0.13

[1] 93 enumeration districts, 1860 census schedules
[2] 115 sanitary districts, 1890 census (Vital statistics of N.Y.C.)

As Warner has indicated in his study of Philadelphia, the rapid rate of growth of cities from relatively small beginnings provided no large stock of existing housing and the rapid multiplication of traditional small-scale occupations in every section of the city created a highly dispersed employment pattern.[5] Certainly the emergence of an ethnic division of labor capable of influencing the location of different immigrant groups had not developed before the Civil War. In 1860 the magnitude and locational significance of differences in the occupational structure of the Irish and German households of Manhattan were not particularly striking. In the ninety-three enumeration districts of Manhattan in 1860, the mean Irish proportions of the total population employed in laboring and domestic service were somewhat higher than their proportionate representation in the occupied population as a whole, while the average German proportions of the total population employed in the clothing trades, crafts, trade and food production and distribution were also somewhat higher than their average representation in the total occupied population (Table 2). However, with the exception of the overrepresentation of Germans in the food trades, the proportionate contribution of Irish and German households to the total occupied population of each division was highly correlated with their proportionate representation in each occupation group (Table 2). It would appear that the overrepresentation of Irish and German households in several major occupational groups was composed of numerically small excesses in each division. Certainly before 1860 the emerging central business district was not the dominant source of immigrant employment, while the small-scale organization and dispersed distribution of most types of immigrant employment reduced the locational effects of an ethnic division of labor.

TABLE 2. Relationship between Ethnic Origin and Selected Occupational Groups, Manhattan: 1860 (by enumeration districts)

	Irish		*German*	
	%[1]	r^2	%[1]	r^2
Laboring	75.9	0.83	18.0	0.83
Domestic Service	69.4	0.86	27.5	0.87
Clothing	50.3	0.86	34.5	0.89
Craft	45.0	0.89	37.1	0.93
Building	52.5	0.86	25.3	0.87
Trade	51.9	0.82	31.4	0.81
Food	39.3	0.80	49.6	0.67
Total Occupied	55.7		30.4	

[1] $\bar{X}$ of total occupied by districts
[2] r^2 of proportion of total occupied and proportion in specified occupation by districts.

Late Nineteenth-Century Patterns

The expansion of streetcar services in the seventies and their electrification in the eighties multiplied the residential alternatives of middle-income people living in central residential locations, while the increased scale of production and distribution and the increased concentration of employment opportunities in the rapidly expanding central business district encouraged the proportionately greater concentration of new immigrant arrivals in central residential areas. . . .

The increase in the volume of foreign immigration necessitated an increase in the areal extent as well as the density of immigrant residential districts, for by the turn of the century these areas housed a major segment of the total urban population. To be sure, this areal enlargement of the immigrant residential districts was in part the result of the relocation of estab-

5. S. B. Warner, Jr., *The Private City: Philadelphia in Three Periods of Its Growth* (Philadelphia, 1968), pp. 49-62.

lished immigrants who could afford improved dwellings and a longer journey to work, but the central immigrant districts also expanded outwards into adjacent residential areas so that the outer limits of the continuous immigrant quarters were often at a considerable distance from the central business district. In 1890, a special census of New York City recorded the maternal parentage of the city's population by relatively small tractlike sanitary districts and, on the basis of these observations, it is clear that far larger proportions of the recently arrived Russian-Jewish and Italian immigrants were concentrated in a limited number of centrally located districts than were Irish and, to a lesser degree, German immigrants a generation earlier (Table 1). Under these circumstances the internal diversity of the extensive and populous immigrant sections assumed impressive dimensions and, in particular, the living conditions of these areas exhibited conspicuous variations in their effects upon the vital rates of their different resident populations.

The Internal Spatial Structure of Immigrant Residential Districts

. . . Although newly arrived immigrants tended to live in more congested quarters than more established groups, the overall death rate of the population of foreign birth was frequently somewhat lower than that of the populations of foreign parentage. The age structures of the newer immigrant arrivals were, however, dominated by vigorous young adults whereas older immigrant groups included larger proportions of both very young and very old people. Thus, although substantial numbers of older immigrant groups had moved into less crowded and often better housing, their more balanced age structures exposed them to the inflationary effects of the very high death rates among infants and older adults.[6]

Age structure alone, however, failed to explain impressive contrasts in the death rates of groups with similar proportions of people of foreign birth and parentage. Russian-Jewish and Italian immigrants, for example, often lived alongside each other in extremely congested quarters and, although the greater prevalence of family immigration among the Jews exposed them to the inflationary influences of infant mortality, death rates among Russian-Jewish immigrants were often the lowest in the city, whereas Italian mortality was generally one of the highest rates. Most observers attributed low Jewish death rates in the congested quarters to the urban ancestry of Jewish people who, unlike most other immigrant groups, had made their adjustments to congested domestic arrangements long before their arrival in American cities. In particular, Russian-Jewish immigrants exhibited an extremely low death rate from tuberculosis, one of the leading causes of death in the congested districts, and this relative immunity was observed among their coreligionists who continued to reside in European cities.[7] Adjacent and often interspersed Italian immigrants suffered from extremely high death rates, and some authorities attributed this great

6. F. L. Hoffman, "General Death Rate of Large American Cities, 1871-1904," *Quarterly Publications of the American Statistical Association* 10 (1906-07):1-75; W. H. Guilfoy, "The Death Rate of the City of New York as affected by the Cosmopolitan Character of its Population," *Quarterly Publications of the American Statistical Association* 10 (1906-07): 515-22.

7. J. S. Billings, "Vital Statistics of the Jews in the U.S.," *Census Bulletin* 19 (1890); L. I. Dublin, "The Mortality of Foreign Race Stocks in Pennsylvania and New York," *Quarterly Publications of the American Statistical Association* 17 (1920-21):13-44.

range in mortality, occasionally within the limits of a city block, to the dietary deficiencies and the unfamiliarity of Italian immigrants with the severity of the American winter.[8] Even longer established immigrant groups exhibited contrasts in their mortality characteristics. Populations of Irish birth and parentage were afflicted with unusually high death rates throughout the nineteenth century. Tuberculosis, in particular, was more prevalent among the Irish than among the German immigrants who had arrived in American cities during the same period.[9] Finally, populations of native parentage which survived within the immigrant quarters frequently exhibited high mortality rates, largely because they were either the oldest or the most impoverished remnants of the earlier resident group.

. . . On the basis of data for New York City and Brooklyn in 1890, it has been possible to demonstrate that high age-standardized death rates and high population density per built-up acre formed an overlapping rather than a superimposed spatial pattern within the immigrant residential universe.[10] Furthermore, the population of Russian-Jewish parentage exhibited a relatively strong association with population density and that of Italian parentage a somewhat weaker association with high mortality. Older immigrant groups demonstrated no clear associations with either high-density or high-mortality characteristics, and the ethnically more diverse populations of districts occupied by long-established immigrant groups probably obscured the frequently publicized association between Irish populations and high mortality.

The spatial implications of these conclusions may be expressed as a descriptive model in which high mortality rates, a high population density, and proportionately large populations of immigrants are considered as circles which occupy largely separate but occasionally overlapping locations within the immigrant neighborhoods (Fig. 1). Areas which are described by different combinations of more than one of the three most widely publicized characteristics of immigrant quarters indicate the effects of distinctive ethnic groups. Area A describes districts in which all three characteristics were present and represents the worst sections of the Italian ghetto, whereas Area B describes districts in which immigrant populations were extremely crowded but failed to exhibit high death rates and clearly indicates the Russian-Jewish ghetto. Area C describes districts where immigrants residing beyond the limits of the congested sections experienced high mortality and expresses the occasionally high mortality of older and frequently Irish immigrant populations. Area D, which combines high mortality and high density, describes remnant and impoverished populations of native parentage.

Congested living quarters were also regarded as a basic cause of not only high urban mortality but also the social disorganization of immigrant populations. It was long assumed that all low income immigrant neighborhoods were afflicted with a wide range of socially pathological behavior which was directly related to the breakdown of the traditional social organ-

8. R. Brindisi, "The Italian and Public Health," *Charities* 12 (1904):483-86; K. H. Claghorn, "Foreign Immigrants in New York City," *Report of the Industrial Commission* 15 (Washington, D.C., 1901):449-91.

9. Guilfoy, "Death Rate," pp. 515-22; Claghorn, "Foreign Immigrants," pp. 460-61.

10. D. Ward, "The Internal Spatial Structure of Immigrant Residential Districts in the Late Nineteenth Century," *Geographical Analysis* 1, 4 (1969):337-53.

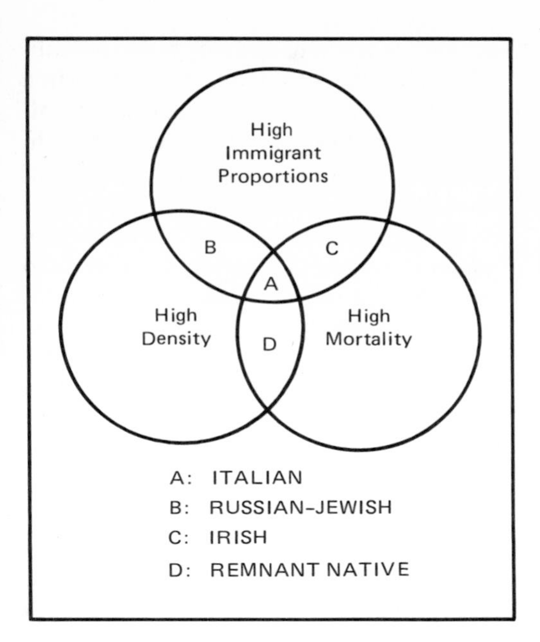

FIG. 1. Components of the internal spatial structure of immigrant residential districts: c. 1900.

ization of rural people in the congested living quarters and impersonal and anonymous social environment of the city. Subsequent revaluations of low-income neighborhoods have suggested that many contemporary observers failed to identify the presence of social organization among immigrant populations, largely because their behavior and priorities were somewhat different from those of suburban or native America.[11] Indeed, most newly arrived immigrant groups were hardly aware of the society of middle- and high-income native Americans to which they were apparently to assimilate, for the society to which they were initially exposed was that of older immigrant groups who had gradually established control of segments of the political and economic life of many cities.[12] Moreover, the ghetto itself, once it had established the institutions and local neighborhood life of a particular immigrant group, in part became a voluntary association, for most immigrants arriving in American cities preferred to spend their early years in an unfamiliar city in a district which housed their fellow countrymen or coreligionists and often their friends and relatives.

. . . Although both legitimate and corrupt forms of political patronage excited popular condemnation, residential concentration also provided larger immigrant groups with their proportionate share of patronage at a time when public welfare was weakly developed.[13]

The positive social attractions and political advantages of immigrant residential concentration were not, however, shared by all immigrant groups nor were they exhibited by all central residential districts. Smaller immigrant groups not only lacked the numbers to support their own institutions but also rarely received their proportionate share of political patronage or of local employment opportunities. Moreover, small immigrant groups tended to be dominated by young single men who eventually hoped to return to their homeland with the assumed profits of their American employment and, consequently, with neither a family structure nor a permanent commitment to residence in the United States, pathological behavior recorded their social

11. W. F. Whyte, *The Street Corner Society* (Chicago, 1943), pp. 94-104, 255-78; H. J. Gans, *The Urban Villagers* (New York, 1962), pp. 3-41.

12. C. F. Ware, *Greenwich Village: 1920-1930* (Boston, 1935), pp. 3-8, 81-126.

13. T. J. Lowi, *At the Pleasure of the Mayor: Power and Patronage in New York City, 1898-1958* (New York, 1964).

rather than their housing predicament.[14] The most frequent manifestations of socially pathological behavior which were associated with central concentrations of immigrants were often confined to those districts which were developed as rooming houses for single people rather than family groups. The age structure, sex ratio, and diverse ethnic characteristics of these quarters clearly distinguish them from those more typical immigrant districts in which one or two large immigrant groups composed largely of families dominated an extensive residential section.

Even the largest and most stable immigrant groups were, however, unable to establish enduring ghettos in those sections of the residential fringe of the central business district which suffered from the continuous invasion of business premises. Since the specialized functional areas of the central business district emerged and expanded at different rates at different times, it is possible to hypothesize that the selective expansion of commercial premises largely determined the relative locations of the variations in the living conditions and social characteristics exhibited by the central concentrations of immigrants.[15] On some margins the extensive invasion of commercial activities followed so closely upon the departure of the original population that the immigrant newcomers had neither the time nor the incentive to establish a stable community. These districts were most frequently occupied by the smallest or poorest immigrant groups along with older and often impoverished remnants of earlier immigrant occupants who had moved on to securer residential locations. Manifestations of social disorganization were thus rooted in the insecurity of residential tenure, frequent population turnover, and the failure of any one immigrant group to establish the institutional fabric of the ghetto. Other margins failed to attract the anticipated commercial developments and, consequently, the immigrant occupation assumed more permanent and stable characteristics. These enduring immigrant quarters not only served the residential needs of the first generation of immigrants but also those of later arrivals. Districts initially occupied by Irish and German immigrants in the fifties eventually passed to Italian, Russian-Jewish, and other later immigrant groups toward the turn of the century.

This discussion of the location and internal spatial differentiation of immigrant residential areas suggests that the first generation of Irish- and German-born immigrants arrived in American cities before either the supply of cheap accommodation or the demand for unskilled labor was concentrated in the central sections of the city. Consequently, although certain sections of the city were identified with a particular ethnic group, these immigrant concentrations housed only a minority of the total immigrant population. Secondly, the majority of immigrants who arrived later in the nineteenth century obtained accommodation and employment in central locations but the outward expansion and changing composition of these areas did not create uniformly undesirable material and social characteristics. The degree of central concentration of ethnic groups was not closely related

14. H. W. Zorbaugh, *The Gold Coast and the Slum* (Chicago, 1929), pp. 142-51; R. A. Woods, ed., *The City Wilderness* (Boston, 1898), pp. 37-51.

15. D. Ward, "The Emergence of Central Immigrant Ghettoes in American Cities: 1840-1920," *Annals of the Association of American Geographers* 58 (1968):343-59.

to the quality of the living conditions nor was the degree of housing congestion closely related to the vital rates of their resident populations. The ghetto, as the areal expression of overlapping concentrations of immigrants, overcrowded housing, and high mortality, occupied areas of quite limited dimensions within the immigrant districts while the blighting impact of the expanding central business district was selective rather than universal. . . .

Race, Residence, and Ideology: Charleston, South Carolina in the Mid-Nineteenth Century

John P. Radford

Despite some recent theoretical statements, it remains generally true, as two historians have recently charged, that "geographers do not give much weight to the ideological components coincidental with spatial change."[1] Nowhere has this been more evident than in geographical studies of urban phenomena, in which ideology has been played down, and in which culturally relative concepts have frequently been used as if they were universal axioms. Those who seek to redress the balance, and to confront the ideological components of spatial change, are faced with severe problems. The shortage of documentation poses difficulties, especially in historical studies. But the major difficulty lies in establishing the existence of direct causal links between ideology, social process, and spatial pattern. It is a chain of events which all the simulation models in the world are unlikely to be able to reconstruct. Yet, however difficult the task, it is an important one, and one which must be attempted. This paper examines some of the spatial concomitants of racial ideology in a mid-nineteenth century city in the American South. Specifically, it focuses on the racial residential patterns of Charleston, South Carolina immediately before the Civil War, and after the end of Reconstruction.

Charleston has been widely regarded as epitomizing the racial residential patterns of the traditional urban South. In the 1920s T. J. Woofter identified old, small, southern cities, and especially Charleston, as having highly scattered patterns of black residence throughout the city.[2] This pattern was contrasted with not only the concentrated patterns of blacks in northern cities but also the clustering of blacks in those southern cities which had no antebellum heritage. Two decades later, E. Franklin Frazier amplified the distinction between two types of southern city.[3] In the older cities most blacks were domestic servants and were interspersed with the white population but in newer cities blacks were often industrial laborers and tended to cluster near to sources of employment. Taeuber and Taeuber also commented on this distinction and identified the dispersed pattern with cities that

1. Haley P. Bamman and Ian E. Davey, "Ideology and space in the Toronto Public School System, 1844-1882," in James T. Lemon, ed., *Internal Relationships within the Nineteenth-Century City,* York University, Dept. of Geography, Discussion Paper No. 11 (1975):9.

2. T. J. Woofter, *Negro Problems in Cities* (Garden City, N.Y., 1928) 37-38.

3. E. Franklin Frazier, *The Negro in the United States* (New York, 1957), p. 237.

Reproduced (with omissions) by permission from the *Journal of Historical Geography* 2 (1976): 329-46.

attained a substantial size before the Civil War when a backyard or alley dwelling pattern would have predominated.[4] Schnore and Evenson confirmed this finding and observed that the relationship between the timing of city growth and residential patterns was still valid in 1960.[5] The authors concluded that "despite the passage of a century since the Civil War, we can be reasonably confident that age of the city is a rather potent factor in affecting its current levels of segregation."[6]

The issue of the origins of so-called "segregated residence" in southern cities is clouded by a tendency to use the term "segregation" rather loosely. If we continue to use the term "residential segregation" at all, a distinction must be made between micro-spatial segregation and macro-spatial segregation. Micro-segregation is separation of residence by lot or block-segment whereas macro-segregation involves the exclusive occupance of whole sections of a city by a particular group. During the middle and late nineteenth century micro-segregation largely gave way to macro-segregated patterns, which became predominant in the early twentieth century. This trend toward macro-spatial segregation was slower in Charleston, South Carolina than in any other major American city. As late as 1940, its racial residential patterns were highly mixed. Taeuber and Taeuber calculated segregation indices for 109 cities using census data for that year, and Charleston had the lowest score, indicating a high degree of residential intermixture of the black and white populations.[7] As the authors pointed out, even this low score revealed an increase in clustering over previous years and recorded a trend initiated before the Civil War. . . .

Most urban theory, rooted in utilitarianism, assumes that urban residential patterns in cities are created by competitive market processes. The allocation of residential space in Charleston, like many other aspects of the life of the city, resulted not from competition but from control. The influence of social control in creating distinctive residential patterns was most clearly recorded in the distribution of the slave population. To Wade the control of slaves in southern cities was enhanced by the dispersed patterns of slave residence which were instigated as a deliberate attempt to prevent the formation of a viable black community.[8] On the plantation a rigid set of rules could be established which not only governed all facets of the lives of the slaves but also reinforced their mental and physical dependence upon their masters. This code could be strictly enforced by means of sanctions and constant supervision on plantations where an isolated location ensured virtually complete control over information reaching the slaves from the outside. Slavery in the urban environment involved the problem of maintaining the isolation of slaves without the "comfortable distances of the plantation."[9] The usual solution was to provide slaves with accommodation on the same lot as the main house, either at right angles to it, or parallel to it at the other end of the lot. The first floor of the accommodation would often be used for storage purposes

4. Karl E. Taeuber and Alma F. Taeuber, *Negroes in Cities. Residential Segregation and Neighborhood Change* (New York, 1965), p. 190.
5. Leo F. Schnore and Philip C. Evenson, "Segregation in Southern Cities," *American Journal of Sociology* 72 (1966):56-67.
6. Ibid., p. 65.
7. Taeuber and Taeuber, *Negroes in Cities*, pp. 37-41.
8. Richard C. Wade, *Slavery in the Cities: the South, 1820-1860* (New York, 1964).
9. Ibid., p. 56.

or as stables. The building faced onto the yard at the back of the main house, the remaining sides of the lot being enclosed by a high wall to form a courtyard. The outside world could only be reached through the main house, or perhaps through a side door. The building plan thus formed a compound which was the architectural expression of the captive status of its inhabitants.

In his portrayal of the urban slave compounds as architectural expressions of racial attitudes, Wade provided a rare insight into the relationship at the microscale between ideology and urban form. This "urban equivalent of the plantation" was not, however, completely successful.[10] In Wade's view, slavery was incompatible with the urban environment, with its manifold opportunities for contact and interaction. In part, the weakening of the institution was associated with an increasing tendency to permit "living out." Slaves, seeking escape from constant surveillance, gravitated to particular parts of the city, and especially its periphery, where "segregated" residential districts were created.

This kind of social and residential control extended beyond the slave population. White social leaders in antebellum Charleston were obsessed with a fear of a slave revolt, but it was the free Negroes of the city who were regarded as the most likely instigators of slave unrest. The free Negro was viewed as a threat to the tight-knit relationship between master and slave upon which the perpetuation of the institution was thought to rest. Despite the oft-recurring references to a few successful and prosperous free Negroes in Charleston, their position in society in the last three antebellum decades undoubtedly declined. The white community viewed the slave conspiracy of 1822, apparently led by a free Negro, Denmark Vesey, as a direct threat to its existence. The immediate repercussions were trials, mass public hangings, meetings of outraged citizens, and ensuing legislation, but the conspiracy also marked the beginning of a new and extended era of repression. The city, in Channing's words, "never again relaxed the outward forms of vigilance."[11] To supplement its sizeable police force the city now established a town guard, a force of 100 men. They were uniformed, trained, and heavily armed, being issued with muskets and bayonets as well as alarming devices such as rattles. Whites as well as blacks were dealt with at the guardhouse, but the list of offenses for which blacks could be held liable was much larger. Slaves and free Negroes were brought to the guardhouse in 1838 for such offenses as: "being out after beating of the tattoo without tickets," "following military companies," "walking on the Battery contrary to law," "bathing horses at prohibited places," and "loitering in retail shops."[12]. . .

Racial Residential Patterns in 1860

By 1860, after three decades of mounting crisis and ensuing response, Charleston had reached the height of its secessionist fervor. During these years the city's reputation was based upon the preservation of a particular way of life in which white supremacy was axiomatic. On the eve of the Civil War, Charleston was a city of some forty thousand people (Table 1), with a built-up area which stretched from the southern tip of the peninsula to Line

10. Ibid., p. 61.

11. Stephen A. Channing, *Crisis of Fear: Secession in South Carolina* (New York, 1970), p. 45.
12. Charleston City Council, *The Mayor's Report of the Proceedings of the City Authorities from September, 1838 to August, 1839* (Charleston, 1839), p. 66.

TABLE 1. Population by Race, 1860 and 1880

	1860	1880
White	23,376	22,699
Non-white	17,146	27,285
Total	40,522	49,984

Source: Eighth and Tenth Censuses of the U.S.

Street (Fig. 1). Of the eight wards into which the city was divided, the four to the north of Calhoun Street had been annexed to the city in 1850.

To determine the racial residential patterns of Charleston in 1860, a 10 percent systematic sample of free households taken from the manuscript schedules of the Eighth Census of the U.S., was mapped (Fig. 2A-C). Whereas the white population was quite evenly distributed throughout the city, the free Negro population had a more northerly bias. It has occasionally been observed that the free Negroes were better represented in the city's Upper Wards than below Calhoun Street.[13] Since the federal census manuscripts distinguish between free *mulatto* and free *black* a further observation can be made: the free black was largely confined to the Upper Wards. Whereas only 40 percent of sample white households were north of Calhoun Street, the Upper Wards accounted for three-quarters of the mulattoes and 86 percent of the blacks.

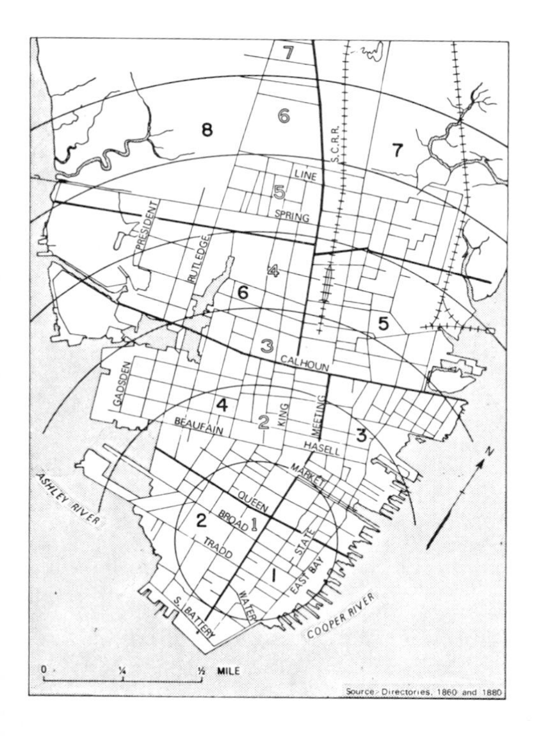

FIG. 1. Charleston in 1860—showing streets, the eight wards, and seven concentric zones.

Apparently there is no way in which the distribution of slave households can be plotted using the U.S. census of population. The slave schedules give the number and names of slaves owned by each owner, but the addresses are not given, and no other source gives this information. A census of 1861[14] did, however, enumerate slave *houses,* and these are mapped in Figure 2D. The slave houses were widely dispersed throughout the city and recorded the coexistence on numerous city lots of a streetfront house with slave quarters at the rear. There was, however, some clustering of the slave houses, particularly on the eastern portions of wards four and six. The mill lots of Chisholm's Mill and Bennett's Mill were also points of concentration.[15]

Ideology and Residence

Free black residence in Charleston in 1860 was, then, largely confined to the Neck. It is possible that this peripheral location represented a squatter settlement of rural in-migrants, but the growth of

13. See, for example, Taeuber and Taeuber, *Negroes in Cities,* pp. 45-49.
14. Frederick A. Ford, *Census of the City of Charleston, South Carolina, for the Year 1861* (Charleston, S.C., 1861).
15. In the case of mill lots, the Ford census provides numbers of slaves rather than slave houses.

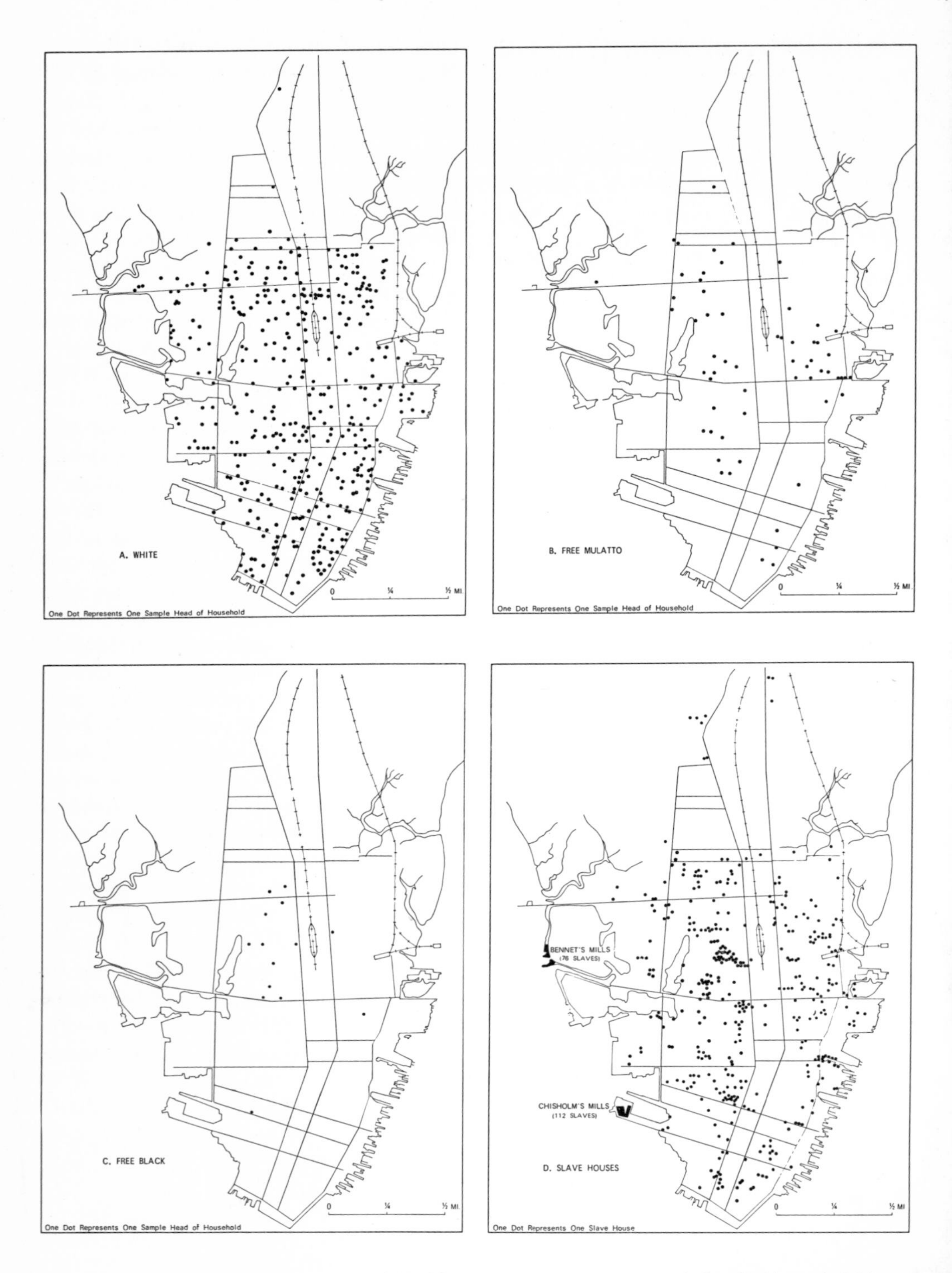

FIG. 2. Place of residence by race, 1860. (One dot represents one sample head of household.)

the residential areas on the Neck took place at a time when the population of the old city was *decreasing,* and there is strong evidence of a flow from the center to the edge of the city. The compilers of a census conducted in 1848 observed that the decrease in the population of the city since 1840 could be accounted for by the movement of slaves and free Negroes to the Neck[16] which had not been annexed at that time. These authors emphasized the "pull" of the area north of Calhoun Street, notably the cheap lots and lower taxes. The Neck held considerable attraction for the slave who had acquired the freedom to "live out." Here he could live in the company of his own choice, beyond the surveillance of his owner.

Although some of the city's inhabitants were attracted to the Neck, others were virtually forced there for the "suburb" on the center of the Neck contained a large number of city rejects. Evidence exists of a "push" from within the city itself and the settlement of the Neck was in part a consequence of attempts of those in power to make the city a safer and pleasanter place for themselves. The motives for these attempts lie in the value system of a white elite which was both the arbiter of taste and the center of social power. This elite was dominated by, and to a large extent composed of, Low Country planters. Charleston had long been the focus of antebellum plantation society in Tidewater South Carolina. . . .

Wertenbaker observed that, whereas in Virginia, Williamsburg was the center of planter civilization and Norfolk the center of the mercantile interests, in South Carolina both rôles were performed by Charleston.[17] In the nineteenth century Charleston became relatively less important as a mercantile center and more prominent as a focus of the planter interests. When the Tidewater planters came to Charleston they brought with them a set of moral precepts and ideas as to what Charleston should be. Their interests were in health, esthetics, and leisure, and increasingly they regarded the pecuniary activities of the merchant with distaste. Moreover, they possessed the affluence and authority to impose their interests upon the city. . . .

The tastes of the elite strongly influenced the city's morphology. The main outdoor focus was the Battery at the tip of the peninsula. Here, as one visitor observed, one could during a summer evening see "almost every one of any notability in Charleston."[18] The houses at the edge of the Battery park were highly regarded not only because of the views which they commanded, but also because of their exposure to the salubrious ocean breezes. The limited amount of available space and the opportunity to build new and more luxurious houses encouraged many planters to choose sites further up the peninsula, usually close to the water. Patios and terraces often stretched out on filled land into the Ashley and Cooper rivers. Here, delicately balanced between the "country fever" prevalent as close as the upper part of the Neck, and the strangers' disease (yellow fever) which periodically threatened to emanate from the wharves, the planters entertained in lavish style.

In contrast, the greater part of Charles-

16. J. L. Dawson and H. W. DeSaussure, *Census of the City of Charleston, South Carolina, for the Year 1848* (Charleston, 1849).

17. Thomas Jefferson Wertenbaker, *The Old South: The Founding of American Civilization* (New York, 1942), p. 14.

18. William Ferguson, *America by River and Rail: Notes by the Way on the New World and Its People* (London, 1856), p. 114.

ton Neck long remained a *terra incognita* to the elite.[19] It had a reputation as an unhealthy area, the source, among other things of "bilious, or as it was familiarly termed Neck fever." The dread of this fever "so pervaded the minds of the citizens that to sleep on the Neck between the first of June and frost was considered tantamount to ordering one's coffin."[20] The city dumped much of its garbage on the Neck and much land was reclaimed in this way. One report noted that a large area of the upper city east of King Street had been filled in with rubbish and "scavenger's offal." Half of this area had been built upon by 1870.[21] Reports issued in the 1870s testify to a long-standing neglect of the area. The City Registrar's report of 1870 noted the inadequacy of the drains in the upper part of the city, which resulted in much of the seventh and eighth wards being submerged after heavy rains. The water stayed until it evaporated, causing "malarial fevers during the autumnal months, and catarrhs, pneumonia and other diseases incident to the winter season."[22] . . .

The threat of fire did as much as the elite's conceptions of health and esthetics to encourage the demolition of inhabited alleyways. The white community lived in constant fear of slave revolt and it was widely assumed that arson would be the major threat.[23] Security against fire was incompatible with the presence of large numbers of free blacks within the city for two main reasons. First, free blacks were seen as the potential instigators of arson and organizers of slave revolts. Secondly, few free blacks could afford housing constructed with other than cheap and highly combustible materials. The city authorities had long tried to limit the construction of wooden buildings, but legislation had proved ineffective, largely because of the high cost of brick and stone in the area. In the aftermath of the fire of 1838, which was widely believed by whites to have been the work of black arsonists, a special committee under the chairmanship of C. G. Memminger recommended a total ban on the construction of wooden buildings.[24] Despite the objections of a few "self-styled friends of the poor," within two weeks of the fire, the mayor ratified an ordinance making it illegal to build any wooden or frame building. Since prior to 1850, the city extended only as far north as Calhoun Street, the effect of the ordinance was to confine the construction of cheap houses to the Neck. Many well-maintained wooden buildings antedated the ordinance survived in the city, but many of the cheaper houses were

19. It was described thus in a cutting from the Charleston *Courier* pasted in the diary of Jacob Schirmer (Ms. South Carolina Historical Society). See also the *Charleston Mercury,* June 22, 1860.

20. Ibid. A more scientific approach to disease in nineteenth-century Charleston is found in: Joseph Ioor Waring, M.D., *A History of Medicine in South Carolina, 1825-1900* (Columbia, 1967).

21. Health District No. 5 Report, *City Registrar's Report for 1867* (Charleston, 1867), pp. 80-81.

22. City Registrar's Report, *Annual Reports of the Offices of the City Government to the City Council of Charleston for the Year Ending December 31st, 1870* (Charleston, 1871), p. 40.

23. The powerfulness of the association between the two threats—arson and revolt—is evident in the tactics which were used during fires. In 1838 the city authorities decreed that, "except for those necessary to carry and guard the caisson, the city guard instead of being required to attend fires should on every alarm repair to the guard house under arms." Charleston City Council, *The Mayor's Report of the Proceedings of the City Authorities from the 4th September, 1837 to the 1st August, 1838* (Charleston, 1838).

24. Report of Mr. Memminger offered to the City Council on 22nd May 1838. *Memorial and Proceedings of the City Council on the Subject of Securing the City from Fires* (Charleston, 1838).

TABLE 2. Numbers of Brick and Wooden Houses, by Ward, 1861

Ward	*Brick houses*	*Per cent of total*	*Wooden houses*	*Per cent of total*	*Total*
1	498	77.3	146	22.7	644
2	251	40.0	377	60.0	628
3	606	54.1	515	45.9	1,121
4	620	45.2	751	54.8	1,371
5	99	13.2	652	86.8	751
6	79	8.0	907	92.0	986
7	16	3.7	424	96.3	440
8	10	1.3	741	98.7	751
Total	2,179	32.6	4,513	67.4	6,692

Source: Ford (1861).

progressively removed, often as part of alley-clearing "improvements," and were not replaced. As Table 2 shows, there were, on the eve of the Civil War, sharp differences between the Lower and Upper Wards in the numbers and proportions of brick and wooden houses.

The Free Black As Outcast

The use of physical improvement schemes to displace blacks in Charleston was one in a mounting series of pressures against the free Negro in South Carolina. In a society with otherwise clear divisions of class and caste, the free Negro had a loosely defined place, and as white apprehension at attacks upon the caste system mounted sharply in the last three antebellum decades, the distinction between free black and slave grew narrower.[25] Within Charleston, this increasing apprehension was manifested in the residential patterns of the city on the eve of the Civil War. The free Negroes and especially those regarded as free *blacks* were viewed with increasing suspicion. The free black in fact became a virtual outcast and his position at the edge of the city reflected that status. The existence of cheap accommodation outside the old city boundary, viewed by some writers as a point of attraction, was itself a function of decisions made by an elite which preempted the healthiest and most attractive sites and supported legislation which discouraged the persistence of cheap *unallocated* housing in the city proper. The slave, whose housing was usually provided and whose presence was largely desired, remained. The free mulatto was to some extent displaced. The free black was largely pushed out of the old city. Ironically, the intermingling of slaves who were living out on the Neck and the free Negroes who had been forced there produced the very situation which slaveowning whites had carefully avoided in the old city. In the view of these whites, this blurring of the institutional boundaries of slavery posed a grave threat to the safety of the city. Moreover, the intermingling was taking place on the edge of the city, beyond the area patrolled by the city guard and outside the jurisdictional limits of the city court. It was this state of affairs which prompted the annexation of the Neck in 1850. The sole justifications for annexation appearing in the preamble of the enabling legislation are the pro-

25. Channing, *Crisis of Fear*. See also Marina Wikramanayake, *A World in Shadow: The Free Black in Antebellum South Carolina* (Columbia, 1973).

vision of "a more effectual police" and the avoidance of "a conflict of jurisdiction."[26]

Residential Patterns in 1880

Traditional interpretations of the postwar Reconstruction era in the South have emphasized corruption and disruption, and portrayed radical changes in the relative status of white and black.[27] In Charleston, because of the wartime destruction of large parts of the city, the virtual abandonment of the area below Calhoun Street in response to enemy bombardment, the abolition of slavery, the postwar immigration of thousands of recently freed rural blacks and the financial ruin of much of the elite, the persistence of the old residential patterns would appear unlikely. Yet recent interpretations of Reconstruction in South Carolina have noted the failure of that venture to impose lasting social change.[28] This is consistent with those studies of black residential patterns which have stressed the persistence of scattering in old southern cities well into the twentieth century.[29] Among historians of race relations, meanwhile, opinion is divided on whether "segregation" was imposed as an immediate reaction to the abolition of slavery, or whether it was a phenomenon which appeared only in the 1890s.[30]

The residential patterns of Charleston in 1880, reconstructed on the basis of census data, provide a datum from which changes which occurred during the War and Reconstruction period may be described. A 10 percent systematic sample of households drawn from the census manuscript schedules was mapped, and the racial patterns (Fig. 3A-C) are so scattered that any suggestion of a trend toward a pattern of macro-segregation by 1880 can be dismissed. Although the residential patterns were not drastically altered, some changes did occur between 1860 and 1880. A comparative classification of households according to street-front or alley location (Table 3) suggests that the antebellum decline in alley populations was reversed. Presumably the

26. An Act to Extend the Limits of Charleston. Charleston: December 1849. Reprinted in: Mayor Courtenay's Annual Review, *Charleston, S.C. Yearbook, 1881* (Charleston, 1882), p. 351.
27. For a review of traditional and revisionist accounts of Reconstruction, see Kenneth M. Stampp, *The Era of Reconstruction* (New York, 1969).
28. For example: Peggy Lamson, *The Glorious Failure: Black Congressman Robert Brown Elliott and the Reconstruction in South Carolina* (New York, 1973); Martin Abbott, *The Freedmen's Bureau in South Carolina: 1865-1872* (Chapel Hill, N.C., 1967); Carol K. Rothrock Bleser, *The Promised Land: The History of the South Carolina Land Commission, 1869-1890* (Columbia, S.C., 1969).

29. Taeuber and Taeuber, *Negroes in Cities,* p. 190; Schnore and Evenson, "Segregation."
30. Compare: Joel Williamson, *After Slavery: The Negro in South Carolina During Reconstruction, 1861-1877* (Chapel Hill, N.C., 1965), pp. 274-99; and C. Vann Woodward, *The Strange Career of Jim Crow* (2nd ed. rev.; New York, 1966), pp. 25-26. Tindall itemizes some of the aspects of life in South Carolina in which discrimination practices varied greatly. George Brown Tindall, *South Carolina Negroes: 1877-1900* (Columbia, S.C., 1952), pp. 291-302.

TABLE 3. Intra-Block Distribution of Sample Heads of Household, by Race, 1860 and 1880

	1860			1880		
	Street	*Alley*	*Other*	*Street*	*Alley*	*Other*
White	408	16	2	417	16	2
Mulatto	58	4	0	147	14	2
Black	13	2	1	447	57	11
Total	479	22	3	1,011	87	15

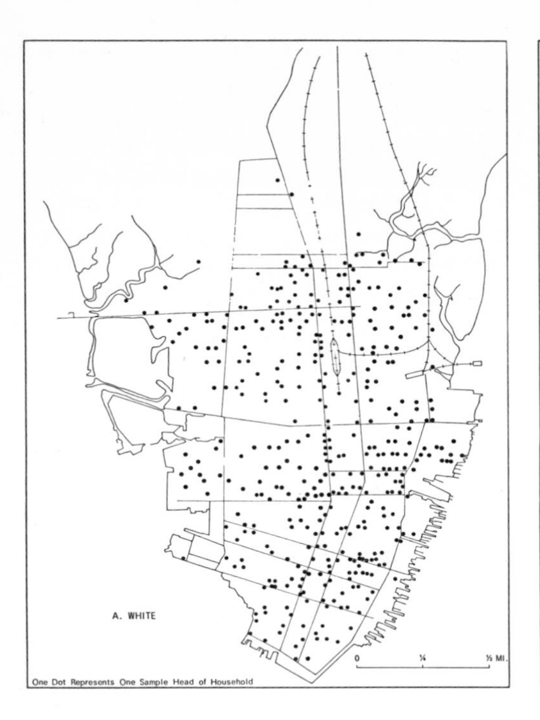

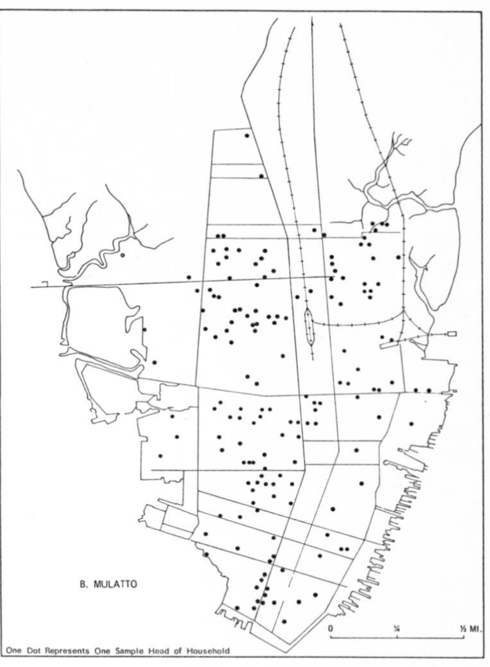

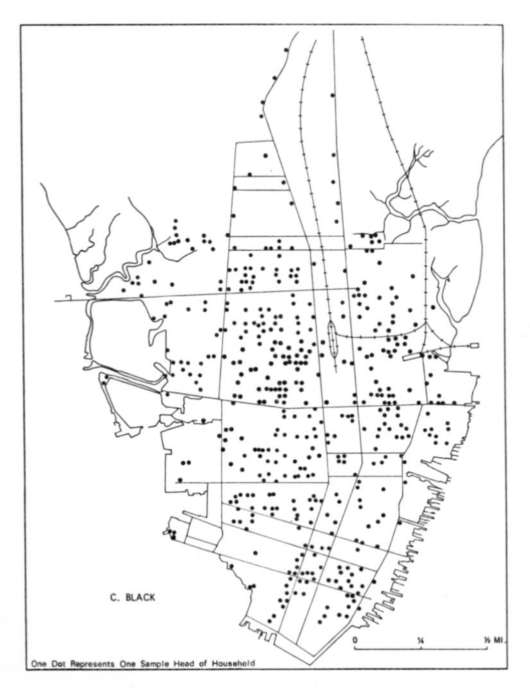

FIG. 3. Place of residence by race, 1880. (One dot represents one sample head of household.)

city's elite were unable to prevent the reoccupation of the alleys by blacks at a time when recently freed slaves were crowding into the city. The number of white alley households remained relatively stable and, consequently, there was a southward shift in the center of gravity of the black population, but only a small lateral movement of whites (Fig. 4).

. . . Aggregate patterns of white residence thus remained largely unchanged over the two decades of war and reconstruction. There was some redistribution of the nonwhite population, but no radical changes. It is possible that more detailed changes would be revealed by analysis of small areas of the city. Nevertheless, the creation of a group of freedmen within Charleston, and the in-migration of large numbers of formerly rural freedmen, scarcely altered the overall residential structure of the city. Visitors

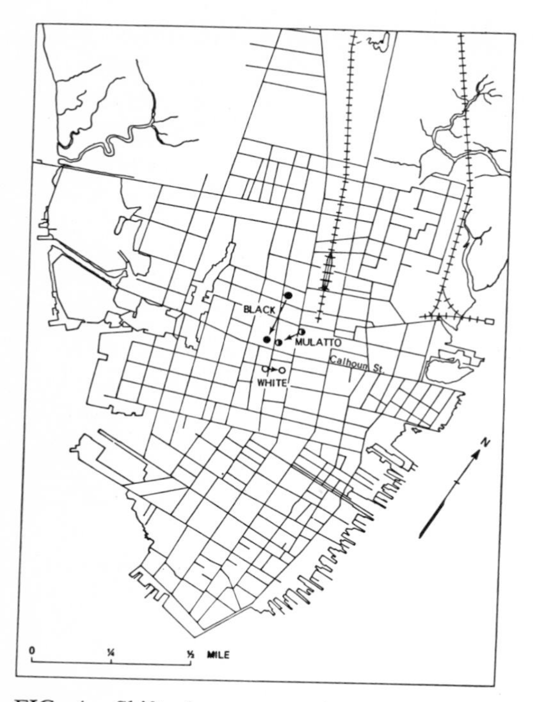

FIG. 4. Shifts in centers of gravity of the sample populations by race, 1860-1880.

in 1880 were just as struck by the "proximity and confusion so to speak of white and negro houses"[31] as they had been before the War, and their observations are consistent with recent comparative studies of segregation in southern cities.

This failure of the Civil War and Reconstruction to produce a clear alternative to the carefully contrived residential patterns of the antebellum era lends support to recent studies which have found a high degree of social and ideological continuity in South Carolina between 1860 and 1880.[32] The antebellum attitudes in Charleston survived Reconstruction, and so too did the antebellum residential patterns. It was not until much more recently that backyard residence and backyard attitudes toward blacks disappeared.

Conclusion

The elite regarded the presence of free blacks within antebellum Charleston as incompatible with the city's continued existence as a safe, clean, healthy, and pleasant place in which to live. During the last three or four antebellum decades, the Low Country planters, who formed Charleston's elite, imposed a value system on the city which survived the Civil War and Reconstruction. The southern planters presided over a society in which prestige was directly related to the ownership of rural land, and in which the normal behavior pattern of the mass of the population was deferential. Planter ideology, including powerful notions of social control, permeated the whole of Charleston's existence. In particular, a curious amalgam of esthetic taste, medical ignorance, and racial myth affected the evaluation and allocation of residential space within the city. In comparison, those market forces assumed to be dominant in nineteenth-century U.S. cities were insignificant. The main process was residential control, not those competitive mechanisms which are fundamental to the theoretical frameworks within which studies of cities in the United States are frequently cast.

31. Edward Hogan, "South Carolina Today," *International Review* 8 (1880):105-19. Quoted in Tindall, *South Carolina Negroes,* p. 295.

32. According to Cooper the post-Reconstruction leadership in South Carolina was fully dedicated to antebellum ideals. William J. Cooper, Jr., *The Conservative Regime: South Carolina 1877-1890* (Baltimore, 1968). Martin Abbott (*Freedmen's Bureau*) has shown that the impact of the Freedman's Bureau on the status and condition of the black population was slight. Carol Bleser (*Promised Land*) has documented the failure of the South Carolina Land Commission to introduce significant land reforms in the 1870s and 1880s. Peggy Lamson (*Glorious Failure*) has traced in the life of a black South Carolina congressman the failure of the experiment in racial equality which seemed to promise so much in 1867.

There is no indication that Charleston was a "typical" southern city; indeed, the evidence suggests that mid-nineteenth-century Charleston epitomized rather than typified contemporary southern society. Whether the cities of the South constitute a distinctive group which may be viewed in contrast to those of the rest of the United States is open to debate. Yet, while reaffirming Warner's observation that U.S. cities, "have grown up within American culture, not apart from it,"[33] it is important to stress that American culture has not been homogeneous, and that values apart from the dominant ideology of urban industrial progress have found tangible expression within the nation's cities.

---

33. Sam Bass Warner, Jr., *The Private City: Philadelphia in Three Periods of Its Growth* (Philadelphia, 1968), p. 6.

The Evolution of American Suburbs: A Geographical Interpretation / *Peter O. Muller*

Whereas the nation's suburbs have only recently emerged as a dominant metropolitan force, they are not a distinctively new type of urban settlement. Development of the city fringe extends back to the dawn of urbanization, and the modern American process of suburbanization—the sustained growth of city edges at a rate faster than that of central areas—has been in evidence for the last century and a quarter.

Since 1850 a series of new urban forms, built up in stages during eras marked by certain intrametropolitan transport innovations, have appeared in suburbia, and their evolution is the major product of the modern history of the American city.

The American Rural Ethic and Suburban Evolution

Central to an understanding of the evolution of suburban forms in America is a set of values and beliefs deeply ingrained in the American national character and native culture: the so-called *rural ideal,* which "pulled" Americans toward the outskirts. The philosophical roots of this ideal lie in the Jeffersonian perception of democracy, particularly its interpretation of the agrarian doctrine of the eighteenth-century Enlightenment. In Jefferson's view the least sinful life is to be found in a small agrarian community of equals governed in the interest of the entire population. Only the country provided a life "in the fruits of the soil, in green growing things, in the healthy human family, and in the freedom from arbitrary political and social constraints." Later commentators also praised the frontier spirit, which promoted cooperation among neighboring families in the settlement of new urban land (Tuan, 1974, p. 236).

In addition to these "pull" factors, suburbanization trends have been reinforced by "push" factors. The fear of being overwhelmed by the growing disorder and complexity of urban life has given rise to a city escapist mentality. This thread, by no means exclusively American, can be traced back through Franklin's Philadelphia to Ceasar's Rome (Tuan, 1974, pp. 228-30). More recently, this need for local identity and security amidst rising urban chaos has been abetted by refusal to share residential space with newly arrived immigrants and minority groups.

The Early History of Suburbs

In the long history of suburbs, a dual role has characterized the evolution of urban perimeter settlements. On one hand, the city fringes were perceived by the wealthy as desirable retreats for country living in

Reproduced (with omissions) by permission from *Urbanism Past and Present* 4 (1977):1-10.

ancient Mesopotamia, classical Athens and Rome, renaissance Florence, and eighteenth-century London; on the other, they were regarded as the domain of society's misfits, its poor and other less-than-fully civilized elements (hence "*sub*-urb"). By the late middle ages, these fringe settlements had acquired an additional function as sites for warehousing and manufacturing activities. Soon many were being embraced both symbolically and functionally by the urban economy through the tearing down of city walls. Most European cities of this period spawned peripheral *faubourg* ("fore-settlement") districts of factories, inns, and houses of entertainment. These multiple functions also typified American suburbs through the first half of the nineteenth century, and French-settled New Orleans even had proper faubourgs on its perimeter. Flight from the city occurred in colonial times (encouraged in Philadelphia and elsewhere by developers actively promoting outlying residential properties), as did the rise of a prevailing negative image of suburbs resulting from their concentrations of social outcasts, brothels, and obnoxious industries. The last, nevertheless, played a significant role in urban economic growth since many of the settlements which sprouted around such large centers as Boston and Philadelphia performed important commercial and commodity production functions for the central town. This geographical interdependency proved to be of vital importance later when these urban centers expanded, by incorporating the outer nodes and their activities, to form the complete city.

Intraurban Transportation and the Stages of Suburban Growth

The suburbs of preindustrial America, however, did not begin to fit the rural ideal until industrialization began to cause deterioration in the central cities. The "romantic" suburb movement envisioned the urban periphery as the ideal location (Thorns, 1973, p. 65). There, one could hold a well-paying city job and yet live in a semirural home, a "refuge" to which one daily retreated for "refreshment" and "mental recruitment." . . .

Middle-income urban residents, barred from the new suburbs by the high cost of commuting, attempted to re-create the rural ideal within the city. The new Chicago which arose from the ruins of the catastrophic 1871 fire contained many elements of the later middle-class suburban ideal. For a time at least, Chicago became "a city in a garden" characterized by a dispersed population, relatively low residential densities, and the widespread use of detached single-family dwellings.

Modern suburbanization, as we have suggested, developed early in the second half of the nineteenth century. Two new factors brought about the transformation of earlier peripheral settlements: more efficient means of intraurban transport; and the beginnings of residential segregation in the American city (Singleton, 1973, p. 45). Since transportation technology has been a significant force in shaping suburban spatial structure for the last century (see Holt, 1972; Tarr, 1973), developments in urban transport go a long way toward explaining the growth of modern suburbs. . . .

Walking-Horsecar Era

Prior to the 1850s, the American city was a small, tightly compact urban settlement in which walking was the dominant mode of movement. Since people and activities were concentrated within a few minutes' walk, the pedestrian city's internal spatial organization consisted of a loose mixture of homes, shops, and work-

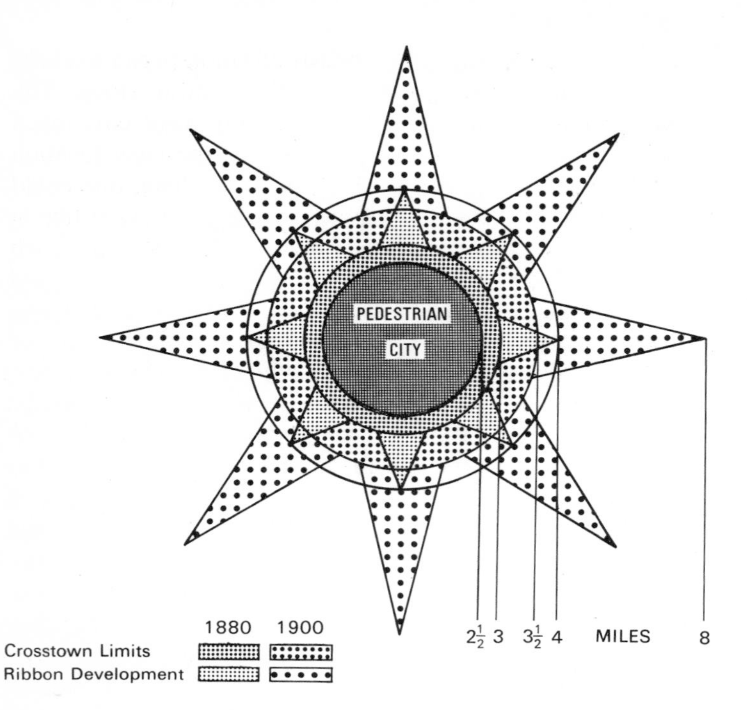

FIG. 1. Generalized sequence of the expansion of streetcar networks in American cities, 1850-1910. From *Cities and Immigrants: A Geography of Change in Nineteenth-Century America* by David Ward. Copyright © 1971 by Oxford University Press, Inc. Reprinted by permission.

places. The population was fairly homogeneous and few cleavages in urban social space existed, though the wealthy did seek the most prestigious locations. These latter also had relative freedom of movement in horse-drawn carriages and, after the 1830s on, newly built railroads.

By mid-nineteenth century most large cities had rail suburbs, but the high cost of both outlying housing and train fares together with the extra commuting time meant that only the affluent could afford them. . . .

Morphologically, these early rail suburbs—really *exurbs* in today's terminology—consisted of a linear pattern of discrete nodes isolated from the city as well as each other. Walking distance from each railhead determined the extent of local development, which usually consisted of a compact residential center and a few shops. Otherwise the suburb was totally dependent on the city.

For the less affluent segments of urban society, access to a less citified residential setting depended upon advances in transport technology. Horse-drawn omnibuses were introduced as the first mass transit innovation in the 1820s, but these stagecoach-like vehicles were too slow and clumsy; street railways offered the best hope and numerous experiments were conducted in cities after 1830. While the street steam engine was a failure and most later cable car systems proved impractical, horse-drawn streetcars were successful and became widespread after mid-century. Although these fixed-rail horsecars were only slightly faster than pedestrian mobility (up to 5 mph), they encouraged urban expansion and home construction to a distance of three miles from downtown. Horsecar lines followed both radial and lateral crosstown routes. Because of superior accessibility, transportation arteries emanating from the city core encouraged both higher residential densities and the precursors of commercial strips. At the same time, however, crosstown lines enabled the development of land in between the arteries and the city maintained its more or less circular shape. These now accessible fringe areas became the *horsecar suburbs* and were used nearly exclusively for new and better residences (Warner, 1962), (Fig. 1). . . .

Middle-class families moved to the horsecar suburbs, and the relocation of these longer-term residents quickly began to erode the fairly uniform society of the pedestrian city. Thus, social and geographical stratification and segregation of economic classes within the early industrial metropolis had begun. Soon thereafter, the American city was locked into a residential spatial structure dominated by closed social cells, wherein ability to pay and quality of one's residential environment went hand in hand.

Electric Streetcar Era

The major turning point in the history of American suburbs occurred in 1887 with the introduction and subsequent rapid diffusion of the electric streetcar invented by Frank Sprague in the city of Richmond (see Krim, 1967). Higher average speeds of 15 to 18 mph—three times that of horsecars—permitted the range of commuting to increase significantly so that the urban development radius could now be feasibly extended outward for distances of up to ten miles from the city center. Thus, in most cases, at least five times the surrounding area of the horsecar era now came potentially within thirty minutes' travel of downtown. A period of vigorous street rail network expansion ensued in most cities; Boston, for example, more than doubled its urban trolley network, from 212 to 445 total track miles between 1887 and 1904 (Ward, 1964, p. 485). Inside the city, the existing net of radial and crosstown routes was intensified, thus facilitating access to areas outside the central business district. The electric trolley, however, made its greatest impact along the new light rail traction lines which were quickly extended from the city into the surrounding countryside; by the early 1890s a new era of middle-class streetcar suburbs had arrived. . . .

These developments in the electric streetcar era inevitably affected the shape of the American metropolis. Its characteristic morphology was that of a central city extended by fingerlike corridors thrust outward along trolley routes and their parallel utility service lines. Moreover, the electrification of railroads and interurban lines permitted more frequent stopping, and the addition of more closely spaced stations resulted in the coalescence of older discrete nodes into a continuous corridor. The total pattern was one of a distinctly star-shaped metropolis with elongated corridor development in sectors containing public transportation and empty interstitial space between them. Development within streetcar corridors was typified by a continuous strip of largely commercial land use which lined both sides of the tracks. Behind them were gridded residential streets, paralleling the tracks to the usual depth of a few blocks on either side. Detached dwellings on rectangular plots lined these streets, with house façades often imitating those of the rich. Beyond the few-block-wide development corridor, open space, often dotted with small market gardening farms, was available to all for recreation. . . .

The overall pattern of residential segregation took the form of concentric belts in which income rose with increasing distance from the city center. The sharp social cleavages of the low-income inner city were expressed geographically in a set of distinct ethnic neighborhoods. The next band of outer neighborhoods, the former horsecar suburbs, consisted of fairly inexpensive housing which was in the process of filtering down from the middle class to moderate-income working-groups. This blue-collar advance into the urban fringe was made possible by the improved transit network and the beginning of factory decentralization along rail axes toward the urban fringe. Beyond the former horsecar suburbs came the middle-class streetcar suburbs. The outermost suburbs were dominated by upper-income groups with their elegant mansions and newly formed country clubs. . . .

Problems arose in the effort to maintain a level of suburban public services commensurate with a good quality residential environment, particularly after 1900 when hopes of metropolitan government ended with the demise of the industrial city's annexation movement, which in the late nineteenth century was the predominant method of city growth. After the turn of the century, the annexation movement subsided considerably as the changing social geography of the big city made its union with the increasingly powerful suburbs less attractive. To offset the lack of a complete range of local public services, many suburban municipalities pooled resources in intermunicipal special service districts to handle schools, hospitals, police and fire protection, water supply, and sewage disposal. However, these attempts only temporarily solved the problem of providing a level of suburban public services adequate for a rapidly growing population. The central difficulty in maintaining a quality residential environment, then as now, was the failure to develop a viable set of cooperative suburban governments which could effectively plan for, and respond more broadly to, the changing needs of their residents.

Important changes in suburban economic geography also occurred during the electric streetcar era. In many of the nation's suburban rail corridors, the beginning of urban manufacturing decentralization was giving rise to both reverse commuting and a growing number of satellite industrial mill towns. Factories had continued following the railroads outward as they discovered that profitable sites for assembling raw materials and distributing manufactures were not limited to the central city. The centripetal force once exerted by downtown rail terminal locations had been more than offset for certain industries by centrifugal factors at the close of the century. Among the latter were the growing shortage of adequate space as the central business district expanded, the subsequent land value spiral which drove up site costs enormously increasing traffic congestion, and such other factors as higher taxes and nuisance legislation. . . .

References and Further Reading

General works on suburban history and historical geography are: Kenneth T. Jackson, "The Crabgrass Frontier: 150 Years of Suburban Growth in America," in R. Mohl and J. Richardson, eds., *The Urban Experience* (Belmont, Cal.: Wadsworth Publishing Co., 1973), pp. 196-221; J. John Palen, *The Urban World* (New York: McGraw-Hill, 1975), pp. 147-75; Joel Schwartz, "The Evolution of the Suburbs," in P. Dolce, ed., *Suburbia: The American Dreams and Dilemma* (Garden City, N.Y.: Anchor Press/Doubleday, 1976), pp. 1-36; Yi-Fu Tuan, *Topophilia: A Study of Environmental Perception, Attitudes, and Values* (Englewood Cliffs, N.J.: Prentice-Hall, 1974), pp. 225-44; *John S. Adams,* "Residential Structure of Midwestern Cities," *"Annals of the AAG*

(Association of American Geographers) 60 (1970):37-62; James E. Vance, Jr., "California and the Search for the Ideal," *Annals of the AAG* 62 (1972):185-210; James E. Vance, Jr., *Geography and Urban Evolution in the San Francisco Bay Area* (Berkeley: University of California, Institute of Governmental Studies, 1964); G. H. Singleton, "The Genesis of Suburbia: A Complex of Historical Trends," in L. H. Massotti and J. K. Hadden, eds., *The Urbanization of Suburbs* (Beverly Hills; Sage, 1973), pp. 29-50; and D. C. Thorns, *Suburbia* (London: MacGibbon and Kee, 1972).

Eighteenth- and nineteenth-century suburbs of the Walking-Horsecar Era are treated in: Kenneth T. Jackson, "Urban Deconcentration in the Nineteenth Century: A Statistical Inquiry," in L. Schnore, ed., *The New Urban History* (Princeton: Princeton University Press, 1975), pp. 110-42; David Ward, *Cities and Immigrants* (New York: Oxford University Press, 1971), pp. 125-45; K. H. Schaeffer and Elliot Sclar, *Access for All: Transportation and Urban Growth* (Baltimore: Penguin Books, 1975), pp. 8-33; Glen E. Holt, "The Changing Perception of Urban Pathology," in K. Jackson and S. Schultz, eds., *Cities in American History* (New York: Knopf, 1972), pp. 324-43; and Joel A. Tarr, "From City to Suburb," in A. Callow, ed., *American Urban History,* 2nd rev. ed. (New York: Oxford University Press, 1973), pp. 202-12.

Turn-of-the-century suburbs of the Electric Streetcar Era are discussed in: Sam Bass Warner, Jr., *Streetcar Suburbs* (Cambridge, Mass.: Harvard and MIT University Presses, 1962); David Ward, "A Comparative Historical Geography of Streetcar Suburbs in Boston and Leeds, 1850-1920," *Annals of the AAG* 54 (1964):477-89; Harlan P. Douglass, *The Suburban Trend* (New York: Century, 1925) and now available in reprint from Arno Press; Graham R. Taylor, *Satellite Cities: A Study of Industrial Suburbs* (New York: D. Appleton, 1915) also available in reprint from Arno Press; Tarr, "From City to Suburb"; and Schaeffer and Sclar, *Access for All.*

Suggested Additional Reading

In addition to the general works cited at the end of the Introduction, the following references elaborate many of the themes raised in this section.

A. Regional Urban Systems

Borchert, John R., "American Metropolitan Evolution," *The Geographical Review* 57 (1967):301-32.

Conzen, Michael P., "A Transport Interpretation of the Growth of Urban Regions: An American Example," *Journal of Historical Geography* 1 (1975):361-82.

Crowther, Simeon J., "Urban Growth in the Mid-Atlantic States," *Journal of Economic History* 36 (1976):624-44.

Duncan, Beverly, and Stanley Lieberson, *Metropolis and Region in Transition* (Beverly Hills, Cal.: Sage, 1970).

Earle, Carville, and Ronald Hoffman, "The Urban South: The First Two Centuries," pp. 23-51 in B. A. Brownell and D. R. Goldfield, eds., *The City in Southern History: The Growth of Urban Civilization in the South* (Port Washington, N.Y.: Kennikat Press, 1975).

Earle, Carville V., "The First English Towns in North America," *Geographical Review* 67 (1977):100-135.

Gottmann, Jean, *Megalopolis, The Urbanized Northeastern Seaboard of the United States* (Cambridge, Mass.: M.I.T. Press, 1961).

Higgs, Robert, "The Growth of Cities in a Midwestern Region, 1870-1900," *Journal of Regional Science* 9 (1969):369-75.

Muller, Edward K., "Regional Urbanization and the Selective Growth of Towns in North American Regions," *Journal of Historical Geography* 1 (1977):21-40.

Pred, Alan R., *Urban Growth and the Circulation of Information: The United States System of Cities, 1790-1840* (Cambridge, Mass.: Harvard University Press, 1973).

Rubin, Julus, "Urban Growth and Regional Development," pp. 3-21, in D. T. Gilchrist, ed., *The Growth of Seaport Cities*

1790-1825 (Charlottesville: Published for the Elentherian Mills-Hagley Foundation by the University Press of Virginia, 1967).

Taylor, George R., "American Urban Growth Preceding the Railway Age," *Journal of Economic History* 27 (1967): 309-39.

B. The Internal Structure of the City

Barton, Josef J., *Peasants and Strangers: Italians, Rumanians, and Slovaks in an American City, 1890-1950* (Cambridge, Mass.: Harvard University Press, 1975).

Blumin, Stuart M., *The Urban Threshold: Growth and Change in a Nineteenth Century Community* (Chicago: University of Chicago Press, 1976).

Bowden, Martyn J., "Downtown through Time: Delimitation, Expansion, and Internal Growth," *Economic Geography* 47 (1971):121-35.

Conzen, Kathleen N., *Immigrant Milwaukee; 1836-1860: Accommodation and Community in a Frontier City* (Cambridge, Mass.: Harvard University Press, 1976).

Fales, Raymond L., and Leon N. Moses, "Thünen, Weber and the Spatial Structure of the Nineteenth Century City," pp. 43-74 in Franklin J. James, ed., *Models of Employment and Residence Location* (New Brunswick, N.J.: Rutgers University Press, 1976).

Feinstein, Otto, *Ethnic Groups in the City: Culture, Institutions, and Power* (Heath, 1971).

Frisch, Michael H., *Town into City: Springfield, Massachusetts, and the Meaning of Community, 1840-1880* (Cambridge, Mass.: Harvard University Press, 1972).

Glabb, Charles N., and A. Theodore Brown, *A History of Urban America,* 2nd rev. ed. (New York: Macmillan, 1976).

Glazer, Nathan, and Daniel P. Moynihan, *Beyond the Melting Pot,* 2nd ed. (Cambridge, Mass.: Harvard University and M.I.T. Presses, 1970).

Groves, Paul A., and Edward K. Muller, "The Evolution of Black Residential Areas in Late Nineteenth Century Cities," *Journal of Historical Geography* 1 (1975): 169-92.

Hareven, Tamara K., ed., *Family and Kin in Urban Communities, 1700-1930* (New York: Franklin Watts, 1977).

Hoover, Edgar M., "The Evolving Form and Organization of the Metropolis," pp. 237-84 in Harvey S. Perloff and Lowden Wingo, Jr., eds., *Issues in Urban Economics* (Baltimore: Johns Hopkins University Press, 1968).

Jackson, Kenneth T., "The Crabgrass Frontier: 150 Years of Suburban Growth in America," pp. 192-222 in Raymond A. Mohl and James F. Richardson, eds., *The Urban Experience: Themes in American History* (Belmont, Cal.: Wadsworth Publishing Company, 1973).

Osofsky, Gilbert, *Harlem: The Making of a Ghetto: Negro New York, 1890-1930* (New York: Harper and Row, 1966).

Pessen, Edward, "The Social Configuration of the Antebellum City: An Historical and Theoretical Inquiry," *Journal of Urban History* 2 (1976):267-306.

Pred, Alan R., "Manufacturing in the American Mercantile City: 1800-1840," *Annals of the Association of American Geographers* 56 (1966):307-38.

Sennett, Richard, *Families Against the City: Middle Class Homes of Industrial Chicago, 1872-1890* (Cambridge, Mass.: Harvard University Press, 1970).

Thernstrom, Stephen, *The Other Bostonians: Poverty and Progress in the American Metropolis, 1880-1973* (Cambridge, Mass.: Harvard University Press, 1976).

———, *Poverty and Progress: Social Mobility in a Nineteenth Century City* (Cambridge, Mass.: Harvard University Press, 1964).

Vance, James E., Jr., "Housing the Worker: The Employment Linkage as a Force in Urban Structure," *Economic Geography* 42 (1966):294-325.

Warner, Sam B., Jr., *Streetcar Suburbs: The Process of the Growth of Boston, 1870-1900* (Cambridge, Mass.: Harvard University Press, 1962).

Contributors

John L. Allen	Department of Geography, University of Connecticut, Storrs.
Robert F. Berkhofer, Jr.	Department of History, University of Michigan, Ann Arbor.
Martyn J. Bowden	Department of Geography, Clark University, Worcester.
Andrew H. Clark	Department of Geography, University of Wisconsin, Madison. (Deceased.)
Michael P. Conzen	Department of Geography, University of Chicago.
O. Fred Donaldson	Formerly of the Department of Geography, University of Washington, Seattle.
Joseph A. Ernst	Department of History, York University, Downsview, Ontario.
Francis X. Femminella	Department of Sociology, State University of New York, Albany.
Philip J. Greven, Jr.	Department of History; Rutgers, The State University; New Brunswick.
John C. Hudson	Department of Geography, Northwestern University, Evanston.
Wilbur R. Jacobs	Department of History, University of California, Santa Barbara.
Terry G. Jordan	Department of Geography, North Texas State University, Denton.
James T. Lemon	Department of Geography, University of Toronto.

David Lowenthal	Department of Geography, University College, London.
Donald W. Meinig	Department of Geography, Syracuse University, Syracuse.
H. Roy Merrens	Department of Geography, York University, Downsview, Ontario.
Robert D. Mitchell	Department of Geography, University of Maryland, College Park.
Richard L. Morrill	Department of Geography, University of Washington, Seattle.
Edward K. Muller	Department of History, University of Pittsburgh.
Peter O. Muller	Department of Geography, Temple University, Philadelphia.
William N. Parker	Department of Economics, Yale University, New Haven.
Allan R. Pred	Department of Geography, University of California, Berkeley.
John P. Radford	Department of Geography, York University, Downsview, Ontario.
John G. Rice	Department of Geography, University of Minnesota, Minneapolis.
Morton Rothstein	Department of History, University of Wisconsin, Madison.
David Ward	Department of Geography, University of Wisconsin, Madison.